Field Methods in Archaeology

SEVENTH EDITION

Thomas R. Hester

University of Texas at Austin

Harry J. Shafer

Texas A & M University

Kenneth L. Feder

Central Connecticut State University

Mayfield Publishing Company

Mountain View, California
London • Toronto

Library of Congress Cataloging-in-Publication Data
Hester, Thomas R. 1946–
    Field methods in archaeology / Thomas R. Hester, Harry J. Shafer,
Kenneth L. Feder. -- 7th ed.
        p.   cm.
    Includes bibliographical references and index.
    ISBN 1-55934-799-6
    1. Archaeology--Field work.   I. Shafer, Harry J.   II. Feder,
Kenneth L.   III. Title.
CC76.H47   1997
930.1'--dc20   96-27313
                                                                                CIP

Manufactured in the United States of America
10   9   8   7   6   5   4   3   2

Mayfield Publishing Company
1280 Villa Street
Mountain View, California 94041

Sponsoring editor, Janet M. Beatty; production editor, Carla L. White; manuscript editor, Beverly DeWitt; text designer, Richard Kharibian; cover designer, Jean Mailander; art manager, Robin Mouat; manufacturing manager, Randy Hurst. The text was set in 9/12 Palatino by Fog Press and printed on 50# Finch Opaque by R.R. Donnelly & Sons Company. *Cover photo:* Excavation at the Wilson-Leonard site in central Texas. Copyright © 1997 Thomas R. Hester

Text, photo, and illustration credits appear at the back of the book on page 424, which constitutes an extension of the copyright page.

C O N T E N T S

PREFACE

Cluster of Olmec figurines (Offering No. 4), excavated by Robert F. Heizer at La Venta, Tabasco, Mexico, in 1955. Photo courtesy Robert F. Heizer.

This book, appearing now in its seventh edition, is a direct lineal descendant of *A Manual for Archaeological Field Methods*, edited by the late Professor Robert F. Heizer in 1949. That initial spiral-bound edition had fewer than 100 pages, with chapters written mainly by students, and it was designed to be a field manual for Central California archaeology. It was published by National Press of Millbrae, California, as were several revisions, until 1975 when Mayfield Publishing Company took its place.

The book has gone through several editions, with the first hardcover version published in 1958. Major restructuring was done for the edition published by Heizer and Graham (1967), which became the most widely used field methods book in North America. The sixth edition, by Hester et al.

(1975), further expanded the book's scope and coverage and sought to deal with some of the criticisms of the 1967 edition.

The present volume has been extensively reorganized and rewritten. Although Professor Heizer died in 1979, he had given Hester a "marked-up" copy of the 1975 edition, annotated with errors and with some ideas for its later revisions; a number of these have been incorporated here. Although we have eliminated many of the older and more obscure references for which he had great fondness, we continue to cite selected older references because we feel they are important in giving a sense of history of field methods to beginning students. Heizer always viewed the book, in its later incarnations, not as a manual on "how to do archaeology," but rather as a guide to the approaches that archaeologists have used in surveying, excavating, and documenting sites of various kinds.

Thus, we wish to dedicate this seventh edition to the memory of Professor Heizer. He did extensive fieldwork in California, the Great Basin, and Mexico. Perhaps his most challenging fieldwork was at the Olmec site of La Venta in 1955; it was certainly the place where he made his most cherished field discovery—a ritual grouping of standing Olmec figurines shown on page ix. A detailed description of how this feature was discovered and the careful reading of its stratigraphic placement can be found in Drucker et al. (1959:152–161).

ACKNOWLEDGMENTS

With a volume of this scope, and with the many people who have contributed to its development, it is literally impossible to express our thanks to each individual. Numerous students and staff members have been of invaluable assistance. In addition, a number of colleagues have aided by providing references, illustrations, and other assistance. These include (alphabetically) Elizabeth Andrews, Stephen L. Black, David L. Carlson, Michael B. Collins, Darrell Creel, E. Mott Davis, Paul Goldberg, John A. Graham, Jessica Johnson, Donald R. Lewis, Robert J. Mallouf, Joseph Michels, Paul

Storch, Dee Ann Story, David Hurst Thomas and the American Museum of Natural History, Alston Thoms, David Van Horn, and many members of the staff at the Texas Archeological Research Laboratory, the University of Texas at Austin.

Then, there are our valued collaborators (including some who stuck with us from the 1975 edition), who have contributed their expertise and knowledge to this volume. For some, it must have seemed that their chapters were always returning to them, year after year, for updates required by the incredible pace of archaeological developments. How they remained cheerful and helpful is a mystery, but indeed a credit to their scholarship. The chapters written by these authors reflect just how diverse archaeology has become, the broad parameters within which archaeologists plan and execute fieldwork in the field, and the vast literature that characterizes the discipline at the end of the twentieth century.

There have also been, over the past decade, more than a dozen reviewers of the book, sometimes reading groups of chapters, sometimes confronted with the whole thing. They have offered us much useful advice, and perhaps more important, most have expressed the belief that such a book is indeed necessary. We have tried to address as many of their concerns as possible, and we thank them for their efforts. Among their number are J. M. Adovasio, Mercyhurst College; Mary Beaudry, Boston University; Colin Busby, Basin Research Associates; Richard I. Ford, University of Michigan; Sylvia Gaines, Arizona State University; E. B. Jelks, Illinois State University; Rosemary A. Joyce, University of California, Berkeley; W. Frederick Limp, Arkansas Archeological Survey; Barbara Mills, University of Arizona; Timothy R. Pauketat, University of Okla- homa; Jerome C. Rose, University of Arkansas, Fayetteville; James Schoenwetter, Arizona State University; David Hurst Thomas, American Museum of Natural History; Nicholas Toth, Indiana University; Gail Wagner, University of South Carolina, and Gary S. Webster, Pennsylvania State University.

Jerrilyn McLerran, archaeologist and editor, stepped in at the last moment to do a final overhaul of the chapters, searching out redundancies, correcting style and grammar, ferreting out the missing references, and otherwise providing invaluable help. We are deeply in her debt. Her calm approach and thoroughness are tremendously appreciated.

The staff at Mayfield has been tremendously helpful, and we sincerely thank Carla White, production editor; Robin Mouart, art editor; Marty Granahan, rights and permissions editor; and Bev DeWitt, a great copyeditor.

We reserve, however, all of the superlatives that we can muster for Jan Beatty, senior editor for Mayfield Publishing Company. Her patience and endurance are unmatched, given the length of time it took to pull this volume together. We tested her faith many times with assurances that the book would indeed, someday, be finished. But whether she believed us or not, her continued support and necessary prodding kept the project moving forward, and her goal of seeing it published before the end of the millennium has been accomplished. Words cannot express our gratitude to her for sticking with us.

Finally, we thank our families for their tolerance and encouragement during the preparation of this book.

THOMAS R. HESTER
HARRY J. SHAFER
KENNETH L. FEDER

This seventh edition of *Field Methods in Archaeology* is dedicated to the late Robert F. Heizer (1915–1979). With *A Manual of Archaeological Field Methods*, a guide of fewer than 100 pages published by National Press of Millbrae, California, in 1949, Heizer began the editing of a series of field methods volumes. Though originally intended as a field manual of Central California archaeology, interest in this review of field techniques led to expanded versions of the book, including the 1967 edition with John A. Graham (National Press, Palo Alto) and the 1975 edition by Hester, Heizer, and Graham (published by Mayfield, the successor to National Press). Heizer saw these books not as manuals of how to do archaeology, but rather as guides to the many different approaches that archaeologists have used in surveying, digging, and documenting sites of various kinds in different regions. He also felt that extensive citations were critical in order to expose both students and professionals to a broader literature on field archaeology and its history. Given the breadth of coverage—and the length of the bibliography—in this edition, we think he would be pleased.

Robert F. Heizer (1915–1979).

1

Introduction

Thomas R. Hester

Archaeology has undergone profound methodological and theoretical changes since the
publication in 1975 of the sixth edition of *Field
Methods in Archaeology* (for a succinct overview
of changes in field methods, see Haag [1986]).
Although this is a book on "field methods," we
have tried to incorporate numerous examples of
these new directions. Despite the book's New World
emphasis, we have also attempted to provide information useful for fieldwork in any part of the world
on the sites of both hunters and gatherers and complex societies. As Chapter 2 illustrates, the many
different kinds of archaeology are being practiced
these days by an amazing array of specialists.

CONTEMPORARY ISSUES

Cultural resource management (CRM) archaeology,
just underway in the mid-1970s, has dominated
American archaeology in the 1980s and 1990s

(Adovasio and Carlisle 1988) and is also conducted
in other parts of the world (for its impact on British
archaeology, see McGill 1995). CRM, or "rescue,"
archaeology seeks to deal with the effects on
archaeological sites of construction done under
state or federal permit (Knudson 1986). The authors
have been involved, at various levels, in this work
and have tried to integrate CRM goals with what
we continue to believe are solid field methods.
McHargue and Roberts (1977) have published a
field guide for "conservation archaeology," but it is
now rather outdated. A number of paper-length
syntheses and monographs specifically relating to
method and theory in CRM archaeology have also
been published (see Chapter 2).

Site formation processes have also attracted
much attention in recent years, in large part as a
result of Schiffer's (1987) study. Formation processes must be viewed, in many cases, in a broad
geomorphological perspective; we recommend a
recent volume by Waters (1992) as an easy-to-read

guide to the subject. In addition, Courty et al. (1989) introduce geological micromorphology to the study of site-deposit accrual. The whole issue of deposition is also part of soil science and the evolution of landscapes (Holliday 1992). Indeed, geoarchaeology and other things "geo-" are at the forefront of archaeology today; for example, geophysical site detection methods are common (with two examples being the work of Sheets [1992] and Roosevelt [1991]), along with forms of remote sensing (e.g., Donoghue and Shennan 1988).

Site destruction and concerns for site preservation are a major issue in contemporary archaeology and the focus of a considerable literature. The subject is often intertwined with CRM studies. Of equal concern is the rapid disappearance of sites at the hands of relic collectors and pothunters (Figure 1.1). We are pleased to see that in many states the number of avocational archaeologists is increasing dramatically and that they are deeply involved in site protection (Patterson 1988)—and also that the Society for American Archaeology, through its Don E. Crabtree Award, has provided annual recognition to outstanding avocationals in the New World, with awards since 1988 having gone to both Americans and Canadians.

Public education is clearly one key to halting the looting of sites, and all archaeologists—professional, avocational, and students—need to be involved in talks to civic clubs and school classes and in the writing of articles and books that convey the results of archaeological fieldwork (and the importance of those results) to the general public (e.g., Shafer 1986). The public also needs to be cured of its infatuation with the "mystical" side of archaeology (for excellent efforts in this cause, see Feder [1990a] and Williams [1991]). Many states have introduced an Archaeology Awareness Week (in Arizona and Texas, this has been expanded to Archaeology Awareness Month!). Archaeologists should do everything possible to support and expand such efforts. I am unaware of similar observances in other countries but hope that they will be developed as part of public education.

Another approach to site preservation is the purchase and protection of sites through the pri-

vately funded efforts of the Archaeological Conservancy, an organization that clearly deserves much support. Write for membership information to 5301 Central Avenue NE, Suite 218, Albuquerque, NM 87108-1517.

In addition, there is a growing literature on the value of the "site" as an archaeological concept (Dunnell and Dancey 1983). Ebert (1992) has articulated his concerns about overemphasis on "sites" and a lack of concern with the archaeological record elsewhere in the landscape. Foley (e.g., 1981) has also written extensively on "off-site" archaeology.

Also a highly sensitive issue today is the handling of human remains and associated grave objects. In the United States, grave furnishings, sacred objects, and burials may be subject to reburial under the terms of the Native American Graves Protection and Repatriation Act, enacted by Congress in 1990, and through laws passed by individual states. This issue has led to considerable acrimony between some Native Americans and some archaeologists. Additional details are presented in Chapters 2 and 11.

THE BURGEONING LITERATURE

The number of archaeologists, the number of archaeological projects, and the number of archaeological publications have increased dramatically in recent years. There is little one can do to keep up with the literature, especially the so-called gray literature resulting from some CRM projects. Efforts have been made to organize the burgeoning CRM and traditional archaeological literature through the compilation of archaeological bibliographies (e.g., Anderson 1982; Ellis 1982; Heizer et al. 1980; Weeks 1994), the publication of abstracts (either nationally, *Abstracts in Anthropology,* or by state, e.g., *Abstracts in Texas Contract Archaeology*), and by assembling archaeological encyclopedias (e.g., Fagan, in prep.; Evans and Webster, in prep.; and the multivolume *Enciclopedia Archeologica* to appear in Rome in the late 1990s). Although our editors would doubtless have preferred that the Refer-

Figure 1.1   Potholes representing looting activity at a rockshelter in the lower Pecos region of southwestern Texas.

ences Cited section of this book be much briefer, we have created a rather formidable listing, one we hope will serve as a useful reference tool.

This revision of the *Field Methods* lineage is but one of a number of field guides. We note in particular Joukowsky (1980), an effort that has broad coverage but is based largely on excavations in the Mediterranean region; Fladmark (1978, and numerous printings thereof), which has a step-by-step orientation and much attention to logistics; Dancey (1981), a small volume that admirably integrates goals, formation processes, and research design with field methods; Barker (1982), focusing largely on British archaeology but with approaches to field methods that can be used at many sites; Newlands and Breede (1976) on Canadian field methods; and Dever and Lance (1978), a handbook for the excavation of Bronze and Iron Age sites in the Middle East.

There are also notable, and more specific, contributions, such as Dillon's (1989) *Practical Archaeology*, with chapters ranging from field mapping to site survey by muleback! A popularly written volume including much about field and lab methods is McIntosh's (1986) *Practical Archaeologist*. Local societies are also preparing field and lab manuals; one that I have used in several field schools is by Hemion (1988). Finally, fieldworkers ought to look at *Australian Field Archaeology* (Connah 1983). Although specific to Australia, its 19 chapters cover a vast array of topics, including terrestrial photogrammetry, aerial photography, geoarchaeology, rock art recording, and report writing and publication—subjects of interest to archaeologists worldwide.

The illustration of archaeological finds, so critical to any report, is covered in several guides, especially Addington (1986), Adkins and Adkins (1989), and Dillon (1985).

ARCHAEOLOGY AND ARCHAEOLOGISTS

As the reader will learn, there are many definitions (and kinds) of archaeology. And, the vast majority of the public has little knowledge of what an archaeologist does. At cocktail parties, you invariably meet a few people who "always wanted to be an archaeologist" (but became physicians or lawyers because they knew they "couldn't make any money doing archaeology"). And, of course, most others you meet will think that you study dinosaurs and fossils. My youngest daughter, having grown up with an archaeologist, with his messy office and frequent absences for fieldwork, wrote the following unsolicited definition of an archaeologist some years ago and left it on my desk. The typewriter is gone now and the word processor is running, but the other aspects are aptly stated:

> *The Archaeolgist:*
> A person with a lot of files, books, flints, artafacts, pictures, drawers. Well, he has a hole lot of things. He goes on digs a hole lot. He has a typewriter; he uses it all the time. I should know, I'm a daughter of a archaeolgist.
>
> *Amy Hester*
> *Age 8 (1985)*

One final note about who archaeologists are and how archaeology is done. Our advice—indeed our warning—to the reader of this and similar books is that field archaeology cannot be done "cookbook" style. Fieldwork requires much advance planning and the ability to modify strategies in the field if conditions warrant. We intend this book to provide some guidance in certain areas of major concern in field archaeology. We also point out in many of its chapters that the key ingredient to a successful field project is to be a careful observer, a diligent recorder—and always to be *thinking* about what you are doing in the excavation of irreplaceable resources.

GUIDE TO FURTHER READING

Field Methods

Barker 1982; Dancey 1981; Dillon 1989; Fladmark 1978; Haag 1986; Joukowsky 1980; Sharer and Ashmore 1993; Thomas 1989

Contemporary Issues

Adovasio and Carlisle 1988; Ebert 1992; Knudson 1986; Schiffer 1987; Sheets 1992; Waters 1992

CHAPTER

2

Goals of Archaeological Investigation

Harry J. Shafer

What are the goals and objectives of archaeological fieldwork? How do they relate to those of the discipline itself? An ultimate goal of **archaeology**—and an appropriate definition for the discipline—is the study of human behavior and cultural change in the past (Trigger 1989:371). Such a broad definition allows for the distinction of several kinds of archaeology, each with its own set of goals. Archaeology, not unlike the cultures and societies under its focus, has undergone many changes over the past century; with each change, new goals have replaced or amplified old ones (Trigger 1989:370–411).

KINDS OF ARCHAEOLOGY

As recently as two decades ago, archaeology taught in American universities could conveniently be divided into studies of the classical world, pre-historic archaeology, and historical archaeology. Today, however, these divisions hold less-distinctive meaning because the more eclectic goals of anthropological archaeology and studies of human ecology have greatly influenced the aims of classic and historical archaeology. We think it is appropriate to outline some of the differences in the goals of various subareas of archaeology.

In America, or in Americanist archaeology, prehistoric and historic archaeology are usually taught under the discipline of **anthropology,** which is the study of humankind in the broadest sense. Archaeology, which concerns itself with the remains of the human past, is one of the subdisciplines of anthropology that studies the development of human culture through time. The advantage archaeologists have is in the depth and breadth of the material record, the large blocks of time within which they may examine culture change and development.

Archaeology of the Classical World

In the United States, archaeologists who specialize in the classical world, or **classical archaeologists,** are usually associated with classics or art history studies. They generally are art historians or classics scholars who use the methods and techniques of archaeology to recover the art and architectural remains of classical civilizations. Classics scholars take advantage of the ancient written records and texts in Greek, Latin, Sumerian, and Egyptian to help them document and understand these ancient civilizations. Working with these scholars are art historians who use art styles and architecture to understand the past (Figure 2.1).

The goals of classical archaeology are by its nature historical in orientation, focusing on details of architecture, recovery of art objects, the tracing of art and architectural themes, and the development of written language. Classical archaeologists in the past have dealt primarily with only portions of the civilizations they were studying by excavating palaces, temples, theaters, and royal cemeteries. The goals of classical archaeologists today, however, are more encompassing, including interdisciplinary approaches to study all facets of the ancient civilization in question (Bass and van Doorninck 1982; Gualtieri et al. 1983; Wiseman 1983).

The contributions of classical archaeology to the study of ancient history, art, and architecture are many. Archaeology today owes much to art historians and classics scholars for deciphering the ancient written records and thus opening new fields of awareness and understanding of the classical world. These archaeologists also lead advances in the study of art, architecture, and by necessity, the development of conservation and restoration techniques for architecture, frescoes, mosaics, metals, clay tablets, and other artifacts.

Figure 2.1   The Hellenistic theater at the classical archaeological site of Ephesus, Turkey.

Prehistoric Archaeology

Prehistoric archaeology is an awkward term usually defined as the study of societies and remains without the benefit of the written record (Figure 2.2). *Prehistoric,* meaning quite literally "before recorded history," includes the entire depth (ca. 2–3 million years) and breadth of human culture before recorded history. Because recorded history began 6,000 or so years ago in some parts of the world but not until the twentieth century in other parts, the term *prehistory* is awkward.

Because the greatest block of human culture history occurred before the invention of writing, however, most archaeology is concerned with the study of the human past prior to historic witnesses. The basic methods and techniques applied to prehistoric archaeology are the same as those used in historical and nautical archaeology because all three share problems of establishing and maintaining contextual integrity.

Historical Archaeology

Historical archaeology is the study of colonial and postcolonial settlements, generally within historical or anthropological frameworks. In the United States, it is an area of scholarly research that has developed since the 1940s. Scholars realized, for

Figure 2.2 Hinds Cave, a large prehistoric rockshelter site in Val Verde County, Texas.

example, that the development of American culture had left a material record amenable to archaeological study much in the manner of prehistoric archaeology. Historical archaeology, however, is global and comparative with regard to colonial and postcolonial studies (Falk 1991); for example, there are parallel developments of historical archaeology in Australia (Allen 1978), South Africa (Falk 1991), and the West Indies (Armstrong 1990).

In the New World, historical archaeology is concerned with the time period from the sixteenth to the twentieth centuries (Figure 2.3). Its goals may be either anthropological or historical in nature—or both. Among the broad topics covered under historical archaeology in the United States, for example, are the remains of European colonial period (Noel-Hume 1982), Spanish mission period (Farnsworth and Williams 1992), and plantation period (Armstrong 1990; Orser 1988; Singleton 1985) settlements; historic shipwrecks (Bass 1988); sites of historical events such as battlefields (Bond 1979; Scott et al. 1989); and postcontact Native American sites (Shafer et al. 1994). Historic sites may be identified through material remains, historical sources, or oral histories (i.e., interviews with living informants).

Historical sites are investigated mostly using the methods and techniques of prehistoric archaeology but with some significant additions, such as the use of historical documents and oral histories. Historical documents, however, record only specific kinds of information about the past, and oral histories are sometimes affected by faded recollections over time. Archaeology can be used to round out the information known from historical documents and sources and can provide a more complete documentation and understanding of historical events (Deetz 1977; Noel-Hume 1982; Scott et al. 1989). Conversely, because specific details and dates can be verified through the historical records, historical archaeology has a great potential for testing anthropological and archaeological theories and documenting the processes of culture change (Deagan 1991; Deetz 1977, 1991; Deetz and Dethlefsen 1965; South 1977a, 1977b). Although the more immediate goals of historical

Figure 2.3 View of excavations at the eighteenth-century Spanish colonial mission site of San Bernardo, Guerrero, Coahuila, Mexico.

archaeology may appear to be purely historical in nature, more often than not they involve ecological, subsistence, functional, or sociocultural problems.

The journal of the Society for Historical Archaeology, *Historical Archaeology*, serves as a scholarly outlet for studies in this subarea. This journal is a recommended reference for students interested in exploring the depth and breadth of historical archaeology.

There are areas of specific interest within historical archaeology that appropriately have their own goals, methods, and techniques. These are industrial archaeology and nautical or underwater archaeology.

Industrial Archaeology. Unlike in other subfields of archaeology, digging is rarely necessary in **industrial archaeology.** The primary goal in fieldwork is precise recording—drawing, mapping, and photography—of standing structures and ruins. Although the techniques and skills of industrial archaeology generally require training in engineering, architecture, and architectural history (Starbuck 1994), any technically trained archaeologist with expertise and interest in American culture would feel at home in this subfield.

The Society for Industrial Archaeology was founded in 1971; membership is especially strong in the northeastern industrial areas of the country and in the western mining regions of California and Nevada (Starbuck 1994). Recent books and monographs on the subject include Council et al. (1991), Gordon and Malone (1994), and Rolando (1992).

Nautical or Underwater Archaeology. The subfield of **underwater** or **nautical archaeology** is defined on the basis of the environment of deposition, not so much on the approaches or goals of its practitioners. Although often thought of as "shipwreck archaeology," nautical archaeology includes not only shipwrecks but submerged architecture, such as portions of the seventeenth-century English port city of Port Royal, Jamaica (Hamilton 1984; Figure 2.4) and many other cultural/historical features including prehistoric sites (Arnold 1989, 1992; Muckelroy 1980). The techniques of documentation and recovery are much the same as those used on land but adapted to the underwater environment (Bass and van Doorninck 1982; Dean et al. 1992). New developments in sonar and magnetometer technologies along with improved approaches in photography and computer graphics have greatly enhanced the tools of the nautical archaeologist.

Recovering data from under water is a delicate task requiring specific skills and equipment. The goals of underwater archaeology are often historical in orientation, in part because of the relationship of the site to historical documents or known events. Ancient shipwrecks, for example, represent time capsules that possess unique potential in studying the past civilizations of which they were once a part. The subject matter of underwater archaeology, however, extends to studies of ancient trade, commerce, colonial expansion and settlement, shipbuilding technology, navigation, and weaponry and warfare, as well as to the examination of submerged prehistoric archaeological sites for cultural resource management and salvage purposes.

Prehistoric archaeological sites are sometimes encountered in underwater contexts (Dunbar et al. 1989; Muckelroy 1980). These kinds of sites require standard approaches to working under water; the technology of recovery is basically the same as for any other underwater site, but the goals of the

Figure 2.4 Two divers, breathing on hooka (a Turkish acronym used by divers to refer to surface-supplied air), recording finds on the brick floor of a building that sank in the 1969 earthquake at Port Royal, Jamaica.

research are structured in the paradigms of prehistoric archaeology.

Removing materials from waterlogged contexts has been problematic, but great advances in material conservation have been made in treating artifacts recovered from waterlogged environments. These advances benefit the field as a whole (Hamilton 1976) because waterlogged sites also occur in terrestrial situations (Daugherty 1988; Doran and Dickel 1988; Purdy 1988), but in these cases the archaeologists work above water.

ANTHROPOLOGICAL ARCHAEOLOGY: A CHRONOLOGY OF CHANGE

American archaeology, which is deeply rooted in anthropology, has undergone several major changes in philosophy, methods, and techniques over the past century. Each of these developments brought about shifts in goals for fieldwork and theoretical interpretations. For convenience, Willey and Sabloff (1993:8–10) label these periods of change cultural-historical era, processual era, and postprocessual era.

Cultural-historical Era

Much of American archaeology during the first half of the twentieth century was concerned with developing culture histories by classifying thousands of artifacts and sites and ordering them in time and space. The goal of these activities was mainly the identification of **cultural norms,** the abstract rules that regulate human behavior; these so-called **normative archaeologists** devoted much energy to defining the typical example of an artifact or a site and compiled trait lists to define a culture; variability was often explained as outside "influence" or "ceremonial." Cultures were defined and compared on the basis of similarities and differences in material traits.

The cultural-historical approach produced an enormous body of material, which was ordered using a multitude of descriptive and classificatory schemes (the Classificatory-Descriptive period defined by Willey and Sabloff [1993:96–121]; Figure 2.5). Its proponents often claimed that the nonmaterial aspects of culture (such as social organization, religious beliefs, etc.) were beyond the means of archaeological inquiry.

Although the cultural-historical era of American archaeology was seen by some archaeologists of the 1960s as a kind of dark age, excellent building blocks were established in many areas of the New World in the form of chronologies and temporal and spatial frameworks. Regional patterning among archaeological assemblages and major prehistoric cultural systems (for example, Hopewell and Mississippian in the east and the Anasazi, Mogollon, and Hohokam in the Southwest) were initially defined during this period.

To build secure chronologies, it was also necessary to develop sound stratigraphic controls and reliable dating methods. The advent of **dendrochronology,** or tree-ring dating, enhanced the development of superbly dated sequences in the American Southwest; stratigraphic studies, ceramic seriation, and cross-dating provided excellent working chronologies in the Southeast, Mesoamerica, and South America.

The direction of prehistoric archaeology began to show a major shift in the 1950s. It moved beyond building culture histories to establishing environmental contexts and ecological contexts against which the culture change observed in the chronologies could be compared. As Gibbon (1984:7) defines it, **cultural ecology** is "the view that sociocultural systems are adapted for exploiting particular portions of their environment through the use of certain technologies, and that the form of a sociocultural system is in large part determined by the ecological conditions to which it is adjusted." The archaeological studies of Starr Carr by Clark (1954), the Jarmo project directed by Robert Braidwood (Braidwood and Howe 1962), MacNeish's (1970) Tehuacan Valley project, and the work of Hole et al. (1967) in the Deh Luran Plain are classic examples of this trend toward ecological and multidisciplinary studies. The initial emphasis of cultural ecology is the relationship between human adaptations and the environment and a better understanding of the human-land relationship. This new goal, together with a plea to seek contextual and functional relationships in the archaeological record by W. W. Taylor (1948), amounted to a change in direction before the theoretical storm that hit American archaeology in the 1960s brought about the most dramatic switch in goals that the discipline has yet witnessed.

New or Processual Archaeology Era

The most punctuated change in the goals of American archaeology can be credited largely to Lewis Binford and his paper "Archaeology as Anthropology" (1962). In this study, Binford, influenced by the teaching of anthropologist Leslie White, employed both a cultural materialist and a systems approach in the analysis of Old Copper culture artifacts from the Midwest to show how intangible aspects of human culture could be inferred from the material remains of the past.

Binford, like many of his colleagues, found the traditional emphasis on typology and chronology building essentially dead ends and challenged his colleagues to go beyond these goals and bring archaeology more in line with cultural materialists' approaches in anthropology. **Cultural materialism** stresses the relationship between environment and technology and assumes that technology is the most determinant factor in cultural evolution

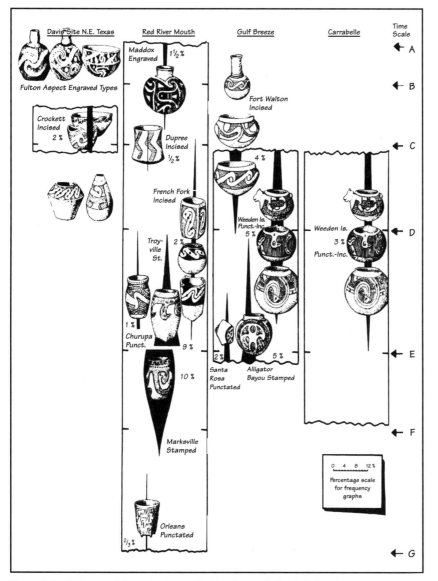

Figure 2.5   Pottery seriation chart compiled by James A. Ford during the Classificatory-Descriptive period in American archaeology.

(Gibbon 1984:7–8). In this view, it is through technology that a cultural system articulates with its environment. Gibbon (1984:8) states that "as cultural materialists, archaeologists attempt to trace the presumed causal connections running from ecological systems through technology and its organization in economic systems to the sociocul-tural system and culture itself." Cultural materialists further assume that social organization and ideology are adaptive responses to technoeconomic conditions (Harris 1968:240).

Above all, Binford introduced the philosophical debate over whether archaeology could be a science and stressed the need for archaeologists to become more scientific in deriving inferences about the past (Binford 1965; Binford and Binford 1968; see also Watson et al. 1971, 1984). Binford's influence on the field was dramatic and widespread; the result became known as "new" archaeology.

With new archaeology came the philosophy of **logical positivism,** which advocated a deductive reasoning process and hypothesis testing to define laws of human behavior. The philosophy of logical positivism could be used to formulate predictive statements about the past. This explanatory approach introduced a new paradigm, or theoretical framework, into American archaeology, with its own research methods and procedures (Willey and Sabloff 1993).

The popularity of a rigidly applied, cookbook version of logical positivism in archaeology has waned in the past decade, but the concern to establish a firm scientific foundation for archaeology whereby results are verifiable and models are tested with independent data sets has not (Gibbon 1984; Watson et al. 1984). Cultural histories, for example, are no longer rejected outright as unscientific and invalid.

> In this prehistoric archaeological paradigm [of processual studies], data are used inductively to generate temporal and spatial frameworks that define the past. In this way, cultural historical interpretations provide the foundation for deductive inquiry designed to identify specific causes of cultural change or stability. Variations within the cultural historical framework may be identified, and "normative" cultural concepts may be used to describe these changes, but only rigorously tested propositions can identify the causes of change and thereby begin to explain cultural process [*Sharer and Ashmore 1979:535*].

General systems theory is another borrowed and modified concept that became popular with the new archaeology. In this light, a culture was viewed as an open system conditioned by outside stimuli. Binford (1965:205) described a culture as "an extrasomatic system that is employed in the integration of a society with its environment and with other sociocultural systems." He also defined three subsystems of a culture (technology, social

organization, and ideology) and the material correlates of each (which he termed *technofacts, sociofacts,* and *ideofacts*). His aim was to show how the Old Copper artifacts could have functioned as sociofacts or technofacts within an otherwise Archaic cultural system.

That the field was ripe for change is indicated by the suddenness of the popularity of this new archaeology. Theory building took precedence over excavation and site reporting. What were formerly questions about the past became problems and hypotheses to be tested against independent data using a hypothetico-deductive reasoning process following philosopher Carl Hempel's (1965, 1966) model of scientific explanation. Inductive reasoning, whereby a conclusion is drawn on the basis of a set of observations, had typified the traditional approach to archaeology; this was now no longer in vogue. The historical reconstructions of the cultural-historical era were considered irrelevant and unscientific. The mere fact-finding typified by traditional archaeologists was rejected as a meaningful goal of research. Out of the new archaeology in the 1960s, a new goal emerged: to search for **nomothetic laws** (i.e., scientifically defined general laws) of human behavior (Flannery 1973; Watson et al. 1971), so that lawlike statements about past human behavior could be formulated (see Dunnell [1983]; Flannery [1973, 1982]; Hole [1978]; and Renfrew and Bahn [1991:432] for critical evaluations of this approach).

Another contribution of new archaeology was in assuming a systemic view of culture in the analysis of archaeological data (Hole and Heizer 1977:254–259, 358–361). Culture can be viewed in two conceptionally different ways. As Hole and Heizer (1977:255) note, the anthropological view assumes that a cultural system is composed of interrelated, interdependent parts (Figure 2.6). The ecological view of a culture system, on the other hand, sees a culture as analogous to an organismic system, possessing the same properties and affected by the same processes as all life systems (Clark 1968:43–130; Hole and Heizer 1977:356–361; Watson et al. 1984).

Binford (1965) saw the systemic approach, which stressed the interrelationships between com-

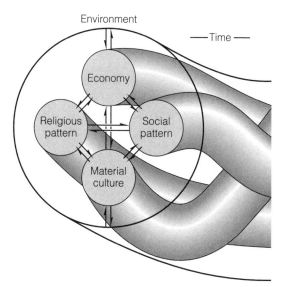

Environment

——Time——

Economy

Religious pattern

Social pattern

Material culture

Figure 2.6 A schematic model: subsystems of a socio-cultural system in dynamic equilibrium.

ponent parts, as an alternative to the normative approach, which viewed culture as a set of shared ideas or norms. In the systemic approach, the cultural system became the subject of study, and data from a site or sites were used to test hypotheses or models regarding change within the system. Consistent with the systems approach, **regional studies,** defining both cultural and environmental variability, and **settlement patterns** (Willey 1953), the study of spatial distribution of ancient settlements and activities, became popular in designing research in the era of the new archaeology.

Overall, new archaeologists were concerned with cultural process, that is, an evolving set of conditions that leads to change from one state to another. **Processual analysis** in archaeology examines the variables or factors that cause changes in the state of phenomena (e.g., from bands to chiefdoms, from chiefdoms to states, or from raw material to manufacture of finished product to discard (Hole and Heizer 1977:358–359; Schiffer 1987:13–46).

The gap between the material record and high-level theories or laws of human behavior was soon realized in the era of new archaeology and was the focus of attention by both Lewis Binford and

Michael Schiffer. Binford (1983b:48, 49) moved to help fill this gap by gaining a body of knowledge, or **middle-range theory,** on how the archaeological record was formed. Binford saw that such a body of knowledge was needed to improve the reliability of inferences made about the past.

Schiffer's solution to the tension between data-oriented and theory-oriented archaeologists at the onset of the era of new archaeology was another perspective on middle-range theory. It involved application of the notion of process to the study of material culture, or what Schiffer termed **behavioral archaeology.** Behavioral archaeology bridged the gap between ideographic and lawlike components by emphasizing the context and behavioral transformation of material culture as it flows throughout a cultural system (Schiffer 1987).

Both Binford and Schiffer have made enormous contributions toward advancing knowledge about how the archaeological record was formed, which have led to more sophisticated approaches in deriving inferences about the archaeological past. Greater understanding about the formation of the archaeological record opened the door for new methodologies and levels of study. For example, Schiffer pointed out two kinds of transformation processes that affect archaeological data: cultural or behavioral (discussed earlier) and natural. Inquiries into the natural processes gave rise to the subdiscipline **geoarchaeology,** the study of geomorphic processes as they pertain to the archaeology and paleoenvironments of a region (Waters 1992). The relationship between geology and archaeology had been of concern for some time, especially in Paleoindian studies (Haynes 1990), but the new levels of inquiry brought about by the focus on natural processes stimulated broader applications of geologic and geographic principles to landscapes and deposits holding archaeological data.

Other changes in methodologies and technology were stimulated by the new archaeology. For instance, beginning in the 1960s, computers became an essential tool of archaeological data retrieval and analysis (see Chapter 5). Field recovery and documentation methods were altered to accommodate the use of computers as analytical tools. The question of adequate and unbiased sampling came to the forefront, especially with the implementation of statistical procedures in data analysis. Many archaeologists became concerned with the effect of sampling strategies and sample size on the reliability of results (Ragir 1975; also see Chapter 3). Quantitative sampling for a broad body of data collected explicitly for computer-aided research changed field methods and strategies.

Before the 1970s, archaeologists focused on archaeological things (finished artifacts, features, architecture) and saved only "representative" samples of bone, debitage, and other bulk material. In the systemic approach, however, archaeologists emphasized quantitative sampling of each material class. Interdisciplinary expertise in archaeology increased as a result of ecological approaches in which past environments and their relevant material evidence (faunal, floral, geological) were encountered.

New sets of questions were being asked of archaeological data, necessitating changes in field methods and strategies; new methods and technologies—ones not available in previous decades of archaeology—were employed for soils analysis, faunal studies, analysis of human remains, recovery of pollen and plant macrofossil remains, dating, and artifact analysis. Interests in subsistence behavior, diet, and formation processes, and the ethical responsibilities of reporting on the whole material record recovered through fieldwork, have given rise to other subdisciplines—among them, **zooarchaeology,** the study of faunal remains from archaeological contexts (see Chapter 13); **bioarchaeology,** the study of human remains; and **paleobotany,** the study of plant remains from archaeological contexts (see Chapter 12).

Important goals of new archaeology were to develop a set of theories that linked the material past with human behavior and to understand the formation of the archaeological record. This approach sought to define the various cultural or behavioral and natural processes that together created the archaeological record that is present today (Binford 1983a:19–30; Schiffer 1983, 1987). The material remains that constitute the archaeological record are themselves in a dynamic environment

(Schiffer 1987). As Binford (1983a:19) notes, the only way we can understand the meaning of artifacts and other materials and how they are arranged is by obtaining knowledge about the dynamic processes or human activities that created them. Likewise, Schiffer (1976:4) in his strategies of behavioral archaeology proposed a similar relationship that linked the past and present with regard to material culture and human behavior.

In this effort, archaeologists have turned to **ethnoarchaeology,** the study of living peoples who make and utilize materials found in the archaeological record (Binford 1978b; Gould 1980; Hayden 1979; Yellen 1977a). Using both ethnographic observations and **experimental archaeology,** replicating prehistoric artifacts and features to understand the techniques and processes of their formation (Coles 1973; Ingersoll et al. 1977; Whittaker 1994), is at the heart of Binford's (1983b:48, 49) middle-range theory.

According to some archaeologists, the era of the new archaeology has passed (Dunnell 1983; Hodder 1986; Hole 1978; Trigger 1989). The two decades of debate left a positive legacy in several respects:

1. The debate resulted in a shift toward developing a science of archaeology (Gibbon 1984; Watson et al. 1984).

2. With a theoretical slant toward cultural ecology, the questions being asked in archaeology are more complex and encompassing than before the era of new archaeology.

3. Field methods of American archaeology now stress eclectic sampling strategies geared to maximizing data recovery for both problem generation (or cultural resource assessment) and problem solving.

4. Archaeologists are more explicit in their statements of research aims and methods.

5. Archaeologists are more conscious of sampling bias and sampling for complementary data for interdisciplinary studies.

6. Archaeologists are more aware of the relationship between archaeology and anthropology and the role archaeology plays in the study of culture change and process.

Postprocessual Era

The field of archaeology is once again going through a testing period of new theoretical approaches and paradigms. The cultural-historical approach was based on the comparative analysis of archaeological data to delineate temporal and spatial patterns. Broad cultures were defined based on a normative view; although the procedures of inquiry followed general scientific principles of hypothesis testing, the hypotheses were largely based on existing models of cultural norms. Processual archaeology focused on the relationships among the subsystems or variables of a cultural system, identifying feedback processes that stimulated culture change, and on the process of change itself, both behavioral and transformational. Both the cultural-historical and processual views examined ancient cultural systems from an outsider's perspective, irrespective of the belief systems and worldviews of the people being studied, and emphasized technology and material culture.

In this era of **postprocessual archaeology,** alternative views are currently being debated. The stimulus behind this paradigm shift is remarkably similar to that which brought about new archaeology: recognition of the inherent weaknesses in the existing paradigm (Cordell and Yannie 1991; Earle 1991). Preucel (1991a:1) sums up the postprocessual view quite succinctly: "the unbridled optimism and self-confidence of the 1960s processual archaeology are gone, and in their place is a more cautious, self-conscious archaeology that is struggling to find its place within the postmodern world."

Despite the plethora of approaches that have been introduced in the era of postprocessual archaeology, the mainstream of archaeology maintains the strengths of the cultural-historical and processual eras with some additions taken from postprocessual developments. Most significant, perhaps, is the addition of cognitive and symbolic aspects to interpretation and explanation (Flannery and Marcus 1983). Likewise, social and ideology factors are now recognized as active forces of change. These aspects of culture were not emphasized as forces of change in the processual era, although they were seen as integral parts of cultural systems.

Postprocessual archaeology was born out of a general dissatisfaction with the then-current state of archaeological method and theory (Preucel 1991:4). As defined by Ian Hodder (1986:181), one of its strongest European proponents, postprocessual archaeology "involves the breaking down of established, taken-for-granted, dichotomies, and opens up study of the relationships between norm and individual, processes and structure, material and ideal, object and subject." It stresses, among other things, the ideological aspects rather than the more technological, determinist or materialist interpretations, and it attempts to view cultural process from an insider's perspective. Postprocessual archaeology also assumes that mental structure, belief systems, and their respective institutionalized codes and symbols guide a culture's lifeways and adaptations. Symbolic/ideological factors can have causal significance, a point not addressed in processual archaeology, and the importance of an object includes both how it was used and how it was viewed. The main elements of postprocessual archaeology are perhaps best illustrated in the goals of contextual archaeology.

Contextual archaeology is an interpretive position that claims all understanding is historically and culturally situated (Johnsen and Olsen 1992). It holds that all aspects of an archaeological culture need to be studied to understand the significance of each part (Hodder 1982, 1986:121–155; Trigger 1989:349–350). The earliest notion of contextual archaeology, defined then as the "conjunctive approach," can be traced to Walter Taylor (1948:150–200). Taylor felt that the function of an artifact could best be determined on the basis of its context and association with other items. The more recent application of the concept according to Hodder (1986:143), states that "each object exists in several relevant dimensions at once," the totality of which defines its context. Contextual archaeology draws on a direct historical approach, using archaeological as well as nonarchaeological data such as oral traditions, linguistics, and comparative ethnography to formulate holistic models of prehistoric cultures. The outsider-insider dichotomy is best illustrated in the distinction made by contextual archaeology of two main types of meaning: functional interrelations and the structural content of ideas and symbols (Johnsen and Olsen 1992).

Functional interrelations are derived from knowledge of the human and physical environments; **structural interrelations** assume that cultures are systems of symbols in a highly structured matrix. The goal of these approaches is to identify the structures of context, thought, and symbolism and to determine how they shaped the ideas in the minds of the people who created the archaeological record (Renfrew and Bahn 1991:426–430). Archaeologists assume there are recurrent patterns of thought in different cultures and that these mental patterns are expressed in the material culture (Arnold 1983).

Another alternative view of postprocessual archaeology is that of **critical theory.** Critical theorists would argue that all inquiry is politicized; the social and political contexts of doing archaeology influence the kinds of questions we ask and the kinds of answers we frame even in our attempts to do objective science (Renfrew and Bahn 1991:430). Consequently, some archaeologists have moved away from processualism to a more relativist position. This alternative gives credence to a variety of approaches for explaining culture change (Hodder 1986:156–181; Trigger 1989:379–382). One important contribution of critical theory is its exposure of yet another area of bias in our procedures that influences our results. Probably nowhere is this more evident in Americanist archaeology than with the subjects of gender and, in cultural resource management, the determination of archaeological site significance, as discussed later in this chapter.

The **archaeology of gender** is a relatively new development, first considered in processual archaeology with the delineation of work space in archaeological communities (Binford 1983:144–194). Feminist thinking over the past two decades has profoundly influenced sociocultural studies, including archaeology. The gender issue has become a goal of postprocessual archaeological theory and practice, ranging from the topics of class formation, political power, organization of produc-

tion and units of production, and uses of space to the development of technologies (Conkey and Gero 1991). The edited volume by Joan Gero and Margaret Conkey (1991) entitled *Engendering Archaeology: Women and Prehistory* provides a broad perspective on gender in archaeology (also see Wylie 1992).

Modern archaeologists use diverse approaches and employ a variety of perspectives that depend on their specific research interests (Preucel 1991:14). Some insight into the diversity of interests and approaches to postprocessual archaeology in the Americas can be found in the edited volume by Robert W. Preucel (ed. 1991) entitled *Processual and Postprocessual Archaeologies: Multiple Ways of Knowing the Past.* The healthy proliferation of goals has served to broaden the growth and relevance of the discipline.

Another important shift in archaeological goals evolved as the result of federal legislation. Following a long developmental period that came to fruition in the 1970s and 1980s, this refocusing changed the way Americanist archaeologists think about archaeological sites. Before the 1970s, archaeological sites were narrowly viewed as places to plan excavations to fill in gaps of knowledge. The emphasis was on the *kinds* of information the site might contain. The new focus, not entirely contradictory, shifted attention to assessing the *significance* of a site or district with regard to the region's and the nation's archaeological heritage. This shift brought about a new subfield in American archaeology, cultural resource management.

Cultural Resource Management and Salvage Archaeology

Legislation passed in the 1960s and 1970s had a direct effect on the goals and directions of Americanist archaeology. The National Historic Preservation Act of 1966, and Section 106 as operationalized by Title 36 Code of Federal Regulations Part 800 enacted in 1974; the National Environmental Protection Act of 1969; Executive Order 11593 in 1971; and the Archaeological and Historical Preservation Act of 1974 resulted in a boom in contract or salvage archaeology (King et al. 1977).

Reservoir salvage archaeology, whereby selected cultural resources are excavated before they are lost during construction projects (Figure 2.7), was instituted in the 1930s as part of the Works Progress Administration (WPA). After World War II, the program of reservoir salvage continued, administered by the Smithsonian Institution River Basin Surveys Program. After the passage of the Reservoir Salvage Act in 1960, the National Park Service assumed the administration of the reservoir salvage program, providing block grants for participating institutions for the next decade.

Figure 2.7 Reservoir salvage excavations at the Devil's Mouth site, Val Verde County, Texas, before construction of the Amistad Dam and Reservoir.

The legislation of the 1960s and 1970s not only provided many millions of dollars for salvage and contract archaeology, but it also made contracts available to private firms as well as to museums and institutions of higher learning. The result was a new subarea of archaeology, **cultural resource management (CRM) archaeology** (popularly called **contract archaeology**). CRM archaeology includes among its goals: (1) managing the archaeological record by establishing and monitoring cultural inventories, (2) assessing site significance by determining the research potential and cultural value of each site and determining which sites should be saved or excavated through salvage archaeology and which ones will be sacrificed to impending construction projects, and (3) protecting and preserving cultural resources.

The second goal, assessing the significance of archaeological sites, introduces the potential for strong bias in the management process. Assessing the research value of a site or area requires a background in anthropological archaeology theory, regional archaeology, and archaeological priorities. Assessing the cultural value requires that the concerns of all people affected by the management decisions be intelligently and efficiently treated (King et al. 1977:103–104). Ultimately, what is recovered and what is not are determined on the basis of the cultural and research values plus budgetary constraints and construction deadlines if destruction is imminent. Rarely are all interests served in the process.

Firms responding to requests for proposals (RFPs) submit their project bids, and the awards are often granted to the lowest bidder. This introduces a "profit motive" into project planning that can conflict with and threaten the basic ethics and priorities of the discipline. CRM firms are required to meet specific contractual obligations as well as to perform broader research-oriented functions within the scope of a finite budget. It is the inclusion of the contract goals, such as inventorying, assessing, and preserving archaeological sites, that separates CRM from its predecessor, salvage archaeology.

The archaeological profession found itself ill-equipped to handle the legalities of federal and industrial contracts. Definitions of what constituted a professionally qualified archaeologist and standards of professional ethics were unavailable to contracting agencies and to members of the profession. The Society of Professional Archaeology (SOPA) was formed to help provide public accountability for and to lend reputability to the profession (McGimsey 1985).

The bulk of archaeology done in the United States today is carried out by the personnel and planners of CRM archaeology, a group Watson (1991) labels as almost an archaeological proletariat. Data recovery is generally standardized following state and federal guidelines. Despite the fact that CRM archaeology is producing most of the archaeological data being collected today, however, its interpretive potential has yet to be realized. CRM archaeology lies at the farthest distance intellectually from the theater of debates in archaeological theory (Watson 1991); one obvious reason is its project-specific goals.

Like its ancestor WPA archaeology, CRM archaeology is providing an enormous amount of new archaeological data that awaits synthesis. A major problem of contract archaeology, the result of budget constraints, is in the dissemination of results to colleagues (Hester 1981; Renfrew 1983). Another problem is that the scope of the investigations tends to be project specific; five projects in one area (such as segments of land designated for strip mining) may be contracted to five different firms from five distant headquarters. This piecemeal approach is a two-sided coin: On the one hand, it hinders communication, information flow, the benefit of experience, and ultimately, archaeology. On the other hand, multiple contract firms may in some instances provide variety in views and methodology that can benefit the field.

CRM archaeology has provided a wealth of new data on many previously unknown regions of the country, particularly large tracts of federal lands. CRM projects have made many highly significant contributions to American archaeology, especially in field methodology, where new methods and technology such as penetrating radar and electronic data management systems are being tested.

Native American Graves Protection and Repatriation Act of 1990

The Native American Graves Protection and Repatriation Act of 1990 (NAGPRA) was a carefully negotiated agreement between Native American organizations, archaeologists, museums, legislators, and other interested parties. The passage of this act prompted vigorous debates at the theoretical, legal, and ethical levels, resulting in yet another paradigm swing (see also Chapter 11). At issue are the rights to the study of Native American prehistory using the material remains. The extreme positions in the debate are clearly drawn: One side believes that the archaeological past belongs to Native Americans. Proponents argue that Native Americans should have control of what is studied,

how it is studied, and the final disposition of the material (Zimmerman 1994). At the other extreme are those who argue that repatriation is a threat to scholarly scientific study of American prehistory and the processes of cultural adaptation, development, and change—and to the discipline itself (Meighan 1994). The majority of Americanist archaeologists, however, find themselves somewhere between these extreme views. A healthy dialogue between archaeologists and Native American organizations is becoming more a practice than an exception (Allison 1996; Spector 1994).

NAGPRA compliance processes are currently underway and have resulted in the reburial of scores of archaeologically excavated human skeletal materials and associated cultural remains. Repatriation of Native American human remains is in process nationwide. Ethical debates continue, however, and focus on those remains that are clearly prehistoric and more often than not have no demonstrable tribal descendants (Lovis 1996). The peopling of North America was one of the more dramatic events in human history; this event and the processes that followed are certainly—and at the very least—worthy of scholarly scientific study inclusive of Native American interests.

GOALS OF ARCHAEOLOGY TODAY

The modern goals of most American anthropological archaeology retain aspects of cultural-historical, new, and postprocessual archaeology. These goals stress the need to establish temporal and spatial controls on the materials under study as well as to explain how the observed patterns and the archaeological record were formed (Binford 1971, 1983a:13–18; Fagan 1991a:43–45). These goals, as stated by Sharer and Ashmore (1993:35) are

1. To consider the *form* of archaeological evidence and its distribution in time and space.

2. To determine past *function* and thereby construct models of ancient behavior.

3. To delimit the *processes* of culture and determine how and why cultures change.

4. To understand cultural *meaning* through the context of symbols, values, and worldview.

Form

The first goal, form, is the description and classification of the material evidence that archaeologists uncover. It is an outgrowth of the cultural-historical approach and is **diachronic**—that is, focused on change over time—in perspective. Comparative studies of the material evidence allow archaeologists to develop models of artifact assemblage distribution through time and space.

It is through the study of form that site, regional, and areal **chronologies,** the ordering of cultural assemblages through time, are modeled. It is not possible to study function or period in time, process, or meaning without knowing the time and spatial limits of the culture under study. A sound culture chronology requires that collections be ordered and classified with regard to temporally and spatially sensitive artifact styles or other recognizable characteristics that serve to differentiate archaeological assemblages. The archaeologist constructs a framework tracing the historical development of cultural change by building local or regional sequences and even relating these to broader patterns and beyond.

Function

The second goal, determining function based on the study of form and association, focuses on knowing how things were used to understand the ancient behavior represented in the archaeological record. Function is both **synchronic**—that is, it focuses on a specific period of time—and **holistic**—it assumes that all aspects of a culture or cultures fit within the context of their environment (Braidwood and Howe 1962; Clark 1954; MacNeish 1970). A systemic approach, one that allows the archaeologist to order and divide the mass of data into meaningful units for analysis, is essential to achieving this goal.

It is through a combined study of form and function that models of lifeway reconstruction are made possible. Reconstruction of past lifeways involves modeling the cultural system or network of systems under study as far as the archaeological record and inferences about the past will permit. It usually involves reconstructing the past environment through ethnobotanical, faunal, and geoarchaeological studies; working from a well-defined cultural chronology; settlement pattern studies that examine the variation in settlement over the landscape through time and space; analysis of subsistence and dietary practices by incorporating zoological, ethnobotanical, skeletal, technological, ethnoarchaeological, and functional studies; and residential and mortuary studies to discern variability in social organization, complexities in the social system, and health. A past lifeway cannot be reconstructed from the excavation of a single site, although each site can provide both unique and comparative data. It is necessary to frame research at least on a regional scale to discern temporal and spatial variability, particularly in an environmentally diverse region.

Process

The third goal, understanding cultural process, is an attempt to explain how and why cultures change through time based on study of the material record. The whole record of human existence is used to explain the variations of the past. The study of culture process became a major goal of the new archaeology.

Meaning

The fourth goal, a postprocessual contribution, is perhaps the most difficult to achieve because it generally requires some basic knowledge of symbols and the worldview of the culture being studied. Sources of contextual data for symbols include inferences derived from a direct historical approach using ethnographies and oral histories. Applications of historical meaning to prehistoric examples are based on subjective judgments, but the strengths of these inferences, like any others in archaeology, are weighed on the appropriateness of the data and contexts from which they are derived.

GUIDE TO FURTHER READING

Goals (General)

Braidwood and Howe 1962; Clark 1954; Hole et al. 1967; MacNeish 1970; Taylor 1948; Trigger 1989; Willey and Sabloff 1993

New Archaeology

Binford 1962, 1965, 1983a; Binford and Binford 1968; Flannery 1973; Gibbon 1984; Renfrew and Bahn 1991; Schiffer 1987; Waters 1992; Watson et al. 1984

Postprocessual Archaeology

Gero and Conkey 1991; Hodder 1986; Preucel, ed. 1991; Trigger 1989

Historical Archaeology

Allen 1978; Armstrong 1990; Deagan 1991; Deetz 1977; Deetz and Dethlefsen 1965, Falk 1991; Farnsworth and Williams 1992; Noël-Hume 1982; Orser 1988; Scott et al. 1989; Shafer et al. 1994; Singleton 1985; South 1977a, 1977b

Industrial Archaeology

Council et al. 1991; Gordon and Malone 1994; Rolando 1992

Research Design and Sampling Techniques

Harry J. Shafer

The purpose of archaeological fieldwork is to acquire new information within the context of a program of research. Archaeologists do not simply go into the field and wander about in hopes of chancing upon some important find. Scientific research projects today range from goal-specific one-day ventures to long-term projects covering many field seasons. These projects are designed to accomplish specific goals or objectives, which may range from the assessment of the data potential or scientific significance of a particular site, geographic locale, or region; to surveys in a geographical or cultural region; to intensive excavations at a site or a series of sites in a region. The archaeological research design justifies the fieldwork and describes what is to be done; this requires much thought and careful planning. The sampling methods detail how the fieldwork as described in the research design is to be successfully carried out.

RESEARCH DESIGN

The **research design** states the strategies of the proposed research and defines the goals of the project; it is a guideline that describes step by step how the project is to be carried to completion. Guy Gibbon (1984:60) lists three functions of a research design. It:

1. Delimits the goals of a research project by clarifying the actual questions that archaeologists and other scientists want answered.

2. Provides more focused approaches by determining through trial formulation which goals and procedures will most economically, effectively, and objectively answer the questions that have been posed.

3. Minimizes error through the use of appropriate sampling methods and standardized collection and excavation procedures and

through the control of other extraneous variables that might adversely influence the outcome of a project.

A research design is analogous to the formal description of a scientific experiment and can take the form of a research proposal to the National Science Foundation or the National Endowment for the Humanities.

Research designs are an integral part of contractual agreements in CRM archaeology. Most RFPs from contracting agencies are written in accordance with state or federal guidelines and provide explicit outline requirements for research designs. Some RFPs provide more flexibility than do others. Any research design must be sufficiently flexible to allow for some restructuring or shifting of priorities in the field. When formulating a research design, one general rule of archaeological fieldwork should be kept in mind: expect the unexpected. A research design that is written too specifically and adhered to like a contract (as is sometimes the case with formal research designs in contract archaeology) can seriously encumber the intended goals of a project when the unexpected occurs.

Excellent examples of project research designs are those for the Dolores Archaeological Program (Kane et al. 1986; Robinson et al. 1986), the Roosevelt Platform Mound Study (Rice 1990), and the Roosevelt Rural Sites Study (Ciolek-Torrello et al. 1990). In these complex interdisciplinary projects, the programs were outlined in explicit detail, specifying the goals of the fieldwork, "mid-level" or analytical studies, and syntheses. Sharer and Ashmore (1993:151–156) provide a general model of a research design that outlines seven principal stages: formulation, implementation, data acquisition, data processing, analysis, interpretation, and dissemination of the results (Figure 3.1).

Formulation

The research problems or hypotheses to be tested through the fieldwork are defined in the formulation stage. Relevant background research that

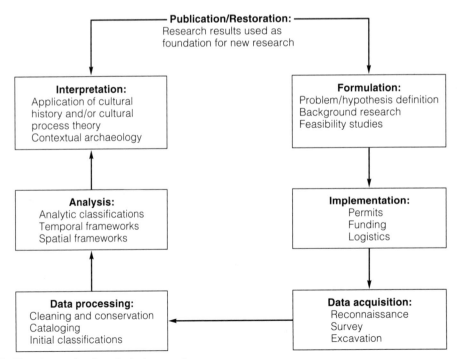

Figure 3.1   The stages of archaeological research.

reviews the history of the archaeological, geological, and any other studies pertinent to the problem supports these objectives. It is always advisable to visit the area of proposed research to investigate and familiarize oneself with the local conditions, initiate local contacts, and assess the overall feasibility (i.e., field logistics, time and budget constraints, and overall practicality) of the project.

Implementation

To implement the fieldwork, the necessary permits (if required), permission, and funding must be in hand, and any problems with field logistics must be resolved. Research on federal lands in the continental United States or on many state lands and in foreign countries requires some form of antiquities permit. Both foreign and domestic antiquities laws and customs vary and change often. The policies in effect in the state or country where the research will be conducted must be addressed by the investigator.

In the United States, it is essential to follow the guidelines of the Native American Graves Protection and Repatriation Act of 1990 and applicable state laws. Antiquities permits not only grant permission to work in the area in question but also specify where and how the specimens collected are to be housed and curated. Permission to conduct the work, whether on foreign, public, tribal, or private lands, is necessary before most foundations will release research funds to the investigator. Consultation with the appropriate Native American group before fieldwork has now become a requirement for most prehistoric archaeology in the United States.

Resolving logistics problems is crucial for any archaeological field project. No project, regardless of its goals, can be successful without proper field facilities (housing, board, and transportation) for the staff and crew. Poor morale as a result of unhealthy conditions or irresponsible leadership can threaten or doom a field project (and the director's career). The health, safety, and comfort of the field staff and crew are of paramount importance and deserve a top priority in planning and implementing field research. It is advisable (if not

required) that staff members carry health and accident insurance coverage (see Chapter 5).

Few projects describe their field camps (see Adams 1987), but larger projects include a camp director on the staff. The camp director's responsibility is to see that cooks are hired, food is kept in supply, fresh water is available, meals are nutritious and on time, and camp facilities (showers and latrines) are maintained. The camp director removes the headaches of camp logistics from the project director, whose time is better spent directing the fieldwork.

Data Acquisition

The research design also specifies the methods and techniques of data acquisition, whether reconnaissance, survey, or excavation. Sampling strategies will vary in accordance with project goals, region, nature of the investigation (i.e., survey or excavation), and site visibility and are discussed at length in the following section. For surveys, it is important to define the area to be investigated—its environmental characteristics and diversity—particularly noting physiographic or geomorphic situations that may affect the sample or the expected distribution of archaeological sites. Important points to consider include: how the reconnaissance or survey will be carried out, including how much of the area will be covered; how the sample units are to be defined and what methods of coverage will be used; and what strategies will be employed for data collection (for a discussion of survey methodology, see Chapter 4).

The approaches and standards to be used in excavation should be stated explicitly. For example, the research design should describe how the horizontal and vertical controls will be established and maintained throughout the project. Establishing permanent horizontal and vertical data points is advisable to maintain consistency from season to season and in the overall data collection. Standardized sampling units (i.e., 1-x-1-m or 2-x-2-m horizontal units excavated on a grid system by natural levels or in 10-cm or 20-cm arbitrary levels) help to provide comparable and quantifiable data sets. The research design should also state the methods of data collection, including screen size and collecting procedures to be used (see Chapter 5).

Data Processing

The research design should also specify how the field data will be processed and maintained for analysis and future reference. Achaeological artifacts may be processed either in the field laboratory or in a processing laboratory at the sponsoring institution or museum. Laboratory processing usually involves cleaning, sorting, and labeling the field specimens to preserve the provenience and contextual data. Artifacts are usually cataloged with field reference numbers; photographs or drawings may also be part of the documentation for certain artifacts. Preliminary analysis may be conducted on artifacts in a field lab. Although they require additional logistical consideration, such as waterproof storage and work space, field laboratories have the advantage of providing constant feedback to the field directors and staff with regard to what is being found. Field strategies and priorities may be altered in accordance with findings revealed during laboratory washing and sorting.

When field specimens are bagged and shipped directly to a museum or laboratory facility for processing and cataloging, the results often are not seen by the field staff for weeks or months. Separation of the laboratory from the field operations delays or eliminates feedback, opening the door for possible missed some field opportunities (see Chapter 5).

Data Analysis

The results of the field data analysis are intended to provide the information sought to shed light on the research problems or to test the hypotheses stated at the beginning of the research design. The objectives of the analysis, which data sets will be examined, how, and for what purpose should therefore be spelled out. Analysis of an eclectic body of field data usually involves sorting into material categories and employing one of several taxonomic approaches to facilitate description and define the ranges of variability within any data set.

These steps are necessary to relate the data to the contextual parameters established for the site or region, to define patterns of distribution in time and space.

Interpretation of Data

When writing a research design, it is rarely possible to know what the investigations will reveal, but archaeologists generally have their expectations. When a given research project addresses specific problems or hypotheses, the data generated by the field research must be synthesized and evaluated in an attempt either to test the proposed hypotheses or to investigate the problems or questions posed.

Interpretations must logically follow the analysis of the data used to examine the research questions and not simply be a restatement of what the researcher wanted to find. It is incumbent upon the researcher in any scientific study to describe and provide access to the basic data generated in the study in a manner that allows other researchers to examine it and derive their own conclusions independently.

Dissemination of the Results

The research design should anticipate the intended method of dissemination of results. Ultimately, the outlet or outlets often depend on the nature of the fieldwork, the volume of data accumulated, and the relevance of the findings in terms of broad or regional implications.

The efforts, findings, and experience of the archaeologist are lost unless the results of the research are disseminated to colleagues in the field. Unreported field data or analyses that go unfinished may represent tragic losses of irreplaceable data. The medium of dissemination is usually publication in the form of an article in a national, regional, or local journal; a monograph in a series; or a book. Specific research findings can be presented formally at a professional meeting as a paper or a poster session. Journal articles are often the medium for reporting ancillary findings or methodological approaches generated during the course of the research.

It is to the benefit of the field and usually the researcher to publicize summaries of the project or its findings in the popular media. Press releases by local or regional newspapers or through university media services potentially reach broad audiences via wire services. Admittedly, such releases occasionally misstate or misquote the authority but do acquaint the general public with important research projects and their findings.

SAMPLING METHODS

The inferences archaeologists make about the past are based in part on what is observable in the archaeological record, what is observed, and knowledge about how that record was formed. Archaeologists rarely have the opportunity to recover all material items contained within a unit of study, such as a region or site. Instead, they base their interpretations and explanations on observations of **samples.** Archaeologists customarily examine a segment of the record and generalize based on the assumption that the observed sample is representative. The validity of inferences about the object of study (region, site, segment of a site) depends on the sample observations' being mathematically representative of the whole (O'Neil 1993). Archaeological sampling is concerned with examining a portion of the archaeological record under study (region, site, stratum, etc.).

Compromises must be made as to how much to collect or sample when it is not possible or feasible to sample the entire universe of study. It is, after all, the information derived from the analysis of the sample on which the inferences about the whole are based. As D. H. Thomas (1978:232) states: "Fruitful archaeological research will always begin by generating samples, and culminate by generalizing about the population from which the sample was drawn. Archaeological field work should not be aimed at recovering populations, and archaeological analysis should not be aimed at generalizations about samples."

How can one be sure that the sample observed is representative of the whole and is not skewed by sampling bias? The best measure is to devise a sampling strategy that eliminates the chance of bias whenever possible; this can be accomplished by having a basic understanding of *what* is being investigated and *how* to best go about investigating it to permit accurate generalizations. Such an approach also forces visualization of the whole phenomenon that is the focus of study, whether it is a region, a site, or a complex of rooms or mounds within a site.

All archaeological study areas must be defined in time and space. The study area is the **sampling universe,** that is, the bounded area of investigation. There are two ways to approach sampling of this universe: nonprobabilistic (contextual) sampling and probabilistic (statistical or quantitative) sampling, which includes a variety of random sampling methods.

Nonprobabilistic Sampling

Up to the 1970s, most archaeological work used **nonprobabilistic sampling.** In this sampling approach, no effort is made to provide a basis of comparison for the amount of material recorded or collected; the primary emphasis is on presence or absence of material. This by no means suggests that nonprobabilistic sampling is automatically bad. Nonprobabilistic samples can be used to provide quantitative estimates. It's just that there are no means for measuring the accuracy of those estimates.

Nonprobabilistic sampling provides contextual information about an area, features, or a site. For instance, a hypothetical reconnaissance trip is made into a little-known valley of western Mexico. The locations of mound sites and features on the landscape are noted, the potential logistical problems involved in conducting a more-intensive survey are estimated, and site localities in fields and road cuts are visited to make collections (or grab samples) of diagnostic pottery and lithics. This is an example of nonprobabilistic sampling. Important contextual information can be gained from such a reconnaissance trip, particularly if the intent is to gather information for a major grant proposal or planning session. Such fact-finding visits, however, although they may reveal the presence of

Middle Preclassic pottery, provide no means of measuring the intensity of occupation for any period of time or the patterns of site location within the valley system.

Nonprobabilistic surveys, or reconnaissance projects, can provide useful information on the conditions of the archaeological sites in a region and an indication of the culture history in a short time and at low cost. A reconnaissance is especially appropriate when the archaeologist is unfamiliar with the setting, vegetation and environmental conditions, and site visibility. Nonprobabilistic surveys can provide information on where certain sites are located but not where all sites will be found or in what proportion (Flannery 1976a). Sampling in such instances is based on personal judgments or informal criteria such as accessibility or visibility.

In site excavations, nonprobabilistic data may be collected from shovel or auger probes, test pits, or exploratory excavations; excavation of selected cultural features or units such as hearths, burials, rooms, or mounds; or even by selectively placed block excavations made at the judgment of the field archaeologist. These kinds of explorations are often time saving and essential. In fact, data gathered by salvage (rescue) archaeology, such as house features or burials encountered in potential construction areas, are nonprobabilistic in nature. Such projects can provide useful information for designing excavation and sampling strategies.

Nonprobabilistic samples have been accumulated over the years in most agricultural regions of the United States by academic archaeologists, state or federal registries, and avocational societies. Most are records and collections accumulated individually, but together they provide excellent sources of information on the culture history of a particular region or site. Because these data were not systematically collected, they are rarely amenable to quantitative studies. Nonetheless, they are very important in identifying regional problems and in developing plans for examining those problems with more systematically acquired information. Archaeologists should not overlook the potential of such collections and archives (Meltzer 1986). To ignore such potential data could

seriously bias a segment of the region sampled by quantitative measures (e.g., Bonnie Hole's [1980] critique of Schiffer and House [1975]; also see Flannery [1976b]).

Until the 1970s, the most obvious archaeological sites were chosen for investigation and were dug until "adequate" samples were obtained for study. An adequate sample may have been a 5-ft square column 10 ft deep, 10 rooms or pit structures, or half the site. Many of these samples provided an accurate indication of the cultural stratigraphy, house types, etc., and the selection of sites and amounts excavated were often determined by skilled excavators (see, for example, Cosgrove and Cosgrove 1932; Kidder 1924; Newell and Krieger 1949; Wauchope 1966; Webb and DeJarnette 1942).

Many situations do not require probabilistic sampling (Flannery 1976a; Thomas 1978), and in such situations, it should not be imposed. Although the sampling methods of J. A. Ford (Ford 1951; Phillips et al. 1951) to provide comparable units of measurement for pottery collections made during a surface survey have been maligned for not being random in a statistical sense (Ragir 1975), the Lower Mississippi Valley sequences based on ceramic seriation have largely stood the test of time, probably because they were large enough to be sufficiently representative to document meaningful trends in ceramic attributes.

In summary, nonprobability samples are fine as a beginning. They can permit the framing of hypotheses that can then be supported or negated with specifiable degrees of confidence by probabilistic sampling.

Probabilistic Sampling

Probabilistic sampling techniques are based on the theory that the samples collected are related in mathematical terms to the population sampled. In probabilistic sampling, there is a basis for measuring the precision of the samples. The sampling universe is subdivided into **sample units,** which may be natural units (such as environmental zones) or arbitrary units (such as equal-size grid squares, or quadrats, and transects; Sharer and Ashmore

1979:96–105). Each unit or each combination of units has an equal chance of being selected (which is not the case in nonprobabilistic sampling).

The advantages of probabilistic sampling are that we can estimate the degree of bias and precision, specify the error rates, and generalize to unsampled areas with known confidence. The collection of all possible sample units or elements in the sampling universe constitutes the **target population;** the **sampled population** is that collection of elements from which the random sample is actually drawn. The character or nature of the target population determines the most feasible sampling strategy. The target and sampled populations may be one in the same. For instance, if a grid is superimposed over a site, the total number of grid squares also represents the population from which the percentage of units actually sampled is drawn.

Often, however, the target and sampled populations are different. For example, one may wish to know the diameter of all hemispherical Classic Mimbres bowls. The target population—in this case, Mimbres bowls—is capable of being precisely defined. The random sample is drawn from a smaller segment of the target population, which may be all Mimbres bowls housed at the Peabody Museum (because it is not possible to select a random sample of all extant bowls).

Once the sample population within the sampling universe is determined, the archaeologist must decide what percentage of that population will constitute a statistically viable or representative sample for projecting probability statements about the total universe. In situations that require investigation of all the sampling units, such as a 100 percent or full-coverage survey of a specifically defined tract of land, there is obviously no problem if the objective is to record all visible archaeological sites. But some regional surveys cover enormous land areas, and it is practical to survey only a portion. What are the best methods of selecting sample units and determining how much to sample?

Cluster Sampling. Each sample unit in archaeological fieldwork will likely contain a cluster of elements (such as pottery, lithics, burned rocks, etc.) (Binford 1975; Cochran 1963; Kintigh 1984; Mueller 1975; Ragir 1975; Read 1975). Krumbein (1965:143) defines **cluster sampling** as "a procedure by which more than one individual in the population being sampled is taken at each randomized position." A cluster of elements is taken from each unit selected on a random basis. Cluster sampling includes any instance where the sample units are defined in terms of *space* rather than *items.* Any sample based on quadrats or test pits is a cluster sample because not artifacts but the space or areas in which they are found are being selected. Clusters cannot be enumerated, whereas items within clusters can be counted and sampled directly. The spacing between sample units is random, but the spacing between elements within the cluster is not random. Cluster sampling is essential in archaeological situations where the frequency distributions between elements is being measured over space. For example, a grid system of 1-m units is superimposed over a site, and artifacts are collected from the surface and plotted according to grid location. The grid squares represent clusters within which the frequency of distribution of each item is plotted. Such a distribution map may show the nonrandom densities of artifacts and activity areas. Applications of cluster sampling in site investigations are illustrated in Binford et al. (1970), Redman and Watson (1970), and Winter (1976).

Nested Sampling. In nested sampling, each sampling level is nested within a higher level (Krumbein 1965:144). Ragir (1975:293) provides the following example of nested sampling:

> This system can be illustrated in areal sampling where, for example, the study area may include several townships as the top level, a random sample of square mile sections within the townships as the second level, a sample of archaeological sites located within the sections as the third level, and cluster samples of grid units on the sites as the fourth level. This kind of sampling is very useful when questions of regional scale of variability are part of the archaeological study.

When a variety of elements of unequal size and proportion are being collected, nested sampling is often essential. Also, a regional approach involves nested sampling: sites are selected for excavation, and then areas within sites are selected to excavate. If the collection is large, only some of the material recovered may be selected for analysis (e.g., examine 10 percent of the debitage for evidence of expedient use-wear). Objectives may include excavating several pueblo rooms whose ruins were used as a midden area by later generations. The midden will contain large quantities of animal bone, sherds, lithics, and botanical remains. Although it is unnecessary to use a screen smaller than ¼ inch to recover the needed pottery sample, that screen size is too large to recover a faunal sample as representative as one would want (Shaffer 1992b; see Chapter 13). Likewise, it would be too time-consuming to conduct flotation procedures on the excavated portion of the midden overlying the architecture; a measured volume of matrix would have to be drawn to recover a sample of botanical remains.

Selecting a Random Sampling Method.   A significant amount of archaeological literature has accumulated over the past two decades on probabilistic sampling techniques at both the regional (e.g., Chenhall 1975; Fish and Kowalewski 1990; Hill 1966; Mueller 1974, 1975; Plog 1976; Plog et al. 1978; Ragir 1975; Redman and Watson 1970; D. H. Thomas 1978; Warren and O'Brien 1981) and site levels (Binford et al. 1970; Brown 1975; Flannery 1976b, 1976c; Redman 1974; Redman and Watson 1970; Whalen 1990; Winter 1976). The more acceptable sampling approaches for probabilistic surveys under ideal conditions where 100 percent coverage is not feasible are based on random sampling and include simple random, systematic random, systematic unaligned, and stratified random sampling techniques.

Proper selection of a probabilistic method requires certain knowledge of the data. The archaeologist must realize in each of these sampling strategies for surveys, however, that one is sampling land units, not archaeological sites (Whalen 1990; Chenhall [1975] also discusses the problem of nonequivalence of land units and archaeological sites). One must not assume that the land units are going to correlate with archaeological sites, or that

all archaeological sites are going to reflect the same adaptive strategy. The same caution holds true with culturally modified landscapes that have assumed a nonrandom structure. Such examples could include the culturally modified landscape in and around a Mesoamerican monumental center or that around a modern urban landscape in which an archaeological survey is required. In these instances, sampling strategies based on **conditional probabilities**—that is, prior knowledge of where sites or features are, or are not, likely to occur—are used to help design an appropriate sampling strategy (Thomas 1986:111–114).

Simple Random Sampling.   The sampled population or data universe must be totally accessible in **simple random sampling;** given this assumption, the segment of the data universe (i.e., n units out of N units are chosen; the ratio of n/N is the sampling ratio) is selected at random using a method that randomizes the selection procedure (Figure 3.2). The amount sampled is determined on the basis of how many observations one wishes to make and the size of the number of possible observations in the data universe.

The purpose of randomizing the selection is to ensure that each sample unit has an equal chance of being selected. For example, assuming that the data universe is a specifically defined geographic region and the problem is to gain a representative sample of the site variability in the region, the archaeologist may choose to sample 20 percent of the region by using equal-size quadrats. The area is gridded, the number of grid units is defined, and the units are numbered serially from one to n. The size of the grid is an arbitrary decision based on the size of the sampling unit desired; grid size can significantly affect the representativeness of the sample. The sample units are then selected by some random procedure, such as a table of random numbers (Arkin and Colton 1963:142).

The random numbers shown in Table 3.1 are a tabulation of six random digits arranged into rows and columns (Press et al. 1988). The analyst selects a page at will, and may read the rows or columns horizontally, vertically, or diagonally. One may select the numbers in order, or only every other random digit, in pairs, or in triplicates of digits if one is numbering units from 000 to 1,000. There are no standard rules for using a table of random numbers. The underlying principle is randomness; other than that, details vary with the data, population, and research questions.

Experimental surveys on paper have demonstrated that simple random sampling is usually not the best approach to regional survey or even for site testing (Binford 1964; Flannery 1976b; Jelks 1975; Plog 1976; Redman and Watson 1970). It is, however, extremely easy to set up a simple random sample. The problem is that by mere chance, one portion of the region or site may be either missed or overrepresented. This is not a failure of random sampling per se, which assumes no significant variation within the population. If variations, such as spatial differences within the region, are expected, however, and if information on these differences is desired, then simple random sampling is not the best approach to use. Also, as Binford (1975) warns, simple random sampling is inappropriate when the universe being sampled is structured, as many archaeological sites and settlement patterns tend to be (especially those with architecture). More appropriate ways of ensuring a better representative coverage are the systematic random sample, the systematic unaligned sample, and the stratified random sample.

Systematic Random Sampling. In **systematic random sampling,** the first sample unit is selected by some randomizing procedure and all other units are chosen by a predetermined procedure, such as every fifth unit, every third unit, etc., depending on the desired fraction size (Figure 3.3). Use of this technique guarantees more uniform coverage of an area than would likely occur with simple random sampling. Ragir (1975:291) discusses the statistical advantages of systematic random sampling but also appropriately does not recommend its use in most archaeological situations.

The technique is appropriate in situations where vertical deposits appear homogeneous, such as in a shell midden (Cook and Heizer 1951), pollen profiles, or lithic debitage deposits (e.g., Colha, Belize [Hester and Shafer 1984; Shafer and Hester 1983]) where the intent is to detect dietary, ecological, or technological shifts depending on the constituents of the deposits. The sample taken would be a column arbitrarily or naturally divided into units. Samples are taken at systematic increments along the column.

Sharer and Ashmore (1993:96) note potential problems of bias with the use of systematic random sampling in horizontal excavations where features were themselves systematically arranged. For example, where postholes of a prehistoric rectangular house were spaced at approximate intervals,

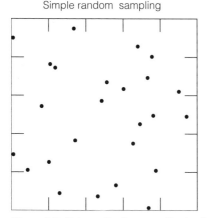

Simple random sampling

Figure 3.2 Schematic diagram of test units selected by simple random sampling.

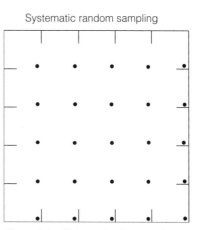

Systematic random sampling

Figure 3.3 Schematic diagram of test units chosen by systematic random sampling.

TABLE 3.1
An Example of a Table of Random Numbers

438170	064408	518310	125094	885750	541655	153827	384880
506189	964171	185601	437477	810761	754556	158191	037791
817369	226980	159268	639024	241775	931317	600698	632674
566727	425322	190512	102932	679371	822200	025784	489170
436800	921385	340209	993907	159620	103856	149568	544490
830398	422980	099337	993189	317382	305967	062356	155129
508476	735920	665506	695183	880611	522423	574126	218075
722491	783775	353034	147849	429885	634161	091413	848697
014562	501165	637937	509043	065043	085892	901765	512838
920003	163266	078749	510918	054476	043058	144953	137541
906308	067457	117612	407195	876891	036534	352958	560405
411444	622247	451332	609018	167738	040178	823644	485635
627207	862669	637617	671041	868600	133574	585386	632749
191237	133593	557746	788397	534906	959324	052762	216920
871259	554959	501173	078683	298164	278784	477641	740385
174686	559771	676400	713567	415542	566115	058950	663519
465864	572690	701737	341046	014812	045302	927321	482097
945568	990889	031462	724388	140428	009379	605881	295914
966304	359474	776090	230143	846146	691680	181150	193959
895378	219497	425820	728936	406829	005085	488225	519205
578276	261330	567329	650705	057337	830198	421218	213367
560721	295648	244199	114544	940463	850296	624762	030622
481128	325076	595546	660672	918469	171299	249966	136780
109616	851051	308154	370697	230497	170332	086565	380515
166121	118623	375092	948608	104767	801264	985469	943556
308886	537518	682074	573091	643178	047434	392147	175050
140454	025885	694354	536787	724794	644240	468504	123752
355597	591595	386321	797752	719973	106685	550633	610944
566591	949577	754584	468375	976358	664735	242921	185030
794271	898215	489062	497520	039982	976951	445256	428055
348570	863584	577890	403253	043854	444785	868359	763072
078985	264754	130800	346373	077773	350483	233282	910069
483792	560982	751177	779532	215739	313439	030147	055956
413508	034657	705228	711986	345566	791856	580959	394614
164994	037860	211456	875447	083730	137854	237245	838661
964805	069165	055844	402037	248150	813954	677197	494257
069547	196028	840773	157798	972253	476911	594988	849310
207727	196946	579080	249434	320930	589730	583340	470500
646375	836096	599144	364116	161349	397059	690900	455489
813107	215714	770562	833920	538714	397445	957565	596825
169056	255463	354131	988330	617410	075357	695477	265735
935961	882826	996568	232275	383972	032431	257106	159149

Note: Based on algorithms in Press et al. (1988).

Systematic unaligned sampling

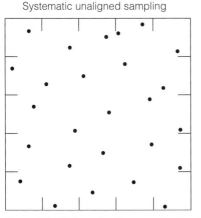

Figure 3.4 Schematic diagram of test units chosen by systematic unaligned sampling.

Stratified random sampling

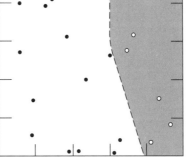

Figure 3.5 Schematic diagram of test units chosen by stratified random sampling.

one's test pits may be systematically placed to miss each posthole or hit each one, giving a biased coverage either way.

Systematic Unaligned Sampling. An alternate to systematic random sampling is the **systematic unaligned sampling** method. In this approach, the sample population is divided into large blocks, and then one smaller block within each larger block is chosen at random. For example, a site is divided into 5-×-5-m blocks and one 1-×-1-m square is chosen at random within each 5-×-5-m block (Figure 3.4). The goal of systematic unaligned sampling is to cover all areas within the sample population.

Stratified Random Sampling. The precision of a sample is based on two factors: sample size and variability of the population. Stratifying the population into classes, each constituting an independent sampling universe, is one way of improving the precision of the sample. Simple random samples are then drawn from each universe using the procedures described earlier (Figure 3.5).

Again using as an example a regional survey, the region may be divided into strata following environmental zones, soil zones, or some other means of ensuring more thorough areal coverage (Figure 3.6). Each zone or stratum is then sampled in the desired proportion (20 percent or whatever).

The goal of stratified sampling is to minimize variability within the sampling strata. In site excavations where random samples are desired, the site may arbitrarily be divided into four quadrants, with each quadrant representing a stratum (Redman and Watson 1970); units are then randomly chosen from each quadrant, guaranteeing a more representative coverage of the area than that which might be provided by an unstratified random sample.

Flannery's (1976a) discussion of this method and an early debate on the use of random sampling (e.g., Mayer-Oakes and Nash [1964] cited in Flannery [1976a]; also see Jelks 1975) are worth noting. Mayer-Oakes and Nash conducted an experimental survey using William Sanders's survey map of the Teotihuacan Valley in Mexico. They stratified the universe into even "strata," or environmental zones. A 0.6-km-square grid was superimposed over the universe and a 20 percent stratified random sample of grid units was drawn for the study. The debate about the appropriateness of the stratified random sample technique hinged on the fact that Teotihuacan did not show up in the sample. Those archaeologists interested only in finding sites viewed the method with skepticism. However, the proportion of each type of site in each temporal phase that fell in the chosen squares was almost identical to that represented in Sanders's 100 percent survey of the valley. As

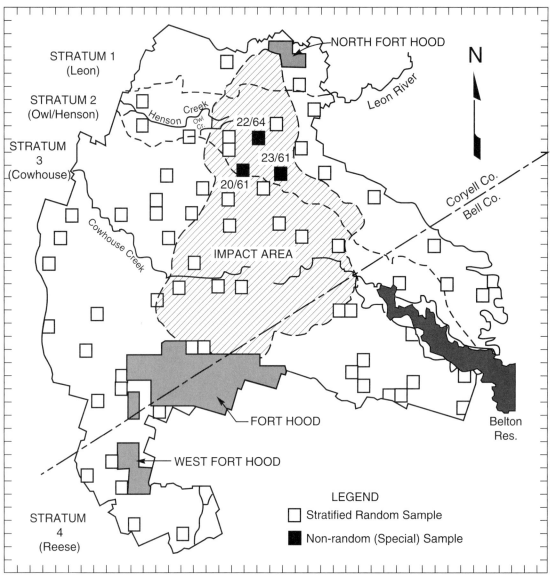

SA1-80EM-5.2

Figure 3.6 Gridded survey area at Fort Hood, Texas, showing location of 1-km squares selected by random sampling and of nonrandom units selected to fill in known critical gaps missed by random sampling.

(Flannery 1976a:135) emphasized, "probability sampling is *not a discovery technique,* it's just the best way to get a *representative* sample of sites if you can't go for the whole universe" (emphasis his).

Sampling within artifact classes may also follow any of these procedures—simple random, systematic random, or stratified random. For example,

if one wanted to do a paste analysis of 20 percent of the sherds from a population of 1,000, one method would be to lay out all of the sherds, number them serially from 1 to 1,000, and select 200 sherds using a table of random numbers. Another would be to select the first sherd on the basis of a random drawing and then every fifth sherd thereafter to produce a systematic random sample. Still a third method would entail ordering or stratifying the sherds by provenience lots and selecting a random sample from each lot.

Sample Fraction and Sample Size

How much of an area should one cover to gain a representative sample? How many sherds is enough to provide a clear picture of ceramic patterning? In area surveys, choice of the sample fraction and sample size may be based on several factors (Mueller 1974; Plog 1976), including size of the survey area, time available for fieldwork, accessibility, nature of the archaeological data, and mathematical considerations.

Sample fraction is the *percentage* of the sampled population (i.e., the total number of units available for sampling) that is observed or tested; **sample size** is the *number* of observations made. For example, if a 20 percent sample—the fraction—is desired and the survey area is 1,000 km², a single 200-km² block—the sample size—would constitute a 20 percent sample. Surveying in small blocks (such as twenty 1-km² blocks), however, would provide more accurate coverage because a greater number of observations would be made (Read 1975).

Plog et al. (1978) stress the importance of balancing the sample size with the sample fraction but caution that designing many small quadrats into survey coverage may be impractical due to the time required or the ability to locate and define the parameters of the quadrats in the field. If the quadrat is smaller than the site (e.g., a 1-km² quadrat falling in a 6-km² Maya site), the site boundaries will be inaccurate. Also, if the quadrat is smaller than a related group of sites, questions about social interaction may be impossible to address. Balancing sample size with the sample fraction is a compromise between what is desirable and what is feasible in the field; it is much easier to achieve balance in the laboratory, where one has a greater control of and access to the data universe. D. H. Thomas (1978:237) stresses the importance of sample size:

> The point is not whether the best ultimate fraction is 0.4 or 0.04. As Cowgill (1975:262) and as

every textbook on sampling strategy forcefully points out, the critical issue in sampling is not **fraction** at all, but rather **the absolute size of the sample.** In very large areas, a relatively low fraction is perfectly acceptable: when the area is small, the sampling fraction must be larger. There is not—and cannot be—an "optimum sampling fraction."

Determining the appropriate sample size in excavation depends on the types of questions addressed in the research design and the classes of material the archaeologist is specifically emphasizing in the research. An archaeologist is obligated to collect and account for all physical data generated from excavation. For instance, if the issue is one of establishing a ceramic chronology through test pit excavations at various sites, all materials (lithics, ceramics, faunal remains, human remains, etc.) encountered should be treated appropriately. The archaeologist's interest is going to be on what constitutes an adequate ceramic sample for his or her purposes; the investigator will not be concerned with an adequate lithics or faunal sample because he or she is not addressing all possible questions related to the material remains being uncovered.

If one is interested in studying the variability in house mounds and must excavate an appropriate number to provide for probability statements, the work may yield tens of thousands of sherds, many times over what may be considered an adequate or representative sherd sample. A large sherd sample creates major time and labor problems related to recording and documentation of the sample, but some quantitative analytical methods are necessary to address complementary problems of type-variety, vessel function, structure function, household assemblages, breakage frequencies for each type of vessel, activity patterning, disposal patterns, and so forth.

Very large samples are obviously unwieldy and sometimes have to be sampled in the field even before laboratory processing and labeling. Although a count of all sherds may not be possible or feasible, quantitative measures are necessary to estimate the total density of material elements in each type of deposit. For example, a stratified random sample of all sherds drawn from the excavation of a house mound or a plaza mound group can provide both the contextual and the quantitative data needed for form and function studies. Such a procedure would not necessarily compromise the excavation of architecture, which often involves the removal of both in situ and mixed deposits.

In site excavations of that sort or in survey situations where large quantities of materials are encountered, we recommend some kind of nested sampling strategy that allows for sampling of all deposits for a variety of material data, from architecture to pollen. We urge, however, the use of methodological restraint to preserve the cultural context of the sample rather than compromising it to some probabilistic sampling strategy (see Sampling Realities, later in this chapter).

Another real problem in field archaeology concerns selection of the study collection to be retained in those situations where 100 percent of the collection simply cannot be saved. Given field situations where enormous sherd collections are amassed, such as in Mesoamerica, decisions may have to be made regarding which sherds are retained for further study and which ones are left at the field laboratory. All pottery is usually sorted following customary type-variety procedures (Gifford 1960; Smith 1979), and taxonomic and provenience data are recorded. A sample of rim sherds and other diagnostic sherds are selected to be cataloged and kept for further study. For these cataloged samples to have statistical validity, they must have been excavated in a quantifiable and systematic fashion and must be selected for further study by some random procedure.

The key to appropriate field sampling is using foresight and good judgment. A recovery technique appropriate for obtaining a quantifiable sample of pottery may not be at all applicable to collecting faunal remains. It is unlikely that faunal materials collected incidentally while obtaining a pottery sample will be representative or even quantifiable if a large screen size is used (see Grayson [1984] for suggestions regarding quantitative sampling of faunal remains). Precision field sampling takes time, but the results provide unlimited analytical potential.

Sample Units

Several factors determine the size and configuration of the sample units for surveys and excavations. There are several options available; for example, Plog (1976) and Plog et al. (1978) discuss some of the options in regional surveys. The archaeologist must weigh the decision on the basis of prior knowledge of the area, land accessibility, field time, and logistics. He or she may choose to use quadrats or grid squares, transects, or block samples (Redman 1974). In any case, the survey area must be defined within a frame of study. The size of the quadrat or grid unit is conditioned largely by the number of observations one wishes to make within the time limits of the fieldwork.

In regional surveys, quadrats may be the least desirable of the three kinds of sampling units. Although quadrats provide a means of randomizing the sampling, the opportunity of missing vitally important data by chance spacing of sample units exists.

Transects are usually placed across the region of study and when completely surveyed, document the full range of archaeological sites and spacing between sites. The placement of transects can be randomized (Plog 1976), ensuring an unbiased sample. Also, transect samples can provide data that permit prediction of the total site population. Transect samples can be applied to deeply stratified sites (see Flannery 1976c for an excellent application of this approach), which pose the greatest challenge to archaeologists with regard to precision sampling.

Large block samples, although providing a more detailed database on the spatial patterning of sites in a region, limit the number of observations one can make throughout a region.

Accessibility to land may be beyond the archaeologist's control. A strategy of surveying all accessible land may be the only compromise available between the ideal and the real situation (Blake et al. 1986).

Another factor affecting sampling is surface visibility. For example, sampling for surface evidence of occupation or activity in a tropical forest may be limited to surveying only freshly burned milpa plots or plowed fields. Technically speaking, sampling in these situations would be biased for those lands where farming is possible or was practiced at the time of the survey. In such situations, the population of sampling units is beyond the control of the archaeologist. One approach to sampling rain forest habitats is that employed in surveying in and around Tikal (Haviland 1969; Puleston 1974; Rice and Puleston 1981). That method was to sample four survey strips extending out from central Tikal (Figure 3.7). Each strip was 500 m wide and 12 km long, and the findings were used to define the settlement extent and density. The settlement information was also used as a basis for estimating the population density at Tikal (Haviland 1969).

Surface Collecting

Largely because of cultural resource management projects, the most common method of artifact data gathering practiced today in most areas of the United States is surface collecting. No other body of collected data is more apt to be skewed, yet major management and mitigation decisions are based on interpretations of the observed sample. Surface collections can provide valuable data on site conditions, temporal periods, site function, material density, spatial variability, and artifact patterning, among other things. As such, they constitute a valuable source of data not to be overlooked. Surface collections are skewed, however, and their literal interpretation can lead to gross misjudgments of the archaeological record.

To use surface collections to generate reliable inferences, an understanding of the geological setting and physical circumstances involving the exposure of the materials is essential. Single-function activity areas, although they may be present, would likely be masked by the debris from other activities on deflated surfaces or blowout areas frequented by many peoples in the past (Binford 1982; Varner 1968). Surface collections gathered from plowed surfaces of an alluvial terrace will yield artifacts of the last occupation episode of the site

but may not be indicative of many earlier deposits buried beneath the surface. Hence, on the basis of the hard evidence, such a locality can be considered indicative only of the period or periods represented on the surface, but it cannot be ruled out as a locality for earlier occupation merely on the basis of negative physical evidence.

Surface collections during regional surveys should be planned in a systematic fashion that allows for quantitative analysis (Flannery 1976c). Surface data collection will depend on the respective levels of analysis designed into the project. Systematic collecting procedures for each site should be incorporated and followed to permit intersite comparisons. Cluster sampling would be an appropriate strategy where designated size units are surface collected for all elements represented (sherds, lithics, burned rocks, etc.). Such a collecting procedure could yield data on the temporal and spatial patterning of the elements included in the surface sample.

Artifact collecting should be included in the research design in most areas. While noncollecting policies often provide a superficial level of information suitable to achieving certain CRM aims, leaving artifacts in known site/feature contexts may encourage relic collecting by tempting tourists, hikers, and relic hunters with exposed collectible artifacts. Such policies may result in the loss of verifiable contextual and quantitative data that could have been saved in well-documented and curated surface collections; such collections provide opportunities for later examination of the artifacts for information not sought in the original CRM survey. Like any research strategy, however, the decision to collect or not to collect must be weighed against local or regional circumstances and land management policies.

Intrasite surface sampling for preexcavation studies yields valuable information that helps guide excavation strategies and greatly improves the quality of field data. Case examples of the positive application of intensive surface sampling before excavation are those of Binford et al. (1970), Flannery (1976c), and Redman and Watson (1970). Knowledge of the region and kind of site being

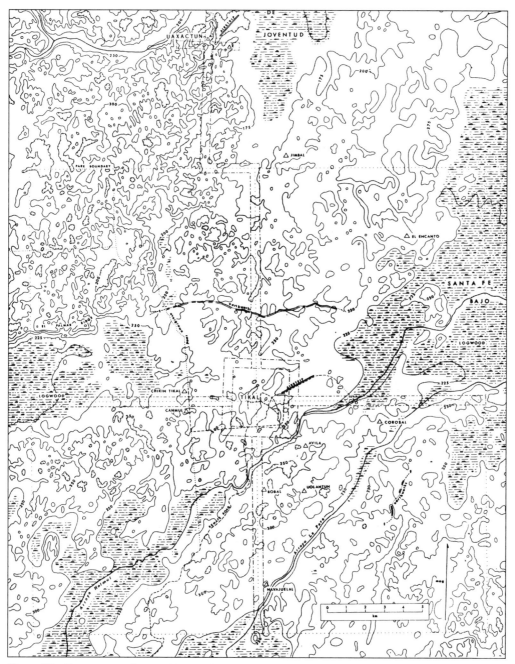

Figure 3.7   Transect sampling used in sustaining area survey around the ancient Maya site of Tikal, Guatemala.

sampled is essential to establish the working assumptions necessary to interpret the meaning of the patterning that may be detected or delineated through the survey. Without prior knowledge of the phenomenon under investigation, one may be led to draw very inappropriate conclusions, especially if the patterns result from the survey rather than from human behavior.

Careful surface sampling may also reveal discrete activity areas or structured use of space. Although clustering of certain elements may be meaningful statistically, interpretations are best advanced with caution and common sense. Careful excavations and analysis can detect discrete activity areas (for instance, see Frison 1982; Odell 1980); such features are structured composites of archaeological materials and are best examined by near–total exposure rather than by sondage or trenching techniques.

Patterning of surface material also may result from differential erosional patterns of the sediments within which the archaeological materials are contained. For example, blowouts in arid environments are caused by wind erosion of the sandy mantle containing the archaeological materials. The heavier artifacts are redeposited on more resistant surfaces in concentrations created by noncultural processes (Waters 1992:185–213).

Excavation Sampling

Sampling designs have shifted greatly over the past three decades, along with the changes in the theoretical paradigms that guide archaeological research. And we can be assured that change will continue as our knowledge of the past becomes more precise. Two examples illustrate how a better knowledge of the processes that created the archaeological record can affect strategies for sampling that record.

The first example is J. N. Hill's (1966, 1970) strategy for excavating Broken K Pueblo, which has been praised for its innovativeness (Figure 3.8). Hill chose to use the pueblo as his sample frame and each room as a sample unit. A near–50 percent random sample was selected for excavation, and rooms were selected randomly for excavation. Inferences on such aspects as sociocultural patterning and room function were based on the excavated sample. In hindsight, a more appropriate strategy might have been to stratify the rooms based on cultural units, such as clusters of rooms built as a unit as determined by wall bonding patterns, and to design an excavation procedure that would allow examination of a random sample of

room suites or room clusters rather than of rooms. Such a strategy would have allowed for more precise statements regarding temporal change within the pueblo and room suite or household variability and, at the same time, would have preserved the functional context of each room. Room function and suite alignment changed through time (Rock 1974; Shafer and Taylor 1986). Pueblo rooms are usually units within a culturally defined set or room suites that may conform to actual households (Rock 1974; Shafer 1982; Wilcox 1975) and therefore constitute a structured universe not amenable to random sampling at the room level. In fairness to Hill, he (1970:21) acknowledged that two nonrandomly different size classes of rooms existed, which would call for stratifying the room sample based on size, but this was not recognized until after the simple random sampling strategy had been initiated.

Rockshelters pose specific sampling problems. A sampling strategy designed to obtain chronological information may destroy rather than discover site structure and spatial patterning (Binford 1975). These kinds of sites are literally palimpsests of households and activity areas structured within a naturally defined space. Household space is predictably structured (see Binford 1983a:144–192; Shafer 1982; Wilk and Rathje 1982) for both ethnographic and archaeological examples. Using Binford's clearly illustrated examples of residential space use among hunters and gatherers as a model, the structure of activities inside a rockshelter would expectedly mirror that around a temporary residence. Structured space use within a rockshelter may be maintained through repeated occupations, although the specific location of activities at any one time may shift as deposits accumulate within the shelter and the amount of available space is either increased or reduced. An example of repeated use of space was noted at the stratified site of Hinds Cave in southwest Texas, where the same spaces in the site were used for sleeping, cooking, and latrines over several thousand years (and many separate occupations) (Shafer 1986; Shafer and Bryant 1977) (Figure 3.9).

Traditional sampling strategies for rockshelters usually include trenching or some form of block

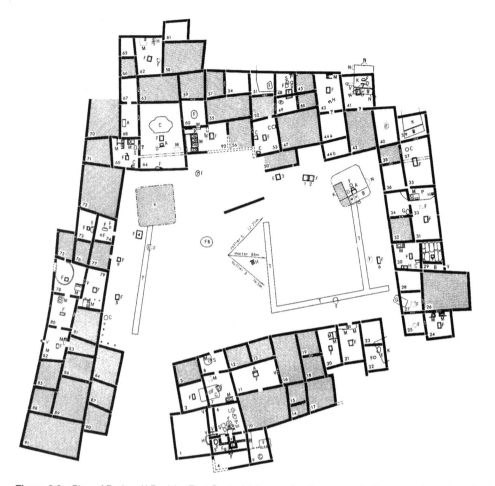

Figure 3.8 Plan of Broken K Pueblo, East Central Arizona, showing excavated rooms selected randomly.

excavation to obtain a vertically stratified sample; the trench would be placed where the deposits are thought to be the deepest. Such sampling strategies destroy the spatial integrity of the deposit. For an excellent example of excavating stratified rockshelter deposits, see Flannery et al. (1986).

A fruitful approach to the excavation of a rockshelter showing signs of habitation is to begin with the assumption that the confined sheltered space was a household much like a pithouse. Defining the sequence and chronology of occupations is as important as defining the spatial variability in activity patterning. The shelter could be sampled in such a way that both temporal and spatial patterning can be defined within the space of the rockshelter.

Another sampling challenge is presented by large, deep open sites. Unlike rockshelter settings that have definable parameters, the various superimposed boundaries for stratified alluvial or colluvial sites compound the problem of acquiring a quantifiable sample. The problem stems from the fact that one simply does not know how many separate activity surfaces or settlements are represented through time, how clear the boundaries are between them, and the horizontal extent of each. Even along streams, where cultural deposits are separated by sediments from slope erosion or overbank flooding, the geological separation of the cultural deposits does not necessarily divide individual settlements; it merely divides composite accumulations, each of which may be that of sev-

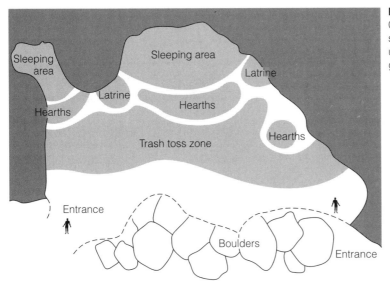

Figure 3.9 Floor plan of Hinds Cave, Val Verde County, Texas, showing interpretation of space use and activity areas based on the general location of cultural features.

eral settlements. Deep sites with superimposed culture-bearing deposits or architecture simply do not allow for probabilistic sampling, although there are nonprobabilistic methods that can be adapted to deep-site excavations.

Flannery (1976c) provides one method of sampling deeply stratified locations. Brown (1975) addresses the issue of sampling deep sites squarely and is recommended reading for anyone considering deep-site sampling. Brown (1975:169) outlines these general procedures for sampling in deep-site excavations:

1. Collect information relevant to the number, depth, and extent of the subsurface archaeological zones within the site limits (that is, make stratigraphic probes).

2. Create a first-order sample stratification of the site sample space.

3. Excavate the set of sample test excavation units.

4. Classify sample units for each layer to recover activity categories held in common among the set of layers.

5. Expand the excavation as a result of creating a second-order sample to improve on the representation of activity types in each layer.

An implicit example of this approach applied to a large, multicomponent site is provided by Bruseth and Martin (1986). Open-air settlements are also more variable than, for example, rockshelters with confined space in terms of structure placement and function. When these kinds of archaeological deposits are buried, the sampling problems are compounded. Sites with deflated surfaces that contain features and artifacts of multiple occupations also pose serious sampling dilemmas (see Binford 1982 for excellent insight into the archaeology of repeatedly used locations), as do sites in eolian environments (Leach et al. 1994; Mauldin et al. 1994). Therefore, it is an advantage to know the formation processes of a site to design an appropriate sampling strategy (see Chapter 10).

SAMPLING REALITIES

The basic idea of probabilistic sampling is to increase precision in comparisons between and within sites (Brown 1975). The probabilistic sampling defined in statistics texts represents ideal situations where accessibility to the target or sampled population is assured. In archaeological fieldwork, complete access to broad areas of coverage for regional problems is rarely possible because of differential land ownership and access, depth of deposits, visibility due to vegetation, and logistics. Probabilistic sampling problems are compounded in large, deeply stratified, multicomponent, and multifunctional sites found in settings of sediment accumulation around the world (see Brown 1975; Flannery 1976b). Therefore, not all archaeological situations are amenable to probabilistic sampling.

The decisions archaeologists make with regard to sampling affect the quality of their data and the accuracy of their inferences and those of others who use the same database thereafter. The challenges are enormous, and unfortunately, they have rarely been dealt with satisfactorily. This is partly the result of inexperience with sampling in archaeology and of the fact that only in the past three decades have archaeologists been asking questions about the past that go beyond How old is it? We now want to know How many? How much? and Is site A different from site B? If we cannot survey or excavate completely, then sampling is the only hope of measuring the precision of our predictive statements about regions or sites.

To summarize, then, in choosing an appropriate sampling strategy for archaeological fieldwork, there are basically seven decisions to be made:

1. The first choice is what kinds of archaeological data are to be collected. This involves selecting and specifying the items (objects that can be counted and sampled directly) that are to be gathered.

2. The next question is what sampling approach best fits the goals of the research design. To facilitate the search for patterns and frequency changes among items, items must be sampled in clusters (areas defined in terms of space, such as gridded units, test pits, or excavation blocks).

3. If cluster sampling is used, the next decision is the size/shape of the sampling unit.

4. Next, the type of cluster sampling appropriate to the project—simple or nested—must be decided. In situations where all items in each category are collected or counted as they occur within the cluster, the cluster sampling is simple. In situations where sub-sample units are necessary within larger sampling units to collect items that occur in high frequency or that are small and require

finer mesh or more time-consuming recovery methods (such as flotation or pollen analysis), a nested cluster sampling approach is called for.

5. Depending on the types of information desired, the sampling strategy can be either probabilistic or nonprobabilistic. If an assessment of the contextual variability within the sampling universe is needed, then nonprobabilistic approaches might be the better choice. On the other hand, if the aim is to define patterning within the archaeological universe under study, then probabilistic sampling will be required.

6. If the sampling strategy is to be probabilistic, then the question of how to control for bias must be answered. Alternative probabilistic methods include simple, systematic, systematic unaligned, and stratified random sampling strategies.

7. Whatever the sampling strategy selected, it is also necessary to decide the sampling fraction (what percentage of the whole is to be sampled) and the sample size (how many items comprise an "adequate sample").

Archaeologists should realize that the accuracy of their interpretations of the archaeological record rests on how representative the sample is. They should always be aware of how a sample was collected before accepting or rejecting any interpretations based on it.

GUIDE TO FURTHER READING

Research Design

Gibbon 1984; Sharer and Ashmore 1993

Sampling Methods

General: Binford 1975; Binford et al. 1970; Brown 1975; Cowgill 1975; Flannery 1976a; Mueller 1975; Redman and Watson 1970; D. H. Thomas 1978, 1986

Regional: Blake et al. 1986; Chenhall 1975; Fish and Kowalewski 1990; Hill 1966; Mueller 1974; Plog 1976; Redman and Watson 1970; Whalen 1990

Site: Binford et al. 1970; Brown 1975; Flannery 1976a, 1976b; Flannery et al. 1986; Whalen 1990; Winter 1976

CHAPTER

Site Survey

Kenneth L. Feder

As stated in Chapter 1, archaeology can be defined as the recovery and study of the material remains of societies and cultures. It is that branch of anthropology that focuses on the things people made and used—often, though not always, because those material remains are all that is left of a now extinct society.

A key assumption in archaeology is that these material remains reflect both directly and indirectly on the culture that produced them. In other words, there is a comprehensible relationship between the "hardware" left behind by a culture and the culture itself.

People do not ordinarily behave randomly but follow patterns established within their societies. Tool manufacture, hunting practices, house construction, religious worship, village location, and so on, are behaviors that tend to conform to societal patterns, standards, or requirements. Behavior follows rules established within societies and,

therefore, is patterned. Because the archaeological record is, at least, an indirect reflection of that behavior, the archaeological record also is patterned and reflects, through an often complex process, the behavioral patterns that led to its formation (Binford 1978a, 1978b; Schiffer 1972, 1975a, 1975b, 1976; Yellen 1977a).

Just as behavior itself is not random, human beings do not behave randomly in space; that is, they do not use the landscape randomly (Hodder 1978; Jochim 1976; Zimmerman 1977). The locations of urban centers, farming villages, seasonal encampments, hunting camps, mining towns, quarries, burial grounds, and so on, are all selected on the basis of cultural and practical requirements. Considerations almost certainly include features of the natural environment: food resources, topography, fresh water availability, ease of transportation, and the availability of other material resources. Other factors are culturally based and may include defensibility of an area, proximity to other members of the society, and even religious considerations.

Depending on the subsistence base of a given group, its relations with neighbors, local environmental variables, and historical factors, people use a landscape in a spatially ordered way, leaving patterned distributions on that landscape. The term for a spatially ordered system of land use is **settlement pattern.** The settlement pattern represents the way in which a particular group of people utilize the landscape. The archaeological reflection of that settlement pattern is called by William Marquardt and Carol Crumley (1987:7) the "**landscape signature**," defined as "the material imprints left on the earth's surface by particular constellations of human groups." The landscape signature of a region consists of the geographical locations of cities, towns, villages, fishing camps, hunting sites, quarries, transportation features and facilities, shrines, burial grounds, and so on, as well as the use of space within such locations. The landscape signature is, therefore, a material representation of the cultural pattern of the use of land and space.

GOALS OF SITE SURVEY

Common goals of archaeological site survey include illuminating a landscape signature and detecting and comprehending a settlement pattern. Often, to obtain that desired result, archaeologists initially focus on an intermediate goal: the discovery of sites, the examination of the spatial boundaries of sites, and the identification of general distributions of material within sites. A **site** is any discrete, bounded location where humans lived, worked, or carried out a task—and where physical evidence of their behavior can be recovered by the archaeologist.

Some have called into question the usefulness and even the validity of the site concept as it is ordinarily used. For example, Dunnell (1992) maintains that the archaeological record does not consist of geographically discrete locations where artifacts, ecofacts, and features are found. Instead, he views that record as virtually continuous across the landscape, reflecting the broad and geographically continuous use of that landscape by human groups.

In this regard, Marquardt and Crumley (1987:2) point out that a significant problem results if archaeologists design strategies to search for sites, when the term *site* is defined narrowly as a place where people lived or buried their dead. As they point out, within the "landscape signature" of an area, there are unoccupied or infrequently occupied places that are difficult to discern archaeologically because so few material remains were deposited. Unoccupied areas of ceremonial significance, mountain passes through which human groups traveled, short-term encampments, and even uninhabited buffer zones between different groups of people are all part of a pattern of land use but may be invisible to archaeologists surveying an area by applying techniques designed to find only discrete, dense accumulations of settlement refuse.

In a similar vein, Ebert (1992) makes the point that focusing on the "site" obscures the actual nature of landscape use by past people. He uses the following analogy (Ebert 1992:245–246): The site concept implies that the archaeological record is a series of discrete snapshots of the past. In this view, each site is a separate photo in time. In Ebert's view, the archaeological record is actually a single, lengthy, time-exposure photograph, a picture with infinitely overlapping images. Some parts of the image are brighter—these would be distinct locations used more intensively (what we call sites)—but the image is nonetheless nearly continuous and ubiquitous, and a focus on those "bright spots" distorts our understanding of a pattern of land use.

Nonsite-based "landscape" or "distributional" archaeology has become popular in the American Great Basin and the southwestern United States, as well as in parts of Africa. This is almost certainly the result of environmental factors. In these areas, the pattern of land use was dispersed and continuous because the features of the landscape that attracted humans tended to be more dispersed. With fewer deeply stratified sites and with a higher proportion of surface sites of different ages mixed together across the landscape, it is apparent why such a perspective might be useful in these geographic areas.

In other regions—the northeastern United States, for example—the archaeological record is more clustered into distinct "sites" because the features of the landscape that attracted human use were themselves discontinuous or more clustered, and different time periods often are separated stratigraphically. Here too, however, a landscape or distributional approach is of great utility because it reveals more of the landscape signature of a region, provides a more representative sample of elements of land use, and thus, provides a clearer view of an entire settlement pattern rather than focusing only on the discovery of the archaeologically richest locations (Dewar and McBride 1992; Feder and Banks 1996). Elsewhere, Crumley et al. (1987) have applied with great success a landscape approach in their survey of the Burgundy region of France.

Although here we will continue to use the entrenched concept of the "archaeological site," it must be said that landscape or distributional archaeologists make an important point for all archaeologists conducting surveys. Our focus should be not on the discovery of sites (in the narrow sense of village locations) but on the broad question of how human groups used the landscape. We should not let apparent clustering of remains in some discrete locations obscure the fact that people likely perceived and used their regions quite broadly. Survey strategies designed for finding only expansive, densely clustered archaeological remains (i.e., village sites) may guarantee that such clusters are all we find and that we miss significant elements in a land-use pattern. Densely occupied villages, if they exist within a pattern of land use, are likely to be only one element within that pattern. This must be kept in mind when developing a survey strategy for any given region; we need to look intensively across the entire landscape to decipher the nature of a complex pattern of land use by past people (Dewar and McBride 1992).

Although ultimately our hope may be to illuminate a landscape signature and reconstruct a settlement pattern, the immediate goals of particular surveys will depend on a number of factors. Sometimes, particularly if sites or landscapes are endangered by development or land modification and if the area is small, the goal of a survey may be to discover *all* archaeological remains in a given locality. For example, in a survey conducted as a part of a U.S. government–mandated environmental impact statement, the desire may be to find all sites or all remains because they are in danger of destruction as a result of a federally sponsored or licensed project involving road construction, flood control, pollution abatement, and so on.

Often, however, it must be recognized that, given time and physical constraints, cost, and labor limits, it is unreasonable to hope to discover all archaeological evidence in a particular region. Site surveys are sometimes designed to locate a *representative sample* (see Chapter 3) of materials within the boundaries of a research area. Thus, though not all sites or remains will be detected, the sample of those that are, it is hoped, will reflect proportions representative of the population in the region. Proportions here means the relative percentages of sites (defined as any place used by people) of different ages, sizes, functions, artifact assemblages, and microenvironmental locations. Within the framework of a survey conducted not as a result of an immediate threat but within the context of long-term planning, a representative sample of sites may be sufficient. For example, a survey funded by the U.S. Department of the Interior through a State Historic Preservation Office in the Survey and Planning Grant program may involve an assessment of the archaeological sensitivity of a town, watershed, or state forest (Derry et al. 1985). Though there may be no imminent danger of site destruction, future development plans can take into account such a general assessment of an area's archaeological sensitivity based on a sample of sites.

SURVEY PHASES

Whatever the specific goal of a project, site survey often proceeds in two phases: reconnaissance survey and intensive survey. The United States Department of the Interior, which sponsors many archaeological surveys and has established policies and guidelines concerning surveys mandated as a result of federal environmental protection legislation (Derry et al. 1985; King et al. 1977), defines the goal of a **reconnaissance survey** as follows:

to provide a general impression of an area's historic properties . . . it should make it possible to identify obvious or well-known properties, to check the existence and condition of properties tentatively identified or predicted from background research, to identify areas where certain kinds of properties are likely to occur [36 CFR Part 64].

An **intensive survey** is defined by the same department as:

a systematic, detailed field inspection. . . . The surface of the land and all districts, sites, buildings, structures and objects of possible archaeological value are inspected. . . . Systematic subsurface testing is conducted if necessary [36 CFR Part 64].

BASIC CONSIDERATIONS IN SITE SURVEY

In one sense, in either an archaeological reconnaissance or an intensive survey we are not searching for sites directly but for what McManamon (1984a) calls the "**constituents**" of sites: categories of archaeological remains. As enumerated by McManamon (1984a:228), these include artifacts, features or facilities, anthropic soil horizons, chemical anomalies, and instrument anomalies. We'll look at each of these in sequence.

Artifacts

Artifacts, simply, are objects modified by humans. Under the heading "artifact" we include tools and the debris from their manufacture (Figure 4.1). Artifacts can be further characterized as being portable objects, to distinguish them from enormous and complex phenomena like architectural remains. Also, floral and faunal remains resulting from human activity can be classified as artifacts in a separate, equivalent category called **ecofacts** (Binford 1964), although some may be organic remains that exhibit no evidence of intentional modification. So, because artifacts constitute a constituent of sites, one of the clues being looked for in the process of site survey is, simply, the presence of artifacts.

Features or Facilities

Features or **facilities** are commonly defined as concentrations of artifacts and/or organic residue (ecofacts), as well as structural remains. A feature is considered to be the archaeological reflection of some activity or set of activities: stone tool manufacture, hide working, pottery making, cooking, burial, trash disposal, metal working, and so on. Features commonly consist of spatially defined clusters of artifacts and/or ecofacts (Figure 4.2). Food remains—including animal and vegetal materials as well as charcoal from fireplaces—and human waste can become concentrated at human habitations at discrete disposal areas or across the living floor of the site. Concentrations can result in the formation of consolidated deposits of trash. These features are called **middens** (Figure 4.3). Some features may be apparent on the ground as mounds or depressions. In some cases, vegetative indicators may be present; soil chemistry in the matrix of a feature may have been altered as a result of the concentration of chemicals, causing anomalous patterns of plant growth.

Anthropic Soil Horizons

As a consequence of common activities, human beings deposit organic refuse in the soil. **Anthropic soil horizons** (or **anthropogenic soils**), therefore, are horizontally and vertically circumscribed concentrations of organic residue: shell, bone, burned wood, and other plant or animal remains.

Chemical Anomalies

Also as a consequence of common activities, human beings can change the chemical constituency of the soils underlying their habitations, creating **chemical anomalies.** Through disposal of waste material, artificial fertilization of crops, and concentration of organic trash as in the case of anthropic soil horizons, the levels of certain chemicals and elements (most notably compounds of phosphorus and nitrogen [Eidt 1973:206]) can become greatly enriched in local soils. Under certain environmental conditions, these chemicals do not leach out of the soil

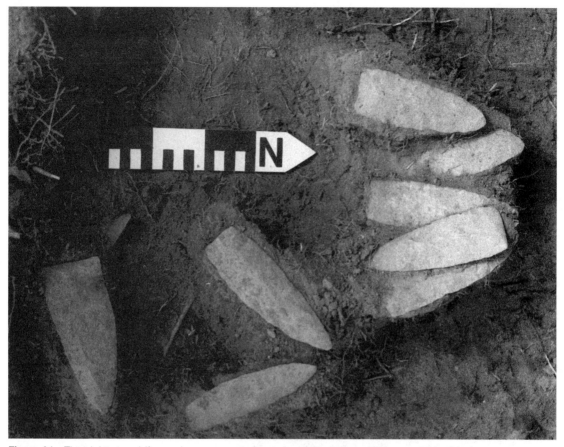

Figure 4.1   The eight stone bifaces shown are part of a cache of 30 similar artifacts—portable objects made and used by people—excavated at the "Glazier Blade Cache" site in Granby, Connecticut.

and can be detected by the archaeologist looking for sites (Cook and Heizer 1965; Eidt 1973, 1984; Hassan 1978).

Instrument Anomalies

Human activities, including pit or trench digging, wall construction, and fire, can result in slight anomalies in soil resistivity to an induced electric current (Carr 1982; Clark 1970) or in variations in the magnetic characteristics of the soil (Aitken 1970). Both are classified as **instrument anomalies.** Though ordinarily used within the context of intrasite investigation, electrical resistivity surveying, proton magnetometry, and even ground-penetrating radar can be used in a site survey program, as is

Figure 4.2   The platform of stones shown above was used to roast deer meat; burned wood and fragments of deer bone were found in the soil between the stones. The platform is an archaeological feature.

Figure 4.3 A midden. The darkly stained layer is caused by decayed organic material in the interior of the midden through which this excavation unit passed.

discussed under "Field Methodology" later in this chapter (Parrington 1983; Weymouth 1986).

FACTORS IN SURVEY DESIGN

So, a program of archaeological site survey involves the search for the constituents of archaeological sites: artifacts, features, anthropic soil horizons, chemical anomalies, and instrument anomalies. In designing a survey program to detect the presence of these constituents, at least three factors must be taken into consideration: environmental, cultural, and practical. Schiffer et al. (1978) label these factors, respectively: visibility, obtrusiveness, and accessibility.

Visibility

The **visibility** of archaeological remains can be defined as "the extent to which an observer can detect the presence of archaeological materials at or below a given place" (Schiffer et al. 1978:6). Visibility is largely a factor of the local environment. Areas with little or no vegetation, minimal geological deposition, or rapid rates of erosion present the researcher with an environment with *high* visibility. Archaeological materials, if present, may be readily apparent on the surface and are not obscured by vegetation, leaf litter, or soil deposits. On the other hand, areas with significant plant growth, relatively speedy rates of geological deposition, and minimal erosion present the archaeologist with an environment with *low* visibility. Archaeological materials may be buried under many feet of geological deposits, or they may be hidden by thick jungle undergrowth or leaf litter. Sites can be covered over by volcanic activity, by a river's flood deposits (alluvium), by lake (lacustrine) deposits, by erosional materials from higher elevations (colluvium), by wind-borne (aeolian) sediments, or by sea level rise.

A treeless expanse affords high visibility to above-ground remains. On the other hand, a tropical jungle where survey transects must often be cut by machete through thick vegetation can render otherwise obvious surficial remains virtually invisible, even to surveyors directly on top of them. Environments with differing degrees of visibility present the researcher with different challenges, and strategies for site detection will vary greatly.

Obtrusiveness

The **obtrusiveness** of archaeological site constituents can be defined as the archaeological or cultural "visibility" of the materials produced by the society. Deetz's (1968:285) "threshold of archaeological visibility" is the equivalent of Schiffer et al.'s (1978) obtrusiveness. Put another way, obtrusiveness is the ease with which the materials produced by a people can be discerned by the archaeologist. Factors contributing to obtrusiveness of a given archaeological manifestation include presence or absence of architecture, production of monumental works, durability of materials used in construction and tool manufacture, degree of sedentism, and population density.

Ordinarily, cultures that produce architectural edifices out of durable materials create archaeological sites that are more obtrusive than those that do not construct buildings or that work in nondurable materials. Similarly, cultures that produce monumental works like pyramids, ziggurats, or megalithic monuments result in sites that are more obtrusive than those that do not.

Beyond this, other cultural factors can have a great impact on how obtrusive an archaeological site is. For example, the degree of sedentism of a given group can have an effect. Occupation of a settlement for a very short period usually results in a sparse scattering of artifacts, whereas settlement occupation over a long period generally produces a denser accumulation of archaeological materials. Clearly, a denser concentration of artifacts is more obtrusive than a small scatter. Similarly, a large population will likely produce a larger archaeological deposit than will a small group. A larger deposit will be more obtrusive and, therefore, easier to detect.

There is, of course, an interaction between the two variables of degree of sedentism and population size in terms of the obtrusiveness of the archaeological remains produced. A large, permanent population will almost certainly produce a site with high archaeological visibility, whereas a small, nomadic group ordinarily will not. On the other hand, even a group present for a very short period of time but comprising a large number of people can produce a highly obtrusive archaeological site. For example, at Little Big Horn National Park, Montana, the battlefield where Custer and his men were defeated by an enormous force of Sioux Indians is a highly obtrusive historical archaeological site, though the use of the area was short term (Scott et al. 1989). The battle was brief, but it involved thousands of individuals.

Also, it should be added that the factors of visibility and obtrusiveness are interactive (Figure 4.4). Thus, a substantial, sedentary population engaged in large-scale architectural projects in durable materials in an area without dense vegetation and generally slow processes of geological deposition—as was the case, for example, in many areas of ancient Egypt or the American Southwest—will produce highly visible, highly obtrusive sites (Figure 4.5a). By comparison, small, nomadic bands of people building small, temporary shelters of nondurable materials in areas with fast-acting processes of geological deposition and thick vegetation—as was the case, for example, in prehistoric New England—will produce sites with both low visibility and low obtrusiveness (Figure 4.5b).

Elsewhere, large, dense populations constructed monumental works in fairly durable materials but in areas with very thick vegetation. Thus, a group like the prehistoric Maya of Mesoamerica

Figure 4.4 Archaeological site survey strategies appropriate to differing levels of archaeological visibility and site obtrusiveness.

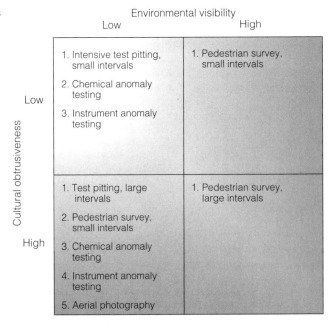

Environmental visibility

	Low	High
Low	1. Intensive test pitting, small intervals 2. Chemical anomaly testing 3. Instrument anomaly testing	1. Pedestrian survey, small intervals
High	1. Test pitting, large intervals 2. Pedestrian survey, small intervals 3. Chemical anomaly testing 4. Instrument anomaly testing 5. Aerial photography	1. Pedestrian survey, large intervals

Cultural obtrusiveness

Figure 4.5a Cliff Palace at Mesa Verde, Colorado, is a highly obtrusive site in an area with high archaeological visibility.

Figure 4.5b The Beaver Meadow Historic District in Barkhamsted, Connecticut, contains 19 unobtrusive prehistoric sites in an area with low archaeological visibility. Strategies for finding sites with differing characteristics will necessarily vary.

Figure 4.6 The Maya site of Chichen Itza, with its stone temples is highly obtrusive, but it is located in Yucatán low forest where archaeological visibility is low.

produced archaeologically obtrusive remains in areas with very low visibility (Figure 4.6). On the other hand, small, nomadic bands like the Shoshone in the Great Basin and the ancient hunter-gatherers in some parts of Texas produced sites of low obtrusiveness, but their sites are highly visible because the local environment tends not to obscure even ancient sites or erosion has worked to expose their remains (P. A. Thomas 1978).

It also must be considered that there will be variability within an individual group's settlement pattern in terms of visibility and obtrusiveness of remains. The fact that some sites within a settlement pattern are in highly visible areas and are at the same time highly obtrusive in no way guarantees that all elements of the land-use pattern will be the same. In other words, sites of differing function within the same archaeological culture can vary in how visible and obstrusive they are to the archaeologist surveyor. A complex state society may produce large urban sites in broad, open areas where visibility is high. Size, density, and durability of structural remains likely will render such sites highly obtrusive. On the other hand, these same people may use other areas of their realm for hunting or for ceremonial activities. Sites resulting from these activities may be located in areas of low

archaeological visibility, and the resulting small clusters of artifacts may lead to the obtrusiveness of such sites being quite low. Neglecting to even look for these more-difficult-to-find kinds of sites will produce an incomplete picture of the land-use patterns of the archaeological group.

It should be clear that archaeological survey strategies must take the factors of visibility and obtrusiveness—and their complex interplay—into account. The approach to finding sites will vary depending upon these key factors (McManamon 1984a).

Accessibility

The final factor to be considered here is **accessibility,** a purely practical consideration. Schiffer et al. (1978) include under this category the effort required to reach a particular survey area, the climate and how it can affect the efficiency of a crew of surveyors, the terrain, the biotic environment (the presence of dangerous animals or insects), the presence or absence of roads, political upheavals, and patterns of land ownership.

Though of a practical nature, considerations of accessibility are by no means insignificant. Surveying for archaeological sites in the wilderness of

Alaska is quite different from surveying in an urban setting. Survey crew efficiency is invariably a factor of temperature and humidity, whereas crew health and safety (see Chapter 5) can be affected by many factors. In some world areas the presence of terrorist groups, drug producers, and even illegal traders in antiquities can render archaeological survey quite dangerous (see "Some Hazards in Fieldwork," Chapter 5). Finally, site survey can be quite easy in areas where large landholdings are in the hands of a government that supports such research, but it can be quite difficult where landholdings are small and in the hands of many different owners, some of whom, for whatever reasons, do not wish to have archaeologists conducting survey work on their property.

Finally, we can here add a subcategory labeled "research accessibility." In the United States, many archaeological surveys are conducted through cultural resource management. Thus, survey funding often results from federal or state regulations requiring that archaeological resources be considered in the preparation of environmental impact statements. A survey may be funded to determine the potential impacts on archaeological sites of road construction, sewer placement, gravel operations, or flood control projects. In such cases, the geographical boundaries of a given archaeological research project may be drawn not on the basis of ecological or anthropological considerations, but may be contractually mandated on the basis of the delineation of the zone of possible impacts. It is rare that a highway right-of-way will correspond to some theoretically justifiable research area. Zones we might wish to test may not be included in the boundaries of the project. In such cases, we often will have no choice but to wait for another time and for additional funding to allow for the research accessibility of areas beyond the contractually mandated boundaries of our research universe.

BACKGROUND RESEARCH

Within the context of the visibility of archaeological remains in a given area, the obtrusiveness of those remains, and their accessibility, the archaeologist develops a survey design. As stated previously, the first step involves a reconnaissance survey. Dincauze (1978) emphasizes the importance of background study, including identification of local informants, and environmental factors, including bedrock and surficial geology (geomorphology), as variables in designing a site survey. When planning a survey, there are many questions to ask: How do we select an area to investigate? How might we divide up the region before we begin fieldwork? On which areas might our energies be more usefully focused? How might we differentiate sites on the basis of their location relative to local environmental characteristics? We begin our surveys not with shovels and trowels but with maps, pen, and paper.

Literature Review

When initiating a survey program, it is wise to ascertain what is already known about the research area before implementing the field methodology. Certainly, a careful perusal of the archaeological literature (if any) on the area may permit identification of sites already discovered and investigated. Many universities, museums, and in the United States, State Historic Preservation Offices and Offices of State Archaeologists often possess large databases with site information collected through regional surveys, cultural resource management projects, and contact with avocational archaeologists and other local informants.

Local Informants

Beyond this, in many parts of the world there is a local body of knowledge about archaeological remains—a kind of folk-archaeology—that is often, though not always, available to the archaeological researcher. In many parts of the United States, for example, there are small but dedicated groups of amateur or avocational archaeologists who know of the location of sites. Sullivan (1980:185–238) and Folsom and Folsom (1993:373–383) provide useful listings of amateur archaeological groups in the United States and Canada, many of which publish newsletters and bulletins detailing local archaeological investigations. Serious enough about arch-aeology to join a group and participate in its activities, most members of amateur archaeological societies are more than willing to share their information with professional archaeologists. Some of these amateurs have been collecting artifacts and information for many years and have an enormous database on site location—commonly, they are more knowledgeable about a local area than is the trained archaeologist. Their information is often quite useful and accurate; for example, Barber and Casjens (1978) were able to field-verify 85 percent of the sites reported to them by amateur archaeologists in one survey project in Massachusetts. It should be said that, at least until fairly recently, a large proportion of sites known to professional archaeologists in the United States had first been reported by amateurs.

Another category of local informants has been called "accidental archaeologists" (Feder and Park 1993:131). These people are not really archaeologists and may have no interest in archaeology but, though not actively looking for archaeological sites, have come upon remains accidentally. Where sites are in areas with high visibility, landowners, hikers, road survey crews, field geologists, and others may come upon above-ground remains. In areas with lower visibility as a result of geological deposition, those who turn over or move large amounts of earth as part of their occupations may have exposed archaeological materials: examples include farmers plowing their fields, construction workers excavating for a foundation, and water company workers putting in a water main.

In many parts of the United States as well as in other countries, it is extremely worthwhile to attempt to contact avocational archaeologists as well as those who have come upon archaeological materials accidentally. In areas where there is a substantial human population and where activities have involved moving substantial amounts of soil, it is common for residents to have found artifacts but to not be aware who might be interested in their information and who to contact.

Reaching out to local residents to let them know who to talk to about archaeological artifacts discovered on their property can be an important

preliminary step in a survey. For example, in the Farmington River Archaeological Project in Connecticut (Feder 1981), we made it a common practice to send questionnaires to local farmers who owned substantial acreage, asking if they had come upon archaeological remains while plowing their fields. Though many landowners had no knowledge of archaeological remains, the percentage that responded positively made the effort more than worthwhile. In his report of his research in Connecticut, McBride (1984:58) suggests contacting a 10 percent sample of all town residents; face-to-face surveys can also be useful in obtaining information and, more important, gaining the trust of local landowners.

Clearly, this step in archaeological survey cannot and need not be applied everywhere. In largely uninhabited areas—for example, in national forests in the United States—park rangers may be excellent sources of information, having walked over large sections of the areas under their care, but human population densities ordinarily are too low to make a questionnaire sent through the mail very effective. On the other hand, in a recent survey conducted by the author (Feder and Banks 1996), a questionnaire mailed to residents living on the periphery of a 3,500-acre game refuge in Connecticut resulted in valuable information concerning prehistoric sites in the refuge, so such surveys should not be ruled out. The potential for questionnaire surveys producing valuable information simply must be assessed on a case-by-case basis.

Making yourself available to local historical societies, school groups, senior citizens' organizations, scouting groups, library groups, and the like can help in establishing contacts with knowledgeable local people who are often willing to share information. Obviously, where such organizations do not exist, this kind of outreach is far more difficult. In many parts of the world, there is very little in the way of such an in-place information network; there may be no telephone directories or few people with telephones; and mail service may be poor to nonexistent. This may make the kinds of personal and direct contacts that work so well in some parts of the world rather problematic if not impossible. Nevertheless, where possible, reaching out to local people with a high potential for having encountered remains allows us to salvage information that might otherwise be lost.

Although the information provided by amateur and accidental archaeologists often does not fulfill the necessity of representativeness discussed in Chapter 3, it can be valuable in providing a database concerning the kinds of remains that might be expected in an area to be systematically surveyed.

History and Ethnohistory

In some areas, historical and/or ethnohistorical sources may provide important clues concerning site location. In the Farmington Valley in Connecticut, for example, there is a series of documents related to the transfer of land from the Tunxis, the local Indian group, to the English settlers of the valley in the seventeenth century (Feder 1983). These treaties, signed by resident Indians and immigrant Englishmen, detail property boundaries and include locational information for seventeenth-century Indian villages. Following treaty descriptions of the location of a Tunxis village at a place called Indian Neck and referring to historical maps of the area, we were able to isolate the most probable location for the village and verify its existence through field research.

Ethnohistorical research, in addition to providing specific site locations, also serves as a valuable source of general information concerning aboriginal settlement patterns. Thus, although not in every instance providing specific site location data, ethnohistory can supply information about the ways in which a historical group utilized the landscape—in other words, its settlement pattern (Thomas 1973). This knowledge can be used when deciding how and where to focus one's energy in the field.

Environmental Variables

Schiffer et al. (1978:5) list some of the environmental considerations that surely affected land-use patterns: the presence of water, firewood, chippable stone, building materials, minerals, and native metals, as well as the gentleness of relief. To this could be added factors of soil fertility, defensibility, and ease of transportation and trade.

As Dincauze (1978:54) has stated concerning background environmental information, we are interested in "what . . . the data mean in terms of resources available to human populations in a given area." In selecting an area for examination, deciding how to divide the area into manageable units for the intensive phase of the study, as well as trying to understand why sites were located where they were, we need to consider the constellation of environmental variables that would have rendered an area attractive to human settlement or exploitation. Although some factors are common to all human groups, it should be noted that the significance of various aspects of the environment varies with different human groups and their varied adaptations.

Certainly different areas within a region provide, to varying degrees, water, fuel, food resources, and the raw materials needed to construct shelters, as well as the tools necessary to extract a living from the environment. Equally certainly, land-use patterns are, at least in part, predicated on such practical considerations as how far it is to fresh water, how abundant is the local plant and animal food base, how close by are construction materials, where lithic/clay/metal/wood resources are to be found, how abundant is heating or cooking fuel (ordinarily wood), how fertile and tillable is the soil, how steep is the slope of the immediate area, and other such factors.

For example, no human group will choose to live in an area where water, fuel, food, or shelter is not available or cannot be made available at a given culture's level of technology—specifically, their ability to move resources from those areas where they are abundant to those areas where they are not available. In one study, in a sample of 133 sites in North Carolina, for example, Robertson and Robertson (1978:30) showed that 88 percent of the sites were within 200 feet of a freshwater source.

In some cases, a single environmental factor may be the ultimate determinant of site location. We know, for example, that until fairly recently among the modern !Kung San people of the Kalahari Desert in southern Africa, the single factor of freshwater availability in the form of permanent springs controlled village location (Lee 1984). In other areas, an interplay of variables rather than a single determinant may be the key to site location. For example, of the 133 sites in the above-mentioned North Carolina study, 81.4 percent were not only within 200 feet of a freshwater source (and less than 100 feet above the water source) but were also situated on land whose slope did not exceed a 15-degree angle (Robertson and Robertson 1978:34–35).

Of great use to archaeologists in the United States in assessing the local environment are United States Geological Survey (USGS) 7.5-minute, 1:24,000 quadrangle maps (see Chapter 9). These maps depict stream drainage, topography, and modern cultural features. The USGS also produces quadrangle maps of surficial deposits and bedrock geology. Other maps are available on the state level from environmental agencies, transportation departments, and natural resource agencies. Though somewhat dated, Makower and Bergheim's (1990) *The Map Catalog* provides a valuable listing of map availability. The book also contains a series of appendixes with addresses for federal and state map agencies in the United States, as well as a short listing of international map sources.

Beyond this, many states in the United States have complete coverage by aerial photography, commonly with a scale of 1 inch to 1,000 feet. Often, aerial photographs can be examined at state libraries or environmental agencies. Maps and aerial photographs allow the archaeologist to examine the research area as a whole and can be extremely useful in designing the intensive phase of research. As Lyons and Scovill (1978:9) point out, aerial photographs can provide key background data for a regional survey, including vegetative zones, physiographic regions, and gross soil changes across the region being studied. Using aerial photographs, archaeologists can target areas where sites are most likely to be located based on environmental conditions revealed by these images and previous archaeological work in the area. An abundance of aerial

photographs are available on the state and federal level in the United States (see Chapter 9). The level of aerial mapping varies greatly from country to country, however.

When deciding on areas to test for archaeological remains, though, one cannot presume that human groups settled or utilized as part of their pattern of land use only those areas that seem sensible from a modern, practical, or economic standpoint. Not all human activity is economically driven or practically based. For example, Dincauze (1968) has shown that the location of one category of sites in Massachusetts, cremation burials dating to between about 5,000 to 3,000 years ago, are sometimes located in areas decidedly *unsuitable* for human habitation or economic exploitation. Some burial sites seem to have been chosen precisely for their isolation and lack of suitability for habitation (Dincauze 1968:12).

A further consideration concerns long- and short-term environmental change. Rivers meander, springs dry up, quarries become depleted, sea level rises and falls. Areas suitable for habitation today may not have always been so, and areas unlikely to attract human settlement today may have been far more attractive in the past.

It is important when designing a research strategy to consider the spatial patterning of resources that would have affected a human group's land-use decisions and settlement pattern. It is equally important to remember, however, that people do not make mechanical decisions concerning land use on the basis of rigid economic considerations—and that survey strategies should not be based on such a spurious assumption.

FIELD METHODS IN SITE SURVEY

Keeping in mind our discussion of visibility, obtrusiveness, and accessibility, as well as the kinds of background information available for an area, we can now discuss the field methodology of intensive site survey, including pedestrian survey, subsurface survey, chemical survey, and remote sensing through instrument anomaly survey and aerial survey. The utility of each of these techniques in a given situation is a reflection of site visibility and obtrusiveness.

Pedestrian Survey

Pedestrian or **foot survey** involves, quite simply, walking over the surface of a region and visually inspecting that surface for the constituents of archaeological sites. Usually, features and architectural remains are recorded and artifacts recovered, though some suggest leaving artifacts in place, at least during the initial survey phase of research (Davis 1978). This practice is problematical, however, because collectors have been known to follow archaeologists into an area to collect the artifacts marked and left in place.

Clearly, pedestrian survey is most effective in those areas where visibility is high. Where geomorphic processes have not acted to obscure surface remains, where such processes have acted to expose buried remains, and where vegetation is sparse, archaeological sites can often be detected by simple visual inspection.

Even in areas where visibility may not be optimal, if remains are highly obtrusive, pedestrian survey may be a very effective way to locate obvious above-ground remains. Also, even where visibility is low *and* obtrusiveness of the archaeological remains is also low, vegetation patterns may be discerned that are caused by variations in soil chemistry resulting from buried anthropic soils or culturally produced chemical anomalies.

Often in a pedestrian survey, crew members will arrange themselves in what is called a **transect** (a linear survey unit) across the landscape and simply walk over the region to be investigated (Figure 4.7). In some cases, the area to be surveyed is gridded into sections, with surveyors assigned to particular grids that they are to walk over in the search for surface remains. There is no one standard for intensity of pedestrian surveys, so there is no universally agreed upon standard for how widely spaced the surveyors should be. Where above-ground architectural remains are present in an

(b)

Figure 4.7 Using a sighting device (an alidade—see Chapter 10), a baseline is established for a pedestrian survey in a wooded area (*a*). In another pedestrian survey (*b*) archaeology students walk the furrows of a freshly plowed field.

environment with high visibility, the spacing of surveyors can be fairly wide, with little risk of missing site indicators. On the other hand, as the distance between surveyors is increased, the possibility grows of missing visible but unobtrusive archaeological remains—for example, a small surface lithic scatter. Schiffer et al. (1978:13) suggest that where remains are highly obtrusive in an area of high visibility, surveyors can be spaced at as much as 100-m intervals, whereas even in areas of high visibility, spacing might have to be as little as 2 m to detect the entire population of unobtrusive sites. According to Chartkoff and Chartkoff (1980:65), the Forest Service in California suggests 10 m as the preferred distance between crew members in a pedestrian survey. Lightfoot (1986) utilized 10-m intervals between crew members in a pedestrian survey he conducted in Pinedale, Arizona. Derry et al. (1985:39), in a publication of the National Parks Service, suggest a spacing of between 5 and 15 m.

As Chartkoff and Childress (1966) point out, the spacing of surveyors not only has a great impact on site discovery but also on survey cost. They calculate the cost in time for a pedestrian survey where crew members are placed at intervals of 20 ft and 132 person-hours per square mile. In another study in California, Chartkoff and Chartkoff (1980:66) calculated the cost in time for surveying a square mile when crew members were placed at 200-ft intervals at 9 person-hours.

Pedestrian survey can also be quite effective in areas where there has been a great deal of erosion. Even in areas with generally low visibility, unobtrusive sites may become visible and detectable through surface walkover where erosion has exposed ancient strata. For example, though the remains of most extinct prehistoric hominids are covered by many meters of geological deposition, initial evidence of their presence is usually discerned by pedestrian survey. Working in the Afar region of Ethiopia, for example, paleoanthropologist Donald Johanson and his team discovered the remains of the 3.18-million-year-old fossil called Lucy—now categorized as *Australopithecus afarensis*—by pedestrian survey (Johanson and Edey 1981). By consciously selecting areas like the Afar region and Olduvai Gorge, where erosion has exposed ancient sediments, paleoanthropologists take advantage of natural "excavations" in their search for sites. Rivers cutting channels, wind moving sediment, waves eroding beach deposits, and so forth, may expose old surfaces or ancient strata.

Even burrowing animals like gophers, badgers, and armadillos can bring archaeological objects to the surface, where they can be identified through pedestrian survey. This is fairly common, for example, in sand mantle areas in Texas (Fox and Hester 1976). A site in Connecticut, Woodchuck Knoll, is named after the mammal in whose backdirt artifacts were initially discovered. Overgrazing by cattle is another process by which animals may expose buried sites.

Human beings also move around quite a bit of earth, exposing buried soil layers and bringing up ancient material (Mallouf 1987). The simple act of plowing in agriculture can expose archaeological remains. McManamon (1984a) suggests that walking plowed fields is still the most common technique of site survey in the American Midwest. The ability of the plow to bring up artifacts within reach of the plow blade is one reason why farmers are often such valuable sources of site location information, as mentioned previously. Archaeologists, both professional and amateur, take advantage of this and often walk up and down the furrows of plowed fields, scanning the turned-over soil for site indicators. In some instances, artifact type and location are recorded and specimens are left in place for more-detailed subsequent field analysis. Often in the disturbed context of a plowed field, artifacts are picked up and bagged, and features and anthropic soil horizons are recorded. Surface collection of plowed fields is more effective in site discovery after a rainfall, which tends to wash the dust off artifacts, making them much easier to see against the background of darker, muddy soil.

Walking plowed fields is such a common procedure for finding archaeological remains in areas where visibility is otherwise low that some archaeologists have attempted to plow unplowed areas expressly in an attempt to find sites (Trubowitz 1976, 1981). Other techniques used to increase the visibility of archaeological remains include raking, forest clearance, and soil removal with heavy equipment. Ordinarily, however, where sites are buried, archaeologists have to dig to find them.

Subsurface Survey

Where visibility is low, particularly as a result of relatively quick acting geomorphic processes of surficial deposition, and where site obtrusiveness also is low, a regimen of subsurface testing almost always is necessary for the discovery of buried archaeological remains (Feder 1990b; Kintigh 1988; Krakker et al. 1983; Lightfoot 1986; Lovis 1976; McBride 1984; McManamon 1984a, 1984b; Nance and Ball 1986). **Subsurface testing** involves, in one way or another, digging holes, bringing up the dirt, and inspecting it for visible constituents of archaeological sites (artifacts, ecofacts, features, anthropic soil horizons).

There are various methods of digging holes and bringing up the soil: soil corers, hand augers, power augers (Assad and Potter 1979), posthole diggers, shovel test pits, and machine-aided trenching. Where these have been compared in terms of their utility in locating archaeological sites, test pits invariably have been shown to be the most effective—and most expensive—technique available (Casjens et al. 1980; Chartkoff 1978; McManamon 1981a, 1981b, 1984a, 1984b, though they clearly have their detractors [Shott 1989]).

Shovel test pits are usually between 25 and 100 cm on a side, though 50 cm seems to be the most common (McManamon 1984a). The larger the pit, the easier it is to examine stratigraphy and to look for otherwise hidden anthropic soil horizons. The pits are shovel dug, with the soil matrix ordinarily dry-screened through ¼- or ⅛-inch-mesh hardware cloth.

Just as there is no one standard for the distance between crew members in a pedestrian survey, test pit placement patterns vary greatly (Figure 4.8). In a survey of forested uplands in western Connecticut, Feder (1988) used a test pit interval of 25 m. McBride (1984) initially utilized a 20-m interval in the Lower Connecticut River Valley and later decreased that interval; and on Shelter Island, New York, Lightfoot (1986) excavated pits at 10-m intervals. Pits are commonly placed in straight-line transects, though other patterns have been used; Kintigh (1988) suggests that a hexagonal lattice of pits is effective. Again, there is no one method that

Figure 4.8 A line, or transect, of test pits excavated at regular intervals across the floodplain of the Farmington River in Connecticut. In this case, all soil was passed through hardware cloth.

necessarily is best under all circumstances. A number of factors—including the depth of material, surrounding terrain, nature of the soil matrix, level of funding, and project goals—must be taken into account.

Once a site has been recognized through test pitting, it is marked—with surveyor's flagging tape in forested areas and surveyor's pins elsewhere—and additional pits may be excavated to determine site size, boundaries, and general patterns of artifact or feature distribution (Chartkoff 1978). Often in this process, additional test pits are excavated in several directions from the original test pit where archaeological material was first identified. These pits are commonly placed at shorter intervals, perhaps only 3–5 m apart (Chartkoff 1978:51), or even less (McBride 1984). Also useful in determining the extent of a site in some areas is mechanical trenching (Anyon and LeBlanc 1984; Frison and Todd 1986; Waters 1986). Using test pits, power augers, and mechanical trenching techniques, the spatial extent of the site can be determined, features can be located, and stratigraphy can be assessed.

In another approach to the initial testing of a site's spatial parameters, Hoffman (1990) has shown that **close interval core sampling** can be useful in determining site dimensions and intensity of use within sites. He took a series of small-diameter (¾ inch) cores less than 2 m apart within known sites and found a close correlation between the presence of soil staining in the cores and archaeological features. Although this seems to be an effective, relatively quick, and inexpensive method for assessing the distribution of anthropic soils within the boundaries of sites, Hoffman admits that it is not an appropriate method for finding sites in a regional survey: the cores need to be too closely spaced, and the existence of stained soils alone is not sufficient to determine the presence or absence of a site.

It is also common for the region being surveyed to be segmented according to local environmental characteristics recognized in the reconnaissance phase of the study. In the survey mentioned earlier, Feder (1988) divided his region into major river floodplains, small stream terraces, areas with significant bedrock exposure, and general uplands. McBride (1984:59) divided the Lower Connecticut Valley into three sampling strata: floodplain, terrace, and uplands. Lightfoot (1986:491) divided his study area into two major zones: coastal and interior. Carlson et al. (1986), in surveying the Fort Hood Military Reservation, divided the area into uplands, intermediate slopes, and lowlands.

Test pit transects can be placed entirely within these zones, or they can be oriented to crosscut the zones. Coverage can be random in areas where there is no knowledge concerning the probable location of sites. Feder and McBride both used a stratified random sample in their surveys (see Chapter 3 for a discussion of sampling procedures) as part of their strategy to sample the different zones within their research areas consistently. Lightfoot, on the other hand, employed a judgmental sample, basing test pit coverage on expectation of site discovery—more pits were placed in those areas where sites were expected based on background research. McBride (1984:67) varied the intensity of test pit placement during the course of his research, greatly decreasing test pit intervals from his initial 20 m to as little as 5 or even 2 m on those landforms that previously produced archaeological material. Handsman (1990) has shown that in western Connecticut, where the late prehistoric and early historic settlement pattern includes small

"wigwam clusters," a test pit interval of greater than 5 m results in some sites being missed entirely. In such a case, test pit intervals of 20 or 25 m would detect only a fraction of the sites actually present and might lead to a gross underestimation of prehistoric and historic population. Casjens et al. (1980) agree that flexibility should be maintained in a testing program to allow for the judgmental selection of some areas for testing or for increased density of testing in particular areas based on subjective criteria. As McBride (1984) points out, however, although this allows for a greater degree of site recovery, it also renders statistical analysis problematical.

Virtually all techniques of subsurface investigation are labor intensive. We, as yet, have no technology that allows us to image subsurface material and identify archaeological remains, at least not on a regional scale (see the remote sensing sections of this chapter). Dowsing for archaeological remains (see Aitken 1959 for a skeptical discussion) and so-called psychic archaeology (Jones 1979; Schwartz 1978, 1983) both have been attempted but represent nothing more than wishful thinking (Feder 1990a).

Comparison of Methods. Test pitting, because of the amount of soil moved in each unit, represents the most labor intensive approach in an already expensive process (McManamon 1984a:262–268). It must be stated, however, that in a side-by-side comparison of the ability to locate buried artifacts by a number of subsurface testing methods (3-cm soil corers, 10- to 15-cm augers, 25- to 30-cm divots, and 25- to 75-cm-wide shovel-dug test pits), McManamon (1981a, 1981b) shows that shovel-dug test pits are by far the most effective method. At known sites, whereas only 1 percent of the cores taken contained artifacts, 45 percent of the larger auger tests and 78 percent of the shovel test pits contained artifacts (McManamon 1981a:204, 1981b:47). The implication is that where sites are being looked for, you are far more likely to detect them by test pitting than by the other methods of subsurface testing.

Therefore, where the constituents of archaeological sites are buried by geological deposition, subsurface testing is necessary. It would appear that shovel-dug test pits offer the greatest likelihood of site discovery, especially for relatively shallow sites. For deeper sites, especially those covered by several meters of overburden, machine-aided testing, including use of a power auger or backhoe, may be needed.

Test-pitting Effectiveness.   Nance and Ball (1986) have assessed the effectiveness of test pit surveys. They define two parameters of such surveys: intersection probability and productivity probability. **Intersection probability** is the likelihood that a test pit in a transect or some other pattern of pit placement will be placed within the boundaries of a site. Intersection is a necessary concomitant of site detection. They go on to assert, however, that sites may have "empty spaces" in terms of their archaeological constituents. According to them, therefore, the mere fact that a test pit is placed within the boundaries of a site is not a guarantee that archaeological material will be recovered or even that the fact that the test pit is within a site's boundaries will be recognized. They define **productivity probability** (called by the clearer term **detection probability** by Shott [1989]) as the likelihood that, once within the boundaries of a site, a test pit will, in fact, bring up archaeological material.

The intersection probability in a given instance is largely a product of test pit interval and site size. The productivity probability in a given instance is a product of test pit size, artifact density, degree of artifact dispersion or clustering, and the methods used in inspecting the test pit (Nance and Ball 1986:460).

Obviously, the more closely spaced test pits are, the greater the likelihood of site intersection. In a survey conducted in Michigan, Lovis (1976:370–371) determined that the mean minimum dimension of sites was 30 yd and intuitively suggested a test pit interval of 25 yd for a high rate of site discovery. Kintigh (1988) simulated a test pitting program, showing that the probability of site intersection increases dramatically when the interval between test pits approximates the mean diameter of the sites being found (Figure 4.9). Krakker et al. (1983) came to the same conclusion.

With this in mind, most researchers are agreed on one point: test pitting is an effective—though expensive—procedure for locating large sites with high artifact densities (Kintigh 1988:706; Krakker et

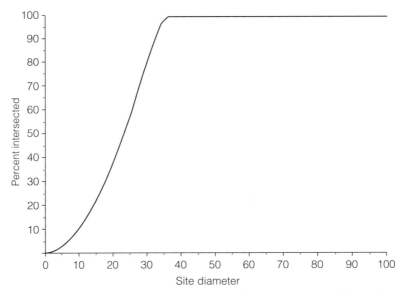

Figure 4.9   Site intersection curve (from Kintigh 1988). This graph shows that as test pit interval approaches mean site diameter, an increasing percentage of the sites present will be discovered.

al. 1983; Nance and Ball 1986:479). As sites decrease in horizontal extent and as artifact density decreases, test pit density necessarily must increase to the point at which the financial or labor limits of any survey would quickly be reached.

On a more optimistic note, in a survey project on Shelter Island, New York, Lightfoot (1986) has shown that an intensive test-pitting regimen can detect a wide array of sites, including spatially small sites with low artifact densities. Similarly, McBride's (1984), Feder's (1988; Feder and Banks 1996), and Handsman's (1990) work in Connecticut has shown that with the application of time and effort, test pitting can illuminate aspects of settlement patterns not previously known, including the presence of spatially small sites with low artifact densities.

On the other hand, Shott (1989) is certainly correct in maintaining that test pit surveys will rarely, if ever, find all sites; but then again, as Nance and Ball (1989) and Lightfoot (1989) have said in response to Shott's criticisms, no archaeological discovery technique is 100 percent effective. And, as pointed out at the beginning of this chapter, the best we can expect from many regional surveys is a representative sample of sites. A test-pitting regimen can be designed to ensure the representativeness of the sample, and we should be able to estimate the site population present (Krakker et al. 1983:480).

Important is Kintigh's (1988) reminder that we need to be flexible in designing our subsurface sampling strategy. As we better understand variation in site size, artifact density, and degree of clustering in a given region, we need to alter our strategies of test pit placement. Shott's (1989) suggestion that forest clear-cutting and surface inspection should replace test pitting in regional surveys seems neither justifiable nor realistic. Test pitting is far from perfect, but it is by far the best methodology currently available for the discovery of buried sites.

Chemical Survey

As mentioned previously, two of the constituents of archaeological sites as enumerated by McMana-

mon (1984a) are chemical and instrument anomalies that result from human activity. Theoretically, it should be possible to conduct site surveys in areas with low visibility by searching for such anomalies. Beyond this, such an approach might be more cost-effective than test pitting because it can be far less labor intensive.

In terms of a **chemical survey,** certainly not as much soil (in most cases, very little soil) needs to be moved to collect samples for analysis for anthropogenic anomalies as needs to be moved in searching for artifacts, features, or soil horizons (Eidt 1973, 1984). Soil test kits, available through various science supply services, are relatively inexpensive, and samples can be processed relatively rapidly (Eidt 1973; Hassan 1981).

Essentially, human activity involving the concentration of organic residues can result in the concentration of their chemical by-products—in particular, compounds of phosphorus, nitrogen, calcium, and carbon—in the soil. Other compounds, including those of mercury and iodine (Dincauze 1976:96–98) may also be important. However, chemical testing is not a simple process, and as McManamon (1984a:237) points out, "no widely applicable single value exists for any of these elements that conclusively indicates the presence or absence of a site." Beyond this, sites can often be missed entirely. In one application (Cook and Heizer 1965), 38 percent of a sample of 13 known sites showed no anomalous chemical levels at all.

Remote Sensing: Instrument Anomaly Survey

Surveying for instrument anomalies involves detection from the surface of archaeological features at some depth without the movement of soil. These surveying methods fall under the category of **remote sensing.** Instrument surveys using the proton magnetometer, electrical resistivity meters, and ground-penetrating radar can be compared to noninvasive diagnostic medical procedures like a CAT scan (Thomas 1989). Where previously a surgeon might have had to conduct exploratory surgery to determine the cause of an illness, the CAT scan can, in effect, let the physician look inside the patient without cutting him or her open. In archaeology, a procedure like proton magnetometry can, in effect, let the archaeologist see under the surface of the ground without having to excavate pits. Some archaeological remains have a characteristic magnetic "signature." Thus, the technique can be used to determine the presence of artifacts, features, or anthropic soil horizons.

A number of geophysical tools have been employed in archaeological survey. As enumerated by Weymouth (1986), these can be divided into procedures that employ passive techniques and those that use active techniques. Among the former are magnetic surveying techniques; the latter include seismic sounding, acoustic sounding, electromagnetic methods, resistivity surveying, and the use of ground-penetrating radar.

Passive Procedures.   Among the most successful of the instrument anomaly techniques, **magnetic** **surveying** involves the use of a device called a **proton magnetometer.** This device measures the strength of the earth's magnetic field at the surface. Under optimal conditions, when this device is pulled over a flat, uniform surface above a homogeneous soil matrix, the earth's magnetic field is uniform across that surface. Any deviation from the homogeneity of the soil matrix alters slightly the earth's magnetic field; magnetometers detect these deviations from the earth's otherwise uniform magnetic field. As Weymouth (1986:343) lists them, the following archaeological features can cause highly localized, slight variations in the earth's magnetic field that can be detected by a magnetometer: trash pits and middens, ditches, walls and foundations, hearths, burned structures, and bricks. Technically, these features have a different magnetic susceptibility than the surrounding soil, leading to slight alterations of the earth's magnetic field as it passes through them (Figure 4.10).

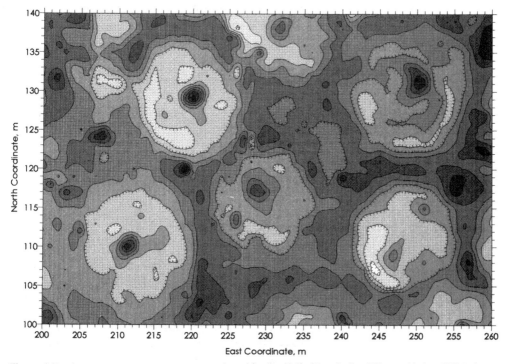

Figure 4.10   A proton magnetometer map produced for the Knife River Indian Villages National Historic Site. This map depicts a small portion of magnetometer survey at the Big Hidatsa Village. The larger circular features represent the magnetic anomalies produced by earth lodges. The small circular anomalies within each of the larger features are fire hearths.

Active Procedures. In another highly successful approach, **electrical resistivity surveying,** a current is passed through the soil. The resistivity or conductivity of the soil depends on a number of factors related primarily to water content, ion content, and soil structure. Variations in these factors can result from the presence of buried archaeological remains or from previous human activity, and consequent variations or anomalies in soil resistivity can be identified. Specific archaeological features that can alter soil resistivity from that of sterile or nonarchaeological conditions include structural remains like foundations or walls. Beyond this, any human activities that result in either the compaction or the loosening of soil can alter soil resistivity. Compaction of soil can result from road or path construction. Loosening of soil occurs in pits, cellars, middens, and ditches (Weymouth 1986).

In the use of **ground-penetrating radar,** an electromagnetic pulse is released into the ground. As is the case in air radar, the return time of the electromagnetic pulse after it is reflected back to the radar receiver is dependent upon the density and distance (in the case of ground radar, depth) of whatever the pulse encounters. As Weymouth (1986) indicates, ground-penetrating radar works best when there are abrupt rather than subtle discontinuities in the electrical properties of the subsurface. Ground-penetrating radar has been successfully employed in the location of buried walls, foundations, and houses with highly compacted floors.

Unfortunately, as McManamon (1984a:234) points out, instrument anomaly analysis turns out to be of limited value in regional surveys because the site constituents these methods are designed to detect are relatively rare and tend to be highly clustered within sites (thus making their detection on a regional level problematical) and also because their detection necessitates the detailed study of off-site areas to provide a baseline for site versus nonsite readings. As Weymouth (1986:312) indicates, instrument anomaly surveys are most useful in the determination of the "content and limits" of known sites, not in the location of unknown sites.

There have been, however, some instances in which the search for instrument anomalies resulted

in site detection where test pitting had failed. For example, Thomas (1987) recounts the search for Santa Catalina, the most important Spanish mission in sixteenth- and seventeenth-century Georgia. Proton magnetometry was quite useful in pinpointing the location of the mission. In a large-scale magnetometer survey in the valley of San Lorenzo in Mexico, 80,000 readings were taken in the search for monumental stone sculptures produced by the Olmec culture. Seventeen such monuments were found in this application (Breiner and Coe 1972).

As yet, however, these cases are exceptional. It might be argued that in Thomas's case, he was not conducting a truly regional survey. He knew the general, somewhat limited area where the mission would be found, and it was just a matter of filtering out the specific locations where it wasn't. His was an exciting application of the technique, but although chemical testing, electrical resistivity surveying, proton magnetometry, and subsurface radar can contribute to a program of site survey, they cannot often replace the mechanical subsurface search for artifacts, features, and anthropic soil horizons. They are of far greater use in the detection of buried features within known sites (Carr 1982; Parrington 1983; Weymouth 1986).

Remote Sensing: Aerial Survey

It is sometimes the case that surficial archaeological remains and anomalous vegetation patterns are too subtle to be seen at ground level. The vertical scale may be too small and the horizontal scale too large to permit recognition of cultural features. One sometimes needs, literally, to get a "bird's eye view" of an area to discern subtle changes in ground surface elevation, as well as vegetation color and growth patterns, to detect the presence of archaeological remains. Sometimes, images in the visual light spectrum cannot indicate the presence of archaeological remains, but infrared images or even radar can. All of these techniques fall under the heading of **aerial survey** (Lyons 1977; Lyons and Avery 1977; Lyons and Ebert 1978) (Figure 4.11). Aerial survey can include aerial photography, thermography, and radar imaging.

Figure 4.11 Aerial photo of Pulltrouser Swamp showing a pattern of ancient Maya raised agricultural fields. One significant contribution of aerial photography is in providing a unique visual perspective of an archaeological site or region.

Aerial photographs can be black and white, color, or infrared. Photographs can be taken from planes at high or low altitudes and even from satellites. Cameras can be mounted to take photographs vertically (straight down) or obliquely (at an angle to the ground). Photographs can be taken under various lighting conditions, from the sun being directly overhead to it being low on the horizon.

These variables in aerial photography produce images of varying use to the archaeologist. Aerial photographs often are used in detecting archaeological remains of great size or patterns of land modification on a large or even regional level (roads or irrigation networks, for example). On the other hand, where archaeological visibility and obtrusiveness are high, even small-scale archaeological features may be discernible in aerial photographs. Photographs taken with sufficient overlap (60 percent; see Chapter 9) can be interpreted three-dimensionally by the use of stereo pairs,

an inexpensive viewing device consisting of two lenses (one for each eye). Using stereo pairs and standard 1:20,000-scale photographs taken by the Army Corps of Engineers covering most of the United States and large parts of Central America, exposed features as small as 5 m across and less than 1 m high can be detected.

Photographs taken when the sun is low on the horizon can display shadow effects resulting from minor topographic anomalies, indiscernible on the ground, that were caused by ancient, largely eroded land modification features like ridged agricultural fields, irrigation channels, or roads.

Infrared photography can be useful in detecting differences in the amount of heat being reflected off vegetation; patterns may be the result of buried archaeological remains impeding (as in the case of a buried wall) or encouraging (as in the case of an anthropic soil horizon) plant growth (D. R. Wilson 1982). Differential patterns of vegetation detected from the air were used by Parrington (1983) to trace ancient irrigation canals and fields in the American Southwest.

Sheets and Sever (1988) used infrared aerial photography, in another example, to study the patterns of ancient footpaths in northwestern Costa Rica. Narrow, sinuous features, unrecognized on the ground, were discovered in the photographs. Sheets and Sever were able to investigate the degree of contact between different ancient settlements using these photographs.

Beyond photography, there are a number of new, high-tech procedures being applied in archaeological survey. Sheets and Sever (1988) also produced data on the pattern of ancient footpaths using a **laser** mounted in a plane. The laser was used to measure precise differences in the height of the land surface and in vegetation, detecting the very small and otherwise indiscernible topographic characteristics of the footpaths. Adams et al. (1981) used **side-looking, airborne radar (SLAR)** in a study of ancient Maya raised fields and canals. The radar can do what optical photography cannot—it can penetrate heavy vegetation covering a region. Adams et al. (1981) were able to discern intricate patterns of canals and raised fields, contributing to a reassessment of Maya agriculture.

So, remote sensing through some form of aerial reconnaissance can be quite useful when, as a result of scale, pedestrian surveys are simply ineffective at discerning the subtle patterns produced by archaeological remains and where visibility is low because of vegetation. Of course, however, in all applications of remote sensing, it still is necessary to verify the results on the ground.

PRACTICAL CONSIDERATIONS

To this point, the focus has been on the theoretical and methodological questions raised by site survey. It is important to discuss, if only briefly, the practical considerations of conducting a survey. Although a detailed discussion would necessarily address regional differences and the particulars of a pedestrian or a subsurface survey, there are some general suggestions that apply to virtually all survey projects.

For example, Figure 4.12 contains a short checklist of supplies and equipment useful in a survey. Not all crew members need all of these items, but all should be available to the crew as a whole.

Beyond this, standardized forms for record keeping are essential. Whether the survey is a pedestrian or a subsurface one, as Dincauze (1978:57) points out that "one person's idea of what is important [to record] is very different from everyone else's." A general test pit form used in the Farmington River Archaeological Project in Connecticut appears as Figure 4.13, and a specialized form used in a pedestrian survey at a large known site, Teotihuacan, in Mexico, appears as Figure 4.14.

While conducting a site survey, consistency in site location designation is crucial, but it is unfortunately lacking in many cases. Where public land surveys were carried out (primarily in the American Midwest), sites can be located by **township, section, quadrant,** and **quarter section** (see Chapter 9). But because large areas of the United States, not to mention the rest of the world, have not been divided up into these types of zones, this method is of limited application. Some prefer to designate

Basic equipment carried by survey crew

Single-lens reflex camera, film
Cloth or paper bags for collecting specimens
Large steel or cloth measuring tape (110 feet/30 meters)
Small steel pocket tape (10 feet/3 meters)
Machete for clearing undergrowth
Pointed-end shovel
Portable sifter with 1/4- or 1/8-inch hardware cloth
Mason's pointing trowel
Whisk broom and paint brush
Pencils
Compass
Ruler and protractor
Scale to be used in photographs
USGS topographic map of area, UTM counter, and other
    maps
Notebook with graph paper for preliminary mapping
Test pit forms/clipboard
Knapsack

Figure 4.12   Supply checklist for archaeological surveyors.

site location by longitude and latitude. A more precise and effective method is based on the Universal Transverse Mercator (UTM) system. On the USGS quadrangle maps (which will be discussed in detail in Chapter 9), grid ticks have been placed at 1,000-m intervals north and south, creating a series of boxes 1,000 m on a side. Scales are available to divide up the large boxes into successively smaller boxes. A site can be located in the UTM system to within a few meters (see Chapter 9). Some states, however, do not yet have UTMs recorded on all of their USGS quadrangle maps. Global Positioning System (GPS) instrumentation now allows locations to be determined extremely accurately in the field (see Chapter 9 for a detailed discussion of GPS).

Finally, site survey information is of little use if it is not recorded somewhere and the data made accessible to researchers. More and more states and organizations are instituting computer data banks of site information. These extensive data banks provide for some degree of data consistency, at least within the state, because everybody generally has to fill out the same forms (Figure 4.15).

Consistency in data recording enables researchers to incorporate into their analysis larger data sets, including information collected by other

Farmington River Archaeological Project
Nepaug and Great Pond Forest Survey

Forest: _____

Transect: _____

Testpit #: _____

Forest Section: _____

Stratigraphy: Provide general information concerning the natural stratigraphy of the pit and specific depth of artifacts, ecofacts, and/or features.

_____

0–10 cm
_____
10–20
_____
20–30
_____
30–40
_____
40–50
_____
50–60
_____
60–70
_____
70–80
_____
80–90
_____
90–100
_____

List Artifacts:

List Ecofacts:

Features:

Additional Comments:

Name _____   Date _____

Figure 4.13   One example of a unit level record used by surveyors to record information derived from each test excavation.

TEOTIHUACAN SITE SURVEY RECORD

1. SITE NUMBER _____   2. Aerial photo _____   3. Previous site designation _____
4. MUNICIPIO _____   5. Village _____
6. Type of holding: Ejido plot []; Pequeña propiedad []; Hacienda []; House plot []; Other _____
    Unknown [].   7. Type of cultivation: Humedad []; Temporal []; Riego []; Flood water [].
8. Setting _____
9. Location (in re other sites) _____
10. DESCRIPTION OF SITE (Streets, block?) _____
    _____

11. Area _____   12. Height _____   13. Depth _____.
14. Vegetation: Milpa []; Barley []; Bean []; Cut alfalfa []
    Uncut alfalfa []; Nopal []; Fallow []; Uncultivated [];
    Other _____   Tepetate depth _____
15. Topography _____   16. Soil _____
17. Amount of erosion _____   18. Terracing _____
19. Modern buildings, roads, walls, etc. _____
20. STONE: a. Very abundant []; Abundant []; Moderate [];
             Sparse []; Very sparse []; Absent [].
          b. Relatively uniform distribution []; Localized [];
             Variable [].
21. OTHER EVIDENCES OF CONSTRUCTION: Cut stone []; Lajas []; Tepetate []; Adobe []; Other _____.
    (X = Present, A = Abundant, M = Moderate, S = Sparse, N = None, Absent)
22. CONCRETE AND PLASTER FRAGMENTS: Concrete []; Plaster []; Painted plaster [].
23. FLOOR []; Wall []; Staircase []; Drain []; Wall fixture (in situ) []; Mural []; Almena []; Column []
    Other _____   Comment _____.
24. MANO []; Metate []; Mortar []; Pestle []; Plaster smoother []; "Plumb-bob" []; Wall fixture [];
    Other (Fire God, etc.) _____.
25. OBSIDIAN: Blades []; Scrapers []; Points []; Cores []; Knife []; Waste []; Other _____.
26. BASALT: Tools []; Cores []; Chips []; Other stone (Chert, Slate) _____.
27. CERAMICS: a. Very abundant []; Abundant []; Moderate []; Sparse []; Very sparse []; None [].
    b. Figurines: Tzac []; Micc []; Tlam []; Xol []; Met []; Puppet []; Toltec []; Aztec []; Other
    pre-Cl []; Other or unknown _____   c. Candeleros: Common []; Other []
    3-pronged burner []; Handled cover []; Censer []; e. Thin orange []; San Martin orange [];
    Red lipped olla []; Nubbins []; Wedge rims []; Stamped []; Plano-relief []; Stucco []; Talm.
    Incising []; Foreign _____.
    Adorno []; Comal []; Miniatura []; _____ []; _____ []; f. Special Sample _____.
28. Phases: Tzac []; Tlam []; Xol []; Met []; Oztotic []; Coyo []; Maz []; Azt []; Other pre-Cl [].
29. BURIALS _____
30. COMMENTS _____
    _____

31. SKETCH MAP []. PHOTOS []. CONTINUATION SHEET(S) [].   32. CODE _____   33. RECORDER_____
34. SURFACE COLLECTION BAG NO. _____   35. OTHER BAG NOS. _____   36. DATE _____

Figure 4.14   Site survey record form designed specifically for Teotihuacan.

HISTORIC RESOURCES INVENTORY
PREHISTORIC ARCHAEOLOGICAL SITES
HIST-7 NEW 9/77

STATE OF CONNECTICUT
CONNECTICUT HISTORICAL COMMISSION
59 SOUTH PROSPECT STREET, HARTFORD, CONNECTICUT 06106

FOR OFFICE USE ONLY

Town No.: | Site No.:

UTM

QUAD:

NR: ☐ ACT ☐ ELIG. ☐ NO | DISTRICT ☐ Yes

SR: ☐ ACT ☐ ELIG. ☐ NO | ☐ No

IDENTIFICATION

1. SITE NAME | STATE SITE NO. | CASH NO.

2. TOWN/CITY | VILLAGE | COUNTY

3. STREET AND NUMBER *(and/or location)*

4. OWNER(S)

5. ATTITUDE TOWARD EXCAVATION ☐ Public ☐ Private

6. USE *(Present)* | *(Historic)*

DESCRIPTION

7. PERIOD
☐ Paleoindian ☐ Early Archaic ☐ Early Woodland ☐ Contact
☐ Middle Archaic ☐ Middle Woodland ☐ Unknown
☐ Late Archaic ☐ Late Woodland ☐ Other *(Specify)*

8. DATING METHOD | C-14 ☐ Intuition ☐ Other *(Specify)*
COMPARATIVE MATERIALS

9. SITE TYPE | OTHER *(Specify)*
☐ Quarry ☐ Camp ☐ Rockshelter ☐ Shell Midden ☐ Cemetery ☐ Village ☐

10. APPROXIMATE SIZE AND BOUNDARIES

11. STRATIGRAPHY | OTHER *(Specify)*
☐ Surface finds ☐ Plowed ☐ Not stratified ☐ Stratified ☐ Major Disturbance ☐

ENVIRONMENT

12. SOIL

| USDA SOIL SERIES | | CONTOUR ELEVATION | SLOPE % |
| TEXTURE | OTHER *(Specify)* | | ACIDITY |

SLOPE %: ☐ 0–5 ☐ 5–15 ☐ 15–25 ☐ over 25

TEXTURE: ☐ sand ☐ clay ☐ silt ☐

ACIDITY: ☐ less than 4.5 ☐ 4.5–5.5 ☐ 5.5–6.5 ☐ 6.5–7.3 ☐ 7.4–8.4

13. WATER | NEAREST WATER SOURCE | SIZE AND SPEED | DISTANCE FROM SITE | SEASONAL AVAILABILITY

14. VEGETATION | PRESENT | PAST

CONDITION

15. SITE INTEGRITY
☐ Undisturbed ☐ Good ☐ Fair ☐ Destroyed

16. THREATS TO SITE
☐ None known ☐ Highways ☐ Vandalism ☐ Developers ☐ Other *(Specify)*
☐ Renewal ☐ Private ☐ Deterioration ☐ Zoning ☐ Unknown

17. SURROUNDING ENVIRONMENT
☐ Open Land ☐ Woodland ☐ Residential ☐ Scattered Buildings visible from site
☐ Commercial ☐ Industrial ☐ Rural ☐ High building density
☐ Coastal ☐ Isolated

18. ACCESSIBILITY TO PUBLIC–VISIBLE FROM PUBLIC ROAD
☐ Yes ☐ No

(over)

Figure 4.15 Connecticut Historical Commission prehistoric site record form. Use of standardized site record forms, which are then housed at a state historic preservation office, state archaeologist's office, or state museum, facilitates dissemination of a consistent archaeological database. Placing the forms on-line and providing access through the Internet makes the data even more widely available to researchers.

19. PREVIOUS EXCAVATIONS	BY WHOM/AFFILIATION	DATE
☐ Surface Collected		
☐ "Pot hunted"	BY WHOM/AFFILIATION	DATE
☐ Tested	BY WHOM/AFFILIATION	DATE
☐ Excavation	BY WHOM/AFFILIATION	DATE

RESEARCH POTENTIAL

20. PRESENT LOCATION OF MATERIALS

21. PUBLISHED REFERENCES

SIGNIFICANCE

22. RECOVERED DATA *(Identify in DETAIL, incl. features, burials, faunal material, etc.)*

23. ARCHAEOLOGICAL OR HISTORICAL IMPORTANCE

PHOTOGRAPH

PHOTOGRAPHER

DATE

VIEW

NEGATIVE ON FILE

*Place
35mm contact print
here*

ADD'L INFORMATION

REPORTED BY:	NAME	ADDRESS	
	ORGANIZATION		DATE

FOR OFFICE USE ONLY

FIELD EVALUATION

COMMENTS

archaeologists. Derry et al. (1985:41–46) enumerate the key information that should be recorded as each site is identified: site name, number designation, location (general as well as UTMs), owner, site type, site description, site size, surrounding environment, site integrity, stratigraphy, kinds of remains (a listing of artifacts, ecofacts, features, structures), significance, bibliographical references, and name of recorder (see also Chapter 6). The office of the state archaeologist, the state museum, the state historic preservation office (SHPO), and university research units are all obvious repositories for site survey data. Derry et al. (1985:99–103) provide a listing of SHPOs.

It should be added that one problem does result from having an accessible, regional survey database, particularly when the data repository is a government office: the information may potentially become available to unscrupulous people interested in looting sites for their archaeological remains. As a result of the federal Freedom of Information Act, site survey files, including detailed site maps and the UTM coordinates of some very important sites, could be open to whomever wished to see them. Beyond this, the archaeological community is concerned about the wishes of landowners who, although often very cooperative with professional archaeologists, do not necessarily want the locations of sites on their land made available to the general public. As a result of these concerns, the federal Freedom of Information Act was amended in 1976 to exempt precise site locations, allowing the Secretary of the Interior to withhold location information for sites listed on the National Register of Historic Places. Similarly, the state legislature in Connecticut passed a bill exempting site location information from the state Freedom of Information Act. Other states have also responded to this potential threat to site integrity.

GUIDE TO FURTHER READING

Survey Methods and Design

Dincauze 1978; Ebert 1992; King 1978; McManamon 1984a; Plog et al. 1978; Schiffer and Gumerman 1977; Schiffer et al. 1978

Regional Approaches

Barber and Casjens 1978; Carlson et al. 1986; Casjens et al. 1980; Chartkoff and Chartkoff 1980; Crumley and Marquardt 1987; Derry et al. 1985; Dewar and McBride 1992; Ebert 1992; Foley 1981; Marquardt and Crumley 1987; McManamon 1984b

Sub-surface Testing

Kintigh 1988; Krakker et al. 1983; Lightfoot 1986, 1989; Nance and Ball 1986; Shott 1989

Remote Sensing

Adams et al. 1981; Carr 1982; Donoghue and Shennan 1988; Ebert 1984; Eidt 1973; Lyons and Ebert 1978; Parrington 1983; Walker 1993; Wilson 1983

5

Methods of Excavation

Thomas R. Hester

There are many reasons for carrying out arch-aeological excavations and many ways to determine the appropriate techniques to use. In contemporary archaeology, the emphasis is on area (or block) excavation, as this provides an excellent way to examine behavioral and contextual relationships. In this chapter a wide range of other excavation methods are reviewed. Some are largely outdated and have become part of archaeology's history. But, in certain cases, variations of these techniques may be applied in modern field research. Flexibility remains a key consideration and the archaeologist should be aware of all approaches to excavation. Although consistency in field techniques is desirable, the ability to adapt methods to newly developing field problems should be paramount. As Sir Mortimer Wheeler (1956:81) said "The experienced excavator, **who thinks before he digs,** succeeds in reaching his objective in a majority of cases."

TOOLS AND EQUIPMENT FOR FIELD ARCHAEOLOGY

The number and variety of implements used in archaeological investigation throughout the world are practically limitless. So many special or unusual conditions are likely to be met in the course of excavation that even a bare minimum of equipment must necessarily include an assortment of tools. Subject to the limitations imposed by money, convenience of transportation, and storage in the field, the more the better is a sound general rule.

There are now some companies that offer tools specialized for the archaeologist (see Appendix B). Individual, prepackaged "dig kits" can be purchased, a real boon to the student preparing for a field school! The "complete archaeologist" can obtain rubber kneepads (or leather/felt ones if you prefer), a leather belt-pouch for your trowel, and the "archaeologist's work vest" with pockets and clips and a backpack pouch to hold the pencils, small tools, and other items that are always needed in the field.

Large Tools

Large or expensive tools and special equipment are usually supplied by the institution sponsoring the dig or by organizations that rent or lend them. For example, field vehicles (vans, Suburbans, pickups, and jeeps) will vary depending on the size of the project crew, the nature of the terrain, and the ability of the project to support them (see Dillon 1982). Boats are sometimes used for surveys and for transporting crews and supplies to excavation locales (Meighan and Dillon 1982). For clearing the site for excavation, several kinds of tools may be needed, including weed-hooks, rakes, hoes, and machetes. A chain saw and gasoline-powered "weed-eater" will speed the process. Screening equipment, also generally supplied by the sponsoring institution, is discussed later (see "Screening Excavated Deposits").

In the last analysis, excavation consists of moving earth; hence, the shovel is the trademark of archaeology and perhaps its most indispensable tool. Long-handled, round-point standard No. 2 excavating shovels are recommended as basic. Square-point shovels are useful in excavating sandy deposits, and many archaeologists find them valuable for cleaning excavation unit floors in the search for post molds, rodent burrows, and other features. Spades are very useful for cutting sod, especially when working in lawn-covered areas where the sod has to be replaced after excavation (this is quite common in historic archaeology); scoops can be useful in removing fill from narrow trenches, and they can come in handy for backfilling. Long, narrow-bladed sharpshooter shovels are useful for digging shovel tests.

Ordinarily, enough shovels should be provided so that every member of the digging crew has one. Shovel handles should be sandpapered occasionally and treated with linseed oil. Conditions and methods for using shovels and other tools are discussed in greater detail below.

Heavy, sharp, stout-handled "railroad" picks are often used, though lighter-weight miner's picks or short-handled pick-mattocks are easier to handle and are preferred by some archaeologists. Because picks can cause considerable damage to artifacts, they are generally used only to loosen calcareous, highly compact, or stony deposits too hard for shovels to penetrate. They are nevertheless essential where such deposits occur. A heavy pick swung with both hands represents considerable force, and workers should be cautioned not to strike themselves in the foot and not to hit other workers who may be nearby, particularly behind them. Where paid labor crews are used, workers usually specialize in the use of pick, shovel, wheelbarrow, or the like, often becoming very skillful and efficient with their chosen tool.

Hand Tools

Certain smaller implements are also considered essential (Figure 5.1). Excavators may have to furnish themselves with one of each because the sponsoring organization may not supply these tools.

Trowels are used for careful excavation, especially to uncover and excavate in the immediate vicinity of artifacts or features and wherever larger tools might damage or displace materials. A 4.5- to 5-inch Marshalltown or Goldblatt brand pointing trowel is by far the best. Both brands are made of excellent steel, with the blade and stem of one piece. They are expensive but worth the investment. Cheap trowels will bend and break, and more-flexible mason's trowels and garden trowels are inconvenient. Some excavators find a rectangular-bladed margin trowel (such as the 5-x-2-inch Marshalltown variety) to be a useful adjunct to the common pointing trowel. A rigid, fine-point, wood-handled **ice pick** is also useful, for exceptionally delicate excavation in exposing features, recovering artifacts from hard deposits, dealing with fragile materials, and such. Sharpened and honed **splints** of bamboo or wood are also valuable tools in cleaning burials and features, and some archaeologists also include **dental picks** and **tweezers** in their tool kits. **Root clippers** are needed to trim the floor and walls of units.

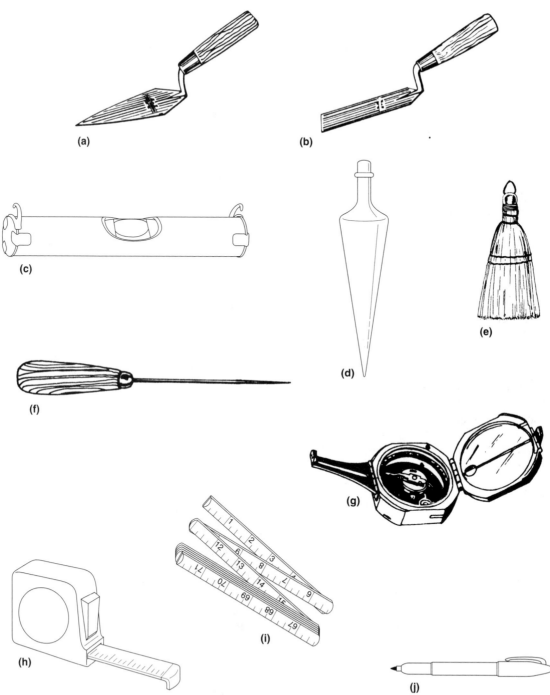

Figure 5.1   Selected hand tools used in archaeological excavations:
(a) pointing trowel, (b) margin trowel, (c) line level, (d) plumb bob, (e) whisk
broom, (f) ice pick, (g) Brunton compass, (h) tape measure, (i) folding wood
rule, (j) Sharpie marking pen.

Paint brushes 2 inches or less in width are very useful. They are helpful in brushing away loose earth in delicate work, such as exposing burials and features and preparing them for photography. A heavy brush and a metal or sturdy plastic **dustpan** can be used to collect dirt at intervals when careful exposure is being done. Occasionally, a whisk broom may be more convenient than a paint brush for removing loose earth. **Measuring tapes** are indispensable during the excavation process, as well as for laying out grids and test pits during the initial phases of the fieldwork. A 2- or 3-m hand tape that can be clipped on your belt or stuck in your pocket is a must. Tapes that are 30 or 50 m in length should also be included in any field project. Steel or fiberglass tapes are superior to cloth ones, though more expensive, and must be cared for by oiling and cleaning. Whitefaced tapes are the easiest to see and thus are the least likely to be misread. Metric **folding wooden rules** are also handy during excavation. **Plumb bobs** and **string line levels** are crucial for plotting artifact locations and measuring depths.

Compasses are indispensable in site surveying, but they are also useful for determining the orientation of burials and features and for recording the location of nonpermanent datum points once excavation has begun. A Brunton **pocket transit** is very useful for most archaeological purposes. A Silva Ranger compass or a Suunto KB-14 compass is sometimes more flexible for mapping. Other useful items include enough **blank forms** to record all data likely to be obtained: a field notebook (some waterproof brands are available), artifact slips, feature and burial records, site survey sheets, photographic record sheets (and the necessary cameras, of course; see Chapter 8), and field catalog sheets. Graph paper will be needed for mapping. Large numbers of bags—cloth, strong paper, and plastic (especially the "zippered" type)—are indispensable. Metal-rim **tags** or linen tags with copper-wire or string ties are handy for labeling or closing cloth bags and for labeling cataloged objects. **Felt-tipped pens** are excellent for marking paper bags because the lettering is bold and permanent. Artifacts and other materials recovered are generally kept in small sacks during the course of excavation; large

bags are used for burials and features. Plastic **vials** and kraft **boxes** of various sizes are useful for storing small artifacts. Whenever possible, cardboard **cartons** are used to store materials and to protect them during transport by automobile; all freight shipments should be in wooden boxes.

Stakes (or sections of lightweight concrete reinforcing bar ["rebar"]), are needed for laying out the site grid before excavation and as local datum points in measuring thereafter. Wooden stakes can often be made at the site, but it is safer to take them along, if there is room. They should be at least a foot long, and stakes 1-x-2-x-24 inches (or even 30 inches) are recommended (some archaeologists use long, 100-penny nails or galvanized spikes). Usually, a small **sledgehammer** is needed to drive in the stakes. Metal-rim tags with tie strings should be included for marking the stakes according to their coordinate location; they can, alternatively, be labeled with a broad-tipped marking pen. Last, plenty of **pencils** should be on hand.

The items described above should be considered a minimum equipment list; a number of additional implements, described below, will often be useful. With a little ingenuity, a great many other implements can be improvised in the field to meet special conditions. Additional equipment necessary in surveying, mapping, preservation of material, and other tasks is discussed in Chapters 7 and 9.

Other Handy Implements

Before photographing a feature, a stratigraphic profile, or a skeleton from a burial, the archaeologist will want to remove any residual loose earth and dust. A **bellows** or a **bicycle tire pump** may be very useful for this purpose; use an **ear syringe** on delicate specimens. The advantage of such instruments, if properly handled, is that they will not disturb fragile or lightweight objects. A **pocket magnifying glass** or "loop" (7X to 20X) is handy for examining small objects on the spot.

A **hand sprayer** of the type commonly used to spread solutions on garden plants may be used to spray water on a wall or cleared flat surface to bring out color distinctions that are otherwise faint or invisible. Light spraying of this sort can be done immediately before photographs are taken to achieve greater contrast (Bruce-Mitford 1956:236; Hole and Heizer 1973:Figure 45).

Thin **plastic sheeting** can be used to shelter an excavation and the excavators from the rain (Borden 1950) and to cover the units overnight. In many areas, the sheeting can help hold moisture in, keeping the units from drying out and thus making excavation easier the next morning. Santure (1990:11) reports the use of straw, as mulch, covered by polyethylene sheeting to keep deposits from freezing during the excavations at the Norris Farms 36 cemetery site in Illinois.

When working in dry caves or rockshelters (or in dusty crawl spaces), a **respirator** or filtered dust mask is essential.

Field recording is enhanced with a **permanent-ink pen,** especially those of the Sharpie brand. **Flagging tape** in various colors also comes in handy to mark corners of units, datum stakes, or survey instrument locations.

If constituents from the excavation, such as burned rocks, are to be quantified before discarding, a **spring scale** with an aluminum pan that can be suspended from a tree limb is very useful.

First aid kits should be at every excavation, along with **"freeze kits"** for snakebites or, more likely, wasp and bee stings. Insect sprays and ant poison are often needed at sites; be cautious in using these materials because some of these substances can be toxic. **Hats** or caps should be worn by all, along with **sunscreen;** overexposure to the sun can cause health hazards, such as basal cell carcinomas. **Gloves** should also be used, especially by students new to the rigors (and blisters) of fieldwork.

APPROACHES TO EXCAVATION

Once a site has been selected for excavation, the major problem confronting the archaeologist about to begin work is precisely where to dig. In the past, this crucial question was often answered by intuition or by selecting an area that "looked rich." More recently, various random and systematic techniques have been devised for sampling a site to see which areas seem to merit further exploration. The particular technique used depends upon the research design of the excavation project (see Chapter 3). These techniques are not without their problems (such as "blank spots" not covered by random sampling), but they do undeniably eliminate subjective bias in deciding where to dig.

Many contemporary excavation projects are preceded by geomorphological studies so that ancient landscapes can be better understood and site formation processes determined. Remote sensing (see Chapter 4) can also play an important role at some sites. Martin et al. (1991) used a magnetometer and an electronic conductivity sensor at sites in north-central Texas. Although both were able to detect buried features of fire-cracked rocks, the magnetometer provided more information, such as the nature of the disturbance and episodes of repeated use, that the feature had undergone (see Scollar et al. 1990 for more detail on this type of remote sensing).

In addition to these techniques, archaeologists have more-traditional approaches for locating an area within the site with the most potential for excavation, and thus deciding precisely where to concentrate their efforts. Unless sufficient advance information is available about the contents of the site (e.g., from the techniques noted above or from looting, damage from construction, or deep erosional cuts), exploratory or test excavations are usually carried out. These often take the form of shovel tests, test pits (*sondage,* Struever 1968b; or "telephone booths," Flannery, ed. 1976), or narrow trenches (Skinner 1971:167). Whether their location is chosen by a computer or by the excavator, at random, by intuition, by logical reasoning from survey evidence, or by a combination of the five, such preliminary excavations can provide information on the composition and stratification (and culture history) of a site, locate areas of activity or concentrated deposits within it, and thus serve as a guide for later, more-extensive excavation.

Most archaeologists will be interested in learning more about the nature and depositional history of the soils in the site area. For such purposes, Deetz (1967:13–14) has suggested digging a "control pit" in a spot away from the area containing cultural remains, although under some circumstances on- and off-site soil samples can be collected with a hand auger (Cook and Heizer 1965:29). In some sites, geomorphological studies require the excavation of long backhoe trenches for comprehensive studies.

Sir Mortimer Wheeler (1954:84–85) says of the test pit (his "control pit") system:

> This is the supervisor's own special charge, and upon it the accuracy of the general digging in large measure depends. . . . Its purpose is to enable the supervisor, with a minimum disturbance of the strata, to anticipate the nature and probable vertical extent of the layers which are being cleared by his main gang. It is a glimpse into the future.

Although archaeologists once shunned the use of machines and heavy equipment, these have become commonplace, especially when a site is doomed for destruction. The archaeologist must decide where excavations should be focused and what the stratigraphy and geomorphology of various parts of the site—which cannot be hand-excavated—will look like. Backhoes, "ditch-witches" (Odell 1992), and other trenching machines have proved invaluable in this regard, giving the archaeologist an early glance at the characteristics of a site and thus guiding the development of the best exca-

vation plan possible (e.g., Black and McGraw 1985; Condon and Egan 1984).

Mechanical earth augers can also be used to get a view of the nature of site deposits (Assad and Potter 1979; Percy 1976; Stockton 1974). Portable, handheld mechanical augers can penetrate only to about 3 ft. However, Whalen (1994:31) reports the use of a bucket auger to define buried features before excavation at the Turquoise Ridge site in western Texas. Howell (1993) used a similar auger at sites in Veracruz, Mexico, and found them to be very useful in areas where thick vegetation prevented surface collections of sherds, as well as for indicating the stratigraphy and depth of dense occupational deposits.

Hydraulic coring of archaeological sites (Figure 5.2a,b) has become a commonly used technique for geomorphological studies, as well as for tracking stratigraphic units across deeply buried sites and gauging the vertical extent of occupational debris in such sites. Stein (1986, 1992) has written on the advantages of coring, noting that continuous stratigraphic samples can be taken with a core. Schuldenrein (1991) advocates the use of coring as a means of rapidly detecting sites in culture resourcement management studies, and Hoffman (1993) has used close-interval coring to determine internal site structure and artifact density.

One must be very careful in the use of heavy machinery, but there are many instances where spe-

(a)

(b)

Figure 5.2 Coring at archaeological sites: (*a*) deep-coring with truck-mounted core; (*b*) auger-coring.

cial circumstances require such equipment (as in testing terrace deposits for buried occupations) or where machinery is an integral part of the research design (e.g., removing sterile overburden to allow broad horizontal excavations). Van Horn et al. (1986) and Van Horn (1988) have described their use of such equipment at two California sites. At site LAn-59, a Case 1835B Uni-loader with a backhoe and bucket loader was used to excavate the remains of this doomed site (Figure 5.3a). This was done after a 10 percent hand-excavated sample had been obtained. Excavation was by stratigraphic levels, although absolute depths of artifacts could not, of course, be recorded. Deposits were placed by the tractor into 6-×-10-ft screens (Figure 5.3b) where the soil was water screened. At site LAn-61, it was determined that a 10 percent hand-excavated sample would be too costly. Thus, an excavation program was worked out in which the site was dug in 10-cm arbitrary levels—9 percent by machine, 1 percent by hand. A John Deere tractor with a backhoe and loader was able to remove a single 10-cm layer at a time, but the excavators switched to a smaller Case 1835B Uni-loader because it was more maneuverable. Again, large screens and water screening were used to process the excavated deposits: ⅛-inch screen maximized recovery. Van Horn et al. (1986) believe that the use of this machine in the sandy matrix of this site was in many ways superior to hand excavation, and they

noted both the accuracy and speed with which the excavation proceeded. The Uni-loader could remove 15 m³ of deposit per day (all put through ⅛-inch screen), whereas hand excavation removed 2.5 m³ per day. "Hard" features such as hearths survived machine excavation and could be recorded in place; "soft" features were usually damaged or destroyed.

Condon and Egan (1984) used a D8 bulldozer at a site to blade an area in order to expose and record feature data that would otherwise have been destroyed. Similarly, Brown et al. (1982) were able to use a small bulldozer to gradually blade away deposits between two areas of hand-excavated hearths at Texas site 41LK67. In this intervening area, the blading of six strips disclosed 30 additional rock cluster features.

Esarey and Pauketat (1992) illustrate the use of a backhoe (with a toothless bucket) to open a large area at the Lohmann site in Illinois (Figure 5.4a,b). After mechanical stripping, shovel scraping was then used. The shovel scraping allowed "100% identification of subsurface features" within the excavation blocks (Esarey and Pauketat 1992:15). Similarly, in a CRM salvage excavation in Illinois, Esarey and Santure (1990) combined road-grader scraping and shovel scraping to expose large portions of agricultural villages along an Illinois highway right-of-way.

Thoms (1994) used a front-end loader to scrape or blade a site surface "in order to locate and

(a)   (b)

Figure 5.3 Mechanically aided excavation at site LAn-59, California: (a) removing the deposits with a front-end loader; (b) water-screening.

(a)

(b)

Figure 5.4 Exposure of subsurface at the Lohmann site, Illinois by (*a*) mechanical stripping with a backhoe and (*b*) shovel scraping.

(a)   **(b)**

Figure 5.5 Blading a site surface before excavation: (*a*) very shallow scraping or blading with a front-end loader to expose feature locations; (*b*) hand-excavated block exposing features found through blading.

recover possible features and artifacts." Hand excavation was also done, and was accelerated by the blading process (Figure 5.5a,b). The use of this approach was part of a detailed research design; before blading, the site was first surveyed at 1-m intervals with a proton magnetometer and each anomaly found was scanned with a metal detector, then probed to detect rock concentrations. Next, 13 backhoe trenches were excavated and profiled, and data from these were used to select a location for the combined blading/hand-excavation episode (Thoms 1994:54).

Special planning in the use of mechanized techniques has to be done for very deeply buried sites.

For example, the Zilker Park site (41TV1364) in Austin, Texas, was to be cut by a massive trench for a wastewater line. The site deposits were estimated to be at least 6 m deep and to date back perhaps 11,000 years. The use of a backhoe to sample a site of this depth was not possible—it just could not dig deep enough. So, the excavators (Ricklis et al. 1991) used a large trackhoe that could reach depths up to 6 m. They excavated the trench in 40-cm trench-long horizontal levels and screened 30 full hand-shovel loads through ¼-inch mesh; 5 hand-shovel loads were put through ⅛-inch mesh. This allowed vertical sampling throughout the 6 m of cultural and ecological (e.g., snails) remains. The trackhoe trench profiles were used to study the depositional processes at the site, to record archaeological lenses, and to obtain sediment samples for radiocarbon dating (see Chapter 14). Such an approach provided a controlled sample and made possible a realistic evaluation of this site for planning purposes by city engineers. Of course, trenches or any other deep excavations must be shored according to engineering standards to ensure crew safety (Figure 5.6a,b).

SITE EXCAVATION TECHNIQUES

Once an area of a site has been chosen for excavation, the archaeologist must choose the appropriate excavating method. The choice depends on the type of site being investigated and on the specific goals of the expedition. For example, Thomas (1983) began work at Gatecliff shelter, Nevada, using "vertical" techniques—test pits and trenches—to obtain a stratigraphic sequence. He next moved to a "horizontal excavation strategy" to excavate and record short-term, intact occupational surfaces within the deposit; deep, open-area excavation was used to explore the remainder of the deposits (Figure 5.7a–d).

Many methods of excavation are available and can be used in combination as well as singly: trenching; the strip method; quartering; architectural units; area and large-area, or block, excavation; and stripping, to name only some of the standard methods we discuss here. Selection of any of these techniques depends on the research design and the nature of the site deposits.

Trenching

Trenching has been used to obtain cross sections of sites and is particularly important in stratigraphic interpretation because it provides a single, long vertical profile. In addition, trenches can expose buildings buried under later structures (Figure 5.8).

Sometimes, as reported by Flannery (ed. 1976), long profiles can be recorded from fortuitous "transects" or trenches cut through mounds, as in the

(a)

(b)

Figure 5.6 Shoring of trench so that it can be safely excavated and profiled: (*a*) wooden shoring installed; (*b*) iron bars add reinforcement at bottom of trench.

case of vertical cutbanks created by the removal of earth for adobe brick at sites in Oaxaca. At San José Mogote, a stratigraphic "transect sample" was made possible by cleaning the profiles of an adobe-brick maker's cutbank over 99 m long (later this

(a)

(b)

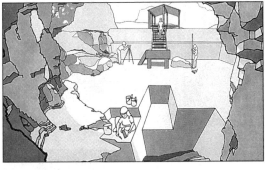

(c)

(d)

Figure 5.7 Approaches to the excavation of Gatecliff shelter, Nevada:
(*a*) initial test pits; (*b*) area excavations opened from initial testing;
(*c*) excavation across all deposits after removal of large roof-fall blocks;
(*d*) deep excavation at the site, terraced for safety.

was connected with another adobe cutbank, creating a "continuous cross section of the village some 192.5 m long . . . [containing] more than a dozen house lenses with floors, and many associated middens, pits and burials" (Flannery, ed. 1976:72)).

Excavation of trenches can be accomplished in a variety of ways. Most common is a linear interconnected series of pits, usually excavated in arbitrary or stratigraphic levels. The term *trench* can also be applied to variously shaped rectangular test pits dug in a site. Trenching can be done by power machinery if sterile overburden is being removed to expose buried cultural remains. As indicated earlier, narrow trenching may be used as a sampling technique in the search for houses, cemeteries, or activity areas to be exposed by area excavation. John E. Clark (personal communication 1996) used a lengthy, hand-dug trench in Chiapas, Mexico, to identify a Formative era ball court.

At certain historic sites where only the approximate area occupied by a fort or mission building is known, the excavator may decide to dig a series of narrow exploratory trial trenches in the hope of encountering foundations, bases of walls, a stockade line, or the like. Once something is known of the location of certain features (identifiable perhaps from illustrations of the original structures) and the extent of the site area, excavation of that area can begin.

In sites where extensive features such as structures are encountered, excavation by trench alone will not give a sufficiently extensive view of the situation. For example, Haury's (1937) sectioning of the great canal at Snaketown yielded the desired information on the size of the canal and its history of use over a long period of time. But in the large ball courts at the same Snaketown site, a trench, though revealing a cross section of the court at one

Figure 5.8   Use of a trench to explore a mound. This trench cuts east-west through the center of Operation 2012 at Colha, Belize. It has exposed stratigraphy related to construction in Late Preclassic times, overlying a plaster-surfaced Middle Preclassic building (seen at the bottom rear of the trench). Note the 2-m stadia rod scale.

point, failed to provide all the data needed on the structure.

Strip and Quartering

In another excavation approach called the **strip method,** often used in mound and barrow excavation, digging begins at the edge of the area to be excavated, and work continues straight through the site in strips—that is, the face of the deposit is exposed in successive parallel cuttings usually 5 ft wide. If a feature is encountered lying partly in one strip or section and partly in the next, it is left on a pedestal while the one strip is excavated and not fully exposed until the excavation advances to the other strip. Then, as the feature is brought into full view, it is noted and removed and the pedestal of earth on which it rested is excavated (see Perino 1968:Figure 30). As each section of the mound is exposed, a stratigraphic profile is drawn so that the construction of the entire deposit can later be determined. Illustrations of this excavation approach are presented by Atkinson (1953:Figure 10), Cole (1951:59, Plate 5A), Perino (1968), and Wheeler (1954:94–95, Figures 18, 19).

An alternative technique is **quartering,** or the **quadrant method,** where the mound is laid out into four quadrants by balks 3 or more ft wide. Excavation of each quadrant proceeds systematically, and the coordinate balks preserve the contour and stratification of the deposit. (For further details see Atkinson 1953:59; Clark 1947:97; Kenyon 1961: Plate 7; and Wheeler 1954:95.)

Jelks and Tunnell (1959:8) describe the quadrant excavation of a mound in eastern Texas:

> A stake was placed near the center of the mound and a grid of 5-foot squares was established which tied in with the centrally located stake. Then each quadrant of the mound was excavated separately. Beginning at the top of the mound, an entire quadrant was taken down by regular vertical intervals, usually of 0.5 feet each. The floor of the excavation was cleaned and examined after each level was removed, and measured drawings were prepared to record any zoning or occupational features that were observed in the excavation floor. The four profiles radiating in the cardinal directions from the central stake were always left intact until measured drawings had been prepared.

Architectural-unit Excavation

In digging mounds on Santa Catalina Island, Georgia, Thomas (1989) first cleared the mounds of all vegetation. The crew then laid out a metric grid system (2-×-2-m units) with the baselines placed along cardinal directions. A permanent datum point (a brass marker in a concrete base) was placed on the perimeter of the site, away from the mound. Next, a contour, or topographic, map was made of the mound. Photographs were taken before excavations commenced. Thomas's first objective was to determine mound stratigraphy and to sample the deposits for artifacts and organic materials for radiocarbon dating. Thus, the first excavation (Figure 5.9) was a trench of four contiguous 2-m-square units, begun at the end of the mound and cutting to the center (two units were dug carefully with trowels). This test trench was dug down to sterile sand. Once the results of the testing were analyzed, a crew returned to the

(a)   **(b)**

Figure 5.9 Excavations at McLoed Mound, Santa Catalina Island, Georgia: (*a*) initial test trench; (*b*) opening up the excavations from the initial exploration.

mound. Digging resumed in the form of large blocks of contiguous units (Figure 5.10), mapping in all cultural materials for a better horizontal perspective. In the case of each mound excavated by Thomas, at least 50 percent was left undug.

Observable **architectural units** or features such as house depressions, pithouses, or rooms in Southwestern American ruins (cf. Deetz 1967:17; Fitting 1973; Shafer 1982) may be used as excavation units. Even so, however, it is wise to establish systematic horizontal and vertical controls in excavating them. Also, if many rooms or other architectural features are present at a site, there must usually be some process for selecting the rooms to be excavated. Hill (1967) used probability sampling in such a situation at Broken K pueblo, Arizona.

Area Excavation

Area excavation, by which is meant the orderly exploration of a sizable expanse of a site, allows the

archaeologist to obtain a larger (and more meaningful) sample of artifacts, features, activity areas, and other buried remains than trenching or other less-extensive methods. Area excavation is usually *but not always* done within a grid system (Figure 5.11). The grid system (see Chapter 9) allows each unit to be excavated so that a wall or balk can be left between adjoining squares. The balk preserves, until the very end of excavation, the stratigraphic profile on all sides of the excavation unit (Figure 5.12a,b). (The careful preservation of balks is shown in the excavations of Atkinson 1953:42–43; Bruce-Mitford 1956:Plate 8A; Goodwin 1953: Figure 8; Kenyon 1961:Plate 8; and Wheeler 1954.)

"Horizontal" information is vital to modern anthropological archaeology, providing data on site structure, behavioral units, patterning related to social phenonema, and artifact concentrations. Archaeologists should work for broad exposure of buried cultural remains, using **large-area excavation,** or as some have called it, **block excavation.**

(a)

(b)

Figure 5.10 Excavations at McLoed Mound, Santa Catalina Island, Georgia: (*a*) continued expansion of the excavations, exposing a central tomb (light area near center); (*b*) completed excavations.

Block excavation may be undertaken as one phase of an overall excavation plan. For example, at the Deshazo site, a Caddoan village in east Texas, Story (1982) used backhoe trenches, test pits, and ultimately block excavations in her field strategy. The continuing horizontal exposure of Unit 1 at the site provided evidence of three overlapping house outlines (Figure 5.13a,b).

Another example is reported from the Pumpkin site, South Carolina (Charles 1995). An area

22-x-90 m was stripped down to the red clay subsoil. This led to the exposure of more than 500 features, including post molds and pits. Features were marked with flagging pins until they could be carefully exposed, mapped, and sampled (Charles 1995:8).

In rescuing the Norris Farms 36 site, a prehistoric Native American cemetery in Illinois, Santure (1990) describes the use of a metric grid placed over the entire site, with excavation then proceeding

Figure 5.11 Area excavation using a grid system as exposure of deposits is expanded by shallow machine stripping (upper part of photo), site 41LK67, southern Texas.

(a)

Figure 5.12 Area excavation utilizing balks, which are left in place to help record both (*a*) cultural features (shown in the profiles) and (*b*) natural stratigraphy.

(b)

Figure 5.13a Area excavation exposing a Caddoan house floor at the Deshazo site in eastern Texas.

in 3-×-3-m units, further subdivided into 1-×-1-m squares. Balks (30 cm wide) were preserved around each 3-×-3-m unit to map sediment deposits revealed in the profiles. Shovel scraping was used to expose features and burial pit outlines and to remove sediment in the gravel fill above the burials; the excavators switched to trowels just before the human remains were encountered. With this combination of approaches, an area of 2,078 m² was exposed (Esarey and Santure 1990:9, Figure 3.5). Because the site had to be dug during the winter, a portable fiberglass-covered frame building, heated by the sun and a kerosene heater, was used.

As noted above, area excavation may or may not involve a grid layout, and balks may or may not be preserved. At the Wilson-Leonard site, a deep, stratified site in central Texas, Michael B. Collins (personal communication 1996) worked from a preexisting grid but developed a large, open area excavation to sample Paleoindian occupation surfaces near the bottom of the site (Figure 5.14). The chief value of large-area, or block, excavation, according to Struever (1968b), is that it "provides a broad expanse of living surface enabling recovery

of the total population of cultural items resulting from activities carried on in that particular precinct" (Figure 5.15). Black et al. (1993) have excavated the Higgins site in central Texas using an area approach, but rather than recording by grid coordinates, they used an EDM (electronic distance measurement; see Chapter 9) with an attached small recording computer with keyboard. Locational data were entered, and at the end of the day, the disk was downloaded into field laptop computers and backed up on a floppy disk. This system, called a Total Data Station, is flexible enough to record the finds being made by a crew of 8–10 people.

Biddle and Kjolbye-Biddle (1969:211–213) report the use of what they call "open-area" horizontal excavation at Winchester, England, covering in detail the techniques and problems of this kind of excavation. The advantage of this approach, according to the authors, is that "an overall view of the horizontal is always obtainable"; the disadvantage is that it is difficult and "requires . . . great site discipline and well-trained workers." Another aspect of block, large-area, or open-area excavations is that they require a lot of time and money.

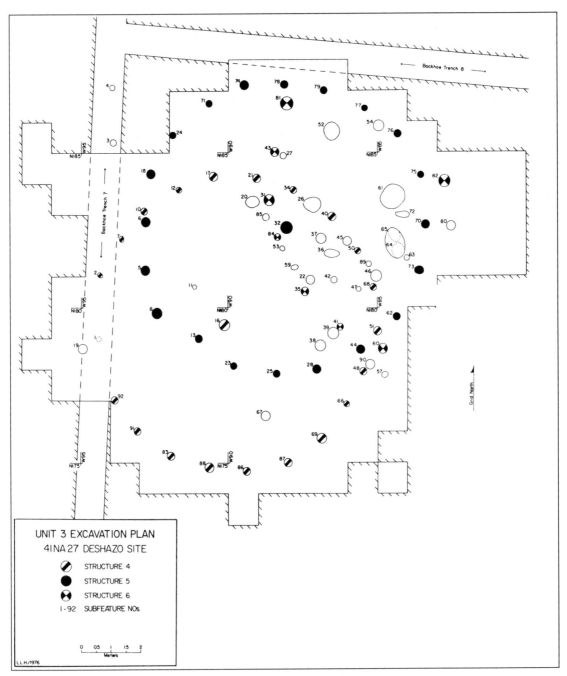

Figure 5.13b   Plan showing overlapping house phases at the Deshazo site.

Figure 5.14 Area excavation at the Wilson-Leonard site, central Texas.

Figure 5.15 Area excavation, exposing features and in situ cultural materials at Lamu, Kenya.

Stripping

Stripping excavations have been used to remove large areas of overburden to expose stable land surfaces bearing living floors, houses, or other cultural features (see Binford et al. 1970). This kind of excavation may be the third phase in the excavation of a site, the first phase being test pitting and the second phase being "block" excavation (Binford 1964). Stripping can be costly, because it usu-ally involves power machinery. However, it is a most valuable excavation technique, permitting archaeologists to examine very large areas and to sample a greater number of phenomena within a site (see Brown et al. 1982) (Figure 5.16). Shovel stripping can also be used to trace features that are buried at shallow depths. Some archaeologists feel that shovel stripping is abused when plow zones are stripped without screening the excavated deposits.

Figure 5.16 Area excavation, exposing shallow hearths. Grid stakes left in place. Site 41LK67, southern Texas.

(a)

Figure 5.17 Excavations at Mound C, George C. Davis site, eastern Texas: (*a*) view of mound before excavation; (*b*) clearing of treasure-hunter's trench, exposing undisturbed mound fill and burial pits.

(b)

What we have provided here is but a brief review of certain major approaches to excavation. So many considerations can affect the plan of an excavation that archaeologists rarely use exactly the same system twice. The best approach to the excavation of a site is a flexible one, allowing the excavator to take advantage of the techniques that will best elucidate the problems under investigation. Adapting techniques to the site at hand is up to the individual in charge of the excavation. As an example of modifying excavation techniques to fit the situation, Figure 5.17 shows excavations in Mound C, a large Caddoan burial mound at the George C. Davis site in eastern Texas. A huge trench had been cut into the mound early in the twentieth century by treasure hunters. The excavator, Dee Ann Story (University of Texas at Austin), used power machinery to clear most of this trench, then a crew with shovels and trowels to locate the edges of the disturbed area. In the process of recording the stratigraphy exposed by the treasure-hunter's trench, Story recognized and excavated large burial pits.

EXCAVATION METHODS

The process of actual digging, like the process of deciding on the location of excavations, varies with the character and content of the site and the research objectives of the excavator. Here again a number of alternative systems are available. The critical factor, no matter what method is selected, is that horizontal and vertical control be carefully maintained. And, as always, flexibility is critical to good excavation.

Vertical-face Methods

Occasionally a unit or a contiguous series of units is dug entirely as a **single vertical face.** This is equivalent to the "slicing" procedure once used for excavating in the Mississippi Valley and other parts of the eastern United States (see Ford 1963:9, Plate 1). One clear disadvantage with this method is that materials may fall out unseen, and if they do, their location is lost forever. This kind of excavation also makes it exceedingly difficult, if not impossible, to trace horizontal relationships of artifacts and features.

Gunn and Brown (1982:59–61) have modified this approach, developing a technique they term the **control face** (Figure 5.18):

> This most basic concept literally dictates trowel movements in the hands of the excavators. All excavation, whether it be following a strata contact, an occupation floor, or removing a rodent disturbance, is done against a vertical control face. . . . A control face . . . is composed of a vertical *cut,* the material being removed; a horizontal *surface,* the material being left; and the *contact,* the perpendicular juncture between

the cut and the surface. An excavator normally works against a two-to-five-centimeter deep control face, which extends across his square. Moving his trowel conformant with the strata, the excavator slices off a defined amount of the control face with each pass, systematically moving across the meter unit. Each slice moves the contact back a few millimeters exposing more of the surface and removing more of the cut. In addition to giving the excavator a clear perception of the materials to be removed and those to be left, the control face allows the supervisors to readily check the accuracy of the excavator's efforts.

Gunn and Brown (1982:59) used the control face technique as a part of a **control front:**

> As with the trowel, the movement of the crew needs to be coordinated in a systematic manner. A control front is composed of a line of control faces crosscutting adjoining excavation units. Excavators aligned in this manner are encouraged to pay close and constant attention of the progress of excavation by their flanking comrades. The spirit of cooperation engendered by the excavators on the control front not only spurs efficiency but leads to constant communication on matters of density of artifacts, vertical locations of artifacts, facies changes in lithology and pedogenic development, and field analysis of interesting distribution patterns. Such discussions insure cross-referencing of unit excavation notes and avoid problems of correlating occupation floors and lithologic contacts from square to square after the fact.

Level-stripping is a widely used variation of the vertical-face system. It consists of excavation in a staggered series of vertical faces, from 6 to 12 inches or more in height, at successive depths and looks in cross section like a flight of steps (Lloyd 1963:Plate 2; Martin et al. 1947:Figure 1). The result is that levels, rather than coordinate squares, are excavated as discrete units by the workers assigned to them. This method, perhaps better termed **step-trenching,** is particularly useful in digging large mounds. For example, Lamberg-Karlovsky (1974) describes and illustrates step-trenching as used at Tepe Yahya.

(a)

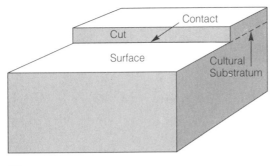

(b)

Figure 5.18 Control column (photo) and control face excavation techniques: (*a*) Circled numbers in the photo identify (1) a line of chert flakes, (2) a defined substratum, (3) rodent disturbance, (4) insect dung deposits, (5) constant volume sample area, and (6) crayfish disturbance. (*b*) A control face is composed of a vertical *cut*, the material being removed; a horizontal *surface*, the material being left; and the *contact*, the perpendicular juncture between the cut and the surface.

Unit-level Method

The **unit-level method** is undoubtedly the most common method of excavating sites that show little stratigraphic variation (Figure 5.19). Here the technique is to dig each pit, defined by the lines of the grid system, vertically as a discrete unit, always completing one before beginning another. The digging is done in a succession of separate arbitrary levels, each 5, 10, or 20 cm (or 3, 6, or 12 inches) deep; the excavation of each level is also completed before the next is begun. The thickness of the arbi-

Figure 5.19 Beginning an excavation unit using arbitrary levels. Upper level of 10-cm thickness is being removed from unit and screened.

trary level depends on the research design and the character of the deposits at the site. Unless there are extenuating circumstances, level thickness should be consistent across the site. Deposits from each unit level are screened to recover chipped stone artifacts, potsherds, animal bones, mollusk shells, debitage, and other items that were not collected or recorded at the moment of discovery.

The unit-level technique is best employed in sites with no visible stratification and in projects emphasizing chronology or culture history. There are many such sites in North America. For example, in California shell middens, there are lenses of mollusk shells interspersed with layers of earth, but these are usually very localized occurrences that run for a span and then disappear. The nature of these small lenses in such sites is clearly shown in illustrations published by Schenck (1926:Plates 36, 37).

In North American sites like these shell middens, workers have become accustomed to digging in arbitrary levels within the unit-level system. The British archaeologist Sir Mortimer Wheeler (1954:53) bemoaned the use of this "outworn system, with its mechanical unit levels," and Pallis (1956:326) also objected to excavation by arbitrary levels or merely recording depth of finds from a

datum-line as "substitutes for actual stratification." No archaeologist will disagree with Wheeler's or Pallis's insistence on visible stratification as the surest means of accurate and meaningful recovery (and subsequent interpretation) of data. In fact, Stein (1992) reports her efforts in using natural stratigraphy in shell midden excavations. But the fact remains that there are many instances where the archaeologist must deal with a deposit that does not contain such stratification, and in these situations, the excavator must turn to a mechanical method of vertical control.

For example, see the cave deposit without visible stratigraphy in Iran illustrated in Hole and Heizer (1965:Figure 10). Or note the remarks of MacNeish (1958:33), who writes: "The deposits [of Nogales Cave, Mexico] contained no definable strata, and all the material from the surface to the bottom of the excavation was one stratum of grey powdery ash and refuse. Occasionally a short lens of white ash or charcoal could be discerned, but none was extensive enough to define as zones." Evans and Meggers (1959:8) have shown why some Amazonian sites lack evidence of clear-cut stratigraphy, as the result of heavy precipitation and leaching.

Indeed, not all of Wheeler's British colleagues decry the method of "metrical stratigraphy," as witnessed by this statement by Burkitt (1956:235): "Where there is no obvious stratigraphy but more than one industry is present . . . uniform layers of 6 to 9 cm thick [are] removed." An example of the history of the controversy over the use of "metrical" versus "natural" stratigraphy can be found in an extended discussion by Phillips et al. (1951:240–241) in which they call attention to the problem of finding cultural differences in unstratified deposits and distinguish between the terms *stratigraphy* and *stratification* (for the latter, see Chapter 10).

Archaeologists continue to have strong feelings about the use of arbitrary levels. One reviewer of the draft for this book wrote, in 1993, that he/she had never used arbitrary levels in test pits or other excavations. Another reviewer that year took just the opposite approach, commending the discussion of arbitrary levels and wondering if we were not being too defensive! After all, most archaeologists use both approaches. The comments of Praetzellis (1993:85) are perhaps most appropriate: "Arbitrary excavation will continue to be a valuable tool when it is used with an understanding of site structure and not as part of an inflexible archaeological orthodoxy."

In practicing metrical stratigraphy, accurate depth recordings of finds are obviously essential. Where the occupation deposit is thin, very small differences in the depth at which objects lie may have meaning. Indeed, in a deposit without visible stratification, these minute distinctions may be the only means whereby the worker can recognize and separate successive occupations (see Bruce-Mitford 1956:273). It is also important when excavating by arbitrary levels to watch for evidence of disturbance. For instance, intrusive pits and rodent burrows will contain fill that ordinarily dates from a more-recent time than the level into which the pits and burrows penetrate, though rodents can also pull up fill from earlier strata (see Phillips et al. 1951:290–291; see also Bruce-Mitford 1956:Figure 43 for graphic, and classic, illustrations of much-disturbed stratification; in addition, Bocek 1992 has noted the lateral displacement of cultural materials by rodent burrowing).

The use of arbitrary levels and stratigraphic excavation can be combined. For example, in digging rockshelter deposits in which natural stratigraphy would be expected, it is sometimes useful to subdivide the units on an arbitrary basis (e.g., in 10-cm levels; see Flannery et al. 1986; Thomas 1983) to ensure tighter vertical control over excavated materials. Hester and Heizer used 15-cm levels to remove thick Early Archaic strata at Baker Cave in southwest Texas (Chadderdon 1983).

Natural-stratigraphic-level Method

Excavation by **natural stratigraphic levels** involves peeling off the visible strata in a site deposit. We illustrate this technique by reference to several published reports. Keller (1973) began his excavations at Montague Cave, South Africa, by making some preliminary cuts, the profiles of which indicated stratigraphy so complex that arbitrary levels would have been unsuitable. One 6-inch level in one of the test cuts yielded microliths from one side of the square and much older hand-axes from the other. Obviously the strata dipped so that a single-level cut into different zones would have caused mixing of the artifacts of different occupations. Thus, the major excavations were done by "natural" units, but with one further provision, as Keller (1973:8) states:

> However, within these "natural" units we encountered concentrations of artifacts that appeared to represent material deposited during a single occupation and so were called occupation horizons or surfaces. The occupation horizons were termed "cultural" units until it became apparent that the layer containing them was equally as cultural in its formation as the horizons themselves.

Keller also provides a useful discussion regarding the differentiation between "natural" and "cultural" depositions at a site. (For further comments on natural stratigraphy, see Chapter 10.)

Other examples of excavation by visible stratigraphic levels at cave and rockshelter sites can be found in monographs by Aikens (1970; Hogup Cave, Utah), Alexander (1970; Parida Cave, Texas), and Jennings (1980; Cowboy Cave, Utah). At Parida Cave and similar sheltered sites along the Rio Grande in Texas, the cultural deposits are extremely complex, but if carefully excavated, they can yield much anthropological information (see Chadderdon 1983; Collins 1969:2–4; Word and Douglas 1970:8, Figure 5) (Figure 5.20). Determined efforts by T. R. Hester and K. M. Brown to use stratigraphic levels in a section of Baker Cave, Texas, proved extremely confusing, until the excavation profiles revealed that strata had been interrupted, contorted, and even reversed by a pre-

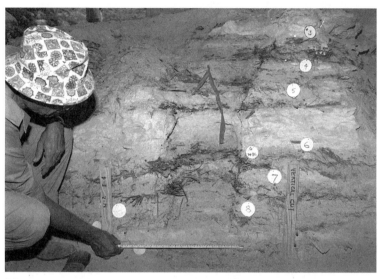

(a)

(b)

Figure 5.20 Excavating by stratigraphic (natural) levels, Baker Cave, southwest Texas, 1976: (*a*) profile view showing stratigraphy; (*b*) excavation proceeding by natural levels; a fiber layer is being exposed.

historic pit-hearth sequence going back, in one spot, several thousand years.

Many open sites are also amenable to excavation by natural stratigraphic layers. The **isolated block** method is sometimes used when stratigraphy is visible. The method entails digging a square trench to isolate a block or pillar of deposit; the stratification thus exposed on all four sides of the block is carefully recorded, and the block is then peeled layer by layer. Classic examples of this technique are provided by Bird (1943:253–257), Chadderdon (1983), Schmidt (1928:258–259), Smith (1955:13–14, Figures 82 and 83), and Webb and DeJarnette (1942:95–98, Figure 27, Plate 142). At times, the block can be "isolated" on three sides, allowing stratigraphic levels to be excavated (Figure 5.21).

Although open sites in the southeastern United States have usually been excavated by arbitrary levels, Morse (1973) excavated the Brand site (a Dalton "butchering station" in Arkansas) by natural stratigraphy. By peeling off the visible stratigraphic layers, Morse was able to expose in situ working floors at the site (see Morse 1973:24, Figure 2). At the Belcher Mound in Louisiana, Webb (1959) recognized in his preliminary investigations that the mound was stratified, with at least four habitation levels. Abandoning the traditional "vertical cake-slicing technique," Webb proceeded to excavate each habitation level as a natural unit.

Bison-kill sites in North America provide other instances of excavation by natural zones. Kehoe (1967) exposed the stratigraphy of the Boarding School Bison Drive (Montana) in test excavations in 1952. Later, in 1958, excavation was done by "layer stripping rather than by arbitrary levels" (Kehoe 1967:13), using the profiles of the 1952 test cut as a guide. Dibble (in Dibble and Lorrain 1968:19) relates the excavation technique used at Bonfire Shelter, Texas:

> The nature of the deposits at this site . . . provided an opportunity for prime reliance on a "natural level" excavation technique. After preliminary exploratory test had made gross outlines of the deposits . . . reasonably clear, further excavation by arbitrary levels was abandoned. Proceeding in descending order of stratigraphic

(a)

(b)

Figure 5.21   Excavations at Baker Cave, southwest Texas, 1985: (*a*) isolated block shows stratigraphic profile, (*b*) levels are peeled away by stratigraphic layers.

occurrence, four culture-bearing deposits were excavated primarily as vertical units.

Whether the excavator uses arbitrary levels or natural strata will of course depend on the internal structure of the site and the problems being investigated. As mentioned earlier, it may at times be advisable to combine the two methods (for example, a thick natural zone can itself be excavated in arbitrary levels), use other techniques, or even devise new ones. In the notes and ultimate publication of any excavation, excavation methods should be carefully recorded so that future workers will know how the materials were recovered.

SCREENING EXCAVATED DEPOSITS

Sifting excavated earth through screens (Figure 5.22a,b) enables the archaeologist to recover many materials that might otherwise be overlooked (leading to considerable bias in the sample obtained from a site). Each digging crew may have a number of sizes and grades of screens for use under varying circumstances. Screens of ¼-inch mesh have commonly been used, but these can often allow tiny flint flakes, animal bones (Shaffer 1992b), and other minute forms of archaeological evidence to be lost. Thus, fine-screening (with ⅛- or ¹⁄₁₆-inch mesh) has become a part of most modern excavations (e.g., Gordon 1993; Shaffer and Sanchez 1994; Thomas, 1983, 1985; Whalen 1994).

In sites where preservation of plant and animal remains is particularly good, a ¼-inch screen can be set over an ⅛-inch screen (Figure 5.22b). The larger items can be collected rather quickly from the top screen, and then small bones, seeds, and other tiny items can be collected from the ⅛-inch mesh (Chadderdon 1983; Flannery et al. 1986). The residue on the lower screen can also be scooped up for later sieving through graduated geological sieves and subsequent careful picking back at the lab.

Aten (1971:15) combined fine screening with "water screening" in processing deposits from coastal middens of mucky (or hard, when dry) clay, using a small gasoline-operated pump to wash deposits through ¹⁄₁₆-inch mesh screen. This technique provided excellent recovery without damaging or destroying such materials as the bones of small animals, as can sometimes happen with dry screening. Indeed, water screening has become a common technique in many excavations (Figure 5.23). Van Horn and Murray (1982) used a water-screening system that employed a sodium bicarbonate solution to get 100 percent recovery from clayey soils. They warn, however, that the effects of this process on radiocarbon samples (i.e., charcoal or other organics in the deposits) are not known. Other examples of water screening may be seen in Diamant (1979:210–217), Highley (1986:Figure 25b), and Shutler et al. (1980:Figure 1.8). Some water-screening systems use nested screens, involving

(a)

(b)

Figure 5.22   Screening: (*a*) at an archaeological site using ¼-inch mesh screen on sawhorse screen stands; (*b*) at Baker Cave, Texas, 1976, using ¼-inch mesh set over ⅛-inch mesh below.

Figure 5.23 Screening of archaeological deposits using low-pressure water screening through ⅛-inch mesh.

¼-, ⅛-, and 1/16-inch screens. However, in some situations, water screening can be destructive, harming fragile bones and plant remains. Ingbar (1985) has provided a comparison of the fine-screening of soil samples to obtain seeds and other plant remains for paleobotanical research at Gatecliff shelter, Nevada. He experimented, using geologic sieves, with dry-screening, flotation, and wet-screening. He found dry-screening the most effective, wet-screening less so, and flotation a distant third. However, he warned that these results may be specific to his project and the nature of the Gatecliff shelter deposits.

At the British Camp shell midden, Stein et al. (1992) washed the excavated sediments through four nested screens. They were, from top to bottom, 1-, ½-, ¼-, and ⅛-inch (Stein et al. 1992:Figure 3). Materials from the upper two screens were

field-sorted, and those from the smaller mesh screens were taken to the laboratory. They reported that 90–95 percent of the fish bone in the shell midden was removed from the ⅛-inch (3-mm) screen.

Archaeologists have also used screening to determine the quantitative composition of an archaeological deposit. Beginning in 1945, workers at the University of California (Berkeley) carried out a program of screening large samples of refuse deposits, sorted the screenings into components (such as bone, shell, obsidian, rock), measured the relative amounts of each, and used the quantitative data to gain insight into the economic and industrial activities of prehistoric hunter-gatherers. These studies resulted in a considerable literature, summarized in Heizer (1960:95–96).

If a limited amount of screening is planned, small hand screens with cross-braced legs are most convenient (Figure 5.24). These may be made up in several sizes so they will nest together for more convenient transportation. Larger screens (often 3-×-5 ft) resting on sawhorses permit a greater volume of earth to be processed, yet are easy to move as excavation progresses. In some large-scale excavations, screens are mounted in metal frames supported by flexible steel bands that allow vigorous shaking. Screens can also be suspended from tripods, where vigorous shaking will quickly process the excavated soil. "Shaker screens" that are rocked by a motor on a carriage have been found to be useful (Bird and Ford 1956; Diamant 1979; Story 1982: Figure 12), and other forms of mechanized screening have been proposed (e.g., Bird 1968; Guerreschi 1973; Michie 1969). Junius Bird devised a "dump sifter" at Gatecliff shelter (Thomas 1983:22–23) to speed the processing of sterile deposits. Earth was dumped down a ramp covered with ½-inch screen, and any soil that did not pass through the screen was examined on a sorting table at the end of the ramp. Perino (1981:Figure 9) has illustrated a "rocking screen" situated in a frame on ball bearings; it is said to be three times faster than conventional screening. Hunt and Brandon (1990) report the use of agricultural grain cleaners for mechanical screening of site deposits. These screening drums (Figure 5.25) process the soil rapidly, and the tumbling does not damage artifacts during the process.

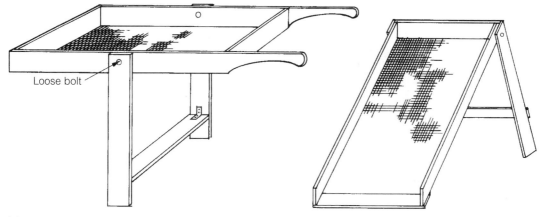

Loose bolt

(a)

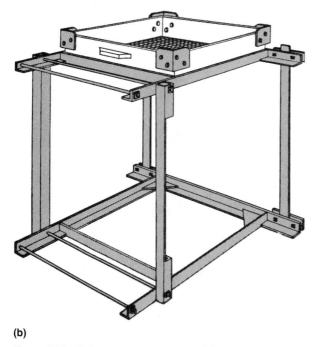

(b)

Figure 5.24   Various screening devices: (*a*) hand screens; (*b*) MacBurney shaker sieve.

The number and kinds of screens provided for an excavation depends on the character of the site and the goals of the research project, but two or three hand screens (¼-inch and ⅛-inch) would probably be a minimum for any site. One example of adapting the screening process to site-specific situ-ations involves the use of a "sorting board" at Colha, Belize. In Maya lithic workshops comprised wholly of debitage and tools broken in manufac-ture, the density of the debitage is so great (up to 5 million pieces per cubic meter; Hester and Shafer 1992), the usual ¼-inch screen is impractical. Thus,

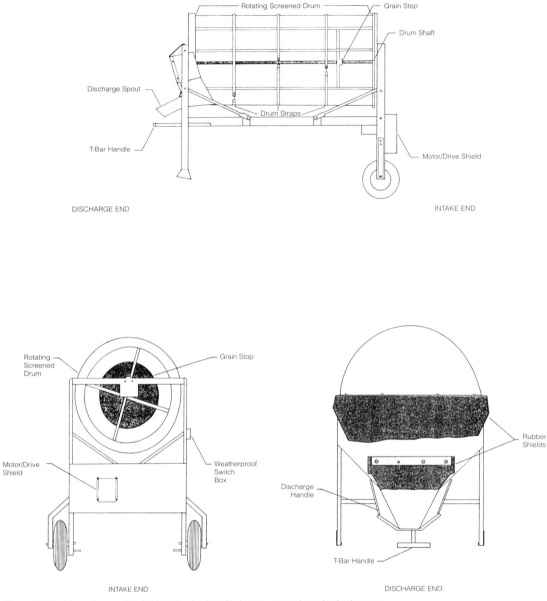

Figure 5.25   Use of a mechanical grain-sieving device as an archaeological screen.

we used a sorting board built much like the traditional screen to examine the flake debris and extract broken formal tools (to study and quantify the debitage, we used column samples removed from the profiles). A modification of the sorting-board technique (Figure 5.26) involves covering half of the screening frame with ⅛-inch mesh. Thus, in digging Early Postclassic midden deposits, the large sherds and lithics could be picked up off the sorting-board portion, and the rest of the deposit screened at the other end to collect faunal remains.

Figure 5.26 Use of a sorting-board/screen. Part of the 3-x-5-ft frame is a wooden sorting board from which large objects can be removed; then, the soil is pushed onto the ⅛-inch mesh that covers the other half for screening.

Moving the excavated dirt from the unit to the screen usually requires wheelbarrows or buckets (either galvanized or heavy rubber buckets work well). The buckets are also useful as water containers if very hard and dry deposits have to be "softened up" or if features must be cleaned and carefully prepared for recording and photography (or if units have to be bailed out after a rain!).

Finally, it should be emphasized that most contemporary archaeologists collect matrix samples, sometimes as column samples (Figure 5.27a), sometimes as constant volume samples (e.g., Thomas 1985:74), or sometimes as microstratigraphic samples (Figure 5.27b). These are not screened in the field but are taken to the lab for a variety of analyses, including fine-screening for faunal and botanical remains, flotation, constituent analysis, and micromorphological studies. At Baker Cave, Texas, the entire fill of a 9,000-year-old hearth was bagged and transported to the lab (Hester 1983). Fine-screening with geologic sieves produced an amazing array of tiny animal bones (including those of 16 species of snakes!), charred seeds, flint chips, and more. More than half the sample was saved for analysis in the future.

(a)

(b)

Figure 5.27 Taking samples from an excavation: (a) removing column samples from a profile; (b) extracting microstratigraphic samples.

EXCAVATING A "TYPICAL" UNIT

The earlier discussions of excavation techniques have been fairly general. To give a clearer picture of practical application of these techniques in the course of ordinary excavation, we think it worthwhile to describe the steps in the process of digging a "typical" excavation unit (Flannery et al. 1986 provide a readable and detailed account of the excavation process, as used at Guila Naquitz Cave, Oaxaca). The proper or customary use of the tools mentioned earlier in the chapter is also addressed further here.

A "typical" unit means one that shares all or most of the characteristics commonly found in excavation in an area. In the real world, such a unit is rarely encountered; most will exhibit at least one special or unique feature. This typical excavation unit, let us say, is 2 m square, and its limits are defined by the intersecting lines of the coordinate system. Its four corners are marked by stakes, each bearing a label (tag, flagging tape, or writing on the stake) giving its coordinate location. The sides of the unit are marked with taut string tied to each corner stake.

Important Considerations

Three considerations should be kept in mind at the beginning of every excavation: cave-in prevention, recording accuracy, and corner-stake preservation. The danger of cave-ins is a real problem in very soft, unconsolidated, or wet site soils. Shoring of units and trenches must sometimes be done, both for crew safety and to comply with federal OSHA requirements (see Figure 5.6). Cave or rockshelter deposits, often loose and relatively uncompacted, have a tendency to slump, and there are recorded instances of archaeologists being killed by the collapsing walls of deep trenches. As a general rule, in any excavation likely to be carried to a depth where there is danger of slumping, the walls of the pit or trench should be sloped inward, or battered, to ensure their stability. Sampson (1975) used stepped walls to protect against collapse of a large

unit dug into the "living clay" of the Caddington site in England (see also Thomas 1983 for an example from a Nevada rockshelter). The dangers of cave-in are evident when you consider that a 10-ft-deep trench (with backdirt on one side) will dump 10 tons of dirt into the unit in the event of a collapse.

Because of the wall slopes—or other wall modifications designed to ensure safety—not all of the deposit contained within a unit as defined on the surface will actually be excavated. The earth lying between the theoretical and actual limits of the unit may, however, be removed when an adjoining unit is excavated. In such cases, care should be taken that materials recovered within this remainder are located, for the record, within their correct unit, according to the site map. Be sure to record in the field notes both the surface and base dimensions of grid (or pit or trench) units that have been excavated with sloping, or battered, walls. You or the reader of your report may want to calculate the cubic content of the deposit excavated, and these measurements will be essential. The depth to which excavation will be carried in any unit can often be determined in advance from its position on the site and indications from nearby excavations. Keep in mind that a decreasing volume of earth is removed as you go deeper (in a unit with sloped walls); this can create problems in comparing and interpreting artifact densities—and in making comparisons between levels across the site.

Remember that the stakes marking the corners of excavation units must be used to record the position of all materials subsequently recovered; their location must therefore be carefully preserved. One way of doing this is to leave the stakes standing on top of substantial columns of earth, which are not to be excavated until the stakes can have no possible further utility. Again, because these columns will lie partially within four separate units, the location of materials eventually recovered from them should be carefully determined. Columns that obstruct the excavation of a burial or some other feature whose exposure is required will, of course, have to be removed.

Obviously, the excavation of any unit must begin with a careful examination of the surface.

The presence of surface finds is a signal that all deposits within the unit, from the surface down, must be examined. Where sterility has been absolutely determined (in earlier test cuts), the surface layer can be dug off with a shovel and thrown aside without examination. It should be remembered, however, that even though a surface layer is "sterile" in that it does not contain cultural material, it is still an important element in the depositional history of the deposit. The same, of course, is true for buried sterile layers separating cultural deposits.

Before excavation begins, you should photograph or make a plan drawing of the unit surface. You should also certainly have the surface contours plotted on your overall site map.

The Excavation Itself

When all sterile matter, if any, has been removed from the top of a unit, the business of actual archaeological excavation begins. In our "typical" excavation unit, this is done with a combination of trowel and shovel. Depending on the goals of your excavation, you may want to carefully scrape down the deposits, using the shovel to move the loose dirt into buckets and then to a screen. When using arbitrary levels, some excavators like to cut a narrow trench along one wall, perhaps to a depth of 10 cm, and then systematically work across the unit with trowels and shovels. This makes it easier to maintain the bottom of the arbitrary level. If an artifact or other object to be recorded is revealed, its location should be plotted immediately, before excavation is resumed.

During the course of excavation, the loose, excavated earth is removed from the unit at fairly frequent intervals and is processed through a screen (see "Screening Excavated Deposits" earlier). Although the earth from the excavation can be thrown directly into a screen, it may also be carried by buckets or in a wheelbarrow to the screen for sieving. As each level, natural or arbitrary, is completed, the floor of the unit should be scraped clean and carefully inspected for evidence of cultural features or natural disturbances such as tree roots or rodent burrows. The walls (profiles) of the unit

should be inspected for evidence of disturbance, pits, soil changes, and so on. Because of this, unit walls should be kept as vertical as the soil deposits will allow (remembering the safety warnings about cave-ins). Neat, vertical walls are important in the process of careful excavation and recording.

Much excavation in North America is conducted in the manner just outlined, in which each unit is dug downward in successive natural or arbitrary levels to the base of the site. However, features such as hearths, pits, and post molds that require refinements or modifications of technique are often encountered in the course of excavation. Some of the special techniques employed in recovering various types of features are discussed in Chapter 7. If a feature or an object cannot be exposed without further large-scale excavation, it should be carefully protected while that excavation is in progress. Trained excavators develop, before long, a "touch" or "feel" so sensitive that the slightest contact with an object is often sufficient for them to release pressure and avoid breaking it. Many experienced workers can tell, from contact, whether they have struck bone, burned clay, or stone.

As noted earlier, the trowel is usually used in combination with shovels or other excavation tools. Trowels should be employed to work through site deposits that contain an abundance of artifactual materials (flint, potsherds, etc.), and shovels are then used only to remove the soil already examined. At those excavations where every attempt is made to leave artifacts in place until they can be plotted (Figures 5.28 and 5.29), work is done almost entirely with trowels. When artifacts are encountered, they are carefully exposed and their in situ positions are plotted on a plan of the unit. This approach permits a precise examination of the spatial relationships among artifacts, debris such as burned rocks, features, and other buried evidence.

In some areas, where the average land contour is near sea level or the water table is very near the surface, groundwater may be encountered during excavation of a unit. Alluvial deposition may have elevated the surface of the ground, and a corresponding elevation of the groundwater level may immerse portions of the site deposit. Gasoline-

Figure 5.28 Excavating a grid unit. Here, at site 41LK201 in southern Texas, students are excavating in 1-m square units; note the string outlining the units and the use of trowels and dental picks to expose bison bone in situ; note labeled unit bag at upper right.

powered pumps can be used to remove the water as it seeps in. A simple hand pump of the diaphragm type (costing about $300) can remove 40 gallons of water per minute; we have used this type of pump successfully in swamp-margin excavation units in Belize.

In his classic study of field methods, Wheeler (1954:56) describes how, at Arikamedu, India, he excavated to a depth of 11 ft below the water table by keeping the water out of the pit with pumps. During excavations in 1991 at the Gault site in central Texas, high water tables and seep springs combined to inundate the excavations unless two water pumps were running at all times. A deep part of a backhoe trench, cut for stratigraphic and geomorphological studies, served as a "sump." One pump pulled water from this sump for use in water-screening the gummy matrix.

Figure 5.29 Excavating a grid unit. Here, at site 41LK201, a recording grid is placed over the unit for accurate and fast plotting of in situ cultural materials.

Whenever possible, units are excavated down to the base of the site or, in other words, to sterile subsoil. (The difference between midden deposit, usually relatively dark in color, and subsoil, normally lighter, is often quite distinctive.) However, such lower deposits cannot safely be presumed sterile until examined with care (i.e., until they are found to be wholly lacking in any evidence of human utilization—no flakes, sherds, burned rock fragments, etc.). To ensure that the bottom of site deposits has been reached, the excavator should take one quadrant of the unit deep into the presumed sterile stratum or use an auger to probe even more deeply.

EXCAVATING SPECIAL SITE TYPES

Certain types of sites demand special considerations and techniques. They include water-saturated sites, caves and rockshelters, and structural remains.

Water-saturated Sites

The excavation of water-saturated sites, such as Ozette and Hoko River, Washington (Croes and Blinman 1980) and Hontoon Island, Florida (Purdy and Newsom 1985), requires a wholly different approach to archaeology. At Hoko River, excavators first used "on-shore coring" to determine the depth and remaining extent of the site. Next, excavation was done via "hydraulic techniques"—with carefully adjusted hose nozzle pressure. Using a grid pattern of units, individual squares were cautiously exposed; artifacts were mapped via three-dimensional coordinates, tagged, and recorded in otherwise traditional fashion, although the preserved vegetal materials, basketry, wooden artifacts, and fishing lines had to be delicately bagged for prompt removal to a field laboratory for treatment (at Ozette) with polyethylene glycol to force out the water (see Chapter 7).

Caves and Rockshelters

The excavation of cave and rockshelter sites involves a great many special considerations not applicable to open sites and thus requires specialized techniques. Limited space, lack of light, the distinctive character of the deposits, the problem of dust, and especially the far better preservation of perishable cultural materials in dry caves are all factors that profoundly affect methods of excavation. Cave excavation can be hazardous. Bats can carry rabies, loose sections of ceiling can be dislodged and fall, and dust can cause serious respiratory difficulties. An exhaust fan run by either a gasoline engine or an electrical generator, dust-filter masks, artificial lighting (Heizer and Napton 1970:Plates 8–11), and timber cribwork to prevent cave-ins (Harrington 1933) may be necessary. At Hidden Cave, Nevada, Thomas (1985:70) had his crew wear surgical masks (Figure 5.30) to keep from inhaling large amounts of dust particles (he had wisely had the deposits checked for the presence or absence of valley fever [*Coccidioidomycosis*], whose spores can be spread through dusty excavations). Excavators also used wood plank walkways through the cave to keep from stirring up the dust. But the dust was so bad that a specially built ventilation system eventually had to be installed. Hidden Cave was also very dark, and the generators that operated the ventilation system did double duty by also supplying power for a lighting system. Other gear and specialized techniques may be necessary if exploration is part of a cave investigation (see Steele and Hissong 1984).

Caves containing evidence of human occupancy occur in many areas. In drier regions, these sites may yield normally perishable materials such as plant leaves and other plant parts, wood, leather, coprolites, and the like (their preservation in the field is often a problem; see Chapter 7). Good discussions of rockshelter excavation strategies are provided by Flannery et al. (1986), MacNeish (1975, 1978), and Thomas (1983, 1985). For example, MacNeish's work in the Tehuacan Valley of Mexico

Figure 5.30 Excavating cave deposits, wearing surgical masks to minimize dust hazards, at Hidden Cave, Nevada, 1979.

first utilized a "blitz crew" to put test pits in rockshelter sites. Test pits could then be connected as a trench, as he did at Purron Cave (MacNeish 1975:69). This trench provided a profile from which 17 different stratigraphic zones could be identified. The rockshelter floor was then staked out in grid fashion and cross-trenches of connected 1-m-square units were dug. These provided profiles from which adjacent squares could then be dug by natural levels, stripping away the defined stratigraphic zones. When natural levels were impractical, 20-cm arbitrary levels were used. Excavations proceeded by "alternate squares" (Figure 5.31), which permitted MacNeish (1975:73) "great control of the stratigraphy." A critique of MacNeish's excavation approach in the Tehuacan Valley has been written by Kowalewski (1976), and it is useful to compare the differing views on the excavation strategies that were used.

Archaeologists and students planning rockshelter and cave excavations could usefully consult the following references, which contain further information on the methods and problems involved: Aikens (1970), Chadderdon (1983), Collins (1969), Cressman (1942), Cressman et al. (1940), Flannery (1986), Heizer and Krieger (1956), Heizer and Napton (1970), Jennings (1980), Lehmer (1960), Logan (1952), Loud and Harrington (1929), Movius (1974), Shafer and Bryant (1977), Steward (1937),

(a)

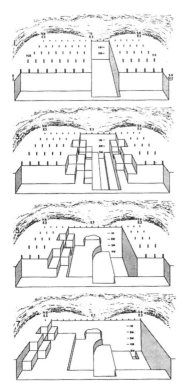
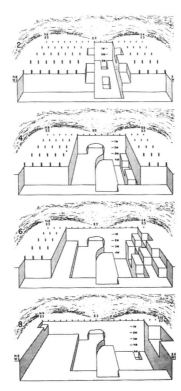

(b)

Figure 5.31 Excavating Purron Cave, Mexico, using the alternate-square method. As shown in the photograph (*a*) and the isometric drawing (*b*), the cave was dug first by cutting a trench through the deepest deposits. Next, 1-m squares were excavated in an alternating fashion (thus leaving 1-m balks to help trace stratigraphy). These began at the trench walls and moved away from it while following horizontal strata exposed in the deposits.

Thomas (1983, 1985), Word and Douglas (1970), and Zingg (1940).

Structural Remains

Structural remains found at sites (such as those standing structures at many Mesoamerican sites) and those discovered during excavation are of great interest and significance. Simple structures constructed largely of perishable materials may leave only minimal traces, usually post molds, behind. Excavators must therefore be constantly alert for these traces—postholes, wall trenches, hearths, and packed earthen floors.

Once recognized, such remains rarely present problems that cannot be dealt with adequately by standard field procedures, if these are perceptively applied; the remains will usually be treated and recorded with the same care and in the same detail as smaller features of special importance. Particular attention should be given during the clearing of the floor to any evidence of wall or roof materials. Often, sizable fragments of the walls or roof fall to the floor and are preserved by one or another agency. If the structure burned, charred fragments carefully excavated and recorded may go a long way toward reconstructing what the building looked like. Such remains should be photographed and drawn in situ. Postholes, wall trenches, possible entranceways, evidence of hearths, and other items of importance must be carefully studied and recorded. Cache and storage pits, burials beneath the floors, and subfloor deposits should be diligently sought. The location of all artifacts, animal bones, and other objects found on the floor must be precisely recorded because their distribution may help locate various activities within the structure.

The best procedure for excavating a floor once it has been discovered is usually to remove the overburden to within a few centimeters of the floor, where structural materials begin to appear or, in any case, before floor-level artifacts and features appear. The deposit immediately overlying the floor can then be excavated meticulously with a trowel. If the structure is a pithouse, its existence may be apparent before excavation. In this case, it may be desirable to dig a unit off center until the floor is located. From this unit, a trench or trenches can be dug to locate the walls, which can then be outlined. Overburden may be removed next, and the floor surface deposit finally dissected by careful horizontal digging. If pithouses are suspected but are not evident from the surface, it may be necessary to dig a test pit outside the site area to test the depth and character of the undisturbed subsoil. Test pits can then be dug in a grid to determine where disturbed deposits continue below the expected natural level. This may indicate pithouse fill to be excavated in the manner described. Sometimes a soil auger can locate floors and save digging pits.

In a site occupied over a long period of time, later house pits may cut through earlier ones (Figure 5.32). Such complex situations require the greatest care in the recording of details and a perceptive overall handling of the excavation. Because pits were sometimes dug for clay or other materials and then filled with trash, care must be exercised not to confuse such features with pithouses. In recording all house excavations, coordinate (usually north-south and east-west) cross sections must be drawn and shown on the plan of the structure (Figure 5.33). See Wood (1969:65, 67) for the technique of Plains house and earth-lodge excavation.

Although surface structures can be excavated using a grid system, archaeological sites with very complex structural or monumental remains require highly specialized techniques and methods of investigation. A notable example is the great temple-pyramid at Cholula, Mexico, where more than 5 miles of tunnels were dug through the mass to study earlier structures concealed within the mound (Marquina 1951). Excavating elaborate structural remains may be further complicated by the legal requirement or moral obligation to consolidate or even restore the remains as permanent monuments of ancient peoples and their works (Bernal 1963). Such monuments require carefully trained and thoroughly experienced excavators and excavation procedures that are outside the scope of this general guide.

We complete this section with some very general observations on excavating structures of moderate structural complexity. The presence of such

Figure 5.32 A Mimbres pithouse excavated at the Old Town site in New Mexico. A later surface room was built over the upper right corner after the pithouse was abandoned. Scale is 1 m.

remains is generally indicated by the mounding that results from the collapse of a roof, upper wall, or other superior portions of the structure and the subsequent erosion of the debris. Confronted with a mounded feature, the archaeologist's immediate task is to determine whether it is architectural in nature. Structures built of stone are sometimes obvious from building stones present in the debris of the mound, but features of earthen construction are seldom so evident. Similarly, rubbish heaps form mounds. These will usually turn out to be formless, but because rubbish was often used as construction fill for platforms and foundations, the issue may remain clouded until actual excavation is undertaken. The regularity of the mound form, its alignment or grouping with other mounds, the presence of a nearby borrow pit, and construction patterns in the area will usually provide clues to identification.

The excavation methods to be applied will depend upon the nature of the structure and the way it was built, the specific objectives of the excavators, and the limiting factors of resources at hand versus the magnitude and complexity of the structure. In general, the basic principle in excavating

stone or adobe structures is "work from the known to the unknown." Thus a pit, perhaps 2-m square, is usually dug some distance outside the mound periphery to locate a plaza or court floor, an old ground surface, or an occupational level and to determine the nature of the subsoil deposits. The pit is then expanded into a trench dug into the side of the mound, penetrating first the surface soil and humus of the present mound, then the collapsed and eroded debris from the upper portions of the structure, and finally the base of the structure's exterior wall.

Once this element of the structure has been discovered and exposed by the archaeologist, side trenches may be opened to follow the wall to the left and right. Where construction is not well preserved, the trench should not turn a corner at an especially poorly preserved section of the wall but should continue well beyond the corner before making the turn. From the amount of fallen wall stone and the preserved height and contour of the mound, it may be possible to determine approximately the original wall height. In clearing the walls, any fallen ornamental or decorative features should be noted and carefully recorded. Evidence

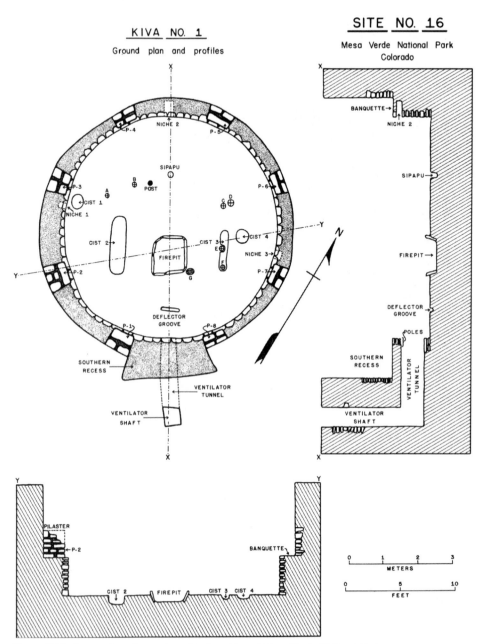

Figure 5.33 Excavation plan and profiles for a kiva at Mesa Verde National Park.

of the original wall facing or surface treatment may be preserved at the base of the wall.

If the exterior walls enclose rooms, these may be excavated next. As discussed earlier, overburden is usually removed to within a few inches of the floor, with the floor zone then carefully exposed by trowel excavation. If the walls are part of a substructural platform, excavation must then turn to the upper terraces or superstructure. These walls are located as before, by trenching in from

(a)

(b)

Figure 5.34 Excavation of a Maya house mound at Colha, Belize: (*a*) using the subop method, the lower wall foundations are found at Operation 2008; (*b*) the perimeter of the house is exposed, and portions of the interior are excavated.

the side of the mound where the upper floor level should be located. If a foundation platform is present, it is usually desirable to sample its fill and to investigate the possibility of earlier construction or an enclosed tomb. Although this is sometimes done by pit excavation from above, the greatest control is maintained when a trench can be excavated in from the side along the base level. In this way, features are exposed where they should be best preserved, and the chance of missing or damaging features is minimized. In excavating foundation fill, the investigator must be careful not to mistake temporary retaining walls and makeshift stairways used in building up the fill for earlier interior construction. Indeed, these construction techniques used in building up the fill should be noted, as Ford and Webb (1956:37–38) and Morris et al. (1931:1:146–148, 204–206) have done.

In carrying out these kinds of excavations, a grid system is often not feasible. There are several other systems that archaeologists have used to keep track of horizontal and vertical proveniences during excavation of structural remains. At the site of Colha, Belize, a system of "operations" (a mound or other major structure has a sequential operation number) and "suboperations" (trenches and other excavation units numbered sequentially) was utilized with great success (see Stock 1980; see also Sharer and Ashmore 1987). The "subops"

exposed architectural features, leading to exposure of the entire building outline (Figure 5.34a,b).

Where construction is of adobe, distinguishing the walls and other structural features from debris composed of the same material can often be painfully difficult. Kidder, who excavated an adobe platform structure at Kaminaljuyu, Guatemala, reports that it was sometimes impossible to see the juncture or separation lines between buildings approached in cross section in a penetration trench. The problem was resolved by having workers use the pointed end of a hand pick for all advance or exploratory work. Because fill did not bond or fuse with the adobe walls it covered, the pick was used to rip dirt loose and pull it forward, causing material to fall away at the cleavage line between fill and wall and exposing the wall (Kidder et al. 1946:27–28, 90, 92). Braidwood and Howe (1960: 40–41) discuss a similar problem in the excavation of touf (loaded-mud) walls.

Although building plans and reconstructions generally seem clear-cut and obvious in published reports, students will find the situation in the field is often quite the opposite: they will constantly face difficult interpretative and procedural decisions of the greatest importance. Even recognizing and interpreting such basic architectural features as walls and floors can be difficult. Where alterations occurred in ancient times, the remains will often

(a)

(b)

Figure 5.35 Excavations at Operation 2035, Colha, Belize: (*a*) view (note looter's tunnel); (*b*) exposing top of pyramid to reveal earlier structure buried under Terminal Classic marl blocks.

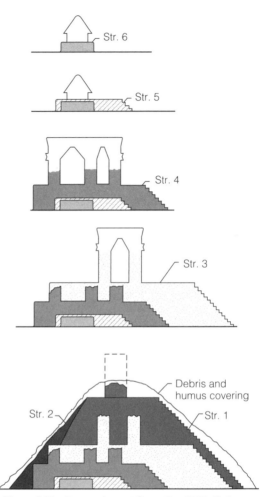

Figure 5.36 Excavations at Operation 2035, Colha, Belize. Profiles indicate the sequence of structures that led to the final phase of this building.

present a confusing array of fragmentary structural features—for example, Structure A-5 Complex at Uaxactun, Guatemala (Smith 1950:15–44, Figures 1–8, 58–81) and North Acropolis at Tikal (Coe and McGinn 1963). It is the excavator's task to retrace precisely the various steps in the sequence of events. A sound knowledge of building methods and patterns in the area will obviously be necessary. For example, Eaton (1994) carried out excavations at Operation 2035, a 9-m-high mound at the Maya site of Colha, Belize. Looters had dug tunnels into the structure, revealing walls of inner, buried buildings.

Through a careful study of the looter trench profiles and then with judicious trenching and opening of subops (discussed earlier in this chapter), Eaton was able to reconstruct the sequence of construction, as well as the changing function of the structure through time (Figures 5.35 and 5.36).

Cultural deposits in architectural remains are also complicated by repeated occupations of a site, especially if the structures are remodeled or become the foundations of later buildings (Figure 5.37). Ancient as well as contemporary rubbish deposits, because they are usually nearby and easier to dig

Figure 5.37   Area excavation of Maya structures and related remains. At Operation 2031 at the site of Colha, Belize, a complicated pattern of house floors, retaining walls, burials, fire pits, caches, and middens from the Middle and Late Preclassic periods was exposed.

in than undisturbed earth, are often used as fill for platforms and foundations. Such rubbish may be scattered about and subsequently incorporated into other deposits or into structures at some distance from where it originally lay. Such disturbed deposits require perceptive ordering through correct interpretation of the structural events; careful and constant attention together with precise recording are required to work out these events and their correlations.

BACKDIRT AND BACKFILLING

Almost invariably, the archaeologist excavates a site under an agreement to restore the land surface. Also, open pits are hazards to ranch and farm animals, as well as to people, wild game, and other creatures, and often may have to be fenced during excavation. In most cases, when the digging is completed, all excavated earth must be replaced in the trenches and pits and the surface left level and smooth.

Backfilling is one of the unavoidable consequences of archaeology, and its ultimate necessity should be borne in mind at all times in the course of excavation. In CRM archaeology, the fieldworker may escape the drudgery of backfilling, because the construction project may involve massive earth-moving after the excavations are done.

A little foresight in the distribution of backdirt may save a great deal of trouble in backfilling. In exploratory excavation, excavated earth is generally piled as compactly as possible on the surface at one side of the unit. Do not see how far you can throw the excavated earth, because it must all be returned to the hole from which it came! To ensure sufficient earth to fill all excavations at the end of the dig, any area on which backdirt is to be thrown should be completely cleared of vegetation or other cover. Otherwise, a considerable amount of dirt may settle and become packed among plants or other matter and be very difficult to move.

Excavated earth should not be put where it covers the surface of units that are likely to be excavated later. Very large piles should be avoided; they are difficult to handle and may necessitate moving the dirt a considerable distance when it is replaced. The main point is to keep a pattern for backfilling in mind at all times during the excavation so that at the end, every pit or trench can be refilled with loose earth piles as near at hand as possible.

The backfill should be packed in so that it will not settle too much during subsequent rains. As the hole is being filled, the earth should occasionally be tramped on and tamped and probed with digging bars and shovels to pack it firmly. Backfilling almost always takes longer than you think. Be sure to allow enough time for it when setting up an excavation schedule, especially if you have a deadline. On the average, for instance, it takes one worker with a shovel a couple of hours to completely refill one 1-×-1-m unit that has been excavated to a depth of 1 m.

A digging crew can sometimes borrow a Fresno scraper from a local rancher (Fitting 1973:7). Hooked to a jeep or a pickup truck, this will fill a site more easily and rapidly than workers with shovels. Large excavations—where the time required for labor to clear, remove overburden, or refill pits and trenches is prohibitive—can often be cleared or filled with a bulldozer or backhoe with a front-end loader secured on hire or loan. A good (and thrifty!) excavator will keep this in mind and, during the course of digging, try to make arrangements to secure such machinery on loan from someone whose interest in the excavation has been cultivated.

Archaeologists often throw bottles and other nonperishable camp debris into the bottom of excavation units prior to backfilling. These serve as markers to any later excavator who might happen to dig in the same spot. Even pothunters sometimes have the forethought to mark their plunderings by placing some modern object in their pits. McKern (1930:443), during his excavations at the Kletzien mound group (Wisconsin), came across a bottle containing a slip of paper bearing the date

"Oct. 11, [18]'96," apparently a record of some early relic-collector's explorations.

SOME HAZARDS IN FIELDWORK

Although it is not our intention to end this chapter on a negative note, it is important to remind students that field investigation can be dangerous. Ordinary city life also has its hazards, as we all know, but they do not prepare anyone for the unfamiliar dangers an excavation offers. Although most archaeologists will not face the perils of an Indiana Jones, there are sometimes problems with guerrillas, smugglers, and most commonly, the climate and foods of a foreign land.

Outside the continental Unites States, there is always the risk of contracting a local disease that, if left undiagnosed or if incorrectly treated, may cause severe health problems. Several diseases can be contracted from eating food prepared in an unsanitary manner. "Traveler's diarrhea" is a common plague and sometimes best countered by large doses of Pepto-Bismol! Water is often contaminated and should always be boiled or otherwise purified if this is known or suspected to be the case (good portable drinking water purifiers are available for under $30, but larger systems are needed to meet the demands of a big field camp). A well-trained local doctor usually can recognize infections and knows how to treat them.

Various prescription drugs and immunizations are often necessary for work in foreign countries. Antimalarial drugs should be carefully considered, in close consultation with a physician. Chloroquine is often recommended, though other strains of malaria (such as Falciparm) require different drugs. Diphtheria-tetanus boosters are recommended every 10 years. A broad-spectrum antibiotic such as tetracycline should be part of your medical kit if the field camp is some distance from medical facilities. Indeed, it is a very good idea to work with a physician to plan the medical aspects of any foreign or remote archaeological project. A member of the field team should be designated to develop and maintain a camp first-aid kit. Staff with CPR training and first-aid skills should be identified. Based on our experience, we would also highly recommend that every crew member have health insurance, either personal or inexpensive group insurance that can be purchased for the duration of the project.

Our comments have focused on fieldwork in other countries, but there are plenty of hazards in doing fieldwork in North America. First of all, whether abroad or in the rural United States, you should behave in a manner that will not offend the local population. This may involve the way you talk or dress; it is best to observe local standards, customs, and courtesies. When digging sites in rural areas, you need to be concerned about potential hazards—rattlesnakes (and other venomous snakes), range cattle, bulls, and rabid wild animals. Snake leggings and snake-bite first-aid kits may be wise investments for certain projects.

Ticks have always been bothersome pests for field archaeologists, and Rocky Mountain spotted fever, spread by the dog tick, has long been a hazard. However, in North America today there is the threat of Lyme disease, which is transmitted by the deer tick and is very common in parts of the United States in the spring and summer seasons. Early symptoms of Lyme disease include a red, circular rash appearing within 2–30 days, fatigue, mild headaches, muscle or joint pain and stiffness, fever, and swollen glands. If you develop such symptoms during or after fieldwork, consult a doctor immediately so that effective treatment can be started.

Valley fever is an endemic disease contracted by breathing dust from soil containing the fungus *Coccidioides immitis* (see Thomas 1985:67). It consists of an unpleasant, though rarely fatal, lung infection (Werner 1974; Werner et al. 1972). The range of this fungus is in a belt from northern California southeast through southern Nevada, Arizona, southern New Mexico, and Texas to the Gulf Coast. Also, cave bats are under suspicion as carriers of rabies. According to Bat Conservation International (July 8, 1996; http://www.batcon.org), there is no direct evidence linking the transmission

of rabies to bat urine or feces. However, histoplasmosis (a respiratory infection caused by the fungus *Histoplasma capsulatum,* which may exist in warm, humid bat habitats) is a concern. Fieldwork in such conditions resquires the use of a respirator that filters out particles as small as 2 microns (Brass 1994; Constantine 1988).

The appearance of hanta virus spread by mice is another concern for archaeological crews. At this time, the virus is found mostly in the American Southwest, but it has spread to moist climes to the East.

Working in dry and dusty caves may lead to serious problems of lung congestion. The Harvard archaeologist S. J. Guernsey reportedly died as a result of such exposure. Fungal spores in caves or sealed cavities (such as burials) can also be harmful. The "Pharaoh's curse" associated with Tutankamen's tomb in 1922 may have been a reaction to severe allergies to mold, fungi, or organic dust in the tomb. It has been suggested that some people associated with that project contracted allergic alveolitis and died of pulmonary insufficiency (C. Stenger-Phillips; Ph.D. thesis, Strausburg University Medical School). Fibrous dust found at some locales can cause pleural mesothelioma, a dangerous disease that could be, although it is not yet known to be, a hazard to archaeologists (Rohl et al. 1982). Camp dangers are common—tripping over tent ropes, eating tainted food, drinking contaminated water, preparing food in dirty field kitchens, falling into the campfire, and the like. Pressure gas lanterns are known to release toxic fumes from the beryllium in the incandescent mantle (Griggs 1973).

As we have already suggested, cave-ins of deep trenches or pits can occur in all kinds of sites, but especially in caves. Several archaeologists have died in cave-ins. Two relic collectors suffocated as a result of a tunnel collapse while digging into a Caddoan shaft tomb (Perino 1981:4). People have had their skulls damaged by heavy double-ended picks wielded by careless co-workers. Unskilled use of axes and machetes has also claimed its share of victims. Guns should also be prohibited in all field camps unless they are needed to defend the camp against dangerous animals or to shoot game for food. Indeed, the director of any excavation has the responsibility to be aware of any illnesses or injuries among crew members that require medical attention as well as to provide and maintain an adequate and clean camp, to insist on good hygiene, and to provide a good diet.

Archaeologists, as a result of the demands of CRM archaeology, have begun to develop excavation safety checklists (e.g., at the Office of the State Archaeologist, University of Iowa). OSHA standards originally led to such plans, but with the ever-increasing number of students in field schools and non-CRM activities, it is incumbent on the field director to ensure crew safety (such concerns include depth of excavations, stability of excavation walls, keeping heavy tools away from edges of units where they might fall into a pit, placement of backdirt, etc.). And the university archaeologist starting his or her first field school should be sure to check with the university's legal staff regarding the existence of, or preparation of, a liability release form.

GUIDE TO FURTHER READING

Barker 1982; Dancey 1981; Dever and Lance 1978; Dillon 1989; Fladmark 1978; Haag 1986; Joukowsky 1980; McIntosh 1986; Sharer and Ashmore 1993; Thomas 1989; Wheeler 1954

CHAPTER

6

Data Preservation: Recording and Collecting

Kenneth L. Feder

The example is given of the blind man asked to study and describe an elephant. Because he cannot see the beast, he needs to use his well-developed sense of touch to gather the data necessary to describe the animal. But each time he approaches the creature and lays his hands upon it, the elephant shyly pulls away. The man realizes that he will never gather the information he needs without somehow stopping the animal from moving. So, he gets a gun. Returning to the elephant, he listens for its motions and then shoots and kills it. Finally, he is able to approach the animal, feel it, and describe it. "An elephant," the blind man states, "is a large, motionless beast that lies on its side and has a gaping hole in its head."

In a sense, archaeologists are faced with this same conundrum; we are like the blind man in the story, and an archaeological site is like the elephant. Archaeological sites are the material representations of a culture. To collect site data we usually need to excavate the material from out of the ground—and in so doing, we destroy the very site we are trying to study. But we have little choice. Archaeological material represents all we have to inform us directly of the lives of past peoples. To get at that material we necessarily apply a destructive technique of data collection—excavation.

In this sense, archaeological sites are analogous to the fossils of extinct animals. Lewis Binford (1964:425) states, "The loss, breakage, and abandonment of implements and facilities at different locations, where groups of variable structure performed different tasks, leaves a 'fossil' record of the actual operation of an extinct society." As Schiffer (1976) points out, behavior does not "fossilize" directly but is distorted by a number of cultural and natural processes.

Just as a prehistoric fossil is not simply a collection of bones, a prehistoric site is not just a collection of artifacts, ecofacts, and features. A fossil is, in this sense, more than simply the sum of its parts; the positioning of individual bones, the juxtaposition of one bone to another, the articulation of different groupings of bones, all provide valuable insights into how the animal stood, moved, foraged or hunted, and defended itself—in other words, how it lived. By the same token, an archaeological site is more than simply the sum of its constituents. The juxtapositions of archaeological remains and the spatial articulations of the constituents of sites all provide insights into how the people at the site behaved.

This is one reason paleontologists do not simply bulldoze their fossils, and would not, even if the bones could survive such treatment. Bulldozing might quickly recover bones, but the positioning of one bone to another would be destroyed—as would the information those spatial relationships provide. Likewise, archaeologists do not simply bulldoze sites. It would be a far quicker way of recovering artifacts, but certainly, the spatial relationships of the materials would be destroyed in the process, along with the information about the culture that left those remains.

Herein lies the paradox. "Noninvasive" techniques in archaeology are in their infancy. We have, as yet, no technique that allows us completely to image the buried remains of an archaeological site. With few exceptions, to study a site we must excavate it and recover the materials. But in so doing, we inevitably destroy the site itself—we are like the blind man who must shoot the elephant to be able to describe it.

It is in our record keeping in the field, however, that we preserve the *information* present in the spatial relationships among the constituents of an archaeological site. Just as a paleontologist eventually removes the bones from their place of discovery, in a sense, taking the ancient animal apart bone by bone, the archaeologist eventually removes many of the archaeological materials—at least the portable ones—from their place of discovery, taking apart the site artifact by artifact, feature by feature. And just as the paleontologist preserves information provided by the articulated skeleton through meticulous record keeping, so does the archaeologist preserve the information presented by the artic-

ulated site, even as he or she is recovering the material and thereby destroying those articulations.

PRESERVING CONTEXT THROUGH RECORD KEEPING

Consider the artifact depicted in Figure 6.1a: a simple stone spear point. If we encountered the point in an archaeological collection, bereft of **site context,** we might be able to examine the point itself to determine the source of its raw material, how it was made, and perhaps how it was utilized. But we wish to know more: What was the context of the tool in its culture? What was it used with? What was its significance in reference to the social or ideological systems of its culture? Spatial context and **association** are key sources of data in our attempt to understand how a given object was used within a particular culture.

Figure 6.1b depicts the same artifact in one context—the spear point is found lodged in the bone of a food animal. Figure 6.1c shows the artifact in another context: in a **cache,** or cluster, of other points awaiting use. Figure 6.1d shows the artifact embedded in the skull of a human being. Finally, Figure 6.1e shows the same artifact, but in a different possible context—as a grave offering to a dead hunter. In each case, the artifact is precisely the same in its material, form, and proportions. But its context is different. Without careful excavation and record keeping, such information would be irretrievable. All we would have is the artifact itself, and a host of unanswerable questions about what that artifact meant. It is, at least in part, our desire to preserve context that renders archaeological excavation so time-consuming.

Measuring Provenience

In Chapters 5 and 9, the process of gridding an archaeological site is discussed. A site grid of 2-x-2-m squares, or 5-x-5-ft squares, or whatever, is the first step in keeping track of spatial contexts at a site. Gridding the excavation allows us to maintain a record of where every item was found to within a unit of a given area.

(a)

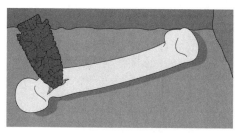

(b)

(c)

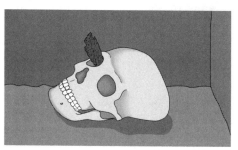

(d)

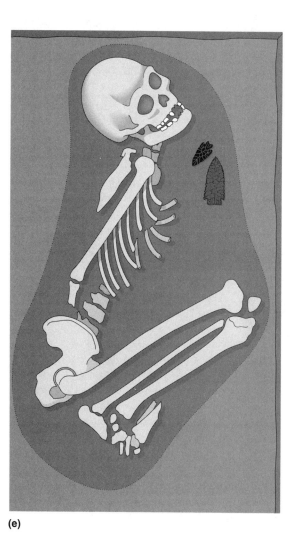

(e)

Figure 6.1   Drawing of the same artifact—a projectile point: (*a*) without a context; (*b*) as a weapon piercing a deer bone; (*c*) in a cache or "bank" of projectile points; (*d*) embedded in a human skull; and (*e*) as a grave offering. In each case, the form and raw material of the artifact is identical. Only the spatial context and associations are different.

Ordinarily, each unit to be excavated is assigned to an individual or a team of diggers. It is essential for each team to have a notebook in which a daily log is kept for recording, in narrative form, all information concerning the excavation of that unit: the discovery of artifacts, ecofacts, features, anomalous stains, and such. A spiral or otherwise-bound notebook with gridded pages (preferably metric) is a good choice. Where high humidity and/or precipitation is a problem, field notebooks with water-resistant pages can be used.

But it is not enough simply to record things at this level of precision. Many human activities are spatially patterned on a scale far smaller or far larger than the typical grid unit of 4 m^2 or 25 ft^2. For this reason, in the process of excavating a site many items initially are left **in situ**, that is, precisely where they were found. The exact measurement of the horizontal and vertical locations of these in situ items—their **proveniences**—are recorded, if not for every single **debitage** (waste) flake or potsherd, at least for complete or broken tools, tool blanks, utilized flakes, sherds above a certain size, and so on. Each site and situation is different, and the level of precision for taking proveniences will differ.

Horizontal Location. In a grid excavation, the four corners of each unit have been located with reference to a fixed **datum** whose precise geographical location may be known (see Chapter 5). In essence, an imaginary sheet of graph paper has been superimposed over the site. There is an **origin** (the 0,0 point on the graph—the site datum) and a series of parallel lines representing the x-axis (ordinarily running east-west) and another set of lines, the y-axis, perpendicular to the x-axis (ordinarily running north-south). The lines are some fixed interval apart (2 m is common), and each excavation unit is delineated by two adjacent lines from the x-axis and two adjacent lines from the y-axis (Figure 6.2). On a graph, each intersection of a line from the x-axis and a line from the y-axis defines a point that can be designated ([x,y]: so many units along the x-axis, so many units along the y-axis). At an archaeological site, each intersection of the x- and y-axes can be similarly designated. At these

points, in the areas to be excavated, a wooden stake can be hammered into the ground. Four stakes will define an excavation unit. Each point marked by a stake will have a unique designation in the grid. Each square is then assigned a unique designator; simply as the result of tradition, the unit may be labeled with the coordinates of its southwest stake (see Figure 6.2).

We can then make a smaller-scaled, imaginary graph within each square to more precisely measure the locations of objects within the units—in other words, to measure proveniences. By using a measuring triangle with bubble levels or two tape measures and a plumb bob, we can measure the precise horizontal location of an object within the square in reference to the southwest stake of the unit. One simply can measure the perpendicular distance of the object being recorded from the south wall of the unit, and then measure its distance from the west wall (Figure 6.3). Or, if the walls taper in with depth, these measurements should be taken indirectly from the southwest corner of the square. This gives us the object's location (ordinarily in centimeters) north and east of the southwest corner of the unit—the location of the southwest stake. Because we also know the precise location of that stake relative to datum, the origin of our imaginary graph, we can easily calculate the location, relative to datum, of an object discovered within a unit. In this way, *all* provenienced objects within a given unit and within all units at the site are precisely located relative to the same fixed point. Thus, the spatial context of everything found at the site relative to everything else can be determined (Figure 6.4). Though the artifacts will be removed, by proveniencing and careful record keeping, we can map the locations of each of those items, creating a permanent record of the spatial contexts of all of them.

It is useful to keep a record (on a 3-x-5-inch card, on a record sheet, or using a spreadsheet or database software on a portable computer kept in the field) of each item so provenienced. Such a record should include the artifact type (spear point, potsherd, clay pipe), raw material, excavation unit, provenience, excavation level, and accession number (discussed later in this chapter).

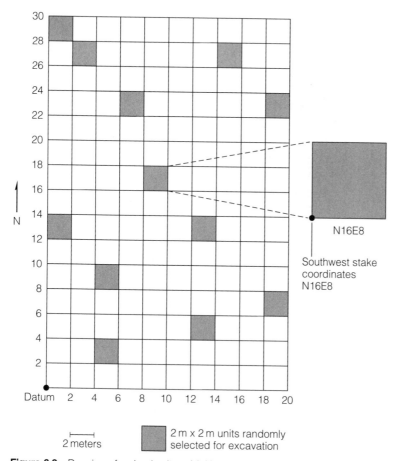

Figure 6.2 Drawing of a simple site grid. Here, excavation units are 2 m square and have been randomly selected on the grid. Datum, the point from which all other measurements are taken, is indicated.

So far, we have been discussing proveniences as they relate to excavation units. There are other **provenience,** or **data collection, units** used in archaeological research. For example, in a surface walkover of an urban site or even a small, historical site with surface remains, a larger grid may be employed. For example, at the eighteenth- and nineteenth-century Lighthouse village site in Connecticut, we first established a grid of provenience units 30 m on a side and walked over the entire village, recording the precise location of surface remains within each of those grid units (Feder 1994). In cases where there are architectural remains, provenience units may be defined by the structures themselves; the provenience or collection unit may be the individual room or other feature. Different kinds of units are appropriate in different circumstances, and provenience units of different scales can often be used at the same site. At the Lighthouse site just mentioned, after using a large grid in our surface walkover, we used a smaller 2-m grid, tied into the larger grid, for our excavation units.

Along with provenience records, particularly where a number of artifacts have been left in situ or in the case of features or architectural remains, photographs can be taken, visually preserving spatial associations within an excavation unit (see Chapter 8). In essence, although we destroy the site

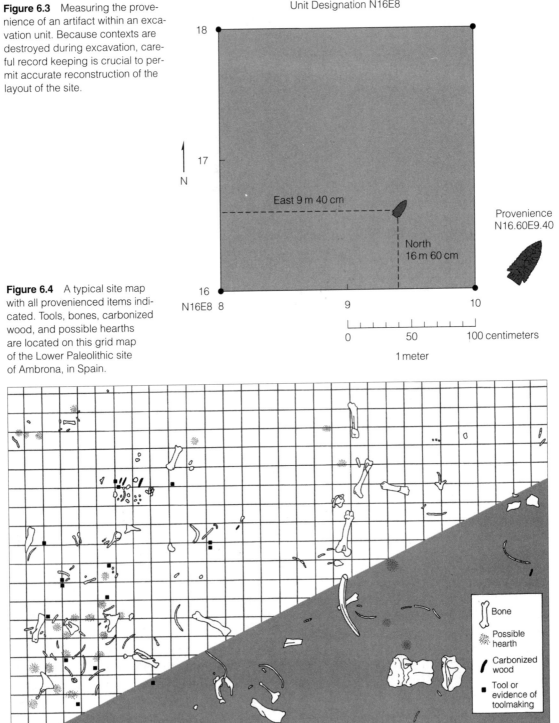

Figure 6.3 Measuring the provenience of an artifact within an excavation unit. Because contexts are destroyed during excavation, careful record keeping is crucial to permit accurate reconstruction of the layout of the site.

Unit Designation N16E8

East 9 m 40 cm

North 16 m 60 cm

Provenience N16.60E9.40

0   50   100 centimeters

1 meter

Figure 6.4 A typical site map with all provenienced items indicated. Tools, bones, carbonized wood, and possible hearths are located on this grid map of the Lower Paleolithic site of Ambrona, in Spain.

Bone

Possible hearth

Carbonized wood

Tool or evidence of toolmaking

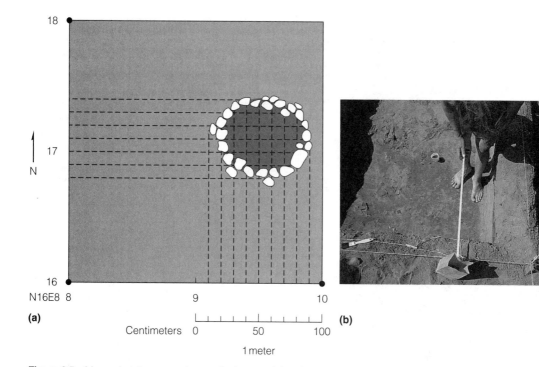

Figure 6.5 Measuring the provenience of a feature: (*a*) a simple hearth characterized by burned earth and a concentration of charcoal and demarcated with stones. Dashed lines represent individual measurements taken every 10 cm from the west and south walls of the excavation unit; (*b*) taking provenience measurements on lithic artifacts resting on a 5,000-year-old living surface.

by excavating it, our record keeping (measuring, mapping, and photographing) allows us to reconstruct it.

For some objects, it is enough to record a single provenience location; for larger artifacts and especially for features and architectural remains, however, a series of locational measurements are needed to define form and boundaries. Again, using the measuring triangle or the two tape measures and plumb bob, we can take a number of measurements to delineate the object or feature on a map of our excavation unit. With the triangle set against one wall of the unit, for example, we can measure the outline of a soil stain by taking readings of the distance of the outline from the western and southern walls of the unit, every 2, 5, or 10 cm along those walls (Figure 6.5). Again, if the walls

taper with depth, provenience can be taken consistently from one corner of the excavation unit (by tradition, but not necessarily, the southwest corner). Obviously, the more closely spaced our measurements, the more precise our drawing can be. It is common practice to photograph each feature, being certain to include a scale; a directional indicator (for example, a trowel pointing north); and a slate or letter board indicating site name, unit designation, feature number, depth, and date (Figure 6.6a).

A useful tool in mapping small features, particularly those consisting of many individual artifacts or ecofacts—for example, a lithic chipping area or a roasting platform—is a **grid frame.** The frame is a wooden or metal square, often 1 m on a side (so it fits easily into a 2-×-2-m excavation unit). String or

(a)

(b)

Figure 6.6 Features are nonportable artifacts, often resulting from a specific activity: (*a*) a stone-lined cooking feature; (*b*) a 1-m-square grid frame with 10-cm increments demarcated by string, useful in accurately measuring and drawing the various elements in a feature.

wire is fastened to the frame at 10-cm intervals to form a grid, as shown in Figure 6.6b. This grid can be placed over a feature to aid in mapping individual objects.

Vertical Location and Extent. Along with the two-dimensional, horizontal location of an artifact or feature, we also are interested in its third, vertical, dimension—for example, the depth of the surface upon which an artifact is resting, the level from which an ancient trash pit was dug, or the depth of a burial.

Ordinarily, as mentioned in Chapter 5, each unit at a site is excavated in layers or levels. The layers can represent natural stratigraphic layers, culturally distinguishable levels, or arbitrary levels of a consistent thickness. Some suggest 3, 5, or 10 cm as a reasonable thickness for each layer peeled back in troweling, but thickness may depend on the stratigraphy at each site (see Chapter 11). While each layer is excavated in each excavation unit, all of the information derived from that layer should be recorded. Along with the previously mentioned unit log, there should be a general site record with a separate section for each excavation or provenience unit. Within each unit's section should be sequential **level sheets** or **unit-level records.** A level or unit-level sheet (Figure 6.7) should contain all essential information concerning an individual level of an excavation unit: site name; unit designation (for example, the coordinates of the southwest stake); starting and ending depth of the level relative both to the surface and to datum; a description of the matrix; a list and count of artifacts and ecofacts; a record of features identified; and a list of photographs, artifact bags, and samples taken. Features can be drawn on level sheets or, more commonly, can be recorded on separate, gridded **feature record sheets** (Figure 6.8).

Just as a general measure of horizontal location needs to be supplemented with precise provenience data, location within a particular level can be supplemented with exact depth measurements for some items. Measuring the precise depth of artifacts may allow the archaeologist to define the **occupation floor,** or living surface, of the site, if the artifacts are, in fact, precisely where the past peo-

TAS FIELD SCHOOL 1990

UNIT LEVEL RECORD

DATE _____ opened

_____ closed

SITE NUMBER 41 _____

Recorder _____

UNIT N _____ W _____   LEVEL _____   BAG # _____

QUAD _____ 1/4 V. CONTROL _____-_____ cm   DEPTH _____-_____ cm

SAMPLES   (#) **RECORDS/NOTES** (✓)

C-14		FEATURE #	
SOIL		PHOTOS:	
SNAIL MATRIX		PLAN MAP (ON	
		REVERSE SIDE)	

EXCAVATOR _____

_____

_____

_____

MATERIALS RECOVERED (✓)

DESCRIPTION	AMOUNT	
CHERT DEBITAGE		
BONE		
MUSSEL SHELL		
LAND SNAIL		
GROUND STONE		
CERAMICS		
HISTORIC MATERIAL		
BURNED ROCK wt in kgs		

SCREEN SIZE   1/4   1/8

PROVENIENCED ARTIFACTS*

UI#	DESCRIPTION	LOCATION	V. CONTROL
		N W	

*SKETCH ALL DIAGNOSTICS ON CONTINUATION SHEETS

LEVEL NOTES (Describe: soil matrix, disturbances, features, etc.)

_____

_____

_____

_____

_____

_____

_____

_____

_____

_____

_____

_____

_____

_____

_____

SOIL COLOR CHART _____ (dry, moist, wet)   AREA SUPERVISOR _____

Figure 6.7   An excavation unit-level sheet. In one approach, when units are excavated in stratigraphic layers, a separate level sheet is prepared for each stratigraphic layer of each unit, indicating site name; unit designator; starting and ending depth; and detailed notes concerning soil, artifacts, and features encountered in the level.

FEATURE RECORD

Feature #: _____   Excavator: _____

Site: _____   Date: _____

Excavation unit: _____

Feature type: hearth _____   earth even _____

                  pit _____   roasting platform _____

                  postmold _____   burial _____

                  cache _____   workshop_____

                  other (describe) _____

                  _____

                  _____

                  _____

Depth feature first recognized: _____ cm below datum

                                        _____ cm below surface

Depth of feature bottom: _____ cm below datum

                             _____ cm below surface

Artifacts recovered within feature:_____

_____

_____

Ecofacts recovered macroscopically: _____

_____

_____

Briefly describe the feature: _____

_____

_____

_____

_____

(Over)

Figure 6.8 It is wise to keep a separate and detailed feature record for each feature encountered. The type of feature records a project requires depends on the kinds of features present.

Feature plan drawing: Draw a detailed, accurate and complete plan of your square and the feature located.

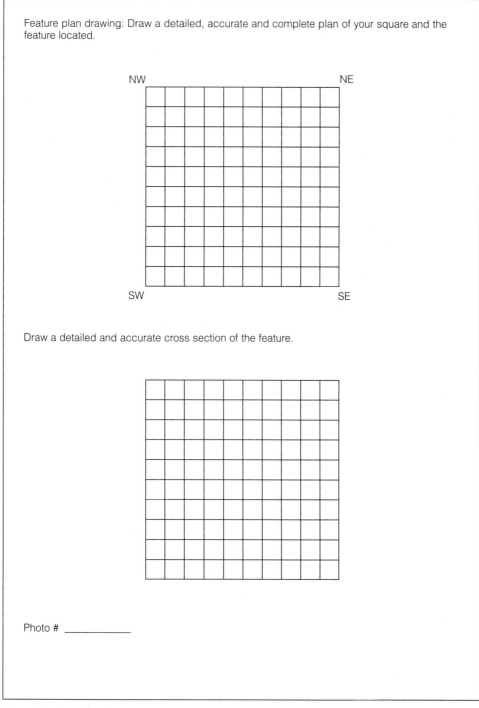

Draw a detailed and accurate cross section of the feature.

Photo # _____

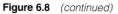

Figure 6.8   *(continued)*

ple left them and not intentionally buried by them (as in a cache) or displaced by disturbance.

Vertical provenience can be measured in a number of ways. What is important is that, however it is measured, we be able to relate all depth measurements throughout the site to a fixed point—a datum—so that all depth measurements can be related to one another. In some cases, just as the exact geographical location of datum may be known, its precise elevation may be known as well.

The precise depth of an object can be measured relative to datum directly through the use of a **transit** or an **alidade and plane table.** With the instrument located at datum or at another point whose elevation relative to datum is known, using a **stadia rod** placed at the soil level on which the artifact is resting or at the top (and then bottom) of a feature, a precise depth measurement relative to datum can be taken. For a detailed description of the use of the transit in measuring vertical provenience, see Chapter 9.

The use of a transit to measure all vertical proveniences can be inconvenient and time consuming, and there are ways around it. Just as we first measure horizontal provenience relative to a fixed point within the square (for example, the southwest stake) and then relate that to the site datum, we can do the same for vertical provenience. When setting up the site grid, we can measure with the transit or alidade the precise level above or below the surface at datum of the ground surface at the four corners of each excavation unit. Then, using a **level line** (a carpenter's bubble on a string) set up either at the base of the southwest stake or attached to a nail at the top of that stake, we can measure depth from below the level string (Figure 6.9). While the string is held taut, the line level is placed about midway between the stake and where the string is being held. When the air bubble in the level is centered, the string is level with the base or top of the stake. Our measurement below the string reflects the depth of the object or feature relative to the stake base or top. Because we know the level of the surface at the base of the stake and can measure the height of the stake if the level is attached to the top, we can relate the depth of every object so measured to the fixed datum

point, regardless of its location in the site. For convenience, the precise level of the stake can be recorded on the stake itself so that measurements of depth within units can immediately be converted and recorded in terms of depth from the site datum.

In the case of a feature, it is important to measure not just surficial and maximum depth, but to draw an outline of it in cross section (see Chapter 5). The third dimension allows for further definition of feature shape and for distinguishing between features with different functions: cooking hearths, refuse pits, storage pits, pit kilns, and so forth (Barnes 1980; Stewart 1977). It also aids the archaeologist in making estimates of feature volume. Features can be excavated in quarters, exposing a number of cross sections, or in halves, usually exposing the longest or widest profile or cross section. Depth measurements can be taken at a series of regular horizontal intervals to produce an accurate drawing of the cross sections of the feature (Figure 6.10).

Recording Stratigraphy

Stratigraphy—the natural and cultural layering of the soil at a site—can provide key information concerning site age, the relative ages of different components of multicomponent sites, local environmental conditions during site occupation, and the extent of natural processes acting on site materials after deposition (Harris 1989; see Chapter 10). Being able precisely to place the occupation level at a site within a vertical sequence of soil layers that may contain datable volcanic ash, major depositional discontinuities resulting from glaciation or deglaciation, evidence of periods marked by increased flooding as a result of wetter climates, or layers resulting from roof falls in cave sites—all can provide temporal and environmental contexts for sites.

When you excavate a site, the very material that contains such information is moved and sifted in the search for site constituents. In other words, stratigraphy as well as context within an excavation unit is destroyed as you excavate. This is why, during excavation, we make it a point to preserve

Figure 6.9 Measuring depth of an occupation level with a line level: (*a*) here at the eighteenth- and nineteenth-century village site known as the Lighthouse and located in north-central Connecticut; (*b*) using a line level, measurements can be taken from a fixed point above the excavated surface. The elevation of the fixed point (the top of the stake as shown in this diagram) is measured relative to the site datum. This allows the depth of any object or layer to be keyed into, at least indirectly, the elevation of the site datum.

(a)

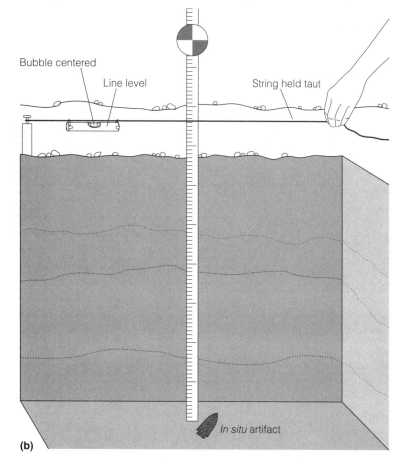

Bubble centered

Line level

String held taut

In situ artifact

(b)

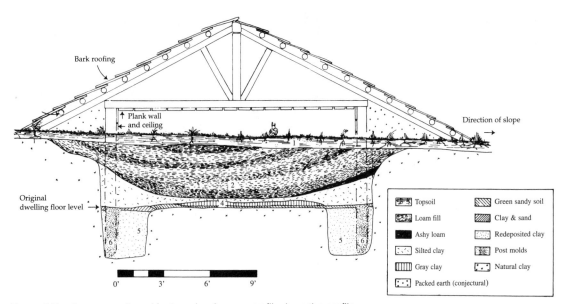

Topsoil

Loam fill

Ashy loam

Silted clay

Gray clay

Packed earth (conjectural)

Green sandy soil

Clay & sand

Redeposited clay

Post molds

Natural clay

Bark roofing

Plank wall and ceiling

Direction of slope

Original dwelling floor level

0'   3'   6'   9'

Figure 6.10 A cross-sectioned feature showing one profile: here the profile of a seventeenth-century structure as excavated (below ground) and reconstructed (above ground) at the Martin's Hundred site in Virginia. Recording a feature's cross-section and quarter-section provides for a detailed reconstruction of feature depth and shape after it has been excavated.

stratigraphic data in the form of **profile records.** In excavations where units are discontiguous, each unit is possessed of four vertical walls, each of which exhibits the stratigraphy of the immediate area. Where units are adjacent to one another, **balks** between them can be left unexcavated, at least temporarily, to preserve a record of soil layering. Because the stratigraphic record is of such great importance, archaeologists tend to be obsessive about maintaining the integrity of profiles, insisting that unit walls be scraped down as flat as is feasible given soil condition to make "reading" the stratigraphy as easy as possible (Figure 6.11).

The kind of soil present in each stratigraphic layer is informative; different kinds of soils form under different environmental conditions, and their natural layering differs widely (Harris 1989). For example, so-called fossil soils represent buried strata that reflect the conditions and plant communities present when they formed. Therefore, the physical characteristics of the soil in each stratigraphic layer in each test pit or excavation unit should be recorded (see Chapter 10) in individual

Figure 6.11 The wall of an excavation unit showing the natural stratigraphy at this 2,000-year-old habitation site in southern New England.

field notebooks, on special forms for this purpose, or on more general site forms.

A standardized **soil triangle** used to distinguish and identify clay, silt, and sand can help in the identification of the kinds of sediments that make up soil strata and can provide insights into how these layers formed and what the environmental conditions were during their formation (Table 6.1). When recording stratigraphy, as well as features or stains, it is important to use a detailed and standardized color scale like the Rock-Color Charts of the Geological Society of America or the Munsell Soil Color Charts available through many science supply houses (see Chapter 10).

Because of the near-universal acceptance that has resulted from its enormous detail and accuracy, Munsell is the preferred scale. The Munsell book is the equivalent of an extremely detailed and accurate paint color chart, providing an objective way to distinguish and label soil color. The Munsell book provides many pages of color chips arranged by **hue** (appearance relative to red, yellow, green, blue, and purple), **value** (lightness), and **chroma** (strength). Because of lighting differences, variations in human color vision, and soil drying, it may be difficult for different individuals to agree exactly—or even for the same individual to be consistent at different times—for the same stratigraphic level. It is also the case that not just a single color chip but a range of chips may seem to be equally good matches for a soil color. As a result, it is far more realistic to assign a range of Munsell designations than an overly precise single label to a soil. This enhances comparability of soil colors across a site and among different fieldworkers. Many fieldworkers take Munsell readings of the same soil both wet and dry to further enhance comparability. Munsell provides us with the best available standard by which soil color can be judged and labeled. By using an objective standard like Munsell, two different individuals should be able independently to come up with the same—or at least a very similar—range of Munsell color labels for the same matrix.

ASSOCIATING RECORDS WITH OBJECTS

Careful record keeping allows for the preservation of spatial context even while archaeological materials are removed from their location of discovery, collected, and taken to the lab. Without careful—some might say obsessive—coordination of recording and collecting, however, it may not be possible to connect records with their recovered artifacts, ecofacts, and features. A great deal of the information recorded will be of limited use.

The problem here results from the difficulty in connecting records to material recovered. Proveniences may be diligently recorded, but how does one associate that information with a given artifact? It would be silly, and often impossible, to record such detailed information on the artifact itself. Instead, we may assign a unique inventory designation to each item—often, but not always, a number. Some archaeologists have used a color code, and computer-generated and computer-readable bar codes are used increasingly. The unique designator—whether numeric, a color, or a bar code—allows us to associate artifacts with the information recorded about them in the site catalog.

Such record keeping begins in the field. For example, materials derived from each collection unit—surface collected or excavated—can be placed together in a container. For example, each level of each excavation unit should have a separate **level bag** associated with it, and all of the small objects recovered from a single level of an individual excavation unit should be placed in that level bag. If the provenience unit is a room floor in an architectural remain, all of the objects located on that floor may be placed in one collection container.

Some archaeologists assign unique designators to each collection container in the field, record these unique designators—for example, numbers in sequence—on each bag, keep a record of the provenience unit represented by each of the bag numbers in a field bag or sack log, and check the bag labels against the log at the end of each day. In this way, an inventory is kept of all the bags from the site, eliminating much of the confusion in the lab when trying to process all of the containers for all of the collection units. A more complete record of these collection-unit containers is kept in the master site record, indicating provenience of the unit, level, associations, date, excavator, and so on. In other cases, each collection-unit container may be stamped with a form or labeled with a tag to be filled out by the excavator that contains key infor-

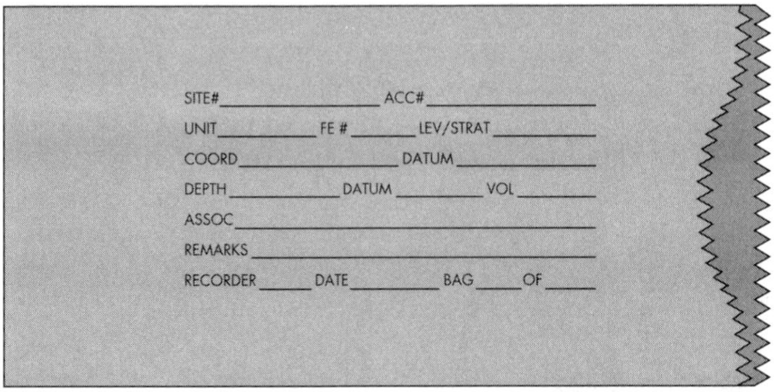

Figure 6.12 A level bag stamp. Use of a stamp to record the data for a collection unit ensures standardization of the information recorded and helps avoid the problem of unmarked bags.

mation—for example, site name, unit and level designation, field specimen or inventory number, date, an inventory of items, provenience, and excavator's name (Figure 6.12). Custom-made rubber ink stamps can be purchased through many office supply firms. Though filling out the label may seem a bother and there is a temptation to wait until later to do it, failure to do so before excavation ends on a given day too often results in unmarked bags and untraceable artifacts. However such records are kept, the most important rule to follow is that each collection unit must have an indelible label. The label may be a simple designator that leads to more detailed information in a master record, or the label itself may record detailed information about the collection unit it marks.

The question arises concerning what to do when an excavation level has not been completed at the end of the workday. One approach is to label the level bag "Incomplete Level" when it is turned in, assigned a bag number, and logged in. The next day, a new bag is used for that level and, when turned in, labeled "Completion of Level" along with all the other information identifying the source of the material (for example, the filled-out bag stamp). This approach eliminates confusion at the lab when materials from different units and different levels are being processed. Another choice when a level is incomplete at the end of the day is simply to postpone logging in the level bag until the level is completed. In other words, the excava-

tor retains the bag and continues to use it in completion of the level the next day.

Ordinarily, materials are further segregated within the collection-unit container. Provenienced artifacts recovered from a unit may first be individually placed in separate, labeled containers. Each container should be labeled either with a designator that refers back to a master record or with a more complete record that gives, for example, provenience unit, level, item identification, provenience, date, excavator, and field specimen or inventory number.

Paper bags or sacks and coin envelopes (useful for holding individual artifacts) are made of paper and held together with glue. As a result, though they are less expensive, they are also less durable, than plastic or cloth bags. Problems of container integrity can arise, particularly in areas where humidity or soil moisture is high or on days when rain falls during excavation. Paper bags and envelopes can fall apart, and records written on them can smear. A staple placed at the bottom fold of a coin envelope is one way of solving part of the problem. Recording information with indelible ink also helps. Some areas, however, are simply too wet for reliance on paper products, and heavy-mil plastic or cloth bags are preferable to paper. Information can be recorded on sticky labels affixed to the bags (but moist conditions can render their glue useless; also, as the glue ages, it becomes less effective and labels can fall off) or placed on cards inserted into the bags. Better still, permanent markers can be used to write on plastic storage bags—some plastic food storage bags have specific areas for label writing. Self-locking bags are useful in the field. The latest generation—with a movable plastic "zipper"—is the most expensive, but by far the most secure and easiest to close of such containers. Heavy (3–4 mil) plastic is preferable. Plastic bags often produce problems with condensation, though. Organic remains can become quite wet in plastic bags, and mold can develop (see Chapter 7). In these cases, "breathable" rigid plastic or cardboard containers may be preferable for long-term storage.

Separate bags, coin envelopes, small boxes, plastic vials, and 35-mm film canisters also are useful containers to protect artifacts, charcoal, bones, shell, snails, beads, or other items that are small or delicate. Stone flakes bagged together can abrade against one another and suffer "bag damage," often destroying valuable use-wear information, so storing each flake in an individual container is necessary when microscopic analysis of wear patterns is planned.

There are other criteria by which material within the level bag can be separated by placing items first in smaller containers. When excavating a 2-m square, for example, one can divide materials by the quadrant within the unit where they were found. In this way, items in the 2-m unit can be placed within a 1-m-square location. Items can also be segregated by raw material or artifact type. This may mean that within each unit-level bag, there will be several other bags: one for each provenienced artifact, one for each raw material collected for each quadrant, and a number of bags containing utilized lithic flakes and delicate potsherds. Also, it is a good idea to segregate large, heavy items from small, delicate ones. It makes little sense to put a large, heavy hammerstone into the same container with fragile items like shell beads, thin stone flakes, or friable metal objects. All of the essential identifying information should be placed on each separate bag; it takes little time to record the site name, unit, item or items enclosed, level, and provenience if applicable. It takes even less time for a small, unmarked container to fall out

of a level bag and become disassociated from its recorded information.

Individual containers should each be labeled with a permanent, waterproof black ink marker. Brands such as Marks-a-lot and Sharpies are quite good, but colored markers should be avoided because they are difficult to photocopy. Pencils, felt-tipped pens, and ballpoint pens may work fine in dry, climate-controlled laboratories. They are, however, terrible in the field, where they run, smear, or fade, often rendering the information recorded with them unreadable. It would be sadly ironic if, after all the labor invested in excavating materials, dutifully measuring their proveniences, and recording the information, all is lost as a result of inadequate writing implements.

Finally, a unique designator—for example, the artifact's **accession number**—should be placed on the container. Accession numbers represent inventory designators for objects recovered at a site. In some cases, each artifact can be assigned a unique number designation. For those working in the United States, the site's **trinomial designation** can be incorporated into its accession numbers. For example, 6LF21-4-65 refers to the sixty-fifth artifact found in excavation unit four at the twenty-first site recorded in Litchfield County (LF) in the state of Connecticut (the sixth state alphabetically). Alternatively, the accession number can relate only to a particular survey project. For example, 96.4.6.65 is the accession number for the sixty-fifth artifact cataloged from excavation unit six in the fourth site found in the 1996 survey. A **field specimen catalog** can be kept where accession numbers are listed sequentially and all associated data are listed: artifact identification and description, horizontal provenience, location in a feature, level, and/or exact vertical provenience (Figure 6.13). In some cases, a field lab number may be temporary, with a permanent accession number assigned later by the final repository of the artifacts; for example, a museum may have its own inventory system. The field catalog records can be maintained at the site on a portable computer; the catalog can then be transferred to a computer at the laboratory.

In many cases, the accession number can be permanently affixed to the artifact itself. To avoid

FARMINGTON RIVER ARCHAEOLOGICAL PROJECT

ARTIFACT CATALOGUE

Site name: _____   Site # _____

Accession #	Artifact description and provenience (if applicable)	Provenience Unit	Level	Excavation date

Figure 6.13 Accession sheet from a site catalog. Individual items or groups of items within categories are assigned inventory numbers, categories are identified, horizontal and vertical provenience data are recorded, and other pertinent information is kept on the accession sheet.

possible contamination, any identifier placed directly on an object should be removable. Calogero (1991), for example, has shown that the chemical constituents of ink used in labeling artifacts can confound the results of the trace element analysis of lithic raw materials. In her study, the titanium in the ink interfered with her measuring titanium levels in the artifact raw materials. Some recommend the application of chemicals (see Chapter 7) that are used to consolidate friable materials as an undercoat and a sealing coat over an identifier. These chemicals are removable, and their use in this way renders the identifier removable as well.

If a label is to be applied to an artifact, it should be placed in an inconspicuous location on the artifact. In some cases, where a detailed analysis of the entire surface of the artifact is planned or when the surface simply cannot be written on, it may be necessary to omit this step, placing the accession number only on the container in which the artifact is stored. When the artifact itself cannot be labeled, it is vital not to disassociate the artifact from the container that carries its designation. With an accession number on the container or artifact and a listing of all the artifacts by accession number in the field catalog, all relevant data can be correctly associated with each artifact.

In many instances, it may not be important or feasible to label every artifact individually. Some urban or complex sites, for example, produce literally millions of artifacts; applying a unique designation to each item can be extremely time-consuming and, in some instances, impossible. Even in smaller sites, the numbers of small artifacts—for example, stone debitage flakes or small pieces of ceramics—are quite enormous. In such instances, a single accession number can be assigned to an entire group of objects—for example, all of the flint flakes recovered from a single provenience/collection unit. The artifact catalog should then indicate the number of artifacts included under the accession number. For example, in a spreadsheet-based catalog consisting of rows and columns, accession numbers are placed in one column, and a separate column is assigned for the number of artifacts or the weight of ecofacts (like charcoal) coded with the same accession number. In a database program

or a HyperCard stack (see "Computerized Record Keeping"), a separate field on each record or card can be used for the number of objects being recorded. A single number designator or bar code is then affixed to the storage container.

Another approach to multiple artifacts of the same type is to affix a range of accession numbers to the container to indicate the number of artifacts inside. Each small artifact is, in a sense, given its own accession number—though it is impossible (but here not important) to associate a particular item with a particular accession number. A quick glance at the accession number range provides a count of the number of objects in the container. On the other hand, in some sites with enormous artifact counts, the number range itself may be too large to be written on the container.

There is no one right way to assign accession numbers to archaeological material, and no one correct way to record them. What is of primary importance is that the process enable the researcher readily and accurately to correlate artifacts with the information recorded for them (site, unit, horizontal and vertical provenience, associations). Flexibility is crucial in designing a record-keeping system for a site or research project. Because by excavating a site, we destroy it, it is only by keeping accurate records that we can preserve the information contained in the site.

COMPUTERIZED RECORD KEEPING

Archaeological record keeping in the field has traditionally been accomplished with paper and pencil, but the computer is replacing these tools to a certain extent. Field notes, a field catalog, maps, field drawings, aerial photographs, artifact illustrations, and so on, can all be stored in a field computer. Because the technology changes so rapidly, it is impossible to provide an up-to-the-minute discussion of computers suitable for data storage and analysis in the field. Nevertheless, it can be said that highly portable notebook and laptop computers weighing 3 or fewer lb and compatible with either IBM or Macintosh operating systems are now readily available. Though prices vary, as this is being written it is easy to find a good machine with a fast processor (100 megahertz or more), plenty of RAM (8, 16, or more megabytes), a sizable hard drive for storage (a gigabyte [1,000 megabytes], 2 gigabytes, and more are available), as well as a floppy disk drive, a CD-ROM drive (at least in some IBM compatibles), a compact keyboard, and a readable screen in the $1,200–$4,000 range. Color screens are available even on some of the less expensive machines. Almost certainly, by the time you read this, faster processors, more RAM, larger hard drives, and additional features will be commonplace; and prices may have dropped further. In purchasing a field computer, other important considerations include battery life (these batteries are rechargeable; depending on the amount of power needed for the tasks being performed, some can power the computer for several hours) and the machine's ability to withstand field conditions.

As in all other cases—and in particular, for a vital field catalog—data backup is essential. Floppy disks are cheap; multiple backup copies should be made regularly of the field catalog, field notes, and all other records. Small, lightweight, portable printers (in the $300 range and even cheaper) are available, and when all else fails, a good hard copy backup can save precious data.

There are a number of different software options for designing a computer catalog or inventory. One possibility is a spreadsheet program (for example, Microsoft Excel or Lotus). In these programs, numerical data or text is input into columns and rows. Commonly, each row represents an individual item—for example, an individual artifact—and each column represents an individual variable—for example, artifact weight. Column width and row height can be manipulated to best accommodate the data being input. The more powerful spreadsheets include various statistical as well as charting and graphing procedures. So, for example, immediately upon inventorying artifacts and inputting metrical data, basic descriptive statistical analyses can be performed. Spreadsheet data often can be exported into more powerful statistical programs, many of which are also based on data placed in

columns and rows. Spreadsheets are easy and convenient methods of data storage, though one may find the column-and-row format a bit too rigid. Also, spreadsheets can become somewhat unwieldy when some variables require much more space than others (for example, a detailed text description will need much more space than a simple measurement). Another disadvantage of spreadsheet programs is that they cannot be used to store graphical images. That being said, they remain a useful option for maintaining a simple field catalog and for at least some preliminary descriptive and exploratory statistical analyses, as well as for producing summary charts and graphs.

Another approach in a computer-based catalog is to use any one of several powerful database management programs. These allow data to be placed in specific fields.

Hypertext language programs are yet another option and allow for highly customized computer-based artifact catalogs. Though there is a bit more work involved in designing the catalog, these programs can produce impressive results, even when used by relative novices. For example, the HyperCard program for the Macintosh platform is based on the metaphor of a stack of index cards. Each card in a stack may represent an individual artifact in an artifact catalog, an excavation unit in a listing of such units, and so on.

The programmer uses a detailed set of tools provided in the program to design the layout of each "card." The stack of cards can be designed with a number of fixed fields, and numerical, text, or graphical data can be saved in each field. If, for example, one HyperCard stack contains the cards with information related to chipped stone tools, each card might contain identical fields for, for example, artifact inventory number, raw material, metrical data, provenience data, a map of the provenience unit, and a photograph of the object—the photograph can be scanned in or input directly using a digital image camera (Figure 6.14).

Hypertext allows you to link cards within the same card stack or in different stacks; then, simply clicking on a linking button takes you to the linked card. For example, a HyperCard artifact catalog stack may be linked to a provenience record stack;

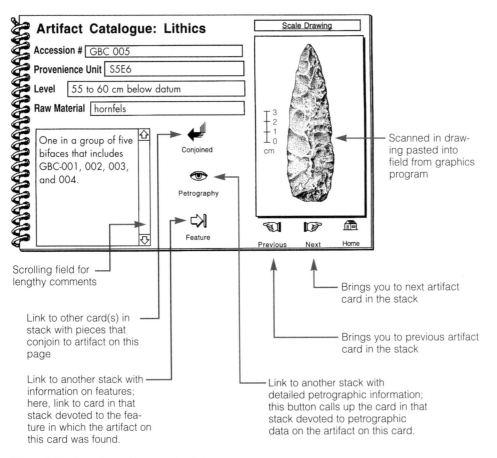

Figure 6.14 Page from a Hypercard catalogue.

by clicking the link button on a particular artifact's card, its provenience data can be called up, perhaps with a map showing the location where the item was recovered. Though the use of a program like HyperCard may involve more work initially, the greater flexibility it provides may make its use the best option for some.

COLLECTION AND PROTECTION OF CERTAIN ARTIFACTS

In addition to the general considerations just discussed for collecting and recording archaeological materials, it is important to address the unique requirements of several different kinds of materials. One important way we can learn about past people is by excavating the material remnants of their lives. But those remnants are often fragile. It would be a terrible irony if, in our attempt to learn about past cultures, we employed recovery methods that destroyed a large proportion of that which has been preserved. As Rye (1981:9) notes in reference to pottery (but it is equally applicable to other categories of archaeological remains):

> Any artifact that has survived burial for hundreds or thousands of years can be assumed to have reached chemical and physical equilibrium with its environment. Excavation immediately places it in a different environment, where a new equilibrium must be attained. For some artifacts, this means very rapid deterioration.

Raphael et al. (1982:3) enumerate the types of deterioration that afflict archaeological specimens: biological, chemical, and mechanical. Biological deterioration results from the action of rodents, insects, fungus, and other microorganisms. Chemical deterioration occurs as the result of moisture, acids and bases in the soil, rusting, and corrosion. Mechanical deterioration includes "breakage, abrasion, and disassembly" resulting from ground pressure, frost-wedging, and careless archaeologists (Raphael et al. 1982:4).

Our goals in artifact recovery and collection, therefore, are to preserve the archaeological material using recovery techniques that result in as little damage as possible and to produce, in our storage, a new equilibrium that will result in the permanent preservation of the material outside of the ground. Activities that address these goals are detailed in Chapters 7, 12, 13, and 14, and some additional comments are offered here regarding preservation of lithics and ceramics.

Lithics

Lithic remains are among the most durable materials archaeologists deal with. Ordinarily, there need be little concern for destruction of stone artifacts in standard excavation and recovery practices. However, lithics present some challenges (Figure 6.15).

The first involves distinguishing tools and debris produced by human activity—**artifacts**—from stone broken by natural processes—**geofacts.** Humans tend to be selective in the stones they utilize to produce chipped tools, focusing on rocks that exhibit **conchoidal fracture,** where the shape and size of flakes can be controlled. Humans usually strike cores at acute angles to produce thin, long flakes, whereas natural processes tend to result in rocks striking each other at right angles. Humans strike rocks in a patterned way; natural processes tend toward randomness (see Luedtke 1992; Whittaker 1994).

It must be said, however, that simpler lithic technologies can result in stone tools and debris that resemble the results of natural processes, and under certain circumstances, nature can produce patterned chipping debris that resembles human activ-

Figure 6.15 Lithic artifact left in situ. This is a finely flaked flint drill, the most intact of four such drills recovered at the 3,000-year-old Wood Lily site in Barkhamsted, Connecticut.

ity. In other words, there are times when the results of human activity are virtually indistinguishable from natural processes of rock breakage. When faced with this sort of a situation, context is key. The archaeologist, with the help of a geologist, must carefully assess other sources of evidence along with the implications of an assessment of the material. Is there other evidence that the stones are part of a cultural assemblage? Are features or anthropic soils present? Is the geological context conducive to the production of naturally patterned chipping debris? Would conferring cultural status on the questionable assemblage contradict well-supported chronologies—the contradiction of which requires a high level of confidence (Haynes 1988)?

Once material has been determined to be of cultural origin, there are some important considerations for treatment. Although stone tools are durable and not likely to break during recovery, some of the evidence that can be present on stone tools is fragile; treatment must be appropriate to preserve such data. Perhaps most obvious is use-wear patterns (Hayden, ed. 1979; Keeley 1980; Vaughan 1985). Consisting of striations, polish, and different kinds of edge damage, these traces often are diagnostic of the function of the tool and the material upon which it was used (Figure 6.16). These traces can be damaged, obscured, or even obliterated by improper handling (Gero 1978; Wylie 1975).

Rough scraping with a trowel of in situ stone tools or flakes should, of course, be avoided during

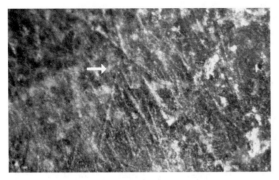

Figure 6.16 Photomicrograph of wear on a stone artifact—in this case, striations on a gouge.

excavation. Beyond this, the environment of post-excavation storage and transport is important. Transporting excavated flakes together in a level bag results in flakes grinding together, producing "bag-damage" (Wylie 1975). Whole tools, and broken tools with intact edges, should be bagged separately before being placed into the appropriate level bag. Beyond this, if there is any indication that flakes exhibit use-wear, or if a detailed microscopic analysis of a sample of flakes is planned, these items also should be bagged separately. Though the number of storage bags or envelopes can increase rapidly, there is little choice other than separate storage to prevent destruction of use-wear information.

Also, both in field treatment and in laboratory handling, there is the question of whether to wash lithic specimens. Certainly, removal of encrusted soil by washing and scrubbing with a soft brush is a time-honored tradition in archaeology. It must be said that to examine patterns of chipping as well as use-wear traces, it is ordinarily necessary to remove material adhering to the artifact. On the other hand, animal and plant residues have been found on sometimes quite ancient stone tools. Careless cleaning of stone tools eliminates such potentially significant information.

Ultimately, the question of whether lithic artifacts should be washed cannot be answered in an absolute sense. The answer depends on the circumstances. Certainly, where residues, in the form of stains or encrustations, are apparent, the artifacts

Figure 6.17 Historical ceramic left in situ at the Lighthouse village site in Barkhamsted, Connecticut. Just being uncovered is a piece of early-nineteenth-century transfer-printed whiteware manufactured in Staffordshire, England.

should be left as is and the residue examined. Even where residues are not apparent, a sample of material should be left unwashed for residue analysis, as well as in the expectation that future technologies may allow us to recover data not presently recognized or recoverable. Such specimens should be stored in chemically inert packing to avoid contamination during storage. See Chapter 7 regarding field and lab treatment of stone tools for residue analysis.

Ceramics

Ceramics present the archaeologist with material that is often chemically durable but physically fragile (Figure 6.17). High-temperature-fired clay, consisting primarily of stable silicates and oxides, tends not to break down chemically even in rather acidic soil, but fired clay objects in the soil are subject to physical breakage as a result of freezing and thawing, root growth, plowing, or careless handling by people (Shepard 1976). Low-temperature-fired clay objects are more problematic. They may reach an equilibrium with their surrounding matrix; once removed, they may begin to deteriorate (Rye 1981). Drying of these ceramics can cause physical damage and may be accompanied by the migration of salts from the interior to the surface, adding to physical damage. The treatment for these conditions is detailed in Chapter 7.

Clearly, ceramics should be handled carefully. Trowels and other tools can damage the surface of ceramic objects, especially nonglazed, low-fired, relatively soft pottery. When small sherds or other ceramic objects are found in screening, care must be taken not to abrade the artifacts against the hardware cloth, obliterating surface decoration or use marks and adding new patterns in the form of screen scratches. Likewise, care should be taken when cleaning a sherd or object. For example, subtle designs from cord marking of a pot may provide information on prehistoric cordage (Hurley 1979), so great care must be taken not to damage sherd surfaces. The question of whether to wash or not to wash all sherds must also be raised. Residues of materials stored or cooked in ceramic vessels may still be present in archaeological specimens. Such residues can be enormously informative, providing direct dietary data. As is the case with lithic artifacts, it is best to attempt residue analysis on at least a sample of the ceramic assemblage before cleaning. Additional details on field and lab treatment of ceramics can be found in Chapter 7.

COLLECTION AND ANALYSIS OF SOIL SAMPLES

As discussed in Chapter 4, human activity can result in the alteration of soil chemistry, often enriching soils, particularly in their phosphorus and nitrogen concentrations (Cook and Heizer 1965; Eidt 1973, 1984). Soil samples can be taken both within features as well as at regularly spaced intervals throughout the site in an attempt to find patterns in chemical concentrations that can be indicative of human activity—primarily in terms of trash disposal or soil fertilization. Field soil test kits are available from most science supply houses. They are also available from companies that sell agricultural research materials. Eidt (1973, 1984) and Hassan (1981) provide useful discussions of procedures for archaeological soil analysis.

Soil samples may also contain microbotanical remains (pollen, phytoliths [see Chapter 12]), macrobotanical items (seeds, nuts [see Chapter 12]), faunal specimens, and other small items including lithic debitage and beads (Adams and Gasser 1980; McWeeney 1989). Soils bearing these materials may be located throughout the site, but commonly these archaeological remains are concentrated in features reflecting human activities like cooking, tool manufacture, burial, and trash disposal. It is often wise to return 100 percent samples of subsurface features and their soil matrix to the laboratory for detailed analysis. This is particularly the case where the features involved cooking or kitchen trash disposal. Here, fragmentary food remains likely are present that can be recovered from the soil matrix, identified, and quantified in terms of contribution to an ancient diet (Jarman et al. 1972; Struever 1968a). Where 100 percent recovery is not feasible, the actual percentage of the feature's volume that was recovered for analysis should be measured and recorded. As indicated previously, soils within sites, even when not within features, may also contain food remains, as well as naturally occurring plant and animal remains that relate to the environment of the area when it was occupied by people. See Chapter 12 for a detailed discussion of the analysis of such paleobotanical remains and Chapter 13 for a similar discussion of the analysis of faunal remains. For excellent guides to collecting macrobotanical remains, see Bohrer and Adams (1977), Pearsall (1989), and Wagner (1988).

Small-scale remains can be extracted from feature and bulk soil matrix by a number of processes. As Wagner (1988) points out, each of the various procedures presents the researcher with certain benefits, each has drawbacks, and each technique is biased toward the recovery of certain kinds of remains and against the recovery of other materials.

Screening is the most commonly used recovery technique and was discussed in detail in Chapter 5. **Flotation** takes advantage of the difference between the specific gravities of archaeological materials and liquids and results in the best recovery rates (see Chapter 12 for additional discussion). However, some macrobotanical remains—maize cobs, for example—can be damaged in flotation, and the technique can be the most time-consuming of all approaches.

Simply, flotation works well as a recovery technique because some organic remains—including many macrobotanical remains—will float in water (or in liquid of some other specific density) and heavier organic remains—like nutshells and bone—and nonorganic artifacts—like stone flakes, pottery sherds, and beads—will sink. In the simplest flotation devices (an example is shown in Figure 6.18), a tub with a .8-mm mesh screen at its base is placed inside a larger liquid-filled tub. Archaeological soil matrix is placed into the smaller tub, whose rim is held above the water level. Some organic materials will readily float to the surface of the water in the smaller tub. A hand-held, fine-mesh (.4-mm mesh) strainer is used to scoop up the **light-fraction** organics that float or are suspended in the liquid. The **heavy fraction** of materials sinks to the bottom of the flotation device, where the materials are caught in the screen at the base of the interior tub. See Pearsall (1989) and Wagner (1988) for detailed discussions of flotation, the different devices available, and the benefits and drawbacks of the various systems.

The heavy fraction requires further processing to separate plant and animal remains, lithics, and other types of artifacts. It can be dried (but not totally; repeated wetting and drying can destroy some organic material like charcoal) and then hand-sorted down to 4 or 2 mm, and then refloated and resorted (Wagner 1988:21). This process can be extremely time-consuming, but recovery rates can be extremely high (Pearsall 1989). Material recovered from different features should be stored separately in glass containers with all salient information recorded on labels placed on the bags: site name, excavation unit, sample number, depth feature designation, date, and quantity.

Regardless of the recovery method used, careful measurements should be taken of the amount of matrix analyzed. This allows for comparison of the amount of material recovered across the site, and ultimately for comparisons among different sites. As noted earlier, where only a fraction of a feature has been analyzed, the size of that fraction (its percentage of the volume of the feature) should be recorded, allowing an estimate of the quantity of the material that might be expected in the feature as a whole.

When feature and bulk soil matrix cannot be processed in the field, the soil can be returned to the laboratory in heavy-duty (4 mil) plastic trash bags for flotation or wet-screening. These should never be overfilled; even heavy-duty bags can break when too much material is placed in them; 10 liters is about the maximum size that can be handled efficiently. Bags should be labeled with tie-on labels, and labels containing the same information should be put in zippered plastic bags that are then placed in the matrix bag. Labels should indicate at least the site name, sample number, excavation unit, depth, quantity (in liters), and feature designation. If the matrix has been placed in more than one bag, the bags should be numbered (i.e., Bag 1 of 2).

The philosophy behind much of archaeological fieldwork is to "save now; worry about what you are going to do with the material later." It is true that material that goes unrecovered often is lost forever—and that worthless material brought back to the lab can always be disposed of later on. The problem is, stored materials like bulk soil samples take up precious lab space. The kinds of samples discussed in this section have great information potential. We simply need to be circumspect regarding how much we bring back to the lab—and realistic regarding how much will actually be analyzed.

ROCK ART RECORDING

Rock art generally can be categorized as either pictographs or petroglyphs. **Pictographs** were made by application of pigment to rock surfaces (Figure 6.19). **Petroglyphs** were made by removal of the exterior surface of rock; the images result from the contrast between the color of the surface and the interior of the rock (Figure 6.20).

Unfortunately, pictographs and petroglyphs often attract graffiti "artists" and other vandals. Preservation and protection of these sites is crucial. Clegg (1983) provides a detailed discussion of rock

(a)

(b)

(c)

(d)

Figure 6.18   Flotation allows for the efficient and thorough recovery of small-scale organic remains from archaeological soil matrix: (*a*) flotation can be accomplished in the field with a manual system using a wooden frame with .5 mm or similar mesh screening; (*b*) the same manual procedure can be undertaken back in the lab. Manual systems rely on the tendency of botanical remains to float in water. Machine aided systems use air or water pumped into a tank or drum from below to force organic remains (including some that might otherwise sink) up to the surface where they can be recovered: (*c*) a pump driven system; (*d*) a system using standard domestic water pressure.

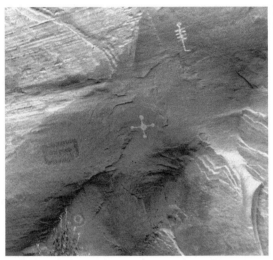

Figure 6.19 Pictograph from Canyon de Chelley in eastern Arizona.

Figure 6.20 Petroglyphs at (*a*) Newspaper Rock in northeastern Arizona and (*b*) Bellows Falls, Vermont.

(a)

(b)

CENTRO CAMUNO DI STUDI PREISTORICI

25044 CAPO DI PONTE   TEL. 0364/42091
VALCAMONICA (BRESCIA) ITALIA   Telex 301504 Archeo [

World Inventory n._____/ _____
Map n. _____
Received on _____/ _____/198 ____
(for CCSP use)

**WORLD INVENTORY OF ROCK ART
IN COOPERATION WITH UNESCO, ICOM, ICOMOS, ICCROM
STANDARD ROCK ART SITE RECORD FILE (RAS)**

(If needed, use additional pages providing titles for each additional item. Underline applicable terms in items II through VI)

I.   LOCATION   CODES
     1. Site Name _____ 2. Site n. _____   _____
     3. Country _____ 4. Map Location/Coordinates _____   _____
     5. State, Province, or Territory _____   _____
     6. Municipality/County or Parish _____   _____
     7. Property Control (ownership/administration) _____   _____
        _____
     8. Other _____

II. SITE DEFINITION
     1. Site Description _____   _____
        _____   _____
        _____   _____
        _____   _____
     2. Elevation _____meters asl. _____3. Site Size (m²)_____(_____ x _____) _____
     4. Total Size of Decorated Areas (m²) _____   _____
     5. Location type: A-cave / B-rock shelter / C-open-air rocks / D-boulders / E-other   _____
     6. Prevailing Site Exposure: North/East/South/West _____   _____
     7. Slope: horizontal/oblique/steep/vertical _____   _____
     8. Archaeological remains I _____   _____

III. GEOGRAPHICAL DATA
     1. Prevailing Topography: mountainous/hilly/flat/other _____
     2. Landform at Site: hilltop/valley/ridge/saddle/other _____
     3. Prevailing Rock: igneous/sedimentary/metamorphic _____
     4. Type of rock: sandstone/limestone/schist/granite/conglomerate/other_____   _____
     5. Type of surface: smooth/smooth with local fractures/rough/very rough _____   _____

IV. GENERAL ASSEMBLAGE CHARACTER
     1. Rock Art Type(s): A-engravings (petroglyphs) / B-paintings (pictographs) / C-high
        and low reliefs / D-other _____   _____
     2. Prevailing Technique   _____
     2a. (engravings): pecked/incised/polished/other_____   _____
     2b. (paintings): brushed/daubed/finger-painted/stencilled/blown_____   _____
     2b1 Color variety: monochrome/bichrome/plychrome   2b2. Prevailing Colors (may use Munsell   _____
        Ref.)__
     3. Number of Figures at the Site: counted _____estimated   _____
     4. Description of the rock art (include period(s) and/or style(s) significance and interpretation,
        if known)_____   _____
        _____   _____
        _____   _____
     5. Estimated Dating: absolute _____relative _____   _____
     5a. References and methods of dating _____   _____
        _____   _____

Figure 6.21   A standardized form for recording rock art data.

art recording in an Australian context. Weaver (1989) suggests the following information be recorded for each rock art site: (1) site name, (2) site location, (3) designs present, (4) colors used (in pictographs), (5) size, (6) type of art (techniques used in production), (7) associated archaeological materials, and (8) vandalism and/or natural deterioration. Rock art record forms are a useful way of maintaining consistency in data collection in a region (Figure 6.21).

V.   QUANTITATIVE TYPOLOGY

Subjects: / Figures:	Anthropomorphic	Zoomorphic	Structures Enclosures Topographic	Tools Weapons Objects	Geometric motifs and symbols	Writing and other signs	Undefined	Total
Clear figures								
Traces								
Total								

These figures are:
precise/approximate/guessed.

Note: If consistent differences in quantitative typology are discerned from one period to another, please provide similar charts for every period.

VI.   CONSERVATION

1. Preservation (state of): excellent/good/mediocre/bad/very bad _____
2. Condition (and agents of deterioration): _____
   A - Geophysical: freeze/thaw/heat/water action/other _____ _____
   B - Physio-chemical: mineral deposits/soluble salts pollution/other _____ _____
   C - Physio-biochemical: lichens/bacteria/roots/other _____ _____
   D - Human: vandalism/development/other _____ _____
   E - Animal: nest/droppings/other _____ _____
3. Conservation of the Rock Art (actions taken and to be taken) _____ _____
   _____ _____
   _____ _____

VII.   CULTURAL DEVELOPMENT

1. Classification suggested: Local/Regional/National/World Heritage _____ _____
2. Cultural Promotion (actions taken and to be taken) _____ _____
   _____ _____
   _____
3. Tourism (state of access) _____ _____
4. Existing facilities _____ _____
5. Availability of displays and other museum concerns _____ _____
   _____
6. Availability of materials for exhibitions _____ _____
   _____
7. Recommendations _____ _____
   _____
8. Bibliography _____ _____
   _____
9. List of Enclosed Documentation (pertinent maps, drawings, photos, data, additional charts,
   etc.)_____ _____
   _____
   _____

VIII.   FURTHER NOTES, EVALUATIONS AND SUGGESTIONS _____ _____
   _____ _____
   _____ _____

Form completed by _____
Signature _____ Date _____ _____
Mailing Address _____ _____
_____

Figure 6.21   *(continued)*

Obviously, photography is an important element in rock art data recording. Because color film deteriorates over time (under the best of circumstances, color transparencies last only 50 years), most archival photography for rock art has been done in black and white; Jim Zintgraff's excellent color documentation of Lower Pecos region rock art in Texas is an exception (Shafer 1986). As Hyder and Oliver (1983) point out, black-and-white documentation often is sufficient for petroglyphs where color is not so important, but black and white simply is inadequate for pictographs or cave paintings where color is an integral part of the image. They suggest using both black-and-white and color photography for all rock art recording. Once magnetic storage media replace film in photography, the problem of color print and transparency deterioration will be eliminated (see Chapter 8).

Hyder and Oliver (1983:97) extol the virtues of natural-light rock art photography (as they state, "the artist painted by it"), though they recognize the necessity of sometimes using artificial illumination. Virtually everyone agrees that images must not be chalked in or enhanced for the photograph. Such enhancing may, in fact, distort the actual image and may damage the art itself. Weaver (1989) suggests that photographic documentation should include the rock art site in its environmental context; all of the rock surfaces that contain art; and individual shots of typical elements and unique designs, as well as vandalized or deteriorated images. Scaled drawings should be made to supplement the photography. Tracings or rubbings are to be avoided because these may damage the art.

Careful recording of pictographs and petroglyphs is one step in the process of saving these sites. The Canadian Rock Art Research Association, the American Rock Art Research Association, and the International Federation of Rock Art Organizations are dedicated to the recording, study, preservation, and protection of rock art sites.

Through standardization of record keeping, an analytically useful database of rock art sites is being produced.

GUIDE TO FURTHER READING

Record Keeping

Dancey 1981; Hester, Heizer, and Graham 1975; Joukowsky 1981; McMillon 1991

Provenience

Atkinson 1953; Feder 1994; Schwarz and Junghans 1967; Wheeler 1954

Recording Stratigraphy

Harris 1979, 1989; Praetzellis 1993

Data Recovery and Preservation

Adovasio 1977; Bannister 1970; Bowman 1990; Dimbleby 1985; Gero 1978; Hesse and Wapnish 1985; Hurley 1979; Pearsall 1989; Pipirno 1988; Raphael et al. 1982; Rye 1981; Shaffer and Sanchez 1994; Shepard 1976; Wagner 1988; Wylie 1975

Rock Art Recording

Clegg 1983; Hyder and Oliver 1983; Weaver 1989

7

THE HANDLING AND CONSERVATION OF ARTIFACTS IN THE FIELD

Thomas R. Hester

The field archaeologist is often confronted with a variety of artifacts that must be conserved and prepared for transport back to the laboratory. In addition, once artifacts are taken to the laboratory, they must be adequately curated for both the analysis and report preparation that follow fieldwork—and for the long-term storage of the collection.

Leechman (1931:131) has admonished archaeologists "to treat every specimen as though it were the only one of its kind in the world." This is advice well worth heeding, because the amount of information that an archaeological specimen can provide is largely dependent on its condition. For example, the careless handling of stone tools and waste flakes in the field and in the lab can create edge damage that can be misinterpreted by the archaeologist as ancient use-wear or that can render the specimens worthless for detailed use-wear studies (Wylie 1975).

Thus, when an artifact is found in an excavation, the exposure, photography, and notebook recording of the artifact (or burials, faunal materials, and other remains) and its context must be followed by certain procedures that will ensure its preservation in the field and later, in the laboratory. Failure to take such precautions will often result in the disintegration, breakage, or loss of important scientific materials.

Planning for field research might involve taking a conservator to the site to get advice on potential problems that might occur. Of course, if your site is one that you know will require many conservation activities, a conservator should be included on your staff. To help you find a conservator, there is a Conservation Services Referral System, available through the Foundation of the American Institute for Conservation of Historic and Artistic Works (1400 16th St, N.W., Suite 240, Washington, D.C. 20036).

Figure 7.1 A hafted Yurok fish knife from northwestern California (P. A. Hearst museum specimen 1-1538): (*a*) the specimen (175 mm long); note fish scales on haft; (*b*) a radiograph of the artifact; (*c*) fish scale extracted from haft (length 5 mm).

(a)   (b)   (c)

GENERAL FIELD PROCEDURES

Field procedures for the care of specimens can be separated into three categories: stabilization, cleaning, and repair. By **stabilization,** we mean that the specimen must be preserved by supporting or strengthening it to reduce the possibility of deterioration. We cover this aspect of field conservation in detail in this chapter.

Cleaning specimens in the field means the very careful and often tedious removal of dirt to facilitate examination, recording, and conservation. We provide a number of suggestions for field-cleaning in this chapter. However, archaeologists must always pay special attention to the possible preservation of residues on (or in) the specimens (e.g., the powdery remnants found in a Maya vessel at Rio Azul, Guatemala, and later identified by specialists as cacao; Hall et al. 1989; Hurst et al. 1989). In addition, there are new techniques that have the potential to extract residues not visible to the naked eye. Visible residues must also be protected for expert analysis (Briuer 1976 and Shafer and Holloway 1979 note the identification of plant parts on stone

tools by microscopic analysis; Hester and Follett 1976 present a study of fish scales imbedded in residues on stone knives from northwestern California; Figure 7.1). In 1983 excavations at the Maya site of Colha, Belize, a sealed Maya cache was found. Within the cache was a sharp-pointed chert blade with a dark stain observable near the tip (Figure 7.2). After the cache items (ca. 250 B.C.–A.D. 250) were recorded and documented, we gingerly placed the blade in clean plastic bags and into a secure box. No further field treatment or handling was done. Later, two scholars were able to independently identify scrapings of this tangible residue as human blood—resulting from a Maya bloodletting ritual that was the focal point of this cache (Potter 1994).

Techniques to analyze surviving residues include lipid or fatty acid analysis (Evershed et al. 1995; Marchbanks 1989) that can identify plant and animal remains absorbed, for example, in pottery; palynological and macrobotanical studies of organic residues (Shafer and Holloway 1979) or the possible preservation of plant opal phytoliths (Piperno 1988); and the identification of plant and

(a)

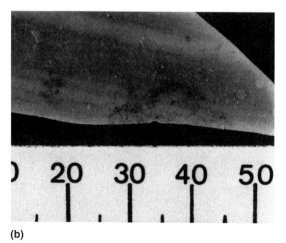

(b)

Figure 7.2 A Late Preclassic Maya macroblade with blood residue at the tip: (*a*) found in strat 55 cache (length, 211 mm); (*b*) close-up near tip, with residue visible (scale in mm).

animal tissues and blood (Garfinkel and Franklin 1988; Hyland et al. 1990; Loy 1983; Loy and Nelson 1986; blood residue techniques are often highly controversial and should not be too quickly interpreted; see Eisele 1994; Fiedel 1996; and Manning 1994 for cautionary notes). The potential of these and other developing techniques may mean not washing or cleaning artifacts in the field but rather postponing that decision until the specimens can be evaluated in the laboratory.

Repair of an artifact in the field, usually with an adhesive, means securing in position separated pieces of the specimen. However, it may often be a better practice to pack fragments separately so that they may be restored in the laboratory under optimum conditions.

In all cases, the archaeologist has to be flexible. The extent to which stabilization, cleaning, or repair is done in the field usually depends on such factors as local climate, the availability of a field laboratory, and the distance of the excavation from a museum with conservation facilities.

The adaptability of conservation approaches is epitomized in the work done by Payson Sheets and his colleagues (Sheets 1992) at the Central American site of Ceren. Buried by a volcanic ashfall around A.D. 600, a group of structures and associated remains have been painstakingly excavated and conserved. Most of the plant remains, for example, are preserved only as casts, having decomposed in the ash and left behind only a hollow space. When such cavities were found by the excavators, a fiber optic–illuminated proctoscope was used to look into the cavity to identify it. Then, a specialist from the National Museum of Health and Medicine developed a dental plaster to fill the void, preserving it as a very tough substance but with minute details intact (Sheets 1992:16). Among the remarkable results was the preservation of an ancient Maya cornfield (Figure 7.3).

A number of publications can be consulted for approaches to conservation, and a major excavation ought to have some of these on hand in the field (e.g., Sease 1994). Journals such as *Studies in Conservation* and *Journal of the American Institute for Conservation of Historic and Artistic Works* should be

Figure 7.3 A clump of 5 maize plants, tied together with 2-ply twine, at the ancient Maya site of Ceren, El Salvador. Excavator Payson Sheets used a fiber-optic proctoscope to recognize maize plant cases in the volcanic ash covering the site; the voids were then filled with dental plaster (see Sheets 1992 for additional examples).

examined for recent developments in field conservation. Other important references include Cronyn (1990), Cross et al. (1989), Dowman (1970), Hodges (ed. 1987), Joukowsky (1980:244–275), Leigh (1978), Payton (1992), Plenderleith and Werner (1971), Raphael et al. (1982), Stanley Price (1984), UNESCO (1968, 1980), and Watkinson (1987). There are num-

erous short papers that deal with specific kinds of materials and conservation approaches. We would note, for example, the use of polyurethane foam for lifting large, fragile objects at the site and the use of spray-foam insulation (Bement 1985) for encasing fragile human bones when removing a burial. Payton (1992) offers additional alternatives.

MATERIALS TO USE AND TO AVOID

Older textbooks, including earlier versions of this one, often recommended materials for use in preserving artifacts in the field. As further study and experimentation have shown, many of those recommendations were wrong. For example, a diluted mixture of Elmer's glue was sometimes suggested as a cheap and easy adhesive to prepare fragile skeletal remains for removal from a burial. This glue was water soluble and could be removed back in the laboratory. However, all white glues that look like Elmer's are not water soluble (and Elmer's itself is no longer water soluble). We learned this through experience at the Maya site of Colha in 1980. A "skull pit" feature, containing 30 decapitated crania, was exposed (Figure 7.4). We had gotten to Central America without a proper preservative, such as polyvinyl acetate (PVA), and used instead, to stabilize the fragile skulls, a water-diluted mixture of white glue. Unfortunately, it was not Elmer's, and it was not water soluble. Though it did its field job of stabilizing the skulls, it was a nightmare for physical anthropologists who later analyzed the skulls. Encrusted dirt was hard to remove, and the skull fragments were difficult to disassemble for better reconstruction; much laboratory effort was required (see Massey 1989).

When faced with stabilization problems in the field—crumbling skeletal remains, fragile baskets or textiles, or other objects that need preservation for recording and possible removal—the archaeologist must consider whether a stabilizing agent or preservative is reversible, because it may be necessary to remove it back in the laboratory. One of the most widely applicable and easily adapted preser-

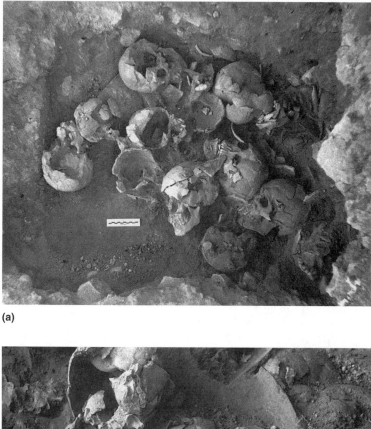

(a)

Figure 7.4 The Skull Pit feature at Op. 2011, the Maya site of Colha, Belize: (*a*) an overview of the Terminal Classic feature exposed; (*b*) a close-up of the feature conserved using the wrong preservatives.

(b)

vatives is polyvinyl acetate (PVA; Union Carbide AYAF grade). The granules can be dissolved in an acetone or ethyl alcohol solution to just about any viscosity (acetone can severely damage the liver and a filter-mask should be worn when it is used;

ethyl alcohol is much safer). Thinner solutions or viscosities are more efficiently absorbed by the material. Never use shellac and alcohol (as recommended in our 1975 edition; see Koob 1984). Also avoid the once-recommended use of beeswax and benzene (or gasoline) for coating wet specimens (however, Paul Storch [personal communication 1986] recommends paraffin and unleaded gasoline to create a mixture for preserving dendrochronological samples). A simple and effective approach is to just wrap string around the wood fragments slated for dendrochronological analysis (Jessica Johnson, personal communication 1996).

If any chemicals are used in the field, records should be kept of the chemicals and the methods by which they were applied. In addition, remember that some chemicals can be toxic and potentially carcinogenic. Use solvent-resistant plastic gloves, wear a protective mask, and make sure the work area is well ventilated.

In addition, there is the time-tested practice in archaeology of using plaster of paris for jacketing burials (see Chapter 11 for a different perspective) or other large features that have to be removed intact. The "slow set" variety of this material mixed with water usually works well. Dowman (1970:77–78) provides details on adjusting the mixture and the setting time that should be allowed (some newer approaches are found in Payton 1992). As will be noted in Chapter 11, some archaeologists (physical anthropologists) do not like the plaster-jacketing method. Indeed, the use of spray-foam insulation (Bement 1985) may be preferable in many situations where bones or features need to be stabilized. Unfortunately, polyurethene foam is not stable and breaks down within a few years (Jessica Johnson, personal communication 1996).

For the field-cleaning of a specimen, various sizes of good-quality paintbrushes (half-inch, quarter-inch, or smaller) should be in the toolkit. They can be used for cleaning the specimen and later for applying a preservative such as PVA. Ear syringes may be useful for gently blowing the dust off fragile matting or textiles. Small sprayers or atomizers are handy both for blowing off dust and for applying thin PVA in mist form. In the dry cave deposits at Baker Cave in southwest Texas, we found a 6,000-year-old basket fragment so fragile that it could not be touched with a fine brush without causing disintegration (Chadderdon 1983). We had to use a small sprayer, holding it a couple of feet above the fragment, to gently blow off the dust.

Then, another sprayer was filled with a thin solution of PVA and held about 3 feet above the fragment, allowing a fine mist to settle on the specimen. Indeed, archaeological conservator Jessica Johnson (personal communication 1996) suggests the use of a fine mist atomizer (available through garden stores) filled with PVA. One shortcut for stabililizing very fragile objects is to use a non-aerosol hair spray (such as the White Rain brand), which also coats the object with a fine mist, stabilizing it to the point that PVA can be applied. However, such hair sprays can be very unstable and may cause problems later for conservators.

FIELD TECHNIQUES FOR SPECIFIC ARTIFACT TYPES

With the preceding observations and general discussion as an introduction, we discuss below some specific field conservation techniques that may be applied to certain kinds of archaeological remains.

Bone

Bone specimens include unmodified animal bones, animal bone fragments, bone artifacts (such as awls or beads), and human remains. Human skeletal materials and their excavation are discussed in Chapter 11. Here our focus is on artifacts of bone and faunal remains (see also Chapter 13). Although faunal specialists prefer that no preservatives be used in the field, some badly deteriorated specimens may be be treated with PVA resin used in 10 percent solution with ethyl alcohol or acetone (see also Singley 1981).

Remember, however, that PVA and most other preservatives will not work properly on damp or wet bones (Koob 1984:98–102; Koob 1986). Another preservative, the polymer or consolidant known as Acryloid B72, is sometimes used and is possibly better absorbed by bone. Sease (1994:11) notes that it can be easily "reversed" (removed from the bone) because it is soluble in acetone and toluene. However, it has been the experience of other conservators that because B72 emulsifies in water, it will probably not penetrate damp bone any better than PVA (Jessica Johnson, personal communication 1996). Indeed, Johnson (1994:227, following Koob 1984) suggests the use of Acrysol WS-24; it penetrates slightly damp bone well and is reversible (using water before the bone has dried and acetone after it has dried). Problems with the use of these and other preservatives is their possible effect on future studies of the bone for stable isotopes or DNA (experimental work in this regard has been published by Tuross and Fogel [1994]). Thus, when field conservation of bone is undertaken, some should be left untreated in the event that such studies are later needed.

Fragile bone artifacts should be cleared of loose dirt and then spray-saturated with a preservative. After that dries, the artifacts can be coated with PVA, with additional coats added to strengthen the specimen. Large, fragile bone (such as bison bone) may also have to be encased in plaster bandaging for safe removal. Storch (1983) has reviewed the various preservatives often used by archaeologists and strongly advises against the use of Duco cement (or other off-the-shelf tube cements), Elmer's glue (or other white glues), epoxies, Gelva-type PVA, spray acrylics, shellac, beeswax, or paraffin in benzene or gasoline.

In packaging bone for transport to the lab, be sure that damp bones are placed in unsealed plastic bags. Dry or preserved bones should be placed in sturdy boxes, padded with cotton (though some conservators have found that cotton sticks to the edges of fragile bone), "bubble pack" (polyethylene sheeting), or other shock-absorbing material. Be careful to provide support for long bones in the packing process. For more details, see Sease (1994) and Payton (1992). Fully label all boxes or other containers with the site number, burial designation, and so on.

In recovering faunal remains from archaeological deposits, it is important that appropriate screening techniques be used (see Chapter 13). If tiny bone is particularly abundant or fragile, large "bulk" samples of matrix ought to be systematically (and volumetrically) collected for more careful processing and sorting back at the laboratory (Hope 1983).

Bones collected individually out of the screen or from the deposit should be bagged or boxed with appropriate provenience labels. Articulated animal skeletons should be mapped before bones are removed. Fragile bone can be isolated on a pedestal and then removed by sliding a shovel beneath the pedestal, encasing the specimen in tissue and aluminum foil, and placing it in a box, to be opened and cleaned at the laboratory. Or the fragile item may be exposed with small hand tools and removed by cutting under it 1 or 2 cm; the object and the soil matrix accompanying it can then be wrapped in tissue paper and covered with aluminum foil to further protect it (Storch 1983:2; see also Sease 1994 and Payton 1992). It is a good idea to then place such fragile materials in an appropriately sized small box, labeled with the necessary provenience data. In the field lab, pack all faunal material together in a separate "faunal" box for transport back to the lab; do not mix bags of faunal remains with lithics or other heavy materials. Large bones may be removed using plaster jackets, as described earlier (Rixon 1976 provides a guide to paleontological techniques for removing bone in a field situation).

Chemical treatment of faunal remains could adversely affect their later use in radiocarbon dating or specialized chemical analysis, and so it is best to keep field treatment of such specimens to a minimum (see Johansson 1987). Soft and damp bone will often harden as it dries, though it should never be exposed directly to the sun.

Once back in the lab, bone can be cleaned by brushing or gentle washing. If encrusted with calcium carbonate, it may be cleaned with a 2–10 percent solution of acetic acid (specimens should be "tested" in advance to see whether this harms materials from a particular site or context; it may dissolve some of the bone). Wash the specimens after the acetic acid has done its work. The use of PVA is recommended for consolidating bone (Hope 1983:127). Again, one must consider whether this or the acetic acid might preclude later chemical analyses of the bone; thus, some nondiagnostic bone should be left untreated for future studies.

Unusual site circumstances will usually demand special considerations. For example, the waterlogged Windover site in Florida yielded human and faunal remains (Stone et al. 1990).

Efforts to stabilize the bone by "slow air drying" led to cracking, splitting, and warping of the bone material. PVA could not be used because the moisture in the saturated bones caused the formation of a white film over the surface. The researchers also found that polyethylene glycol (PEG; trade name Carbowax; Grattan 1988), used previously for conserving waterlogged wood and leather, did not work as well with waterlogged bone. Although PEG stopped immediate exfoliation of bone, this type of deterioration reappeared a year later in the laboratory, requiring the application of PVA to halt the process. In addition, the waxy surface created by PEG obscures important details important in analysis, and the preservative stains the bone a dark color. However, in a later five-year study period, PEG-treated bone remained stable.

The Windover researchers also used acrylic emulsion (Rhoplex AC-33), which is water soluble and can be used to treat wet, water-saturated bone. Koob (1984) recommends a 5–10 percent aqueous solution brushed onto waterlogged bone. Experiments by Stone et al. (1990:183) indicate, however, that the best approach is "an initial soaking of 20 minutes in a 10 percent aqueous solution with 10 minute resoaks for large and dense elements, or for extremely fragile bone." Rhoplex does not discolor bone, and it can be used to treat bone in situ. However, there are no long-term studies available on the stability of Rhoplex, and it is known to be acid. This does not mean that it should not be used but simply that there are unanswered questions about it (Jessica Johnson, personal communication 1996).

Antler

Antler is much like bone, with a spongy interior that is often very fragile when it is exposed. It generally can be treated much like bone (Leechman 1931:140; Sease 1994:44–45). If wet, the artifact should be dried slowly and then coated with a thin solution of PVA. Dry specimens in very poor or decomposing condition may be immersed in a jar containing a thin solution of PVA or Acryloid B72 until the bubbles cease to rise, and then they should be dried and immersed again.

Shell

Shell artifacts and specimens in good, dry condition may be packed immediately for transport to the laboratory. However, specimens that are delicate or flaking should be soaked in a thin PVA solution after cleaning (Sease 1994:83–84 alternatively recommends a 3–5 percent solution of Acryloid B72 in acetone or toulene; Storch 1988:273 advises the use of the less-toxic acetone). Shell that is wet or damp can be immersed in a PVA solution, diluted 1:4 with water; alternatively, Storch (1988:272) recommends Rhoplex AC-33 acrylic emulsion for wet or damp shell. Shells from damp soils may also be sent to the laboratory in a container that preserves their moisture (Tennant and Baird 1985).

Stone

Stone artifacts rarely need special treatment in the field. Chipped stone or obsidian artifacts need, as discussed earlier, careful packaging to prevent edge damage and may require special handling to ensure that residue studies can be carried out later. Washing such artifacts in the field should be avoided; similarly, metates or grinding slabs may also retain identifiable residues and should not be scrubbed until samples have been taken for analysis (see Tuross 1994; Yohe et al. 1991). Pollen washes can rather easily be taken from such surfaces (see Chapter 12).

Stone monuments and buildings in sites of complex societies, such as in Mesoamerica or the Middle East, may require attention if poorly preserved. If the occurrence of features of this nature can be anticipated in the field planning, an architectural conservator should be part of the project staff. Otherwise, a deteriorating stone object of any importance should be left in place, perhaps pedestaled and jacketed, to be sent to the laboratory for proper preservation. Lithiol should not be used, as suggested in the 1975 edition of this guide (Paul Storch, personal communication 1986). Dowman (1970:125) further notes that "it is advisable to let stone objects dry out slowly to prevent rapid crystallization of any soluble salts that they may contain, with the consequent flaking-off of the surface." For details on stone preservation, see Agnew (1984), Ashurst and Ashurst (1988), Clifton (1980), Dowman (1970), Hanna (1984), Hodges (ed. 1987), Price (1984), and Sease (1994:86–88).

Textiles

One of the early efforts in field conservation can be attributed to Sir Flinders Petrie (Drowser 1985:311). After opening an Egyptian tomb, Petrie was faced with preserving elaborate string matting. He used "collodion," cellulose nitrate, the first synthetic plastic, a material that with time becomes very unstable, turns brittle, and peels up (Jessica Johnson, personal communication 1995; see also Selwitz 1988).

In contemporary archaeology, archaeologists dealing with less spectacular but equally important open prehistoric sites, sometimes find textiles occurring as carbonized fragments or as pseudomorphs ("fossilized fabrics"; *C&EN* 1984; Jakes and Holter 1986; Sibley and Jakes 1986). First, we will deal with carbonized remains. These are very delicate and must be treated with extreme care to recover such important information as the weave used in making the basket or textile. A thin solution of PVA may be applied with a sprayer, as noted earlier in the example from Baker Cave. (PVA is a plastic, though, and might possibly affect subsequent radiocarbon assay.) Well-preserved textiles and baskets from dry caves or arid environments like the American Southwest, Great Basin, lower Pecos Texas, Egypt, or Peru (Donnan 1987) should never be cleaned with water. Carefully brush away dust around the textile, then gently loosen it, and support it from underneath when it is picked up. It should undergo minimum handling, and the textile and its support should be immediately wrapped in acid-free tissue and placed in a sturdy container for transport to a laboratory where it can receive attention from a conservator (Sease 1994:91–93). Waterlogged textiles are sometimes found in wet sites (Purdy 1988; see Adovasio 1977 regarding the removal of basketry from wet sites), and these require highly specialized attention as detailed in Sease (1994) and Tarleton and Ordonez (1995).

A conservator should be on-site for these materials. Selected references for textile treatment include Baer et al. (1977), Donnan (1987), Gardner (1979), Jedrzejewska (1972), Sease (1994), and Vigo (1977).

Pseudomorphs, the remnants of textiles on metal objects, should be carefully protected and brought to the attention of a conservator. The pseudomorph is a fabric or textile in which the original organic fiber has been replaced by mineral compounds. In this way, the physical shape of the textile is preserved. Pseudomorphs are usually found in corroded areas of metal artifacts, where fabric has been in contact with the object (for example, on a Hopewell Indian copper ornament dated at A.D. 150). See Sibley and Jakes (1986) for details on these fascinating archaeological phenomena.

Metal

Excellent guides to the cleaning and study of metal objects have been prepared by Biek (1963), Plenderleith and Werner (1971), and Sease (1994); the older guides (such as Biek and Plenderleith and Werner) include some techniques that are no longer used by conservators, however. The conservation of metal artifacts from underwater sites is the subject of a monograph by Hamilton (1976). In that study, Hamilton reports the conservation of Spanish materials from a 1554 shipwreck; his work on hooped barrel guns is shown in Figures 7.5 and 7.6.

Any metal object, particularly those altered by corrosion or rust, must be treated with the utmost care in the field. Do not attempt to remove the corrosion; doing so may destroy the artifact. A trained conservator can sometimes use a scalpel and microscope for mechanical cleaning of metal objects in a field laboratory (e.g., as done by Jessica Johnson [personal communication 1996] for a bronze pin at a site in Turkey).

Sease (1994) suggests that all dirt be cleared from around the specimen; it can then be pedestaled and carefully undercut for removal. Particularly fragile specimens should be placed in a rigid container to protect them until they are

Figure 7.5 Professional conservators remove a Spanish Colonial hooped barrel gun from a vat of molten wax applied as a final preservative coating.

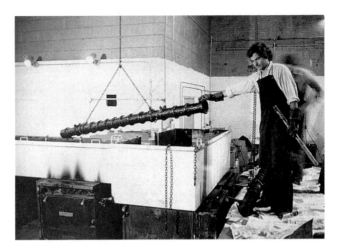

Figure 7.6 Conservators wipe off excess microcrystalline wax from a series of hooped barrel guns dating from the sixteenth century (see Figure 7.5).

treated at the lab. Never place metal objects in plastic bags; moisture will soon accumulate. Do not wash metal artifacts in the field, and do not attempt to repair them with adhesives in a field situation.

Artifacts of iron are often subject to rusting that carries deep into the metal. Treatment of such specimens, as with other metal objects, should be left to a trained conservator. These artifacts are often so badly rusted that little remains but a thin core of the iron, encased in ferric oxide and ferric hydroxides. If, in the field, it is critical to preserve the iron object's shape, let the object dry thoroughly, and soak it immediately in an acrylic solution (like B72), because PVA is slightly acidic to metal.

Lightly corroded specimens of copper, silver, or gold should be cleaned by a conservator. In the field, Bacon (1987) recommends that copper alloy, silver, and gold objects be removed as soon as exposed by excavations and that they be protected from the "ambient environment." The latter is particularly important, because the processes of decay and corrosion—slowed or halted while these objects were buried—resume on their exposure to the air. Copper alloy objects from sites in arid lands often develop bright green powdery spots on the surface, a condition known as "bronze disease" (see Plenderleith and Werner 1971).

If broken or fragile objects are uncovered, Bacon (1987:139) suggests three ways for proper removal. However, before disturbing the objects, be sure to make photographs or scale drawings. Specimens can be isolated on soil pedestals, lifted, and placed in a box or container. Or the object, on its pedestal, can be treated with PVA and a gauze bandage applied over this. Third, the item can be encased in plaster of Paris, with a foil or plastic sheet to separate it from the plaster. Bacon urges that the latter two techniques be used rarely and if used, that the item requires immediate postexcavation treatment by a conservator. When metal objects are removed from the field, special attention should be given to maintaining low humidity and to the use of acid-free materials in packaging. The specimen should not be wrapped but rather placed on a "soft bed of foam or [acid-free] tissue; a similar layer should cover it" (Bacon 1987:140). Do

not field-clean copper objects: adhering cloth or wood residues might be destroyed. Do not remove these objects piecemeal, but rather extract the artifact and its fragments together in a block. Never attempt to remove any corrosion without the advice of an on-site conservator. In short, record and remove the specimen and leave the cleaning and long-term conservation to the laboratory specialist.

Further information on cleaning metal artifacts can be found in Bacon (1987), Hodges (1989), Plenderleith and Werner (1971:270–272), Scott (1983), Sease (1994), and Storch (1986a).

Wood

When wooden objects are found in dry cave contexts, they usually need little preparation in the field, other than light brushing and placement in a stable container to prevent breakage. When insect infestation is suspected, objects might be isolated in polyethylene bags containing Shell no-pest strips or paradichlorobenzene crystals (PDB; see Lewis 1976:65). This kills any boring insects and eliminates the need for fumigation while in the field. Conservators such as Florian (1986) suggest that this approach does not work and that freezing the object is the best approach. There is also a nonaqueous fungicide called Mytox (PL-40S) that can be used if necessary (Paul Storch, personal communication 1986). However, any wooden specimens or other organic remains that may be infested or subject to infestation should be clearly labeled when sent back to the laboratory so that appropriate treatment can be carried out there. If wood needs to be preserved in the field for dendrochronological studies, publications by Bohrer and Adams (1977), Hall (1939), and Hargrave (1936) should be consulted in advance. Figure 7.7 illustrates the field-jacketing of wood posts for dendrochronological samples (using string, paraffin, and gasoline) and the application of plaster bandages to a post sample to allow later study as an architectural sample (Paul Storch, personal communication 1986).

Wet wood or wood excavated from damp soil needs immediate special handling in the field (Lewis 1976:35–40; Purdy 1988). Damp or wet wood must be kept in that condition until it arrives

Figure 7.7 Field conservation of wood-post fragments for dendro-chronological samples; plaster sample near center is being preserved for architectural study.

at the laboratory. It can be packed in a watertight container surrounded by wet crumpled paper, moss, or wet cloth to preserve the humid condition of the specimen. Wood that has lain in water may best be sent to the laboratory in water to which a 10 percent solution of ethanol has been added as a temporary preservative (Paul Storch, personal communication 1986). Polyethylene glycol applied to wet wood serves as a preservative (see Albright 1966; Grattan 1988), but paraffin treatments and the use of alum processes should be avoided because they cause too much shrinking and cracking. The rest of the careful handling needed for damp wooden objects must be done at the laboratory or museum. Recent references to the processing of waterlogged wood objects include Ember (1988), Florian and Hillman (1985), Grattan (1988), Oddy (1987), Rowell and Barbour (1990), Singley (1981), and the volume *Waterlogged Wood: Study and Conservation* (Waterlogged Wood Working Group Conference 1984).

Ceramics

The most definitive coverage of the field conservation of ceramics is by Sease (1994); see also Hodges (1987), Rye (1981), Singley (1981), and Storch (1986b). Potsherds, like stone tools, are often hardy objects and can be bagged in the field without immediate treatment. They may be washed with soft brushes in the field lab; however, close attention should be given to the possible presence of organic residues or charred macrobotanical deposits that could be adhering to a sherd. Field-scrubbing of sherds could also remove or damage fragile surface decorations, slips, or glazes (Rye 1981:111). If use-wear analysis is planned, cleaning should be done in conjunction with the analysis to avoid brush marks or other damage to the sherd surfaces.

Complete or restorable pottery vessels, such as those found in caches or graves, require patient exposure and documentation before they are removed. Never attempt to remove a vessel by lifting it by the rim. Usually, the matrix beneath the vessel must be undercut to free it for removal. Do not remove the soil within the vessel; it will help hold the specimen together while it is removed (in addition, laboratory removal of the dirt from within the vessel can provide possible residue or pollen samples). If the vessel is cracked, gauze strips may be wrapped around it to provide stability and support.

Intact vessels are usually placed in boxes and supported around their exterior with tissue or "bubble pack" for careful transport to the field laboratory. Restorable vessels should be treated likewise, with no effort made to glue together the fragments until after they have been cleaned in the lab. However, the sherds should be wrapped or padded so that the edges are not damaged in transport or storage, making restoration more difficult (Raphael et al. 1982). Fragile, crushed sherds (often shattered vessels or vessel fragments) that are eroded or damp should be pedestaled, lightly brushed, recorded, and then removed by undercutting the pedestal and placing the sherds and matrix in a box or other suitable container.

If sherds or vessels are particularly friable in the field, some consolidation can be achieved by using Acryloid B72 in a 3–5 percent solution. Sease (1994:78) also suggests the use of PVA diluted 1:4 with water to field-treat damp pottery.

Sherds from some sites (arid lands and sites submerged in ocean water) may be heavily impregnated with salts and will require prompt treatment in the field laboratory. Jessica Johnson (personal communication 1995; see Paterakis 1987) suggests soaking such sherds in distilled water. Hodges (1987:144–145) further suggests the use of ultrasonic cleaning (not practical in many field circumstances), and a variety of soaking and heating techniques using static, running, or agitated water. Calcite-encrusted sherds can be cleaned with Calgon in a 10 percent solution of distilled water (Storch 1986b:2). Vinegar or muriatic acid may also be used (Hodges 1987), but some specimens should be tested before any cleaning procedure is applied on a large scale. There are many problems associated with the acid cleaning of pottery. Experiments on ancient Near Eastern ceramics as described by Johnson et al. (1995) using dilute hydrochloric, nitric, and acetic acids all caused physical damage to the sherd's surface. Subsequent studies done by Lippert and Shipp (1995) found that presoaking sherds for two hours and use of dilute (10 percent) acetic or (5 percent) nitric acids can remove salts without damage to sherds. However, this must be followed by soaking over a period of several days to remove the acids.

Although pottery that is very fragile may be consolidated with preservatives like PVA, these do not usually penetrate deeply into the body. Hodges (1987:146) relates techniques that involve either soaking the sherd under reduced air pressure (requiring a vacuum pump and chamber in the field lab) or using "capillary action," where the sherd is suspended above the stabilizing solution so that its bottom edge contacts the liquid. While capillary action draws the solution up into the sherd, the sherd is slowly lowered and more liquid is absorbed.

Special Cases

Special circumstances or site conditions (e.g., wet sites) require specific kinds of conservation measures. Often, experiments must be conducted or a variety of conservation techniques evaluated over several years (Stone et al. 1990). Sites in the Arctic require specific conservation techniques, as detailed by Cross et al. (1989) and Hett (1987). Another special case, archaeological skin materials, are rare but include leather, parchment, and hides. These can occur in sites that are very dry, frozen, or water-inundated (see Peacock 1987). Laboratory curation of skin artifacts is addressed in Reed (1972) and Storch (1987).

A "field guide" cannot anticipate every site situation, nor can it be fully current with the rapid advances in conservation techniques. A good research design should attempt to take into account a site's potential conservation needs before fieldwork begins.

CURATION FACILITIES

Archaeological laboratories, where artifacts are housed, analyzed, and curated for long-term research needs, vary widely in their capabilities. Some are within museums, with well-organized retrieval systems and with conservators and conservation labs in-house. Other "labs" might be in a professor's office, a building that a university cannot use for anything else ("rocks don't need air-conditioning"), or in cramped quarters with artifacts in boxes stuffed under stairways. During the 1970s and 1980s, however, the archaeological community in the United States began to devote more attention to archaeological collections (e.g., Lindsay et al. 1980), perhaps largely because contract archaeology funded by government agencies required a commitment for suitable, long-term curation (archaeological materials are not "stored"—they are "curated" so as to always be available for future research). As a result, many private contract firms began to use "repositories"—often university-based facilities that were recognized as places where specimens could be securely housed and easily retrieved. In the early 1990s, government agencies began to issue curation standards for laboratories housing collections generated through federal contracts and grants. These are compiled in a booklet, *36 CFR, Curation of Federally-Owned and Administered Collections* (Washington, D.C., 1991; available through the National Park Service). Such guidelines and the growing concerns of the archaeological community should lead to improving curation conditions in the years to come.

Ideally, an archaeological curation facility should have adequate space; humidity and temperature controls (e.g., a constant temperature of 60–70 degrees, and a relative humidity of around 40 percent; Bailey 1996:1–2); fire alarm and prevention systems; a security system; a pollution-free environment; analysis and research areas; and acid-free conditions for housing collections (Figure 7.8; and see Young 1992). Both the collections the facility houses and the records that accompany them should be organized for easy access (this is increasingly being done through computerized collection management systems).

All of these concerns are largely outside the scope of a book on field methods. There are, however, some important collection and curation procedures that need to be the concern of the archaeologist whenever fieldwork is planned and designed.

Field Record Considerations

Recording forms, field notes, site survey forms, and the like should always be on acid-free paper.

Maps and plans should be drawn on Mylar, which does not deteriorate during long-term curation. Extremely valuable references, *Preserving Field Records* (Kenworthy et al. 1985) and *Preserving the Anthropological Record* (Silverman and Parezo 1992) offer detailed guidance in developing a program for archaeological records from the field to the archive.

With computers being increasingly used both in the field and in the laboratory, the preservation of data on disks presents a special problem for curation. These kinds of documents have relatively short life spans (e.g., magnetic disks, 5–10 years), and the computer software on which they are based quickly becomes obsolete. Rothenberg (1995) explores this issue and provides recommendations for the preservation of such data.

Various field logs for bags, photographs, radiocarbon samples, and so on, need to be correlated with the items they inventory (e.g., are all rolls of film accounted for and each photograph or slide labeled or identified?) before the "field" portion of a project can be said to be finished. The archaeologist should also anticipate archival requirements that may be mandated by the repository in which the collection will ultimately be housed.

Laboratory Curation Considerations

An understandable and consistent cataloging system should be used for processing artifacts and materials. Check with the laboratory collections manager to see how artifacts should be labeled or tagged for curation after they have been analyzed for publication. Equally important here is the laboratory packaging necessary for the curation of debitage samples, bulk matrix or soil samples, and faunal or vegetal samples. When artifacts are analyzed, keep the analytical categories together; disassembling these back to field proveniences makes future research incredibly difficult. Many laboratories have specific guidelines for the curation (or even the acceptance) of human skeletal remains, and it is critical to be aware of these prior to fieldwork.

In the context of collections curation, prior planning needs to be devoted to the materials

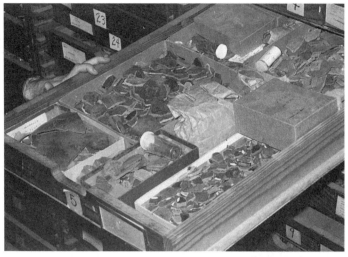

Figure 7.8 Laboratory curation: old and new: (*a*) organic artifacts housed in crowded conditions in wooden drawers (acid-rich); (*b*) new housing of artifacts in acid-free environment.

(a)

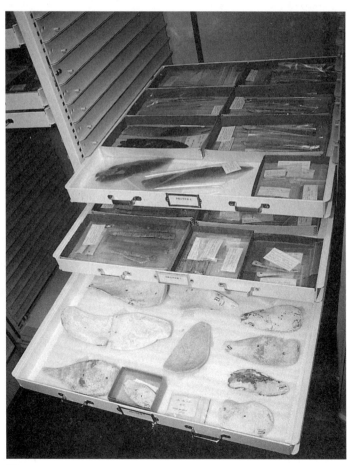

(b)

necessary to properly house the artifacts and records from fieldwork. It may be necessary to budget for acid-free materials (see Bailey 1996)—specimen boxes, packaging cartons, plastic bags, and labels, as well as archival-quality slide and negative holders—as part of any curation agreement with a laboratory. Most repositories now assess one-time fees, often based on the number of drawers used or cubic feet occupied, for housing of collections. This provides funding for proper collections maintenance on a long-term basis. All of these considerations help to ensure the long-term preservation of artifacts and records that result from fieldwork.

GUIDE TO FURTHER READING

General

Dowman 1970; Hodges, ed. 1987; Leigh 1978; Sease 1994

Field Treatment of Various Artifacts

Bacon 1987; Grattan 1988; Hodges 1987; Johansson 1994; Johnson 1994; Koob 1984, 1986; Purdy 1988; Sease 1994; Storch 1987, 1988

Artifacts and Records in the Laboratory

Kenworthy et al. 1985; Lindsay et al. 1980; Rothenberg 1995; Silverman and Parezo 1992; Singley 1981

Archaeological Field Photography

Harry J. Shafer

We have stressed repeatedly that the full and accurate recording of an archaeological exploration is the sine qua non of archaeological analysis as well as the overriding moral and ethical responsibility of the excavator. Photography as a tool in record keeping is of such importance in the field that it is discussed separately in this chapter.

Archaeological photography using still cameras has been the subject of several books; Dorrell (1989), Harp (1975), Howell and Blanc (1992), and Simmons (1969) are among the more recent. Students interested in pursuing the specialty are encouraged to consult these books for a beginning. Also, photography is addressed in conjunction with archaeological techniques in Barker (1983), Dever and Lance (1978), and Joukowsky (1980).

OBJECTIVES OF FIELD PHOTOGRAPHY

The purpose and responsibility of archaeological field photography is to achieve two basic but not mutually exclusive objectives: photo documentation and photo illustration for reporting or publication. Ideally both should be done in color transparencies and black-and-white prints and, where feasible, field-narrated video.

Photo Documentation

The purpose of **photo documentation** is to produce a comprehensive and precise pictorial record of an investigation from beginning to end. This documentation is an essential part of the record keeping and serves to illustrate general field conditions, methods of excavation, mechanical procedures of recording, excavation units, features, special finds, profiles, personalities, innovative techniques, effects of adverse circumstances (such as weather, wall collapses, or vandalism), and anything else that may be deemed important. Photo documentation, like field notes, becomes part of the historical record of the excavation or survey and is an invaluable aid to anyone involved in subsequent analysis and reporting. A general rule to follow in any aspect of field documentation is to assume that someone else is going to be analyzing your data.

In documentary photography—regardless of the type of camera—the photographer is concerned specifically with recording methodology and detail, so the emphasis is on documenting the process of recovery and what is recovered. For example, a sequence of photographs may be called for to record the procedures used in the removal of a series of floors (Figure 8.1a–c) or a series of items superimposed in a pit (such as a burial with pit outline, covering stones, artifacts placed in grave fill or accompanying the burial; or objects vertically stacked in a cache pit) where a single photograph or video shot would not properly document the specific context of each artifact or feature item.

Photo Illustration

The second objective of field photography, **photo illustration,** is to provide images appropriate for use in published reports or public presentations. The photographer's objective in this case is to communicate specific kinds of information to the reader or viewer. The photographic field should be cleared of extraneous debris, including spoil dirt and tools, and should be free of overly contrasting shadows that detract from the central figure in the photograph (Figure 8.2a,b). Many times the documentary photograph and the illustrative photograph are one in the same, but the archaeologist should always be concerned about the purpose of the photograph to achieve the desired results. For example, because information that properly identifies the subject should be included in a documentary photograph, one photograph could be taken with the feature information for site records and another with the information removed for possible report illustration (where the pertinent information could be included in the figure caption). The illustration then would communicate the specific details that the archaeologist desires but would be free of unnecessary clutter.

Although it is not possible to anticipate in each case which photographs will eventually be selected for illustration, the archaeologist usually is aware of special or opportune circumstances that will likely be emphasized in a report. Notable features, rare artifact associations, or architecture are likely to be illustrated. Photographic and video documentation are not ends in themselves but significantly enhance the next stage of archaeological inquiry.

General Purposes

To adequately control photography as a tool of archaeological research, investigators must possess not merely the necessary technical equipment but a thorough understanding based on experience and common sense of the potentials and limitations of field photography and equipment. Given equipment options and recent advances in both photographic and video technology, one need not be a professional photographer to achieve excellent results. Cameras with built-in light meters are now standard, and a variety of accessory lenses can usually be purchased for most popular brands of 35-mm cameras so that many photographic options are available in most situations. Most modern cameras offer various options for automatic exposure control, and some even focus themselves. With only a short course in photography (usually provided by the literature that accompanies a camera purchase) and experimental efforts prior to the fieldwork, the archaeologist can develop a "feel" for both equipment and subjects and should be able to gauge results fairly accurately in advance.

The archaeologist must always bear in mind that photography is an interpretation of reality, not a means of duplicating reality. The photographic process reduces a three-dimensional subject to a two-dimensional depiction. In that process, certain qualities are enhanced; others are diminished. Furthermore, the properties of different films and the use of lens filters can produce various tonal alterations. Pictures may not lie, but photographic reproductions can be entirely misleading unless

Figure 8.1 Series of photographs showing sequence of superimposed floors in a small room at the NAN Ruin, Mimbres Valley, New Mexico: (*a*) small habitation room floor with hearth; (*b*) cobble-reinforced floor of granary; (*c*) storage room floor.

(a)

(b)

(c)

Figure 8.2 Examples of bad and good field photography: (*a*) a poor field photograph of superimposed architecture; note the strong early morning shadows, including that of the photographer; (*b*) much improved view with a north arrow, scale, identifying chalkboard, and subtle shadows.

(a)

(b)

these points are borne in mind and adequately compensated for.

SOME BASIC ELEMENTS OF PHOTOGRAPHY

Although many students have a working knowledge of fundamental photography, it may be helpful to review some of the basic elements of photography as a preface to this chapter. It is not possible to pursue these fundamental aspects beyond the most elementary level, and students should familiarize themselves more fully with these points and others not discussed. The books by Dorrell (1989), Harp (1975), Hawken (1979), Howell and Blanc (1992), Imboden and Rinker

(1975), C. Shipman (1981), and Simmons (1969) all contribute useful details.

Aside from the quality of the equipment used and similar considerations, successfully **exposing** (admitting the proper amount of light to) film depends on the combination of film speed, diaphragm opening (aperture), and exposure time (shutter speed). **Film speed** refers to a film's measured response or sensitivity to light; diaphragm opening and exposure time control the light to which the film is exposed, and they may be either determined by the photographer or calculated automatically by the camera. Automatic cameras make the adjustment based on the film speed (which you must set manually each time you change to a different film) and amount of light determined by an internal light meter.

Film Speed

Film speed is expressed in terms of an **ISO designation** (formerly referred to in the United States as the ASA number). An ISO of 25 or 40 describes a "slow" film, one that requires relatively more light and thus a longer exposure and/or a larger diaphragm opening. Slow films are generally fine-grained, **grain** being the tiny light-sensitive particles of silver that form the negative. Grain is a basic quality of a film's definition, and finer grain contributes to a higher definition of detail in a photograph. Slow fine-grained films are of particular importance to scientific photography. Further, these films are essential where negatives are small because the process of magnification in enlargement also increases the grain.

An ISO of 200 or above describes a "fast" film, one that requires relatively less light and thus a shorter exposure and/or a smaller diaphragm opening. Modern fast films are fine-grained and high-resolution, and they provide many of the same advantages of the older slow films. The added advantage in the use of modern fast films is that the faster exposure time reduces the problem of movement, thus providing a clearer resolution. Improvements in fast films have reduced problems, such as contrast quality, that formerly limited their uses in archaeology. The gradation of black-and-white film, however, is affected by exposure (underexposure increases contrast, other factors being equal). The "best" film is the slowest film that is fast enough to do a perfect job (Feininger 1965:124).

Diaphragm Opening

The **diaphragm,** a variable aperture (or opening) built into the lens of the camera, controls the amount of light reaching the film; the light passes through the **diaphragm opening** itself. Diaphragm opening sizes are expressed in terms of **f-numbers** according to the following scale, which reflects increasingly smaller openings: 1, 1.4, 2.8, 4, 5.6, 8, 11, 16, 22, 32, and so on. Each larger f-number indicates a decrease of one-half in light intensity. These diaphragm settings are commonly referred to as **f-stops,** and the difference between successive settings is called a **full stop.** An intermediate setting—for example, f/3.5—is called a **half stop.**

Exposure Time

The duration of the film's exposure to light—**exposure time**—at any of these settings is regulated by the **shutter,** with its built-in timing device. **Shutter speed** is now measured in fractions of a second by the following series: 1/2, 1/4, 1/8, 1/15, 1/30, 1/60, 1/125, 1/250, 1/500, 1/1,000, and so on. Again, the difference between successive settings is termed a **stop.**

Relationship Between Diaphragm Opening and Exposure Time

When correct exposure data have been determined, an increase in either shutter speed or diaphragm opening must be accompanied by a corresponding decrease (same number of stops) in the other. The strict reciprocity of speed to opening holds, except for an extremely short or an extremely long exposure time. It should be noted also that when the aperture is changed to one with a number twice as high, a fourfold, rather than a twofold one, increase in exposure time is required.

Light Intensity

Most cameras are equipped with fully automated light meters. A **light meter** provides an objective basis for measuring light intensity to determine the correct exposure under existing light conditions. Set at the appropriate film speed (ISO), the meter will indicate the relative amount of light available. Fully automatic cameras make this adjustment provided the light meter is functioning correctly (battery checks are advised before going into the field, and spare batteries should always be carried). Cameras with light meters that are not fully automatic require the photographer to adjust the aperture until the appropriate amount of light is received (usually indicated by a scale in the viewfinder).

With handheld light meters and manual cameras, various combinations of shutter speeds and diaphragm openings may be used to obtain the correct exposure for the given film. Which combination of settings is selected for a manual camera depends on what is being photographed. Fast shutter speeds are employed to "capture" a split moment of action and require correspondingly larger diaphragm openings (i.e., smaller f-numbers). With stationary subjects, slower shutter speeds can be used, resulting in smaller reciprocal diaphragm openings (i.e., larger f-numbers).

There are both advantages and disadvantages to using cameras with built-in light meters. The light meter "averages" the amount of light received regardless of the subject. For instance, if a feature is being photographed in bright sun, the reflection of light from the background can be so intense that it can literally wash out the image of the feature. This can be circumvented in three ways. One is to soften the light before taking the photograph by shading the area framed in the viewfinder. The second is to frame out the bright background by moving in, taking a light reading on the feature, and adjusting the f-stop for that exposure; as you move back, the exposure meter will indicate too much light (or too little in reverse situations), but what appears to be an over- or underexposure may in fact be the "right" exposure for the feature. The third is to take a reading off a **gray card,** a piece of poster board with a standard gray tone that can be purchased at any photography dealer. The gray card provides a mean reading between extremes that allows one to capture the detail in the shadows.

The f-numbers are used to describe the "speed" of a camera lens for its "relative aperture," the measure of its transmission of light; its largest effective diameter is said to be its highest possible speed. Thus an $f/2$ lens is said to be a very "fast" lens, whereas an $f/8$ lens is "slow." Because of certain optical properties, it is often not desirable to use the maximum speed of a lens. Smaller diaphragm openings provide greater depth of field, meaning that objects behind and forward of the object focused on will be sharper. For example, the large diaphragm opening of $f/2$ has very minimal depth of focus; in a photograph where the subject is close to the camera, objects not far behind or forward of the subject will be blurred at that set-

ting. Depth of field increases, however, with increasing distance between subject and camera.

The size of the diaphragm opening also affects the problem of controlling for aberrations in sharpness. At full aperture, most lenses produce negatives with sharpness greatest in the center and decreasing toward the edges. Optimum sharpness is achieved with most lenses when the diaphragm is stopped down two to four stops beyond the maximum opening.

In archaeological photography, where subjects are usually stationary, it is almost always desirable to obtain the increased depth of field and other advantages offered by the smaller diaphragm settings. Because shutter speed must be slowed correspondingly, exposures will often have to be made on a tripod or the unsteadiness of the handheld camera will be recorded by blurring in the photograph. Actually, it is desirable to use a steady tripod even at quite rapid shutter speeds. A good rule of thumb is to use a tripod if at all possible when the shutter speed is 1/60 second or slower.

CAMERA EQUIPMENT

The perfect photographic equipment for any purpose would be technically versatile, simple to use, capable of making photographs of the highest quality, capable of withstanding the dirt and moisture common in field situations, and yet economical to buy and operate. Such ideal qualities do not combine naturally, but adequate compromises can usually be made.

The finest-quality photographs are obtained from larger negatives made from cut or sheet film. Since a large negative allows contact printing, the finished print suffers no loss in quality through enlargement. Contact printing further means the greatest freedom in film choice because film grain will not be increased through enlarging. Finally, the large negative allows maximum laboratory manipulation to enhance picture quality. Generally speaking, we are referring to a minimal negative size of 4-×-5 inches; smaller films will usually require enlargement.

Of the large cameras, the **press cameras** of the Graphic/Graflex type have been the most commonly used in archaeological field photography in the United States. Some 4-x-5 press cameras offer the optimum combination, among large cameras, of versatility, efficiency, and manageable size and, consequently, have been considered the best suited for archaeological fieldwork. Unfortunately, almost all of these cameras have been discontinued in recent years, and they are usually available today only as used equipment; also, few suppliers stock the appropriate size film.

The **view cameras,** the other principal large-camera type, offer almost unparalleled photographic potential but are quite cumbersome and inefficient for general field use.

Among the smaller cameras used in fieldwork, the **twin-lens reflex cameras** of the Rollicord/Rolleiflex or Yashica-Mat type have been very popular among archaeologists. These cameras generally use 120-mm-size roll film to make a 2¼-inch-square negative. Enlargement is almost always required for illustration purposes, but 120-mm film offers a better negative than does 35-mm film, although 120-mm cameras are somewhat more difficult to use than 35-mm cameras. In twin-lens reflex cameras, viewing is done from the top on a ground glass the same size as the actual picture made. The ground-glass image is reflected by a mirror from a view lens (the "twin lens") placed directly above the lens that actually exposes the film. The viewing lens is coupled to the lower lens so that focusing the ground glass image also focuses the photographing lens. Because of the separate positions of the twin lenses and the consequent problem of parallax, however, these cameras are quite poorly suited for close-up work. Furthermore, they have very limited versatility in terms of interchangeable lenses and other accessories. If the 2¼-inch negative is desired, there are several fine single-lens reflex cameras of this size offering great versatility and many advantages.

The high-quality 35-mm, **single-lens reflex camera** offers the greatest technical versatility, excellent portability, very efficient and rapid operation, and great film economy. Also, the 35-mm camera is virtually the only format for producing transparencies. In the single-lens reflex cameras, viewing and focusing are done by means of mirrors and prisms through the actual lens exposing the film. Some cameras are even equipped with automatic focus. Precise framing of the picture is, accordingly, quite accurate—and in some models is absolutely so. This is always advantageous, but it is supremely so in close-up work, where the single-lens reflex is precise, efficient, and very speedy in operation. Furthermore, these qualities are retained when using the many interchangeable lenses offered for the best models. Because 35-mm film is commonly available in 36-exposure rolls—compared with the usual 12-exposure rolls or film packs for the other cameras discussed—the speed and convenience of making a large number of exposures is increased. The use of interchangeable backs on the best models also allows rapid shifting from one type of film to another—for example, from color to black-and-white—an advantage shared by the film packs of the larger cameras.

The single but substantial disadvantage of the 35-mm camera is the small negative size, usually 24-x-36 mm. To preserve maximum definition and clarity of detail with this negative size, it is best to use fine-grained film, small diaphragm openings, and fine-grain developing. Recent improvements in film quality and processing techniques have reduced somewhat the disadvantages of the small negatives.

With all of the cameras just discussed, there is a time lapse between the taking of the photograph and the receipt of the results from a film processing laboratory. The **Polaroid Land camera** is the answer when immediate results are desired. Its instant prints can provide important references for use in the field, but the prints should not be attached to permanent documents or records because of the acids contained in the developing chemicals. These prints do not meet most curation standards for inclusion in permanent reacords.

If the camera equipment includes a 4-x-5 camera, Polaroid Land film holders are available to fit most 4-x-5 cameras and even some 2¼-x-2¼ cameras. Such a combination is highly desirable, because most Polaroid Land cameras are not versatile. The major problem in using a Polaroid is film storage and immediate processing of the negatives in the field. An indoor laboratory environment is highly recommended for Polaroid negatives because during processing, the emulsion is extremely soft and easily damaged.

With the rapid advancements in computer technology, it was only a matter of time before photography and computer technology merged and **digital cameras** became available. This new and quickly evolving technology holds some promise for archaeology, but it is not a panacea. Digital cameras eliminate the use of film and developing time and provide instant images in studio work for editing and critique. It is a technology that has found its niche in publishing—and that may not be limited to studio use. Digital cameras are not something you can simply pick up and throw over your shoulder, though. Most digital cameras require a computer tether, but some come with their own storage devices; either can be taken to situations where computers are in use. Images can be downloaded and transmitted almost instantly. Because of the logistical parameters, digital cameras are best suited for use in publishing in archaeology.

Like any photography, digital images have their limitations. They do not have the resolution or color depth of traditional photography, and the user does not have the latitude or tonal range of film. Digital cameras will not replace traditional cameras and film, or scanners. Because virtually any film image, old or current, can be scanned, the use of traditional cameras will not become obsolete; digital cameras, like any tool, have advantages and disadvantages and enhance the archaeologist's options.

Perhaps the most negative aspect of digital cameras at this time is the cost; they are expensive (prices range up to $40,000), but integrated backs for traditional cameras can cut the cost considerably. Like all new computer technologies, however, the price will likely moderate. A pocket model digital camera with zoom lens capability that can put hundreds of images on its PC card will soon be on the market. The interested reader should consult the magazines *Advanced Imaging* (PTN Publishing Company) and *Future Image Report* (Future Image Inc., Burlingame, California) for updated information and price lists for digital camera hardware.

ACCESSORY EQUIPMENT

If a field camera does not have a built-in exposure meter (such as a 4-x-5 or some 2¼-x-2¼ cameras), a good **exposure meter** is an essential item of photographic equipment. A good-quality cadmium-sulfide meter is particularly recommended because of its great accuracy and remarkable range of sensitivity. Because these meters are battery activated (as are light meters on cameras), it is desirable to obtain a meter with a built-in means of testing battery strength. Although the battery is very long lasting, it is a good idea to carry a spare; likewise, extra batteries are highly recommended for battery-operated camera light meters.

For 35-mm cameras, it is highly recommended that a combination of **lenses** be included in the camera kit, such as a wide-angle (28 mm) lens, a standard (55 mm) lens, and a macro lens for close-up work. Because of the flat field of a macro lens as well as its broad focus range, it is an excellent lens for larger items in addition to close-up work.

A **flash unit** can be extremely useful in many field situations. The most efficient for field use are the compact electronic units. Either the rechargeable cadmium-sulfide units, the C-cell, or the AA-cell battery units may be used in the field. Both C-cell and AA-cell batteries probably are desirable for a long field season in an area without electricity, because some models allow 4,000 and more flashes from one set of C-cells. It should be noted that successful use of flash photography for scientific purposes requires practical experience. As is the case with the other equipment, the student should experiment fully with flash equipment under different lighting conditions before going into the field. A flash extension cord is useful if the flash will be used for side lighting.

The results of flash-illuminated photography are very difficult to predict precisely, particularly when the flash is used for side lighting to emphasize relief. Reflecting natural sunlight into shaded or dark areas can often be an excellent solution to illumination problems. Suitable **reflectors** can easily be made by taping aluminum foil to a flat surface like cardboard or tacking a white bedsheet to a wooden frame. The reflector's size depends on the amount of light needed and convenience in handling.

A **tripod** is essential for exposures less than 1/60 of a second and may be used advantageously, as mentioned earlier, even with fairly rapid shutter speeds. Adequate attention is seldom given to the selection of tripods, but a carelessly selected tripod can cause many headaches in the field. Tripods must be sufficiently sturdy. Careful attention should be given to the locking devices on the extending legs; many locking mechanisms begin to jam, fail to hold securely, or simply are troublesome to use after prolonged fieldwork. A universal or swivel-type head is usually very convenient, but one may be added to a tripod not so equipped; several models are available. A **shutter release** should be used with the camera when it is mounted on the tripod. Spare shutter releases should be carried along because these items often malfunction when laden with dust. The usefulness of other pieces of equipment depends on circumstances and the preferences and habits of the photographer.

In conclusion, it should be noted that although purchase price often determines the choice of equipment, good equipment carefully selected provides so many advantages in the long run that it justifies the greater investment many times over. The best way to save money on photographic equipment is not to buy lower-quality items but to buy high-quality used ones. Purchased from a known and reputable dealer, quality equipment can often be obtained at a savings of as much as half the original price. Lenses, in particular, do not wear out (but they may become scratched or otherwise damaged; some insect sprays, for example, will etch and permanently damage a lens), and many older lenses are superior to newer ones costing much more. Similarly, a 35-mm camera equipped with an f/2.8 lens will be considerably cheaper than one that goes all the way to f/1.4, a lens speed that archaeologists are unlikely to use in any case.

SOME SUGGESTIONS FOR FIELD PHOTOGRAPHY

During fieldwork, certain documentary photographs will have to be made without delay and perhaps with no choice of time or natural lighting conditions. Nothing can be done in these instances but to make the best of circumstances, using ingenuity to overcome adverse conditions and to capitalize on whatever advantages may be present. Other photographs, however, can be taken at any moment over a period of time. In these cases, the subject should be observed (and perhaps photographed) at different times of day to test for the most favorable and effective lighting. Sensitive and delicate features that are being cleared also should be photographed at the end of each workday. During the course of excavations, the archaeologist should take note of the variable lighting produced by the sun's shifting path and the advantages and disadvantages of cloudy conditions.

Early mornings on clear days just before sunrise provide the optimum time for soft, even lighting conditions; such conditions may be preferred for landscape, architectural, or general overview photographs of the excavation. Evenly overcast days often provide the same kind of lighting conditions. Sharp, high-contrast conditions occur in bright sunshine or under bright clouds. Most documentary photography probably should be postponed or planned for early in the morning or later in the day if high contrast is a problem.

Where photographs are of extreme importance, make several exposures at different settings ("bracketing") of the same view as a safety precaution. How much the settings should vary depends on the latitude of the film. Color film has restricted latitude; bracketing exposures should be made at one stop above and below the exposure meter's reading. Most black-and-white films have considerably greater latitude, and a difference of two stops from the meter's reading is usually adequate.

When photographing a feature exposed by excavation, the light meter reading should be made close to the subject to avoid inaccurate readings from reflecting walls or background sky. Following this simple guideline increases the likelihood of getting adequate light and exposure of the feature being photographed.

If 35-mm photography is being used, film expense is a minor aspect of the total cost of the fieldwork, and exceptionally full photographic recording is to be expected. The 35-mm documentation can be supplemented by 2¼-x-2¼ and 4-x-5 cameras, especially where documentation of architecture and landscape views is needed. Also, reserving most shots anticipated for illustrative purposes for the larger negatives will reduce the overall cost yet provide adequate coverage of the field project. No one has ever taken too many photographs. When developing is done, inexpensive proof sheets will serve as a guide to be checked against the negative, of course, for deciding which views to enlarge. These proofs are also adequate for cataloging negatives. In making color transparencies, it is worth bearing in mind that if duplicates are desired, they are best shot in the field rather than duplicated by the laboratory. Color quality will be far superior, and the cost will be less.

Photographic field logs are a very important part of field documentation. Each roll of film should get a unique log number, and a record needs to be kept of each exposure. The log may include such information as photographer, date, number and type of cameras (if more than one is being used), site, feature, direction, time of day, and ISO. Photographs and negatives should be cataloged to correspond with the field photo log. It is also advisable to process film as soon as possible to ensure that you are not caught at the end of the field season without photographs because of a malfunctioning camera.

Use of basic photographic equipment can be mastered quite easily and its latitude will become increasingly familiar with experience. But even the most expensive equipment does not guarantee good pictures. The human behind the equipment has the ultimate responsibility for the results, and experience and mistakes are the best teachers. A few simple tips will help to enhance the usefulness of photographs.

When **framing**—focusing the item of interest in the frame—look around the periphery of the frame before taking the picture for extraneous items that may detract from the subject itself, such as encroaching shadows of individuals standing by (including the photographer's), shadows from profile walls, and the photographer's feet. This rule is especially appropriate for color transparencies, where such detail cannot easily be excluded later in the laboratory.

The quality of any photograph is gauged by its **sharpness,** or its crispness of detail. A fuzzy photograph is not only wasteful of valuable time and resources, it is useless for documentation and illustration. Following several basic procedures will better ensure good photographic results.

Focus is critical. Cameras have definite limitations of focus, but if these are recognized in photographing three-dimensional objects, sharpness can usually be achieved.

Housekeeping is also important. A dirty lens, no matter how expensive, will affect sharpness. Light simply cannot project through solid particles like dust and lint.

The camera must be held steady; **camera movement** is perhaps the single most common cause of fuzzy photographs. Although sharpness is enhanced when the film speed is reduced, slow exposures increase the likelihood of camera movement. A tripod should be used religiously in the field.

Lighting can be used to increase sharpness (such as with an oblique light source) and desired contrast, but lighting can also create undesirable effects if it is extremely reflective or too bright.

FIELD CARE OF EQUIPMENT

Great care must be given to both film and equipment while in the field. Heat, dampness, and grit are the principal sources of damage to film. Film containers should be kept in the shade or some other cool, dry place. In humid areas, a desiccating agent such as a silica gel should be kept in the film container and checked regularly for moisture absorption; the gel will keep the air within the film container dry and, combined with the slight vacuum effect of the container, the air will also stay slightly cooler than that outside. Color film is particularly subject to deterioration; Eastman Kodak Company advises that Kodak color films will keep for two months at temperatures up to 70 degrees Fahrenheit and six months up to 60 degrees.

It may be desirable to store film under refrigeration in a moisture-proof container. If film is so stored, remember that to prevent moisture from condensing on the cold film surface, the film must

Figure 8.3 Excavations in dry environments pose serious problems for cameras and photographic equipment care because of the very fine dust.

be removed from refrigeration well in advance of its use; this allows the film to warm up before it is removed from its container. When exposed film is ready for storage, humidity should first be removed with a desiccating agent. In remote areas with extremely high temperatures, it may be unwise to entrust film to the local postal service.

Camera equipment should also be kept dry and out of the sun except when making a photograph. Dust, dirt, and moisture are the greatest sources of damage to equipment; they not only can foul delicate camera mechanisms, but also can damage or ruin film (Figure 8.3). Plastic bags are often useful in protecting the camera and other sensitive equipment from these dangers. Dust will settle on the camera lens during use in the field, and great care must be exercised in removing it. Optical glass is extremely soft; using a handkerchief to clean a lens may permanently scratch it. Only a camel's hair brush, an air bulb, photographic lens tissue, and lens-cleaning fluid should ever be used. One recommendation for protecting the camera lens is to use an ultraviolet light (UV) filter; these are much cheaper to replace than a lens. Another helpful hint on camera care is to include a box of wet-wipes in the camera bag so that photographers can clean their hands before handling the camera, film, or other equipment.

In sum, the camera bag—which should be a padded, insulated container of leather or some equivalent material (metal is not recommended because it tends to absorb heat)—minimally should contain the following items: camera(s), extra lenses such as a wide-angle and a close-up, extra film, lens tissues, lens brush, flash, extra batteries, UV filters, wet-wipes, north arrow, scales in metric and English system, pencils/pens, and a notepad.

Camera equipment should also be protected from excessive moisture (dew, fog, rains) at all costs. Leaving cameras in the corner of a tent, for example, could be disastrous. The weight of the camera is sufficient to create a catch basin for any rain water that might leak into the tent during heavy rains; the camera(s) would be in the bottom of the water-filled basin. The corrosive effects of moisture will quickly render cameras and light meters permanently inoperable.

SUBJECT MATTER

The subject matter of the photograph often dictates the type of equipment and film, accessory equipment, preparation, time of day, and improvisation needed to obtain the desired results. Types of subject matter include general site views, features and burials, excavation methods and techniques, soil profiles, petroglyphs and pictographs, and artifacts.

General Site Views

Every effort should be made to obtain good overall views of the site at all stages of the investigation: before and after clearing of brush or vegetative cover, at the beginning of excavations, during all stages thereof, and at the conclusion of the work. The photographer should attempt to bring out the shape and height of the site in addition to any special features. Black-and-white exposures of site views or architecture are best accomplished using large-negative film (or a 35-mm wide-angle lens). Placing a person at various effective points for the photographs frequently emphasizes aspects of the site's configuration and provides a feeling of depth. The person serves as a convenient approximate scale and should be engaged in some activity that does not detract from the central interests of the photograph. A few action photos showing people working at routine tasks are very useful not only in documenting the history of the site's investigation and methodologies employed but also for identifying the individuals who are engaged in the work. Such photographs are ideal for public relations and public information reports: these formats customarily call for photos that include people. However, photographs of personnel are secondary in importance to documenting the procedures and findings.

Views that bring out the relationship of the site to the various features of the adjoining landscape are frequently very useful. Take views at a series of distances; carefully judge the most effective distances to emphasize the various features of the site's configuration and relationship to the surrounding terrain. Careful consideration of each photographic view is the only way to obtain a useful photographic record.

A wide-angle lens is often very useful for panoramic views of a site. A moderate length wide-angle lens is much preferred; lenses that take in an extremely wide view may distort perspective so drastically that the photographs will have little value.

Elevated views may be taken simply by climbing a stepladder or a tree on the site. Special devices such as balloons (Bascom 1941; Whittlesey 1966, 1967, 1975), tripod ladders (Allen 1975; Merrill 1941; Piggott and Murray 1966; Sterud and Pratt 1975), the "Swedish turrent" (Straffin 1971), poles (Schwartz 1964), and front-end loaders or "cherry pickers" (machines with hydraulic extension arms to hoist workers) have also been valuable in making photographs from above the ground.

In **photogrammetric recording,** Hood (1977) has suggested the use of a square scale in elevated views of a site or feature. Using square scales increases the value of such views for obtaining accurate plans photogrammetrically from them. Although the excavator rarely has the opportunity to make aerial photographs of the site, the remains may show up on existing aerial photographs, and these may be useful as part of the site records as well as for publication purposes.

Underwater photography poses its own unique set of problems and circumstances. The equipment requirements for underwater work are not difficult to meet as a result of the popularity of diving today. Properly encased cameras of standard sizes and accessory equipment are available at most camera stores and outfitters of diving gear. The needs of photography are much the same as in any other kind of archaeology; if anything, underwater archaeology requires more details in recording the techniques used in documentation and recovery as a result of the frequent need to improvise. The often limited visibility of the site area makes photogrammetric documentation essential in underwater excavations. Bass (1982) and Rosencrantz (1975) describe essential techniques and procedures of underwater photographic documentation.

Features and Burials

Proper cleaning of archaeological features, burials, and architectural elements is an important step in

Figure 8.4 Pit feature containing potsherds, with improvised scale (chalkboard), north arrow (trowel), and chalkboard with identifying information.

the photographic process. Before photographing, the subject should be properly cleaned of loose fill, chaff, and so forth.

Various accessories are usually required in photographing features. These accessories, which should be placed in the feature after it has been properly cleaned, include an arrow (or some other appropriate object such as a trowel) pointing grid north; a scale (metric or English, depending on the system being used at the site) or an object of known size; and an information board (chalkboard, menu board) (Figure 8.4). The north arrow itself may contain a scale. These accessories must be arranged so that they are legible but do not detract from the subject of interest. In extreme cases where macro lenses are used to document minute finds, such as the traces of textiles in a burial, an identification photograph containing the context information may be made from a greater distance before the close-up is taken. When multiple features are photographed, white plastic letters or numbers from a menu board may be placed on the dirt to label each feature. Whatever the procedure, a scale should always be included. It is essential that the

scale be parallel to the film plane or it will be foreshortened and useless; it should also be placed near the main object of the picture and in the same plane as that object.

Photographing smaller features and burial details usually involves making moderate close-ups, at a distance of between 3 m and 10 cm. In such photographs, it is usually desirable to have as much of the picture as possible in clear focus; particular attention must therefore be paid to depth of field. Usually it is effective to focus on an important central item approximately one-third of the distance into the feature and to use a small diaphragm opening (f/11 to f/22, the smaller the better) to achieve maximum depth of field from this point. The range of sharp focus can be checked by using the depth-of-field preview button or scale present on most cameras, and any necessary adjustments can then be made. There are a number of safeguards one can use to ensure an in-focus photograph. If it is difficult to get sufficient depth of field, the photographer may wish to step back and enlarge the frame; although the feature will be smaller, a sharp negative will permit later enlarging in the darkroom while maintaining the desired sharpness; the unnecessary field surrounding the subject can be cropped.

Photographs must show clearly the exact relationship of artifacts to the feature or burial. Care should be taken to minimize distortion of perspective; views from directly above are most satisfactory in this respect, but they may be difficult to make. For some purposes, however, oblique views may be the better perspective to illustrate the relationships of the components of a feature. In addition, views from several perspectives and detailed close-ups of important aspects of a burial or feature are frequently of great value. Photographs showing the relationship of a feature to a broader area of context, for example a room or the feature's place within a block excavation, should also be standard.

When photographing successive levels in a unit, always orient the photos of a layer in the same direction (for example, always facing north) so the series of photos can be more easily compared. Also, because differential drying can produce color changes, get the photo board and camera ready and be prepared to take the photo quickly (especially on windy days) or you may need to spray with a mist of water to even out the moisture.

Burial photographs on black-and-white film are often best made in shade; if a flash is not used, it is often necessary to improvise some means of blocking direct sunlight, for example using dark sheet plastic, cardboard, or whatever may be available. As noted earlier, overcast days often provide the ideal diffused light for photographing certain kinds of subjects; under bright sunlight, the contrast between shaded and lighted areas may be too great. When features are located partially in the sun, it is usually necessary to either shade the entire feature or provide reflected light to the shaded portion in order to even the lighting. Aluminum foil reflectors can be quickly constructed and can be valuable assets when trying to deal with difficult shadows. Bright days with oblique light often provide the greatest challenge to good field photography at locations that are either in the open or under trees.

Excavation Methods and Techniques

A series of photographs illustrating the various techniques used in excavating the site often prove valuable for illustrations in the site report and as records in the site archives. Special effort should be made to illustrate excavation techniques and to document special sampling procedures such as removing archaeomagnetic, pollen, or plaster samples, and dendrochronology specimens.

Soil Profiles

Photographic recording of soil profiles is a particularly important and especially difficult aspect of field photography. If color and texture differences between strata are difficult to distinguish with the eye, they may be even more difficult to bring out in photographs. The cramped space of a trench also may make photographing at the proper position difficult, if not impossible. For purposes of greatest utility and scientific value, the camera should be centered on the profile, with the film plane precisely parallel to the profile wall. A wide-angle lens is often helpful in photographing profiles, but one must be aware of the distortion of scale in using such a lens. Photographing profiles in shadow, in indirect, and in direct light will often yield variable, if not contrasting, results. A slight dampening of the soil with a spray gun filled with water is sometimes quite effective in bringing out contrasts in soil color and texture.

In black-and-white photography, contrast can be heightened by using various color filters or high-contrast films, if available (Secrist 1979). The effect of these filters can be gauged easily after a little practice simply by viewing by eye through each filter and observing the contrast that results. Use of high-contrast films often provides excellent results, but such films limit flexibility because one cannot turn from photographing a soil profile (for which such films are best adapted) to a feature or a site view, where extreme contrasts might be a disadvantage. Secrist (1979) discusses various uses for high-contrast films.

Color transparencies should also be made of profiles; color slides provide an excellent record of

Figure 8.5 Faint petroglyph enhanced for photographic recording by using a washable solution of kaolin and water.

profile detail. As noted earlier, color slides offer an excellent way of revisiting the scene during analysis of field data. Placing the slide under a zoom binocular microscope with light behind the slide will provide a close-up stereoscopic view of the subject. Detail is limited only by the film's grain quality. This procedure can be an important tool in enhancing description and detail during analysis.

Infrared film can often be used to obtain greater contrast than can be secured with regular panchromatic film. Brose (1964), Buettner-Janusch (1954), and Gillio (1970) illustrate and discuss the use of infrared photography in recording soil profiles. Because experimentation is required in its use and its effects cannot be surely predicted, infrared photography must be viewed as a supplement to ordinary panchromatic recording. Detailed technical specifications for infrared film and instructions for its use are to be found in the current edition of the *Eastman Kodak Infrared and Ultraviolet Data Book* available at larger photographic shops (also see Eastman Kodak Co. 1972, 1977).

Petroglyphs and Pictographs

Petroglyphs are made by pecking shallow grooves into a stone surface. They usually appear clearest in photographs taken when the light conditions produce shadows in the peck grooves, which then contrast with the unmodified stone surface. When these lighting conditions are not attainable naturally, side lighting by flash to "rake over" the surface of the stone may provide clear contrast (Knight 1966:63). Colored filters, particularly red, can often be used to increase contrast.

Chalk has often been used in the past to outline or fill in the pecked grooves and thus further emphasize the petroglyphs. The problem is that chalk is an abrasive, may alter the natural state, and is retained in the petroglyphs for quite some time. Kaolin clay or a mixture of water and aluminum powder (Swartz 1963) is preferred to enhance the image, because these soon wash away with the rains without any damage to the rock (Figure 8.5). *Never* use any form of paint or shoe polish to enhance the petroglyphs: either will cause permanent damage.

Pictographs, or rock paintings, require especially thorough recording because of their fragile and perishable nature. Unfortunately, though, because pictographs are often faded or faint in color, adequate photographic records may be very difficult to make. In black-and-white photography, the pictograph will often show up better when the exposures are made in shaded light. Panchromatic film must be used. The use of color filters can often produce very enhanced photographs. With panchromatic film, a color is emphasized by a filter of its complementary color; thus, a green filter is used to bring out red (Webster 1962:Plate V). Dampening pictographs with a water spray may intensify the colors (see Zintgraff's use of this technique in Shafer 1986), but such drastic microenvironmental changes could ultimately damage the rock art and are not recommended. The use of reflected ultraviolet light to bring out faded red ocher and palimpsests of red and white ocher has been described by Webster (1964).

Color photographs or transparencies should also be made of rock paintings. Care should be given to proper lighting conditions to minimize color distortion, and a Kodak Color Bar should be included in the picture as a color standard. Sun reflectors are often effective. Sketches should also be made, and watercolor copies are desirable. A small scale and identifying legend board are essential accessories in petroglyph and pictograph photographs. J. C. Clark (1974) and Gebhard (1960) discuss methods of pictograph recording, and Turpin (1982) and Turpin et al. (1979) discuss mapping rock art sites in Texas with stereophotogrammetry using two Wild Heerbrugg fixed-base stereometric cameras.

Artifacts

The photography of artifacts and excavated specimens, usually for purposes of publication, is a considerably different task from field photography (Dorrell 1989:178–198, 209–237). However, photographs taken in the field camp of special-find artifacts or of artifact samples are sometimes desirable or necessary under restricted logistical situations. Also, it is recommended that fragile artifacts be photographed before being transported to distant analysis laboratories because there is the chance that the artifact will not survive the trip intact.

For artifact photography in the field, it is recommended that the photographer construct an improvised photo laboratory with appropriate background scale, lighting, camera, and tripod. It is wise to anticipate this need prior to fieldwork. Lighting conditions will be a difficult problem to resolve without standard darkroom quartz lamps; mobile quartz lamps (such as a Sun-Gun) can provide considerable latitude for field artifact recording if electricity is available in the field camp.

Preferred cameras for artifact photography were once 4-x-5 and 2¼-x-2¼ negative size, but given the current potentialities of the 35-mm cameras (with the macro lens), they, too, can adequately serve the purpose and are essential if color transparencies are to be used. Natural light, such as indirect sunlight or soft indirect morning or afternoon light, provides the most even source without the worry of shadows. Overcast days are excellent for artifact photography. Use of artificial light often creates shadows, but these can be used to enhance attributes of an artifact's surface, such as flake scars, pitted surfaces, or incised lines, to convey an image of depth.

When photographing an artifact, the operator should be aware of what specifically is to be communicated. For example, one can take a photograph of a chipped stone item on an attractive background but not communicate the details of technology that an archaeologist is interested in conveying. Always include a scale when photographing artifacts. It is a good practice for the archaeologist, if he or she is not doing the photography, to work directly with the photographer so that the necessary information is documented.

When artifacts are photographed in the laboratory, conditions can be controlled precisely, and various photographic devices can be used to facilitate the job. It is usually possible to obtain advice and consultation from professional photographers, if not their services. However, artifact photography is an art unto itself; most professional photographers are concerned with the total picture and not with emphasizing specific attributes of archaeological specimens. Therefore, it is the archaeologist, not the professional photographer, who must decide what is to be emphasized in the photograph.

Useful suggestions on general aspects of laboratory photography are made by Baker (1985), Blaker (1977), Dafoe (1969), Dodge (1968), Dorrell (1989:178–198, 209–237), and Toumey (1979). Problems in photographing translucent lithic artifacts or lithic artifacts with contrasting colors (such as artifacts of white chert on the same plate with items of black chert or obsidian) can be overcome by applying ammonium chloride crystals (Kraft 1971; Weide and Webster 1967; Wilkenson 1968) or simply by coating the surface with a water-based photo retouch medium that can easily be washed off when the photography is completed. Kelemen (1946) and Sanger (1975) discuss other problems and solutions to laboratory photographing of archaeological objects. Baker (1985) addresses the problems of photographing waterlogged artifacts from shipwrecks and other submerged sites.

NEGATIVE STORAGE

Specific attention should be given to the type of negative holders used for archival photographs. Some transparent plastic slide protector pages may actually ruin slides as the acids in the vinyl or polyvinyl chloride plastic leach out. When such leaching occurs, slides have a "wet" look, the result of acid eating the film. One should use only those polyethylene protector pages that are chemically stable and have a pH of 7 (neutral); such material is generally free of peroxides and sulfur and has no reaction to hydrogen ions. Careful selection of negative holders will ensure long life for photographic archives.

FIELD PHOTOGRAPHY: A RECAP

Photography is an essential part of archaeological field documentation and reporting. Full photo documentation of the archaeological setting, excavations, recovery methods, architecture, features, special finds, progress, problems, and personnel provides an invaluable record of the processes of field information gathering.

Photographic equipment, supplies, and at least minimal expertise in their use are a must for any archaeological endeavor. The more requirements placed on documentation, such as those encountered in large excavations, the more emphasis should be placed on obtaining the proper photographic equipment and its optimum use.

Photographs, both black-and-white and color transparencies, are an essential part of the archaeological archives. Although new advancements in video recording and digital cameras for computer imaging are now available to field archaeologists, these new technologies only increase the options available; they do not replace the traditional methods of recording. Photographic film storage is essentially permanent, but the rapid developments in video and computer technologies often leave older programs obsolete and useless.

Photographic documentation of archaeological fieldwork requires some knowledge of camera equipment and film, especially their advantages and limitations, as well as proper care. High-quality equipment alone, however, does not guarantee good field photo documentation. Attention must be given to proper lighting, framing the image, preparation of the scene, and identification and orientation of the photograph through the use of a menu board or something similar, directional arrow, and scale.

Specific subjects require specific attention to detail. For example, landscape scenes, large architectural monuments, and smaller architectural features require different photographic approaches than do hearths, burials, rock art, or artifacts photographed in the natural setting despite the fact that they may all be photographed with the same camera, albeit with different lenses or filters, and on the same role of film.

Field photography must be able to compensate for the shortcomings of field conditions such as improper lighting, composition, or other conditions that cannot be immediately controlled. Lighting can be improved through the use of reflectors or flash equipment. Problems in composition, such as a poor focal perspective, can be improved with elevating devices, and detracting items or elements may be cropped out either by framing or in the darkroom. Laboratory photography of artifacts, however, occurs in a controlled environment where the photographer has enormous latitudes in composition and lighting of the subject.

Only a small number of photographs taken in the field ever appear in publications. The use of photographs in the published report, however, should always be anticipated. All field photographs and negatives are part of the original data record and must be properly labeled and stored in an acid-free environment for future reference and use. Photographs literally capture time and are an invaluable archival source to our archaeological past.

GUIDE TO FURTHER READING

General

Barker 1982; Dever and Lance 1978; Dorrell 1989; Harp 1975; Hawken 1979; Howell and Blanc 1992; Shipman 1981; Simmons 1969

Infrared

Brose 1964; Gillio 1970; Eastman Kodak Company 1977

Artifacts

Baker 1985; Dafoe 1969; Dodge 1968; Dorrell 1994; Kraft 1971; Sanger 1975; Toumey 1979; Weide and Webster 1967

9

Archaeological Mapping, Site Grids, and Surveying

L. Kyle Napton
with Elizabeth Anne Greathouse

This chapter is intended to help beginners, as well as experienced archaeologists, use existing maps, design and construct site control grids, and draft archaeological maps. In addition, we will discuss various types of mapping tools, from tape and compass to advanced electronic surveying systems. We acknowledge that not all readers may have access to some types of advanced instruments, but they might have older, still fully functional equipment. With this in mind, we will review the operation of some of the traditional mapping tools—the plane table and alidade, Abney level, and standard transit—and we will discuss sophisticated Global Positioning and total station surveying systems. In any case, it won't be long, we suspect, before a great deal of today's "advanced" equipment will also be—archaeologically speaking—"archaic."

The information given here can, of course, be only a basic outline. It is not meant to substitute for comprehensive books on surveying (Anderson and Mikhail 1985; Bannister and Raymond 1984; Bell 1993; Bettess 1984; Bodley and Hallas 1978; Brinker and Minnick 1987; Brinker and Wolf 1984; Evett 1991; Moffitt and Bouchard 1991; Sebert 1985; Spier 1970), site layout and excavation (Barker 1982; Brighty and Stirling 1989), remote sensing (Avery and Berlin 1992; Maclean 1994), aerial reconnaissance (Burnside 1985; D. R. Wilson 1982), and cartography (Campbell 1991).

Archaeologists need to know how to use, or "read," existing maps and create ("draft") their own maps. Maps drafted by archaeologists range in complexity from basic "sketch" maps drawn in the field to accompany site record forms to extremely complex maps based on information provided by sophisticated data acquisition systems. The latter include detailed maps of site cultural and natural features (topographic maps), cross sections (profiles), perspective (isometric) views, and thematic (theme-oriented) maps of archaeological sites and features.

Archaeological maps are produced to illustrate site reports, masters' theses, doctoral dissertations, contract reports, and monographs and books describing and interpreting archaeological excavations. Many archaeological site maps are not published in the formal sense of the term, but are **maps of record** that document the progress and results of archaeological investigations. Archaeological maps form an important part of the archaeological database. For this reason, they must exhibit the highest professional standards.

IMAGING TECHNIQUES

Before embarking on an archaeological field project, it is a good idea to become familiar with the types of maps and other graphic resources available for the project area or region to be investigated. All of the continental United States and extensive parts of other countries have been mapped or photographed from the air; every location on earth has been imaged many times by remote sensing satellites. We will first look at current imaging techniques, beginning in space and, as it were, gradually coming down to earth.

Remote Sensing Imagery

Remote sensing is the process of obtaining images of the earth's surface from suborbital and orbital altitudes in various wavelengths of the visible and invisible spectrum (Barrett and Curtis 1992). The principal advantage of remotely sensed imagery in archaeology is that it provides general information pertaining to a very large area, revealing widespread patterns of vegetation and landforms (Avery and Berlin 1992; Avery and Lyons 1981; Limp 1989; Lyons and Hitchcock 1977; Scollar et al. 1990). The U.S. Geological Survey (USGS) initially operated the Earth Resources Observation Systems (EROS) program, which obtains images of the earth by means of conventional aerial photography and by remote sensing from Landsat satellites (Colwell 1983; Cracknell and Hayes 1991). The first of these

systems, Landsat-1, was launched in 1972. Since then, successive satellites have obtained millions of images of the earth. Landsat-4 and Landsat-5 satellites each orbit the earth in 98.9 minutes, completing 14⁵⁄₆ orbits daily. Standard altitude is approximately 438 mi (705.3 km). After 16 days, each satellite returns to its starting point. This process produces coverage of every location on earth every eight days. The area covered by a given Landsat image is 115-x-106 mi (about 185 km east-west by 170 km north-south). Ground resolution (the smallest image that can be detected) of objects or features is about 30 m^2.

The Earth Observation Satellite (EOSAT) Company (Appendix B, 1) maintains Landsat data in a worldwide reference system consisting of some 2.5 million images indexed by two coordinates, which are called **path** and **row** lines. The 233 paths are the north-south orbits of the Landsat vehicles; the 248 rows are the east-west image sequences. Each path/row segment constitutes a full Landsat scene. Using a Landsat coverage index map available from EOSAT, imagery can be obtained by identifying the center of the area of interest by path and row number (Figure 9.1). The principal disadvantage of Landsat imagery is that it is expensive.

Landsat multispectral data are directly applicable to digital geographic information systems (GIS), discussed later in this chapter. Other applications of remote sensing of interest to archaeologists include the enhanced Landsat Thematic Mapper (TM) instrument, which records seven measurements for every quarter-acre of land on earth. This information is available from EOSAT as digital or photographic products.

French-owned satellites *Système Probatiore d'Observation de la Terre* (SPOT) (CNS 1984) include SPOT 3, launched in 1993, which features on-board sensing apparatus that provides images of every point on earth every 26 days, with multispectral or panchromatic spatial resolution (in the panchromatic mode) as small as 10 m^2 (a higher resolution than Landsat). SPOT's equipment also permits imaging of an object or feature from two or more directions, yielding stereoscopic images that create a three-dimensional perspective of terrestrial features (Goodenough 1988). The excellent imagery

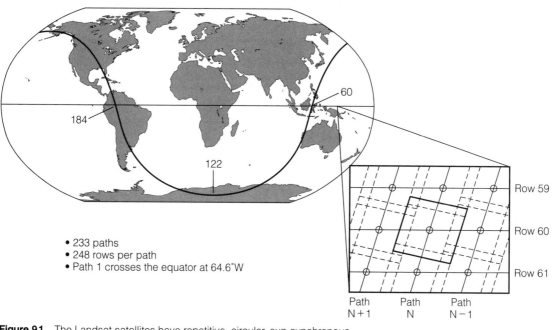

LANDSAT Orbit

184

122

60

Row 59

Row 60

Row 61

Path
N + 1

Path
N

Path
N − 1

- 233 paths
- 248 rows per path
- Path 1 crosses the equator at 64.6°W

Figure 9.1 The Landsat satellites have repetitive, circular, sun-synchronous near-polar orbits, varying in altitude from approximately 696 to 741 km. Landsat-4 and Landsat-5 together offer repeat coverage of any location every eight days. Each trip around the earth takes 98.9 minutes.

provided by SPOT is available directly from archive, but not inexpensively (Appendix B, 1). SPOT imagery has been used in archaeological projects via the Geographic Resources Analysis Support System (GRASS) GIS image processing system (Madry and Crumley 1990; Westervelt et al. 1986) (see "Geographic Information Systems," later in this chapter).

The NASA Large Format Camera Program, launched in 1986, produces stereoscopic images suitable for compilation of topographic maps at 1:50,000 scale, with potential ground resolution images of 3–30 m². This system has great potential for scientific applications (Moffitt and Mikhail 1980).

Remote sensing by radar includes plan-position radar and side-looking airborne radar (SLAR), an active microwave system with ground resolution of 3–30 m². It is useful for mapping land formations, drainage patterns, land under cultivation, and other geographic features (Drager and

Ireland 1986; Drager et al. 1985; Siegal and Gillespie 1980). Some of the many applications of remote-sensed imagery in archaeology are discussed by Avery and Berlin (1992), Avery and Lyons (1981), Baker and Gumerman (1981), Camilli and Cordell (1983), Lyons and Avery (1972), Lyons and Ebert (1978), Sheets and McKee (1994), and Wood et al. (1984).

Landsat data have been used to assist archaeological survey, notably in the Lake Turkana region, Africa (Isaac 1981); at Chaco Canyon, New Mexico (Hayes et al. 1981; Lyons and Mathien 1980), and on the Great Plains (Wood et al. 1984). An outstanding application of Landsat imagery in interpretational archaeology is remote sensing of portions of the Yucatán peninsula: archaeologists and NASA scientists used false-color Landsat imagery to reveal Maya settlements and farmed fields (Adams et al. 1981). For additional information on remote sensing, see Curran (1987), Harris (1987), Lillesand and Kiefer (1987), and Watson and

Knepper (1994). Overviews of remote sensing in archaeology (Ebert 1984; Lyons and Ebert 1978) include detailed examples and comprehensive bibliographies.

Aerial Photographs

Most modern maps are based on photographs obtained from aircraft by special (or conventional) vertical cameras. Aerial photographs are routinely obtained in color, panchromatic (black and white), and infrared. Aerial photographs covering most of the continental United States are available from the U.S. Soil Conservation Service, U.S. Forest Service, Bureau of Land Management, National Park Service, Bureau of Reclamation, and other agencies. County planners often obtain project-specific aerial coverage for roads and urban planning; local civil engineers (surveyors) also require aerial photographs of project areas. Coverage is acquired ("flown") as needed or obtained from archives.

Vertical aerial photographs, including contact prints made from large negatives (9-x-9 inches or about 23-x-23 cm) covering most of the United States, can be ordered from the U.S. Geological Survey (USGS). When the scale of photography is 1:24,000 (to serve as the base for USGS topographic quadrangles, discussed below), the area covered by a single contact print is about 12 mi^2. The USGS publishes index maps that show flight-lines of aerial photo coverage and the central point of each photograph. (The USGS will enlarge prints from whole negatives to four times their original size but will not provide enlargements of portions of negatives.)

Archaeologists can acquire their own aerial views from either fixed-wing aircraft or helicopters using a vertically aimed camera or, for stereoscopic viewing, two cameras. Requirements include fast shutter speed (1/1,000), rapid film advance, fast emulsion-speed film (e.g., minimum film-speed ISO 400/27°), or Kodak High Definition Aerial Color or Infrared film.

Sites should be prepared for aerial photography by laying out markers near the planned photocenter prior to overflight. Marker "panels" can be made of strips of white cloth or wide strips of plastic. Markers should be placed at specific, measured intervals so they will be visible in the photographs. Distances intercepted by the markers are measured and the photographs scaled accordingly. (For example, two markers are placed 30 m apart on the ground; the aerial photographs are enlarged to suitable scale, e.g., 30 cm equals 30 m). There are much more sophisticated methods of scaling aerial photographs (American Society of Photogrammetry and Remote Sensing 1960). It is useful also to install a clearly visible ground marker indicating true north and to identify (panel) reference points such as the site datum (discussed elsewhere in this chapter).

Low-level aerial or overhead photographs can be taken from captive balloons (Whittlesey 1966, 1970, 1977), from photo-towers and special "model" aircraft, or by means of high tripods or other devices (Connah and Jones 1983; Johnson 1983; Straffin 1971:232–234). Applications of aerial photography in archaeology are discussed by Beresford and St. Joseph (1979), Gumerman and Lyons (1971), Riley (1987), St. Joseph (1977), Simmons (1969), Solecki (1957), Willey (1953), and D. R. Wilson (1982).

Terrestrial Photographs and Photogrammetry

Although not always strictly a "mapping" procedure, **photogrammetry,** the science of measurement by photography, can be used to record cultural resources (Slama 1980) such as plan views of features, vertical aspects (elevations), aerial views of structures in the built environment, and roads (e.g., at Chaco Canyon, New Mexico [Hayes et al. 1981]), entire historical districts, and many other types of cultural and natural features. Photogrammetric procedures and examples of recording historic architecture and other cultural features are discussed by Beaton (1983:65–66) and Borchers (1977).

GENERAL MAP TYPES

There are literally hundreds of types of maps available today worldwide; consult *The Map Catalog* (Makower and Bergheim 1990) and *The World Map*

Directory (Maizlish and Hunt 1989) (see also Appendix B, 2). A useful set of maps now available for most of the United States is the *Atlas and Gazetteer Series* produced by DeLorme Mapping (see Appendix B, 3). An example of this series, the *Arizona Atlas and Gazetteer*, consists of 53 "quadrangular" maps covering 43 minutes of longitude and 49 minutes of latitude, an area approximately 40.2-×-56.3 mi (or 64.4-×-90.6 km), at 1:250,000-scale. A major advantage of the *Atlas and Gazetteer Series* is that the borders of each map display tick marks that identify latitude and longitude. Five-minute-interval tick marks are labeled in both conventional and decimal systems; between these are tick marks spaced at one-minute intervals. These maps are very useful for determining your location and that of archaeological sites, using, for example, handheld Global Positioning System (GPS) equipment (discussed later).

In Canada, 1:250,000- and 1:50,000-scale maps are available (British Columbia Surveys and Mapping Branch 1975; MacGregor 1981; St-Onge 1990). The United Kingdom Ordnance Survey (OS) grid divides Great Britain into 100-km-square sections (100-×-100 km), each of which is labeled with two letters. These sections in turn are divided into 1-km-square blocks. The OS Landranger series covers Britain in 204 sheets at 1:50,000; scale 1¼ inches to the mile (2 cm = 1 km). The Pathfinder series, beautifully detailed, offers coverage at 1:25,000; 2½ inches to the mile (4 cm = 1 km) (Bell 1978; Phillips 1980; J. G. Wilson 1985).

Map interpretation and navigating by map ("orienteering") are skills best acquired by practice. Basic procedures are given by Blandford (1991), Jacobson (1988), Kals (1983), Kjellstrom (1994), Radliff (1964), and Randall (1989). A good way to learn how to interpret topographic maps is to practice with a map covering an area with which you are well acquainted, then study maps that show different types of terrain—mountains, deserts, seashores—to appreciate the relationship between observed and mapped natural and cultural features. Instructional sets of topographic maps display different types of terrain, such as volcanic features, alluvial fans, playas, river terraces, and so forth, which can be visualized in stereoscopic effect by means of a suitable viewer (see Appendix B, 4)

(DeBruin 1970; Jackson 1984; MacMahan 1972; Raitz and Hart 1975). "Three-dimensional" **relief maps** made of molded plastic are also useful for visualizing terrain.

To obtain USGS quadrangles covering your area of interest, request from the USGS an *Index to Topographic and Other Map Coverage*, which gives instructions for ordering maps, as well as current prices (see Appendix B, 2). Most American archaeologists use USGS 1:24,000-series topographic quadrangles (commonly known as 7.5-minute quads), discussed below.

USGS TOPOGRAPHIC QUADRANGLES

United States Geological Survey topographic maps are so designated because they display line and symbol representations of natural and man-made features and depict the landforms upon which these features occur. Topographic maps produced in color by the USGS are available in several different scales. The area covered by a USGS topographic quadrangle depends on the latitude and longitude of the mapped area (see "Geographic Coordinate System," below). (Remember, a "small-scale" map covers a *large* area.)

1:250,000-scale Maps (1-×-2-degree Series)

The 1:250,000-scale map series covers the largest area (4,580–8,669 mi^2). At this scale, 1 inch on the map equals 250,000 inches, or almost 4 miles, on the ground. Each map in this series covers 1 degree of latitude and 2 degrees of longitude.

1:100,000-scale Maps (30-×-60-minute Series)

Another type of topographic map issued by the USGS is the 30-×-60-minute intermediate scale quadrangle, a metric 1:100,000-scale series, the principal advantage of which is that 1 cm on the map represents 1 km on the ground. Maps in this series, covering approximately 1,578–2,176 mi^2, are used by the Bureau of Land Management (BLM) and other agencies in the western states. Contours and elevations are shown in meters.

1:63,500-scale Maps (15-minute Series)

The USGS 15-minute topographic quadrangle series maps (informally, "15-minute quads") cover 197–282 mi^2. The 15-minute quadrangle is scaled 1:63,500; 1 inch is approximately equivalent to 1 mi. (USGS topographic maps of Alaska are scaled 1:63,360; 1 inch to the mile.) Although 15-minute quadrangles display more detail than the 1:250,000-scale series, the area covered by 1 mi^2 is only about 1 inch square on the map. Consequently, it may be difficult to plot accurately the position of small archaeological sites. This series, now obsolete and officially abandoned by USGS, has been replaced by the USGS 7.5-minute topographic quadrangle.

1:24,000-scale Maps (7.5-minute Series)

Probably the most widely used USGS topographic quadrangle is the 7.5-minute series, now completed for all parts of the United States except (at this writing in 1996) Alaska. These maps provide much more detail than that given by the 15-minute series: each 7.5-minute quadrangle "enlarges" one-quarter of a 15-minute quadrangle and is scaled 1:24,000; 1 inch representing about 2,000 ft on the ground, somewhat more than 2½ inches to the mile. The area displayed on the 7.5-minute quadrangle covers approximately 49–71 mi^2. The 7.5-minute series provides accurate detail of terrain, vegetation patterns, streams, roads, and many other types of features. These quadrangles are frequently used as base maps upon which archaeological (and other) projects are laid out and site locations plotted.

OTHER USGS MAP PRODUCTS

The National Mapping Program of the USGS also produces many types of special-purpose maps, including **orthophotoquads** that provide "advance" or preliminary coverage of unmapped areas. These aerial photographs are rectified to eliminate image displacements so that the terrain shown is "map correct." Contour lines, survey boundary lines, and other information can be added to these maps on request, but not inexpensively. Other USGS mapping products include advance prints, feature separates, out-of-print maps, maps on microfilm, survey control diagrams, and maps in digital form (US GeoData).

Information Given on Topographic Quadrangles

Each USGS quadrangle is identified by name and other data printed in the lower and upper right-hand corner margins. The names of adjoining quadrangles are printed in small, slanted upper-case letters at each corner and on all four margins of each map. When the area covered by a quadrangle lies entirely within a single county, the county name is printed at the upper right-hand corner of the map, beneath the name of the quadrangle. If a map displays portions of more than one county, the respective boundaries are indicated. Important information printed at the lower left corner of each quadrangle includes the dates of the aerial photography on which the map is based, the year that preliminary copies of the map were checked by USGS field parties, and **coordinate zone** data (discussed below). In the lower right-hand corner of the map is the date of its publication. The date when the map was "updated" by photorevision (if this has been done) is printed in purple. Map users should be aware, of course, that even recently published maps of rapidly developing areas may be out of date, as a result of the length of time—perhaps several years—that may elapse between acquisition of aerial photography and publication of the final map.

Topographic maps issued by the USGS are inspected for accuracy at every stage of preparation. Details in aerial photographs obscured by vegetation are field-checked. The United States National Map Accuracy Standards (Thompson 1988) used by USGS state that for maps on publication scales larger than 1:20,000, not more than 10 percent of well-defined map points tested shall be in error by more than ¹⁄₃₀ inch measured on the publication scale and that for maps on publication scales of 1:20,000 or smaller, that the error shall not be more than ¹⁄₅₀ inch (5 mm)—about 40 ft on the ground on a 7.5-minute quadrangle or 100 ft for a

1:62,500-scale 15-minute quadrangle. Well-defined points are those that are easily visible or recoverable on the ground, such as bench marks, property boundary monuments, right-angle road intersections, and so forth. (Vertical accuracy standards are discussed later.)

Symbols Used on Topographic Quadrangles

Cartographic symbols—"the graphic language of maps"—are conventional, standardized representations of natural and cultural features. The latter are indicated on USGS maps in black, with the exception of freeways, primary roads, and secondary roads, which are red. Improved roads are indicated by solid double lines, farm or back-country roads by broken (dashed) double lines, and trails by single dashed lines. Vegetation is colored green, water blue, urban areas pink, photorevised (unverified) areas purple, and landform contours brown. The section and township lines of the United States Public Land Survey System (discussed below) are shown in red.

Roads indicated on USGS quadrangles by standard cartographic symbols may appear to be scaled wider than they actually are on the ground. For example, an unimproved "back road" indicated on a quadrangle by dashed double lines might "measure" about 50 ft wide on the map, yet the actual road may be only some 6 ft wide. Hence, measurements from depicted roads should be taken from the center of the indicated road, not from its edges. Many types of symbols are used by the USGS to depict natural and cultural features (Figure 9.2).

Contour Lines on Topographic Quadrangles

Contour lines are a cartographic device used on topographic maps to indicate land forms (topography). Changes in elevation are shown by thin, brown contour lines (**isolines**), imaginary lines that connect points of equal elevation. The space between contour lines is called the **contour interval**. On USGS quadrangles, every fifth contour—the **index contour**—is printed wider than the others and is identified by its elevation, given in feet above mean sea level.

Various scales of USGS maps display different contour intervals. On USGS 1:250,000-scale maps the contour interval is 200 ft; on 15-minute quadrangles it is 40 or 80 ft; on most 7.5-minute quadrangles it is 5, 10, 20 ft, and so forth, as indicated on each map. The contour interval is printed on the bottom margin of each quadrangle, beneath the graphic scale. In terms of vertical accuracy, as applied to contour maps on all publication scales, USGS standards specify that no more than 10 percent of the elevations tested shall be in error by more than one-half the contour interval. Thus, on USGS quadrangles with a contour interval of 10 ft, 90 percent of all test points must be within 5 ft (1.5 m) of the actual elevation.

Contours spaced at wide intervals indicate level or gently sloping terrain; closely spaced contours denote steep slopes. Deviations from a repetitive pattern may indicate knolls, ridges, drainages, or other types of landforms. Depressions or hollows are indicated by contour lines with hatch marks (small tick marks) pointing into the depression. The relationship between landforms and contours is shown in Figure 9.3, which gives an oblique ("bird's-eye") view of an ocean bay, river valley, and adjacent low hills. For hints on how to visualize terrain indicated by contour lines, see Campbell (1991), MacMahan (1972), and Robinson et al. (1984).

Elevations on Topographic Quadrangles

Topographic quadrangles published by the USGS give the location of precisely determined points of elevation called **bench marks.** Established in the field by licensed surveyors, bench marks are brass or aluminum disks attached to short, vertical pieces of pipe or affixed to rock outcrops, bridge abutments, or other prominent features (Gatto 1987). Elevation information is stamped on the bench-mark disk. The position of each established bench mark is indicated on USGS quadrangles by an "×" symbol printed in black ink and labeled "BM," adjacent to which are *vertical* numbers giving the elevation of the bench mark. "Spot" elevations of identifiable locations such as road intersections are indicated on USGS quadrangles

TOPOGRAPHIC MAP SYMBOLS

VARIATIONS WILL BE FOUND ON OLDER MAPS

Primary highway, hard surface	
Secondary highway, hard surface	
Light-duty road, hard or improved surface	
Unimproved road	
Road under construction, alignment known	
Proposed road	
Dual highway, dividing strip 25 feet or less	
Dual highway, dividing strip exceeding 25 feet	
Trail	
Railroad: single track and multiple track	
Railroads in juxtaposition	
Narrow gauge: single track and multiple track	
Railroad in street and carline	
Bridge: road and railroad	
Drawbridge: road and railroad	
Footbridge	
Tunnel: road and railroad	
Overpass and underpass	
Small masonry or concrete dam	
Dam with lock	
Dam with road	
Canal with lock	
Buildings (dwelling, place of employment, etc.)	
School, church, and cemetery	Cem
Buildings (barn, warehouse, etc.)	
Power transmisssion line with located metal tower	
Telephone line, pipeline, etc. (labeled as to type)	
Wells other than water (labeled as to type)	o Oil o Gas
Tanks: oil, water, etc. (labeled only if water)	● ● ● Water
Located or landmark object; windmill	
Open pit, mine, or quarry; prospect	✕ X
Shaft and tunnel entrance	◪ Y
Horizontal and vertical control station:	
Tablet, spirit level elevation	BM △ 5653
Other recoverable mark, spirit level elevation	△ 5455
Horizontal control station: tablet, vertical angle elevation	VABM △ *95/9*
Any recoverable mark, vertical angle or checked elevation	△ *3775*
Vertical control station: tablet, spirit level elevation	BM ✕ 957
Other recoverable mark, spirit level elevation	✕ 954
Spot elevation	✕ *7369* ✕ *7369*
Water elevation	*670* *670*

Boundaries: National	
State	
County, parish, municipio	
Civil township, precinct, town, barrio	
Incorporated city, village, town, hamlet	
Reservation, National or State	
Small park, cemetery, airport, etc.	
Land grant	
Township or range line, United States land survey	
Township or range line, approximate location	
Section line, United States land survey	
Section line, approximate location	
Township line, not United States land survey	
Section line, not United States land survey	
Found corner: section and closing	
Boundary monument: land grant and other	□ □
Fence or field line	

Index contour		Intermediate contour	
Supplementary contour		Depression contours	
Fill		Cut	
Levee		Levee with road	
Mine dump		Wash	
Tailings		Tailings pond	
Shifting sand or dunes		Intricate surface	
Sand area		Gravel beach	

Perennial streams		Intermittent streams	
Elevated aqueduct		Aqueduct tunnel	
Water well and spring	o ..... o	Glacier	
Small rapids		Small falls	
Large rapids		Large falls	
Intermittent lake		Dry lake bed	
Foreshore flat		Rock or coral reef	
Sounding, depth curve	*10*	Piling or dolphin	o
Exposed wreck		Sunken wreck	
Rock, bare or awash; dangerous to navigation			

Marsh (swamp)		Submerged marsh	
Wooded marsh		Mangrove	
Woods or brushwood		Orchard	
Vineyard		Scrub	
Land subject to controlled inundation		Urban area	

Figure 9.2 Topographic map symbols used by the U.S. Geological Survey. Some of the symbols are printed in color on the maps (see text).

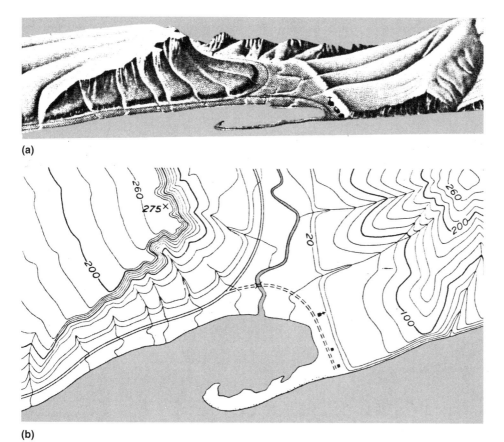

(a)

(b)

Figure 9.3 A river valley and seashore: (*a*) oblique view; (*b*) visualized from above, with elevations indicated by contour lines at 20-ft intervals.

by *slanted* numbers. There are no bench marks or monuments at these locations; nonetheless, spot elevations are accurate within the limits of USGS cartographic standards.

The USGS is in the process of obtaining accurate elevations for all terrain displayed on the USGS 1:24,000-series topographic quadrangles. This is accomplished by means of a regular grid (matrix) of sampled elevation values (DEMs). The sampling matrix is at intervals of 30 m in latitude and longitude. Sampling for the 1:250,000-series topographic maps has been completed.

Direction on Topographic Quadrangles

Topographic maps are printed so that true north (the pole of the earth's rotation) is at the top of the

map. At present the magnetic pole lies in northern Canada some 1,300 km south of the pole of rotation. Hence, throughout most of the United States (and in other countries as well) there are significant differences (locally as much as ± 20 degrees) between true and magnetic north. This effect is called **declination.** In some parts of Canada and the United States (e.g., at present approximately from the Great Lakes to Louisiana) declination is minimized because the magnetic pole and the pole of rotation nearly coincide. (This zone of "zero declination" is called the **agonic line.**)

Printed on each USGS quadrangle is a **declination diagram** showing the relationship of true north, magnetic north (MN), and grid north (GN) at the center of the map when the map was compiled, but the relationship between true and magnetic north has probably changed since the map was

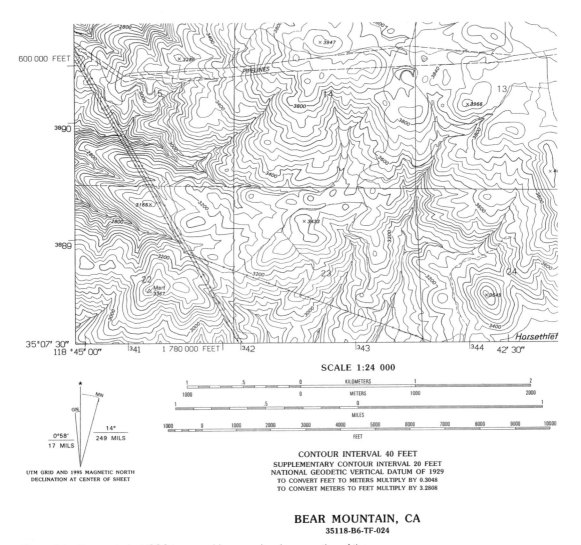

Figure 9.4 Segment of a USGS topographic map, showing a portion of the 7.5-minute Bear Mountain, California, quadrangle.

published. Current declination (**isogonic**) charts (issued at 10-year intervals) should be consulted to determine local declination. (Grid north pertains to the central meridian of a specific grid system; see "Universal Transverse Mercator Grid System" later.) Compass declination can be determined in reference to a particular USGS quadrangle by sighting with the compass along a surveyed road aligned to true north and observing the current degree of declination (see "Compasses," below).

Distances on Topographic Quadrangles

The scale of each USGS topographic quadrangle is expressed in graphic form by **bar scales** printed at the lower center margin of each quadrangle. Bar scales give the relative distances on the map in miles, feet, and kilometers. The use of these scales for measuring distance is generally self-evident (Figure 9.4); for further information consult Muehrcke (1992).

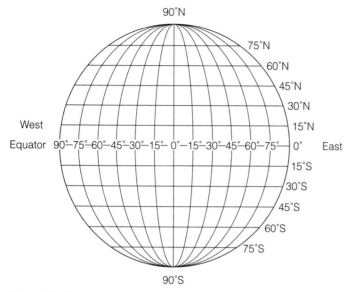

Figure 9.5 The world: latitudes (equator to poles) and longitudes east and west from Greenwich prime meridian.

Locational Reference Systems on Topographic Quadrangles

All USGS topographic quadrangles give information related to several types of locational systems. These include the Geographic Coordinate System ("latitude and longitude"), Universal Transverse Mercator Grid System, United States Public Land Survey System (informally called the "Legal Location" or "Range and Township System"), State Plane Coordinate System, and the Metes and Bounds System. These systems are summarized below.

Geographic Coordinate System (GCS) ("Latitude and Longitude"). The GCS locational system is based on the fact that the earth rotates on its axis every 24 hours; for the purposes of this system, the poles of rotation are considered to be fixed, identifiable points. Arcs of circle (meridians), called lines of **longitude**, are drawn from pole to pole. By international agreement among English-speaking countries, the meridian passing through the observatory located at Greenwich, England, is designated as the first, or **prime**, meridian. Longitude is measured in

degrees of arc, 180 degrees east or west of the prime meridian (Howse 1980). From the equator (zero degrees latitude), parallel degrees of **latitude** are projected in degrees of arc to the North Pole (90 degrees north) and South Pole (90 degrees south) (Figure 9.5).

The latitude and longitude of any location on earth can be determined by means of instruments, such as the mariner's sextant or the land surveyor's transit. (Further information on how this is accomplished is given by Brinker and Wolf [1984:349–351] and Howse [1980].) Using a transit (described below) and equipped with an accurate timepiece or shortwave radio to obtain the exact time at Greenwich (Greenwich Mean Time; now Coordinated Universal Time [CUT]) or using a handheld Global Positioning System receiver, field personnel can determine the position of an archaeological site to within approximately 15 m (50 ft) of its true position on earth when no other reference system is available. At the present time, most American archaeologists do not use the GCS, but it is widely used in Africa, where sites are identified in reference to it (Nelson 1971), and in other countries with few established reference points. The

GCS is becoming more important in American archaeology, however, because most portable Global Positioning System receivers display locational information in latitude and longitude coordinates (see "Global Positioning System," below).

As noted above, the area covered by USGS quadrangles is determined by lines of latitude and longitude. Because lines of latitude converge from the equator to the poles, USGS topographic quadrangles are *slightly* trapezoidal, an effect not particularly noticeable when viewing an individual quadrangle but quite evident when comparing, for example, topographic maps of northern versus southern states.

Universal Transverse Mercator (UTM) Grid System. The UTM system is based on the International System of Units (SI), informally, the metric system. This system establishes a metric grid covering the northern hemisphere from the equator north to 80 degrees north latitude and the southern hemisphere from 80 degrees south latitude north to the equator. (In either hemisphere, grid orientation is to the *north*.) The two polar regions are governed by the Universal Polar Stereographic Projection. The UTM system deals with **point locations.** (Compare this with the USPLSS [discussed below], which deals with area.)

The north and south hemispheres are spanned by a series of 60 sequentially numbered north-south trending zones, each of which is 6 degrees of longitude wide. Each UTM zone is "flattened" by the UTM map projection. A grid of uniform squares is established by imaginary lines spaced 100,000 m apart, creating the basic coordinate reference system. Grid numbering begins in each UTM zone at a point *outside* the zone. This point, called a **false origin,** is located south and west of the area subsumed by the grid (see "Site Datum Point and Site Grid," later). Hence, the coordinates obtained by measurements are always positive numbers, reading from the point of origin *east* ("right") and *north* ("up").

In both hemispheres, UTM readings are always made to the east (**easting**) and to the north (**northing**). To obtain UTM coordinates of a given location, simply measure easting and northing (the

mnemonic device is "read-right-up"). Other methods of determining UTM locations are given by Cole (1977).

To identify the UTM location of an archaeological site in either hemisphere, one need only identify the UTM zone and the position of the site in meters easting and northing. The UTM system is indicated on USGS quadrangles in two ways: older maps display along their top and bottom margins **UTM tick marks** printed in light blue, denoting 1,000-m easting intervals. The accompanying UTM numbers are abbreviated—only the first three digits are printed. Tick marks along the left and right margins of the map indicate 1,000-m northing intervals, identified by numbers consisting of four digits. On recently issued USGS 7.5-minute topographic quadrangles, the UTM grid is delineated by superimposed lines printed in black. Box 9.1 provides information for determining site location on the UTM grid.

The UTM system included on USGS 7.5-minute-series quadrangles permits measurement of the coordinates of a site (on USGS 1:24,000 topographic quadrangles, 1,000 m measures 41.5 mm), but the accuracy of *any* UTM reading will only be as good as the archaeologist's reckoning of where the site is located in the field. Unlike in the USPLSS, there are no UTM-specific, monumented reference points in the field from which measurements can be made from a known (established) point directly to a site. However, using Global Positioning System (GPS) equipment (discussed below), it is now possible to determine accurately the UTM (or other grid) location of a site in the field with an error of between 15 and 100 m (49–328 ft). However, most handheld GPS units will not work in deep, narrow canyons or dense forests because the satellite signals received by GPS units cannot penetrate dense vegetation, landforms, or buildings. (The coordinates obtained by GPS should, of course, be checked in reference to UTM map coordinates.) It may be that in the near future UTM coordinates will be the *only* locational reference entered in many computerized site data control systems, so it is essential to strive for as much accuracy as possible.

We have seen that UTM coordinates locate specific *points*, unlike the USPLSS which, as explained

---

BOX 9.1   DETERMINING THE UTM GRID LOCATION OF ARCHAEOLOGICAL SITES

To determine the UTM location of an archaeological site, you must "read" the east (easting) and north (northing) coordinates of the site location. To accomplish this, you need some basic equipment—the appropriate USGS quadrangle; a sharp pencil; a 36-inch or meter-length metal straightedge; a flat, smooth table; and a UTM coordinate template, or "reader." (The reader can be purchased or made: many archaeologists create a composite reader to measure UTM coordinates and subdivide sections in the USPLSS.)

Because the UTM grid defines square units, the same scale is used to measure both easting and northing. To measure a UTM position, refer to the progressively numbered UTM grid lines or tick marks printed on the margins of each USGS quadrangle. If UTM grid lines are not printed on the quadrangle, experienced archaeologists carefully prepare the quadrangle before making UTM measurements by ruling the essential UTM grid lines directly on the map, guided by the blue tick marks printed along the map margins. Because not every tick mark is labeled on most USGS quadrangles, it's a good idea to rectify omissions by numbering *each* blue UTM tick mark.

To obtain the UTM coordinates of an archaeological site, mark the location of the site on the quadrangle, read meters easting, then meters northing. To read easting, find the UTM line immediately *left* (west) of the site and carefully place the zero mark of the prepared coordinate reader on this line. For example (referring to Figures 9.6–9.8) we can locate the position of the "×" marking elevation 5346. From UTM 761 read *east* ("read-right"). The "×" is located approximately 380 m east of that line; hence, the coordinate is UTM 761380 m easting. (Easting is always a six-digit number.)

Next, measure distance northing to the "×." Place the coordinate reader with zero on the UTM line *below* (south of) the site and read *up* (north) to find the site northing position. In Figures 9.6–9.8 the site is located above (north of) the 4211-m UTM line a distance of 530 m north of that line. Hence, the coordinate is UTM 4211530 m northing. (Northing is always a seven-digit number.) It is necessary to obtain one further piece of information—the UTM **zone** identification, which is found in the information block printed at the lower left-hand corner margin of each USGS quadrangle. Most of California is in UTM Zones 10 or 11; Nevada is entirely within Zone 11. Let's say the site discussed above is in Zone 10. Hence, the full UTM coordinates referring to this site are: Zone 10, 761380 mE; 4211530 mN.

---

below, defines *areas*. Archaeological sites often cover extensive areas. Many site record forms, such as those used to nominate a site to the National Register of Historic Places, require that if the area covered by a site exceeds a certain size (usually 10 acres), it must be identified by enclosing it in a three- or four-sided figure: the full easting and northing UTM coordinates of each corner must be obtained. (To determine acreage, multiply site length by width in feet; divide by 43,560.)

United States Public Land Survey System (USPLSS) (System of Rectangular Surveys). In the 1780s, Thomas Jefferson and others realized that a better means of defining private property was needed to replace the cumbersome, often inaccurate metes-and-bounds survey method (see dis-

cussion later) then in use. Finally, the Continental Congress enacted the Land Ordinance of 1785, which provided for systematic survey of the vast lands north and west of the Ohio River (the Northwest Territories), to encourage their rapid, permanent, and orderly settlement (Estopinal 1989; McEntyre 1986; Pattison 1979).

The USPLSS (often informally identified on site record forms as "legal location") divides the public domain into large segments, each with a vertical **principal meridian** running true north and, at right angles to it, a horizontal **base line.** Today there are 31 principal meridians and base lines in the continental United States and five in Alaska, each of which is named or numbered. The intersection of a principal meridian and its complementary base line is called the **initial point** of survey. The

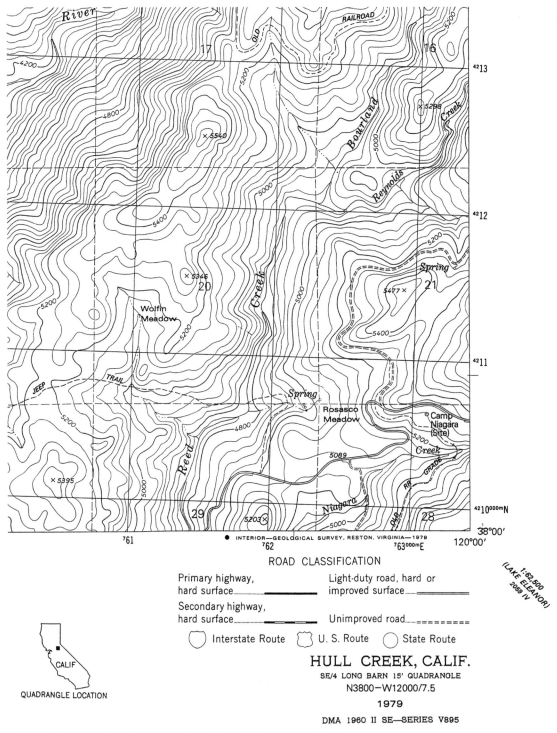

ROAD CLASSIFICATION

Primary highway, hard surface	Light-duty road, hard or improved surface
Secondary highway, hard surface	Unimproved road

Interstate Route   U. S. Route   State Route

HULL CREEK, CALIF.

SE/4 LONG BARN 15' QUADRANGLE
N3800—W12000/7.5

1979

DMA 1960 II SE—SERIES V895

CALIF

QUADRANGLE LOCATION

Figure 9.6   A UTM location. The UTM position of the small "x" (followed by the number 5346) in Section 20 is 761380 mE, 4211530 mN, Zone 10. (Zone number appears at lower left corner of full map.)

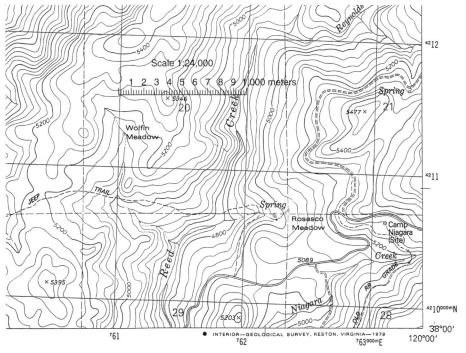

Figure 9.7 A UTM reader is shown, positioned to determine the easting coordinate of point "x 5346": 761380 mE.

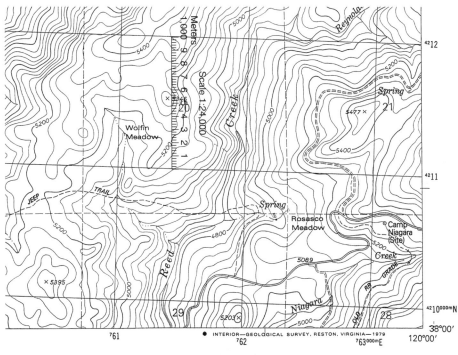

Figure 9.8 A UTM reader is shown, positioned to determine the northing coordinate of point "x 5346": 4211530 mN.

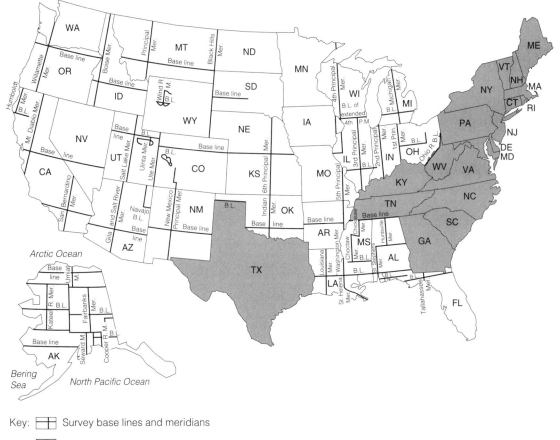

Key: ⊞ Survey base lines and meridians

▓ Excluded areas

Figure 9.9 Areas covered by the United States Public Land Survey System (excluded areas shaded), showing principal meridians and base lines intersecting to form initial points.

latitude and longitude of each initial point is carefully determined by astronomical observations and permanently monumented. All measurements in the Public Land Survey System originate from these initial points (Figure 9.9).

For example, much of the land in California and Nevada is controlled by the Mount Diablo Meridian and Base Line (MDMBL). Measurements in reference to the MDMBL are made from an initial point established in 1851 atop the north summit of Mount Diablo near San Francisco Bay, from which it was (then) possible to see parts of 38 California counties. Land in Idaho is controlled by

measurements from the Boise Meridian; in Montana, in reference to the Montana Principal Meridian; in Arizona from the Gila and Salt River Meridian. (Texas has a similar rectangular system not part of the USPLSS.) The locations of all USPLSS meridians are shown on a special map titled *Principal Meridians and Base Lines Governing the United States Public Land Surveys* (see U.S. Department of the Interior, Bureau of Land Management [USDI/BLM] 1973:60–61).

Beginning at each principal meridian, land is divided into a series of parallel strips 6 miles wide, called **townships.** The first township *north* of the

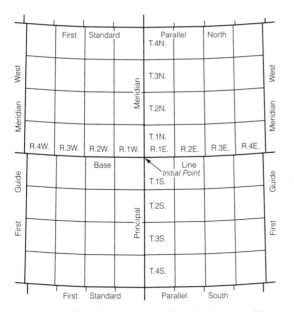

Figure 9.10 Coordinate system of numbering townships, with guide meridians extended north from the base line. Townships are numbered north and south; ranges east and west from the initial point.

BOX 9.2
GUNTER'S CHAIN

The surveyor's or Gunter's chain, devised in 1620 by Edmund Gunter, an English astronomer, is 66 ft long (based on a 16.5-ft rod) (Toscano 1991:155–161). The standard Gunter's chain used in the United States is composed of 100 links, each 7.92 inches long. Using this chain, early-day American surveyors measured 80 chains to the mile (66 × 80 = 5,280 ft) to establish a section corner; 480 chains to establish the corners of a 6-mile-square township. Metal chains are no longer used to measure distance, but many surveyors refer informally to the process of measuring as "chaining" (Uzes 1977), using 100 ft to equal "1 chain." The law prescribes the chain as the unit of linear measure for the survey of public lands (USDI/BLM 1973:13); information on location posters ("k-tags," discussed in the text) is given in chain units—i.e., one surveyor's or engineer's chain equals 100 ft.

base line is T1N, followed by T2N, and so forth; townships *south* of the base line are identified as T1S, T2S, and so forth (Figure 9.10). East and west of the principal meridian are parallel lines that also form strips 6 miles wide. These strips are called **ranges.** The first range east of the Mount Diablo Meridian is R1E, followed by R2E, and so forth, numbered progressively east (or west) from the principal meridian. Range and township lines form units 6 miles square; these are townships. Each township is divided into **sections** 1 mile square. Hence, each 6-mile-square township contains 36 sections, each of which (ideally) covers 1 square mile. In the United States, sections are numbered in sequence beginning at the northeast (upper right) corner of the township, proceeding thence west 6 miles (sections 1–6); thence east (7–12), and so forth, alternately to and including section 36, located in the southeast (lower right) corner of each township. In Canada, sections are numbered from the southeast (lower right) corner of each town-

ship; numbering proceeds progressively west-east alternatively to the northeast corner, section 36. In Texas, the land grant system is based on the Spanish *vara*, equivalent to about 33 (actually, 33.372) inches; 36 *varas* equal 100 ft (Uzes 1977:300).

Townships and section lines are *not* imaginary: they are laid out in the field by surveyors, often with great difficulty (Cazier 1993). Township and section corners are physically marked (monumented) in the field (Figure 9.11). Quarter-corners, sixteenth-corners, and other section subdivisions may also be monumented, depending on the degree of control necessary to define property lines. Surveyors have been working in the American West for nearly a century to complete the USPLSS, but many areas are not completely surveyed. See Box 9.2 for information on chaining.

The importance of the USPLSS for archaeological mapping is the fact that the corners of most townships and sections are physically and permanently established in the field by monuments or

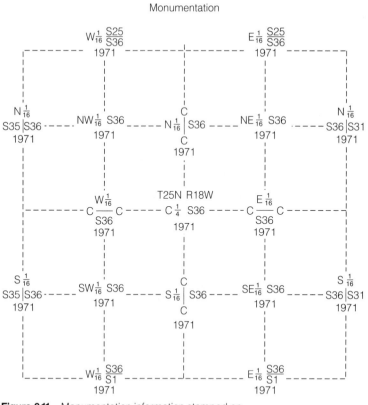

Figure 9.11 Monumentation information stamped on "brass caps" at interior quarter-section corners and all sixteenth-section corners.

markers, informally called **brass-caps.** A standard brass-cap installed by a licensed surveyor is a metal disk approximately 3 inches in diameter made of brass or aluminum. The disk is attached to the end of a piece of metal pipe, which is set vertically in concrete and stands about 1 ft above the surface of the ground. Locational information identifying the monumented position is stamped on the disk.

If a section corner is located in a position occupied by a large tree, the corner is marked by an aluminum tag nailed to the trunk, or by an "x" symbol carved on its south side. If a section or township corner has been established ("found") in the field, its location is indicated on USGS 7.5-minute quadrangles by a "+" symbol printed at the appropriate section or township corner (Figure 9.12).

Township and section corners are sometimes destroyed by erosion or earth-moving machinery, so each monumented corner is referenced by a buried marker, and also by **witness posters** (also called witness points or witness corners) installed near the corner. On some privately owned land and on federal land (national forests, national parks, and BLM land), corners are referenced by location posters called **k-tags.** These small metal signs (4½-×-5 inches), usually yellow in color, are nailed to trees along roads and trails. Printed on each k-tag is a small diagram of a mile-square section. The position of the specific k-tag is indicated by a nail or tack located at the appropriate point on the section diagram. The distance and bearing to the referenced section corner is inscribed on the k-tag. Established section corners and k-tags are

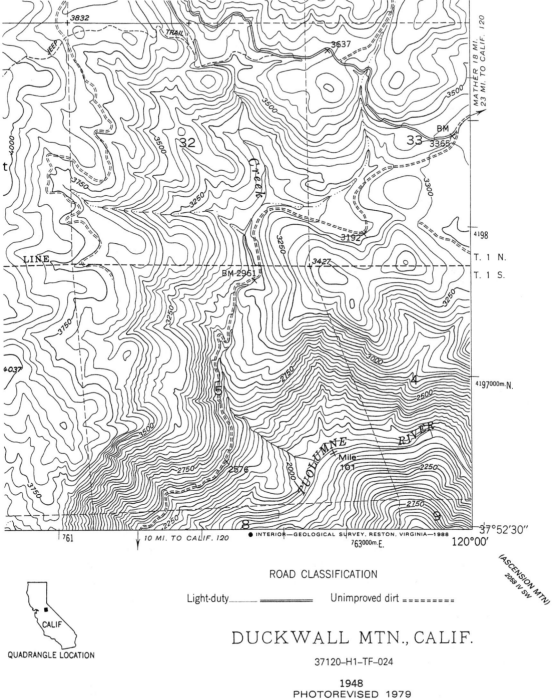

ROAD CLASSIFICATION

Light-duty................ ━━━━━━━   Unimproved dirt ═════════

DUCKWALL MTN., CALIF.

37120–H1–TF–024

1948
PHOTOREVISED 1979
DMA 1959 I NE—SERIES V895

Figure 9.12 Portion of the USGS map of Duckwall Mountain, California, topographic quadrangle, showing irregular section (5) and monumented corner sections 4, 5, 32, and 33. The contour interval is 50 ft.

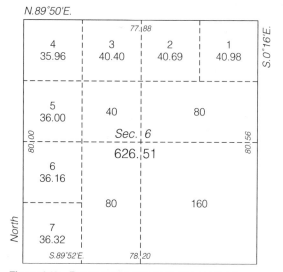

Figure 9.13 Example of subdivision of a section by protraction, showing numbering of "lots" within an irregular section of 626.51 acres (rather than the standard 640-acre section).

extremely important in the western forests, because they help field archaeologists ascertain the "legal location" of archaeological sites. However, k-tag positions are not shown on USGS maps. A site may be located in reference to an established section corner, quarter-corner, or k-tag by taking a compass sighting (bearing or azimuth) *from* the established point *to* the site datum, and, of course, by measuring the intervening distance.

Each **regular section** defined by the USPLSS in theory contains 640 acres "as nearly as may be," as the law states (36 R.S. 2395; 43 U.S.C. 751), but the acreage in some sections varies as a result of converging meridians, steep terrain, and because of the fact that the USPLSS grid system of 6-mile-square townships is imposed on the curved surface of the earth. By convention, the south and east boundaries of each township are normally the governing lines of subdivisional surveys. Any excess or deficiency of measurement or acreage is assigned to sections in the *north* and *west* portions of a given township. For this reason sections along the north boundary of a township (sections 1–6) and those along the west boundary (sections 7, 18,

19, 30, and 31) may be irregular in shape or contain fewer than the prescribed 640 acres (Figure 9.13). Irregular portions of sections, defined as **fractional lots,** are numbered sequentially by licensed surveyors. Use of the USPLSS is explained in Box 9.3.

Many township and section corners remain to be established (monumented) in the field. Unsurveyed lands present a problem for field archaeologists, who often simply rule missing section lines on their maps. This practice is questionable, because fractional lots must be established by licensed surveyors, not by guesswork. If it is necessary to rule section lines on a map, the site record form should clearly state that the "legal location" is only *approximate.*

It is well to remember that surveyors employed by or under contract to the U.S. Forest Service, BLM, or various other federal, county, or state agencies might have completed surveys of areas shown on USGS topographic maps, but even the most up-to-date USGS quadrangles probably will not depict all recently monumented corners. For further information, contact local surveyors or land agencies (see USDI/BLM 1973; U.S. Department of the Interior, Geological Survey [USDI,GS] 1989; U.S. Government, Superintendent of Documents 1991).

State Plane Coordinate System (SPCS). The SPCS is a statewide system coordinated with the North American Datum of 1927 (NAD 27), originally established in central Kansas (Mitchell and Simmons 1977). The SPCS divides the United States into 120 large zones. Any point within a given zone can be located in reference to this system with an accuracy of 1 in 10,000—that is, 1 ft of possible error in 10,000 ft. Measurements in the SPCS are made in the English System. At present the SPCS is in transition to the International System of Units (SI) (the metric system) and is coordinated to the North American Datum of 1983 (NAD 83). Although rarely used by archaeologists, the SPCS is referenced by licensed surveyors and is becoming increasingly important because it is integrated with the UTM grid system (discussed earlier). Many of the SPCS's triangulation points, which are used to determine accurate elevation

---

BOX 9.3   DETERMINING SITE LOCATION USING THE USPLSS ("LEGAL LOCATION")

The area shown in Figure 9.12, upper left, is Section 32, as shown by the large bold number "32" printed at the center of the section. However, there is a Section 32 in *every* township, so you must identify the specific Section 32 by determining the appropriate township and range. Township numbers are printed in red on the left and right margins (**neatlines**) of each USGS quadrangle; range numbers (not shown in Figure 9.12) are printed on the top and bottom margins. In Figure 9.12, the common boundary of Townships 1 North and 1 South is labeled "T. 1 N. and T. 1 S."

For purposes of discussion, let us ascertain the "legal location" of the position of the letter *C* in the word *Creek* in Section 32. Section 32 is in Township 1 North (written as T1N), Range 18 East (written as R18E). Hence *C* is in S-32, T1N, R18E—an area 1 mile square. Next we will need to determine which meridian governs this particular township and range. For various reasons, California has three principal meridians: Mount Diablo (MDM), San Bernadino (SBM), and Humboldt (HM). (The meridian controlling the area represented on a given USGS quadrangle is *not* identified on the quadrangle; other sources must be consulted, e.g., for California, refer to Beck and Haase [1974:Section 60] or contact local county surveyors.) For illustrative purposes we refer to the Mount Diablo Meridian and Base Line.

Having determined the section, township, and range in which the letter *C* appears (and also having identified the appropriate meridian), the location in question has been narrowed to a specific 1-mile-square section. A greater degree of precision is necessary, of course, because a square mile (640 acres) covers a great deal of terrain. The location of *C* can be reduced to a quarter-section (160 acres), then to a quarter of a quarter-section (40 acres), then to a quarter of a quarter of a quarter-section (10 acres). It is desirable to reduce the location at least to a 10-acre area, bearing in mind that a single acre is 208.71 ft on a side.

Section lines are indicated on USGS quadrangles by either solid or dashed red lines, but sections are not further subdivided. Sometimes the positions of quarter-corners are indicated. In Figure 9.12, the north quarter-corner is marked by a "+" symbol. Irregular sections may be divided by licensed surveyors into fractional lots. When archaeologists expediently divide sections for mapping purposes, the results may be invalid in terms of the strict legal description of the property. Archaeologists can approximately subdivide regular sections using a special transparent template (see Appendix B, 5) or by preparing their own 1-mile-square overlay template made of tracing paper or, better, matte drafting film. Using the scale of miles provided on each map, regular sections can be subdivided into four quarters: the upper right quarter is the NE quarter, the upper left the NW, the lower right the SE, and the lower left the SW (see Figures 9.12 and 9.13). In a regular section, each of those quarters consists of 160 acres. Each of those 160-acre quarters can be divided into four segments, each of which covers 40 acres; these are also called the NE, NW, SE, and SW quarters, respectively. Any one of these quarters can be further subdivided into four more segments of 10 acres each, and so forth. Thus, the "legal location" of our point *C* is: "the NW 1/4 of the NE 1/4 of the SE 1/4 of S-32, T1N, R18E, MDM."

---

and distances from point to point, are physically established (monumented) in the field. The SPCS coordinates, however, are *not* displayed by most handheld Global Positioning System (GPS) receivers (discussed later in this chapter).

Each of the 120 zones of the SPCS has its own centrally positioned origin, through which passes its own north-south meridian (Trimm 1966). A **false origin** point is established southwest of each zone, usually 2 million ft west of the central meridian. Coordinates in the SPCS are read east and north in feet from the false origin reference. (The same procedure is used to read UTM coordinates.)

Metes-and-Bounds (MB). Land grants and private property boundaries in the American colonies (the original 13 states) were defined by metes (lengths) and bounds (boundaries), forming areas that often were highly irregular. Metes-and-bounds property boundaries followed streams, ran along ridge crests or other natural features, and often were only vaguely marked by stakes or piles of stones. Landowners sometimes increased their holdings by moving property boundary markers in their favor, resulting, of course, in lengthy disputes and litigation. Early-day surveyors established boundaries of private property using a surveyor's chain (see Box 9.2) and a handheld compass. Modern surveyors continue to survey irregular areas of land in metes-and-bounds, but with transits and other accurate surveying equipment.

LAND INFORMATION SYSTEMS (LIS)

Computer retrieval of land records is a recent development in the automation of land information. The Land Information Systems (LIS) program currently underway in the United States will identify the corners of land parcels by coordinates, such as those used in GCS, UTM, and SPCS (National Research Council 1982). Survey records, ownership status, and resources will also be identified and managed by LIS.

ARCHAEOLOGICAL SITE RECORD MAPS

Many types of maps are produced during archaeological field investigations. Among them are site record maps, site excavation maps, maps for publication, and special-purpose (thematic) maps.

Site record maps are often called sketch maps, and it is indeed true that in the past many site maps were little more than hastily drawn sketches. Although even a "sketch" map may be better than no map at all, it is becoming increasingly important that site record maps conform to standard cartographic principles. With a little time and effort, satisfactory maps can be produced. Basic site record maps that accompany site record forms often are drafted in the field using a minimum of equip-

ment, so we will begin by discussing the basic equipment needed to prepare a site record map.

Information and Equipment Needs

To create an acceptable site record map, one needs at least three vital pieces of information: direction, horizontal distance, and vertical distance. **Direction** is obtained with a handheld compass or by means of surveying instruments, such as the transit. **Horizontal distance** can be estimated by pacing or determined more accurately by taping, stadia, or electronic transit. **Vertical distance** (difference in elevation) is obtained by several methods discussed later (breaking tape, Abney level, electronic transit) and is usually indicated by contour lines.

Determining Direction. Direction is obtained by compass; hence, one of the most important tools for the field archaeologist is a reliable **compass.** With it you can determine the location of archaeological sites and features, orient the position of test units, and align site grids. We will consider four types of compasses: pocket transits, base-plate compasses, handbearing compasses, and digital compasses. There are various models of these basic types. Most are quite accurate; in several, the compass housing provides a useful "straightedge." The compass needle in most of these models is contained in fluid, which reduces (dampens) needle swing. Compasses intended only for use in the Northern Hemisphere will not perform properly in the Southern Hemisphere or vice versa, due to differential attraction of the earth's magnetic field. "International" models can be used anywhere.

One of the primary differences among the types of compasses listed above is the way in which the compass dial is graduated: some compasses give **azimuth readings** (0–360 degrees); other models give **bearings**—the compass circle is divided into four segments, or **quadrants,** each of which covers 0–90 degrees (Figure 9.14a,b).

Several types of compasses have optional features, such as mirror sights and provision for declination adjustment (see below). Mirror-sight compasses have a mirror built into the compass lid. To use this type of compass, hold it open at waist

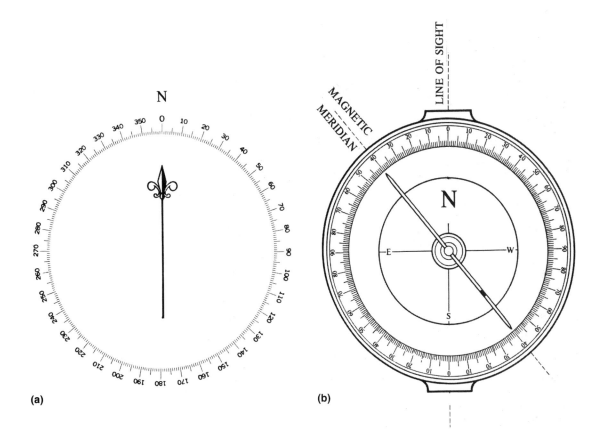

Figure 9.14   Two types of compass graduation: (*a*) 0–360 degrees for azimuth readings; (*b*) quadrants (0–90 degrees) for bearings.

level and rotate your body to line up the north end of the compass needle with a distant object. This type of compass can also be read at eye level by observing the direction indicated by the south end of the compass needle, which is reflected in the compass mirror.

Declination adjustment (declination is the angular difference between true and magnetic north) is a useful compass feature. In some parts of the United States, magnetic declination varies from practically nil (between the Great Lakes and Louisiana) to approximately 20 degrees east in the state of Washington and 20 degrees west in Maine. Declination is an important effect, because if you assume that magnetic and true north are the same in an area where there is significant declination

(say 10 degrees), you might follow a false compass heading, in which case for every mile traveled you could be off course laterally as much as 921 ft (302 m) (tan 10 degrees × 5280 ft). This problem can be eliminated by setting the compass for local declination, per center of the pertinent USGS quadrangle, following the instructions given by the compass manufacturer (see Kals 1983:116 ff.).

A long-time standard of archaeologists, geologists, and foresters, the **pocket transit,** or **cruiser's compass,** is so described because it can be used to read both horizontal and vertical angles. One manufacturer (Brunton; see Appendix B, "General Supply Sources") makes various models of pocket transits: standard, induction-damped (the compass needle comes to rest very quickly), waterproof,

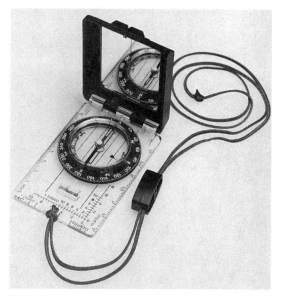

Figure 9.15 Suunto MC-1 base-plate compass open for use. Compass is placed on map and oriented in reference to true north. This type of compass can be adjusted to compensate for magnetic declination.

international (functional in both hemispheres), and a model with an illuminated digital display.

The **base-plate compass** is popular for "orienteering"—that is, for finding one's way cross-country. The Silva Company of Sweden (see Appendix B, 6) makes about a dozen models, as does Suunto of Finland (Figure 9.15). Most base-plate compasses can be adjusted for declination; many have map scales printed or etched along the edge of the base. (For operating instructions, see Box 9.4.)

The **handbearing compass** is designed to be used while being held to your eye. The compass "card," contained in a liquid-filled aluminum or plastic housing, rotates to the direction in which you are sighting. The azimuth (or, depending on the compass model, the bearing) is superimposed by optical illusion on the target or object sighted. This type of compass, made by Suunto (Figure 9.16) and also by Silva, obtains direction rapidly, but the internal compass card cannot be set to compensate for magnetic declination.

TABLE 9.1
Forest Service Pacing Method for Hilly Terrain

Percent Slope	Up		Down	
	Paces	*Skip*	*Paces*	*Skip*
10	6	1	–	–
20	3	1	11	1
30	2	1	6	1
40	1	1	2	1

Figure 9.16 Suunto KB-14/360 handbearing compass in use, held at eye level to obtain azimuth to distant point.

The **digital fluxgate compass,** an advanced type of handbearing compass, is used for both marine and land navigation. One model, KVH Industries' DataScope, electronically obtains and recalls bearings or azimuths and can be set to compensate for magnetic declination. It includes a 5-×-30 monocular and a rangefinder mode. The latter is capable of determining the approximate distance from the user to a faraway target by optically displaying a vertical "stack" of bar-segments, which the user matches against the known height of the distant target. The KVH DataScope also includes a useful chronometer (see Appendix B, 7).

Determining Distance. Approximate distances can be obtained by **pacing,** often not very accurate over uneven terrain but usually better than sheer guesswork. Accuracy of pacing can be improved before departing for a field project by laying out a pace-course on level ground. Mark a point; then, using a steel or fiberglass tape, measure 200 ft (61 m) and mark a second point. Pace this distance (following the methods outlined below) and return to the initial point so that the total distance covered is 400 ft (122 m). Ascertain the number of double steps taken by counting a pace each time your right

foot strikes the ground. (The average double pace is 5 ft.) Divide the length of the course by the number of double steps taken. If you covered the 400-ft course in 80 paces, your average pace is 5 ft.

Some fieldworkers count *each* pace, rather than double paces, and use a pocket calculator to convert their paces to feet or meters. It is advisable to pace using a normal, relaxed gait, not an exaggerated, exhausting stride. Pace will vary, depending on the type of terrain being covered and the type and density of groundcover and, of course, may be affected by whether one is fresh or tired. A method of pacing used by the Forest Service helps to compensate for variations in uphill and downhill pacing. Paces are omitted, depending upon the degree of slope, as shown in Table 9.1.

Over long distances (given fairly level terrain) you can roughly estimate distance covered by elapsed time. On level ground you might cover a mile in about 20 minutes or a kilometer in 15 minutes, but of course this method of estimating distance will at best yield only an approximate value of the actual distance traveled.

Taping is a more accurate approach to distance measurement. Probably the most useful piece of inexpensive equipment for field measurements is the 100-ft-long (30 m) fiberglass open-reel tape. Weighing approximately one pound, the open-reel fiberglass tape is easy to carry and, unlike steel tapes, will not rust. When taping, it must be remembered that distance measured down a slope is *not* equivalent to horizontal distance. If terrain slopes more than 4 degrees, measurements should be reduced to the horizontal. This is accomplished by two methods: the first of these, called **breaking tape,** is to measure short segments of distance while keeping the tape as horizontal as possible (see Box 9.5). The other method, **slope reduction,** involves measuring directly down a slope and reducing slope distance to horizontal distance by trigonometric calculations (see Box 9.6).

Distance can also be measured by the **odometer** of a vehicle—one-tenth of a mile of course is 528 ft (about 161 m)—but this method gives only approximate distances. Variations may occur due to the characteristics of a given vehicle and the type of road surface over which distance is measured. Methods of determining distance that require various types of surveying equipment are discussed later in this chapter.

While in the field you will probably carry only essential equipment because even a lightweight camera, notebook, compass, and tape are subject to one of the unwritten laws of archaeological surveying: "The weight of any object being carried increases exponentially for every mile traveled." These are some of the items that you might need for archaeological reconnaissance:

compass	pocket tape
clinometer	water bottle
altimeter	rucksack
site record forms	felt-tipped
pens	marking pen
cameras, film, tripod	flagging
mapping board	metal tags
base maps (topos)	first-aid items
aerial photos	snakebite kit
pocket stereoscope	field boots

Identifying the Site Reference Point

The first step in mapping a site is to inspect it to determine whether it can in fact be mapped in the time available. Hours, days, or weeks might be needed to map an extensive site, so it is a good idea to estimate the scope of the job beforehand. Sites are usually examined to locate and flag artifacts and features and, if possible, estimate the site perimeter. Some archaeological survey contracts require field archaeologists to mark the perimeter

---

BOX 9.5

MEASURING SLOPE DISTANCE BY BREAKING TAPE

To measure slope distance by breaking tape, one person (the "rear chainperson") handles the tape and records measurements. Another (the "head chainperson") holds the zero end of the tape and unreels it as needed. Taping by breaking tape is accurate, but an unsupported 30-m tape requires a tension of about 20 lb to measure correctly the full 30-m distance. Metal tapes are standardized for use at 68 degrees Fahrenheit. (A 15-degree difference in temperature will result in an error of about 3 mm in 30 m.)

When taping a slope by breaking tape, it is best to proceed downhill. The head chainperson carries a short plumb line or a 2-m rod (the latter is easier to handle). Keeping the tape taut and level, the head chainperson holds the rod or plumbline vertically to establish a point on the ground directly under the zero end of the tape. The tape must be kept horizontal; if the end of the tape is half a meter above or below horizontal, an error of 3 mm is produced: this is not much, but over a long distance, the cumulative error could become significant. Greater error may be introduced by allowing the tape to go slack or caused by lateral pull due to windy conditions. Both chainpersons should position themselves on the right-hand side of the tape and take up any slack in the tape (gently but firmly) before measurements are read. The process of measuring and recording is continued until the desired distance down the slope has been covered. The procedure of measuring distance on a slope by breaking tape sounds simple enough but takes practice.

---

of each site with flagging or wire flags ("pin-flags") and to identify the approximate center of the site with a metal tag or other marker. This point, often called the **site reference point,** is the central point for mapping and also is the point that will be "tied" to the outside world by locating its position in reference to the USPLSS, Global Positioning System (explained later), or other locational system.

BOX 9.6
Obtaining Slope Reduction and Difference in Elevation by Clinometer or Abney Level

You can measure slope distance without breaking tape by means of two special pieces of equipment: a **clinometer** to measure the angle of the slope and a **scientific notation pocket calculator** of the type that displays trigonometric functions. When this method of downslope measurement is performed, the tape is not kept horizontal, but instead parallels the surface of the slope.

The rear chainperson measures the angle of the slope (eye to target) using the clinometer. (Certain types of compasses, such as the Brunton, have built-in clinometers: turn the Brunton on its side to read the angle of incline.) Suunto and other companies make special clinometers that display both degree and percent of slope. Horizontal distance on sloping ground can be ascertained using a Suunto clinometer equipped with a **secant scale:** tape the slope distance, read the secant value, and divide the measured slope distance by that value to obtain horizontal distance.

Other than a clinometer, a good instrument to use for obtaining slope measurement is the **Abney level,** widely used by foresters (Figure 9.17). Optional types of scales for Abney levels include scales calibrated in degrees; percent of slope (one unit on the Abney arc represents a change of 1 ft in elevation for every 100 ft of horizontal distance); or topographic units (one unit on the arc equals 1 ft in elevation for each chain, or 66 ft, in horizontal distance) (R. L. Wilson 1982, 1985). Abney levels measure the angle between the horizontal plane and the slope incline. The horizontal plane is represented by a bubble in a level attached to the Abney; the slope angle is the line-of-sight down the incline to a target, as indicated by the reading on the Abney arc. The Abney level offers an advantage over clinometers in that it has a 5X telescope. Some models are equipped with a useful **stadia reticle** (explained later in this chapter).

As an example of how an Abney level is used, referring to Figure 9.17, let us assume that the measured distance downslope is 30.00 m and the slope angle (determined with an appropriately scaled clinometer or Abney level) is 12 degrees. Using the trigonometric functions of a scientific notation pocket calculator, display the cosine of 12 degrees, which is 0.9781476. To reduce slope distance (SD = 30.00 m) to horizontal distance (HD, unknown), multiply cos 12 degrees (0.9781476) by 30.00 m, which yields 29.344428; hence, HD = 29.34 m, as shown in the following calculator solution:

Find HD (A–B):

HD cos 12°

Enter	Press	Display
12°	cos	0.9781476
	×	
30	=	29.344428

HD = 29.34 m

To determine difference in elevation (DE) in the same configuration, use sin 12°, as shown in the following calculator solution:

Find DE (B–C):

DE sin 12°

Enter	Press	Display
12°	sin	0.2079117
	×	
30	=	6.2373507

DE = 6.24 m

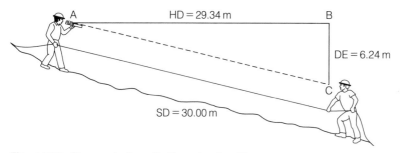

Figure 9.17 Slope reduction with Abney level and tape, showing taped slope distance (SD) (Point A to C) in relation to horizontal distance (HD) (Point A to B) and difference in elevation (DE) (Point B to C).

A prominent natural or cultural feature located on a site in a convenient, central location can be designated as the site reference point, which may be permanent or temporary, depending on the requirements of a given project. (Installation of *permanent* points, such as the site datum point, is discussed later.) Probably the best type of site reference point is an established (monumented) section corner, USGS bench mark, or some other type of survey marker that is part of an established control system. Needless to say, ready-made, convenient datum points are not often found on archaeological sites, so you will probably have to install your own: for example, by driving a metal or plastic stake into the ground or nailing an aluminum tag to a tree trunk. It is important to bear in mind that almost any type of reference point, whether temporary or permanent, affects the site. Hence, permission to install reference points must be obtained from the landowner or appropriate administrative agency. The reference point should be identifiable, but not so conspicuous that it defaces the site or attracts undue attention. Wooden stakes eventually decay or may be pushed out of the ground by frost or animals; steel reinforcing rod (rebar) may quickly rust in alkaline soil. Survey stakes made of polyvinyl chloride are good reference markers. Rust-, rot-, and shatter-proof, these heavy-duty plastic survey stakes are orange or white in color (see Appendix B, "General Supply Sources").

The site reference point serves two purposes: it is the *internal* reference point for mapping the site features, and it is the terminal point of the directions that you provide to guide other archaeologists to the site; hence, it is referenced *externally*. If a section corner or other established survey marker is used as a reference point, its location may be indicated on the pertinent USGS 7.5-minute topographic quadrangle (remembering, of course, that many section corners could have been established since the map was compiled and published). If there is an established survey marker within reasonable distance of a site, locate it, and from it, take compass bearings to the site reference point and, of course, also measure the distance from it to the site reference point—working from the "known" (i.e., a monumented section corner) to the "unknown" (the archaeological site reference point).

Drafting a Site Record Map

Site record maps can be drafted by several methods. One of these, the **radial method,** is performed by standing at a site reference (datum) point. Mark its position at the center of the map form, determine true north and, from the reference point, take a bearing or azimuth to the first feature. Lay out the bearing on the map using a protractor. Pace or tape the distance from the datum point to the feature and scale this distance on the map. (A convenient scale is 1 cm = 1 m.) Plot the details of the

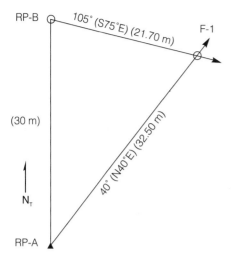

Figure 9.18   Feature 1 (F-1) is located from Reference Point A (RP-A) by laying out a base line (RP-A to RP-B) 30 m long and taking compass readings from both reference points to F-1, which is located approximately at the intersection of the two readings. (Both azimuths and bearings are shown.) The distance from RP-A and RP-B to F-1 can be taped if necessary.

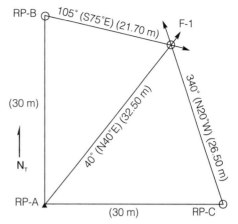

Figure 9.19   Feature 1 (F-1) is located from Reference Point A (RP-A) by laying out a base line (RP-A to RP-B) 30 m long and taking compass readings from both reference points to F-1, the position of which is further defined by taking a compass reading from Reference Point C (RP-C), established 30 m east of RP-A. F-1 lies within a small triangle formed by the three compass readings. Distances can be taped if necessary.

feature on an appropriate form. Return to the site reference point, take a bearing to the next feature, and continue from feature to feature until the site is mapped. Because each bearing originates at the site reference point, mapping from a central point outward to each feature is labor-intensive. However, this method usually reduces cumulative error.

An alternative means of mapping, the **intersection method,** is accurate and (after some practice) usually quicker than the radial method. The location of a feature is ascertained by sighting on it from two or more reference points (Figure 9.18). From the site reference (Reference Point A), lay out a line 30 m long in any direction (if you prefer, oriented true north) and establish Reference Point B. Take bearings on the feature (F-1) from both points A and B. The point where the two bearings intersect establishes the approximate location of F-1. The distances from points A and B to F-1 need not be taped unless great accuracy is required.

The accuracy of points plotted by the intersection method is increased, of course, by taking three

or more bearings (or azimuths) that converge on F-1, forming a small triangle—the surveyor's **triangle of error** (Figure 9.19). If the triangle of error is unacceptably large, one or more of the bearings is probably inaccurate. Triangulation is particularly useful when the feature to be located is inaccessible—e.g., on the opposite side of a river. By means of triangulation, the position of a remote feature can be determined without actually having to measure directly to it. (This procedure is aided by application of a little trigonometry; see Box 9.7.)

Use of the portable KVH DataScope, Haglöf Forestor DME 201, or a comparable device to obtain distance and direction greatly expedites the procedures just described. Briefly, to use the KVH DataScope, stand at the site reference point and take the direction (bearing or azimuth) to each feature. A helper first carries a target to each feature; the approximate intervening distance is determined by using the DataScope's rangefinder mode, which optically displays a vertical "stack" of segments that the user matches against the height of

BOX 9.7

USING HORIZONTAL ANGLES TO OBTAIN THE POSITION OF FEATURES AT UNKNOWN DISTANCES

The compass—and its more complex big brother the transit or theodolite—can be used to lay out horizontal angles, which, with a little trigonometry, allow you to determine the distance from a given point to an inaccessible feature. For example, we wish to know the distance across a river from Point A to Point B (Figure 9.20a). We can use the Pythagorean Theorem to find an unknown side in a right triangle, or a trigonometric ratio using the tangent of the given angle. We can also use oblique angles (Figure 9.20b).

In Figure 9.20a, we wish to determine the length of the unknown side (c). From Point A lay out right-angle line h (30 m long) and establish Point C. From Point C, use a compass or transit to take the azimuth to Point B across the river; in Figure 20a the angle formed is 39 degrees. With one known angle (39 degrees) and one known distance (h; Point A to Point C = 30 m), the distance from Point A to Point B can be computed as follows:

$$\tan C = \frac{c}{h} \text{ or } \tan 39° = \frac{c}{30}$$

Calculator Solution:

Enter	Press	Display
30	×	30.
39°	tan	0.809784
	=	24.293521

$$c = 24.29 \text{ m}$$

In Figure 9.20b, we wish to find the distance E to F across a river. To find E to F, begin at Point E, lay out line E to D (distance 30 m). Use a compass or transit to measure angle E (117 degrees). Then occupy point D, take the azimuth to Point F, and measure the angle (41 degrees). Use the trigonometric Sum of Angles Principle to obtain angle F:

Calculate Angle F:

$$\begin{array}{r} 180° \\ -117° \text{ (Angle E)} \\ \hline 63° \\ -41° \text{ (Angle D)} \\ \hline 22° = \text{Angle F} \end{array}$$

Formula for EF:

$$EF = \frac{(DE)(\sin D)}{\sin F}$$

Calculator Solution:

Enter	Press	Display
30	×	30.
41°	sin ÷	19.68
22°	sin =	52.539

$$EF = 52.54 \text{ m}$$

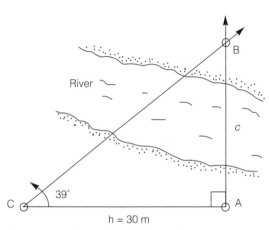

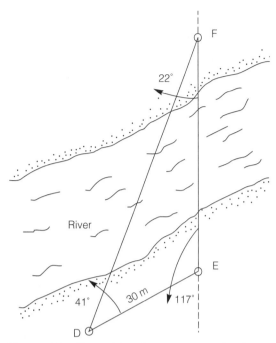

Figure 9.20a Determining distance from a given point (A) to a point at an unknown distance (B) across a river. Point C is established 30 m west of Point A; the angle to Point C is obtained (39 degrees). With one known angle (39 degrees) and one known distance (A to C), the unknown distance *c* (A–B) can be computed (see text). Distance *c* is 24.29 m.

Figure 9.20b Determining distance across a river from a given point (E) along a line of survey to Point F using an oblique angle. To fine E to F, we require angle F. From E, shoot to F (0°); establish Point D 30 m from Point E, Angle 117°; occupy Point D, shoot to F (41°). To compute the distance E–F, the Sum of Angles Principle is used (see text). The distance from Point E to Point F is 52.54 m.

the target in order to determine range (distance) to the target.

The Haglöf Forestor DME 201 consists of two pieces of equipment—a small transponder, which you attach to a camera tripod and position at the site reference point, and a small, handheld measuring instrument. Carrying the latter, proceed in a 360-degree circle around the transponder (from feature to feature). The push of a button displays an accurate measurement from each feature to the transponder. The DME 201 measures in the English system or tenths with, according to the manufacturer, an accuracy of ±1 percent (see Appendix B, 8).

Distance can also be measured with small handheld devices like the Sonin Electronic Distance Measurer, which measures up to 60 ft without a target and up to 250 ft with a target, using a

beam of infrared light. (The line of sight between the sending unit and the target must be direct and unobstructed.) Another useful instrument for measuring distance, inclination, and slope distance is the Criterion Measuring Laser. Depending on the model, the Criterion will compute the distance or the *X-Y-Z* coordinates (explained below) in reference to the target (see Appendix B, Forestry Suppliers, Inc.).

The topography, or landforms, of the site can be indicated by drawing contour lines (discussed earlier in this chapter). Contours can be **interpolated** (approximated) by referring to the contour lines on the appropriate USGS quadrangle and transferring them to the site record map, augmenting local detail by direct observation. Better results, of course, can be obtained by mapping with instruments, discussed below.

When preparing a site record map, keep in mind that each map must display a title block, conventionally but not invariably located in the lower right-hand corner. The title block presents the map's vital statistics: the name and/or number of the site, the map scale, a north arrow, the names of the mapping team, the date, and a key or legend explaining all symbols that appear on the map.

SITE DATUM POINT AND SITE GRID

We have seen (Chapter 4) that before an archaeological site is sampled it is essential to establish a control system to aid in recording the exact location (provenience) of specimens, features, and other phenomena, as well as to guide the process of controlled surface collecting (Redman 1987; Redman and Watson 1970) and site testing (Kintigh 1988; Renfrew and Bahn 1991). The most widely used control system is the site grid, originating from an initial point called the site datum. In this section we will explain how to establish a datum point and lay out a site grid, beginning with small grids constructed with simple equipment and progressing to very large grids laid out with precision surveying instruments.

Establishing the Datum Point

As the major control point for site investigation, the **datum** point has much in common with the site reference point previously discussed. They can be one and the same, except that the datum point usually needs to be *permanent* because it may eventually serve as the reference point for future work at the site. Horizontal and vertical measurements of artifact and feature provenience are taken and recorded in reference to the datum point. Established survey points, such as section corners and bench marks, are sometimes found on or near archaeological sites, but if a permanent marker is not at hand, one can be created with a length of corrosion-resistant pipe set in concrete, PVC pipe filled with concrete, or of course, by installing a "brass-cap" marker affixed to metal pipe.

Each datum should be identified in the field. Licensed land surveyors often monument survey points with a length of metal pipe or reinforcing rod ("rebar"), to which is affixed a plastic cap. The surveyor stamps essential register information into the plastic cap. The datum point should display the name and address of one's affiliation or sponsoring agency. (Many datum points have been obliterated because no one was aware of their purpose or importance.) It's good practice to install auxiliary **witness points** to aid in relocating the principal datum, and to serve as reference points during instrument survey (explained below).

There are two fundamentally different approaches to the placement of the principal site datum point. Some archaeologists install a central datum point; others prefer an off-site datum (or a combination of both). The **central datum,** as its name implies, is located near the center of the site. The grid control system originates at the central datum point and expands outward in all directions. Most grid systems are based on the rectangular (Cartesian) coordinate system. The Y-axis is the meridian; the X-axis, the base line. Measurements are made in each quadrant (NE, SE, NW, SW) originating from the central datum point (Figure 9.21).

Central placement of the datum point has the advantage of making it readily accessible for mapping, but on the other hand, a central datum is often (invariably, it would seem) situated in an area that eventually has to be excavated. Another disadvantage of a central datum is that the provenience of artifacts and features is measured in different directions depending on which quadrant they occupy. For example, in the NE quadrant, provenience might be measured north and east, in the SW quadrant, south and west, and so on, a procedure that might produce errors in recording provenience.

An **off-site datum** is usually placed southwest of the site, well outside its estimated perimeter. The grid system originating from the datum then extends north and east over the entire site. Grid numbering may begin at an arbitrary point—for example, N100 m/E100 m. This is a "false-origin" system, the basis of most geographic coordinate grid systems, such as the UTMS and SPCS. Pro-

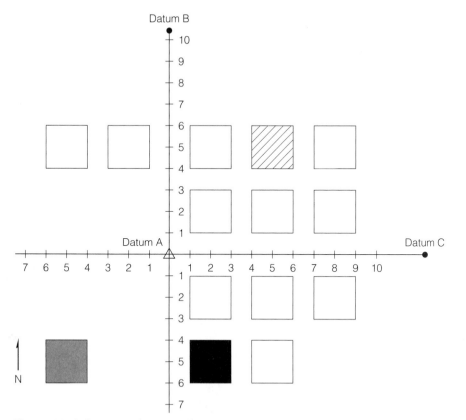

Figure 9.21 Infinite grid with balks. The control point of the black unit is S4/E1. The hachured unit is N4/E4. The gray unit is S4/W4. Note that the site meridian and base lines are protected by leaving an unexcavated 1-m-wide balk on each side of the control lines. The grid is oriented true north.

venience coordinates are n meters north and n meters east of the datum point. These measurements, based on the X and Y coordinates of plane trigonometry, are standard reference coordinates in modern electronic total-station and EDM surveying instruments (described later in this chapter) and can be integrated conveniently with computer graphics data-display programs (Monmonier 1993).

Grid Theory

Before beginning to construct an archaeological control grid, it is important to consider exactly what use is to be made of the grid. Will it identify only a few units needed to control limited collec-

tion of surface specimens, or is it to be used for extensive probability-based sampling? Will the site be sampled by "test pits" or by a series of trenches? These questions are important, because a grid consisting of a datum point and a few key sampling units is relatively easy to construct, whereas an extensive grid with "master" units and internal subunits is labor-intensive and time-consuming to lay out, even using sophisticated surveying equipment, especially if the terrain is undulating or heavily vegetated. (See Box 9.8 for information on expedient gridding.)

At present, many site excavations are based on some form of probability sampling (see Chapter 3). Units from which surface collections will be

BOX 9.8

LAYING OUT EXPEDIENT GRIDS AND PICKET LINES

The key to laying out an expedient grid is to be able to stake a straight line and to "turn" a right angle in relation to that line. A reasonably straight line can be constructed by a two-person team using stakes (surveyor's lathes) aligned by eye. The alignment of stakes is called a **picket line.** Place Stake 1 at the datum point and Stake 3 along the desired line of sight, say at 60 m. While one member of the team sights from Stake 1 to Stake 3, the other installs Stake 2 at 30 m. Stake 5 is then set in line with 2 and 3; Stake 4 is set by eye, and so forth. Picket lines can be offset around obstacles by placing 2 or 3 pickets to the right or left of the line, then returning by offset to the original line. A 90-degree angle can be turned at any point using a surveyor's right-angle prism (see Appendix B, 9), or even by sighting along straightedges nailed firmly together to form a horizontally mounted right-angled cross (Hobbs 1983), a simple device comparable to the *groma*, which Roman engineers used to lay out their celebrated roads (Dilke 1971; Stone 1928).

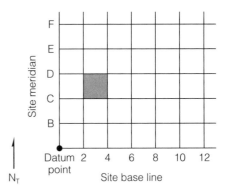

Figure 9.22   Grid in 2-m increments established on a site; grid orientation is true north. The shaded square is Unit C/2.

obtained, or which are to be tested or excavated, are identified by an appropriate sampling strategy, such as stratified random sampling, augmented by purposive or discretionary sampling (Binford 1964; Mueller, ed. 1975; Renfrew and Bahn 1991; Thomas 1989).

Some archaeologists use a letter and number system to identify units: those along the meridian are identified by letter; units along the base line are numbered, or vice-versa (Figure 9.22). Regardless of the system used, the purpose of unit identification is to enable archaeologists to establish the provenience of finds in each unit in reference to the unit control stake without having to refer to the principal datum, which may be located some distance away. The horizontal (north and east) provenience of specimens and features is measured from the unit control stake. Vertical provenience (depth)

is ascertained in reference to the elevation of the unit control stake, in turn referenced to the datum plane (discussed later in this chapter).

Constructing a Small Grid

A small grid—covering, say, 2 m^2, 5 m^2, or 10 m^2—can be laid out using a portable "jiffy right angle" made of wood or light metal, such as aluminum. The wood version is made of three pieces of straight, knot-free 1-x-2-inch batten (furring strips) or similar wood strips available at any lumberyard. Cut each to a length of 2 m, drill and bolt two pieces (arms) together at one end, and using a carpenter's square, position them to form a 90-degree angle. Place the third member at a 45-degree angle across the two right-angled boards, drill holes at each conjoining end, and bolt the angled member to the two arms.

To lay out a 2-m^2 unit, place the corner of the angle on the unit control point. Using a suitable compass, align one arm of the angle to true (or magnetic) north. The other arm, of course, extends east. Level the angle frame and install a unit marker (a stake or spike) at the north and east ends of each arm of the angle. Then invert the angle outward, so that the ends of the arms touch the north and east unit markers, and install the northeast corner unit marker. A good feature of the jiffy right angle is that it can be leveled to compensate for

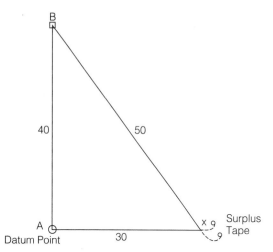

Figure 9.23 Laying out a right angle (as between the site meridian and the base line) with tapes by applying the Pythagorean Theorem. Meridian line A–B is staked; tapes are extended from A and B and adjusted to meet at Point X, which is then staked.

Plane Table Method. Prepare the plane table by setting it up over the datum point. Attach drafting material (discussed below) to the table surface. Center the table over the datum by visual estimate, or use a plumb-bob attached to the end of the tripod column. Level the plane table at a convenient height, using the built-in level or a small carpenter's level. Draw a north-south meridian on the drafting material and, perpendicular to it, an east-west base line. (The north-south line usually runs along the length of the table; the east-west line across it.) Orient the plane table to true north by placing the compass (adjusted for magnetic declination) on the north-south line. (Make sure that metal objects do not deflect the compass needle.)

Place a triangular engineer's scale on the north-south meridian and use it to sight along the north line. Have a helper run the tape out along the north line to the north for the desired distance, say 30 m. (Guide the helper by means of hand signals or radio.) When the correct distance is reached, the helper drives a stake on line as you direct. (If the helper handles the tape and a third person does

slope. The main drawback is its weight, but it can be folded into three parallel lengths for transportation. Its appearance can be enhanced by painting alternate half-meter increments red and white. Lightweight jiffy right angles can be made from metal yardsticks or other materials. As a point of historical interest, this device is not unlike those used in antiquity to lay off a right angle (Mason 1953).

Taping is another method of constructing a small grid. See Box 9.9.

the staking, the process goes a lot faster.) Place grade stakes or wire flags at suitable intervals along the line.

Having established and staked the meridian, "turn" a 90-degree angle to lay out the base line, running east. Simply align the engineer's scale (or alidade, discussed below) along the east-west line on the drafting material and sight along the line—this is a **foresight.** Your assistant places a stake at E30 on the line of sight as you direct. The grid can be expanded indefinitely, but, before moving the plane table, it's a good idea to install as many stakes along the meridian and base line as may be needed.

To expand the grid, mark the datum point with a stake or wire flag, then set up the plane table at a new station, e.g., N30. Orient the table by taking a **backsight** on the stake or marker at the previously occupied datum point. Taking a backsight is accomplished by placing the sighting guide exactly along the meridian and sighting back (south) along it to the datum point marker. Rotate (orient) the plane table so that you are sighting directly at the datum point. Secure the plane table rotation lock (explained below), then turn a 90-degree angle east from N30, tape 30 m east, and establish N30/E30. (The distance from E30 to N30/E30 should, of course, also be 30 m.) Exactly the same procedure is followed to lay out a grid with instruments, e.g., an alidade (which rests on the surface of the plane table) or a transit mounted on a tripod (discussed below).

Constructing Very Large Grids

When dealing with large sites, archaeologists often need to lay out extensive control systems. For example, many archaeological data recovery projects are based on identification and examination of **quadrats**—grid squares that are often 500 m or more on a side (Mueller 1975). Extensive grids can be constructed by establishing a datum point from which a meridian is extended north and a base line extended east. Using a suitable compass (described earlier), control lines can be run across rough terrain and through dense vegetation. The sighting compass is ideal for the job—if the control lines are

oriented to magnetic north or if you adjust the compass to compensate for magnetic declination. Handheld GPS units (see discussion later) can be used to establish the corners and boundaries of quadrats—vegetation and terrain permitting. Grid boundaries can be marked expediently with flagging or by means of a **hip chain,** a device used by foresters to measure and mark temporary lines. The "chain" box contains white or orange biodegradable thread, the maximum length of which is 2,743 m. To define a line, simply attach the end of the thread to a tree or stake and proceed in the desired direction. The hip chain measures the amount (feet or meters) of thread dispensed. The thread line can be augmented at intervals with biodegradable flagging for greater visibility (see Appendix B, 10, for suppliers of hip chain). If the terrain is not heavily vegetated, units can be staked by constructing long picket lines (see Box 9.8 earlier) or by means of a surveying compass or transit, the operation of which is presented in the next section of this chapter.

Electronic Stake-out. Very large grid arrays can be laid out rapidly using electronic equipment receiving locational data from the Global Positioning System, described in the next section. An example of such equipment is the Trimble GPS Total Station, by means of which coordinates of centimeter-level accuracy are calculated. When you occupy each field point, the system displays the coordinates of that point, which you write on the grid stake—an obvious time-saver for subsequent operations, such as controlled surface collecting or site mapping, because a staked and identified grid system is created during a single stake-out operation.

THE GLOBAL POSITIONING SYSTEM (GPS) AND MAPPING

The **Global Positioning System** (GPS), developed by the U.S. military service, is a satellite system for navigation that permits you to determine your (nearly) exact position 24 hours a day, any place on earth, in any weather conditions. The GPS space-based radio positioning and navigation system—called NAVSTAR (**NAV**igation by **S**atellite **T**iming **A**nd **R**anging) or, generally, GPS—consists of a constellation of 24 satellites, each of which orbits the earth twice a day, emitting precise GPS time and position information. A portable (or handheld) GPS receiver obtains signals from four or more satellites to calculate the user's position anywhere on earth. The basis of the system is accurate time: GPS satellites are equipped with atomic clocks (accurate to within 1 second/300,000 years). By measuring the time interval between transmission and reception of satellite signals, the GPS receiver calculates the distance between the user and the satellites and, by means of precise distance measurements, provides a "position-fix" (Leick 1990; Letham 1995; Logsdon 1992; National Aeronautics and Space Administration 1977; USDI/BLM 1991a).

The importance of GPS for archaeology lies in the fact that with this positioning system you can determine exact location coordinates and elevation *in the field* (Bock 1990; Hofmann-Wellenhof et al. 1994). Moreover, these data can be collected by a single individual, carrying a small, lightweight GPS unit (Schulman 1991). For example, when you occupy on-site points, the GPS system obtains the horizontal position, which is displayed as latitude/longitude or UTM, within certain limitations of accuracy (discussed below). Some GPS units also display the approximate altitude of these points (Exon 1993). Data are accessed and displayed rapidly, permitting you to write this information directly on site unit control stakes. The GPS data are collected and stored for future map compilation (Wells 1986).

Absolute GPS positioning accuracy is subject to the U.S. Department of Defense (DOD) 100-m Selective Availability (S/A) policy, under the requirements of which GPS data are randomly degraded so that 95 percent of the Standard Positioning Signals (SPS) (Coarse Acquisition [CA]) codes available to the general public are accurate only to within 49 ft (about 15 m) to 328 ft (about 100 m) of the actual ground position, whereas DOD Precise Positioning Service (PPS) signals available to the military are accurate to within 1 m (Alexander 1992; Kleusberg and Langley 1990). Because of

selective availability, you might arrive within 15 m of a given location on one occasion, but at another time you might only be within 100 m of the same location. The GPS signals available to civilians are randomly degraded in the interests of national defense. Without selective availability, even civilian receivers would be accurate to 15 m. It is likely that the S/A policy will be discontinued in the not-too-distant future, providing 1-m accuracy for GPS receivers used by civilians.

The GPS system is extraordinarily useful for locating archaeological sites in the field. Moreover, it can *relocate* sites (if the coordinates of the site are known) either from previous on-site GPS readings or by means of map coordinates (Crowther 1994). Optimally, you simply enter the coordinates of a site, and the handheld GPS receiver will guide you to that location. It will track your course automatically; indicate the direction you are heading, how fast you are going, and how much farther you have to go; and predict your estimated time of arrival (Magellan Systems Corporation 1992). Most GPS receivers require a short period of time (about 15 minutes) to "initialize"—that is, to obtain initial almanac information from the satellites. This is called "time to first fix," after which position acquisition is very rapid. Some GPS units, such as the Magellan GPS Trailblazer, can track up to 12 satellites and provide accuracy to 15 m. (See Appendix B, 11, for supplier sources for all GPS units discussed here.)

The Trimble GPS Total Station is a compact system that can be carried and used by one person. With it you can obtain centimeter-level *X-Y-Z* coordinates while staking out a point on a site, with obvious savings of field time. The GPS package gives stake-out data, local control (site unit position), topographic detail for contours, and boundary positions to stake out the estimated site perimeter.

The Trimble GPS Pathfinder PRO XL is capable of computing the location of any point on earth in 1 second with an accuracy of less than 1 m (depending on selective availability and local environmental factors). The manufacturer states that with an optional package the user can pinpoint a location to within 10 cm. The system records readings en route in a moving vehicle or on foot. Marine archaeologists will be interested in the system's ability to locate and map objects under water with sonar or side-scan sonars (Samuel and McGeehan 1990). The system works well under most types of forest canopy and also can guide you to return to specific locations, such as section corners or site datum points. Perhaps best of all, the system (instrument pack, antenna, and handheld display unit) is contained in a small backpack that can be transported easily by one person.

Another Trimble package, the pocket-size GeoExplorer GPS, has an integrated six-channel receiver and antenna, offers 2- to 5-m resolution, tracks up to eight GPS satellites, stores over 9,000 three-dimensional GPS positions, and includes a user-selectable map coordinate system display. The unit is powered by four standard AA batteries or a vehicle cigarette lighter adapter. The GeoExplorer GPS is capable of computing positions to a horizontal accuracy of better than 5 m (or 2 m, with averaging of differentially corrected data). Other handheld GPS units include the Trimble Scoutmaster (Figure 9.24), the Garmin GPS 45, and the Sokkia Spectrum GPS.

Handheld GPS units display data in reference to grid coordinates. Some grids used for archaeology are latitude and longitude, Universal Transverse Mercator (UTM) system, and the Ordnance Survey of Great Britain (OSGB). (Most GPS units do not display data for the State Plane Coordinate System.) The standard datum for GPS is the World Geodetic System 1984 (WGS 84); all receivers present locations in terms of WGS 84. (The North American Datum [NAD 83] is, for this purpose, equivalent to WGS 84; however, it is advisable to set the GPS unit to the datum given on the specific map being used.)

Most handheld GPS units provide bearing, true north, and magnetic north modes; some offer plotting and automatic tracking modes, point-to-point calculations, time signals, even the times of sunrise and sunset. Some currently available GPS units include optional download software and input/output formats. Some receivers accept data in ASCII format and connect directly to the computer's RS-232 port.

Figure 9.24 The Trimble Scoutmaster GPS is a hand-held, personal navigational device weighing 14 ounces. It stores 250 locations and displays the user's latitude, longitude and altitude, and UTM coordinates. It can also display locations in reference to the British national grid system (OSGB) and optional TOPO GPS (7.5 USGS) map locations.

The data collected by GPS systems can be transferred to geographic information systems (GIS) databases (discussed later) by means of various software (Davis et al. 1991; Gibbs and Krajewski 1993; Russ 1992). Data can be exported to GIS formats like ARC/INFO, Intergraph, and computer-assisted drafting packages like AutoCAD. With the Trimble GeoExplorer and optional PFINDER software, it is possible to define and collect a full set of descriptive features and attributes of given points (stations) while in the field. You can ascertain the location of a site datum point, for example, and input its description.

Historical archaeologists can use programs such as TIGER 5 (in Atlas GIS), which, based on USGS 1:100,000-series quadrangles, displays street maps of the entire United States, or City Streets for Windows, an electronic mapping program built around an extensive database of metropolitan area maps that includes search, display, and customization capabilities (Gervin 1992). Used with this system is the Marco Polo GPS Type II PCMCIA Card, which provides on-screen latitude and longitude coordinates—and even displays on the system's maps a graphic of a tiny "car" to indicate the user's location (see Appendix B, 12). Street Atlas USA contains on a single CD-ROM a database of every street in the United States, including place names, state boundaries, cities, and points of interest (Appendix B, 3). The EtakMap databases display roads and streets corresponding to the 1:24,000-series topographic quadrangles in urban areas and the 1:100,000 quadrangles in rural areas. Roads are named and classified by type, address ranges, zip codes, and so forth (see Appendix B, 13).

Archaeological sites and their environments can be mapped quickly and accurately using differential GPS to measure control points (Puterski 1992). Custom or archival stereo photographs are optically scanned and the control points are matched with ground features on the photographs. These images are analyzed by computer software to produce a detailed topographic map of the site (see "Computer-assisted Site Mapping," below). The literature on GPS applications is literally and figuratively growing skyward; see Wells et al. (1992).

ARCHAEOLOGICAL SITE PLAN MAPS

Site plan maps display numerous detailed measurements and document the horizontal provenience of specimens and features. Site plan maps should achieve three principal objectives. First, this type of map is one of the principal means of recording details of cultural and natural features. Second, provenience control is obtained by means of a site grid, which is shown on the map in relation to cultural and natural features. Third, the site plan map provides a key to cross sections (profiles), depicting the stratigraphy of the site and the vertical provenience of specimens and features. Site plan maps are often so intricate, however, that an archaeological cartographer or graphic artist must simplify and clarify them for publication. Normally, surveying instruments are used to obtain data for complex site plan maps.

Instruments Used in Site Plan Mapping

There are three fundamentally different "packages" of surveying instruments. One of these, the plane table and alidade, enables archaeologists to draw large site maps on drafting material directly in the field. The second group of instruments includes transits, theodolites, and engineer's levels. These produce accurate data, which are recorded in field notebooks or saved in computer files and used to compile the map in the office, rather than in the field. A third instrument package, developed comparatively recently, is the Global Positioning System (GPS), which, as we have seen, enables archaeologists to lay out site grids, obtain data for topographic maps, plot feature locations, and acquire other data rapidly in the field, with integrated local X-Y-Z coordinates, latitude and longitude, and UTM coordinates.

The place where maps are drafted is important, in view of the fact that if one uses traditional equipment (much of which, as we have said, is still functional), errors made in the field or in data transcription can be detected and corrected on-site, rather than in the office, days or weeks later. Modern surveying and computer technology obtains data on-site, helping to mitigate such problems. It is always desirable, of course, before leaving the field site, to prepare draft versions of maps for careful checking. Increasingly powerful portable ("notebook") computers and portable printers help make this possible, permitting data retrieval and printout, even in remote locations.

Let us compare two traditional instrument systems and consider some of their advantages and disadvantages.

Plane Table and Alidade.   The plane table and alidade outfit consists of a flat, tablelike drawing board mounted on a tripod that has a special swivel head, enabling the operator to level and orient the table. When the table is level and oriented to true north, it can be clamped in place by means of special lock-rings. The alidade, basically a telescope mounted on a flat metal base-plate or blade, rests on the surface of the plane table but is not attached to it (Figure 9.25). The standard alidade

Figure 9.25   Standard alidade on plane table in use in Nevada desert. Plane table tripod is set up over site datum point; site meridian is staked, background.

(often called a "Gurley" alidade, after one of its principal manufacturers) uses the stadia function (tacheometry, explained below) to obtain distance measurements.

With a standard alidade telescope the operator obtains distance measurements by observing the markings on a stadia rod held on the desired point. The distance from the alidade to the rod can be determined with acceptable accuracy by "reading" the markings on the stadia rod. The rod marks are intercepted by two horizontal stadia wires mounted inside the telescope.

To use this equipment, simply set up the plane table, level and orient it over the site datum point, and sight through the alidade telescope to the stadia rod, which the rodperson holds on the desired survey station. Read the stadia interval to obtain the distance to the station. Draw a line along the beveled edge of the alidade base-plate scaled to represent the actual distance and plot the position of the station on the map.

The standard alidade has been succeeded by various types of advanced instruments (Allen et al. 1993), including the self-reducing alidade (Stanley 1952), the David White SA-5 prism alidade (see Appendix B, Forestry Suppliers Inc.), and the Benchmark electronic alidade (Figure 9.26). The last offers electronic distance measuring (EDM) capabilities, including distance measurement, slope reduction, and other features calculated electronically and displayed digitally, in either English

Figure 9.26   Electronic alidade (IRI, Inc.) self-reducing EDM on plane table. Rodperson (left) holds single prism EDM used for mapping of local detail or archaeological site.

or SI units (see "Electronic Distance Measuring Instruments," below).

Transit, Theodolite, and Engineer's Level. Although these instruments serve different functions and vary in design, for our purposes they are considered as a group. **Transits** enable surveyors to measure horizontal and vertical angles with great accuracy and to lay out roads, bridges, buildings, and other types of construction. Standard "mechanical" transits have been succeeded by electronic distance measuring instruments (EDMI), but because many of the older transits and other instruments comprising this group are still service-able, their operation is considered here. Whether standard or EDMI, transits are used in archaeology primarily to establish very large, accurate site grids, lay out horizontal and vertical control networks on large sites, and acquire provenience data on complex structural sites where high levels of accuracy are required (USDI/BLM 1991b).

Using a transit (or a theodolite, or an engineer's level), the instrument operator records the horizontal angle between a reference point (usually but not invariably true north) and the desired survey point. This information is entered in a notebook or stored in a stand-alone notebook computer, or on advanced instruments, in an integrated (onboard) computer module. Using standard instruments, the respective angles from the site datum to a series of survey stations are determined by reading the fine graduations on a vernier scale or scales. Modern instruments compute the angles automatically; the desired information is compiled by onboard electronics, displayed digitally, and stored for subsequent retrieval. Some models of standard transits are equipped with stadia wires or reticles; modern instruments offer EDM.

The transit concept originates in antiquity. The *dioptra* described by Hero of Alexandria, ca. 120 B.C., consists of a pedestal on which is mounted a detachable sighting table equipped with worm gears for adjusting the table in respect to the horizontal and vertical axes (Cohen and Drabkin 1958). The *dioptra* was a very sophisticated instrument for its time (Figure 9.27).

Reduced to bare essentials, the standard (traditional) transit is a telescope mounted on a horizontal circular protractor. The telescope magnifies from 10 to 30 power (most are in the range of 22 to 27X). Inside the telescope are vertical and horizontal "target" crosswires. (Some transits are equipped with stadia wires or a glass stadia reticle.) The telescope is mounted on vertical supports (standards) attached to a circular upper plate on which is a vernier scale. (Some transits have two opposing vernier scales.) This assembly rotates ("transits") horizontally in reference to a circular lower plate scaled from 0 to 360 degrees. The upper and lower plates are fastened, respectively, to inner and outer

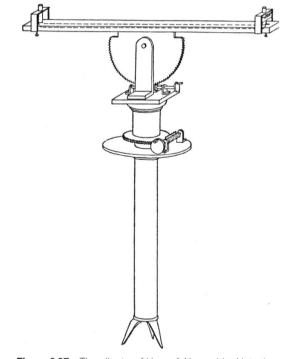

Figure 9.27 The *dioptra* of Hero of Alexandria. Note the geared mechanism to adjust the instrument to any plane between the vertical and horizontal and any position in the plane.

vertical spindles that rotate around the central axis of the horizontal circle. The transit is leveled by means of two small plate vials. Leveling adjustments are made by rotating three (or on some models, four) foot screws that rest on a support plate. The older telescopes are leveled by means of sensitive spirit levels attached to the support plate; modern instruments are leveled by an optical plummet device. Most transits are equipped with a compass, which is mounted between the telescope support standards. The entire transit is mounted on a tripod (Figure 9.28).

Horizontal angles are measured by clamping the lower (horizontal) plate in a fixed position (for example, true north), rotating the telescope (the attached vernier plate moves with it), and sighting along a line (ray) to the target point. The angle between true north and the target point is read by observing the position of the vernier index in refer-

Figure 9.28   Standard mechanical transit. This type of transit is rugged and dependable and can measure vertical and horizontal angles with great accuracy.

ence to the underlying graduated horizontal circle. The angle can be read in degrees on the horizontal circle, and minutes and seconds on the vernier scale. Angles can be used to calculate distance by trigonometry (see Box 9.7).

On older instruments, vertical angles are measured by reading the vertical arc attached to the telescope. This is done by sighting uphill or downhill at a reading on the rod equal to the instrument height, then reading the degrees of angle on the vertical scale and minutes on the vernier. The vertical height of the point sighted above or below the instrument equals:

Slope distance × sin Vertical angle

Many transits are equipped with a stadia reticle for determining distance by tacheometry, but sta-

dia readings obtained by transits are not necessarily more accurate than those obtained with an alidade. Some standard transits permit angles to be read to one-fifth of a second of arc, which is a factor amounting to an error of ca. 1 cm over a distance of 10 km.

It is deceptively easy to describe the use of a transit in general terms and to outline the basic principles of transit surveying, but it is not possible to present here a detailed discussion of how to operate every type of transit, standard or electronic, under all possible field conditions. Comprehensive books on surveying that the reader might consult include Brinker and Minnick (1987), Brinker and Wolf (1984), Evett (1991), Kissam (1981), Moffitt and Bouchard (1991), Pugh (1975), and Ritchie (1988).

The **theodolite** is a precision instrument for measuring extremely accurate angles by vernier readings and distance by stadia. In Europe, the term *theodolite* is more or less synonymous with the American *transit*. In the United States, optical measuring instruments have come into wide use in surveying; these are usually referred to as theodolites; the term *transit* is reserved for standard mechanical transits like those discussed in the preceding section.

Modern theodolites are very compact and streamlined in appearance (Figure 9.29). The vertical and horizontal circles are mounted inside a symmetrical housing. Standard theodolites are leveled by rotating three (or four) footscrews; newer instruments are leveled automatically by an optical plummet. There are no mechanical verniers on modern theodolites. Instead, illuminated micrometers are arranged so that horizontal and vertical angles appear as direct digital displays observed through an eyepiece next to the sighting telescope or are displayed in liquid crystal diode (LCD) windows. Horizontal and vertical degrees are indicated in minutes on two scales; seconds of a degree appear on another, smaller scale. Theodolites permit accurate triangulation, determination of location by astronomical observation, and precise traversing. They are generally more expensive than engineer's transits, but if one is purchasing new equipment, a theodolite might be considered. Most current models of theodolites include or will accept a further refinement, the electronic distance measuring instrument (EDMI), which attaches to standards above the telescope.

The **automatic level** or **self-leveling instrument** is basically an optical system that establishes a level reference plane. Several types of automatic levels have built-in optical systems that allow the operator to view a bubble-level from the telescope sighting position. Taking level sights (for example, in reference to the site datum plane) is accelerated by using an automatic level—one does not spend time adjusting footscrews. Most (but not all) recently manufactured automatic levels include a stadia reticle (ratio 1:100). The horizontal circle is graduated to 1 degree, with vernier reading to 10 minutes. Vertical angles (differences in elevation) cannot be read with levels.

When the automatic level is positioned over the datum point, the level can be rotated in any direction to establish the horizontal datum plane above

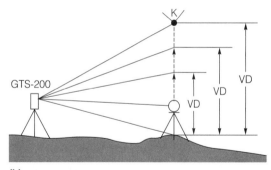

(b)
Remote Elevation Measurement
Height can be measured to points where the prism cannot be placed directly.

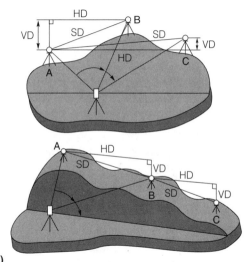

(c)
Missing Line Measurement
Multiple missing line can be drawn between first and last points or last two points.

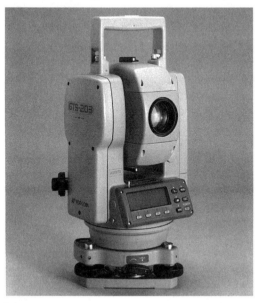

(a)
Figure 9.29   (*a*) A theodolite. TOPCON's Electronic GTS-200 Series Total station instrument provides (*b*) remote elevation measurement, (*c*) missing line measurements, and (*d*) offset. Data are displayed on a four-line LCD. Distances are measured up to 1,400 m with a triple prism array; x, y, z coordinates are calculated.

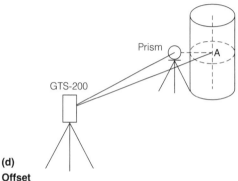

(d)
Offset
For measuring the distance to a point where the prism cannot be placed.

the site. The datum plane elevation is determined by reading the graduations on a survey rod held on the desired point. Inexpensive **construction** or **builder's levels** can be used for distances up to 90 m; the horizontal circle is usually graduated to 1 degree with vernier reading to 15 minutes. Builder's levels and automatic levels can be obtained from suppliers or local equipment rental stores (see Appendix B, 14). It is worth reiterating here that most types of builder's levels or automatic levels cannot be used to read *vertical* angles; moreover, many types of levels are not fitted with a stadia reticle.

Comparative Merits of Plane Table and Alidade Versus Transits. The principal advantage of the standard plane table and alidade system is that the map is created in the field. The outfit is specifically designed for on-site, small-scale topographic mapping, which is exactly what the archaeological mapmaker does. There is, however, a trade-off in plane table mapping—extreme accuracy is sacrificed for the ability to create a map on-site; detail is added by **interpolation** (a cartographer's term meaning "to add detail by estimation").

Mapping by transit, theodolite, or engineer's level is extremely accurate, but mistakes made in the field (even when using electronic equipment) will not necessarily become evident until the map is compiled from the field data. Drastic errors or omissions may be disastrous if it is not possible to return to the field. One way to have the advantages of both systems, of course, is to use an alidade that offers electronic distance measurement (EDM) and other electronic features. A combination of the two systems is particularly effective: an EDM transit or GPS equipment is used to establish the site grid; topographic and archaeological detail is plotted using one or more EDMI, GPS, or conventional plane table outfits.

Instruments for Distance Measurement

There are basically two methods of determining distance with surveying instruments: stadia (tacheometry) and electronic distance measuring

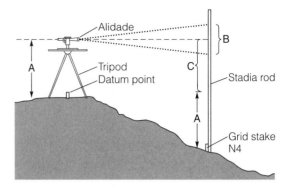

Figure 9.30 Determination of distance and difference in elevation using an alidade and plane table (mounted on a tripod). In the drawing, A identifies the Instrument Height; B the Stadia Interval (dotted lines); C the difference in elevation between the datum plane (broken line) and the Instrument Height. (This figure is subtracted from the datum point elevation to obtain the elevation of grid stake N4.)

(EDM). Both are discussed here because much of the older, rugged, stadia-based conventional equipment is still in use or is available.

By Stadia (Tacheometry). Stadia is a method of measuring distance. The ancient Egyptians probably invented it or, at any rate, used it. Stadia is based on a simple principle: if you look through a hollow tube and sight on a vertical length of rod, you will see only a small part of it when the rod is nearby, but more of it when it is farther away (Figure 9.30).

Stadia measurement by instruments is based on the fact that two very fine stadia "wires" are mounted horizontally a few millimeters apart inside the telescope of an alidade or transit, so that when the surveyor looks through the telescope, the closely adjacent horizontal wires are optically superimposed on the stadia rod. The surveyor observes the amount of the rod intercepted by the two horizontal wires—the observed interval being equivalent to the distance from the instrument to the stadia rod (Figure 9.31). Stadia wires are permanently factory-mounted in the telescope at an exact, carefully determined interval called the

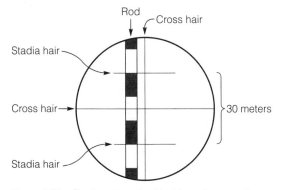

Figure 9.31 Stadia rod marked in 10-cm increments as observed through an alidade or transit telescope. The amount of stadia rod that is visible between the stadia "hairs" (or in modern instruments, etched marks) shows that the stadia rod is exactly 30 m from the instrument position.

K-factor. Most modern instruments have a K-factor of 1:100, so when sighting through the telescope at a stadia rod held at a point 100 ft away, the stadia wires span (intercept) a distance of 1 ft on the rod. (Using a metric rod, approximately 30 cm of the rod is intercepted at a distance of 30 m.) (Some of the older transits used by the BLM and other agencies have a stadia interval of 1:132 for use with the 66-ft chain unit.)

Horizontal stadia intercepts in older instruments are made of very fine wire (even strands of spider web) that extend horizontally across the entire field of view, above and below a horizontal center cross-wire used for leveling. Mistakes can be made if the surveyor confuses a horizontal *stadia* wire with the horizontal center *leveling* wire. Hence, improved surveying instruments offering the stadia feature are usually equipped with short horizontal stadia marks etched on a glass reticle mounted inside the telescope. The stadia marks are horizontal but do not transect the full field of view, whereas the horizontal center leveling mark extends across the entire field of view.

Advantages and Disadvantages of the Stadia Method. The principal advantage of the stadia method is that distance measurements are obtained simply by looking through the telescope and reading the stadia interval while the rodperson holds the stadia rod on the desired station. The stadia interval, multiplied by the K-factor, gives the distance from the instrument to the station. Taping is largely unnecessary. When the stadia method of determining distance is used in conjunction with the triangulation method of finding the position of a feature or station (discussed in a preceding section), the two methods complement each other, and accuracy is increased.

The principal disadvantage of the stadia system, however, is its inherent inaccuracy, which can be introduced by several factors. For example, on older instruments the apparent optical center of the telescope occurs at a point in space slightly beyond the physical center of the telescope. Therefore, apparent stadia distances will be slightly *less* than the actual physical distance. (A correction factor, applicable to the characteristics of a particular instrument as determined by the manufacturer, is usually written inside the instrument case.)

The accuracy of readings obtained by the stadia system also depends to some extent on the user's experience. Graduations on conventional leveling rods are difficult to discern when the rod is far away, and it is very difficult to read accurately the graduations on almost any type of stadia rod on a hot day when heat waves rising from the ground blur and distort the magnified image of the distant rod. It is difficult to take sights into the early morning or late afternoon sun. An inattentive rodperson may move the rod at the wrong time, resulting in an inaccurate reading. Some of these disadvantages can be mitigated by testing the instrument, the stadia rod, (and the rodperson) over known distances and under various conditions before going to the field. An experienced stadia rodperson can make the process of surveying much easier (see Box 9.10).

Electronic Distance Measuring Instruments (EDMI). An **electronic distance measuring (EDM) system** enables one to measure long distances by use of modulated light beams (infrared), microwave, or laser (Rick 1996). Distance is deter-

---

BOX 9.10 SURVEY TARGETS, PRISM RODS, AND RODPERSONS

The person who carries the standard survey target rod is an important member of the surveying team. Proper handling of the survey rod is an art of its own: a skilled rodperson can make the instrument operator's task a great deal easier. The rodperson must be well-informed concerning the tactics of mapping a site. Before mapping a site, it is a good idea for both members of the survey team to inspect the site and decide which points or features are to be mapped. As the two tour the site, they identify points to be mapped and make notes concerning them. Experienced instrument operators sometimes work with two rodpersons, each carrying a target or prism rod.

During the process of surveying, the rodperson places the target or prism rod exactly on each station and holds the rod in a vertical position, which can be achieved by standing with one's feet apart and balancing the rod lightly between the fingers. (A bubble-level device is available that attaches to the rod and assists in keeping the rod vertical; see Appendix B, 15.) It is good practice to hold the rod by its sides so as not to obscure the figures on its face.

An experienced rodperson watches the instrument operator carefully, observes when a sighting is to be made, and positions the rod on-station. When contours are being plotted, the rodperson places the rod close to the line of sight by observing the instrument, thus expediting the process of reading elevations. In heavily vegetated areas the rodperson or assistants may have to deflect obstructing foliage or place the rod in a position where a sighting can be made. The rodperson may have to manipulate the rod to enable a shot to be completed. For example, the rod might have to be "waved" (tipped *slowly* forward and backward along the line of sight) so that the instrument operator can read the exact elevation; "fanned" slowly from side to side so that the operator can locate it in dense vegetation; or "lofted" (elevated) a certain amount to enable a sighting to be made—with the rodperson measuring the additional amount of elevation to add to the reading. (Lofting is done when exact elevations are not required.) In windy conditions, the rodperson must hold the rod as steady as possible for the shot. Conventional leveling rods are difficult to use in stadia surveying. Much to be preferred are special stadia rods that display bold "pennant" or "block E" patterns. These are easily read over long distances under adverse conditions.

Prism clusters, of course, permit accurate sighting over long distances. The handling of prism target rods differs little from conventional target rods, except that the rodperson must be careful not to drop the prism, which is delicate.

---

mined by measuring the amount of time required for a signal emitted by the instrument to reach its target and return. Several EDMI are available; distance readout is given in feet or SI units (meters). The infrared EDMI, the most popular type, ranges from zero to 10,000 ft (about 3,048 m). Microwave EDMs range up to 150 miles, with minimum ranges of 100 ft (30 m). Laser equipment can measure distances from 3 ft to 37 miles (59,546 m). Most of these instruments have an error of less than ± 5 mm (Bird 1989; Price and Uren 1989).

Laser EDMI use one or more prism reflectors to return the signal to the generator. Instruments using microwaves require a transponder to transmit and receive the signal. One of the inherent problems of EDMI is that for all of their great accuracy over long distances, emitted EDM waves or impulses can be reflected or obstructed by dense vegetation and are affected by "noise" generated by heat shimmer. Accuracy of some EDMI decreases at distances of *less than* 30 m. If an EDMI malfunctions or is damaged, it may be almost impossible to repair in the field, whereas one might be able to repair less sophisticated surveying instruments.

An EDMI for archaeological applications is the Topcon DM-A5 (Appendix B, 16), the use of which is the essence of simplicity: turn it on, point it at the target prism (or prism array), touch the "measure" button, and the EDMI measures the distance between the instrument and the target prism. Distance readings are displayed digitally (LCD), with single prism measurements to 2,500 ft (762 m); with three prisms to 3,600 ft (1,097 m). The unit weighs only 2 pounds and has an optional slope reduction calculator.

There are several superior all-purpose surveying systems for those who require extreme accuracy over long distances. These are called **total stations.** Examples are the Topcon GTS-300D-PG series and the Topcon GTS-4/ITS-1 (Appendix B, 17). The latter electronic total station is comprised of a digital theodolite with EDM and an LCD system that displays eight characters to 99,999.999 m. The EDM component measures distances to a one-prism target up to 6,600 ft (about 2,011 m); with three prisms to 8,900 ft (2,713 m); using nine prisms, to 11,800 ft (3,597 m) with an accuracy of ± 3 mm + 2 ppm. The Topcon GTS-4/ITS-1 provides automatic slope reduction measured in meters or feet, corrected for curvature of the earth and refraction conditions. The system offers a 256K RAM card for onboard data collection (capacity up to 5,500 data points including descriptions), which is removable: insert a fresh card to collect additional data. Comparable total station instruments include the Pentax PTS-V series and the Pentax PCS-1S.

Using a combination theodolite-EDM (total station instrument) with self-reducing capability, distance and direction are measured simultaneously and the information is stored in computer memory. Horizontal and vertical angles and slope distance are computed and displayed and, in response to operator-directed commands, the distance and direction coordinates (X and Y) of sighted points are calculated in reference to elevation (zenith angle; Z) or other configurations. The information is stored against accidental loss in solid-state memory devices. The principal drawback in using total station systems is their initial expense.

Another important type of information, topographic data, can be obtained with electronic surveying equipment. Using modern equipment, one sets up an EDMI at a central datum point (preferably but not necessarily of known elevation) and from it obtains and records (by means of the onboard computer) the distance to and elevation of numerous points. The stored data can be downloaded to an office microcomputer or PC. By means of suitable software (e.g., Surfer), the topography (contours) of the surveyed area are calculated by computer and produced graphically by printer or, preferably, plotter (see "Computers and Electronics in Surveying and Mapping").

Radio

The greater the distances involved in surveying, the more important it is for the instrument operator, rodperson, and other members of the survey team to be in contact by radio, either citizen's band (CB) or frequency modulation (FM). The latter is preferable because it greatly reduces extraneous noise. Two-way radio outfits are made with combined headset and voice-activated microphone to permit hands-free operation, a great asset in surveying (see Appendix B, 18).

Helpful Hints. Remember that direct, intense sunlight, rain, fog, dust, and sand adversely affect precision instruments (California Department of Transportation 1984). Set up surveying instruments in the shade and, if possible, avoid the heat of the day. Do not use an instrument downwind from a particularly dusty screening operation; do not leave the instrument standing in a rain or lightning storm or near a highway where the slipstream from passing trucks may topple it. Above all, guard the equipment: do not leave it in the back of a pickup truck or standing unattended in the field.

Lastly, it is strongly and emphatically recommended that beginners learn to use surveying equipment *before* taking it to the field. By all means take courses in surveying if they are available, or consider adding a trained surveyor to your field party: some instruments (e.g., total station theodolites and transits) are highly specialized and, although electronic and wonderfully accurate, may not necessarily be user-friendly to the uninitiated. Advanced types of instruments should, and in some cases must, be operated by well-trained personnel.

Establishing the Site Bench Mark and Datum Plane

When testing or excavating an archaeological site, it is essential to obtain the horizontal and vertical location (provenience) of specimens, features, and stratigraphic units. Horizontal provenience is measured in two dimensions in reference to the **site grid coordinates,** often the X and Y Cartesian coordinates. The third dimension, vertical provenience (the Z coordinate), is measured in reference to the site **datum plane.** The datum plane can be thought of as an invisible ceiling that extends over the entire archaeological site. The depth of stratigraphic units and the vertical provenience of artifacts and features are measured from this overhead plane.

Instrument Height. When you set up a plane table and alidade or transit over a site datum point or bench mark that has a certain ground elevation (say, 100 m), it is evident that the instrument telescope is higher than the ground elevation beneath the instrument. The additional **instrument height** is compensated for by the survey rod, which (so to speak) transfers the instrument height down to the ground elevation. Target rods are available with moveable number-display bands that can be adjusted to compensate for instrument height so that rod readings begin at an even meter.

Site Bench Mark and Datum Plane. The datum plane usually originates at the datum point, provided that the datum point is located on the highest part of the site. However, if the datum point is lower than some parts of the site, it may be desirable to establish a separate **site bench mark** on the highest point of the site. If there is a USGS bench mark on or near the site, so much the better, because the elevation of each USGS bench mark is established, and pertinent information concerning it is given on the bench mark disk. If there is no convenient bench mark, you can establish your own and give it an arbitrary elevation, for example, 100 m.

Two operations are performed using the site bench mark as a control reference. The first of these is to determine the vertical provenience (depth) of cultural and natural features. The second is to map the topography (landforms) of the site by plotting contour lines on the site map. We will explain both operations using the plane table and alidade. (See, however, "The Global Positioning System and Mapping," earlier.)

The plane table is set up, leveled, and oriented over the site bench mark, which is normally on the highest point of the site. The elevations of points below the bench mark can be obtained by taking a series of **radial sightings** and plotting site contour lines. We should point out that these could be two separate operations, because to begin excavation of test units, it is necessary to establish the elevation of each unit control stake. Then, while excavation proceeds, the surveyor can map details of site features and landforms and also plot contour lines.

Plotting Contour Lines

Three "traditional" methods are used to obtain the position of contour lines by direct field survey: the trace contour method, the controlling point method, and the radial method. Because it uses only conventional, nonelectronic equipment, the **trace contour method** is labor-intensive. To find the location of a contour, the rodperson places the rod at a trial location, and the surveyor directs the rodperson up- or downhill until the rod reading indicates the desired contour interval.

The **controlling point method** is useful on archaeological sites that have been gridded. The survey team obtains the elevation of each grid stake and plots this information on the site map. Contours are interpolated using the known elevations of the grid points as controlling points.

The **radial method** is performed by plumbing the plane table over the site bench mark and reading elevations outward (downhill) in the cardinal directions and at 45 degrees in each quadrant. This procedure yields eight "rays" along which points of known distance and elevation are plotted. All points identified as "99 m" are connected with one contour line; all points identified as "98 m" are connected by another line, and so forth. Each contour line connects points of the same elevation; each contour line must close on itself.

Computer-assisted Site Mapping

There is another, much more sophisticated and accurate method of plotting contour lines, accomplished by using stereo pairs of aerial photographs of the site, obtained by project-specific overflight or from photo archives. The stereo pairs are viewed in a contour-plotting imaging system, such as the MPS-2 Micro Photogrammetric System (see Appendix B, 19). Photogrammetry uses two photographs to form a three-dimensional image from which accurate height, width, and depth measurements (*X-Y-Z* coordinates) are recorded (American Society of Photogrammetry and Remote Sensing [ASPRS] 1960, 1985, 1994). The MPS-2 accepts 35-mm and 70-mm photographs and interfaces with a variety of host computer platforms and plotters.

Special computer programs (e.g., Surfer, TNTMIPS, see Appendix B, 20) will automatically generate contours and other landform configurations at user-defined intervals. Traverse PC is a coordinate geometry program that will run on any IBM or IBM-compatible. Data collected in the field are read by Traverse PC and displayed as a traverse, showing each point occupied and backsight, foresight, and side shots (see Appendix B, 20). Maps produced by computer-driven imaging systems are very accurate and display excellent detail. Their production, of course, requires suitable equipment, which, fortunately, is growing increasingly sophisticated while gradually becoming less expensive.

GEOGRAPHIC INFORMATION SYSTEMS (GIS)

The systems that are collectively called **geographic information systems** (GIS) have developed primarily from older computer mapping systems, such as SYMAP (Redman and Watson 1970) and remote sensing technology (Fraser-Taylor 1991; Sage 1990; USDI, GS 1991). The various GIS permutations offer unprecedented opportunities to represent and model geographic and archaeological data (Ehrenberg 1987; Haines-Young et al. 1993; Harris and Batty 1992; Price 1992; Price and Heywood 1994). As Martin (1991) puts it, "GIS not only

potentially offer far greater power for manipulation and analysis of data than had been available with earlier systems . . . but also place greater demands on data accuracy and availability."

There are numerous ways in which a GIS is used (Allen et al. 1990; Hearnshaw and Unwin 1994; Legg 1992; Raper 1989; Ripple 1989). These include mapping, database, and spatial analysis. The first of these applications involves using a GIS for **mapping processing** or display systems. A data set from either the natural or the built environment is represented as a map (referred to as **layer, theme,** or **coverage**), which is manipulated to add, subtract, or combine various data sets, often to produce dynamic output in the form of a new map or graphic, one that displays the original data in a significantly different way or ways than the originals.

The **database** view of GIS emphasizes the importance of a well-designed and implemented database. Applications that record information and are amenable to frequent user-queries are well suited to this approach, but with some GIS presently at hand, it is difficult to execute complex analytical operations requiring the use of many types of geographical data. The third application of GIS involves **spatial analysis,** the potential of which is yet to be fully realized because proprietary GIS software systems available at this writing offer limited functions in spatial analysis.

There are several introductory-level textbooks covering GIS, among which are Burrough (1986), Huxhold (1991), Martin (1991), Peuquet and Marble (1990), and Tomlin (1990); see also Wilson (1990) for an annotated GIS bibliography.

Elements of a GIS

A GIS is composed of five basic elements: data, computer hardware, computer software, "liveware" (people), and procedures. The hardware element consists of various types of computer platforms, such as personal computers (PCs) and microcomputers, high-performance workstations (e.g., UNIX), and mainframe computers. In addition to the standard input, storage, and output devices, special peripherals are required for data input (scanners and digitizers) and output (plotters) and, sometimes, for data storage and processing—the latter potentially affected by the type of display device in use, its resolution, and color spectrum (Antenucci et al. 1991; Madry 1990).

There are many permutations of GIS software. Three basic designs are: file processing, hybrid, and extended designs. The **file processing system** stores each data set and function as a separate file. These are linked together during analytical operations. An example of this type of system used in archaeology is Idrisi. The **hybrid design** stores attribute data in a conventional database management system (DBMS); separate software is used for geographical data. An example of the hybrid design is ARC/INFO (Environmental Systems Research Institute [ESRI] 1986, 1989a, 1989b, 1990). The third type, **extended design** DBMS, stores both geographical and attribute data to provide the required geographical analytical functions. SYSTEM 9 is an example of this design configuration (see Zubrow 1990).

The key element in a GIS is the spatial database, which comprises an integrated collection of data delineating spatial parameters and their attributes. There are two fundamental spatial data models: vector and raster. **Vector digitizing** involves recording (in digital form) information from a source document as points, lines, or areas (polygons). The major problem is that data input often has to be done manually. An example of a vector-based GIS is ARC/INFO. **Raster-based systems** use individual points for processing, creating a "grid" of **pixels** ("picture elements"), which are individually processed and displayed. A well-known raster-based system is Idrisi, a low-cost program that runs on most IBM-compatible PCs. The cell-based modules present geographical features as polygonal units of space in a matrix (lattice grid or array), displayed as a series of X-Y-Z coordinates. There are raster/vector and point-data GIS—e.g., GRASS—which at this writing run under X-Windows and UNIX environments on workstations (Madry 1989; Madry and Crumley 1990).

Archaeological Applications of GIS

For the archaeologist, an appropriate GIS can present data in ways that a few years ago were extremely difficult (or even nearly impossible) to accomplish (Kvamme 1989; Savage 1990). For example, a GIS was used to model prehistoric agricultural productivity over an 1,816-km^2 area in southwestern Colorado (Van West 1993). Spatial variations in human occupation patterns within a given geographical area can be configured by adding a third dimension—time. Thus far, however, most GIS applications in archaeology are management-oriented projects involving quantitative site locational analysis, primarily centered on predictive modeling of site location (Calamia 1986; Zulick 1986) and its ramifications (e.g., Altschul 1990; Carmichael 1990; Kvamme 1989; Madry and Crumley 1990; Savage 1990; Wandsnider and Dore 1995).

Beyond basic data manipulation, GIS has great potential importance for archaeological mapping by amplifying studies of landscape archaeology and catchment analysis (Vita-Finzi 1978). It is becoming increasingly possible to explore effectively past social systems in relation to their environment (Van West 1993), ultimately addressing an oft-espoused if elusive archaeological raison d'être—explanation of cultural change (Binford 1965:203–210).

COMPUTERS AND ELECTRONICS IN SURVEYING AND MAPPING

To meet the increasingly exacting standards of contemporary archaeology, both site record maps and site topographic maps almost invariably must be redrawn for presentation or publication. We use the word "presentation" because of the fact that archaeological maps might not be "published" in the usual sense but might be reproduced as part of a university thesis or included with site record forms in a contract report. The development during the past decade of computer-aided technology for surveying and mapping has made it much easier to produce high-quality maps based directly on graphic or digital data acquired in the field (Mutunayagam and Bahrami 1987). Throughout this chapter, we have referred to the many innovations in surveying, measurement, data recording, and processing that the computer and the electronic age have made possible (Burger and Gillies 1989). The technology of this rapidly developing field changes so quickly, as most of us are painfully aware, that hardware and software discussed today probably will be obsolete tomorrow (Monmonier 1985, 1993). With this caveat in mind, we attempt to convey some impression of the potential of computer-aided surveying and cartography without, we trust, spending too much time on equipment that is already outmoded, or soon will be.

At present, major innovations in surveying and mapping include: acquisition of survey data through EDM, including areal coordinates (X and Y angles) and elevation data (Z angle); processing and display of those data by various types of software; production of the data by computer-driven pen-plotters; reproduction of maps by electrostatic copiers; and, of course, rapid, widespread distribution of information via computer networks, such as the Internet (Newton et al. 1992).

In a typical combined application of the various technologies presently available, the field archaeologist or archaeological surveyor can obtain mapping data by GPS or with an electronic total station theodolite, prism array, and onboard or handheld computer. Essential points can be occupied, and their X-Y-Z coordinates obtained in the field and stored by the computer. At the field office or laboratory, the files are transferred from the field laptop computer to a PC or minicomputer running a computer-aided design (CAD) program, where data points can be labeled, integrated, displayed, and prepared for presentation. The data are printed on monotone or multicolor plotters. All of this technology is currently available; improvements (manifested with mind-boggling frequency) often represent quantum leaps. We recommend consulting journals covering the field or using library data retrieval (e.g., InfoTrac or CARL) to obtain current information.

Cartographic Software

Map data are displayed graphically, manipulated, and presented effectively on screen or sent to a printer or plotter by means of various types of computer software (Grim 1992; Selner and Taylor 1992; Selner et al. 1986). Some of these programs are Surfer, GeoLink, Atlas MapMaker, Atlas Pro, and MapInfo. A powerful and flexible program, Surfer is designed to produce on IBM or compatible PCs high-resolution contour and three-dimensional surface plots from randomly spaced data. The software offers more than 100 options for creating surface or contour plots. Randomly spaced data are converted to regularly spaced, gridded data; labels or titles can be added to the display, and plots can be exported to other programs. Surfer permits labeling of point-elevations on contour maps; surfaces can be plotted and displayed in reference to standard X-Y-Z coordinates. The Surfer three-dimensional program will create "fishnet" surfaces and "skirt" block diagrams (Figure 9.32). Surfer will run under DOS 2.0 or later, requires a minimum of 320K RAM, a Surfer-supported graphics printer or plotter, and an IBM VGA monitor. (A math coprocessor chip greatly increases speed of gridding and plotting.) Later versions include Surfer for Windows (see Appendix B, 20).

Computer-assisted Drafting (CAD)

Technical drawings, such as maps and other archaeological data, can be produced rapidly by means of **computer-assisted drafting (CAD)** packages. Among the many CAD programs for the Windows operating environment are Anvil-1000MD, AutoCAD, Cadvance, Drafix, Pj2 CAD, and DesignCAD 2D. Important features to look for in a CAD package include architectural drawing, which allows the user to create horizontal, vertical, and aligned (angled) dimensions in a variety of styles. The package should also offer mechanical drawing, including curves, hatching inside complex boundaries, and a variety of hachure patterns. Another important feature is data management, enabling the CAD program to generate a list of materials, measurements, and other information pertaining to architectural or archaeological drawings (see Werner and Young 1991).

A PC-based CAD for Windows is AutoCAD Release 12, which requires Microsoft Windows 3.1 or later. AutoCAD provides an impressive array of features for creating architectural and mechanical two-dimensional drawings. Historical archaeolo-

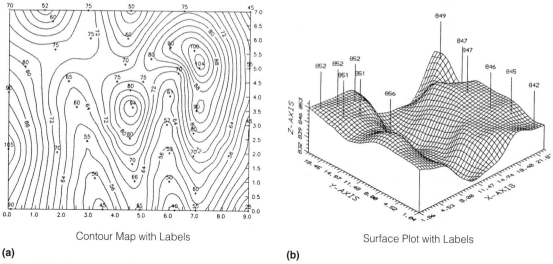

(a) Contour Map with Labels

(b) Surface Plot with Labels

Figure 9.32 Contour map (*a*) and surface plot map (*b*) created by Surfer for DOS. The Surfer program creates surface plots with stacked contours of fishnet surfaces, optional rotation and tilt angles, independent scaling in the *X*, *Y*, and *Z* dimensions, multiple text blocks at any position, angle, color, font and size, and many other attributes.

gists will find the program useful for production of detailed maps of features of the built environment. AutoCAD 12 supports just about everything in the computer world, but its price tag is hefty. A less expensive (and of course less powerful) incarnation is AutoCAD LT, also for the Windows environment, but without digitizer support and other features of AutoCAD 12.

DesignCAD for Windows is not as powerful as AutoCAD but offers many of the same features. Running under Microsoft Windows 3.1 or later, DesignCAD is a robust package, offering fast performance and adequate power for most tasks at a bargain price. It is a reasonable substitute for more expensive, top-end programs. (See Appendix B, 20, for both programs.) Programs for the Macintosh include Dreams, MiniCAD, and ClarisCAD.

Computer Modeling: Thematic Depictions and Virtual Reconstruction

Maps are intended to assist visualization of archaeological data and so to contribute to the interpretation and explanation of archaeological phenomena. Computer graphics techniques are also increas-

ingly being used to reconstruct or recreate prehistoric remains and historical architecture. For example, Peterson et al. (1995) modeled a virtual reconstruction of an excavated pithouse in British Columbia, Canada, using three-dimensional computer graphics techniques to integrate spatial data. Computer modeling permits the viewer to perceive the pithouse from various viewpoints, moving about the structure visually to obtain a better idea of use areas and other interpretational information. Computer imaging techniques extrapolating field data have great potential for clarifying and more effectively presenting artifact distributions, architectural features, and a host of other archaeological data.

MAP PRODUCTION

Let us consider the process of map production from rough draft to finished product. It is vital to think ahead to the final version (or versions) of all types of archaeological maps. Most site record maps are drawn in the field on 8½-×-11-inch paper, the size being dictated by convenience and the fact that many site forms include preformatted "map forms" of that size. Large-scale site maps are needed, however, to plot vital cultural and natural features and provide essential measurements and bearings without "crowding." Large-scale field maps often display intricate technical detail, including survey reference points, contour elevations, bearings or azimuths, and so forth. Such information may be too complex to publish without simplification and reorganization for effective presentation.

Questions to Consider

One of the primary questions to consider at the outset of any project is whether you will need a single copy or multiple copies of the final maps. If multiple copies are needed, what process is going to be used for their reproduction? The final copy of a hand-drawn map can be inked with drafting pens and labeled by means of prepared lettering. Preprinted transfer "pasteup" symbols, once commonly used on maps, have been generally supplanted by computer-generated symbols produced on transfer film by high-quality laser printers.

Will the map or maps be reproduced at the same scale (same size) as the original? Probably the least expensive and most readily accessible reproduction process is the electrostatic copier. Most offices and universities have copy machines that produce same-size copies. Many brands of electrostatic copiers reduce and enlarge copy from 50 to 200 percent in 1 percent steps (increments). Hence, one can draw a site map oversize (say 14-x-16 inches) and use a copier to reduce it to an 8½-x-11-inch format, but not everyone has access to large-format copiers or plotters that are capable of handling oversize maps. Multiple copies of maps and other graphics can be produced by local copy companies using large-format, high-speed reproduction equipment. A single 8½-x-11-inch map can be reproduced in quantities of 1–100 copies or more, usually at modest cost.

Hand-drawn, hand-lettered maps (if well done) can be very appealing (Figure 9.33); they often are a welcome departure from computer-generated maps. The appearance of hand-drawn maps is improved when they are reduced in size; reduction diminishes uneven lines and "shaky" lettering. Reduction is not necessarily a cure-all for poor-quality drafting, but it can improve the appearance of hand-drawn maps. However, reduction may also cause undesirable effects (see "Shading and Pattern Transfers," later).

Can all of the information concerning an archaeological site be displayed on a single map? The more complex the site, the more carefully map presentation must be designed. Work up "dummies" (detailed pencil sketches) of basic map concepts and design. It is usually best to design a *series* of maps that guide the reader through various "views" of the site, beginning with an index map of the country, state, or province where the research was conducted and, in succeeding maps, narrowing the focus to present increasingly detailed information.

Map Drafting Materials

Among the first considerations in laboratory map drafting is the type of material on which to draw the map. Many archaeologists draw field maps directly on matte-surface drafting film. Cartographers also use this material when drafting the final version. Caution is advised, however, because some types of matte-surface drafting film will not accept conventional inks (special inks are available). It is advisable to test samples of various materials to be sure that the desired effect will be obtained. Most art supply stores carry various types of drafting film and paper. Maps also can be produced by scribing on special film surfaces or by photomechanical processes. Although these materials are not often used in the production of archaeological maps, they can be employed to ensure extreme accuracy and registration. (For further information on types of drafting materials, consult Campbell [1991].)

Data Compilation

When site record maps are created using a standard plane table and alidade, most of the carto-

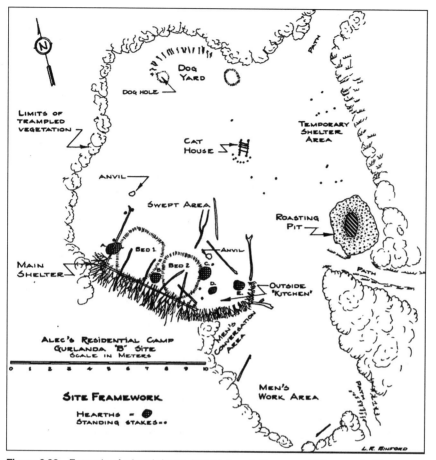

Figure 9.33 Example of a hand-drawn, hand-lettered site map, which appeared in *American Antiquity* 51(3):559.

graphic data are compiled in the field. But, as we have seen, when a transit is used for mapping, one must compile the map from data entered in field notebooks or stored in computer memory. An inherent advantage of the plane table and alidade method of mapping is that one leaves the field with a reasonably complete map, which can be redrawn, enlarged, or reduced as needed.

Data obtained in the field by instrument survey are compiled with the aid of several instruments, one of which, a circular protractor, is used to lay off horizontal angles based on field data. The map can be adjusted to true north during drafting, but it is easy to err when transposing magnetic bearings to true north. Before changing or improving a field

map, it's a good idea to save a file copy of the entire map exactly as the field surveyor recorded the data.

When the map details are compiled, be sure to include a title block; reference grid (USPLSS or UTMS grid); a north arrow, bar-scale, date of compilation, an explanation of symbols, and other information. Many cartographers rule a "neat-line," or border, around the edges of their maps. If the map is to be included in a thesis, remember that most universities have strict requirements regarding size and shape of margins, use of color illustrations, and other aspects of publication: it's a good idea to investigate these requirements before creating final maps (Figure 9.34).

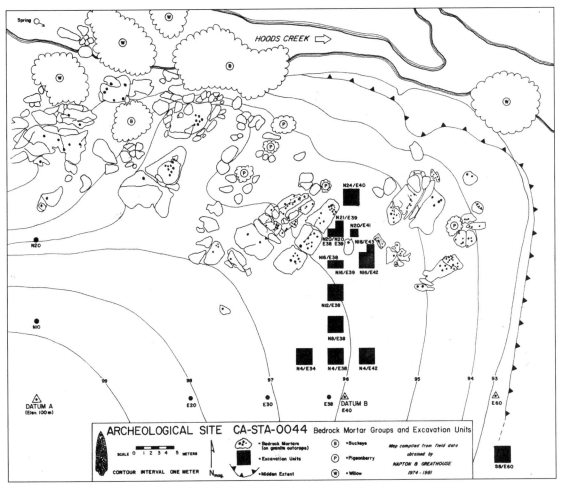

Figure 9.34 Archaeological site map illustrating cartographic data imported from both on-site surveying and aerial photography.

Cartographic Symbols

Symbols help to reduce descriptive labeling that often burdens maps and detracts from their effectiveness. One of the principal shortcomings of many site record maps is that they do not use standard, readily identifiable symbols. Often, features and vegetation patterns are not depicted as seen from overhead, but instead are drawn as though viewed from an oblique angle. "Three-dimensional" houses and trees should *not* be drawn on maps that are intended to depict an area as seen from above.

Standard map symbols used by the USGS are explained and illustrated in color in USGS leaflets

and also on the margin of some maps, e.g., the USGS 30-x-60-minute topographic series. Study these symbols carefully, not only to improve your own maps but to better understand the information presented by USGS quadrangles. A point to remember, however, is that the USGS quadrangles are printed in color. Consequently, the symbols used by USGS may have to be modified to be effective on maps printed in black ink.

There is no universal set of archaeological map symbols, principally because there are so many different types of cultural and natural features, specimens, and stratigraphic contexts. Some of the more commonly used map symbols are found in Ahmed and Almond (1983), Barnes (1990), Bennison (1990), Berg and Greenpool (1993), Maltman (1990), Spencer (1993), and W. S. White (1992). Mapmakers should always explain any unusual or nonstandard symbols that appear on their maps.

Lettering

Hand-lettered maps are rapidly becoming an artifact of the past due to the convenience, legibility, and minimal cost of producing computer-generated fonts. There are literally hundreds of styles of typefaces (fonts) in numerous sizes (points). It is a good idea, however, to avoid using elaborate or unconventional fonts or, for that matter, too many different fonts on one map. Some of the principal methods of producing mechanical lettering are discussed below.

Typing. The typewriter is one of the least expensive (and probably least satisfactory) ways of labeling archaeological maps. Labels can be typed on gummed white paper, cut to size, and attached to the map surface. (Use a carbon ribbon on the typewriter.)

Transfer Letters. A widely used, if rather laborious, method of lettering maps is by means of transfer lettering. Transfer sheets have an assortment of letters printed on backing material. The user transfers each letter in sequence from the backing sheet to the map surface by pressure. Transfer lettering is excellent and easy to use—if the stock is not old and brittle. Care and patience are required. This type of lettering is easy to work with in 18-point type or larger. However, because the letters are applied one by one, they can easily be misaligned. Transfer lettering can be purchased at most stationery stores.

Leroy Lettering. The Leroy lettering system employs templates and a scriber. The latter has three "arms": one fits into a guide-groove in the template; another is tipped with a sharp guide-pin that fits into grooved letters on the template. The third is tipped with an interchangeable pen or pencil point. To create a letter, place the letter guide-pin in the desired template letter and form the character on the map surface. With a little practice, a beginner can produce neat, attractive letters. Some Leroy sets have adjustable scribers that produce slanted, tall, or short letters from a single template.

Kroytype Lettering. The Kroytype lettering system offers a variety of fonts and point sizes engraved on interchangeable disks. Lettering reproduced from these disks is printed on strips of either opaque white paper or transparent material, which is peeled from its backing and applied directly to the map. The user works with complete words or phrases, rather than individual letters, so the process of "pasteup" is expedited. The Kroy DuraType 240 SE or K225 is a computer-controlled machine that produces adhesive-backed lettering in a variety of type styles and point sizes.

Computer Fonts. Most computer word processing and CAD software offers a variety of fonts scalable to size (points). Printing can be added to maps directly via software or printed by laser printers on applique film and transferred to maps.

Shading and Pattern Transfers

Hundreds of styles of shading and patterns are available. Preprinted designs represent geological formations, vegetation patterns, topographic features, and the like. To use transfer film, simply place it on the desired area of the map and, using a very sharp knife, cut the transfer film to conform to the area. Peel the transfer segment from the backing sheet and attach it to the map. Use care, however, because most brands of transfer and shading film are delicate and must be handled carefully, not only during application but when the map is being photographed or copied. (Shading film may eventually break or detach from rolled maps.)

Shading patterns can be produced by hand-applying stippling (dotting) or other types of images. But if you attempt this, it is important to produce a uniform, neat-appearing pattern. The appearance of stippling is often improved by reduction, but shading, whether applied by transfer sheet or by hand-stippling, may "close up" when reduced. If a map is reduced drastically, delicate shading will probably close up to such an extent that the shaded parts may reproduce as dark gray or black. Another problem involving shading patterns is that they are often used indiscriminately to depict stratigraphic levels. Abrupt changes from one shading pattern to another may convey the impression that the stratigraphic layers are quite discrete and well defined, which in fact may not be the case.

Production Considerations

As we have seen, the appearance of hand-drawn maps can be improved by reduction. However, if a map is to be reduced drastically, say from an original of 18-x-20 inches to 7-x-9 inches (to allow margin and binding edge on an 8½-x-11-inch sheet of paper), small print may become illegible and carefully prepared shading patterns may close up to such an extent that they become almost unrecognizable. The solution to this problem is to reduce samples of the desired lettering and shading beforehand, to see what it will look like when it is reduced and printed in final form. Various fonts will "hold" (sustain their appearance) better than others. A point to keep in mind, in reference to university theses and doctoral dissertations, is that when these documents are microfilmed (as they often are), color illustrations, shading patterns, and other fine detail will probably be considerably degraded.

Color Reproduction

Color reproduction, traditionally accomplished by photolithography, is extremely expensive, which is the reason most university textbooks are printed only in black ink. Color reproduction by photolithography requires preparation of color-separation negatives and multiple printing plates, which require either multiple passes through the press or a multicolor press. The advent of desktop publishing with output to inexpensive computer-driven color printers has dramatically increased the possibilities for color illustrations in all kinds of books

and reports. However, some archaeological contract specifications and university thesis standards prohibit use of color illustrations.

Oversize Maps

Maps can be reproduced at almost any size if available plotters or print shops can handle large-format work. Most print shops are limited to the size of paper accepted by their machines; some shops will not copy *any* map, due to copyright restrictions. Some commercial electrostatic copiers can reproduce copy up to 36 or 48 inches wide by any length—but not inexpensively. Oversize maps drawn to accompany university theses can of course be folded to be included in the final bound presentation, but most universities have very exact specifications regarding *how* this is to be done. Oversize maps can be folded and inserted ("tipped in") to theses or included in a pocket or envelope attached to the end papers—depending on university regulations. This process can be costly and laborious, so it is best to make sure that it is feasible from all points of view. Many archaeologists have solved the problem of handling oversize maps by publishing reports in the (U.S.) standard 8½-x-11-inch format; accompanying maps and other graphics are folded and boxed separately. However, to save space, libraries often microfilm oversize maps—with consequent loss of legibility.

PARTING THOUGHTS

From beginning to end of the mapping process, it is wise to plan ahead, asking: How are the data to be acquired? How are they to be compiled? How are they to be reproduced? The more you know about and plan for the data acquisition, processing, and presentation processes, the easier it will be to produce quality maps. Prospective archaeological mapmakers would do well to take courses in cartography and, of course, to study published archaeological maps to see how they are drawn, what symbols are used, and how to present graphic information. This type of knowledge is all the more essential when dealing with architecturally complicated prehistoric sites and the vast array of structures and other features found on historical sites.

GUIDE TO FURTHER READING

Details on Mapping and Map Design

Campbell 1991; Dent 1993; Keates 1989; Raisz 1962; Robinson et al. 1984; Southworth and Southworth 1982

Thematic Maps

Dart 1985; Dent 1993; Tyner 1992

History of Map Making and Sources of Map Titles and Suppliers

Makower and Bergheim 1990; Wilford 1981

History of Surveying in the United States

Barlett 1962; Cazier 1993; Goetzmann 1967; Hughes 1979; Manning 1967; Pattison 1979; Preuss 1958; Uzes 1977; Wheat 1957–1963; White 1983

History of Surveying in the Old World

Breaks 1771; Godlewska 1988; Styles 1970

Evolution and Types of Surveying Instruments

Bennett 1987; Cuvigny 1985; Stone 1928; Toscano 1991

Examples of Classic Archaeological Maps

Black 1967 (Angel Mounds); Carr and Hazard 1961 (Tikal); Leakey 1971 (Olduvai Gorge); Lewis and Kneberg 1946 (Hiwassee Island); Millon 1973 (Teotihuacán); Mosley and Mackey 1974 (Chan Chan); Movius 1977 (Abri Pataud); Sabloff and Tourtellot 1991 (Sayil)

C H A P T E R

10

Stratigraphy

Richard E. W. Adams and Fred Valdez, Jr.

Archaeologists are repeatedly confronted during their excavation careers with maddeningly complex physical situations. In the American West, they may find that a herd of bison was driven into an arroyo and some 190 of them killed and then butchered, leaving a bewildering mass of bones and artifacts, the whole later modified by erosion. That was what Wheat (1972) and his associates encountered at the Olsen-Chubbuck site. In the Middle East, they may find multilayered jumbles of mud-brick walls intermingled with burials, trash, burned-down buildings, all modified by later construction, casual looting, and prehistoric antiquarianism. Dry caves and deserts may yield exquisitely preserved materials and plant remains, but often in the context of dust as fine as talcum powder and sand that runs like water when disturbed. Shell middens in North and South America, geologically rearranged deposits in East Africa, pithouse villages in China, and Maya ruins in

Yucatán all present their own unique problems of excavation.

In all of these situations, however, the basic purpose is always the same—to elicit order from the apparent chaos. A primary means of accomplishing this purpose is stratigraphy. As geology analyzes the strata of the earth, in archaeology the strata, or layers, of archaeological sites are studied for chronology and order. The processes of layering are also a significant aspect for understanding the stratification. For the professional archaeologist, there are few satisfactions to match that of reaching a complete, rational, and tested explanation for a complex stratigraphic problem. It is upon such data that the most important goals of archaeology are based, the studies of cultural history and of cultural process.

Both the stratigraphic principle and the practice of stratigraphy were recognized long ago, perhaps as early as Classic Greece. Then, both principle and practice were apparently lost, not to be rediscovered until the sixteenth century. Relative chronology as observed in geological stratification was presented by George Owen in 1570 (*History of Pembrokeshire*), but not published until 1796. The concept of superposition was first published by Nicolaus Steno (1638–1687) in 1669 (*Prodromus*). William Smith (1769–1839), who recognized a sequence of deposits at Kent's Cavern in England in the 1790s, is also among the earliest rediscoverers (see Thomas [1989] for additional details concerning early stratigraphic efforts). **Metric** or **arbitrary-level stratigraphy** (a technique for dealing with weakly stratified or apparently unstratified sites by establishing levels of arbitrary depth; see Chapter 5) was introduced to the New World probably by Boas through his colleague Manuel Gamio, who excavated in such a manner in 1911 (Adams 1960). Nels Nelson's use of the technique probably stemmed from his Old World experience with Paleolithic archaeology, gained while excavating with Obermeier and Breuil. In 1914 Nelson applied this principle to sites in the Galisteo Basin of New Mexico. Nelson's work was much better publicized than Gamio's and had an immediate impact on fieldworkers.

In his use of arbitrary levels Nelson also applied the "index fossil concept" (from geology) to prehistoric pottery recovered from his stratigraphic units. This system allows for intersite comparisons to less stratified sites. A. V. Kidder used the method in his work at Pecos, New Mexico, and it became standard practice in American archaeology in the 1920s (Willey and Sabloff 1993:103–108).

DEFINITION

Phillips et al. (1951) have provided both a succinct definition of stratigraphy and a useful distinction: stratification is what you find; stratigraphy is what you do with it. To properly understand a site's stratification, an archaeologist must combine the law of superposition with a consideration of context.

As already noted, the term and the basic method come from geology. Some of the basic assumptions, such as uniformitarianism, come from

geology, too. **Uniformitarianism** is the assumption geologists make of uniformity or continuity in the processes that form the strata of the earth. The processes that acted in the past are like those we can observe today. In other words, when volcanoes erupt today, they lay down layers of ash. Geologists assume that ancient volcanoes did the same. An excellent example of ancient volcanic stratigraphic deposition is reported by Sheets (1983, 1992) for the Ceren site in El Salvador (Figure 10.1; see also Sheets and Grayson 1979). Similar are the depositional effects from flooding by rivers (known as alluvial deposits). Deposits laid down by other natural forces include colluvial, aeolian, glacial, and marine deposits.

Archaeologists also assume that human behavior (the force that forms archaeological deposits) is much the same today as it ever was. For example, most modern communities have a dump for their rubbish and garbage. Archaeologists routinely encounter mixed deposits whose likeliest origin seems to be their having served as the trash heap of a prehistoric people. A. V. Kidder, digging into the Andover, Massachusetts, town dump in 1922, found layering and change there that was markedly similar to what he found in the much older trash deposits at the prehistoric Southwestern ruin of Pecos.

PRINCIPLES

There is really only one major principle in archaeological stratigraphy. This is the **law of superposition.** This "law" dictates that under most conditions, the oldest layers are on the bottom and the younger layers are on the top. A sequence of events, physical and/or cultural, producing the layers is represented by the changes from bottom to top. The excavator should also be aware of the possibilities of "reversed stratigraphy," deposits in which normal stratigraphic processes have been disrupted. Such modifications can be caused by the digging of storage pits or graves, animal burrowing, and the like (cf. Hole and Heizer 1973:147; additional examples are provided by Colton 1946; Pyddoke 1961; and Tolstoy 1958).

Figure 10.1 View of stratigraphic deposition resulting from volcanic activity at the site of Ceren, El Salvador.

Even normal stratigraphic conditions, however, do not make excavation simple. Strata may be horizontal, slanting, vertical, deformed, or a combination of these. They may be sharply distinguished from one another by color or consistency or contents, or they may grade very subtly into one another. Preservation contexts range from the best (dry caves and deserts) through architectural stratigraphy and open sites to geological deposits (for example, redeposited materials), usually the worst for preservation. The physical nature can range from talcum powder–like dust to heavy clays and stone.

A relatively new subdiscipline of archaeology, usually called **geoarchaeology,** focuses on the sedimentary processes related to stratigraphic formation and context. Geoarchaeology is built on the traditionally close interaction between geologists (especially geomorphologists), other earth scientists, and archaeologists. For recent studies involving such research, including the analysis of soil sediments, soil formation processes, and the manner in which they can be naturally disturbed, the reader is referred to Courty et al. (1989), Donahue and Adovasio (1990), Gladfelter (1981), Goldberg (1988), Hassan (1978), Holliday (ed. 1992), Rapp and Gifford (1985), Rosen (1986), Shackley (1975, 1985), Stein (1987, 1990), Stein and Farrand (1985), Waters (1992), and Wood and Johnson (1978).

GOALS

Whatever the nature of the site and its strata, the minimal goal of archaeological stratigraphy is to work out the sequence of deposits and to elicit the events producing them. In other words, one aims at producing a depositional history for each excavated sample or group of samples. A middle-range goal of stratigraphic work is to establish a site chronology and culture history by synthesizing the histories of the individual deposits.

The ultimate aim is to establish a regional sequence into which individual events and site sequences are keyed by means of common factors. Usually it is at this point that one can begin considering problems of culture process, although they may be anticipated earlier.

TECHNIQUES OF EXCAVATION, LABELING, AND RECORDING

Test pits excavated by arbitrary levels are usually the first means of revealing stratification in the deposits at a site. During excavation of a test pit, it may or may not be possible to discern the natural levels. However, once the pit is dug, the natural levels may show more clearly on the pit walls or profiles. With excavation, whether of test pits or of the main site, extensive and detailed notes should be kept, including schematic drawings on gridded paper showing features as they appear. These features often fade in both color and contrast after exposure, and it is vital to note them promptly as a guide to the final recording procedure (also see below). Soil color is usually an important aspect of the stratigraphy, and description should be done using the Munsell Soil Charts. Grain size, soil consistency or plasticity, and other characteristics should also be noted for each layer. Grain size ranges from clay to silt to sand.

When a unit has been completely excavated, the walls of the pit should be thoroughly cleaned to make the strata easier to see. If the walls are stable, cutting with a sharp trowel will work; otherwise, a method must be improvised to suit conditions. In dry cave deposits, directed puffs of air from an atomizer may be used for final cleaning. In permanently damp sites such as Star Carr, water jets might help in excavation (G. D. Clark 1974:50). Compressed-air brushes may be helpful at times. Wetting with a back-pump sprayer will often freshen and rejuvenate the colors of dirt for recording. Even at dry sites, the profile may first be cut with a trowel and then carefully sprayed (not with jets) with water. This brings artifacts into sharp relief, and microstrata—for example, a thin layer of sand—may erode or wash out at a different rate, becoming visible. This technique was pioneered in North America at Ozette, Washington (Gleason 1973). Sturdy deposits, such as shell middens, may be safely and effectively cleaned with high-pressure water hoses (Marquardt and Watson 1983:Figure 15.5).

Labeling is necessary at least during the final stages of recording. This may be done by attaching numbered pieces of note cards or metal-rimmed tags to the wall with nails. Other, more ingenious means of labeling include the use of cutout plastic numbers and letters that can be attached to vertical surfaces with nails. The aim is to produce a visual reference system for use during recording. At this point a Polaroid color photograph may be taken to guarantee that something of an objective record is made. The labeling system used will naturally depend on the field system in use by the project. It is very convenient to use label numbers that are also the lot numbers assigned to materials from those layers. Thus the excavator and the artifact analyst (if they are not the same person) can talk more easily about their various conclusions. See

Figure 10.2 Stratigraphic profile at Arenosa Shelter (41VV99): (*a*) upper half; (*b*) section. Note thick layer of flood-laid soil (just above the stadia rod).

(a)

(b)

Figure 10.2 for an illustration of labeled cave deposits at Arenosa Shelter in Texas. Figures 10.3a and 10.3b depict strata labeling at the site of Cuello, Belize, using small attached cards; Figure 10.3c shows the same system in use at an archaeological excavation in Africa.

Stratigraphic recording can be done in a number of ways using some sort of scaled reference system. American archaeologists have traditionally stretched vertical and horizontal strings across the face of an excavation to create a grid, using a line level to establish horizontal levels and a plumb bob

Figure 10.3 Excavation block at Cuello, Belize: (*a*) general view. Note the use of tags to mark stratigraphic layers. (*b*) section of stratigraphic profile at Cuello, with tags marking each identified layer. (*c*) stratigraphic excavation at Kibiro Cutting III in Africa. Note wall tags denoting stratigraphic deposits.

(a)

(b)

(c)

to establish vertical ones. All measurements should generally be metric, and millimeter-ruled paper should be used for scale drawings. However, for many historic sites, the English system makes more sense. Long rolls of grid paper or Mylar that can be cut are preferable to 8½-×-11-inch notebook-size paper. Detailed notes may be made on or at the margins of the scale drawings. For each layer, color, composition, unusual features, and content should be described.

Again, a picture is worth a thousand words (see Chapter 8). Color photographs with Polaroid and 35-mm cameras are absolutely necessary. Because color photos are expensive to reproduce, final and detailed shots should also be taken of the wall with black-and-white film (35-mm and if possible, large-format). Detailed shots may be made in 135 mm, but overall final shots should be made using film no smaller than 120 mm. This allows for enlargement without much loss of significant detail. Although it is frowned upon in some quarters as modifying what one is seeking to record, outlining the strata by lightly cutting lines in the face of the wall with a trowel makes the strata much more distinct and the boundaries between them more visible. More-revealing photographs can then be taken. If this is to be done, however, the unmodified excavated face should be photographed beforehand. A very useful technique involves taking a Polaroid photo of the stratigraphic profile with the profile outlined and writing on the photo itself (with a marker). However, this should be used only as a temporary measure for recording data, and the photo should be copied onto acid-free paper for the permanent record.

Photogrammetry is a potentially very valuable means of recording stratification to scale. The use of this aerial photo and mapping technique in archaeology has been pioneered by Jesse Fant and William MacDonald of the University of Minnesota Messenia Project in southwestern Greece (Fant and Loy 1972). Briefly, two cameras (e.g., 120-mm Hasselblads) are placed at opposite ends of a bar mounted on a bipod. The cameras are aimed so that the photos they produce overlap by about 20 percent. The distance from the film in the cameras to the trench wall is recorded. This information is fed into a device called a second-order stereo-plotter, which uses the two overlapping negatives to make scale drawings, at any scale desired, of the trench wall. Although the technique demands a big capital investment in cameras, it is cheap and efficient when one considers the saving in excavators' time and energy. Stratigraphic profiles can be recorded in a fraction of the time required to draw them by hand, in a more objective manner, and the technique can provide a three-dimensional illustration. The drawback to the method is that no detailed record of the stratigraphy is immediately available. The second-order stereo-plotters are seldom located near enough to the field to be immediately usable. This handicap might be overcome by supplemental use of Polaroid shots and schematic drawings.

Because of the press of field conditions and multiple demands on attention, the archaeologist should have either a form that supplements the stratigraphic drawing or a checklist of data that should be recorded. Either in notes or on a form, cross references should be made to all associated drawings, photos, lot numbers, burials, and any other pertinent data.

Another important aid in recording stratification is a video camera (½-inch VHS or 8-mm). The camcorder systems allow for immediate recording and review of the filmed strata not only with pictures but also with a verbal description. Care should be taken to select or acquire the highest quality equipment when feasible (for example, Hi-8 is recommended for the 8-mm format).

The Harris Matrix system (Harris 1979, 1989) of recording obviates a great many possible problems of complex stratigraphy because it is a method of labeling and recording that can be independent of the field system. Harris argues that features such as interfaces between deposits or the burned surface of a wall are stratigraphic elements and reflect human activity or specific events that must be documented. These events are recorded in systematic fashion and emphasize a depositional history. This depositional history is distinct from determining the relative age of the deposits, as implied by superposition, because the first formation could have been redeposited (as in reversed stratigraphy).

Harris (1979) suggests five basic units of stratification: **natural layers** are formed by the movement of material to the place of deposition through natural forces; **man-made layers** are composed of a deposit or deposits formed by humans, such as house floors or the filling of pits, postholes, and so on; and **vertical strata** refer to upstanding strata, including walls and columns. The next two units, known as **interfaces,** are the surfaces of the various strata and follow a division similar to that just explained: **horizontal feature interfaces** are those located in an approximately horizontal state, and **vertical feature interfaces** are directly tied into vertical deposits or constructions. These should be recognized and numbered as they are encountered. The value of Harris's system is seen in the excavation and subsequent analysis of complex archaeological stratigraphy; in essence, it is a method of diagramming the relationship of the many types of stratigraphy usually encountered in block excavations. Hammond (1991) has applied this system at the Maya site of Cuello. Other applications of this system are found in Anthony and Black (1994), Harris and Brown (1993), and Paice (1991). An illustration of this method is provided in Figure 10.4 from Shaw (1994).

Much of the labeling of stratigraphic units in the Harris system is of artifact-free features. It should be realized that artifact-free strata may contribute crucial information in an archaeological investigation. For example, the Paleolithic sequence of deposits at the rockshelter of Abri Pataud (France) include what are called *eboulis*, layers of sterile materials that mark milder climatic episodes during the Pleistocene (see Laville et al. 1980; Movius 1974).

The **arbitrary-level test pit** is not only the most common but the simplest recording and labeling problem that the archaeologist will face. Should the deposits be deep, rich in artifacts, and distinctly stratified by soil color, however, then it is mandatory to take a sample by **natural-level excavation.** A column is first isolated on three sides by digging three pits with arbitrary levels. The isolated column is then excavated by natural levels, which are correlated with the arbitrary units around it, thus increasing the size of the artifact sample. Examples

of profiles resulting from this sort of excavation at Altar de Sacrificios, Guatemala, are illustrated in Figure 10.5.

An example of interesting and significant stratigraphy excavated entirely by arbitrary levels within a series of adjacent 5-ft squares is the Devil's Mouth site in the Amistad Reservoir of southern Texas (Johnson 1964; see Figure 10.6). This illustration emphasizes, again, a primary aim of stratigraphy, which is to elicit a depositional sequence in its own terms. Johnson's notes and drawings during excavation were undoubtedly kept according to the individual squares excavated but were later correlated, synthesized, and presented in terms of depositional history.

Trenches reveal long stratigraphic profiles. In recording, labeling, and controlling stratigraphic data from trenches, it is important to be aware of the arbitrary nature of the separation between sections of the trench. Essentially the same techniques are used for trenches as for pits, the major difference being the quantity of data to be handled.

Architectural elements within any excavation complicate matters and necessitate distinct approaches. Structures are often excavated by cultural or depositional levels—i.e., the space between two plaster or beaten earth floors or between two walls. However, rooms or open spaces within architectural complexes must be subdivided both horizontally and vertically.

Stratigraphic situations found in association with architecture are the most complex of all and require infinite patience and a distinct recording system. One workable system is to record by strati-units rather than by functionally designated units. **Strati-units** (compare with the Harris Matrix system) are physically distinguishable units that are clearly the results of a single activity. For example, a stone wall is a strati-unit. In contrast, the **functional,** or **interpretative, unit** might include not only the stone wall, but the plaster floor that runs up to it and the ceiling that lies above it, if that survives. In this system, recording is done on the strati-unit level, which in effect is a natural stratigraphic level. The distinction between this and nonarchitectural stratigraphy is that several strati-units may coexist in the same horizontal level.

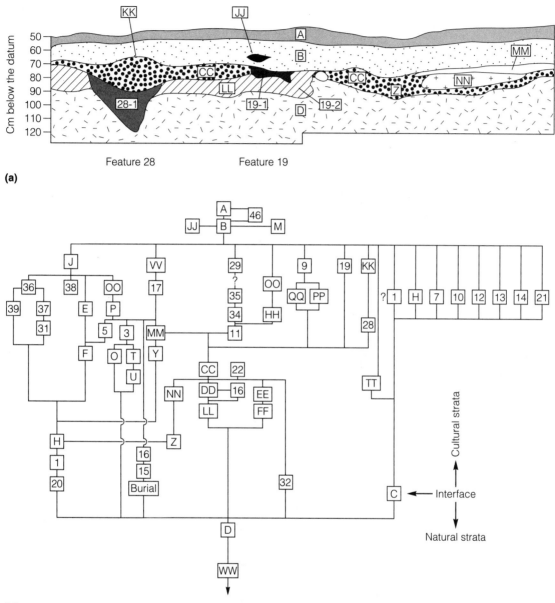

(a)

(b)

Figure 10.4 Complex stratigraphy at the Willowbend site, Mashpee, Massachusetts: (*a*) profile; (*b*) completed Harris Matrix for the site.

An analogy from linguistics may be useful here. The phonetic unit is the smallest *distinguishable* unit (as is the strati-unit), and the phoneme is the smallest *functional* unit (as is the interpretative

unit). Each functional unit is based on interpretation of the physical evidence, which in turn allows an interpretation of an event. This event, the building of a wall and associated floor, also represents a

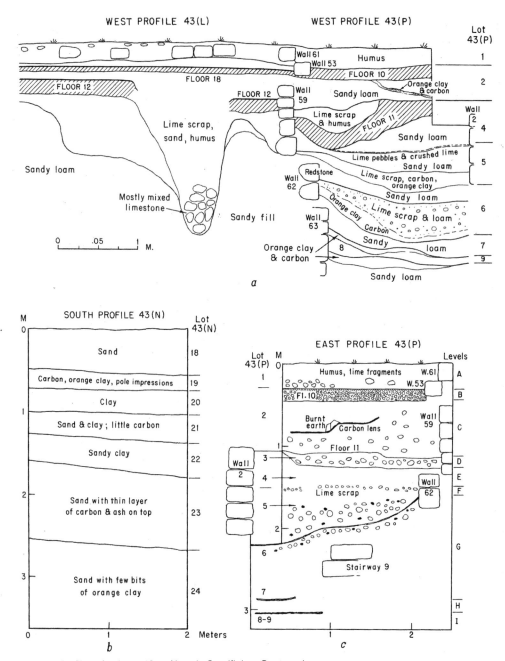

Figure 10.5 Profiles of column 43 at Altar de Sacrificios, Guatemala. This column was first isolated on three sides and then taken out by natural levels. The rich deposits of many types of potsherds in the changing levels were crucial in setting up the Altar ceramic sequence.

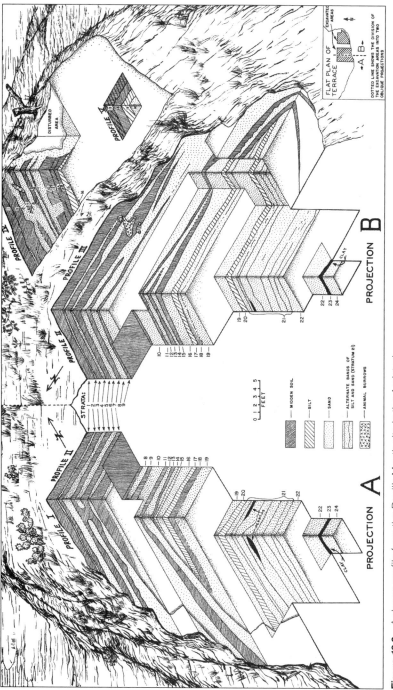

Figure 10.6 A drawn profile from the Devil's Mouth site in the Amistad Reservoir of Texas. Note the technique of presentation and the correlation of deposits from pit to pit.

Figure 10.7 A drawn profile from Operation 2037, Colha, Belize. The system of labeling used here eases viewing and interpretation of the depositional history for this locale.

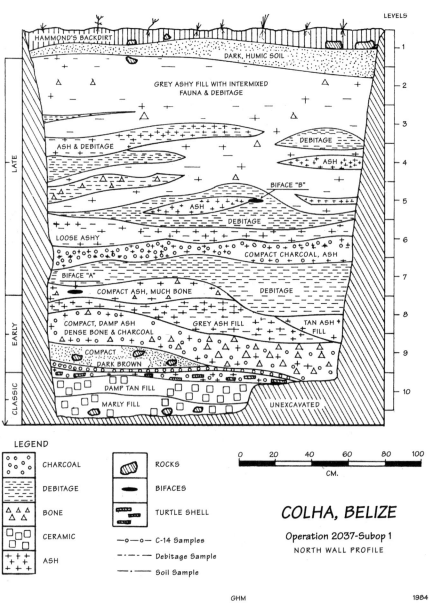

LEVELS

HAMMOND'S BACKDIRT

DARK, HUMIC SOIL

GREY ASHY FILL WITH INTERMIXED FAUNA & DEBITAGE

ASH & DEBITAGE

DEBITAGE

ASH

BIFACE "B"

ASH

DEBITAGE

LOOSE ASHY

COMPACT CHARCOAL, ASH

BIFACE "A"

COMPACT ASH, MUCH BONE

DEBITAGE

COMPACT, DAMP ASH
DENSE BONE & CHARCOAL

GREY ASH FILL

TAN ASH FILL

COMPACT
DARK BROWN

DAMP TAN FILL

MARLY FILL

UNEXCAVATED

LATE

EARLY

CLASSIC

LEGEND

CHARCOAL		ROCKS	
DEBITAGE		BIFACES	
BONE		TURTLE SHELL	
CERAMIC		—o—o— C-14 Samples	
ASH		—·—·— Debitage Sample	
		—·—· Soil Sample	

0 20 40 60 80 100
CM.

COLHA, BELIZE

Operation 2037-Subop 1
NORTH WALL PROFILE

GHM   1984

period of time, which can be designated a "time-span" (Coe 1962:506). If one uses this system of excavation, labeling, recording, analysis, interpretation, and synthesis, one ends up with a depositional history. These depositions may be phrased in either terms of interpretative units or in terms of time spans. Figure 10.7 illustrates the various strata that, together, comprise the depositional history of the structure at Operation 2037, Colha, Belize.

SPECIAL SITUATIONS

Multiple and complex architectural units should be designated by a system using nonsense names. This allows reference to the strati-unit or interpretative unit in notes without the implied sequencing of numbering or lettering. When using a number system, one may number two sequent structures 1 and 2, only to find another structure between them or a building phase off to the side that came between. Rather than using 1a, 1b, and so on, one might use as temporary designators three-letter words like "cow," "zip," "tek," etc. These nonsense tags can be discarded after excavation is finished, and structures can be numbered or lettered in sequence. Figure 10.8 provides an example of a cross section of complex architecture. In the final designation system, it is best to number from the latest to the earliest so that the highest-numbered structural unit is the earliest (Figure 10.9). Then if further excavation uncovers earlier phases, "minus" designations, such as –1, –2, and so forth, can be avoided.

In dealing with large architecture, it is useful to break up an apparently homogeneous mass of fill into manageable units. Structural fill may contain considerable ceramic material from several phases. The stratigraphic evidence from pits and trenches is clearly the only way to order the artifacts within such fill. For example, we know that ceramic complexes given the names Blue, White, Red, and Black are contained within the structure. But we know only the relative age of these complexes (say, that Black is the latest complex, and all the others are earlier) by evidence from undisturbed deposits excavated at another location. This sort of information is most reliable if it is replicated over and over within the segregated blocks of building fill. Those blocks nearest the surface are naturally most open to mixing with material earlier than the Black complex, but segregation of blocks of structural fill will indicate this as excavation proceeds more deeply into the structure (Figure 10.10).

Burials are often found within structures or other deposits, as well as in cemeteries. Artifacts included in burials were clearly in use at the time the person was buried. However, heirloom pieces may have been manufactured long before, or in some cases, depositional circumstances may have "mixed" the finds (see Chapter 11). Sequences based on burial lots may also be faulty if special items were made for the funeral or brought from outside the region to the funeral. The latter may have happened in the case of distant kin groups. Burials are often made under disturbed deposits, and these can date the burial independent of the items contained as offerings. Use of the "not-ear-lier-than" technique in connection with the evaluation of structural fill is a means of determining this information (see, for example, Adams 1971:59–78).

Vertisols (shrink-swell or self-mulching clays) are a bothersome aspect of archaeological and geological stratigraphy in parts of the world, including the south-central United States and parts of Texas (Duffield 1970), Africa, India, and Australia. These soils are especially susceptible to heaving and cracking and carry artifactual material with them, thus disturbing the original stratigraphic situation.

Sandy soil layers and artifacts in them are particularly subject to modifications and displacement due to that common human activity—walking about the living area. Experimental trampling in sandy deposits has displaced artifacts as much as 8 cm vertically (Villa and Courtin 1983), and perhaps as much as 16 cm according to Stockton (1973). Additional data on the vertical dispersal of artifacts via trampling in archaeological sites can be found in Gifford-Gonzales et al. (1985).

There are various activities that also disturb stratification. Although some of these may no longer be considered "special" situations, they are nonetheless acknowledged and discussed here. Examples of disturbed processes include plowing, which tends to move material out of its context both vertically and horizontally. Thus the identified and plotted material becomes unclear in terms of related positioning. Digging and bulldozing can likewise bring deposits to the surface if not completely remove them.

There are many types of turbation (see Wood and Johnson 1978), including animal burrowing, that may disturb deposits below as well as near the surface. Floods may wash layers away and redeposit them in a secondary context, producing a

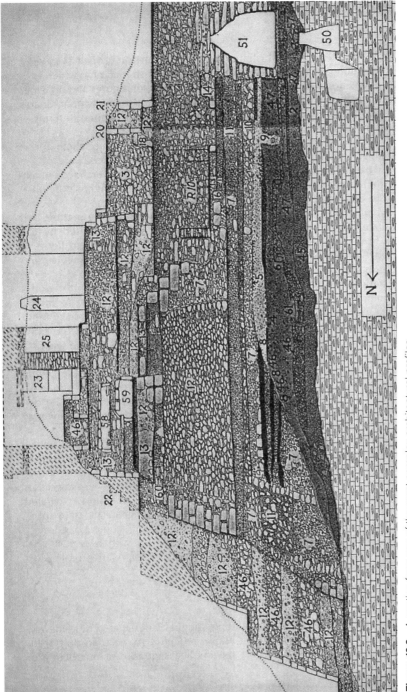

Figure 10.8 A section from one of the most complex architectural profiles in the Maya area, A-V palace at Uaxactun, Guatemala. E. M. Shook produced two detailed cross sections; this is a fragment of one. Shook's extraordinarily accurate drawing is surely a tour-de-force of this kind of recording.

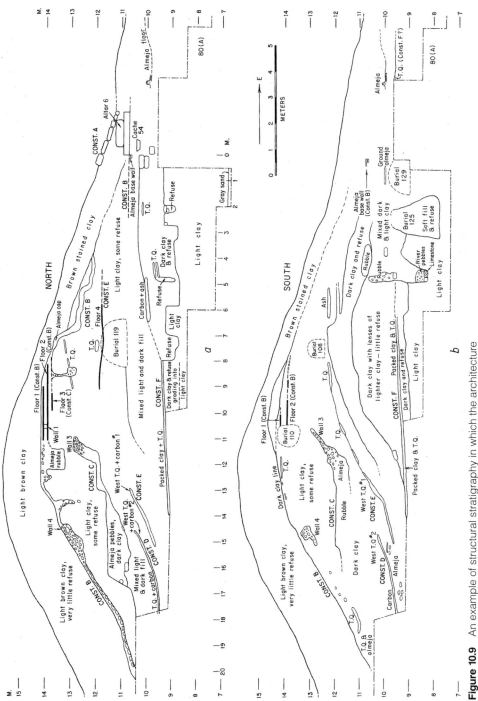

Figure 10.9 An example of structural stratigraphy in which the architecture is largely earthen or clay fill. Structure B-II at Altar de Sacrificios, Guatemala.

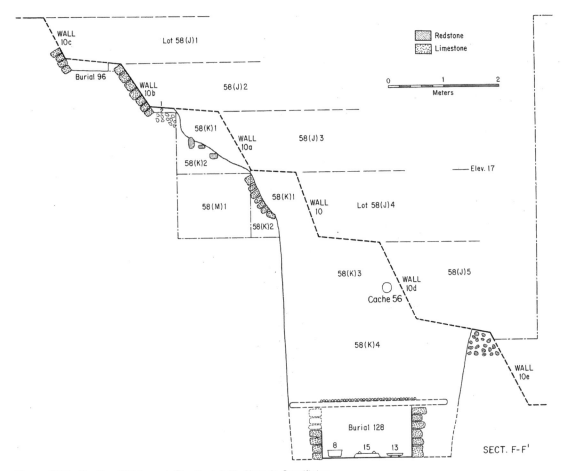

Figure 10.10 Section F-F' through Structure A-III, Altar de Sacrificios, Guatemala. Note the segregation of blocks of structural fill.

stratigraphic situation without any direct relation to cultural activities.

Horizontal stratigraphy is often seen in sites occupying a very large (or long) area. In these situations, the stratification is found across a site rather than vertically. A riverbank, for example, may have been occupied and reoccupied along its length, rather than having experienced continued or continual occupation of the same locality (creating depth). Similar horizontal stratification may be found along with beach formation (DePratter and Howard 1977; Giddings 1966).

Archaeological projects should make every effort to include in the staff a geoarchaeologist or someone with a strong background in geomorphology or soil science. This person can help to make critical distinctions between natural and cultural processes and discern formation and deformation processes (Goldberg 1988).

THE PROBLEM OF SAMPLING

All of archaeology can be viewed as a vast sampling game (see Chapter 3). The reliability of the information gained from stratigraphy is directly related to the size of the sample. In other words, the more you dig, usually, the more reliable your conclusions. And, relatively speaking, archaeologists dig very little. It has been calculated that in the case of a moderately large Maya site, Altar de Sacrificios, only 2–3 percent of the deposits theoretically present were sampled in 15 months of digging. The Jarmo excavations produced only about a 4 percent sample on a relatively small site, one with about 2,000 m^2 of scatter showing on the surface (Braidwood 1974). At the site of Momil in Colombia, the Reichel-Dolmatoffs' (1956) excavations produced a 1/6,000th sample from total theoretical deposits of about 360,000 m^3. Another way the point can be made is that rarely does one get the chance of replicating information by further excavation. The hoary tales of the most interesting finds being made in the final days of a project are true.

One disquieting aspect of stratigraphic sampling is that so much of the information produced is anomalous, confused, and understandable only by means of digging into undisturbed locations with long sequences under them. The latter are statistically rare in any excavation. Thus, a systematic and rigidly based sampling system is not necessarily the best means of *sampling* for stratification; such a system is, however, excellent for *locating* stratification. For purposes of increasing the size and reliability of the sample, however, one must differentially exploit the best-ordered deposits and those with the longest sequences. There is no mechanical cookbook approach to fieldwork that will infallibly yield reliable results. One must approach each situation with a willingness to apply the most appropriate from a full arsenal of techniques ranging from the most subtle and painstaking to the most rapid and narrowly objective oriented.

The archaeologist must approach peculiar and specific situations with technical finesse and theoretical sophistication. Obviously, the extremely detailed and careful approach demanded by a Paleolithic rockshelter (Movius 1974) is not always appropriate for one of the many apartment houses in Teotihuacan. The fact that there are many fewer Paleolithic rockshelters in all of southwestern Europe (about 500) than there are apartment houses (over 2,100) in the single Mexican site of Teotihuacan may influence the approach to the archaeologist's respective stratigraphic problems. How-

ever, these are all finite data and many times represent unique excavation opportunities. How one approaches stratigraphic excavation is, in a sense then, another aspect of the sampling problem.

SPECIAL AIDS

Soil samples from the walls of pits or trenches can be taken for special and/or future studies by various techniques. These materials (samples) may, after specialized analysis, assist with stratigraphic interpretations. The wall should always be cleaned immediately before sampling. A simple technique is to dig out the sample from each stratum with a clean knife or trowel, putting each sample into a sterilized container and labeling the material clearly. Specific extraction techniques may be required depending on the type of sample and its intended use (e.g., see Chapter 12 concerning pollen studies). Another technique is to paint the wall with a vertical stripe of latex rubber or other adhering material. Several coats of the rubber will form a strip sufficiently strong to peel off with samples of the various strata adhering to the underside. The sample side can then be protected by wrapping it with cloth, and the whole thing placed in a box, either whole or in sections (see Chapter 12 for a similar discussion). Methods of removing such sediment peels can be found in Goldberg (1974).

For purposes of faunal and floral analyses, specialists in each field should be consulted concerning the collection of samples to be studied. Because specific techniques of collection and methods of analysis affect the samples, only properly trained (or instructed) archaeologists should attempt the sample collection. For equipment and techniques involved in various sample collecting (and analysis) strategies, see Chapters 6, 12, and 13.

Coring tools, especially hand-operated augers or corers, are useful in testing subsurface deposits when one has reached the bottom of a deep pit. Too many archaeologists have assumed that a sterile lens encountered at respectable depths was the bottom of cultural deposits, only to find through later excavation that the most interesting material lay just below (see Drucker et al. 1959; Johnson 1964).

Using a coring device at Kinal, Guatemala, Scarborough was able to reconstruct the stratigraphy of a water reservoir by reviewing the profiles of the cores (Scarborough et al. 1994). A related technique implemented at Rio Azul, Guatemala, involved a motor-driven coring device, but the dirt in the core was not used or analyzed. Instead, a fiber optic line was dropped down the core hole, and the stratification was observed on a monitor and recorded on tape for future consideration (Valdez and Buttles 1991).

As mentioned earlier, air jets and sprayed water, both run by portable engines, can greatly aid in excavation and in making the stratigraphy more visible. These tools may assist in determining fine distinctions between various strata that are often differentiated by slight color differences or minor textural composition. Air jets may be especially useful in outlining mud-brick architecture, where it is often difficult to distinguish between the matrix soil and the structure.

For European Mesolithic sites, G. D. Clark (1974) recommends securing the collaboration of paleoethnobotanists to make sure that the stratigraphy has been interpreted correctly. Indeed, the older the site and the more dependent the archaeologist is on ecological data to explain cultural matters, the more urgent is the need for cooperative colleagues from the natural sciences. This kind of cooperation and interdisciplinary effort have been demonstrated at a number of archaeological sites worldwide, for example, Adovasio et al. (1978), Goldberg (1988), and Stuckenrath et al. (1982). At the archaeological site of Colha and adjacent Cobweb Swamp in northern Belize, soil formation processes, pollen remains, and artifacts have been used in conjunction to reconstruct and understand the stratification (Jacob 1992; Jones 1994). Soil scientists, a paleoethnobotanist, and archaeologists have worked in harmony in the Cobweb Swamp study. Archaeologists should not attempt to acquire all of the skills necessary to do palynology or a similarly complex analysis. They will not only spend valuable time on a secondary commitment but will find that their analyses carry less weight than if done by an appropriate specialist.

A final comment about archaeological stratigraphy and the information presented here. This chapter introduces the student to stratigraphic situations and the complexity of stratigraphy. Although the "law of superposition" and the Harris Matrix system have been introduced, each are worthy of greater attention and are discussed in much detail elsewhere (Harris 1989; Harris and Brown 1993). Other basic geological principles—such as the laws of original horizontality, lateral continuity, and intersecting relationships—are beyond the scope of this chapter but are mentioned as potential areas of additional study (see Harris 1989; Waters 1992). The role of the paleoethnobotanist, soil scientist, and geoarchaeologist in archaeological investigations is ever-increasing as methods of recognizing, defining, and recording stratigraphy continue to develop.

GUIDE TO FURTHER READING

History of Archaeological Stratigraphy

Adams 1960; Phillips et al. 1951; Thomas 1989; Willey and Sabloff 1993

Recording and Interpreting Stratigraphy

Clark 1974; Harris 1979, 1989; Harris et al. 1993; Johnson 1964; Laville et al. 1980; Movius 1974; Sheets 1983; Smith 1972

Disturbances Affecting Stratigraphy

Bollong 1994; Duffield 1970; Gifford-Gonzales et al. 1985; Sheets 1992; Villa 1982; Villa and Courtin 1983; Wood and Johnson 1978

Stratigraphic and Subsurface Sampling

Goldberg 1974; Scarborough et al. 1994; Stafford 1995; Voight and Gittins 1977

11

Excavation and Analysis
of Human Remains

Joseph F. Powell, D. Gentry Steele, and Michael B. Collins

Virtually all human cultures, past and present, have beliefs concerning the treatment of human remains. Attitudes toward death and dying are reflected in the way that a culture disposes of its dead and the way that human remains fit into both the ritual and daily life of its members. For prehistoric cultures, we must rely on the archaeological record for information regarding treatment of the dead. In the process of excavating, recording, and interpreting human remains and their archaeological context, the archaeologist acts according to his or her culture's own belief system regarding the dead—that, under certain conditions, human physical remains can be used for the benefit of society at large (Ubelaker and Grant 1989). Yet, not every cultural group within the United States agrees with this treatment of remains (Arden 1989). Some feel that human remains should not be the objects of study at all, under any circumstances (Mihesuah 1991). Still others feel that we have learned every-

thing there is to know and that further study of remains is both futile and disrespectful.

Today, the archaeologist is caught in a conflict between preserving the past by documenting all types of archaeological data including human remains and accommodating the belief systems of those with opposing views. Many students of archaeology, having to resolve this conflict on a personal level, want to know what point there is in studying human remains at all (Ubelaker 1989a:1). In this chapter, we attempt to answer this question, beginning with a general overview of the usefulness of human skeletal remains in resolving problems of anthropological interest. We also discuss the techniques for excavating burials and the laboratory techniques for collecting osteological data. Although most of the analytical techniques discussed in this chapter are traditionally performed in the laboratory, many are now conducted in field laboratories as prompt reburial of human skeletal remains becomes more common (see Rose [1985] for an excellent discussion of field analysis protocols). Even if human remains are to be analyzed and curated, it is extremely important for excavators to understand not only how to excavate them, but how excavation can affect subsequent analyses. Improper excavation, handling, or documentation of burials can severely limit the research potential of skeletal remains. Finally, we present some of the legal and ethical considerations of human remains research and some possible solutions to a difficult dilemma.

WHY EXCAVATE HUMAN REMAINS?

From a scientific standpoint, the study of human remains contributes directly to the major areas of archaeological inquiry: understanding cultural and biological history, reconstructing past lifeways, understanding the interplay between biology and culture of human populations, and understanding site formation processes. The skeleton of an individual is a reservoir of information about the individual's culture, environment, and life history, filtered through his or her physiology. As such, the skeleton can provide information related to a number of questions about that individual: What was the sex or biological affinity of the individual? How old was the individual at the time of death? How did the individual die? What did the individual look like? What was the individual's state of health? What did the individual eat? How were the remains of the individual treated by those who survived? Taken as a group, human remains make it possible to reconstruct aspects of biology and behavior that are not available from the study of other kinds of archaeological data. Recognizing this, Saul (1972) and Saul and Saul (1989) describe the study of the human skeleton as "osteobiography."

Being social animals, humans are inevitably members of a social group, a population, and the collective study of the remains of members of that population can shed light on the quality of life of the population. Raising the level of generalization from the individual to the population permits

inquiry into human ecology and evolution. When such questions are raised, it is virtually impossible to separate the impact of the biological world from that of the cultural world on the population. Any change in the quality or style of life will evoke cultural and biological responses, and so closely are the two interrelated that it is commonly impossible to address the one response without addressing the other (Goodman et al. 1988). This is in fact one of the basic tenets of American anthropology.

Because of their value in addressing the above questions, human remains should always be investigated with care and under thorough archaeological controls. The investigator is obligated to be familiar with, and proceed according to, all applicable statutes regarding human remains. Also, it is incumbent on the investigator to take into account the customs, beliefs, and wishes of the society with which the remains are affiliated. Most important, it is the excavator's responsibility to be aware of the nature of anthropological analysis of human remains so that the excavation will recover as fully and precisely as possible the data available in the field setting. It should also be remembered that at times, human remains are excavated using archaeological procedures for forensic rather than anthropological investigations (Morse et al. 1983; Rathbun and Buikstra 1984; Sigler-Eisenberg 1985), and what is presented here applies as much to law enforcement as to archaeological excavation and analysis.

RESEARCH WITH SKELETAL POPULATIONS

An archaeological **skeletal assemblage** is a collection of human remains recovered from an archaeological context. This assemblage is often referred to as a **skeletal population,** defined here as a community of individuals at a given locality who at one time had the potential to interbreed (Mayr 1970). In reality, mortuary assemblages may instead represent **skeletal lineages** (Cadien et al. 1974; Konigsberg 1987), accumulations of individuals from some larger cultural and/or biological unit over a period of several generations. Although generational overlap and incompleteness of skeletal samples can present difficulties for investigators, in many cases human remains representing a number of individuals may be recovered under sufficiently close archaeological controls that the inference that they represent a population is justified. Or, several carefully excavated assemblages may be collectively considered representative of a past biological population (Buikstra 1981; Sciulli 1990a, 1990b). In these instances, the examination of the skeletal material can contribute to the elucidation of many aspects of human biology and prehistory. Given this perspective, there are several lines of inquiry that can be followed in the examination of human remains.

Paleodemography

Paleodemography is an approach to the study of the composition, age structure, survivorship patterns, health status, and genetic makeup of past populations. Because of the scope of this approach, paleodemography integrates several technical fields. The fundamental and, unfortunately, most difficult task of paleodemographic analysis is recovering or assembling an adequate sample of remains to constitute a population (Buikstra and Konigsberg 1985). It must be demonstrable that the individuals whose remains are under examination lived close enough together in culture, politics, social organization, geography, and time to justify their inclusion in a single unit of demographic analysis.

Once a skeletal series has been identified as representative of a population, the individual age and sex data are summarized in age categories that are defined by the research question (though typically these are in 5-year intervals from birth to 50 or more years). Care should be taken that the age and sex determinations are unbiased (Buikstra and Mielke 1985), and fortunately, detection of biased data has become easier (Lovejoy 1971; Weiss 1972, 1973). After compilation, the data are statistically analyzed to produce rates of survivorship and mortality for that population (see Acsadi and Nemeskeri 1970; Asch 1976; Jackes 1992; Roth 1992; Swedlund 1975; and Weiss 1973 for discussions of

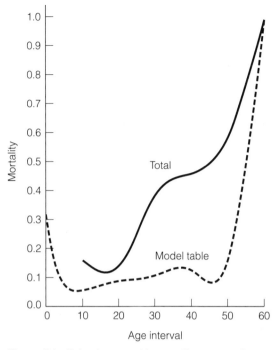

Figure 11.1 Paleodemographic mortality curve and statistically derived model-life-table mortality for a prehistoric Texas population.

methods). These results can then be matched to model life tables that list the parameters of survivorship, mortality (Figure 11.1), fertility, and population growth for mathematical models that are drawn from the census data of living populations (Coale and Demeny 1966; Weiss 1973, 1975).

Once completed, the demographic analysis can be used to address a variety of research issues. It may be possible to link mortality rates to morbid conditions in skeletal and dental remains (Clark et al. 1986; Goodman and Armelagos 1988; Palkovitch 1980). Patterns of mortality, survival, and fertility can be interpreted within a cultural context on an intra- or intersite scale (Buikstra 1981; Buikstra et al. 1986; Konigsberg 1985; Lovejoy et al. 1977; Mensforth 1986). Even cultural behavior such as specialized corpse disposal or intergroup violence can be detected by examining who is missing from the age and sex profile (Blakely and Mathews 1990; Buikstra 1981; Owsley et al. 1977).

Paleodemography is not without problems, however, and critics have been quick to identify the abuse of many of its assumptions (Bocquet-Appel and Masset 1982, 1985; Sattenspiel and Harpending 1983). Other authors, recognizing the methodological and theoretical difficulties of paleodemography, have shown that the methods have research potential if used responsibly (Buikstra and Konigsberg 1985; Buikstra et al. 1986; Jackes 1992; Konigsberg 1985; Konigsberg et al. 1989; Roth 1992; van Gerven and Armelagos 1983). One approach that has tremendous potential for correcting the problems of paleodemography is the comparison of demographic patterns obtained through skeletal analysis against demographic data from written records (Corruccini et al. 1989). Readers should consult the recent overviews by Jackes (1992) and Roth (1992) and edited volumes by Larsen and Milner (1994), Ortner and Aufderheide (1991), Owsley and Jantz (1994), and Verano and Ubelaker (1994) for further information on paleodemographic research.

Paleopathology

Over the past 25 years, research on skeletal populations has broadened our view of the effects of disease on human biology and culture. Reviews of the diagnosis (Mann 1990; Ortner and Putschar 1981; Rothschild and Martin 1993; Steinbock 1976; Zimmerman and Kelley 1982; Zivanovic 1982) and interpretation (see Brothwell and Sandison 1967; Cohen and Armelagos 1984; Eisenberg 1991; Gilbert and Mielke 1985; Goodman et al. 1988; Iscan and Kennedy 1989; Janssens 1970; Kelley and Larsen 1991; Merbs and Miller 1985; Ortner and Aufderheide 1991; Saunders and Katzenberg 1992; Steward-Macadam 1989, 1992; Stewart-Macadam and Kent 1992; Wood et al. 1992) of prehistoric disease processes have been published. The science of **paleopathology** is dedicated to understanding how, where, and why diseases originated and evolved (Armelagos and Dewey 1970; Baker and Armelagos 1988; Buikstra and Cook 1981; Goodman et al. 1988; Lallo et al. 1977; Salo et al. 1994; Stewart-Macadam 1989, 1992), how human biological systems were affected by changes in behavior or environment (Buikstra 1976; Eisenberg 1991; Gregg

and Zimmerman 1986; Jurmain 1990; Larsen 1982; Lukacs 1989; Powell 1985; Schumucher 1985; Stewart-Macadam 1989, 1992; P. L. Walker 1985), and how human cultural systems adapted to, and were shaped by, biological disorders (Kent 1986; Rose 1985). Hundreds of articles have been published on the health of skeletal populations, yet research continues because new techniques, new theoretical approaches, and the reanalysis of collections permit new questions to be asked of these data (Bell 1990; Buikstra and Gordon 1981; Ortner 1991; Wood et al. 1992). Readers should see the edited volumes by Larsen and Milner (1994), Ortner and Aufderheide (1991), Owsley and Jantz (1994), Saunders and Katzenberg (1992), and Verano and Ubelaker (1994) for recent examples of paleopathological research.

Bones and teeth, which are living tissues, are affected by disease in a number of ways. During growth, infection (Kelley 1989; Steinbock 1976), trauma (Merbs 1989), genetic disease (Cook and Buikstra 1979; Dickel and Doran 1989; Turkel 1989), and other direct factors (Stewart-Macadam 1989, 1992; Stewart-Macadam and Kent 1992) can alter bone, leaving permanent defects in hard tissue. Likewise, environmental factors, such as quantity and quality of the diet, can disrupt patterns of normal growth (Goodman and Armelagos 1988; Goodman and Rose 1991; Gregg and Zimmerman 1986; Rose et al. 1985; Skinner and Goodman 1992) and leave a permanent defect in bones or teeth (Figure 11.2). In adults, the skeleton may retain the evidence of childhood disorders and continues to accumulate evidence of current health and behavior (Armelagos et al. 1982; Kennedy 1989; Lukacs 1989). Hard tissues do not record all types of medical disorders, however. Many viral and bacterial infections leave little trace in osteological remains or are difficult to diagnose (Jackes 1983; Ortner and Putschar 1981:222–229), and diseases of the soft tissues (such as gastroenteritis) may not affect bone at all. For a disease to affect bone, it must act directly on hard tissues, affect soft tissues immediately adjacent to bone, or in some way involve bone growth and metabolism, as in the case of anemias (Kent 1986; Ortner and Putschar 1981:251–183; Steinbock 1976:213–252; Steward-Macadam 1989,

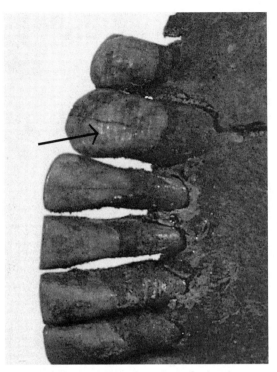

Figure 11.2 Linear enamel hypoplasia. Such paleo-pathology on teeth usually reflects serious illness or malnutrition during tooth formation.

1992). In some instances, the individual lesion may be diagnostic of the disorder. In others, the individual lesions on bone created by different diseases may be similar, and only the distribution of the lesions throughout the skeleton may be diagnostic of the disorder (Hackett 1976).

Under certain environmental and cultural conditions, preserved or mummified soft tissues (Figure 11.3) (Allison and Pezzia 1974; Clausen et al. 1979; Cockburn and Cockburn 1980; David 1985; Doran et al. 1986; Hauswirth et al. 1991; Newell 1984) or stomach, intestinal, or colon contents are preserved in association with skeletal remains (Shafer et al. 1989). In these cases, infections, parasites, and other agents can be researched histologically, biochemically, and in gross form (David 1985; El-Najjar and Mulinski 1980; Peck 1980; Silimperia et al. 1984; Toriabara and Jackson 1982; Zimmerman et al. 1981). The remains of medicines may

also be found in the stomach, intestines, or colon, providing information about the health care practices of the past (Shafer et al. 1989). Recent advances in DNA extraction and amplification techniques have made it possible to directly identify the DNA sequences of infectious microorganisms present in ancient bones and soft tissues (Ortner et al. 1992; Rothschild 1992). In one case, such research was able to show conclusively that tuberculosis was present in the New World before European contact by identifying the DNA of *Mycobacterium tuberculosis* in a pre-Columbian mummy (Salo et al. 1994).

Paleodietary Analysis

Biochemical determinations of diet from archaeological remains (skeletal, generally) recently have provided us with significant insights into the diets of past peoples (Ambrose 1986; Boaz and Hampel 1978; Price et al. 1985; Sillen et al. 1989), complementing the more traditional approaches to dietary analysis. For example, reduced strontium levels in burials whose grave offerings suggest higher social status might reflect differential access to meat, because strontium is incorporated into the skeletal system from plant foods. Numerous studies of trace elements—including not only strontium, but barium, lead, magnesium, and zinc as well—have been used to reconstruct paleodiets (Aufderheide et al. 1981; Francalacci 1989; Gilbert 1985; Lambert et al. 1979; Lambert et al. 1984; Schoeninger 1979; Sillen and Kavanagh 1982).

The relative importance of certain plants—for example, maize—in the diet is also subject to determination from isotopic analysis. Most plants utilize a "C_3" photosynthetic pathway, whereas maize utilizes a "C_4" pathway that transmits to plants a larger proportion of the heavy carbon isotope, Carbon-13. Humans metabolize Carbon-13 and Carbon-12 indiscriminately, with the result that the ratio of Carbon-13 to Carbon-12 in body tissue—including collagen—is proportional to that in the diet. High ^{13}C-to-^{12}C ratios in archaeological samples of human bone collagen indicate that maize or some other C_4 plant was important in the diet. In some cases this proves a more reliable means of

Figure 11.3 Naturally mummified human infant.

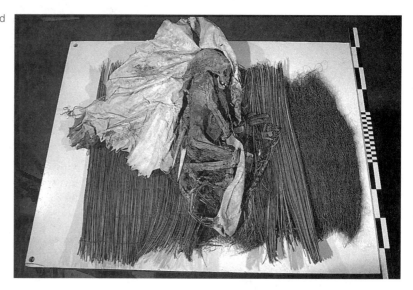

investigating the beginning of maize agriculture than more traditional forms of archaeological inquiry (Burger and van der Merwe 1990; DeNiro and Epstein 1978; Farnsworth et al. 1985; Schwarcz and Schoeninger 1991; Vogel and van der Merwe 1977). Another isotope used in the investigation of prehistoric diets is Nitrogen-15. The ratio of ^{15}N to ^{14}N is felt to differentiate between marine and terrestrial foods (Keegan and DeNiro 1988; Schoeninger and DeNiro 1984; Schoeninger et al. 1983) because ^{15}N is more highly concentrated in marine food chains.

Criticism leveled at isotopic and biochemical studies of prehistoric diet has focused on the fact that bone decay (diagenesis) may destroy the original chemistry of bone and thus create false pictures of past diets (Buikstra et al. 1989; Klepinger et al. 1986; Kyle 1986). The use of preservatives on bone can also greatly affect results (Moore et al. 1989). Further, some critics feel that the metabolism of chemical key markers is not sufficiently understood to make conclusive statements even if the original chemical constituents of the bone are known (Schoeninger and DeNiro 1984; Sillen et al. 1989). Nonetheless, refinements in the field make many archaeologists and biochemists confident

that chemical analyses of bone will provide information on prehistoric diets unavailable from other sources (Price 1991; Sandford 1992; Sillen et al. 1989). Up-to-date information on the problems and successes of biochemical research using human bone can be obtained from the reviews by Price et al. (1985), Sandford (1992), Schwarcz and Schoeninger (1991), and edited volumes by Price (1989) and Sandford (1993).

More-traditional analyses of human remains can also provide clues about prehistoric diets (see the papers in Sobolik 1994). The shift to agriculture was often accompanied by degradation of health in prehistoric populations (Cohen and Armelagos 1984; El-Najjar 1976; Gilbert and Mielke 1985; Larsen and Milner 1994), and the status of health is reflected in the skeleton. However, recent theoretical developments indicate that the association between skeletal health and morbidity in a living population may be more complex than previously thought (Wood et al. 1992). Teeth contain much more direct data on the health status of individuals. For example, dental caries are associated with diets high in carbohydrates (Larsen et al. 1991; Lukacs 1989; Marks et al. 1985; Powell 1985). Abrasion and trauma to the teeth may indicate an abrasive diet, grit introduced during food processing, or a diet with small, hard-to-chew constituents (Comuzzie and Steele 1989; Irish and Turner 1987; Marks et al. 1985; Teaford 1991; Turner and Machado 1983). Nutritional deficiencies or overabundance can produce skeletal lesions, such as scurvy, rickets, or hypervitaminosis (Ortner and Putschar 1981; Steinbock 1976; Stewart-Macadam 1989).

SKELETAL BIOLOGY

In the past, archaeologists and physical anthropologists interested in understanding the nature of biological variation in humans collected vast amounts of metric data from the skeleton (Armelagos et al. 1982; Brace 1972; Lovejoy, Mensforth, and Armelagos 1985). Principally, this information was used to classify races and to analyze variation within a population. Although this field of research has been partially eclipsed by paleopathology and paleodietary analyses, physical anthropologists continue to answer important questions about body size, body proportions, sexual dimorphism, and population variation using skeletal data derived from both historic and prehistoric populations.

As an example, some of the continuing questions raised pertaining to human evolution concern why humans are sexually dimorphic, why they are less sexually dimorphic than many of the other anthropoids, and what the biological mechanisms that cause populations to differ in degree of sexual dimorphism are (e.g., Armelagos and Van Gerven 1980; Brace 1972; Frayer and Wolpoff 1985; Hall 1982). Changes in body proportionality between populations have also been noted and examined in prehistoric North American populations (e.g., Doran 1975; Jantz and Owsley 1984a).

The growth and development of individuals in prehistoric populations have also been major concerns of physical anthropologists. Typically, the rates of growth or development in individuals are used as assessments of the health of the individuals or the degree of adaptive success of the population (e.g., Armelagos and van Gerven 1980; Armelagos

et al. 1982; Hummert and Van Gerven 1983; Jantz and Owsley 1984b; Johnston and Zimmer 1989; Mensforth 1985).

Biological Affinity

One area of research in which skeletal biologists have been particularly active is the study of biological affinity and human phylogeny. At the level of the individual, the question addressed simply may be, To which population did this individual belong? Forensic research in particular has focused on techniques for assigning an unknown individual to one particular biological population or another (Gilbert and Gill 1990; Giles and Elliott 1962; Gill 1984). Although this type of research at the level of the individual has limited utility for archaeologists, there are instances where it is useful.

A more common endeavor is to establish the phyletic relationships of populations to one another. These analyses proceed under the assumption that differences in size and shape of the skeletal features being examined are at least in part genetically controlled and that the application of principles and methods of quantitative genetics or phylogenetics to skeletal populations will provide accurate estimates of the genetic similarities (Conner 1990; Konigsberg 1987, 1990; Konigsberg and Blangero 1993; Relethford 1994; Relethford and Harpending 1994; Relethford and Lees 1982; Sciulli 1990b; van Vark and Howells 1984). These assumptions are well supported by experimental data (Cheverud 1988; Kieser 1990) and mathematical theory (Blangero 1987; Falconer 1989; Hartl and Clark 1989; Relethford and Blangero 1990; Relethford and Harpending 1994; Sokal and Rohlf 1971; Williams-Blangero and Blangero 1989). Biological distances based on metric traits have been estimated for the earliest North American populations (Powell and Steele 1992; Steele and Powell 1992, 1994), for Archaic and Woodland populations in the eastern Woodlands (Harris and Bellantoni 1980; Powell 1995; Sciulli 1990b; Sciulli et al. 1984), late prehistoric groups in the American Southwest (Coruccini 1973), and populations in the Great Plains (Jantz 1977; Key and Jantz 1990).

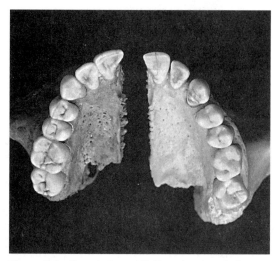

Figure 11.4 Shovel-shaped (*left*) and unshoveled (*right*) upper incisors from populations in Asia.

The same assumptions found in metric studies of skeletal population variation underlie the study of nonmetric variation. Discrete traits of the cranium and teeth, such as the presence of accessory foramina in the cranium or incisor shoveling (Figure 11.4), have been used to characterize populations and indicate their relationships to one another (Buikstra 1976; Conner 1990; Konigsberg 1987, 1990; Lukacs and Hemphill 1991; Ossenberg 1974, 1976; Turner 1985, 1986, 1987, 1990). Again there is support that these features are heritable (Hauser and De Stafano 1989; Nichol 1989); standardized methods for scoring traits are readily available (Hauser and De Stafano 1989; Turner et al. 1991). Similar comparative analyses of populations are being conducted on DNA and proteins of modern populations (Schanfield 1992; Schanfield et al. 1990; Smith and Wilson 1990; Spuhler 1988; Stoneking et al. 1986; Szathmary 1985, 1994; Torroni et al. 1993), and the recovery and amplification of DNA from soft tissue and bone of prehistoric remains indicates yet another way that recovered remains may be studied to provide information on the biological affinity of individuals and phylogenetic relationships of populations (Andrews 1994; Hauswirth et al. 1991; Lawlor et al. 1991; Martin et al. 1993; Pääbo et al. 1989; Rogan and

Salvo 1990; Thuesen and Engberg 1990; Williams et al. 1990).

Cultural Behavior

Because the remains of the deceased are usually disposed of following a rich and complex set of behavioral patterns, their study provides essential data on cultural behavior. Mortuary studies abound in the archaeological literature (Brown 1971; Buikstra 1976; Goldstein 1980; O'Shea 1984; Saxe 1971; Ubelaker and Willey 1978; Whittlesey 1978). The types of grave goods present, their distribution in a site, the position of the body, and the form of corpse disposal all provide keys to understanding how and why past peoples acted. In ossuary sites, where bodies were collected on a regular schedule for ceremonial reinterment, osteological data can be combined with ethnohistoric research to enable us to understand how these sites functioned within a cultural system (Jirikowic 1990; Ubelaker 1974).

Beyond mortuary behavior, the examination of skeletons themselves provides data on daily life and activities. Intentional alteration of the body, for whatever reason, can be detected in hard tissues (Milner and Larsen 1991; Romero 1970; Stewart 1973). Medical procedures, such as **trephination** (removal of part of the skull) or amputation, are cultural behaviors that also affect skeletal tissue (Ortner and Putschar 1981; Steinbock 1976; Zimmerman et al. 1981). Even more mundane activities, such as constant squatting or use of the teeth as tools, can be discerned in skeletal remains (Kennedy 1989; Ubelaker 1979). Human remains may also be modified for personal use, being converted into jewelry, tools, or household decorations (Hester 1969; Seeman 1988).

Perhaps the most striking examples of cultural behavior detected through human remains are signs of interpersonal violence, such as sharp or blunt trauma to bone (Walker 1989). Weapons, whether they be stone projectile points or lead slugs, are often found in or around bone (Figure 11.5) (Prewitt 1982; Rose and Santeford 1985:113; Steinbock 1976). Cut marks on bone are also noted,

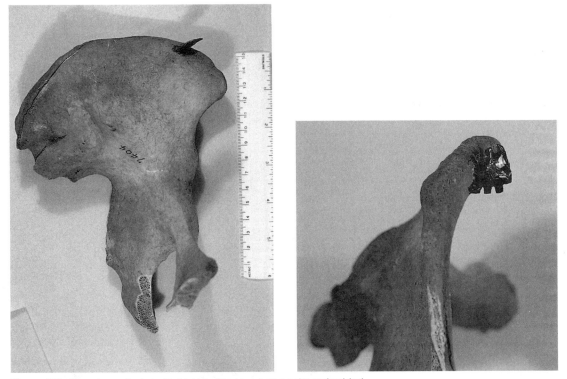

Figure 11.5 Two views of a Late Prehistoric Stockton arrow point embedded in the dorsal side of the anterior iliac crest (pelvis). Site CCo-138, California.

although it can be difficult to distinguish between aboriginal cuts and those caused by an excavator's metal tools; this is one reason metal tools should not be used in exposing burials. Examples of cut marks include dismemberment as part of the mortuary program (Raemsch 1993; Ubelaker 1974), dismemberment as part of intergroup violent behavior or cannibalism (White 1992; Zimmerman et al. 1980), flaying of skin (Massey 1989; Massey and Steele 1982; White 1986), scalping (O'Shea and Bridges 1988; Steinbock 1976), and stabs or cuts from metal weapons during battle (Blakely and Mathews 190).

Taphonomy

Human skeletal remains, both individually and as a population, can provide the archaeologist with valuable information on the processes contributing to site formation. The elements present, their distribution in a site, and their association with features and stratified deposits are all important to interpretations of site formation. The fact that only certain parts of the body (such as the spinal column) are in articulation may indicate that some of the bodies were interred in an advanced state of decomposition (Haglund 1991, 1992; Haglund et al. 1989; Mann et al. 1990; Ubelaker 1974). The effects of burning, weathering, trampling, and other destructive processes acting on bone assemblages have been extensively examined (Binford 1981; Bonnichsen and Sorg 1989; Buikstra and Swegle 1989; Lyman and Fox 1989; Micozzi 1991; Olsen and Shipman 1988; P. Shipman 1981; Shipman et al. 1984; Turner and Turner 1992; Ubelaker and Sperber 1988), and the presence of these factors in a human bone assemblage provides the excavator with additional tools for reconstructing site formation processes. Taphonomic factors are also important to understand because they can affect chemical analyses of human bone (Buikstra et al. 1989; Hanson and Buikstra 1987; Klepinger et al. 1986; Kyle 1986; Lambert et al. 1990; Sillen et al. 1989).

TYPES OF INTERMENTS

Human groups have followed a great variety of burial practices in the prehistoric past. A complete classification of burial practices is beyond the scope of this chapter, and we suggest here only some of the main varieties that may be encountered in the archaeological sites created by noncomplex societies. In more complex societies, individuals may be buried in various (and sometimes quite elaborate) ways depending on their achieved or ascribed social status. For a broad perspective on the study of burial practices, see Brown (1971), O'Shea (1984), and Saxe (1971). For a review of the terminology and categorizations associated with human remains in archaeological contexts, see Sprague (1968).

Primary Interments

In primary interments, the deceased lie in their initial place of repose—either placed in the ground, put in a rock crevice, dropped into a cave shaft or body of water, or placed in a tomb. If buried, the bones lie in the same anatomical relationship (articulation) as when the individual was alive, and the presumption is that the relationships of the skeletal elements to one another have not been altered since the soft tissue decomposed. In dry caves, open deposits, or cold climates, corpses may be found in naturally "mummified" conditions, as in Arizona (Kidder and Guernsey 1921), Nevada (Loud and Harrington 1929), Northern Mexico (Zingg 1940), Texas (Turpin et al. 1986), Kentucky (Neumann 1938), the coast of Peru (Mason 1961; Vreeland and Cockburn 1980), predynastic Egypt (Lucas and Harris 1962:270; Peck 1980), and circumpolar regions.

The body may be in a contracted or flexed position (Figure 11.6), an extended position (Figure 11.6), or a sitting posture and may lie on its face, side, or back. If the exposed bones are carefully studied, the investigator will usually be able to describe the exact position of the corpse at burial. Open-air exposure of such corpses for a time before burial may be indicated by the presence of fly pupae on or around the excavated remains or the observation of carnivore and rodent gnawing on bones (Haglund 1991, 1992); the season in which such exposure occurred is also indicated by the type and stage of pupae and by other factors (Mann et al. 1990).

If the body was placed in water, dropped in a cave, or disposed of in some fashion where it did not decay in a protected environment, then the elements are commonly scattered and may be commingled with those of other individuals. An example of a primary interment where the bones are separated and commingled is a cave shaft ("sinkhole") burial where, over a period of time, bodies are dropped in the chamber but not covered with earth (Bement 1991; Skinner et al. 1980; Turpin 1985); in some sinkhole situations, however, the elements remain in relatively good anatomical relationship (Arroyo de Anda et al. 1953).

Secondary Interments

Secondary interments are those remains where the bones were collected at the primary site of disposal after the flesh had been removed by exposure or by bacterial decay and then were deposited elsewhere, usually in a grave. The bones are not in natural anatomical relationship, and typically some are missing (Ubelaker 1974). Also, individuals may be mixed. The reinterred bones may have been painted, broken, or cut (Collins et al. 1969; Hester 1969; O'Shea and Bridges 1988; Ubelaker 1974). "Trophies" or other dismembered remains also fall into this category (Massey 1989; Massey and Steele 1982; Seeman 1988; Steele et al. 1980; Zimmerman et al. 1980).

Multiple Interments

Single graves containing the skeletal remains of several people are of two main types: those in

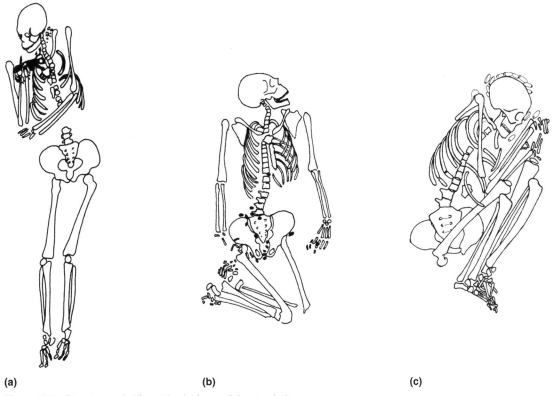

(a)   **(b)**   **(c)**

Figure 11.6 Plan views of different burial forms: (*a*) extended, (*b*) semiflexed, and (*c*) flexed.

which all were buried at once and those in which primary and secondary burials were added over a period of time. The simultaneous group burials are usually taken to result from the death of many people by a single cause, such as massacre, disease, sacrifice, or war (Zimmerman et al. 1980). In the southeastern United States (Sears 1961) and at Coclé, Panama (Lothrop 1937), however, graves have been found containing not only a paramount individual but also retainers or servants or slaves apparently killed to join their master. Examples of this type of mortuary behavior were found at the George C. Davis site (Story 1972) and Cahokia (Fowler 1977). In many Old World megalithic chambered tombs or dolmens—but only rarely in prehistoric sites in the New World, as at San Agustin Acaguastalan, Guatemala (Smith and Kidder 1943)—the same graves were reused as burial chambers over a period of many years. A

method for assigning bones from a mixed collection to individuals by the use of ultraviolet fluorescence is described by Eyman (1965) and by McKern (1958). In such cases, however, it may be better to describe the osteological material as a single group rather than attempting to sort out individuals (for examples, see Marks et al. 1985; Powell 1991; Ubelaker 1974).

Cremations

If the dead were burned, earth may have been thrown over the ashes and cremated bones. More commonly, however, the ashes were sifted; the calcined bone collected and placed in a pouch, basket, or pottery jar (Bowman 1990; Heye 1919; Sayles 1937:Plate 27); and the container buried in a dug pit. At times, as at some sites in California or Arizona, the cremated bones were simply put into the pit and covered with earth (Sayles 1937:Plate 28). Special rectangular clay crematory basins were used by the Ohio Hopewell people (Shetrone 1930) and at the Snaketown site in Arizona (Sayles 1937). In at least one known instance (Bowman 1990), the cremated remains of a single individual were placed in three separate pits; historic sites on the Gulf coast of Texas include the remains of several individuals in a single cremation feature.

Adventitious Remains

Human physical remains are often encountered under conditions suggesting unintentional placement. Teeth, small bones, and the like become displaced from burials and mixed with refuse in occupational sites. In the past, excavators felt that such remains were useless and uninformative. However, appropriate knowledge of taphonomy, the conditions of preservation, and provenience on the part of the bioarchaeologist can provide excellent data from adventitious remains. For example, if an archaeologist notes the presence of numerous anterior teeth in a site's habitation area, these scattered elements may have an important cultural interpretation. Coupled with a lack of other cranial elements associated with these teeth, good preservation of other organic material inside house areas, and a lack of anterior teeth in secondary burials, the bioarchaeologist might infer that the teeth had fallen out of skulls suspended inside habitation areas prior to secondary burial of the skulls in an area away from the habitation.

Individuals sometimes met with tragedy away from their place of habitation, and their bodies were never found by other members of their group. Unlike the intentional burials discussed above, the prehistoric miner who perished when a dislodged rock fell on him in Mammoth Cave, Kentucky (Neumann 1938), was found in the place and position of death, as were some of the Neanderthal individuals of Shanidar Cave, Iraq, who evidently were crushed under great rocks falling from the roof of the cave (Solecki 1963:179, 1975). Such remains by themselves provide a modest amount of information about the population they represent (see Trinkaus 1983) but a good deal about the activ-

ities of that individual at or near the time of death. Patterning in unburied remains can also be indicative of behavior such as cannibalism (Flinn et al. 1976; T. D. White 1992) or other incidents in which burial did not occur even though survivors were clearly present.

EXCAVATING BURIALS

Exposing the Burial

Certain techniques and the observance of certain precautions are helpful when exposing a burial. Not all the problems that might arise in such an excavation can be discussed here; the individual worker's sense and ingenuity must be relied on to cope with special contingencies. In the following discussion, it is assumed that the pit or other feature in which human remains are discovered is being recorded by the same procedures used to document other features (see Chapters 5 and 6). This documentation is critical because the context of the feature containing the remains is often the primary evidence associating the human remains with a particular time period, archaeological culture, or other physical remains.

On uncovering bone in an excavation unit, the excavator should proceed with caution. The excavator should first attempt to determine whether the remains in question are human or nonhuman. Guides such as Ubelaker (1989a) provide discussions of how to distinguish between faunal and human skeletal elements by their size and shape. The best means of making such assessments in the field, however, is for the excavator or someone on the crew to have training in human osteology and faunal analysis (see Chapter 13). If it is not possible to immediately determine whether skeletal elements are indeed human, it is always better to err on the side of caution—to presume that the remains are human until proven otherwise. Excavators should be particularly alert to the presence of human bone when excavating midden deposits because some cultures disposed of subadults and infant remains in refuse areas rather than in those locations typically used for burial of adults. More than once has the skeleton of a human infant been

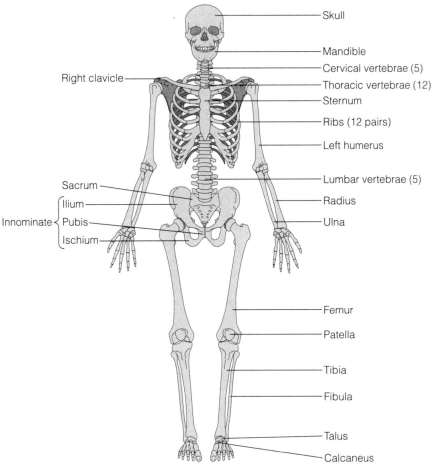

Right clavicle
Skull
Mandible
Cervical vertebrae (5)
Thoracic vertebrae (12)
Sternum
Ribs (12 pairs)
Left humerus
Lumbar vertebrae (5)
Sacrum
Ilium
Innominate Pubis
Ischium
Radius
Ulna
Femur
Patella
Tibia
Fibula
Talus
Calcaneus

Figure 11.7 Articulated human skeleton showing the major bones of the body.

sorted out of a faunal assemblage in the lab rather than in the field because the excavators mistakenly presumed that the bones were not human. The result in such cases is an extreme loss of information about the context of burial and the mortuary treatment of certain segments of a prehistoric society.

As soon as a burial is discovered, the excavator must try to determine the position of the individual. Because of its size and height, the skull is frequently the first skeletal area uncovered during removal of overlying deposits. Several additional points on the skeleton, such as the pelvis, knees, and elbows, must be located to pinpoint the exact position of the individual. This should be done before further exposure is attempted and should itself expose as little of the skeleton as possible to protect it from damage. Knowledge of the form and relative position of the major bones of the skeleton, and the ability to determine the side of the body to which they belong, are necessary for identifying the exposed parts. Excavators of human burials should become familiar with the human skeleton (Figure 11.7), either through classroom training or through the use of texts (Bass 1987; Brothwell 1982; Steele and Bramblett 1988; Ubelaker 1989a; White 1991). Familiarity with the skeleton can save time and effort in planning and executing the removal of human remains.

Trowels, dental probes, and other metal tools should not be used to excavate bone. These items can damage bone, leaving cut marks and scratches that are easily mistaken as signs of mutilation, dismemberment, or other perimortem trauma. Furthermore, metal tools can severely damage or destroy pathological conditions in bone, resulting in a loss of data. When working with bone, the excavator should use soft materials such as bamboo or cane splints (with rounded tips) and wooden dowels. Soft brushes, especially horsehair brushes, are preferred over stiff-whiskered brushes or whisk-brooms. Remember, the bone is softer than the tools being used to excavate it and is quite easily damaged. Also keep in mind that bone in the ground is often moist, which makes it even softer.

One of the most satisfactory methods of exposing a burial is by **pedestaling** it as soon as its position and extent are determined—that is, by leaving the burial embedded in its matrix while the surrounding dirt is cleared away and a level floor established. The height of the pedestal will vary, but 20–25 cm is a minimum. This method not only gives a more convenient working height, but also prevents loose dirt from drifting back onto the burial. However, it may not always be feasible to follow this procedure. Indeed, it should not be used if any trace of the burial pit remains, for such evidence must be preserved. For example, burials in the sterile subsoil of a mound may reveal the grave pit outline by a difference in color and texture between the mound soil and the subsoil (Story 1972; Ubelaker 1989a:14; Webb 1946).

Burials should generally be exposed from the top downward (Figure 11.8). Because it is obviously inefficient to continually sweep loose dirt over previously cleaned areas, it is advisable to expose the central areas first, especially the cavities of the rib cage, abdomen, and pelvis. Once these are cleaned, the excavator can then expose the arms and legs from proximal (closest to the trunk) to distal (farthest from the trunk). The hands and feet consist of numerous small bones that are easily disturbed after they have been exposed; they should therefore be the last areas excavated.

Certain areas within a burial should be given special attention. Nonperishable items of shell,

Figure 11.8   Excavated burial from New Mexico. Note that the burial has been carefully cleaned. A meter stick (scale) with a north arrow is included as is a chalkboard that identifies provenience.

bone, and stone that are worn as ornaments—either strung or on clothing—will remain after the perishable items have disappeared. Therefore, valuable information may be gained by observing the exact location of such nonperishable objects before removing them. For example, necklaces may be indicated by beads or other perforated ornaments found around the neck, shoulders, and upper rib cage; headdress ornaments may be found around the skull, wristlets along the arm, and waistband and skirt ornaments in and around the pelvis. Ornaments or tools were often placed in the hands, and the areas around the hands should be carefully investigated.

That an object is found in a burial pit along

with human remains does not make it a priori interpretable as an intentional grave inclusion. The grave fill may contain site refuse that inadvertently rests next to the corpse at the time of burial. Also, the position of objects can shift within the grave context, making the meaning of their position uncertain. A projectile point found between the ribs of a skeleton buried in a pit that was dug into and then refilled with midden debris could be interpreted as (1) an intentional grave offering that settled into that position, (2) the tip of a projectile that had wounded the individual, or (3) a fortuitous association resulting from the point's having been introduced with the grave fill.

One item first-time excavators often fail to recognize is powdered red or yellow ochre. Occasionally found with burials, ochre or cinnabar may stain the bones a dull brick red or a light yellow color, and it may also tinge the soil surrounding the bones. Where the pigment cannot be collected in pure lumps, a sample of pigment-stained earth will suffice for mineralogical determination.

The burial should also be closely examined for the presence of perishable materials on or around the body. Clothing, hair, connective tissue, and gastrointestinal contents may be well preserved, especially in historic interments (Rose and Santeford 1985) or under certain environmental conditions (El-Najjar and Mulinski 1980; Robbins 1971; Shafer et al. 1989; Turpin et al. 1986). These items are important because they provide genetic and pathological data not available through the examination of skeletal remains alone (Sandison 1980; Thuesen and Engberg 1990). Perishable artifacts found with the burial may also provide clues about the social status of the individual (Binford 1971; Palkovitch 1980; Whittlesey 1978) or the method of interment (Turpin et al. 1986).

The deposits in and around the burial should be sampled for pollen and soil chemistry using the techniques described in Chapters 6 and 12. Soil samples should be collected from within the body cavity, within the burial pit (if such a feature is present), and outside the burial area. Analysis of these samples can provide important information about bone preservation, and such an analysis is a prerequisite for the interpretation of bone chem-

istry data (Hare 1980; Klepinger et al. 1986; Kyle 1986). Pollen and macrobotanical analyses of burial deposits can provide information about the environment at the time of interment and can verify the presence of botanical material incorporated into the mortuary program (Solecki 1975) or ingested as medicine (Shafer et al. 1989). Investigators should pay special attention to the pelvic region while sampling soil because intestinal contents may be adhering to the iliac blade or sacrum. Careful examination and sampling of these areas may provide data that could not be obtained from examination of the skeleton alone.

Multiple graves are not as readily exposed as individual interments. When the remains of more than one individual are in close proximity, added caution is needed to obtain a clear picture of the position of individuals or individual skeletal elements (Ubelaker 1989a:21). The approach will depend on the particular circumstances, but working from the center outward is usually appropriate if individuals are side by side. If they are arranged vertically, it may not be practical to fully expose lower individuals before removing upper ones. More complex situations, such as large ossuaries, may require that the bone accumulation be removed in sequential horizontal sections (Ubelaker 1989a). In such instances, the excavator must be absolutely sure that all burial records, plan maps, and photographs are accurate so that a composite plan can be reconstructed from the records.

Complete cremations obviously present a different problem. The local accumulation of ash, charred wood, and calcined bone usually serves to delimit the area of the cremation, and careful troweling and brushing will define the horizontal limits of the cremation in the surrounding matrix. Once this is done, a vertical profile may be obtained by excavating half the cremation, thus exposing a side view and showing the depth of the ash-and-charcoal lens. The profile may also give clues to the exact cremating procedure, if layering of charcoal and bone appears at different levels. Any bone extending into the profile should be left in place because such elements may indicate the position of the body during cremation. The investigator should also attempt to determine whether the burned bones and ash are from an in-place cremation or have been redeposited from another location. Finally, the excavator must take special care in brushing to ensure that carbonized fragments of normally perishable objects, especially wood, are not discarded.

At one time it was thought that a pile of cremated bones was of no value, under the incorrect assumption that little could be learned from bone fragments. Several studies (Bowman 1990; Brothwell 1982:14–16; Buikstra and Swegle 1989; Gejvall 1963; Powell 1994; Shipment et al. 1984) have shown that detailed examination of burned bone can answer a wide range of questions. The number of individuals present and their sex, age, and even pathological conditions often can be determined by a thorough analysis of cremations. Current studies have shown that the state of soft tissue decomposition, firing temperature, and even body position can also be inferred from cremated remains (Binford 1963; Brothwell 1982:14–16; Buikstra and Swegle 1989; Shipman et al. 1984; Storey 1990; Ubelaker 1989a:35–38). Mortuary data from cremations can then be interpreted in light of regional patterns (Baby 1954; Bowman 1990; Creel 1989; Powell 1994).

Badly preserved bone is difficult to expose and collect (see Wesolowsky 1973:342). Special care in brushing away the enclosing earth lets the excavator record the position and preservation of the bones. Richie and Pugh (1963) describe a special method of photographically recording badly decayed skeletal materials, and use of a video camera in the field also can provide essential documentation. Even decaying osseous material offers relevant information about burial position and accompanying artifacts. Coupled with sampling of deposits around the burial, microscopic examination of the bone, and interpretation of burial stratigraphy, the excavator can gain insight as to how and why the bones have decayed—the **diagenetic process** (Lyman and Fox 1989). Decayed bone is also useful in chemical and isotopic studies.

If time permits, decayed bones should be removed slowly. Before doing so, it is advisable to perform a field analysis of age and sex because the areas that provide these data—the skull and the pelvis—are fragile, easily damaged, and infre

quently recovered intact. In the past, archaeologists used consolidants in the field to maintain the integrity of bone (see Chapter 7). In general, this is not advisable because the addition of preservatives precludes chemical and isotopic analysis. Consolidants should be used only in extreme cases: waterlogged sites (Doran and Dickel 1988; Stone et al. 1990) or unique skeletal specimens that are too badly fragmented or decayed to remove and reconstruct in the laboratory (Weir 1985). Guides such as Lamb and Newsom (1983), Stone et al. (1990), and Storch (1983) provide lists of appropriate consolidants and should be consulted before using any consolidant in the field (see also Chapter 7). In any case, the excavator should retain some untreated elements, preferably from a variety of localities and bone types. This will ensure that chemical, isotopic, and histological studies can be performed without fear of contamination. A rule to follow in using consolidants or preservatives is that whatever chemicals are added to the bones should be completely removable without damage to the specimen. Few, if any, consolidants applied in the field meet this rule. When consolidants are applied to skeletal remains, careful records should be kept of the types of materials and procedures used. These records should be included with the field notes and other burial documentation, and copies of these records should be kept with the curated bones. This ensures that later investigators, especially those conducting biochemical, histological, or radiometric analysis of the burial, will be aware of all phases of conservation that might affect their results.

Burial Records

The documentation of burials follows the same principles and general procedures used for any other kind of archaeological feature. Written as well as visual records are needed, and most organized field projects have some type of burial data sheet (Figure 11.9). When properly completed, such forms ensure that basic information about each burial is recorded. Because anatomical information about human remains is needed, burial documentation requires that an experienced person be

TEXAS A&M UNIVERSITY

NAN RANCH BURIAL FORM

Site no. _____ Burial no. _____ Feature no. _____ Field Sack no. _____

1. LOCATION
   a. Room _____
   b. Horizontal _____
   _____
   c. Depth from surface _____
   d. Depth from datum _____
   e. Depth from floor _____

2. GRAVE DIMENSIONS
   a. Max. Length _____ Dir. _____
   b. Max. Width _____ Dir. _____
   c. Depth (at bottom) _____

3. GRAVE TYPE
   a. Surface _____ c. Cist_____
   b. Pit_____ d. Other _____

4. BURIAL TYPE
   a. Extended _____ e. Reburial_____
   b. Flexed_____ f. Cremation _____
   c. Semiflexed _____ g. Part. Crem. _____
   d. Other _____

5. BURIAL DIMENSIONS
   a. Max. Length _____ Dir. _____
   b. Max. Width_____ Dir. _____
   c. Thickness _____

6. DEPOSITION
   a. Position _____
   b. Head to _____

7. STRATIFICATION
   a. Inclusive_____ c. Disturbed _____
   b. Instrusive _____

8. AGE
   a. Infant (0-1) _____
   b. Child (1-6) _____
   c. Adolescent (6-12)_____
   d. Sub-Adult (12-20)_____
   e. Adult (20-50) _____
   f. Old Adult (50+) _____

Recorded by _____

Excavated by _____

9. SEX
   a. M _____ F _____ INDETERMINATE_____

10. PRESERVATION
    a. Tissue: Yes _____No _____
    b. Bone: Poor_____ Fair _____ Good _____

11. COMPLETENESS
    a. Head _____
    _____
    b. Cranial Deformation _____
    c. Post-cranial _____
    _____

12. ASSOCIATIONS
    a. Ceramic _____ FS no. _____
    b. Jewelry _____ FS no. _____
    c. Lithics _____ FS no. _____
    d. Textiles_____ FS no. _____
    e. Adobe sealing grave ____Fea. no. _____
    f. Stones covering grave ____Fea. no. _____
    g. White precipitate in grave _____
    h. Other _____

13. SAMPLES
    a. Pollen _____FS nos. _____
    b. Flotation _____FS nos. _____
    c. Tissue _____FS nos. _____
    d. Other _____

14. SOIL OR FILL TYPE _____
    _____

15. PHOTOS _____

16. NEG. NOS. _____

17. REMARKS _____
    _____
    _____
    _____
    _____
    _____

18. PRESERVATIVE applied to bones _____
    _____

Date _____

Figure 11.9   Burial recording form for field use.

present or that careful reference be made to an appropriate manual (i.e., Bass 1987; Steele and Bramblett 1988; White 1991). The burial should be thoroughly photographed with black-and-white and color film (preferably with more than one camera) and described in writing at successive stages during its exposure (see Chapter 8). As noted earlier, video cameras can also be used to document the burial and details of the excavation procedure. Still photographs can be captured from the videotape and reproduced in a variety of media.

Once the burial is fully exposed, it should be carefully drawn to scale (Figure 11.10) and once again photographed with a scale, north arrow, and unit/feature designation clearly visible. These visual documents should show as much of the human remains and associated artifacts as possible, as well as any visible aspects of the grave pit, tomb, container, or other context. Written descriptions of these factors as well as other pertinent observations also should be made. Location, orientation, matrix, and stratigraphic position should be noted along with any anatomical observations, such as missing or displaced elements. If the excavator is competent to do so, it is advisable that he or she note the age, sex, and health status attributes of the human remains as part of the burial records. However, demographic variables and health data should be reanalyzed in the laboratory after the skeletal remains have been properly cleaned.

Sketches and photographs may seem to duplicate each other, but one cannot be certain of the quality of a photograph until it is developed and printed. If one or more photographs should be ruined, the sketch may be the only record of a given stage in the excavation or of a certain artifact's original position. Instant-developing film can provide a partial safeguard, and the use of Polaroid positive/negative instant film provides both a print in the field and a negative for later laboratory printing. Small details and especially artifacts are often difficult to identify in burial photographs taken under adverse conditions. These are easily identified in a sketch, which makes it a necessary supplement to photography. Conversely, reliance on drawings alone has the disadvantages that rarely can all of the details be illustrated and

that extremely detailed illustrating is quite time-intensive. Methods for drawing accurate plan views of features and artifacts are discussed in Chapter 6.

Removing the Burial

After the burial is exposed, recorded, and photographed, it should be removed to safeguard the skeleton and associated artifacts. Care must be taken to avoid breaking the bones while removing them from the matrix. This is accomplished best by completely undercutting each bone with a bamboo splint and lifting it all at once. Any bones on top must be removed first. Gradual and overall pressure is necessary on the larger bones to prevent snapping. Each bone is cleaned as thoroughly as possible (and practical) as it is removed, and the dirt is left in the burial pit for later screening. The skull and the pelvis are the most difficult to remove and must be handled with great care. After freeing the skull from the matrix, effort should be made to very carefully remove matrix inside the skull through the foramen magnum (the large opening at the base of the skull for the spinal cord). Calcareous matrix left to harden in the skull can damage bone through a "rattle" effect; clay matrix inside a skull can expand or contract, causing the bones of the cranial vault to crack or break. In rare instances when brain tissue or its residues may be preserved in the braincase, retrieval of the cranial contents should take place in the laboratory.

At the time of removal, certain bones should be placed in their own paper bags and appropriately labeled for element, side, burial, and site number (e.g., "Right *Os Coxa*, Burial 12, site 41GV125"), as well as the date of excavation and the excavator's initials. The sternal end of the fourth rib, the *os coxae* (specifically, the auricular surface of the ilium and the symphyseal area of the pubis shown in Figure 11.11), and the skull can all be used for determination of age and sex (Iscan et al. 1984; Lovejoy, Meindl, et al. 1985; Meindl and Lovejoy 1989; Meindl et al. 1983; Phenice 1969; Steele and Bramblett 1988) and should receive special treatment. In the case of the fourth rib, which is used in age assessment, vital information will be lost if the archaeologist fails to separate and label this ele-

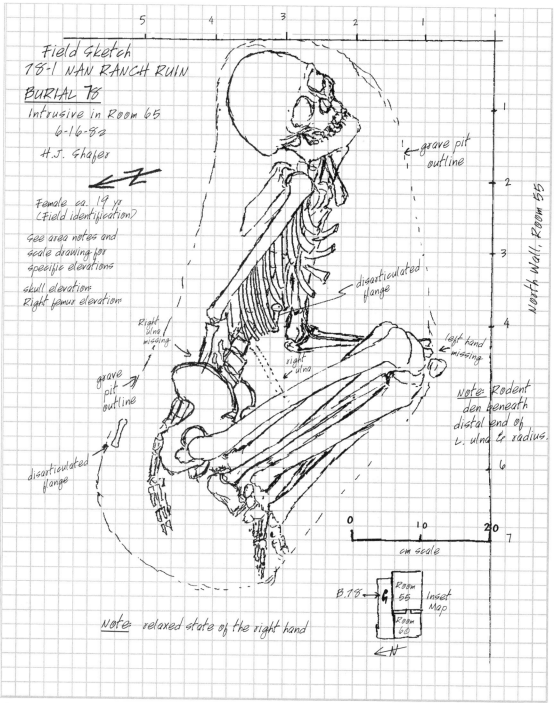

Field Sketch
18-1 NAN RANCH RUIN
BURIAL 78
Intrusive in Room 65
6-16-82
H.J. Shafer

Female ca. 19 yr
(Field identification)

See area notes and
scale drawing for
specific elevations

skull elevation=
Right femur elevation=

Right
ulna
missing

grave
pit
outline

disarticulated
flange

grave pit
outline

disarticulated
flange

right
ulna

left hand
missing

Note: Rodent
den beneath
distal end of
L. ulna & radius.

North Wall, Room 55

Note: relaxed state of the right hand

B.78 →

Room
55

Room
60

Inset
Map

cm scale

0   10   20

Figure 11.10 Typical plan view sketch of a flexed burial.

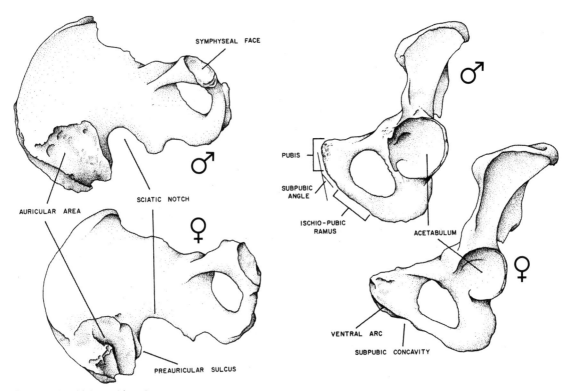

Figure 11.11 Male and female *os coxae*.

ment, because it is difficult to specifically identify central ribs if the set of ribs is incomplete or fragmentary (Steele and Bramblett 1988:140).

At one time it was thought that the removal of the entire burial feature, matrix and all, was a preferred method for burials that were not easily freed from their matrix or those on which more thorough documentation was required. Archaeologists would sometimes expose a large pedestal of matrix containing the burial, encase it in a plaster jacket, and undercut the jacketed block with a large board or sheet of plywood so that the burial could be excavated in the laboratory. Although certain situations may require this method (see Dockall 1995), we feel that it is not advisable for most human burials. Burials are easily damaged either during transport of the block or by the jacketing process itself. The method is also expensive and time-consuming in the field and greatly increases the cost and time of

laboratory analysis. In rare instances, such as when bones are extremely fragmented, individual skeletal elements or areas of the body can be encased in commercial polyurethane spray foam insulation. This material is light, easy to transport, and can be removed with acetone (Bement 1985; Dockall 1995). Dockall (1995) describes a method for removing burials as a block that is superior to the traditional plaster of Paris technique. We stress that this must be considered a last resort for the removal of bone and should be used only when other methods have failed.

Cleaning and Packing

If bones are relatively free of matrix, they should not be washed in the field. This prevents possible chemical contamination of the bone and ensures that organic materials adhering to bones, such as blood, clothing, pollen, phytoliths, and preserved DNA, are not altered or damaged through contact with water. It also prevents damage to bone through excessive handling and harsh scrubbing. However, in some situations (for example, burials from clay deposits) it is necessary to wash bone in the field after careful examination for adherents such as cloth, matting, or red ochre. If hard and calcareous, adherent matrix can be removed much more easily immediately after exposure than after it has dried. A tub or bucket or water, brushes, and bamboo splints are usually sufficient to clean bones in the field. Each skeleton must be kept separate while being washed. Bones and teeth should never be submerged because they will absorb water, causing cracking. Instead, drops of water can be dribbled onto the bone, or a damp soft brush can be lightly applied. Scrubbing of bone should be avoided because this can remove more delicate features and evidence of medical disorders. Teeth should be washed in a mixture of water and alcohol to prevent cracking from water absorption. Drying is best done on screens to facilitate drainage and in the shade to prevent cracking and peeling. Bone should never be packed until it is thoroughly dry, to prevent mold growth and to keep packing materials from adhering to the bone (newspaper stuck to a wet bone is extremely difficult to remove!). Certain bones should be cleaned only by someone knowledgeable in skeletal analysis; these are the pubic symphysis and the delicate bones of the face. Mending of broken bone should not be done in the field unless it is necessary to prevent further damage during transit. Again, washing and excessive handling of bone in the field can be detrimental to subsequent analysis; such work should be done in the laboratory.

The age, sex, and medical disorders of a skeleton become clearer after the bones have been removed and properly cleaned, and the critical areas examined. Because field determinations of sex, age, medical disorders, and so on, are often done hastily and by nonexperts, they should always be checked in the laboratory by qualified specialists, and these more accurate findings attached to or filed with the burial record made in the field. Field determinations of age and sex are most useful when the bone is poorly preserved or when excavating large cemetery or ossuary sites in which preliminary demographic data can be used in directing further excavation. For example, in large cemetery sites, it is useful to determine whether burials are spatially arranged by age or sex variables so that subsequent excavation can take such patterning into account.

Wooden boxes, made to size, are the ideal containers for skeletons, both in the field and for shipment to the laboratory. They afford far more protection than cardboard cartons, and they do not fall apart when they get damp. Once made, they will last for years of fieldwork. The ends should be made of ½-inch to ¾-inch stock; the sides, top, and bottom, of ⅜-inch stock. Experience has shown that the following inside measurements are adequate for the skeletons of normal adults: 66 cm (26 inches) long, 28 cm (11 inches) wide, 22 cm (8½ inches) deep. A number of smaller boxes may be provided to accommodate the skeletons of children and for fragmentary or partial skeletons. If it is not feasible to construct or purchase wooden boxes, heavy-duty cardboard containers of the same dimensions can be used if measures are taken to protect the boxes from dampness.

The burial number, skeleton catalog number, and other pertinent data should be written in indelible marker on the box or on a card placed inside the box. Cards tacked or glued to the box are often lost during transit. To be on the safe side, it is useful to tie an identification or reference tag to a long bone as well. Long bones can be wrapped separately in sheets of Styrofoam packing material or acid-free paper. The cranium, the mandible, the vertebrae, fragmentary bones, and the bones of each hand and foot should be placed in separate paper bags and labeled (e.g., "Bones of left hand, Burial 12, site 41GV125"). This will ensure against the loss of small bones, teeth, fragments, and other such items. Shredded paper or Styrofoam "packing peanuts" are a nuisance, both in the field and in the laboratory. Sheets of packing foam or crumpled acid-free paper provide adequate protection, are easy to obtain, and are recyclable.

In packing, the cranium should be placed at one end, the heavy long bones such as femorae, tibiae, and humerii packed next, and the lighter bones placed on top. These recommendations apply, of course, to skeletal material in a fairly good state of preservation. Friable or poorly preserved bones require additional packing material with adequate support. Wet bone should be field-treated and dried (following Stone et al. 1990) before packing. Rapid desiccation of wet bone, however, can be extremely destructive and should be avoided.

OSTEOLOGICAL ANALYSIS

In this section, we discuss the types of analyses that are typically performed on human remains once they come in from the field. It is imperative that archaeologists be familiar with the types of laboratory investigations that can be conducted if human skeletal remains are properly excavated, documented, and handled in the field. The following discussion provides the reader with basic references for field determinations of age, sex, and health status. Those interested in more detailed discussions should consult the references sections of the papers cited here. Useful general references include Bass (1987), El-Najjar and McWilliams (1978), Iscan and Kennedy (1989), Krogman and Iscan (1986), Reichs (1986), Steele and Bramblett (1988), Stewart (1979), Ubelaker (1989a), and White (1991). With the advent of state and federal legislation requiring reburial of remains, Buikstra and Ubelaker (1994) have developed a standardized protocol for analyzing human skeletal remains, so that data from various investigations can be compared with minimal difficulty. Expansions of this standard system are underway as of this writing. Computer database programs, such as the FACS system (Shaffer and Baker 1992) and others currently under development, can be used for the storage and management of bioarchaeological data.

Determination of Sex

To determine the sex of an individual, bioarchaeologists rely on the basic differences in reproductive anatomy, size, and overall shape that are reflected in skeletal remains. Two main areas, the pelvic region and the skull, are discussed here in terms of subjective assessments of structure. Quantitative methods of analysis utilize measurements of the skull (Giles 1970), the pelvic region (Kelley 1979; Taylor and DiBennardo 1984), the bones of the feet (Steele 1979), long bones (Black 1978; Stewart 1979), and teeth (Kieser et al. 1985).

The bones forming the pelvis—two *os coxae* and the sacrum—are the most reliable indicators of sex in skeletal remains. In females, the iliac blade flares broadly, the sacrum is broader, and the greater sciatic notch is larger and wider (see Figure 11.11). The body of the pubis is narrower, the dorsal (internal) surface of the pubis is often pitted, and there is a laterally curving line at the inferior (lower) border of the pubic symphysis (the "ventral arc") in females (Phenice 1969; Suchey et al. 1979).

In the skull, determination of sex is more problematic. Here, sexually dimorphic features reflect relative differences in size and robusticity, features that tend to overlap greatly in most human populations. A large female from a robust population can be mistaken for a male from a gracile population. Sex determinations from the skull are therefore accepted with greater caution unless the researcher has had previous experience with that particular population and knows the range of variation for males and females.

In general, the skulls of males are more robust and the structures of the face and jaw more prominent. Males have large browridges, large mastoid processes, more prominent external occipital protuberances, square chins, and gonial angles that approach 90 degrees (Figure 11.12, *top*). In females these features are less robust, the gonial angle is obtuse, and the frontal bone more vertical than in males (see Figure 11.12, *bottom*). A more in-depth review of sexual dimorphism in the skull is presented in Bass (1987), Brothwell (1982), Keen (1950), Krogman and Iscan (1986), Steele and Bramblett (1988), Stewart (1979), Ubelaker (1989a), and Wienker (1984).

A useful technique to facilitate assigning sex to individuals in a large skeletal series is to seriate the assemblage (Acsadi and Nemeskeri 1970). The most masculine and feminine elements in a series

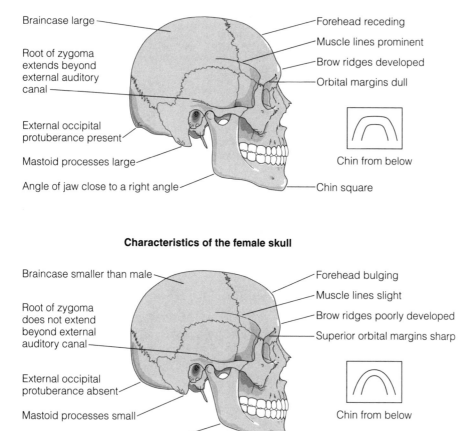

Characteristics of the male skull

Braincase large

Root of zygoma extends beyond external auditory canal

External occipital protuberance present

Mastoid processes large

Angle of jaw close to a right angle

Forehead receding

Muscle lines prominent

Brow ridges developed

Orbital margins dull

Chin from below

Chin square

Characteristics of the female skull

Braincase smaller than male

Root of zygoma does not extend beyond external auditory canal

External occipital protuberance absent

Mastoid processes small

Angle of jaw obtuse—over 125°

Forehead bulging

Muscle lines slight

Brow ridges poorly developed

Superior orbital margins sharp

Chin from below

Chin rounded

Figure 11.12   Male and female crania, lateral view.

can be used for rating other remains along a continuum of variation. Each feature (e.g., brow size, sciatic notch width, etc.) is assigned a score from –2 (most feminine) to +2 (most masculine) based on the extremes in that population, and the average score for all features is used to assign a sex to that individual (Acsadi and Nemeskeri 1970). Thus, the determination of "masculine" and "feminine" features can be tailored to the range of sexual dimorphism in a given population.

Determination of Age

Age determination techniques vary depending on the general age of the individual. In subadult

remains (i.e., those younger than 15–20 years at death), osteologists rely on the relative state of maturation of bones and teeth to assign ages. In adults, in whom maturation is completed, researchers must rely on the gradual deterioration of certain features, changes that are sex-specific.

During intrauterine development and throughout infancy, the cartilage model of the skeleton begins to ossify at a number of sites. The appearance of these centers of ossification and the stage of development of bones can be used to assign ages to fetuses, infants, and subadults. An extensive list of measurements and statistical predictions of age from subadult skeletal dimensions is available in Fazekas and Kosa (1978), with additions by Kosa

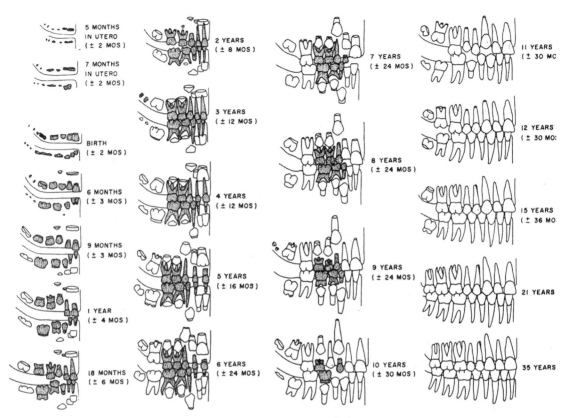

Figure 11.13   Tooth formation chart derived from Native American populations.

(1984) and Ubelaker (1989b).

One of the most frequently used methods of age determination in subadults is dental maturation. Subadult remains can be matched to charts, such as those of Schour and Massler (1944) and Ubelaker (1989a), that illustrate the relative state of development and eruption of the deciduous (milk) and permanent (adult) teeth as a means of determining age (Figure 11.13). Other techniques rely on the completion of crown and root formation (Moorrees et al. 1963a, 1963b; Schour and Massler 1940).

A second method for age determination in subadults is long-bone growth. Subadult long bones consist of the diaphysis (shaft) and epiphyses (articular ends) that eventually unite to form the mature bone (see Hancox 1972 for a discussion of bone growth). The number of epiphyses varies

between bones, and the rate of epiphyseal closure varies from site to site within and between bones (Figure 11.14). Using this information, it is possible to determine the age of subadults with some accuracy by examining the state of epiphyseal closure in various elements (Krogman and Iscan 1986).

In adults, the cessation of growth marks the beginning of other gradual, age-related changes in the skeleton. In the skull, the junctures between the bones, known as sutures, begin to fuse. This process is quite variable and should be used only to obtain a general age range for an individual. Krogman and Iscan (1986), McKern (1970), and Meindl and Lovejoy (1985) describe techniques for age determination from suture closure.

The pubic symphysis is the most reliable and best studied indicator of adult age. Like other adult age changes, the morphogenesis of the pubic

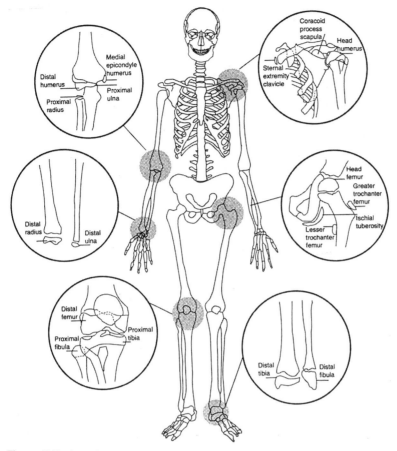

Figure 11.14   Location of epiphyses in the subadult skeleton.

symphysis varies between the sexes, so that a reliable sex determination is required before assigning an age with this technique. The techniques of McKern and Stewart (1957), Gilbert and McKern (1973), and Suchey et al. (1984) are typically used. Although the method of recording and scoring the observations differs among analysts, all rely on the billowed surface of a young individual being obliterated as secondary bone is deposited on the symphyseal surface, followed by degradation of the smoothed symphysis. These methods are accurate for individuals between the ages of 17 and 50 years. Older individuals can be assigned to a 50+ age category, but accurate age assessment is problematic.

In many burials, the fragile *os pubis* is missing or badly fragmented and cannot be used for age assessments. A more durable osteological structure like the auricular surface of the ilium should instead be assessed (Lovejoy, Meindl, et al. 1985; Meindl and Lovejoy 1989). In general, the auricular surface, like that of the pubic symphysis, changes from a billowed, finely grained appearance to a rugged, porous topography surrounded by arthritic lipping and other signs of degeneration.

The sternal end of the fourth rib is another indicator of age. The method devised by Iscan et al. (1984) uses a three-component scoring system like that used for the pubic symphysis by McKern and Stewart (1957) and Gilbert and McKern (1973). The depth of the pit at the sternal end, the pit shape, and the rim/wall configuration are all scored on a 0–5 scale, the sum of which can be checked against average ages in a table.

Microscopic changes in adult bone composition, even in highly fragmentary remains, can also be used for aging. The normal process of remodeling of the bone cortex (the thick, hard exterior) consists of bone-removing cells (osteoclasts) cutting longitudinal tunnels (haversian canals) through bone. These haversian canals are then gradually filled with bone from bone-producing cells (osteoblasts), creating circular "osteons." New osteons are formed at random among existing ones, so that with increasing age the number of fragmentary osteons also increases. By sectioning a bone and counting the number of existing and fragmentary osteons, an estimate of age is obtained (Ahlqvist and Damsten 1969; Kerley and Ubelaker 1978; Singh and Gunberg 1970; Thompson 1979).

Other methods of age determination include estimates based on dental attrition (Brothwell 1982; Lovejoy 1985; Molleson and Cohen 1990; Scott 1979; Walker et al. 1991). Basically, techniques based on examination of teeth assess the rate of attrition at the time of death between the first, second, and third molars, each of which erupts at 6-year intervals. The bioarchaeologist must take into account cultural practices—dietary and culinary practices and use of teeth in daily activities—when estimating the age of an individual using dental attrition methods.

Each of the above methods has limitations and each has been abused, requiring caution on the part of the analyst (see Buikstra and Mielke 1985 for a cautionary note on age and sex determinations). With many of the age assessment techniques outlined, an exact age cannot be determined even under the most cautious and careful of examinations; however, it may be possible to place an individual within an age category. The following are suggested bone-age categories, following El-Najjar and McWilliams (1978) and Steele and Bramblett (1988):

Fetal	Conception to birth
Infancy	Birth to 2 years
Early Childhood	3–5 years
Late Childhood	6–12 years
Adolescence	13–24 years
Adulthood	25–49 years
Old Adulthood	50 years or more

Other methods of categorization, such as 5- or 10-year age groupings, may be preferred where large collections can be seriated. The data on age and sex can then be used in paleodemographic analyses for the determination of population structure, health, and behavior (Acsadi and Nemeskeri 1970; Buikstra et al. 1986; Kunstadter 1972; Weiss 1973).

Metric Data Collection

Measurements of the cranial and postcranial bones are best carried out in the laboratory. Special equipment, such as osteometric boards, sliding and spreading calipers, coordinate calipers, and head spanners, is needed to obtain metric data. Before metric data can be recorded, broken bones must be reconstructed, a time-consuming process that should be conducted only by those familiar with human osteology. Reconstructions should proceed only when the metric data are a primary research objective or when time allows. Metric data from a single individual, out of the population context, are of relatively little value except in forensic determinations of age, sex, and biological affinity. The lab analyst must weigh the costs in time and effort of reconstruction against the information to be obtained from the metric data.

Cranial measurements are the most frequently used in forensic analysis, although the skull is highly susceptible to postmortem degradation and is rarely recovered intact. Long bones are also commonly measured and the data used in studies of sexual dimorphism or population variability (France 1983; Hamilton 1982). One use of long-bone measurements is in the estimation of living stature. Intact long-bone measurements may be entered into regression formulae for a variety of populations (Genovés 1967; Trotter 1970; Trotter and Gleser 1952, 1958, 1977) provided that the researcher knows the sex and biological affinity of the remains. Fragmentary long bones may also be used to estimate stature (Brooks, Steele, and Brooks 1990; Simmons et al. 1990; Steele 1970; Steele and Bramblett 1988; Steele and McKern 1969), though the stature ranges are broad. The measurement of teeth can be used not only for sex estimation as discussed earlier, but also for evaluating genetic affinity (Groeneveld and Kieser 1987; Lukacs and Hemphill 1991; Sciulli 1990a). Standard measurement procedures for cranial and postcranial elements have been outlined in the following works: Bass (1987), Howells (1973), and Steele and Bramblett (1988). Dental measurement procedures are outlined in Kieser (1990) and Moorrees and Reed (1954).

Paleopathology

Once the bones have been inventoried, measured, and assigned an age and a sex, the bioarchaeologist should begin to scrutinize them for signs of medical disorders. Misalignment of bones or the presence of a bone callus suggests a healed trauma (Figure 11.15). The presence of porosity and pitting in the cranium and orbital roof may indicate active or remodeled anemia (porotic hyperostosis). Striated or "woven" bone on the exterior of bone shafts is also common, indicating infection between the bone and the surrounding membrane, the periosteum (Figure 11.16). More severe infections in bone can produce swelling, macroporosity, and abscessing. Arthritis appears as bony out-

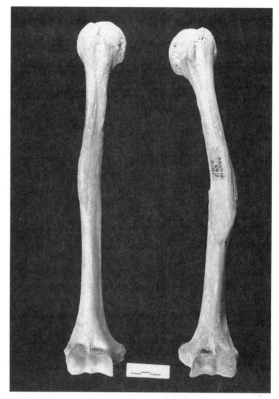

Figure 11.15 Healed fracture in a left humerus from a historic Native American burial in Texas.

Figure 11.16 Infection of the periosteum (periostitis) in an adult femur.

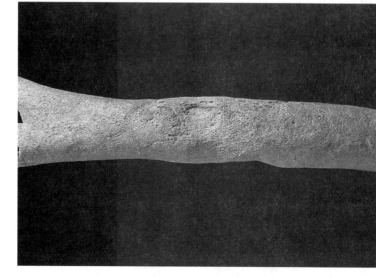

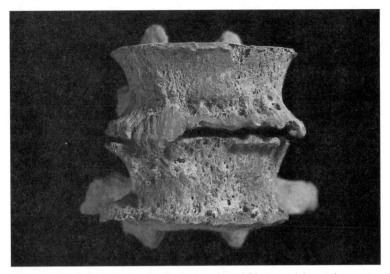

Figure 11.17 Arthritic lipping (vertical osteophytosis) in two adult vertebrae.

growths at the margins of vertebrae (Figure 11.17), lipping around articular areas, and polishing or erosion of the joint surface. Many medical disorders consist of fragile structures that are easily destroyed by careless excavation or harsh cleaning; the excavator in the field has as great a responsibility for the recovery of information on medical disorders as does the bioarchaeologist in the laboratory for recording that information. When making diagnoses of medical disorders, it is suggested that researchers consult Mann (1990), Ortner and Putschar (1981), Steinbock (1976), Zimmerman and Kelley (1982), and Zivanovic (1982). For recent information on theoretical interpretation of paleopathological data, readers should consult Cohen and Armelagos (1984), Goodman (1993), Ortner and Aufderheide (1991), Stewart-Macadam and Kent (1992), and Wood et al. (1992).

Biological Affinity

One of the most difficult tasks in the lab is the assignment of human skeletal remains to a particular biological and/or ethnic group. The range of variation in one human population broadly overlaps with others, making a positive assignment of an unknown individual to a particular geographi-

cal population problematic. Anthropologists trying to deal with this problem in North America have focused on characterizing three major biological groups: American Whites (caucasoids), American Blacks (negroids), and American Indians (mongoloids). In spite of the difficulties and generalizations, there are situations in which knowledge of the biological affinity of remains is helpful. For example, at Spanish mission sites in the southwestern United States, Native Americans and Europeans were often interred in the same cemetery and in a similar fashion. In this case, the archaeologist might want to know which of the graves contained Native Americans in order to learn how native peoples adopted or modified typical European mortuary practices (see Ricklis 1994). The reader should be cautioned that accuracy in determining biological affinity is dependent on the investigator's experience with the techniques and on his or her familiarity with the population in question.

The skull provides metric and nonmetric clues about the affinity of a particular set of remains. Giles and Elliot (1962) and Gill (1984, 1986) have provided morphometric guides to racial assessment based on dimensions of the skull and face. By taking the correct measurements and entering them into statistical formulae, a set of remains can be assigned to one of several major groups or used to explore the role of social interactions in generating biological variability (Key and Jantz 1990; Powell 1995; Sciulli 1990b). The drawback of these techniques is that human remains from archaeological sites are rarely well-preserved enough to make all of the necessary measurements. A more common approach is to make a subjective assessment of the skull and face. Rhine (1990) and Brues (1990) have provided criteria for the skull; other authors (Bass 1987; Steele and Bramblett 1988:58–59; Ubelaker 1989a:119–120) provide similar criteria. Subjective and objective criteria for biological affinity in postcranial elements (Gilbert and Gill 1990) are discussed in Krogman and Iscan (1986) and in the volume edited by Gill and Rhine (1990).

LEGAL AND ETHICAL CONSIDERATIONS

During the 1980s, professional archaeologists began creating policies and guidelines for the treatment of human remains that they felt met the needs of Native American groups who wished disinterred remains to be reburied (Mihesuah 1991) and of those groups (including anthropologists) who advocated long-term curation and study of prehistoric human remains (see Buikstra and Gordon 1981 and Ubelaker and Grant 1989). The Society for American Archaeology (SAA), the primary professional organization for archaeologists working in the New World, formulated its policy on human remains in 1986. This organization felt that it was the archaeologist's "ethical responsibility 'to advocate and to aid in the conservation of archaeological data'" as specified in the society's bylaws. However, "the concerns of different cultures, as presented by their designated representatives and leaders, must be recognized and respected" (SAA Executive Committee 1986:7). The society advocated maintaining skeletal collections in a dignified manner for use in legitimate scientific and educational purposes. Disputes over reburial and repatriation of human remains "must be resolved on a case-by-case basis through consideration of the sci-

entific importance of the material, the cultural and religious values of the interested individuals or groups, and the strength of their relationship to the remains in question" (SAA Executive Committee 1986:7). Various views on both sides of the reburial issue and discussions of ethical problems associated with human remains research can be found in Buikstra and Gordon (1981), Deloria (1992), Dockall et al. (1996), Goldstein and Kintigh (1990), Klesert and Andrews (1988), Layton (1989), Powell (1994), and Rose (1985).

Several state and federal agencies have legislative mandates regarding the removal, study, curation, and reburial of human skeletal remains recovered from archaeological sites; a review of these is presented in Ubelaker and Grant (1989). Nearly half the states have laws that protect burials, and many states have adopted sweeping reburial policies (Carnett 1991). As a result, the field has seen increasing movement toward cooperative interaction between living descendants and archaeologists (Klesert and Andrews 1988; Powell 1996; Rose 1985; Smith 1984). Because most repatriation legislation is complex, under current adoption or revision, and varies from state to state, students and professionals should stay abreast of the local legislation in their area and federal legislation concerning human remains in their region of research. The most recent change in the repatriation issue has been the passage of federal legislation, in November 1990, in the form of Public Law 101-601, the Native American Graves Protection and Repatriation Act. As noted in Chapter 2, this legislation regulates the excavation of human skeletal material and associated funerary objects on federal or tribal lands. It also mandates that federal agencies and institutions (those receiving federal funding) inventory their collections and contact descendant groups regarding repatriation and reburial.

The issue of reburial causes concern among anthropologists about conducting one-time studies of skeletal samples, because one-time studies are antithetical to the scientific method. In a review of publications on skeletal remains, Buikstra and Gordon (1981) found that of 228 existing skeletal series that have been reexamined, 84 (37 percent) were used to check previous results. Of these 84 studies, only 6 (7 percent) confirmed the conclusions of the original investigation. The remainder altered the previous conclusions (62 percent) or produced results that were unclear (31 percent). As pointed out earlier in the chapter, the advent of new technologies makes the potential for skeletal research quite high. For example, 50 years ago recovery of genetic material from preserved tissue and the determination of diet from bone chemistry were unknown. No one can predict the types of research that will be available in the next 50 years. Buikstra and Gordon (1981) note that 144 (63 percent) of the 228 reexaminations of existing osteological collections were directed toward new research problems, a trend that will in all likelihood continue. Therefore, the investigative potential of new technology, coupled with the need to check and recheck results, makes the reburial issue a concern for bioarchaeologists.

Research must proceed, however, with reburial of some or all of the remains of any given site a probability. Standardized data collection protocols are now available (Buikstra and Ubelaker 1994) that will enable bioarchaeologists to amass a much more useful and comprehensive database regarding the biology of past peoples. Rose (1985) developed a field protocol for the same-day excavation, documentation, and analysis of human remains from historic cemeteries; this protocol has been used effectively in other similar field situations (Dockall et al. 1996) and may become more commonplace in the near future. Other noninvasive methods of recording, such as computer-aided tomography, radiography, and digital imaging (Santulli et al. 1996), may offer a permanent record of some types of skeletal data. Casting of materials may also be a solution. Unfortunately, these techniques are expensive and financially out-of-reach for most museums and universities. In situations where reburial is to occur, bioarchaeologists must be as painstaking as possible in their work, use standardized data collection procedures (Buikstra and Ubelaker 1994), check their work against that of other colleagues, and record every possible kind of data before reburying human remains. Perhaps the best solution is to work in conjunction with

descendant communities and to incorporate them into the research design and execution of the project. Such cooperation may ultimately lead to a better understanding of the importance of bioarchaeological investigations and a greater appreciation of the people whose ancestors are being studied (Powell and Dockall 1995).

The interpretive potential of archaeologically recovered human remains is high, and anthropologists must be ever alert to opportunities for improving our ability to recover and interpret these data. It is, after all, the fact that our species evolves culturally and biologically that makes our existence unique, and nowhere is there a more pertinent database on human evolution than in well-preserved human remains from well-documented archaeological contexts. The excavator's responsibility is to be aware of the use of human skeletal remains in archaeological investigations, to excavate human remains with care and respect, to keep abreast of federal and state legislation regarding the excavation of human remains, to conduct the most thorough investigation possible of those remains, and to be sensitive to the concerns of the living individuals to whom those remains are linked. Only then will the biocultural past be preserved for our future.

GUIDE TO FURTHER READING

Attitudes Toward Excavating Skeletons

Carnett 1991; Ubelaker and Grant 1989

General Skeletal Biology

Bass 1987; Buikstra and Ubelaker 1994; Iscan and Kennedy 1989; Steele and Bramblett 1988; White 1991

Paleopathology

Mann and Murphy 1990; Ortner and Aufderheide 1991

Paleodemography

Buikstra and Konigsberg 1985; Verano and Ubelaker 1992

Bioarchaeological Methods

Grauer 1995; Powell et al. 1991; Owsley and Jantz 1994; Saunders and Katzenberg 1992

CHAPTER

12

Excavation and Recovery of Botanical Materials from Archaeological Sites

Richard G. Holloway

Botanical remains—pollen, phytoliths, seeds, bark, leaves, wood, charcoal, fibers, and other plant materials—are an important class of artifactual materials recovered by archaeologists during the excavation of sites (Bryant and Dering 1994; Pearsall 1989). Through the recovery, identification, and analysis of plant materials, archaeologists are able to reconstruct many aspects of prehistoric and historic cultures. This information provides critical clues to such important topics as the types of plants used as food, kinds of shelters that were constructed, woods that were selected for making tools, and the variety of natural environments that were available for exploitation.

The careful recovery of plant remains from sites is only the first step, yet it is one that is often not well understood by the archaeologist. In many instances, plant remains from sites are collected, identified, and then merely listed in tables at the end of the site report. The ideal approach, of course, is to incorporate and integrate the botanical information into the interpretation of the archaeological data.

This chapter discusses the various types of botanical remains most often recovered during the excavation of archaeological sites, along with the potentials and limitations associated with the interpretation of those types of remains. In addition, other critical aspects associated with the development of the discipline and the sampling, quantification, analysis, and interpretation of a wide range of botanically significant remains are examined. A recent useful discussion of sampling strategies for paleobotanical specimens (such as flotation, bulk sampling, scatter sampling) is presented by Lennstrom and Hastorf (1992) based on their fieldwork in Peru. Other appropriate references are listed at the end of the chapter.

MATERIAL TYPES

Pollen

In recent years, archaeologists have become increasingly aware of the potentials of fossil pollen (Figures 12.1 and 12.2), although some view it as a panacea for providing information about many cultural and environmental phenomena. Bryant and Hall (1993) have reviewed the sampling and interpretation of the pollen record. As recently as 20 years ago, few archaeologists routinely collected pollen samples, but today it is common for most sites to be sampled for these types of materials. Sometimes samples are also collected from bog or lake deposits near archaeological sites in hopes that the resulting fossil pollen record will offer clues concerning the regional paleoenvironmental record. For example, Fearn and Liu (1995) report core sampling at Lake Shelby, Alabama, near an archaeological site; and Jacob (1995) has done similar paleoenvironmental coring at swamps adjacent to Maya sites in northern Belize (Figure 12.3).

A major problem with the use of palynological data is its inappropriate use to infer paleoenvironmental conditions based entirely on samples collected from levels within archaeological sites (Bohrer 1968; Schoenwetter 1962). By definition, an archaeological site is a disturbed area and thus presents a biased and distorted view of the natural pollen rain caused by the actions of the prehistoric populations. Environmental reconstructions are extremely important to the interpretation of archaeological sites, but these must be based on the analysis of the pollen and plant macrofossil remains from nearby dated sections of relatively undisturbed sediments as well as from sediments within the archaeological site.

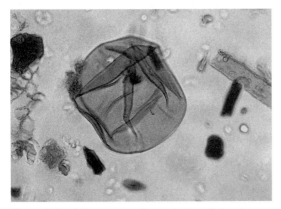

Figure 12.1 A *Zea mays* pollen grain from Cobweb Swamp at Colha, Belize.

Figure 12.2 A cluster of pollen grains characteristic of the mix often found in pollen samples showing a variety of background pollen.

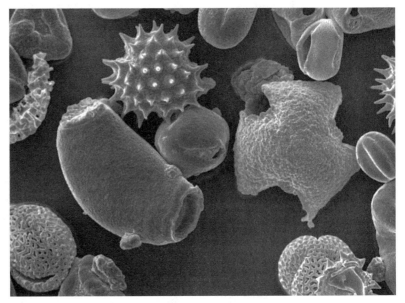

Figure 12.3 Evidence for environmental or manmade changes in local plant communities may be found in pollen cores taken from nearby bogs, swamps, or lakes. A pollen core is being extracted from a freshwater swamp at Burrell Boom, Belize, to test for vegetation changes created by the ancient Maya.

Under ideal conditions, fossil pollen samples can provide a variety of information about the site or sites under examination. For example, pollen collected in midden areas often indicates what types of plants were being collected and utilized for food or other economic purposes by the prehistoric cultures. Fossil pollen found in floor sediments is used to suggest potential types of room utilization (Hill and Hevly 1968), and scrapings collected from the inside surfaces of ceramic vessels often contain fossil pollen from the plants that were stored in or eaten from those vessels (Bryant and Morris 1986). Scrapings from the surfaces of grinding stones such as manos and metates often contain the whole or broken fragments of pollen that adhered to the surfaces of seeds ground into flour, and analyses of sediments adhering to the inside surfaces of basketry can sometimes suggest functional uses of those artifacts.

Ceremonial practices, such as using pollen in burial rituals (Leroi-Gourhan 1975), can often be detected in the soils directly beneath or on top of skeletal materials recovered during archaeological excavations. Other types of data can be inferred from the recovery of fossil pollen in human coprolites (Bryant 1974a, 1974b; Williams-Dean 1978), an application discussed later in this chapter. A relatively new area of investigation is centered within the field of nautical archaeology. Containers such as amphorae are beginning to be routinely examined palynologically for clues of their contents (Jones and Weinstein 1996).

Pollen analysis of soils from nearby prehistoric agricultural fields can sometimes help archaeologists infer the extent and type of cultigens that existed during the occupation of a given site (Dimbleby 1985; Weir 1976). Also, in some cases, the fossil pollen data from these locales can aid in determining when the shift to agriculture began at a particular site (Dimbleby 1985; Iversen 1941). There are limits, however, to the utility of pollen analysis in this type of investigation. As Edwards (1979) has observed, a 1-cm-thick pollen sample may represent as much as 25–30 years of deposition, more than enough time for the entire sequence of forest clearance-agriculture-regeneration to have occurred. Kelso (1994) has used palynology to study historical rural landscapes in Pennsylvania. Percolating groundwater carries down pollen from the surface, and in areas where there is slow soil development, as at the Great Meadows site that he studied, the pollen profile can distinguish preagricultural forests, the clearance of the forests, and the introduction of cultigens.

The paleoenvironmental setting and the chronology of vegetational changes likewise often can be reconstructed using fossil pollen data. However, careful collection and interpretation of these samples are critical if the data are to be useful. Under ideal circumstances, one should seek a nearby lake (e.g., Fearn and Liu 1995) or bog locale that can provide samples free of the altering effects often inadvertently introduced by human activity. As noted earlier, archaeological sites are often a less-reliable source of fossil pollen data for reconstructing the paleoenvironment because they often contain not only the normal windblown pollen types of the regional vegetation but also additional pollen types resulting from human economic activities within the site. Thus, although it is not advisable to use data recovered solely from the archaeological site for paleoenvironmental reconstruction, data from within and without the site area do complement each other.

In spite of the utility of fossil pollen data from archaeological sites, a cautionary note is in order. Pollen grains do not always preserve equally well in all types of archaeological deposits (King et al. 1975). Experimental data (Holloway 1981) show that sites located in areas where severe soil oxidation occurs, where soil microbial activity is strong, where soil alkalinity is high, and where the soils are repeatedly wetted and dried throughout the year yield very little fossil pollen. Areas within sites containing a high concentration of charcoal

(i.e., hearths, certain types of pits, areas of ash concentrations) tend to restrict the ability of palynologists to recover fossil pollen. Hearth areas, often the preferred sampling locale by archaeologists, are especially noted for their lack of pollen content, primarily because the pollen originally present is often incinerated along with the wood, and thus any pollen recovered must be considered to be of postoccupational origin. In addition, this pollen is extremely difficult to concentrate and to clean of unwanted charcoal fragments.

A systematic research design for all pollen sampling should be established as part of the overall research design (Bryant and Holloway 1983). This provides the archaeologist with a means for statistically investigating the palynological component of the site. Accommodations can be made, of course, for specialized features and/or artifacts, but these are generally sampled separately. Not all of the collected samples need to be analyzed, but all too often, the very samples we need to complete our analysis are the ones that were not collected.

As Miksicek (1987) has noted in reference to macrobotanical remains, archaeological sites are, as a rule, notoriously undersampled. This is equally true of pollen sampling. However, it is no longer acceptable to collect a single set of samples and attempt to interpret the range of variability represented in the excavation units from that one site sample. That variability of pollen assemblages within discrete site areas does exist has been previously demonstrated (Cully 1979), and thus it is imperative that multiple samples for pollen analysis be taken from each unit. Because human activity is patterned, we can fully expect to see pollen evidence of this either in specific-area use or, on a smaller scale, in compartmentalization of the available space within an area.

Sampling the Overall Pollen Rain. It is the job of the project botanist to provide an environmental framework within which to interpret the material culture and adaptations of the archaeological population. To accomplish this task, the botanist must become familiar with the contemporary biotic communities of the region. To repeat an earlier admonition, the establishment of a paleoenvironmental framework is best accomplished at relatively undisturbed locales outside the influence of the archaeological site. But, this is only a portion of the research. To interpret the pollen record, the present range of variation of both extant plant communities and their constituent pollen rain must be ascertained. Although some information is available in the literature, especially as a result of the efforts of the CLIMAP (1981) project, basic raw data, especially in the western United States, are still lacking for most areas. Therefore, the botanist/palynologist must conduct a modern ecological analysis of the area to obtain data from surface pollen samples, which can then be applied to the analysis of the paleoenvironmental record.

In new research areas, additional problems are encountered. An adequate reference collection of local plants is essential to any researcher. These collections should include all types of materials, such as pollen, seeds, wood and charcoal, leaves, and fibers. At least one complete specimen must be collected and a "voucher" (sample) placed in a herbarium or botanical reference collection. Techniques for collecting plant specimens can be found in standard plant taxonomy textbooks (Porter 1967) or field guides (Smith 1971). These collections should be multipurpose—extensive enough to meet the needs of both the palynologist and the paleoethnobotanist. If different individuals are employed in these roles, every effort should be made to coordinate this aspect of the field research to reduce duplication of effort.

Sampling Archaeological Sediments. Pollen assemblages are extremely useful in delineating habitation floors, especially in sites representing sedentary populations. However, extreme care must be observed in the collection of such samples (Lennstrom and Hastorf 1992). Cully (1979) has clearly shown that a composite sample consisting of a number of "pinch" samples collected from several locations within the room most clearly represents the pollen rain present in that room, a method previously shown to be statistically valid by Adams and Mehringer (1975). Cully's (1979)

experiment also showed that floors should be sampled immediately upon exposure to minimize contamination from atmospheric pollen. To serve as both control samples and sources for identification of background pollen, samples should be collected from the fill directly above each floor as a matter of course.

For example, in the excavation of Southwestern Puebloan sites and in sites in the Near East (Kelso and Good 1995), the excavation unit is often a room or a roomblock. Under these circumstances, multiple pollen sampling sites within each room are requisite. Column samples should be taken at designated areas within each grid unit superimposed over the room (e.g., the northwest corner of each 1-x-1- or 2-x-2-m square). This procedure ensures adequate sampling of the entire site. Again, not all of these samples need to be analyzed, but they will be available if needed.

Ideally, an archaeologically trained palynologist should be at the site to direct the actual sampling. Box 12.1 provides general procedures to follow during profile sampling. Samples removed from the fill of rooms should be taken no more than 2–3 cm above the floor surface (and preferably closer to it). This increases the correlation between culturally derived pollen assemblages (floor) and the naturally deposited assemblages (fill) immediately after human abandonment. Just as one sample from a floor does not accurately reflect the pollen assemblage, one sample from fill cannot characterize the natural pollen deposition. It is strongly advised that a series of composite fill samples be collected in the same manner as proposed by Cully (1979) for floor samples.

In sampling rockshelters or open sites, a different strategy is necessary. Pollen columns can accurately reflect the pollen deposition in these areas. Normally, 10-cm soil-sampling intervals are used, although this spacing is not sacred and can be adjusted for local conditions (Figure 12.4). Likewise, changing the lateral placement of samples to accommodate changes in the thickness of the sedimentary levels is desirable. If there is one inviolate rule in pollen sampling, it is that under no circumstances should a single pollen sample cross-cut sedimentary divisions (see Box 12.1, item 7). Again,

Figure 12.4   A vertical series of soil samples collected from the bottom up are taken to test for changes in the pollen spectrum through time. Here palynologist Vaughn Bryant stands in front of a pollen column sample from a deep profile at the Lubbock Lake site, Texas.

numerous columns taken throughout the site are preferable to a single column.

A common sampling technique used to obtain pollen sequences from bogs or swamps is coring. Figure 12.3 showed the extraction of a pollen core from a Central American swamp.

Sampling Artifactual Material. A third major form of pollen sampling involves analysis of utilitarian vessels and uses essentially a presence-absence approach. Vessels of many forms often contain sufficient residue to allow inferences about what was stored or processed in them. Suspected storage vessels can be examined for polliniferous

BOX 12.1
Procedure for Collecting Pollen Samples from Site Profiles

1. Clean the outer surface of the excavation pit profile before sampling.

2. Always use a clean trowel or other type of digging implement.

3. Collect between 0.5 and 1.0 liter of material. This ensures a sufficient sample size for a second analysis if necessary.

4. Carefully clean the sampling tool before collecting each new sample.

5. Always use a sterile, leakproof container for each soil sample. If the sample is damp, add a few drops of fungicide or 100 percent ETOH to prevent microbial activity that could destroy pollen in the sample.

6. Correctly label each sample with a permanent-ink pen.

7. Whenever possible, sample within one stratum of the profile rather than mixing strata in a single sample.

8. Start sampling from the bottom of the profile and work toward the top to ensure that material falling from the upper strata will not contaminate samples collected from the lower strata.

9. Move the trowel laterally, following the plane of the stratum. This also prevents contamination between strata.

10. Avoid taking samples from hearths or from any archaeological features that appear to have been burned or that contain large amounts of ash and charcoal. Avoiding charcoal-rich layers is important because charcoal is often impossible to remove from samples during laboratory processing, and pollen is often destroyed in areas that have been burned.

residues (Bryant and Morris 1986), as can vessels whose charred exterior surfaces indicate probable use in food preparation. Bryant and Morris (1986) have demonstrated that samples recovered from the interior surfaces of these vessels probably relate to deposition during use and not to subsequent filling. In any event, these and other categories of information (i.e., pollen washes from metates, analysis of sediment within the strands of basketry, etc.) need to be incorporated into the sampling design before excavation.

Pollen washes of suspected ground stone implements are another excellent source of samples but present additional problems. Ideally, the artifacts should not be washed before they are submitted to a palynologist. Generally, a low recovery of pollen can be expected from these artifacts, but even a small assemblage can provide evidence of plant-processing activities. If the archaeologist prepares the samples, an estimate of the surface area washed should be included (see Chapter 7). This provides a method for relating the pollen concentration values to a standard unit of measure, allowing for comparison between different artifacts. Without these data, the pollen assemblages merely reflect the number of grains present on a given artifact, often precluding meaningful comparisons among artifacts.

Phytoliths

Inorganic crystalline structures (**phytoliths**) are common in the stems, roots, and especially leaves of many plants. Because most phytoliths are composed of either amorphous hydrated silica (opal) or calcium oxalate, they are of great potential value to archaeology because they are not subject to the same types of degradation processes that destroy organic plant remains such as wood, seeds, leaves, or pollen. In addition, the soils of every type of archaeological site should contain phytoliths from the plants that were introduced to the site by humans. The potential of phytolith analysis in archaeology has been discussed by Dunn (1983), Pearsall (1989), Pearsall and Piperno (1993), Piperno (1988), Rapp and Mulholland (1992), and Rovner (1983).

Extraction and analysis of phytolith assemblages from archaeological soils show potential usefulness in interpreting the paleoecology of sites. These types of analyses have generally been applied to those sites located in the western portion of the United States (Lewis 1979; MacDonald 1974; Rovner 1980), but a few sites in the eastern United States have also been examined (Carbone 1977). The majority of studies have focused on the opal silica forms of phytoliths. Those composed of calcium oxalate have received somewhat less attention. Jones and Bryant (1992) have examined the calcium oxalate phytoliths from selected species of the Cactaceae from Texas.

Phytolith analyses have been used to address questions about prehistoric agriculture. With initial studies focusing on the taxonomic identifications of cereal grains (Baker 1960; Blackman 1968, 1969; Miller 1980; Prat 1948; Twiss et al. 1969). Specific types of plant utilization have been investigated by Pearsall (1978, 1982a, 1982b), Pearsall and Piperno (1993), Piperno (1984, 1985, 1988), and Roosevelt (1980). Phytoliths have also been used in analyses of diet (Armitage 1975; Baker 1961; Bryant and Williams-Dean 1975), and remains from tool surfaces have been investigated by Kamminga (1979), Del Bene (1979), and Shafer and Holloway (1979). Wilding (1967) has demonstrated the potential of using phytoliths for radiocarbon dating.

Although overall, preservation of phytoliths is better than of organic microfossils, phytoliths are not totally indestructible; they can be broken down and destroyed by mechanical abrasion and/or geochemical activity (Rovner 1983). Generally, however, phytolith remains are adversely affected only in highly alkaline sediments. In an experimental study, Krauskopf (1956) showed that preservation is independent of pH up to a pH of 9.0. Above this level, chemical dissolution is quite rapid.

As with pollen and other organic fossils, differential preservation is a problem affecting phytoliths. Experimental studies indicate that tree-derived particles are affected much more rapidly than are grass- or herb-derived specimens (Wilding and Drees 1974). Unfortunately, these and similar problems are not normally addressed in the analysis of phytoliths from archaeological sites.

Attempts have been made to systematically describe the morphology of phytolith remains (Rapp and Mulholland 1992; Twiss et al. 1969). Piperno (1984, 1988) describes eight variants of

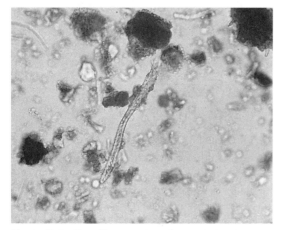

Figure 12.5   Plant fiber, starch grains, and phytoliths are part of the residue matrix left on this stone tool from Hinds Cave, Texas—evidence that the tool was used to process plants.

cross-shaped phytoliths on the basis of size and external morphology. By examining the proportions of the variants in an assemblage, Piperno (1984) was able to demonstrate the presence of pre-ceramic maize at the Ladrones site in central Panama. The phytolith data were also supported, in this case, by subsequent botanical analyses. Brown (1984) has published a morphological key to some of the grass phytoliths in the upper Midwest. Bozarth (1985, 1986) has investigated the morphology of phytoliths from a variety of domesticates including *Cucurbita, Phaseolus*, and *Helianthus.*

Sampling for phytoliths can be conveniently conducted along with sampling for pollen. However, because separate extraction procedures are necessary for pollen and phytoliths, a slightly larger soil sample is needed to accommodate both types of analyses. Phytoliths can also be found in organic residue on stone tools from dry caves (Figure 12.5).

Wood and Charcoal

Charcoal is found scattered throughout the deposits of many archaeological sites. The partial burning of wood (charring) leaves behind this inert substance, which remains preserved in sites where often all other organic debris has been destroyed. For decades, archaeologists either discarded the charcoal fragments or, in later years, saved them only for conducting radiocarbon or dendrochronologic dating (see Chapter 14). More recently, however, archaeologists are finding that the careful collection and analysis of charcoal fragments can provide a wealth of information about ancient cultures and the natural environments in which they operated.

As a matter of course, all charcoal concentrations encountered during excavation should be collected in total. Samples of all charcoal material that is to be submitted for either radiocarbon or dendrochronologic dating should first be identified as to species by a specialist. In the case of dendrochronologic-dating samples, identification before submission will ensure the best possible results. Charcoal can also be obtained from the screened portions of each level as well as from flotation methods. It is recommended that all charcoal recovered from the ¼-inch screen be retained for possible future study. For the most part, these pieces should be large enough for species identification.

The woody portions of plants are composed of specialized cells (such as tracheids, vessel elements, and parenchyma rays) arranged in distinctive patterns (Esau 1965). The distribution and configuration of these cellular patterns are uniform within a given species and often similar among members of the same plant family. This type of uniformity often allows the precise identification of a wooden fragment or of the charcoal fragment that results when the wood is burned. Although the cellular structure of wood is sometimes contorted and altered during the burning process, sufficient clues usually remain for an accurate identification of a charcoal fragment.

Manuals of procedures for the identification of charcoal remains are virtually nonexistent, but other types of reference materials are available. For example, Hough's *Encyclopedia of American Woods* (Harrar 1957) contains thin sections of many woods of North America, and these can be photographed and used as reference materials. A computer-assisted wood identification program (Wheeler et al. 1986) is available, and the *International Association of Wood Anatomists Bulletin* is an excellent source of photomicrographs for comparisons.

Routine identification of archaeologically derived wood and charcoal is based primarily on the analysis of transverse and secondarily longitudinal and radial sections of specimens. The method is quick, inexpensive, and precise enough for identification at least to the generic level (Leney and Casteel 1975). More precise species identifications are sometimes possible but require maceration techniques or embedding and thin-sectioning (Barefoot and Hankins 1982; Dale 1968).

The types of potential archaeological information that can be derived from either wooden or charcoal fragments are manifold. Wood remains can provide clues as to the types that were selected to make tools, weapons, ceremonial items, house structures, rod and slat armor, boats, and, of course, for firewood. Charcoal fragments can often be linked to any of the just-mentioned uses when the archaeological context is consistent with such an interpretation. Most often, however, charcoal fragments are restricted to those recovered from fire hearths, where their main interpretive value relates to the types of wood that were burned as fuel.

Firewood use is an important aspect in the interpretation of an archaeological setting. Prehistoric peoples sometimes burned whatever wood was available, seeming not to discriminate between different plant taxa in their local environments. In other cases, they apparently found that certain types of wood produced better fires because the wood burned longer, burned hotter, or produced less smoke and soot (Asch et al. 1972). Such a selective process is evident in the charcoal fragments recovered from Mimbres Mogollon sites, where analysis has shown that piñon pine was the main source of firewood (Minnis 1981a). Later, as the local population of piñon pines decreased as a result, perhaps, of their use for building construction and firewood, the people were forced to turn to juniper wood, which they seemed previously to have considered an inferior type of fuel. Recognition of this switch in firewood preference suggests environmental conditions at the time of site occupation and also alerts the archaeologist to search

for other indications of this type of early "energy crisis." As Smart and Hoffman (1988) have observed, the total assemblage of woods utilized at a site represents the cultural selection process. The analysis of wood types from various features also provides clues to the selection of taxa for specific purposes (Smart and Hoffman 1988). Thus, it is imperative that multiple samples be taken from similar feature types.

As mentioned above, charcoal fragments can provide evidence about the paleoenvironmental settings during site occupation. In the case of the Meadowcroft rockshelter, the majority of the charcoal was derived from deciduous trees in an area thought to be a boreal forest, suggesting that the ancient cultures were either extremely selective in their choice of firewood or that the paleoenvironment may have been a deciduous, rather than a boreal forest (Volman 1981). Often, evidence from charcoal remains offers the only clues to the paleoenvironment. In areas of south Texas, for example, the soils are not conducive to the preservation of pollen and other types of plant macrofossils. Thus, charcoal recovered from archaeological sites constitutes the only support for the hypothesis that the mixed mesquite (*Prosopis*) and riparian communities have been established in the area for at least the past 6,000 years (Holloway 1986).

Seeds

Seeds, or plant propagules, can be found in the soils of almost all archaeological sites. In many rockshelter, desert, or Arctic sites, seed preservation is generally ideal and their remains are plentiful. In other types of locales with repeated wetting and drying of the soil or in areas where soil microbial activity is intense, recovery is generally limited. The degree of weathering of the recovered assemblage is an important criterion to consider, especially when attempting to assess the reliability of that assemblage (Minnis 1981b; Toll 1981).

How best to collect and sample seeds from sites and the selection of an appropriate analysis method are major problems for both archaeologists and paleoethnobotanists. Miksicek (1987) and Van der Veen and Fieller (1982) have discussed the advantages and disadvantages of various types of sampling techniques currently used. Miksicek (1987) notes that some approaches call for the excavated sediments to be screened and/or subjected to flotation to obtain an accurate seed sample from each cultural horizon. Alternatively, when a method of random sampling is used, the problem centers on how to determine the sampling locales and on how much sediment should be collected from each excavated square or level. Based on field and laboratory experiments, Miksicek concluded that most archaeological sites are undersampled for botanical remains, and what remains are found are generally overanalyzed in the laboratory, a position echoed by Van der Veen and Fieller (1982). Although not specifying precisely how much of a site should be sampled or exactly how much sediment should be collected for adequate seed analysis, Miksicek does state that the most essential criteria to consider are that a large number of soil samples be collected from horizontal and vertical locations within a site and that all examined samples be analyzed in a similar manner before any types of meaningful patterns or statistical distributions can emerge. As Bryant and Hall (1993:278) have stated, "It is better to collect too many samples than not enough."

The point should also be made that the components of features or seed caches be collected in total. These can then be subsampled by the paleoethnobotanist during analysis. This is especially effective in areas, such as southern New Mexico, where recovery of charred plant materials is extremely poor. There, processing of several liters of soil can result in a sample of less than 100 ml. Thus, in these areas, processing of large amounts of soil is preferable to recover the rarer types of materials—i.e., the types that can provide a more-complete inventory of prehistorically available taxa. For example, suppose that a single seed of a particular taxon was recovered from the processing of 5 liters of soil. If only a single liter of that soil had been processed, it is very unlikely that the particular seed would have been recovered, and thus, the information provided by that taxon would not be available. Processing larger quantities of soil matrix can mitigate this potential problem (Dean

1993). However, the archaeologist must balance potential recovery with the increased costs of longer processing times and more analysis associated with this procedure.

Sampling of floors, middens, and fill deposits requires a different strategy. Under normal conditions, a column-type sampling procedure is best. Generally, a predetermined volume of sediment is taken at designated intervals, much the same as when sampling for pollen. It is important to record the volume so that samples can be compared using unit volume measurements, which are useful for both within- and between-site comparisons in the same region.

The same set of sampling procedures can be used when sampling for either microfossil or macrofossil plant remains (see Box 12.1). It is generally easier to take a single column sample for all types of later analyses. Of necessity, this will increase the size of the individual samples. Samples for microbotanical analyses (pollen and phytoliths) should be bagged separately from those taken for macrobotanical analyses, but they should be taken from the same levels in the column.

An equally challenging question focuses on trying to determine which recovered seeds represent materials deposited during site occupation and which represent later contaminants. Keepax (1977) describes four major factors that she feels cause seed contamination in archaeological sites: (1) careless collection of sediment samples from the excavation sites; (2) aerial contamination of site sampling surfaces caused by seeds blowing into the site area; (3) cross-sample contamination caused during the seed flotation process; and (4) pre-excavation contamination of site sediments caused by surface plowing, rodent burrows, earthworm activity, and drying cracks in the soil surface. As a solution to these contamination problems, she suggests that researchers should discard all noncharred seeds that are recovered because they may represent potential contaminants (Keepax 1977). Certainly there is merit in this approach, yet in some cases uncharred seeds may represent the majority of the originally deposited noncontaminant materials. For example, Keepax's technique may work well in the temperate regions of the world, where experiments have shown that modern seeds can move downward in sediments from the surface to depths of 1 m or more, although most contamination occurs within the upper 50 cm (Keepax 1977). Also, in these same regions, destruction of buried organic materials is intense; therefore, one could safely assume that originally deposited uncharred seeds would not have remained preserved. On the other hand, in dry rockshelters found in arid regions or in peat bogs, the environments of deposition are often so ideal that seeds that are thousands of years old still look as fresh as ones recently shed by the plants. Thus, unlike in soils where organic destruction is intense, uncharred seeds from these more-favorable deposits often form the basis for subsequent data analysis (Bohrer 1972; Dering 1979; Helbaek 1969).

Recently Minnis (1981b) has addressed a similar problem by examining the differences in the number of taxa recovered when charred vs. non-charred seeds are counted. Although some uncharred seeds may be prehistoric, especially in sites in the American Southwest, the majority are a source of contamination in one form or another. All other factors being equal, the inclusion of uncharred seeds serves only to increase the noise level, effectively reducing the understanding and interpretation of the assemblage.

Minnis (1981b) further suggests that upon analysis, we may discover that some seed types show a tendency to be associated with particular types of features. This type of analysis relates directly to an earlier problem—sampling. There is absolutely no hope of obtaining information on the distribution of seed remains using the typical sampling strategies—usually a single column removed for flotation analysis—employed by archaeologists.

Coprolites

Human fecal remains (**coprolites**) are often found in archaeological sites located in semiarid, arid, or Arctic regions of the world (Reinhard and Bryant 1992). Rapid desiccation or freezing of fecal samples prevents destruction and preserves them for thousands of years. Although coprolites can yield some of the most important clues about the diet and nutrition of prehistoric groups, only recently have they been systematically collected from archaeological sites and analyzed.

Harshberger (1896, 1898) was one of the first to recognize the potential wealth of information that could be obtained through the analysis of human coprolites. He suggested, for example, that the undigested seeds, pieces of plant fiber, and fragments of animal bones found in the fecal remains of prehistoric man could be used as evidence of the types of foods that were gathered and eaten. Between 1896 and 1960, only a few archaeologists such as Jones (1936), MacNeish (1958), and Wakefield and Dellinger (1936) conducted limited excavations and analysis of coprolites from various sites in the United States and Mexico. During the 1960s, Callen (e.g., 1963, 1967) and Callen and Cameron (1960) opened a new era in coprolite analysis through their discovery of new analytical and quantitative methods. As a result of their work, many more archaeologists now recognize the importance of coprolite studies and have made a greater effort to recover coprolites and provide for their analysis.

What types of data are potentially recoverable from human coprolites? To answer this question, an understanding of the types of materials contained in coprolites is essential. As explained by Fry (1985), coprolites contain food residues, intestinal secretions, digestive secretions, bacteria, parasites, blood residues, occasionally gallstones and enteroliths, and so forth. Thus, given the extensive variety of the constituent parts, analysis of fecal materials requires the most extensive background and is the most difficult subfield of paleoethnobotany to pursue.

Much of the recent work on coprolites has been conducted in the desert areas of the U.S. West. Bryant (1974a, 1974b, 1974c), Holloway (1984), Riskind (1970), Stock (1983), and Williams-Dean (1978) have analyzed a number of specimens from Texas. Studies in the Great Basin have likewise been extensive. Among the first to investigate the Great Basin deposits were Heizer (1967, 1970) and Napton (Heizer and Napton 1969). Later, Fry (1970, 1976, 1978, 1985) investigated specimens from

Danger and Hogup caves in Utah and Frightful Cave in Nevada. Coprolites from Hogup Cave (Kelso 1976), from Nevada's Lovelock Cave (Napton and Kelso 1969; Napton and Heizer 1970), and recently, from Dryden Cave in Nevada (Holloway n.d.) also were analyzed.

Materials recovered from coprolites can be separated into three broad categories: plant, animal, and inorganic. Plant remains such as pollen have been used to infer diets (such as consumption of flowers) (Williams-Dean 1978), to determine seasonality (Bryant 1974a), and to make limited inferences concerning paleoenvironmental conditions (Schoenwetter 1974), although caution is urged in this last regard. Holloway (1984) has recently inferred the medicinal use of plants from the analysis of coprolites dating from the Late Archaic period in West Texas. Seeds, fibers, and leaf fragments from coprolites are useful indicators of the types of foods eaten and how they were prepared. Coprolite studies by Callen (1967) revealed that millet seeds used by ancient Peruvians were ground on milling stones before they were eaten. Callen (1967) also found that maguey leaves in the Tehuacan Valley of Mexico were roasted before being eaten. Another plant indicator of diet often found in coprolites are phytoliths. Sometimes when certain plants such as cactus and agave are chewed for their juice, the only remaining bits of evidence of this dietary item are the microscopic phytoliths (Bryant and Williams-Dean 1975).

Evidence of animal remains in coprolites take the form of hair, bone, shell, feathers, chitin, scales, and parasites. When meat is eaten, it is generally so well digested that no visible traces are recovered in the coprolites. Instead, one generally finds only very tiny fragments of undigested materials. Each of the just-mentioned coprolite inclusions can be used as evidence of the types of animal foods eaten. Often, hair, feathers, and scales remain attached to meat or fish during the butchering and cleaning process. Small fragments of bone and shell are also sometimes inadvertently swallowed during the consumption of eggs, shellfish, or meat. Insect chitin is not digestible; when found in coprolites, it indicates that insects such as grasshoppers, ants, grubs, and termites formed a portion of

human diet in the past. In addition, the eggs and/or protozoan cysts of certain endoparasites and remnants of ectoparasites are sometimes present in coprolites, offering indications of the health of these aboriginal groups (Fry 1976; Samuels 1965). Under certain circumstances, the presence and amount of occult blood can be determined from dried specimens (Williams-Dean 1978).

The inorganic component of coprolites includes dirt, small pieces of grit, and occasionally small chips of stone. Callen and Cameron (1960) suggest that high levels of dirt in some coprolites may reflect its use as seasoning, its adhering to foods, or its having been eaten in times of famine to fill the stomach. Small chips of flint, obsidian, and chalcedony have also been found in human coprolites (Fry 1970) and suggest the practice of using the teeth to retouch artifact edges (Hester 1973) or the inadvertent swallowing of tiny chips detached from artifacts used during butchering.

Most important, the wealth of information that is potentially recoverable from human coprolites makes their careful collection and subsequent analysis essential. After all, although other types of data recovered from the excavated soils of sites, such as bones, seeds, leaves, and wood fragments, can provide circumstantial evidence of diet, health, and food preparation methods, only coprolites can provide direct qualitative evidence.

Any coprolites, or even suspected coprolites, should be collected and stored separately, labeled, and sent to the laboratory for verification. Final identification and analysis should be left to a specialist trained in the study of these types of materials. Often, in the excavation of dry cave shelters, extensive lenses of these remains may be found. Extreme care should be exercised during the excavation of these materials. Note the existence of fiber or vegetational lenses that may be interspersed between the coprolites; these may represent separate depositional events. The profile containing the coprolites should be carefully mapped for later reconstruction of the depositional sequences. Specimens should be carefully marked as to position within the deposit. Although the coprolite layers may extend only a few feet in thickness, the careful excavation and recording of the lenses may demonstrate an accumulation of several thousand years.

Collection of as many coprolite specimens as possible across a horizontal area is equally important. All suspected specimens should be collected for later synchronic studies. Just as the analysis of a single projectile point or pottery type is insufficient, the analysis of a single coprolite does not accurately reflect the diet of a population. The synchronic analysis of coprolites provides much-needed information concerning the overall diet and seasonality of the population. The days of collecting a representative sample and discarding the remainder are, it is hoped, behind us.

The laboratory methods and procedures used in coprolite analysis are beyond the scope of this textbook, but several points need to be made concerning actions that should be taken by the archaeologist to aid the analyst. Once the fieldwork has terminated, all coprolites should be photographed and weighed in the laboratory. This should be done before any sampling of the individual specimens. Records should be kept of any types of plant or animal remains embedded in the coprolite surfaces. Also, descriptions of the shape and appearance of the coprolites, including both longitudinal and transverse measurements, are important. If the archaeologist is doing the sampling, it is imperative that a longitudinal subsample be sent to the analyst. This will ensure a representative sample of macro- and microfossil remains within the fecal specimen. Also, this longitudinal sample will alert the paleoethnobotanist to any differences in the specimen that might suggest the possibility of more than a single meal being represented. As Williams-Dean (1978) has demonstrated, different-sized particles pass through the digestive system at varying rates. Thus a transverse subsample will perhaps yield a somewhat biased database.

Matrix and Fiber Analysis

Analyses of matrix and of fiber samples of vegetal materials have proven to be of exceptional value, especially in dry cave shelters of the American Southwest. Dering and Shafer (1976) performed

Figure 12.6 Epidermis fragment of sotol (*Dasylirion* sp.) extracted from the organic residue left on a stone tool from Hinds Cave, Texas, indicating the tool was used, among other things, to process sotol for food.

analyses on four matrix samples from Gobbler shelter in southwest Texas. In addition to recovering and identifying leaves, seeds, and fruits, the authors were able to identify plant remains of agave, sotol, and yucca by the cuticular cell arrangement. Although they concluded that any seasonal interpretation made on these data would be tentative, Dering and Shafer conclusively demonstrated the utility of examining matrix samples. Often in such cases, enough of the plant material is preserved to allow species determinations, which are useful in determining both seasonality and paleoecologic relationships with some precision.

Such fibers can also be detected on stone tools from dry caves. Shafer and Holloway (1979) found sotol (Figure 12.6) on a tool edge, indicating its use in processing this plant.

Fibers constitute another potential, largely untapped source of paleoethnobotanical information. The difficulties involved in assigning fibers to a taxonomic category are compounded by the lack of comparative morphological and anatomical data. Most archaeological reports deal with the analysis of weaving techniques (Adovasio 1977; Andrews and Adovasio 1980) and not with the process of identification. Bell and King (1944), however, were among the first investigators to propose a method for the identification of leaf fibers from four taxa of the Liliopsida. The method they employed included the use of sectioned material, and they devised a key to the four genera based on the observed morphological differences. Several papers on the identification of fibers in basketry are available (Hendrickson and Felger 1973; Kistler 1969), but unfortunately, most papers deal only with the analysts' interpretation and not their methodology.

Fibers are produced in many different regions of the plant and are normally elongated in shape. Fiber walls are thickened by deposition of lignin, which helps preserve the fiber because lignin is very resistant to the decay process; there is little variability in the overall shape and morphology of these fibers, however. As such, they represent a continuing problem to the analyst attempting identification. At present, most identification is based on morphological comparisons between the fibers recovered archaeologically and those from vouchered reference specimens. The lack of descriptive morphological keys to various fibers has severely hampered the utility of these botanical data. Recently, however, two publications have attempted to alleviate this problem. Parham and Gray (1982) and Catling and Grayson (1982) have provided manuals for the identification of plant fibers. This type of research is promising, but a great deal of taxonomic work is still necessary.

Whole leaves were often utilized for the production of artifacts like sandals and mats. These types of materials can be positively identified, but the techniques for doing so are expensive both in terms of laboratory equipment and time, often involving embedding and thin-sectioning or the use of epidermal peels to study the cuticular patterns of the leaves. Of necessity, these procedures must be conducted by specialists under laboratory conditions, but the archaeologist must be aware of the possibilities to ensure adequate sampling of the remains.

PROCESSING METHODS

It is not cost-effective to ship large quantities of soil matrix to the laboratory when the organic remains will be separated and the inorganic material discarded. Thus, separation of organic materials from inorganic by flotation is most effectively handled if the process is included as part of the fieldwork. This reduces the quantity of materials to be shipped to small, lightweight components. Pearsall (1989) and Wagner (1988) provide excellent summaries and reviews of flotation methodology for paleobotanical studies. Illustrations of flotation techniques can be found in Chapter 6 in Figure 6.18a–f.

Several methods of flotation are currently in use; the archaeologist should use the technique that is best suited to environmental conditions. In areas where water is readily available, a simple method of water flotation works extremely well. Struever (1968a) has described the Apple Creek Method, which entails placing a galvanized tub with a screen bottom in a stream. The soil samples for flotation are poured into the tub, the lighter materials float on the water surface, and the heavier artifacts (such as bone, sherds, and flakes) are caught in the bottom screen. The screen size used must be small enough to retrieve the smallest-sized seeds (Struever 1968a). Window screen should not be used, and Wagner (1988) recommends using a screen with 0.8-mm-sized openings or smaller. Struever (1968a) also points out that the screen size is to some extent conditioned by the soil type at the site. The proper screen size can be determined experimentally in the field. The lighter fraction is generally removed by scooping with a wire strainer covered with a fine mesh material such as cheesecloth or gauze.

Water separation can also be conducted in small basins or drums, but obviously the quantity of soil processed and the speed of the separation are reduced. In utilizing these variations, additional problems of mixing samples, removal of sediment, and so on, become issues.

The materials can also be removed chemically. A solution of zinc chloride can be used to separate plant and animal remains effectively. However, because this is an expensive procedure, it is usually restricted to separation of the light fraction after it has been separated from the heavy fraction by water.

Several mechanical flotation devices that operate by forcing water or solvent in an upward direction are available. The lighter organic materials are thus separated and usually routed to a catchment area for consolidation. Variations of this approach can be seen in the descriptions by Davis and Wesolowsky (1975), French (1971), Jacobson (1974), Limp (1974), and Williams (1973). Pendleton (1979) describes an apparatus suitable for field sorting, which is modified from the froth-type machine originally described by Jarman et al. (1972). Pendleton's (1979) procedure is effectively a combination of water and chemical separation by use of kerosene (150-ml/sample in a 35-gallon tank) to coat plant remains, thus increasing their buoyancy. The seeds and organic particles are washed into a series of interlocking collection screens, which separate the materials. One drawback to the use of any chemical extraction procedure is that once a chemical such as kerosene (or any other hydrocarbon) is used, the sample becomes useless for radiocarbon dating purposes. Thus, this type of system cannot be applied when radiocarbon samples are anticipated.

GUIDE TO FURTHER READING

General

Ford 1979; Hastorf and Popper 1988; Pearsall 1989; Smith 1971; Simpson and Ogorzaly 1986

Pollen Analysis

Bryant and Holloway 1983; Dimbleby 1985; Traverse 1988

Phytolith Identification

Piperno 1988; Rovner 1986

Seed Analysis

Adams 1980; Martin and Barkley 1973

Wood and Charcoal Identification

Barefoot and Hankins 1982; Panshin and DeZeeuw 1980; Parham and Gray 1982

Coprolite and Diet Analysis

Bryant 1974; Gilbert and Mielke 1985; Smith 1985

CHAPTER

13

Basic Approaches in Archaeological Faunal Analysis

Barry W. Baker, Brian S. Shaffer, and D. Gentry Steele

The fundamental aims of archaeology are to understand the history of humanity, how past humans behaved, how this behavior changed over time, how humans acquired the resources they needed to survive, how human societies changed, and how humans have evolved as biological organisms. **Zooarchaeology** is that subdiscipline within archaeology that focuses on interpreting human behavior, ecology, and evolution from the examination of animal, or faunal, remains. Typically, though not always, these faunal assemblages are recovered from archaeological context.

Zooarchaeology is a relatively new field, particularly in North America. It was not until the late 1970s that the first historical review of North American zooarchaeology was published (Robison 1978). As a new field, the study of animal remains associated with archaeological sites or human activities has been given several titles, including zooarchaeology, archaeozoology, osteoarchaeology, and faunal analysis (Beck 1983; Bobrowsky 1982;

Hesse and Wapnish 1985; Lyman 1982b; Olsen and Olsen 1981; Schramm 1982). Even today, no one title for this field has been accepted by all researchers.

In spite of the recency of the coalescence of the discipline, individual scholars have been reporting analyses of faunal remains from archaeological sites since the nineteenth century. Cope (1875) listed 17 species of vertebrates from a site in Maryland. Fewkes (1896b) reported on Pacific coast shells from archaeological ruins in Arizona, and Eaton (1898) discussed fauna from an archaeological site off the Atlantic coast. It is notable that two of the basic interests of zooarchaeologists, reconstructing the prehistoric human diet and the human use of faunal remains as material goods, are reflected in these early works.

Early papers that began to establish zooarchaeology as a discipline include Wintemberg's (1919) "Archaeology as an Aid to Zoology," Merriam's (1928) "Why Not More Care in Identification of

Animal Remains," and Hargrave's (1938) "A Plea for More Careful Preservation of All Biological Material from Prehistoric Sites." Gilmore (1946, 1949) published two important papers entitled "To Facilitate Cooperation in Identification of Mammal Bones from Archeological Sites," and "The Identification and Value of Mammal Bones from Archeological Excavations," respectively. However, it was not until after World War II that researchers in North America began devoting more than a cursory interest to the field. Most noteworthy during the early part of the postwar period were the contributions of John E. Guilday, Stanley Olsen, Paul Parmalee, and Theodore White (see Bogan and Robison 1978, 1987; Dawson 1984; McMillan 1991; and Morris and McMillan 1991 for citations to their extensive contributions).

The broad scope of zooarchaeology makes it impossible to summarize all of the methods and techniques used in faunal analysis or to discuss in detail their limitations. Not all forms of analysis can be applied to all sites, nor will all investigators have the skills to conduct research in all areas. The approach taken here is to present an introduction to common research questions addressed by zooarchaeologists and to provide beginning students with an overview of the broad scope of the literature available. Five commonly recognized areas of zooarchaeology will be discussed in more detail, including data collection, taphonomy, the reconstruction of past human diets, seasonality studies, and paleoenvironmental reconstruction.

FAUNAL ASSEMBLAGE COMPOSITION

Typically, a faunal assemblage recovered from an archaeological site consists of the hard parts of the skeleton and dentition of vertebrates and the shells and opercula of mollusks (snails, freshwater bivalves, marine shells). Softer tissues including exoskeletons of invertebrates (e.g., crabs, shrimp, and insects), fish scales, bird feathers, muscle, ligaments, tendons (sinew), skin, hair, gut, and brains have also been recovered from some archaeological sites. As examples, the fleshy remains of bison and

mammoth have been found in permafrost and in anaerobic muds in Alaska as well as Eurasia (Sutcliffe 1985).

Soft tissue of mummified animals found in dry caves has been reported from Texas (Steele et al. 1984) and the Southwest (Olsen 1985:35–39), and feathers have been recovered from archaeological sites in several regions of North America (Gilbert et al. 1985), as have egg shells (Brooks et al. 1990), hair (Bonnichsen and Bolen 1985; Ryder 1980; Weir 1982), fish scales (Casteel 1976), and insect remains (Elias 1994; Sutton 1988, 1995). A faunal assemblage may also consist of trace fossils or ichnofossils. These include scats of animals and other indirect evidence such as footprints, animal burrows, and chew marks (Gautier 1993).

COMMON RESEARCH TOPICS

The identification of those animal remains present in an archaeological site fails to address the complete data set that zooarchaeologists use to explore questions of human and animal behavior, ecology, and evolution. One of the paramount sets of questions concerns the role that animals played in human diets (Kennedy and LeMoine 1988; Lyman 1982a). Analysts are interested in how animals were procured, when and where they were hunted, and which habitats were exploited and how frequently (Smith 1975; Styles 1981). Attempts have also been made at reconstructing the nutritional contribution of animals to past diets (Gilbert and Mielke 1985; Klippel and Morey 1986; Parmalee and Klippel 1974; Reitz et al. 1980; Sobolik 1990, 1994; Wing and Brown 1979). Determining if animals of a certain age range or sex were preferentially procured is also of interest (Amorosi 1989; Wilson et al. 1982). Researchers may attempt to determine if the same animals were hunted throughout the year and in the same fashion.

Zooarchaeologists are interested in knowing how animal remains were modified by both human and nonhuman processes, where these activities occurred, and how they may affect assemblage interpretation. Animal remains can often shed light on site formation processes. Thus, the condition and the context of the faunal remains within the site is equal in importance to knowing which animals were present (Hesse and Wapnish 1985:59–62; Lyman 1994b; Meadow 1978; Steele 1990).

Another set of questions involves the sorts of social and cultural behavior associated with the procurement and processing of animals and their use. Topics of hunting patterns, butchering practices, food processing habits, and patterns of food distribution typically have been addressed (Binford 1981; Coon 1971; Davis and Reeves 1990; Hudson 1993; Isaac 1978a; 1978b; Lyman 1977, 1982a, 1987a; Muñiz 1988; Stiner 1991; Vehik 1977). One fascinating issue involves the role of scavenging and hunting in early hominid populations (Blumenschine 1986, 1988; Nitecki and Nitecki 1987; Shipman 1986). Taphonomic studies, including those that seek to distinguish marks on bone left by early hominid butchering practices from those caused by bone-chewing carnivores, are important to this question.

Analysts are also interested in knowing how animals were used as nonfood items, such as for clothing (Reed 1972), structures (Armitage 1989; Klein 1973:89–109), trade or commercial goods (Crabtree 1990; Creel 1991; Lightfoot 1979), and ornaments and tools (Campana 1989; MacGregor 1985; S. L. Olsen 1979, 1989; Shaffer 1990; Steele 1988).

Often, ethnographic and ethnoarchaeological studies are used to understand the diverse cultural exploitation, use, and dispersion of animal remains (Hudson 1993). Some researchers have even suggested that it may be possible to identify specific culture groups from bone breakage and dispersion patterns (Yellen 1977b).

Animal domestication and pastoralism are topics widely addressed by Old World investigators (Angress and Reed 1962; Crabtree et al. 1989). Domesticated animals can provide a constant and large food source and also an alternative source of energy, thereby increasing the carrying capacity of the local environment. Many zooarchaeologists have devoted their professional careers to questions of animal domestication and pastoralism (Boessneck 1969; Chang and Koster 1986; Clutton-Brock 1981; Davis 1981).

Traditionally, North American zooarchaeologists have not emphasized domestication studies, though domesticated animals were part of North American human ecosystems. Throughout North America, there is prehistoric evidence of the domestic dog (Morey 1992; Olsen 1985). Later, in historical times, the horse became of immense importance to many groups of North American Indians (Wilson 1924). In addition, in the American Southwest the turkey was kept, either as a domesticated animal or a penned wild animal (McKusick 1986).

At North American historical sites, typical zooarchaeological topics include the relative importance of wild game versus domesticates, seasonality, bone distribution patterns, animal husbandry, and how animals were butchered and used for food and tools (Crabtree 1985; Crader 1990; Jolley 1983; Landon 1996; Lyman 1977). Also, attempts have been made at identifying ethnicity, social complexity, and social status from historic fauna (Crabtree 1990; Huelsbeck 1989; Langenwalter 1980; Lyman 1987b; Schulz and Gust 1983).

To fully understand the range of human behaviors that occurred at a site, the adaptations that humans made to given regions should be ascertained. It is important to reconstruct the environments within which they lived and the seasons when those environments were inhabited or exploited. Various studies of animal remains can provide important information on when sites were occupied (Bernstein 1990; Monks 1981).

One of the major sources of information about past environments is the remains of animals that lived within them. Because many animals live in very specific habitats, the identification of a given animal at a site may provide detailed information about that area's past environmental history. In conjunction with complementary lines of evidence, zooarchaeologists often attempt to reconstruct paleoenvironments by reconstructing the animal community of a given time period (Davis 1987:61–74; Evans 1972; Graham et al. 1987; Grayson 1981a, 1987; Lyman 1986).

Finally, zooarchaeologists are interested in the biology of the animals themselves. What did the animals look like (Purdue 1983, 1986)? How much morphological variation was there within a given species (McDonald 1981)? What was the status of their health, and what pathological conditions did they have (Baker and Brothwell 1980; Baker and Shaffer 1991b; Brothwell 1991; Miles and Grigson 1990; Rothschild and Martin 1993; Siegel 1976)? How have their geographic ranges changed through time (Dillehay 1974; Grayson 1987; Livingston 1987; Lyman and Livingston 1983)? What osteological effects has domestication had on animal biology (Davis 1981; Tchernov and Horwitz 1991)? What was the relationship of past human-wildlife competition for resources (Neumann 1984, 1989)? What can be learned of past animals from genetic and blood residue studies (Allison 1990; Dolzani 1987; Loy 1983)? Vertebrate paleontologists and zoologists, as well, often rely on data from archaeological faunal assemblages (Clutton-Brock 1978; Graham et al. 1987; Lundelius 1967, 1979).

With increased interest in the effects that modern humans have on the environment, the field of "applied zooarchaeology" may soon come into vogue. Trace element analyses of archaeological faunas could be compared with modern specimens from the same area to address questions of localized pollution and environmental change.

From this short review, it is apparent that zooarchaeologists are interested in all aspects of the animal remains and traces of animal remains from a site, not just the most complete, the rarest, or those animals thought to have been used for food. To the zooarchaeologist, even the bits and pieces of broken animal remains can often provide substantial information about past behavior and change.

DATA COLLECTION

Before an analysis is undertaken, the primary goals of the project archaeologist or principal investigator must be considered. Until recently, archaeologists frequently requested only minimal dietary information, including short descriptions and lists of animals present. Though species lists may be important in their own regard (Lyman 1986), questions explored today require much more detailed information if they are to be resolved. Historically,

faunal analysts were biologists, paleontologists, or zoologists with little training in archaeological method and theory. Today, increasing numbers of faunal specialists are themselves archaeologists, with specialized training in faunal research. Thus, researchers will no longer want only species and bone counts but will require in-depth analyses on many aspects of the sample (Smith 1976).

As with other archaeological materials, faunal remains are more informative if interpreted within specific archaeological context (Figure 13.1). Minimally, the zooarchaeologist requires detailed provenience information, feature descriptions, information on soils and soil chemistry, site formation processes, recovery methods and sampling strategies, a site plan view, stratigraphic profiles, correlations of dates with specific unit-levels and features of the site, and other relevant information. Essentially, all information relevant to the project archaeologist for the interpretation of the site will be pertinent also to the zooarchaeologist.

Furthermore, the zooarchaeologist (as an archaeologist and anthropologist) needs a clear research design, with questions that can be potentially answered by the assemblage (Binford 1964; Hesse and Wapnish 1985:15–17). Working together, the zooarchaeologist and principal investigator can structure the analysis to meet project goals. Emslie (1984), Gamble (1978), Meadow (1980), Reitz (1987), and Wing (1983) provide basic reviews for archaeologists of information that will enhance faunal interpretations. Archaeologists anticipating the recovery of faunal remains from their sites are strongly encouraged to review these works and to consult with a zooarchaeologist before starting the project.

Box 13.1 lists the types of background information the zooarchaeologist needs to enhance faunal interpretation. Required information will vary depending upon the site, the research design, and the personal preferences of the zooarchaeologist. As Meadow (1980:65) has stated, "The most important contribution an archaeologist can make to the success of faunal analysis is to be willing to maintain a dialogue with the specialist so that the concerns of both parties are expressed and acted upon before it is too late to do anything about them."

Figure 13.1 Excavation of faunal remains at site 41HY209T, Central Texas: (*a*) overall view of excavation; note faunal remains being exposed; (*b*) close-up of carefully excavated faunal concentration.

(a)

(b)

Sampling Strategies

A consideration of methods used in the recovery of faunal materials is of primary importance in the interpretation of animal assemblages (Grayson 1981b, 1984; Payne 1972). To emphasize this point, several studies have documented biases in the use of various screen sizes in recovering vertebrate and invertebrate assemblages (Casteel 1972; Clason and Prummel 1977; DeMarcay and Steele 1986; Dye and Moore 1978; Gordon 1993; Meighan 1969; Nagoaka 1994; Payne 1972, 1975; Shaffer 1992b; Shaffer and Sanchez 1994; Struever 1968a) (see Chapter 5). To reduce this problem, fine-screening, water-screen-

ing (Figure 13.2), and flotation methods can add significant information over the standard use of ¼-inch screens (Casteel 1972:383–387; DeMarcay and Steele 1986:250–264; Payne 1975; Prevec 1985; Shaffer 1991:118–120; Stewart 1991; Thomas 1969; Wing and Quitmyer 1985). Tables 13.1 (pg. 305) and 13.2 (pg. 306) present data from screening experiments of modern comparative animal skeletons, conducted to predict what elements might be recovered from ⅛-inch and ¼-inch screens for various-sized animals. This information is useful for predicting screening bias against various-sized mammals. As can be seen, ¼-inch screening greatly biases samples against small animals.

BOX 13.1   FAUNAL ASSEMBLAGE BACKGROUND INFORMATION

1. Person for zooarchaeologist to contact when questions arise.

2. Site number and/or name.

3. Site location (state, county, city, map coordinates, etc.).

4. When was the site excavated and by whom?

5. Is the site single- or multicomponent?

6. Type of site (kill site, habitation site, shell midden, etc.)?

7. Component date(s), methods of determination, and specific provenience from which datable material was recovered.

8. Site environment (near streams, lakes, hillside, vegetation, etc.).

9. Geology of the site area, including hydrological information.

10. Will any additional environmental specialists or statisticians be consulted during the course of the site analysis? If yes, please provide contact information.

11. Were all faunal remains collected from the site (this includes snails, shells, "unidentifiable" bone fragments, etc.)?

12. Information on recovery methods used: including sampling strategy, screen sizes, wet or dry screening, etc., and where applied.

13. Were units excavated in arbitrary or stratigraphic levels?

14. Information on the number of units excavated, their size and depth, as well as the number of levels excavated per unit. A map and list of units would be extremely helpful.

15. Were pH, soil chemistry, or any other related tests conducted at the site? If so, please indicate the provenience of the samples and the test results.

16. If known, how was the site area used in the past and at the time of excavation (pasture, cattle pen, forest, homestead, etc.)?

17. List any disturbance(s) noted during excavation and the units and levels most affected (mechanical disturbance, such as grading or road construction; bioturbation, etc.).

18. What features were found at the site? Please include provenience information and a description of each feature identified.

19. Which features had faunal remains associated with them? Are feature numbers indicated on the sample bags (field sacks)? Please provide a feature list, and indicate the association of each feature with stratigraphic or excavation units.

20. Were any faunal remains removed from the sample for testing (e.g., for dating or isotope studies)? If yes, list the specimens removed with their associated provenience.

(continued. . .)

Figure 13.2 Water screening for recovery of faunal remains. Deposit is being washed through ⅛-inch mesh at site 41LK201, southern Texas.

BOX 13.1, *continued*

21. Has the faunal sample been divided in any other way? That is, does your submitted sample consist of all the faunal remains recovered from the site (this includes bone and shell tools, faunal ornaments, grave-good fauna, mollusks, animal burials, etc.)?

22. Have any of the faunal remains been treated with glue or preservative, either in the field or in the laboratory? If so, which specimens, and what type of preservative?

23. May the faunal analyst treat specimens in poor condition with preservative? (Such treatment may affect future radiocarbon dating and some chemical analyses.)

24. May the analyst pull specimens with cut marks, pathologies, etc., and bag them separately?

25. Were any human or animal burials found at the site? If so, please indicate provenience and provide associated field notes, photos, and burial forms.

26. If the faunal report should be presented in a specific format style, please indicate the guidelines to be followed.

27. May photographs be included in the faunal report? If so, up to how many photos and of what size?

28. Please make copies of photographs or slides of the site available to the analyst, especially those that include faunal remains.

29. List any research questions you specifically wish the faunal analyst to address.

30. Where will the faunal remains eventually be curated?

31. Include a site plan, topographic map, and stratigraphic profile. These will provide additional information that will aid in the proper interpretation of the faunal remains.

32. Include an explanation of any lot or provenience systems used and an inventory of the bags or field sacks submitted, along with their associated lot numbers.

33. Provide any publications that may already exist on this site including grant and contract proposals, draft copies, and preliminary reports. If you plan to compare this site with other archaeological sites, it would be helpful if the faunal analyst were made aware of such references so that faunal assemblages can be compared.

34. What word processing and database management software (and versions) do you use?

35. Please keep the zooarchaeologist informed of new developments and reference material as you encounter it. Although some of this information may not yet be available, the more information you provide, the more relevant and detailed the analysis can be.

However, fine-screening (including ¹⁄₁₆-inch screens and smaller) can be expensive and time-consuming (Barker 1975:62; DeMarcay and Steele 1986:260; Payne 1975:16–17) and in some cases may not add significant faunal data (Baker et al. 1991:142–145). In addition, archaeological sites containing shell middens or other dense deposits of mollusks may pose problems of their own in terms of faunal recovery and sampling strategy (Anderson 1973; Kent 1988:19–27; Klippel and Morey 1986; Meighan 1969; Muckle 1994; Stein 1992; Waselkov 1987:150–153).

With limited time and funds, it is best to excavate less material, but screen it more thoroughly to reduce biased samples. One common sampling strategy is to use a series of nested screens including ¼-inch, ⅛-inch, and ¹⁄₁₆-inch mesh sizes (see Chapter 5). Flotation and bulk samples should also be taken where appropriate. In all cases, the zooarchaeologist should be provided with detailed information on the volume of earth excavated from all blocks, levels, and features of the site. Volumetric data can often be used to address questions of site bone density and rates of deposition.

TABLE 13.1

Weight and Measurements in Ascending Order by Lowest Weight for Taxa Presented in Table 13.2

Reference Number	Taxon	Weight (g)	Length (mm)	Femur[1] (mm)
1. Least shrew (*Cryptotis parva*)		4–7	56–64	7.0
2. Pygmy mouse (*Baiomys taylori*)		7–9	51–64	9.3
3. Evening bat (*Nycticeius humeralis*)		7–9	36–38	13.1
4. House mouse (*Mus musculus*)		11–22	81–86	12.2
5. Shorttail shrew (*Blarina* sp.)		11–22	76–102	9.1
6. Deer mouse (*Peromyscus maniculatus*)		18–35	71–102	15.1
7. Mexican pocket mouse (*Liomys irroratus*)		34–50	102–127	22.2
8. Kangaroo rat (*Dipodomys ordii*)		42–72	102–114	24.6
9. Eastern mole (*Scalopus aquaticus*)		57–140	114–165	13.0
10. Valley pocket gopher (*Thomomys bottae*)		71–250	122–178	19.0
11. Wood rat (*Neotoma albigula*)		135–283	190–216	33.6
12. Thirteen-lined ground squirrel (*Spermophilus tridemcimlineatus*)		140–252	114–165	29.0
13. Red squirrel (*Tamiasciurus hudsonicus*)		198–250	178–203	40.5
14. Mexican ground squirrel (*Spermophilus mexicanus*)		198–340	171–190	30.4
15. Mink (*Mustela vison*)		198–340	228–266	54.7
16. Gray squirrel (*Sciurus carolinensis*)		340–726	200–250	52.2
17. Spotted skunk (*Spilogale putorius*)		363–999	230–340	46.4
18. Cottontail (*Sylvilagus auduboni*)		600–1,200	300–380	65.2
19. Ringtail cat (*Bassariscus astutus*)		900–1,130	360–410	63.8
20. Muskrat (*Ondatra zibethicus*)		908–1,816	250–360	43.6
21. Jackrabbit (*Lepus californicus*)		1,300–3,100	430–530	106.2
22. Red fox (*Vulpes fulva*)		4,500–6,700	5,600–6,300	132.6

[1]Femur length is based on greatest length (Driesch 1976:84–85).
Note: After Shaffer and Sanchez (1994:Table 1).

Ideally, sampling strategies should be developed in collaboration with the zooarchaeologist and other investigators who will conduct specialized analyses. This interaction should begin at the grant-writing and proposal stage. It is also best if the faunal analyst can participate in the excavation or visit the site several times throughout the fieldwork phase.

Once samples reach the laboratory, it is often necessary to subsample the faunal assemblage for analysis purposes. Limited time and funds often make it impossible to identify all of the remains during the first phase of analysis (Levitan 1983, 1984). It should be realized, however, that subsampling may result in significant information loss (Turner 1984). Subsampling decisions are best made with a knowledge of information that has been provided by other faunal assemblages from the same area and with specific research questions in mind.

TABLE 13.2

Results of Screening Tests on Controlled Samples with ⅛-inch and ¼-inch Mesh Screens. (Taxa keyed with Table 13.1.)

Taxon:	1	2	3	4	5	6	7	8	9	10	11	12	13	14	15	16	17	18	19	20	21	22
Cranium	EQ	EQ	EQ	EQ	EQ	EQ	EQ	EQ	EQ	EQ	EQ	EQ	EQ	EQ	EQ	EQ	EQ	EQ	EQ	EQ	EQ	EQ
Ramus	–	–	E	E	E	E	E	E	E	EQ	EQ	EQ	EQ	EQ	EQ	EQ	EQ	EQ	EQ	EQ	EQ	EQ
Atlas	–	–	–	–	E	E	E	E	E	E	E	E	AA	EQ	EQ	EQ	EQ	EQ	EQ	EQ	EQ	EQ
Axis	–	–	–	–	E	E	E	E	E	E	E	E	EQ	E	EQ	EQ	EQ	EQ	EQ	EQ	EQ	EQ
Cervical	–	–	–	–	–	E	E	–	E	E	E	E	E	E	EQ	EQ	EQ	EQ	EQ	EQ	EQ	EQ
Thoracic	–	–	–	–	–	E	E	E	–	E	EQ	E	E	EQ	EQ	EQ	EQ	EQ	EQ	EQ	EQ	EQ
Lumbar	–	–	–	–	–	E	E	E	E	E	EQ	EQ	EQ	EQ	EQ	EQ	EQ	EQ	EQ	EQ	EQ	EQ
Sacrum	–	–	–	BB	–	–	BB	E	BB	BB	BB	EQ	BB	EC	EQ	EQ	EQ	EQ	EQ	EQ	EQ	EQ
Caudal	–	–	E	–	–	–	–	–	E	–	–	EQ	EQ	E	E	–	E	–	–	E	E	EQ
Scapula	–	–	E	E	–	E	E	E	E	EQ	EQ	EQ	EQ	EQ	EQ	EQ	EQ	EQ	EQ	EQ	EQ	EQ
Clavicle	–	–	–	–	–	–	–	–	E	–	–	–	–	–	–	–	–	–	–	–	–	–
Sternal segment	–	–	–	–	–	–	–	–	–	–	–	–	–	–	E	E	E	E	E	E	EQ	EQ
Manubrium	–	–	–	–	–	–	–	–	E	E	E	E	E	E	E	E	E	E	E	E	EQ	EQ
Rib	–	–	–	–	–	–	–	–	–	–	–	–	–	–	E	E	–	E	E	EQ	EQ	EQ
Humerus	–	–	E	–	–	E	E	E	EQ	E	EQ	E	EQ	EQ	EQ	EQ	EQ	EQ	EQ	EQ	EQ	EQ
Ulna	–	–	–	–	–	E	–	E	E	E	E	E	E	E	EQ	EQ	EQ	EQ	EQ	EQ	EQ	EQ
Radius	–	–	E	–	–	–	–	E	E	E	E	E	E	E	EQ	EQ	EQ	EQ	EQ	EQ	EQ	EQ
Carpals	–	–	–	–	–	–	–	–	–	–	–	–	–	E	E	E	E	E	E	–	E	E
Metacarpals	–	–	–	–	–	–	–	–	–	–	–	–	–	–	–	E	–	–	E	–	E	EQ
Pelvis with fused sacrum	–	–	–	EQ	–	–	EQ	EQ	EQ	EQ	–	–	EQ	–	–	–	–	–	–	–	–	–
Innominate	–	–	E	–	–	E	E	–	–	–	EQ	EQ	EQ	EQ	EQ	EQ	EQ	EQ	EQ	EQ	EQ	EQ
Femur	–	–	E	E	–	E	E	E	–	EQ	EQ	EQ	EQ	EQ	EQ	E	E	E	E	E	E	E
Patella	–	–	–	–	–	–	–	–	–	–	–	E	E	–	E	EQ	EQ	EQ	EQ	E	EQ	E
Tibia	–	–	–	E	E	–	–	–	–	–	–	E	EQ	E	EQ	EQ	EQ	EQ	EQ	EQ	EQ	EQ
Fibula	–	–	–	–	–	–	–	–	–	–	–	E	E	E	EQ	EQ	EQ	EQ	EQ	EQ	EQ	EQ
Tibiofibula	–	–	–	–	–	E	E	E	E	E	EQ	–	–	–	–	–	–	E	–	E	E	E
Metatarsals	–	–	–	–	–	–	–	–	–	–	–	E	E	E	E	E	E	E	E	E	E	E
Astragalus	–	–	–	–	–	–	–	–	–	–	–	E	E	E	EQ	E	EQ	EQ	EQ	E	EQ	EQ
Calcaneus	–	–	–	–	–	–	–	E	–	EQ	E	E	E	E	EQ	E	EQ	EQ	EQ	E	EQ	EQ
Other tarsals	–	–	–	–	–	–	–	–	–	–	E	–	–	–	–	–	–	–	–	E	E	E
Sesamoids	–	–	–	–	–	–	–	–	–	–	–	–	–	–	–	–	–	–	–	–	E	E
Proximal phalange	–	–	–	–	–	–	–	–	–	–	–	–	–	–	E	–	–	–	–	E	E	E
Middle phalange	–	–	–	–	–	–	–	–	–	–	–	–	–	–	–	–	–	–	–	–	E	E
Distal phalange	–	–	–	–	–	–	–	–	–	–	–	–	–	–	E	–	–	–	–	–	E	E

Key: A = Element not present for tests; B = Sacrum was recovered, fused to the innominates; C = Sacral body segments were unfused and not recovered in ⅛-inch tests; E = Element recovered by ⅛-inch mesh (shaded blocks indicate recovery only by ⅛-inch mesh); Q = Element recovered by ¼-inch mesh; EQ = Element recovered by ⅛-inch and ¼-inch mesh; – = Element not recovered by either screen size.

Note: From Shaffer and Sanchez 1994:Table 2.

Field and Laboratory Treatment of Specimens

Because of the varied nature of faunal assemblages and their differential states of preservation, it is difficult to recommend a single approach to be taken in the treatment of archaeological faunas. Also, faunal analysts may disagree on whether specimens should be bagged separately or if each specimen should receive a separate catalog number (Rea 1986). It is best to consult the analyst who will be working with the material for his or her views on excavation, cleaning, conservation, labeling, and sorting.

Generally, the same precautions taken in the treatment of human skeletal remains apply to faunal remains (see Chapter 11). During excavation, care must be taken to reduce bone damage. It is better to leave matrix adhering to the bone than to damage the specimen while removing the dirt (Huelsbeck and Wessen 1982:224). A basic knowledge of skeletal anatomy can help you predict where the remainder of a partially exposed bone lies. This helps reduce mechanical damage during excavation.

The use of preservatives in the field should generally be avoided. Only apply preservatives in situations where the faunal materials cannot be recovered relatively intact and when their intact recovery will enhance research or exhibit value (see Chapter 7 for information on products). The addition of preservatives to bone in the field often results in the recovery of surrounding matrix. This greatly increases laboratory processing and cleaning time. Excessive use of preservatives can also obscure important morphological and taphonomic features of the bone. Investigators should realize that preservatives may also contaminate specimens and interfere with various dating and isotopic analyses. Alternatives to preservatives include block lifting, plaster or spray-foam jacketing, and controlled drying (Bement 1985; Dockall 1995; Johnson 1994:229). Other discussions of conservation can be found in Koob (1984) and Storch (1983, 1988).

If animal burials or articulated skeletons are encountered in the field, they should be recorded in a standard detailed manner using photographs, notes, and feature and burial forms. Emslie (1984) provides examples of faunal catalog forms and nonhuman burial forms that can be completed in the field.

Mandibles or skulls recovered with teeth should be packaged individually so that loose teeth do not become separated from their sockets. Similarly, fragile elements such as skulls, bird sternae, and poorly preserved specimens should be packaged individually so they are not crushed by other elements after being bagged and returned to the laboratory for analysis. Fragments of the same element, or articulated elements, should also be packaged separately from the rest of the sample to facilitate later reconstruction.

In cleaning specimens, be aware that animal teeth may provide important dietary or paleoenvironmental information through phytoliths or insect parts lodged in tooth fissures or dental calculus (Akersten et al. 1988; Armitage 1975; Wing 1983:10). If analysis is expected to proceed along these lines, it is best to leave such specimens unwashed. Excessive washing and cleaning can also leave marks on the bone that may be mistaken for butchering marks or animal chewing. For additional discussions of the field/laboratory treatment of faunal remains, see Allen (1986), Emslie (1984), Henry (1991), Hesse and Wapnish (1985:51–68), Rea (1986), Storch (1988), and Wing (1983).

Animal Identification

The identification and recording of specimen attributes form the basis upon which interpretations are made (Butler and Lyman 1996; Driver 1992). For accurate identifications, collections of modern comparative specimens must be available for use (Beck 1981:364; Coy 1978:143; Davis 1987:32–35; Olsen 1971:2–3). This process may appear overwhelming to the beginner, but identification skills develop with time and repetition. Recent articles outlining techniques in the establishment of modern comparative collections include De Wet et al. (1990), Dirrigl (1989), Matthiesen (1989), and Maiorana and Valen (1985).

Due to the fragmented condition of bone and shell, or lack of element uniqueness, not all specimens can be identified to species. Therefore, many elements are identified to more general taxonomic categories, such as genus, family, order, or class. There is no one-to-one relationship between specimen size and its potential for identification. Commonly, very small and even fragmentary rodent teeth can be identified to species, whereas relatively large bone-shaft fragments may be classified only as "large mammal."

It is better to be conservative in reporting taxa identifications, thereby ensuring that identifications are correct (Ziegler 1975:186), than to make unsure species or subspecies identifications. Definitions and discussions of the term *identifiable* are provided by Driver (1982:203), Gustafson (1972:54), Hesse and Wapnish (1985:54–55), Lyman (1979b:23–24), and Ziegler (1973:5, 7–8).

Many osteological and anatomical guides are available to aid in the identification of archaeological faunas. A few are listed here, primarily with emphasis on North American taxa. Guides should be used only as aids to identification, not in place of comparative material (Davis 1987:32–33; Gilbert et al. 1985:i; Reitz 1987:32). By far the most commonly used guides are those associated with mammals (Boessneck 1969; Brown and Gustafson 1989; Crabb 1931; Fisher 1942; Ford 1990; Gilbert 1980; Glass 1951; Hepworth 1974; Hildebrand 1955; Hillson 1986; Lawrence 1951; Olsen 1960, 1964, 1982; Schmid 1972; Torres et al. 1986; R. Walker 1985).

Examples of avian reference material include Gilbert et al. (1985), Hargrave (1970), McKusick (1986), S. J. Olsen (1968b, 1979a, 1979b), Schmid (1972), and Wolfenden (1961). Herpetological sources include Auffenberg (1969, 1976), Feuer (1970), Holman (1981), and Olsen (1968a). Identification of fish elements can be aided by Cannon (1987), Casteel (1976), Courtemanche and Legendre (1985), Harkonen (1986), Kozuch and Fitzgerald (1989), Morales and Rosenlund (1979), Mundell (1975), Olsen (1968a), Rojo (1991), and Wheeler and Jones (1989). Several useful invertebrate guides are also available (e.g., Hulbricht 1985; Kent 1988; Parmalee 1967; Pennak 1989; Starrett 1971; Turgeon et al. 1988; Vaught 1989), though mollusk taxonomy is often problematic.

Traditionally, species identification has involved comparison of the skeletal morphology of archaeological specimens with elements of known, modern taxa. More recently, investigators have undertaken the analysis of biochemical data to make animal identifications (Lowenstein 1985; Yohe et al. 1991). Such continued research is likely to provide exciting information on highly fragmented assemblages, traditionally considered unidentifiable.

Data Recording

Associated with faunal identification and analysis is data recording. Using computer technology, the process is more efficient than the hand tabulations performed prior to the 1970s (Campana and Crabtree 1987; Gifford and Crader 1977; Shaffer and Baker 1992; Wijngaarden-Bakker 1986). Reviews of recent computer-associated zooarchaeological coding systems are provided by Baker and Shaffer (1991a) and by Shaffer and Baker (1992). Typically, numeric or alphanumeric codes are used to record information including provenience, taxa name, element, portion of element, side, age, and sex (Figure 13.3 and Table 13.3). Taphonomic questions can be addressed by recording breakage, burning, weathering, cut-mark, gnawing, and cultural modification information.

When adopting or developing a faunal coding system, several important factors must be considered. First, the coded data should be easy to decode, preferably electronically. This is readily handled by many database management software packages. The data should also be easily sorted, allowing comparison of multiple variables. In addition, the codes themselves should be easy to use and apply. The system or process must be flexible enough to be expanded, depending upon the research design, the type of site being analyzed, and the attributes encountered. Different user views of the data must be possible, including calculation of abundance measures such as MNI (minimum number of individuals) and MNE (minimum number of elements).

In recording faunal data, it is best to use standardized terms and measurements. Driesch (1976)

| | | | | | | | | | | | | FAUNAL ATTRIBUTE CODING SHEET
Codes follow Shaffer and Baker (1992) Version 3.3 | Page 32 of 116 |

	Site #: 41DT11		Name: Spider Knoll				Recorder: Brian Shaffer				Date: 2 Aug 1993

LOT	QTY	TXN	EL	PE	SD	AC	A	BK	B	G	CT	COMMENTS
141	54	70060						1	3			
141	20	70060						3				
141	1	93470	473	901								
142	17	40200	701									
142	1	76200	210	755	2			1				
142	1	89650	32	216				1	3			
142	1	94200	30	275	2	32		1				
144	1	91800	200	639	1			1	3			smaller than coyote
144	1	94350	32	203				1				
145	2	88151	20	157	1			1				
147	1	90000	30	234	1							
180	1	45550	740	301	3							
191	1	93700	300	601		07		1				see Brown & Gustafson for criteria
379	33							1				
381	1	32400	210	745	2			1				
415	1	94200	180	660	2			3				cut-distal lateral end

NOTES: Box Number 2

Key: QTY=quantity. TXN=taxon. EL=element. PE=portion of element. SD=side. AC=age criteria. A=age. BK=breakage. B=burning. G=gnawing. CT=cut.

Figure 13.3 Faunal attribute coding sheet.

and Morales and Rosenlund (1979) present guidelines for recording measurements of animal remains, should osteometric analysis apply to the research design (Boessneck and Driesch 1978). Such guides are by no means the last word on these topics, but they are extremely useful. Standardized anatomical nomenclature guides useful in data recording include Baumel (1979), International Committee on Veterinary Gross Anatomical Nomenclature (1983), Peters (1987), Roemer (1956), and Rojo (1991).

Quantification

Once specimens have been recorded, data manipulation and analysis can begin. Animal and element abundance are typically quantified at an early stage in interpretation. In recent years, numerous methods of quantification have been used (Casteel

and Grayson 1977; Lyman 1994a). The most common measures of animal abundance include number of identified specimens (NISP) and minimum number of individuals (MNI). For addressing taphonomic issues (discussed later), measures of minimum animal units (MAU) and minimum number of elements (MNE) are commonly used. The two most common measures, NISP and MNI, are briefly described here.

NISP is simply defined as the number of specimens identified for a given taxon. A taxon can be a species, genus, family, and so on. NISP is subject to a number of problems (Grayson 1984; Reitz 1987:33–34), primarily the interdependence of specimens. That is, dozens of broken specimens may all be from the same element or animal, providing an inflated appearance of taxa abundance if bone or specimen counts alone are considered. In addition, the strict use of NISP as a quantification technique

TABLE 13.3

Summary of Data Converted from Codes in Figure 13.3

Lot	Qty	Taxon	Element	Portion of Element	Side	Breakage	Burning	Comments
141	54	Mammalia (Medium/large)	Indeterminate	Fragment		Angular	Charred	
141	20	Mammalia (Medium/large)	Indeterminate	Fragment		Spiral	Unburned	
141	1	Artiodactyla (Medium)	Proximal abaxial sesamoid	Complete or nearly complete		Unbroken	Unburned	
142	17	Testudinata	Shell	Fragment		Angular	Unburned	
142	1	*Sylvilagus* sp.	Pelvis	Acetabular end of ischium	Right	Angular	Unburned	
142	1	Carnivora	Tooth, perm./decid. ind.	Cheek tooth		Angular	Charred	
142	1	*Odocoileus* sp.	Permanent tooth	Lower M1 or 2	Right	Angular	Unburned	
144	1	*Canis* sp.	Ulna	Semi-lunar notch only	Left	Angular	Charred	smaller than coyote
144	1	*Antilocapra americana*	Tooth, perm./decid. ind.	Enamel fragment		Angular	Unburned	
145	2	cf. *Microtus pinetorum*	Mandible	Horizontal ramus with diastema	Left	Angular	Unburned	
147	1	*Procyon lotor*	Permanent tooth	Upper PM4	Left	Unbroken	Unburned	
180	1	Colubridae	Dorsal vertebra	Complete or nearly complete	Axial	Unbroken	Unburned	
191	1	*Cervus* sp.	Proximal phalange	Complete or nearly complete		Angular	Unburned	see Brown & Gustafson 1989 for criteria
379	33	Vertebrata	Indeterminate	Fragment		Angular	Unburned	
381	1	*Bufo* sp.	Pelvis	Acetabular end of ilium	Right	Angular	Unburned	
415	1	*Odocoileus* sp.	Humerus	Distal end	Right	Spiral	Unburned	cut-distal lateral end

assumes that all taxa and elements are equally identifiable and that recovery rates for specific taxa and elements are consistent (Reitz 1987:33). However, NISP is not subject to problems of aggregation, element siding, fragmentation description, or many of the other problems associated with MNI (Grayson 1979, 1981b, 1984).

The **minimum number of individuals (MNI)** count for a given assemblage or taxon is typically defined as the greatest number of individuals represented by duplication of elements. In addition, factors such as age (Bökönyi 1970:291–292) and element size (Klein and Cruz-Uribe 1984:27) may also be considered when determining how many animals are represented in an assemblage. Grayson (1979, 1981b, 1984), Lyman (1994a), and Reitz (1987) provide recent reviews of MNI calculations.

Grayson (1984:92) suggested that MNI should be used only "as a part of a wider ranging analysis based on the number of identified specimens." This is because MNI suffers from varying aggregation methods that can produce differing results (Casteel 1977; Grayson 1973, 1978, 1984). For example, MNI can be calculated for different cultural levels, for arbitrary levels, or for a site as a whole. Because of the many ways of computing MNI, comparison of MNI values from different sites or assemblages may be difficult if differing quantification methods were used. The methods used to calculate MNI should always be reported with the analysis.

There are other problems to consider when using MNI counts. Foremost is that MNI is dependent on sample size (Grayson 1979, 1981b, 1984). A small sample is less likely to accurately reflect the abundance relationship of all of the taxa deposited in the site. MNI values alone also tend to overestimate the dietary importance of small taxa. The presence of 10 freshwater mussel shells and 1 deer from a site, for example, should not be interpreted as meaning that mussels were more important in the diet. In this case, the deer could potentially provide much more meat. Despite these concerns, MNI is one of the most common quantification methods used because its limitations can often be overcome by careful excavation and analysis (Reitz 1987:35).

TAPHONOMY AND FACTORS AFFECTING FAUNAL ASSEMBLAGE COMPOSITION

Ideally, the zooarchaeologist wishes that the faunal remains be in the exact condition and location they were in when last modified by humans. However, this is rarely the case. Once bone is discarded, it is subject to innumerable destructive forces of nature. Therefore, it is vital in terms of reconstructing past human behavior to be able to distinguish between those modifications an assemblage has undergone as a result of human behavior and those made by other agents.

The field associated with processes of animal degradation and methods for differentiating human forms of postmortem alteration from nonhuman forms is called **taphonomy** (Efremov 1940), a field shared with all paleontological sciences. Efremov (1940:85) defined taphonomy as "the study of the transition (in all its details) of animal remains from the biosphere into the lithosphere." Examples of important taphonomic works include Andrews (1990), Behrensmeyer (1975), Behrensmeyer and Hill (1980), Binford (1981), Binford and Bertram (1977), Bonnichsen and Sorg (1989), Brain (1981), Johnson (1985), Koch (1989), Lyman (1994b), P. Shipman (1981), Weigelt (1989), and T. D. White (1992).

Taphonomy is founded on two basic observations. First, animal remains are degradable. They can be reduced in mass, structure, and composition by cultural, mechanical, chemical, and biological means. And second, degradation commences when the animal dies and continues throughout the history of the specimen. If taphonomic processes can be understood, in terms of a specific faunal assemblage, more meaningful statements on environment, human subsistence, and other topics can be made.

Taphonomists interested in the processes of the degradation of faunal remains and subsequent information loss have recognized several stages in the transformation of a living community of animals to the point at which a few remnant pieces of a few individuals are recovered, analyzed, and reported (Clark and Kietzke 1967:111–129; Davis 1987:22; Gifford 1981:387; Hesse and Wapnish 1985:19–20; Klein and Cruz-Uribe 1984:3–4; Meadow 1980:67). Following Klein and Cruz-Uribe (1984:3–4), with additional modifications of Davis (1987:22), Gifford (1981:387), Hesse and Wapnish (1985:19), and Meadow (1980:67), these stages may include: (1) the life assemblage, (2) the death assemblage, (3) the deposited assemblage, (4) the fossil assemblage, (5) the sample assemblage, (6) the recorded assemblage, and (7) the interpreted assemblage.

The **life assemblage** represents the entire living community of animals present in their "natural" proportions. The second stage, the **death assemblage,** represents that subsample of the life assemblage that has died and whose remains are available for collection by various taphonomic agents. The third stage, the **deposited assemblage,** constitutes those elements that "come to rest at a site" (Klein and Cruz-Uribe 1984:3). Taphonomic agents that may assemble bones at a given location include (but are not limited to) humans, carnivores, rodents, and hydraulic activity. The next stage, the **fossil assemblage,** includes those elements of the deposited assemblage that survive until they are collected by the researcher. The **sample assemblage** refers to remains that are actually collected by the archaeologist in the field.

In addition to those discussed by Klein and Cruz-Uribe (1984:3–4), two other stages must also be considered. Although these are not taphonomic stages in the strict use of the term, they do reflect successive information loss. The first of these is the **recorded assemblage** (similar to Davis 1987:22; Gifford 1981:387; Meadow 1980:67). This assemblage is composed of those faunal elements that are actually identified and recorded in some manner as the first step in studying the remains. It is often impossible for the zooarchaeologist to place all of the faunal remains that were initially recorded within strict archaeological context. Therefore, site interpretations are often made on a subsample of the recorded assemblage. This final stage is the **interpreted assemblage,** reflecting the actual specimens from which site interpretations are made (similar to Davis 1987:22, Gifford 1981:387; Hesse

and Wapnish 1985:19; Meadow 1980:67). Grayson (1979) and Lyman (1982a) have noted that with each successive taphonomic stage, it becomes more and more difficult to accurately reconstruct the composition and nature of the previous assemblage.

At various stages, faunal material can be physically added, deleted, or reduced in some fashion by both human cultural activity and natural forces. Consequently, many zooarchaeologists have focused on differentiating human patterns of bone modification and destruction from nonhuman patterns (Behrensmeyer 1975; Binford 1981; Brain 1981; Haynes 1980, 1983; Hockett 1991; LeMoine and MacEachern 1983; Schmitt and Juell 1994; P. Shipman 1981; Steele 1990; Thomas 1971).

Nonhuman Factors Affecting an Assemblage

As faunal remains pass through these transformation stages, there are taphonomic forces that affect the distribution, assemblage composition, and rate of decomposition of the remains at a given site. These may be broadly divided into nonhuman and human forces. Examples of nonhuman taphonomic forces that destroy or reduce bone include gnawing and trampling by animals, weathering, root etching, acidic soil degradation, and water transport (Fisher 1995; Gordon and Buikstra 1981; Lyman and Fox 1989). Movement of materials at a site can occur by processes such as slumping, water transportation, and movement by animals. Once materials are buried, additional movement can be caused by heaving of the soil during freezing and thawing, burrowing animals, or the growth of tree roots.

In addition to the above factors, the question of fortuitous faunal association—the possibility that at least some of the faunal remains accumulated as a result of animals dying at the site or being transported there by forces other than human activity—must be considered. Traditionally, many small taxa, such as gophers, prairie dogs, and ground squirrels, have been assumed to be noncultural because of their burrowing nature. However, numerous ethnographic accounts attest to their use by North American aboriginal peoples. Therefore, specific taxa and sites must be evaluated on an individual basis to determine the most likely faunal accumulating agents (Hockett 1991; Schmitt and Juell 1994; Shaffer 1992a; Shaffer and Neely 1992).

Similarly, the presence of large animal remains must be scrutinized. For example, modern cattle remains have been recovered from prehistoric sites, and even a mastodon tooth fragment was recovered from an early ceramic site along the Texas coast (Baker et al. 1991:141). Also, carnivores and raptors may deposit animals in archaeological sites through scats or regurgitated pellets.

Differential preservation represents an additional nonhuman factor that may affect the nature of a faunal assemblage. The bones of fish, birds, reptiles, and amphibians are more fragile than those of mammals and tend to preserve less readily. In addition, the skeletons of reptiles and amphibians possess more cartilage than do the skeletons of the other vertebrate classes, as a result of their characteristic indeterminate growth. This further hinders their preservation and identification potential and may result in a bias against the presence of their remains at a site. Even within an individual animal, different bones may survive longer than others based on their density (Lyman 1984).

Animal disturbance is another major biological factor that moves materials within a site. Small invertebrates, such as earthworms and ants, are known to effectively move soil. Larger vertebrate animals like rodents may also move material within a site (Bocek 1986; Chew 1978; Erlandson 1984; Wood and Johnson 1978). Badgers, canids, armadillos, and turtles are common burrowers, as are humans. At a large cemetery, humans may bury hundreds of individuals and, in the process, be a major disruptive force to previous occupation horizons within the site.

Bone breakage also continues to occur during the fossilization process. Bone within a site can be broken by both mechanical and biological means. The weight of overburden can crush poorly supported bone within a site, and compressive forces at a site can exacerbate the breakage. Both plants and animals can also break bone. Roots of large shrubs and trees penetrating the soil of a site are known physically to break bone that they encounter, and animals gnawing on bone they encounter while burrowing through the site reduce the bone assemblage.

Human Factors Affecting an Assemblage

Human activity that may bias a given faunal assemblage must be considered as well. The burning of bone by humans, for example, may either increase or decrease a bone's preservation potential, depending on the degree to which it is burned. Bone that is burned white, or calcined, tends to become chalky in appearance and may weather easily. Bone burned black (charred) often preserves better than unburned bone in areas of lower soil pH.

Humans may further the process of bone reduction through such activities as butchering and marrow and grease extraction (Noe-Nygaard 1977). During disarticulation, bones are commonly cut with stone tools, contributing to the reduction process. The breakage of bone by humans, commonly resulting in spiral fractures, also contributes to degradation of faunal remains. Many times, bone breakage is intentional for the removal of marrow or grease (Binford 1978b, 1981; Vehik 1977; Zierhut 1967). Bone may be further processed by grinding, either as bone meal or with the entire carcass (Yohe et al. 1991).

Although humans are not the only taphonomic agents that produce spiral fractures, marrow and grease extraction commonly result in spirally broken bone. Additional human activity that may have influenced the composition of the faunal assemblage centers around the consumption and use of animals away from the site. Fauna that served as food or tools may not be incorporated into the assemblage.

RECONSTRUCTING HUMAN DIET AND SUBSISTENCE

The topics of subsistence and diet are frequently addressed in archaeology, with faunal assemblages often forming much of the data set. Typically, the term **subsistence** is used to refer to a general lifeway, including the collecting, processing, and consumption of food items. Common questions raised by archaeologists about a past people's subsistence include: What animals were consumed? Where were they collected? Which parts were consumed, and by whom? When and where did these various activities take place? More narrowly, subsistence reconstruction attempts to identify the exact nature of what was consumed—that is, the past diet. Surprisingly, of all the subsistence topics that can be addressed, this basic question is typically the one that zooarchaeologists have the most difficulty answering.

Often, investigators can be very specific about which environments were exploited, how various animals were disarticulated and processed, which meat-bearing elements were transported to home bases, what specific taphonomic factors affected the assemblage, and so on. In the end, however, we can never know the exact role these animals play in the diet, because we can never know the full scope of what was consumed, by whom, where, and over what period of time. This is because faunal samples come only from specific sites, and not from the total universe within which animals were consumed or used.

The animal remains from an archaeological site, then, may represent at least a portion of the faunal contribution to the diet. The starting point for reconstructing this contribution is the site taxa list. At one time, all animals recovered from archaeological sites were commonly considered cultural in origin, primarily representing human dietary refuse. As the previous discussion on taphonomy has shown, this assumption has proven inappropriate. As studies of animal behavior, geoarchaeology, and taphonomy have progressed, it has become apparent that almost any taxon may be intrusive into an archaeological assemblage. Concomitantly, recent studies have also shown that many small taxa once thought to be primarily intrusive may, in fact, be cultural (Jones 1984; Shaffer 1992a; Sobolik 1993; Stahl 1982; Szuter 1988; Yohe et al. 1991).

Once a taxa list representing the potential fauna consumed has been established, determinations of the relative importance of taxa may be even more problematic. The animals must be evaluated to determine whether they were brought to the site by humans and whether they represent food refuse. Some of the taxa included in the faunal list may be cohabitants of the site, such as dogs, rodents, or small reptiles. If that is the case, they may or may not have been food items. Thus, determination of human dietary items must rely on other lines of evidence. For example, butcher marks may suggest that animals were processed for food.

Dogs occupying a site present another problem. The products of their hunting activities may have been brought back to the site either as food for later consumption or in their digestive tract, later to be defecated at the site. Also, animals may have occupied the area of the site after it was abandoned by humans. In that case, they would not have been food refuse.

Animals inhabiting sites after human abandonment is a common occurrence at rockshelters. In sandy soils, burrowing animals commonly intrude on buried sites. Here the difficulty lies in recognizing the temporal sequence of occupation, for if these same burrowing animals were available during the time of site occupation, they may well have served as a food resource.

Other issues must also be considered. Are all of the remains brought to the site by humans represented in the recovered assemblage? As an example, the smaller and more fragile bones in a site are subject to more rapid deterioration simply because of their smaller bone mass. Therefore, more of the larger taxa and mature individuals may be preserved in many faunal assemblages. Similarly, if a surface site has been subject to water erosion, the smaller and lighter elements may have been washed away. Finally, scavengers at a site, either contemporaneous with the humans or later occupants of the site, may have fed off the human refuse left behind, destroying those pieces of evidence of the human diet. As previously discussed, recovery methods may also select against smaller animals.

Identifying those animals that represent human dietary refuse is confounded by a further series of problems. Factors including food taboos, differential distribution and consumption of food, and the nonfood use of animals (skins, sinew, bone tools, etc.) by humans makes it impossible to assume that all of the cultural faunal remains represent portions of food that was consumed.

Quantification methods also affect which taxa appear to have been more important culturally. As Lyman (1982a:372) noted, "To assume the most abundant taxa in an archaeological fauna were preferred for their food value may be at best tenuous, and at worst incorrect." Given these points, dietary reconstruction, although a high research priority of zooarchaeologists, must proceed with caution (Schmitt and Lupo 1995).

After identifying which animals in an assemblage were utilized by humans, the next logical questions are these: (1) From what habitats did humans collect these resources? (2) How did they procure the resources? and (3) How were the resources processed? Determining from which habitat any one species was procured is dependent on an ecological analogy in which one assumes the behavior and ecology of the species today was the same in the past as it is today. Thus, if an American pronghorn is recovered from a site, the assumption is that it was hunted in a grassland environment. By evaluating each taxon's habitat preference, it is possible to develop a model of where the fauna was procured.

Determining how fauna was procured is often based on cultural materials associated with kill sites, but not in all cases. For instance, the locations where mass kills of bison have been found often help to determine how they were driven. As another example, very small culturally obtained fish remains from a site suggest the fish were netted or poisoned, rather than caught individually on a line.

How animals were processed may be indicated by an examination of the remains in context at a kill site. Also, the examination of cut marks on bone may indicate patterns of dismemberment. In summary, although this information may often be difficult to discern from an examination of the faunal remains, the bones and shells may provide the only lines of evidence available to address these questions.

ESTIMATING SEASONALITY

Archaeological sites often represent relatively short periods of time, especially hunter and gatherer sites, which may represent only a seasonal home or single episode of activity. However, many sites represent several seasons or years. Such is the case at Puebloan sites or base camps. Determining whether a site was occupied during a single season, multiple seasons, or year-round is a goal of seasonality studies.

The season(s) of the occupation of a site is not always clear from the faunal sample. The term *season* may not represent an actual chronological period but rather, a period of specific weather. For example, spring weather does not occur at the same time every year in a given location and may vary from region to region. Seasonal variations may cause spring to occur in the April–June or the February–March time period. Thus spring events may reflect a five-month range in some areas.

One of the oldest and simplest methods for estimating seasonality is by the presence or absence of seasonal animals, such as herpetofauna, insects, and migratory fish, birds, or mammals. The basis on which such interpretations are made is noting when these animals are "seasonally available" in modern environments. This requires an in-depth knowledge of a taxon's habits or migratory schedules. It also presumes that the specimens upon which the seasonality estimate is based were animals that were killed and eaten during site occupation and did not occur naturally.

Aging techniques, such as tooth eruption, dental growth lines, tooth wear, and epiphyseal fusion, can be used to estimate seasonality when the birthing period and schedules for these events are known. For estimations based on epiphyseal fusion data, it is necessary to know the season or month a species is born and the age at which different elements within the species fuse (Monks 1981:185–187), as it is for tooth eruption and wear. Work using teeth to estimate seasonality has been conducted with several species of mammals, including artiodactyls, carnivores, rodents, and insectivores, with varying degrees of success (Gordon 1984, 1991; Hillson 1986:208–222).

Incremental structures have been used to determine seasonality in aquatic taxa such as mollusks and fish. Mollusks produce annular rings in their shells. By measuring ring distance, the season of the death of the animal can often be estimated (Aten 1981; Carlson 1988; Claassen 1986; Davis 1987:83–86; Kent 1988). Fish vertebrae, scales, and otoliths (Artz 1980; Casteel 1976:31–35, 65–71, 78–83; Monks 1981:199–200; Wheeler and Jones 1989:154–161; Yerkes 1987) can be used in a similar way. With catfish, pectoral spines have been used (Brewer 1987; Hoffman 1989; Morey 1983).

In cervids, the growth, maturation, and shedding of antlers can be used to determine seasonality (Monks 1981:190–191). Another method is the measurement of oxygen isotopes in marine shells (Davis 1987:86–90). As the sea temperature rises, the ratio of ^{16}O to ^{18}O is reduced. Careful studies of changes in the oxygen isotopes can provide good indicators of ambient water temperature, thereby providing seasonal indicators.

PALEOENVIRONMENTAL RECONSTRUCTION

Faunal remains may also contribute significantly toward reconstructing past environments in which humans lived. Although paleoenvironmental reconstruction of the climatic environment surrounding a site requires evidence from many disciplines, faunal remains may play a major role in this endeavor. For example, one of the main presumptions about late Pleistocene environments is that winters in many locations in North America may have been milder than they are today, with the summers cooler. This model of reduced seasonal differences is based on evidence that during the late Pleistocene, many Mesoamerican-derived vertebrates had a much more northerly distribution than they do today, whereas northern fauna in turn had a much more southerly distribution. Thus, at a particular site, the disharmonious mixture of northern and southern fauna is possible because northern fauna (limited in their southern distribution by warm summers) and southern fauna (limited in their northern distribution by cold winters) could

co-exist in a climatic regime with reduced seasonal extremes (Graham and Lundelius 1984; Lundelius 1989). In this example, the taxa are used as discrete attributes. In other words, their presence or absence is used as evidence of range expansion or reduction, rather than using the relative frequency of numbers of animals of individual taxa as evidence of shifts in climate. The frequencies with which animals are recovered from a site are thought to be too easily affected by factors other than just climate (Grayson 1981a).

Grayson (1981a), then, has argued that in paleoenvironmental reconstructions, taxa should be treated as attributes and not as variables. Examination of frequency changes of taxa through time or geographic location can provide specific data, but such counts are not likely to be demonstratively valid (Grayson 1981a:29). This is because so many factors can affect assemblage composition, including human selectivity, human processing activities, element density, and various taphonomic factors.

Grayson (1981a) has suggested that a suite of taxa be used in making paleoenvironmental reconstructions. This is also the preferred approach for seasonality estimates. Basing such reconstructions on a single animal leaves them suspect. However, if several taxa are used, especially in comparison with such other lines of evidence as botanical data, then more accurate reconstructions can be made.

Data that can be used to reconstruct paleoenvironments may be derived from wildlife habitat data or from incremental structural data from fish (Casteel 1976; Chaplin 1971; Wheeler and Jones 1989) or mollusks (Claassen 1986; Davis 1987:85–90; Kent 1988). For a given assemblage, examination of the natural habitats of all of the taxa represented will provide insight into the habitats exploited by humans. However, taxa with wide ecological ranges cannot provide niche-specific information. Taxa with narrowly defined habitat ranges can provide more-specific environmental information.

ETHICAL CONSIDERATIONS

As with the analysis of human remains, investigators should be aware of ethical concerns in zooarchaeology. Numerous state and federal permits are required, for example, to possess and maintain modern comparative animal collections. Typically, these permits must be updated annually. In processing recently dead animals for their skeletons, international, federal, state, and local health and safety regulations must be followed. If conducting academic research, investigators should be aware of all applicable university regulations governing the use of animals in research. Guidelines established by the Ad Hoc Committee on Acceptable Field Methods in Mammalogy (1987) should also be followed if live mammal specimens are collected for comparative purposes. Dirrigl (1989) has provided an excellent review of curation and animal preparation standards. In addition to addressing these concerns, archaeologists have an obligation to the archaeological faunal assemblages themselves.

As alluded to previously, many archaeologists traditionally perceived faunal assemblages as troublesome, secondary data sets. "What should we do with these boxes of bones?" is a question that continues to be echoed. It is not uncommon even today for archaeologists to inquire whether faunal assemblages can simply be discarded after analysis is complete. The issue of permanent faunal curation is of great concern among the zooarchaeological community. The International Council for ArchaeoZoology (ICAZ) drafted the following resolution:

> Given that faunal remains from archaeological sites of all periods are subject to analysis from many and varying points of view and using different methods, all faunal remains recovered from archaeological sites must be retained and stored in such fashion as to permit restudy of the material in the future, particularly by individuals other than the original investigator [Meadow 1980].

Even researchers who would never discard such assemblages often request that zooarchaeologists curate the material. Ideally, faunal remains should be permanently curated following applicable federal and local guidelines and in association with all other material from the site or at the same locale. Copies of any reports and data associated with the

faunal remains should be curated at the same repository. Many zooarchaeologists now require that decisions concerning the curation of faunal remains be made and agreed upon before they will accept a project.

Faunal analysis has progressed dramatically over the past 30 years. Researchers now address a multitude of complex issues concerning the behavior and evolution of past humans and animals. Foremost in addressing these topics is the proper excavation, recording, laboratory treatment, and analysis of archaeological faunal assemblages. Early and continued interaction between the faunal specialist, and the project director and field personnel is vital to the ultimate success of the faunal analysis. In addtion, such interaction stimulates discussion and often raises new and important questions and insight into the behavior of past humans.

GUIDE TO FURTHER READING

Bibliographies on North American Zooarchaeology

Bogan and Robison 1978, 1987; Kock 1989; Lyman 1979a; Olsen 1961a; see also *Zooarchaeological Research News* (beginning in 1982)

Old World and Worldwide Bibliographies and Databases

Angress and Reed 1062; Müller 1991; Stampfli and Schibler 1991

Major Texts on Zooarchaeology

Brothwell et al. 1978; Chaplin 1971; Clason 1975; Cornwall 1956; Davis 1987; Hesse and Wapnish 1985; Klein and Cruz-Uribe 1984; Olsen 1971; Read 1971; Ryder 1969; Ziegler 1973

Research Designs and Approaches to Zooarchaeology

Beck 1981; Bonnichsen and Sanger 1977; Brain 1974, 1976; Brewer 1992; Clason 1972; Daly 1969; Driver 1982,

1992; Emslie 1984; Gamble 1978; Gilmore 1949; Grayson 1973; Grigson 1978; Huelsbeck and Wessen 1982; Legge and Rowley-Conwy 1991; Lyman 1979b; Meadow 1980; Olsen 1961b; Parmalee 1985; Payne 1972; Reitz 1987, 1993; Steele 1989; Uerpmann 1973; Wing 1983; Wing and Brown 1979:111–142; Ziegler 1975

Journals Emphasizing Zooarchaeological Studies (some include topics related to the human skeleton)

Anthrozoologica; Archaeofauna; ArchaeoZoologia; Canadian Zooarchaeology; International Journal of Osteoarchaeology; Journal of Archaeological Science; Journal of Ethnobiology; Ossa; Zooarchaeological Research News

CHAPTER
14

Chronological Methods

Thomas R. Hester

The study of the past is concerned with the sequence of human activity and events through time, and to understand the past, we must know what cultural evidence is earlier and what is later. **Chronology,** the temporal ordering of data, is not an end in itself, but the necessary prerequisite to understanding the sequence and processes of events in prehistory.

The purpose of this chapter is to acquaint the reader with some of the major dating methods currently available to archaeology. These are constantly being upgraded and refined, and noted here are some important concepts that have developed about the precision, or in some cases the lack thereof, of certain techniques. Retained from the 1975 edition are some earlier references so that the reader will have an idea of the history of some of these dating methods. Where appropriate, suggestions are offered on how samples for specific dating techniques should be collected in the field.

There are several excellent introductory archaeology texts on the market that can provide the reader with even more details about major dating methods in contemporary archaeology (e.g., Fagan 1991b; Sharer and Ashmore 1993; Thomas 1989). We especially recommend the paper by Wintle (1996) for its review of current and developing dating techniques that will be "relevant" for the twenty-first century.

Of course, many dating methods are highly specialized or are so specific that they cannot be applied to all sites. However, in planning fieldwork, archaeologists need to be aware of what techniques are available to them, the kinds of samples that should be collected, the time span appropriate to the technique, and the limitations of the results that certain dating techniques will yield. Many methods are applicable only to certain types of sites or kinds of materials. Dry-cave or shelter sites, deposits formed in swampy areas, deeply buried finds of geologic antiquity, and pottery-producing sites each offer certain possible avenues for determining their relative or absolute chronologic position. Techniques that yield exact dating in years are few, but many methods reveal changes in the natural environment that can indirectly indicate the age of the associated cultural remains. The quantitative estimate of this age (i.e., in terms of years ago) will then depend on the opinion of experts who are familiar with the causes for and the tempo of such environmental changes.

Refinements of old methods, new applications, and the development of new dating techniques, taken together with the large and growing literature on chronological methods, all help to make this subject one of the largest and most difficult in archaeology. Literature on major dating techniques is cited in the discussions that follow in this chapter. You can keep abreast of new developments in dating through such journals as *Archaeometry, Science, Nature, American Antiquity, Journal of Archeological Science,* and *Journal of Field Archaeology.* In addition, there are extensive bibliographies in Heizer et al. (1980:277–305) and Ellis (1982:35–130).

METHODS FOR ABSOLUTE (CHRONOMETRIC) CHRONOLOGY

There are now several methods, some still in the developmental stages, that yield absolute dates for archaeological remains. In this section, the most commonly used physical and chemical techniques are described, along with a brief review of historical approaches.

Dendrochronology

Tree-ring dating, in which annual growth layers of trees are counted and matched with known environmental changes, can give the year when a tree was cut. Development of a reliable tree-ring chronology is attributable to the astronomer A. E. Douglass in about 1913. The potential of the method was appreciated much earlier, in the eigh-

teenth and nineteenth centuries (see Campbell 1949; Heizer 1969:53–58), but the technique was not developed until the time of Douglass's research. A very readable account of the early development of dendrochronology is provided by Hitch (1982), and a popular account of the technique is offered by Trefil (1985).

Only certain woods (and only in certain areas) are reliable for dendrochronological analysis, and only well-preserved wood or sizable pieces of charcoal can be used. The rings observed in such charcoal, or in timbers used in archaeological structures, have to be correlated to a "master sequence" in order to be dated. Such a sequence must be anchored at a known date. For example, in Douglass's pioneering work, he developed a tree-ring sequence beginning with modern trees and extended it back in time, until overlap rings could be recognized in wooden beams found in ancient Southwestern ruins. The sequence now goes back over 2,000 years.

Douglass (1929) and Glock (1937) have outlined the essential method of dendrochronology (see also Baille [1982] and Stahle and Wolfman [1985]). Bannister and Smiley (1955:179) have listed the four basic requirements for dendrochronological research:

1. There must be trees that produce clearly defined annual rings as the result of a definite growing season (e.g., in the arid Southwest, where there is highly seasonal rainfall).

2. Tree growth must be principally dependent upon one controlling factor.

3. There must have been an indigenous prehistoric population that made extensive use of wood.

4. The wood must be well enough preserved so that it still retains its cellular structure.

Most applications of dendrochronology have been in the American Southwest, where pine (along with fir, juniper, and oak) was used extensively in the region's prehistoric cultures. Lists of tree-ring dates for the American Southwest have been published, and the *Tree-Ring Bulletin* of the

University of Arizona provides updated information on dendrochronological research in the Southwest.

However, dendrochronology has expanded beyond its initial goal of providing a chronological framework for the prehistoric American Southwest. Indeed, the technique has become more widely important for its role in helping to calibrate radiocarbon dates. The world's oldest living tree, the bristlecone pine (*Pinus aristata*) grows in the White Mountains in eastern California. A continuous sequence of annual rings going back over 8,200 years has been recovered. This sequence cannot be used for direct dating of archaeological materials because wood of the bristlecone pine has not been found directly associated with archaeological materials. At the same time, this tree, through its 82-century record of growth, has been extremely important in the calibration of radiocarbon chronology.

Additionally, the techniques of dendrochronology have been applied to other tree species in North America, often with very good results. For example, Weakley (1971) used juniper, ash, and hackberry to obtain dendrochronological information for prehistoric South Dakota sites. Red cedar and bald cypress have been found useful for dendrochronology in the southeastern United States (Stahle and Wolfman 1985). A 1,600-year-long chronology is possible in the Southeast using bald cypress, and there is a possibility that the chronology and environmental reconstruction can be extended back into the mid-Holocene (Stahle et al. 1985; Stahle et al. 1988). Historic log buildings have been dated by dendrochronology (Stahle 1979), and research with live oak has potential for dating historic structures and other archaeological remains (Joel Gunn, personal communication 1986; Jurney 1986). Historic climatic patterns can also be studied through tree-ring analysis (Stahle 1990).

Dendrochronological dating has also been extended to Europe, where the sequence goes back at least 7,000 years. Becker and Delorme (1978) describe the use of oak to develop tree-ring chronologies for medieval and prehistoric sites in central Europe. Fletcher and Dabrowska (1976) used tree-ring examination to date the timbers found in a sixth-century well, discovering that their age was as early as A.D. 280–300. An overview of dendrochronology for Europe is found in Fletcher (1978).

Long-term tree-ring records can also be used to reconstruct ancient climatic patterns. The recurrence of drought in the Great Plains has been examined by tree-ring data collected in Iowa, Oklahoma, Montana, and Wyoming (Stockton and Meko 1983). A similar study focused on annual precipitation patterns between A.D. 1680 and 1980 in the American Midwest (Meko et al. 1985). It is likely that such studies will be an increasingly important part of tree-ring research in coming years.

Radiocarbon Analysis

Radiocarbon dating, variously referred to as carbon-14, C-14, or ^{14}C dating, was developed by Willard F. Libby (1955) as a spin-off from atomic research during World War II. The general public thinks that almost anything can be radiocarbon dated, when actually only things that are organic— that once lived—are possibly subject to analysis of this sort. Some archaeologists think that radiocarbon dating is the final solution to most of their chronological needs when in actuality there are uncertainties about the method and its results that must be carefully considered. These caveats aside, radiocarbon dating remains the most widely used chronometric technique in modern archaeology, with its range now extending back about 75,000–100,000 years. We will explore some of the issues surrounding radiocarbon dating and dates in this section. For more detailed descriptions of the method, its techniques, and its problems and potential, the reader is referred to Bowman (1990), Gillespie (1986), Mook and Waterbolk (1985), Taylor (1987), and Taylor et al. (1992). A bibliography of radiocarbon-dating literature has been published by Polach (1988).

E. Mott Davis, long the director of The University of Texas at Austin Radiocarbon Laboratory, has summarized the basic analytical processes involved in **radiocarbon dating** as follows (Davis 1973):

Figure 14.1 View of a radiocarbon laboratory. In this photograph, the technician is feeding carbon dioxide into a reaction vessel to convert it to lithium carbide, a step in the process of conversion to benzene.

The radiocarbon technique is based on the fact that in living tissue there is a stable ratio of ordinary carbon (carbon-12) to radioactive carbon (carbon-14, also called C14 or radiocarbon), the ratio being about a trillion to one. When the organism dies the radiocarbon gradually disappears through radioactive decay, and the decay takes place at a set rate, expressed mathematically by a figure called the "half-life." Since the rate of decay is known, ages may be calculated by comparing the amount of C14 in the carbon of the sample to be dated (the "unknown") with the amount that occurs in the carbon of living tissue (the "modern").

There are more than 40 university-based and commercial radiocarbon laboratories in North America that accept samples for dating. The university laboratories are often engaged in long-term research on radiocarbon problems or in providing dating services to archaeologists from within their institution (Figure 14.1). Most will accept outside samples, but there can be a considerable wait for results. Commercial laboratories can sometimes offer a wider range of services, including the processing of samples of varying size, and usually a quicker delivery date. The 1995 price of a conventional radiocarbon date from a leading commercial laboratory was about $235. Special handling, dating of smaller-than-usual samples, and so on, all cost considerably more.

As discussed in a later part of this section, radiocarbon laboratories accept a wide range of organic remains for dating (Table 14.1), and they often require that these be submitted within a cer-

TABLE 14.1

Organic Materials Used in Conventional Radiocarbon Dating
(see also Pollach et al. 1983:Table 1). Weights are in grams.

Material	Minimum Weight	Optimum Weight	Approx. Amt. Needed (optimum dry weight)
Charcoal			
clean	2–5	10–20	A handful
dirty	3–5	20–50	A double handful
Wood	3–5	30–100	A piece 2 sq cm × 30 cm
Cloth or paper	3–5	30–100	A piece 30 cm on each side
Shell	5–40	100–200	Varies considerably; consult your local laboratory
Limestone (plaster)	5	50–100	Consult a radiocarbon specialist
Bone	20–100	1,000	2 lbs of untreated material
charred	200–500	1,500–3,000	
collagen	100–300	800–3,000	
apatite	500	1,000	
Peat	10–70	100–200	A small bagful
Soil (humates)	500	1,500–2,000	Two medium-size bagsful
Seeds	10	10+	
Grass or leaves	5	35–50	
Flesh, skin, or hair	5	45	

tain weight range for a meaningful date to be obtained. However, beginning about 1977, radiocarbon researchers announced a new technique for dating very small samples of organic material (Muller 1977). This permits dating of sites and materials that could not before be dated because of inadequate sample size. Termed **accelerator mass spectrometry** (AMS) or **particle accelerator radiocarbon dating** (Hedges 1983; Hedges and Gowlett 1986; Taylor et al. 1984), the new techniques permit not only the dating of samples in the milligram to microgram range, but also the possible extension of radiocarbon analyses much farther back in time—perhaps to as much as 45,000–65,000 years ago. Good syntheses of this advance include Taylor (1987, 1989, 1991), Tuniz (1986), and Wintle (1996:128–129). One example of the application of the technique was at Guitarrero Cave, Peru, where minute samples of organic remains were used to date some of the earliest textiles in the region to around 10,000 years ago (Lynch et al. 1985). Similar studies of small samples can be done by enrichment of the ^{14}C isotope (see Browman 1981). Even tiny amounts of organic material from rock art have been successfully dated (Russ et al. 1990).

Collecting Samples in the Field. The best samples are those found in situ, properly noted and recorded, and that can be linked to meaningful associations (such as a living floor, a specific artifact type, etc.). A clean trowel or pocket-knife blade, perhaps aided by tweezers, should be used to pick up the material. Handling charcoal or other organics with the hands might lead to contamination from body oils, although laboratory pretreatment will usually remove these (Davis et al. 1973). The sample should be placed in a clean aluminum foil pouch or in a plastic or glass vial or clean polyethylene bag. Some archaeologists prefer not to use plastic bags for fear of contamination, but radiocarbon specialists have told us that this fear is unwarranted. If the sample is wet when collected, it should be allowed to dry thoroughly before it is packed for storage or shipping. However, be careful that during the drying process the sample is not contaminated by blowing dust or other airborne materials.

The collected sample should be clearly labeled (e.g., with a marking pen, directly on the aluminum pouch) and, to be doubly safe, placed in a cloth or paper collecting bag; and make sure this is also fully labeled. It is critical that as much information as possible about a collected radiocarbon sample be recorded at the time of collection, including possible associations, evidence of disturbance (if any), expected significance of a date from the sample, and so on. Be sure to record the name of the person making the sample collection, exact position and depth within the specific excavation unit and level, the name and number of the site, the method of collecting the sample, any preservative treatment to which the sample may have been subjected (it is best not to use preservatives on any anticipated ^{14}C sample), the condition of the sample when collected, and the planned place of curation. If possible, any carbonized plant or wood species should be identified prior to dating. Finally, when the sample is submitted to a radiocarbon laboratory, all of this information may be needed again to fill out a laboratory sample form that will serve as a record of the assay.

In general, it is best to try to collect as much of an organic material as possible if radiocarbon dating is anticipated. Indeed, as much charcoal as possible should be collected, even if the amount exceeds that needed for dating. The remaining charcoal might be used for wood species identification. Often, during field collection of charcoal, some soil is commonly mixed with the organic material. This can give a false impression of the weight of the charcoal collected; once the sample is cleaned at the laboratory, the amount of residual charcoal can be disappointing.

In collecting AMS samples, J. Hester (1987:449) cautions that "microstratigraphic techniques" are necessary. Small samples must have tight proveniences and clear association with what is being dated. He further warns the field archaeologist to carefully watch for burrows, tree-root cavities,

ancient soil stumps, and soil cracks, as well as human factors such as the digging of pits, to ascertain the context of small charcoal samples.

Radiocarbon-dating specialists warn against the use of preservatives on human or other bone that might eventually be considered for dating purposes (Murray Tamers, personal communication 1986). Bones coated with Gelva or similar preservatives are ruined in terms of their potential for radiocarbon analyses.

Increasingly, archaeologists are using soil for dating purposes. The organic constituents (humates, humic acids) can be extracted and can thus provide an avenue for estimating the age of cultural remains found within specific soil formations (Haas et al. 1986). Some of the considerations important to the field archaeologist in the dating of soils have been summarized in Hall et al. (1987:37):

> To be suitable for geochronometric dating, a deposit or soil must meet certain requirements to which are added additional requirements when these techniques are to be used in archaeological inquiry. Radiocarbon dating of organic-rich deposits produces satisfactory results when the organic content is of the same age as the deposit being dated, which is ordinarily the case with pond or lake deposits. Streams, particularly low-energy ones, on the other hand, may dislodge and transport clayey, organic-rich deposits from an earlier time and redeposit them without expunging the organics. If these are then dated, the apparent age will be greater than the true age of the later deposit. Stream deposits that contain organic matter suitable for accurate radiocarbon dating result from the cleansing of clastic particles of older organic materials and the depositing of these with coeval organic materials. Soil humates are also suitable for dating, but it must be remembered that these date the products of pedogenesis which necessarily are more recent than the earth materials in and on which the soil formed.

Soil samples should optimally be 1,500–20,000 g in weight. They should be collected as horizontal lines across a profile face, rather than as the traditional "column sample" cube often taken by archaeologists from a unit wall (Salvatore Valastro, personal communication 1993).

In Table 14.1, we have listed estimates of the amount of specific organic materials needed for a standard radiocarbon assay. These estimates are derived from Beta Analytic (a commercial radiocarbon firm in Florida), from conversations with Salvatore Valastro of the Radiocarbon Laboratory at the University of Texas at Austin, and from Huebner (1991) and Pollach and Golson (1966:26).

Other materials than those listed in Table 14.1 can sometimes be dated by the radiocarbon method. Lime mortar has been dated in this fashion by Folk and Valastro (1976), and Michels (1973) reports that iron smelted by wood or charcoal fuels has been dated by some laboratories (see Fleming 1977:79–83 for additional details on the application of radiocarbon dates obtained from iron specimens).

Evaluating a Radiocarbon Date.   The radiocarbon dating technique is based on the rate of radioactive decay (of the ^{14}C isotope), a gradual disappearance that takes place at a set rate termed the **half-life.** Earlier radiocarbon research used half-life figures different from those of today, so archaeologists have to take note of this when using dates published in the 1950s and 1960s. Most laboratories today use the "Libby half-life" of 5,568 ± 30 years, although recent research has suggested that a half-life of 5,730 ± 40 years may be more accurate. In fact, dates determined using the 5,568-year half-life can be converted to dates based on the 5,730-year half-life by multiplying the former reported radiocarbon dates by 1.029. As noted earlier, conventional radiocarbon dating may go back as far as 60,000 years; it can date more-recent materials up to a limit of about 300 years ago.

Archaeologists often have problems in determining the meaning of a radiocarbon assay. Too often, it is interpreted as a simple calendrical statement. The radiocarbon age of a sample as reported by the laboratory might read, for example, "2000 ± 50 years B.P." First of all, "B.P." means "before present"; some years ago, A.D. 1950 was set as the fixed point for calendrical conversions, and thus, 2000 B.P. subtracted from A.D. 1950 would yield a "date" of "–50," or 50 B.C. However, what about that ± figure tagged on to the end of the "date"? This is the standard deviation, or one-sigma error, possibly present in the assay. In other words, there is a 2-in-3 chance that this radiocarbon date falls somewhere between A.D. 0 and 100 B.C. (+50 years or –50 years); further, there is still a 1-in-3 chance that the true "date" falls outside that range. This illustrates one reason why a single radiocarbon date from a site should be used with caution, and why a series of assays from several samples for a site provides a more predictable estimate of the site's true age.

Calibration of Radiocarbon Dates.   To further complicate the issue, it has been learned over the past two decades that the carbon-14 content of living organisms has not been uniform or constant over the millennia. There have been variations caused by sunspots, cosmic radiation, the burning of fossil fuel, and changes in the earth's magnetic field through time. All of these can serve to alter the radiocarbon years reported through a laboratory assay.

Fortunately, the correlation of radiocarbon dates and the tree rings of the long-lived California bristlecone pine have permitted radiocarbon specialists to develop **calibrations** for radiocarbon assays (Suess 1980). With the bristlecone pine data, systematic deviations in the amount of atmospheric carbon-14 have been charted as "calibration curves" (Pearson 1987). Thus, we are presently able to make some significant corrections in radiocarbon dates by use of calibration tables published by Stuiver et al. (1993). These calibrations are continuing to be refined through time and the reader must be aware that corrections in radiocarbon dates must always be considered before they are published and interpreted. For example, recent efforts have been made to calibrate radiocarbon dating, beyond the dendrochronological calibration, through uranium-thorium dating of sea corals (Stuiver 1990). These studies have suggested that some radiocarbon assays may be off as much as 3,800 years.

Earlier, we alluded to the need to have carbonized plant and wood identified prior to radiocarbon assay. Plants with a C_4 pathway need corrections provided by the ^{13}C isotope which can be obtained on request from the laboratory.

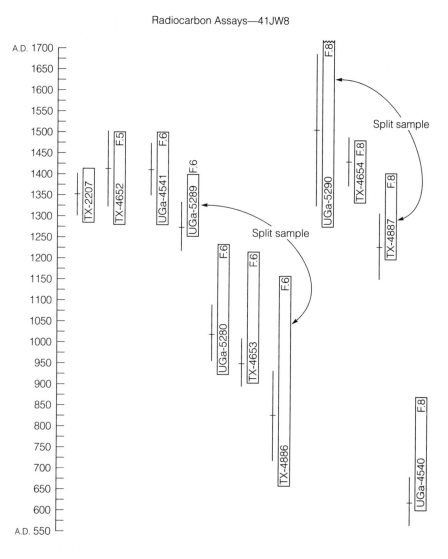

Figure 14.2 Display of radiocarbon dates from an archaeological site.

Publishing Radiocarbon Dates. When a radiocarbon assay from a laboratory is published, several factors must be included: the laboratory name (usually there is a standard abbreviation), the laboratory's sample number, ¹⁴C and ¹³C data (to be used for calibration purposes), the B.P. date and its standard deviation, the A.D./B.C. date based on the most current calibration available, the type of organic material dated, and the provenience (under this should be included not only site and unit/level data, but also interpretation and discussion—what the date means, what its importance is, and

how it conforms to, or deviates from, the archaeologist's expected date).

Most archaeologists publish the date and then refer to it in the text using its calibrated midpoint (the "calendar date"). Some archaeologists argue, quite correctly, that the date should be discussed as a *range* of time (within the one-sigma 2/3 or 68 percent accuracy, or by expanding the range to 2-sigma and thus getting a 95 percent accuracy in terms of the time range within which the sample will date; Figure 14.2). By all means, the name of the calibration program used in addition to a full citation of it should accompany the publication of the assay.

Other Problems in Radiocarbon Dating.
We have already noted that there are several kinds of contamination that might affect an organic sample that is to undergo radiocarbon analysis. Archaeologists should be careful to remove any visible possible contamination, such as rootlets, before the sample is submitted. Standard sample procedures in the radiocarbon laboratory should remove the remaining rootlets. Hassan and Ortner (1977) have also noted that calcite inclusions in bone radiocarbon samples can skew the assays that are obtained.

But what about "old wood"—the use by prehistoric peoples of older woods in hearths and in construction—collected by archaeologists in later years as well-provenienced samples that should "date" the prehistoric activity with which they were associated! For example, in arid regions where well-preserved rockshelters are found, there is the potential that inhabitants of the site might have used wood of much greater antiquity simply because it was preserved and available in the rockshelter. Or in recent sites, the use of older wood can produce widely divergent dates from samples collected within the same hearth (Black 1986). A detailed study of the "old wood" problem has been published by Schiffer (1986).

It is a fair warning to the reader that the vagaries of radiocarbon dating—sample collection, laboratory analysis, interpretation of dates, and so forth—are many and complex. Black (1986:155) has summarized what we believe to be a good approach for archaeologists who look to radiocarbon analysis to provide them with absolute chronologies:

> Most archaeologists have never taken the time to understand how radiocarbon dating really works. Previously, this author used radiocarbon dates rather carelessly; if a date "looked right," it was used uncritically, if not it was ignored or explained away. In order for radiocarbon dating to live up to the "optimistic plaudits" mentioned, the tool of radiocarbon dating must be used for what it is rather than for what we archaeologists would like it to be.

Toward this end the following suggestions are offered:

(1) Archaeologists should take time to carefully investigate the radiocarbon laboratories to which he or she sends samples. The pretreatment methods, equipment calibration standards, and counting times used by a given laboratory can seriously affect how the date will come out. If samples are to be split and sent to two laboratories, it behooves the archaeologist to make sure that both laboratories use essentially identical methods, or else the results are liable to be inconsistent.

(2) Archaeologists should work more closely with radiocarbon scientists at all stages of the process, from the field circumstances to the final interpretations. Each feature, component, or site is unique and should be treated as such.

(3) Radiocarbon laboratories should provide as standard information the processing details for each sample. Some laboratories make a standard practice of this, many others do not. Most information could be summarized in three to five pages. The pretreatment variation, the sample count times, and any problems in processing for each sample should be reported to the archaeologist.

(4) . . . a detailed comparative study needs to be made of the radiocarbon laboratories that provide data to archaeologists. This study would reveal which procedures are and are not producing reliable results and would provide a means to evaluate and compare data received from various radiocarbon laboratories.

Electron Spin Resonance

Ikeya (1978, 1986) and Ikeya and Miki (1980) have described a technique which they term **electron spin resonance (ESR) dating** (see Aitken 1990). ESR measures radiation-induced defects or the density of trapped electrons in bone and calcite materials. These materials can include stalactite, stalagmite, and other cave deposits, as well as human and animal bone and gastropods (Goede and Hitchman 1987). Research at McMaster University (Canada) indicates that tooth enamel seems to be among the best materials for ESR, particularly when there are thick enamel layers (see Bower 1989), though cranial fragments have also been used (Bower 1988). Wintle (1996) further adds that the ESR technique is best suited for teeth or other materials with biological origins (such as coral).

ESR shares some similarities with the thermoluminescence method described later, but it is a far simpler technique and essentially nondestructive. Thus far, it appears to have a range of 500–1,000 years ago to about 1 million years. Human and animal bones from sites in Japan, Germany, and Greece were dated by Ikeya and Miki (1980) and from sites in France by Schwarcz and Grun (1988). The evolution of hominids has been dated using ESR (Grun and Stringer 1991). Evidence of a hearth has been dated at Petralona Cave, Greece (Ikeya and Poulianos 1979). At Kebara Cave, Israel, Porat et al. (1994) used ESR on burned flint (see also Garrison et al. 1981) and found good agreement with thermoluminescence dating of similar materials (see the following section). In addition, ESR holds great promise for dating biological materials (see Aitken 1985:211–213) and Quaternary sediments containing archaeological deposits (Henning and Grun 1983).

Thermoluminescence

Thermoluminescence, hereafter referred to as TL, has been on the archaeological scene for quite some time, but its application has greatly increased in the past 15 years, resulting in a large body of literature (Wagner et al. 1983; Wintle 1996). Although TL is used primarily for relative dating, sophisticated developments in the process have produced absolute, chronometric dates. Although many of the archaeological applications have involved pottery, TL theoretically (and in some cases, practically) can be applied to any ancient burned materials— among them, heated rocks, flints, and soils (for example, TL can be used to determine if a prehistoric chert artifact was heat-treated as part of the manufacturing process [Melcher and Zimmerman 1977]).

Dr. Donald R. Lewis (University of Texas at San Antonio) has provided the following succinct summary of the **TL technique:**

Thermoluminescent (TL) dating provides a measure of the age of pottery and other ceramics from about 50 years to more than 20,000 years. The accuracy in good circumstances is approximately ±7 percent of the age. The accuracy increases with increasing age of the sample. For some types of sample material, ages of millions of years have been determined. The reported "age" is the length of time since the object was heated to a fairly high temperature (3500 degrees C or greater). If the material has never been heated, it is the time since the formation of the presently existing solid structure, that is, the actual clay mineral crystals, the obsidian glass, or the limestone rock from which the artifact was fashioned. These ages are usually of more interest to the geologist than the archaeologist. This technique has also been used successfully to date heated lithic objects, bricks and kilns, molding sands, stone hearths, soils, and the age of formation and growth of travertine deposits and stalagmites and stalagtites. In general, TL dating and carbon-14 dating are not applicable to the same materials. Dating procedures can use very small samples of materials (10 mg or less), although better accuracy results from larger samples. TL is frequently used for artifact authentication. Here the actual age is not determined, only whether the thermoluminescence observed is consistent with that expected from an object of the presumed age. Samples of the object for TL dating are normally taken by drilling a small hole (typically 2-mm diameter) in one or more inconspicuous locations. The cuttings from the drilling are used for dating. For pottery sherds, portions of the sherd are carefully crushed to provide the sample. Usually several sherds from each level are dated. Extreme care in sample collection and handling are essential for valid TL dating. TL dating is based on the fact that all material on earth continually receives a low level of radiation from the radioactive elements in the environment. Many solids store a fraction of this energy, producing a steady accumulation of stored energy with time. The stored energy can be released by heating the solid, and the emission of light which accompanies this energy release is called thermoluminescence. A particular sample can glow only once when heated, because the heating has emptied all of the accumulated energy. As a sample is being heated, the TL intensity increases and decreases in a regular, repeatable pattern characteristic of the sample. The graph of TL intensity variations produced by the increasing temperature of the sample is called a glow curve. Three different kinds of measurements are needed to determine the age of an object from TL:

1. The natural TL of the object, measuring the accumulated energy.

2. A determination of the rate at which the object has been receiving radiation from the environment.

3. A measure of the amount of TL produced by known amounts of radiation.

The second quantity is the most difficult to determine accurately, and is the greatest source of uncertainty. Usually a thermoluminescence dosimeter is placed in the location from which the object was removed to monitor the external environmental radiation. Alpha radiation counters are used to determine the uranium and thorium in the sample, and a chemical analysis for potassium determines the radiation from that source. Not all pottery or ceramics or minerals emit thermoluminescence. It is sometimes found that objects which have been fashioned or used by man have not been heated to a high enough temperature to anneal out all of the stored energy previously accumulated in the material from which the object is made. For these reasons, each object must have a preliminary series of qualifying measurements to assure that a valid TL date can be obtained.

Abundant details on TL can be found in Orme (1979) and in a thorough summary by Aitken (1985; see also Aitken 1989, 1990).

TL dating is such a fast-changing field that we will simply list here a series of archaeological dating efforts, using TL, in recent years. These should give the reader an idea of the kinds of TL dating

applications that may be possible (see also Aitken 1985). Thermoluminescence dates are published on a regular basis by *Ancient TL,* at Washington University, St. Louis.

Material Dated	*Reference*
Fired clay	Zimmerman and Huxtable 1971; Sampson et al. 1972
Burned limestone	Martini et al. 1986
Quartz	Parenti et al. 1990
Burned flint/chert	Huxtable and Aitken 1986; Aitken 1989; Valladas and Valladas 1987; Debenham 1994
Bronze	Fleming and Fagg 1977
Loess (soil)	Rowlett and Tandarich 1985

In a final example, TL dating was used by Valladas et al. (1987) to date a Neanderthal burial at Kebara Cave, Israel, at 60,000 ±4,000 years ago, thus contributing to the debate over the evolution (or the lack thereof!) of Homo sapiens to Neanderthal (see Wintle 1996:126). Later research combined radiocarbon dating and TL to date the Upper Paleolithic at the site to 42,000–46,000 years ago (Bar-Yosef et al. 1996).

A comparison of radiocarbon dates and TL dates is provided in a study by Bell (1991). This study used hearths in Australia.

Related to TL is a developing dating technique called **optically-stimulated luminescence (OSL)**. It uses laser technology to date the emissions from quartz and feldspar grains in archaeological sediments; it has the potential to date in the range from 100 to 100,000 years ago (Smith et al. 1990). According to Wintle (1996:132), OSL has been used to firm up the early human occupation of Australia at ca. 60,000 years ago.

Potassium-argon Dating

Potassium-argon dating was developed by scientists at the University of California, Berkeley, in the 1950s, and it has been of utmost importance over the past three decades in dating the remains of the earliest human fossils in East Africa. **Potassium-argon dating** is based on the process whereby a radioactive isotope of potassium decays into argon gas. When rocks are superheated, as in a volcanic flow, any gases built up since the last time the rocks melted are released into the atmosphere. This sets the "atomic clock" to zero. When the rocks solidify again, radioactive potassium proceeds to decay and argon builds up in the rock at a fixed rate, much the way sand accumulates at a fixed rate at the bottom of a freshly overturned hourglass. We can collect samples from volcanic flows, heat them to a very high temperature, collect the argon gas that is released, measure it, and determine how long that amount of gas would have taken to accumulate through radioactive decay based on the known half-life of 40,000 years. This gives us a date for the volcanic flow. If we find archaeological materials in stratigraphic association with the flow, we can apply a date to those materials relative to the date of the flow—before a certain date when the materials are beneath the flow, after a certain date when they are above the dated flow, or bracketed between two dates when the materials are stratigraphically positioned between two flows. Thus, at localities like Olduvai Gorge, the age of fossils and of sites that were occupied during periods of volcanic activity can be dated through associated lava flows. A detailed review of the potassium-argon dating method can be found in Fleming (1977; and see also Wintle 1996:124–125).

A new technique using laser microprobes is referred to as **laser argon-argon dating** (Kelley et al. 1994). It has been used to date geological horizons at early hominid sites (see Wintle 1996:129). In addition, small samples of artifacts can be sourced to their original geologic outcrop with this technique (e.g., a Neolithic stone ax from the Stonehenge area; Kelley et al. 1994). Paul Goldberg (personal communication 1995) reports that the argon-argon (40 Ar/39 Ar) technique has been used at the site of Birket Ram in Israel for dating of sediments. Argon-argon dating also helped refine the dates for the famous hominid find, "Lucy" (Wintle 1996:127).

Uranium-series Dating

A system of dating based on the decay of uranium radioactivity sequences ($^{238}U+$, $^{235}U+$) has been known for some years but has had limited archaeological applications (Schwarcz 1982; Schwarcz and Blackwell 1992; Taylor 1991). The uranium content in bone has produced absolute dates that later proved worthless because of groundwater contamination of the bone. Uranium-series dating has also been applied to the dating of carbonate materials; and a lead isotope (^{210}Pb), also a member of the uranium series, has a short half-life (22 years), which makes the technique useful in authenticity studies (for example, of seventeenth-century paintings; Fleming 1977:108–109). Recent applications include uranium-series dating of travertine deposits associated with prehistoric archaeological remains (Schwarcz 1980), dating of human skeletal remains from the Del Mar and Sunnyvale sites in California (where dates of 11,000 and 8,300 years, respectively, were obtained, in marked contrast to much older dates provided by amino acid dating, discussed later in this chapter), and the analysis of late Pleistocene fossil animal tooth enamel that indicates potential for a variant of the uranium-series method (known as **uranium disequalibrium dating**) to provide dates ranging from 10,000 to 300,000 years (McKinney 1977). Other examples come from the dating of fossil hominid remains at Swanscombe, England, at 326,000 B.P. (Szabo and Collins 1975) and of fossil bones from European alpine caves (Leitner-Wild and Steffan 1993). The use of mass spectrometry may allow uranium-thorium dating to reach back 600,000 years. For additional details, see Wintle (1996:126–127).

Fission Track Dating

Many natural glasses (like obsidian) and minerals contain decaying uranium atoms that emit alpha particles as they decay. In about one atom per every two million that decay, spontaneous fission occurs. The decay rate is constant and can be determined by counting the **fission tracks** in the material—a greater number of tracks are found in older samples. This technique has had limited use in archaeology, but it has the potential to provide dates between 100,000 and 1,000,000 years of age. Like potassium-argon dating, it can be used with the volcanic-associated human materials of East Africa, and like the uranium-series method, it has potential for use in authenticity studies. Important references for the method include Fleming (1977) and Aitken (1990). Rowe (1986:18) summarizes three potential archaeological applications for the technique:

> 1) natural glasses or crystals whose formation time corresponds to an activity of archaeological interest . . . ;
> 2) man-made glasses, recent material in which uranium has been added for coloration, and older material in which uranium is a natural constituent of the raw materials that make up the ceramic; and
> 3) natural glasses or crystals known to have been reheated.

A more sophisticated application of fission-track dating, known as **isothermal plateau fission-track (ITPFT)**, may develop greater accuracy for the technique in the twenty-first century (Wintle 1996:130–131).

Obsidian-hydration Dating

Much has been written on the subject of archaeological dating by calculating the time required to produce a **hydration layer** (depth to which water absorbed through the surface has penetrated) of a given thickness on obsidian artifacts or debitage (Clark 1961; Friedman and Smith 1960). A comprehensive review is provided by Freter (1993).

Suffice it to say that the thickness of this hydration layer depends on how long the article has been buried, the temperature conditions to which it has been subjected since burial, long-term changes in soil humidity (Wintle 1996:127), and the petrographic nature of the obsidian itself. Variable hydration rates have been devised depending on climatic conditions within a latitudinal range. By applying these appropriate rates, the age of an obsidian implement can be calculated. Obsidian

implements exposed on the soil surface and subject to strong diurnal and seasonal temperature and moisture changes are not suitable for dating. Among the general accounts published of the theory, the techniques employed, and the results secured are Fleming (1977), Michels (1973, 1986), Michels and Tsong (1980), Michels et al. (1983), and Taylor (1976).

Luckily for archaeological dating, there have been marked improvements in obsidian-hydration analysis since the previous edition of this book (Hester et al. 1975:271–272). Indeed, it is now used in many regions as a reliable **chronometric** (absolute) dating technique. Even a single sample can provide a date, if both chemical composition of the sample and site temperature have been determined. A number of laboratories conduct trace element research on obsidian, and that can provide the chemical composition data needed for dating. Further, there are now thermal implantation cells that can be placed at sites to provide a direct measurement of temperature at an archaeological site. The implanted device is left in the site soils for one year. A substitute for soil temperature is known air temperatures at a locality, which can then be used in a special chemical temperature integration equation to determine an effective hydration temperature. However, there are other variables that may play a part in the accuracy of an obsidian-hydration date, including relative humidity (Friedman et al. 1994; Ridings 1991) and soil pH (Freter 1993).

The hydration "layer" or "rim" on an obsidian artifact is measured by transmitted light, under optical microscopy. It involves cutting a slice or wedge of material from the obsidian artifact; this is then mounted on a microslide and ground down, by lapidary means, to less than 100 microns (Figure 14.3).

Obsidian-hydration dating, when it is possible given the occurrence of obsidian artifacts and the necessary controls on composition and temperature variables, is of great appeal to archaeologists in that it is much less expensive than other dating methods. Additionally, if soil temperatures have been established for a nearby site, it is possible that this process will not have to be repeated at your site. An example is the obsidian-hydration analysis done for the site of Colha, Belize. We had obtained

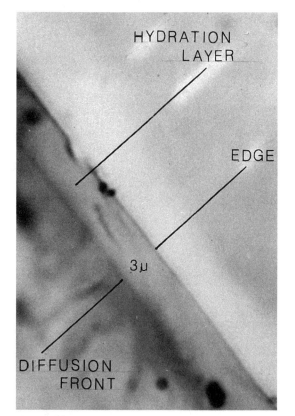

HYDRATION LAYER

EDGE

3 μ

DIFFUSION FRONT

Figure 14.3 Obsidian-hydration analysis. Microscopic view of the edge of an obsidian artifact and the hydration layer. According to Michels (1986:98), "the optical phenomenon that appears as a result of hydration is a measurable luminescent band."

the data on geologic sources through a collaborative research program at the Lawrence Berkeley Laboratory. However, for purposes of MOHLAB's chronometric studies of our obsidian, we did not have site temperature data from Colha; fortunately, the laboratory had this for the site of Cuello, about 20 miles away. Resulting obsidian-hydration dates for the Early Postclassic at Colha, for example, correlated very closely with radiocarbon dates we had available, suggesting that indeed both source and temperature variables were controlled for in the Colha sample. The obsidian-hydration dates provided a much finer resolution of Early Postclassic chronology (A.D. 1000–1250) at the site than was possible through radiocarbon dating.

Obsidian-hydration dating can measure the age of specimens as recent as 250 years ago or as old as 120,000 years. It is possible that dates of up to 500,000 years ago can be obtained.

There are numerous published applications of chronometric obsidian-hydration analysis: from East Africa (Michels et al. 1983), Ecuador (Bell 1977), the American Southwest (Findlow et al. 1975), the western United States (Ericson 1981; Hughes 1984; Minor 1980), and Mesoamerica (Freter 1993).

Finally, artifacts made of glass (as early as 1600 B.C. in Egypt and Mesopotamia) often acquire annual weathering layers that can be measured for chronological purposes (Brill 1961). A study by Lanford (1977) provides more detail on this approach, particularly with reference to nineteenth- and twentieth-century American glass. For American archaeologists, it is possible that this application of the hydration technique might be useful for historic-period sites.

Archaeomagnetic Dating

In a handbook written by J. L. Eighmy (1980:13), the **archaeomagnetic dating** technique is summarized as follows:

Archeomagnetic dating depends on independently dated master records of changing virtual geomagnetic poles. With such data, [a] burned feature can be measured for its fossilized magnetic direction, this direction compared to the master record and an age assigned to the feature.

Before field archaeologists can rely on archaeomagnetic dating, they must know: (1) how the master record was independently dated, and (2) because the changes depicted in the master record are regionally specific, whether a master record developed in one region can be applied to others (Eighmy 1980:13). Thus, the rates of change in the earth's magnetic fields can be measured, and their variability, from time to time, can be documented. In burned features in archaeological sites or associated with sites, there are fossilized magnetic minerals that assumed the direction of and reflect the intensity of the earth's magnetic field when the feature was burned or fired in ancient times. Thus, in situ baked clay fire pits, rock-lined hearths, pottery kilns, brick or earthen ovens, and iron-smelting furnaces are all potential candidates for obtaining archaeomagnetic dates. If the feature is of a clay that has been reheated (used again after its original firing), however, the magnetic readings will likely be different and application of this dating technique would be useless.

If the archaeomagnetic master curves described above by Eighmy are adequately controlled, this technique has the potential to provide dates accurate to within 30 years. Presently, it can provide dates as early as 2,000 years ago (Burlatskaya and Braginsky 1978). Collection of archaeomagnetic samples is a precise task, requiring the use of non-magnetic molds and plasters, a Brunton compass, and a great deal of background knowledge on specific techniques for extracting the sample. Thus, archaeomagnetic sampling is best left to specialists, although a detailed step-by-step methodology is available in Eighmy (1980).

For good summaries of archaeomagnetic dating, see Eighmy (1980), Eighmy and Klein (1990), Eighmy and Sternberg (1991), Tarling (1985), and Wolfman (1984). The technique has been used for dating cave paintings in Spain (Creer and Kopper 1974), late Pleistocene hearths in France (Barbetti et al. 1980), ancient canals in the American Southwest (Eighmy and Howard 1991), and refinement of dating techniques in the western United States (Verosub and Mehringer 1984). Another application of archaeomagnetism is the study of the thermoremanent magnetism of burned rocks in prehistoric features. Ascertaining whether the rocks have been in place since they were last fired or whether they have been moved and jumbled should help to shed new light on the function of such features in antiquity (this research is being spearheaded by Wulf Gose of the University of Texas at Austin; see Collins et al. 1990; Kappelman 1993).

Amino Acid Dating

Amino acid dating refers to a method of measuring the slow change (or **racemization**) of the amino acids of organisms. Aspartic acid is the amino acid most commonly found in bones; it has thus been the focus of research surrounding this technique. Theoretically, the measurement of aspartic acid racemization (AAR) should permit dating of bones from a few thousand to several million years of age. Unfortunately, racemization rates vary considerably depending on environment, especially fluctuations in temperature—and these variables are very difficult to control for in obtaining meaningful dates. The best dates have come from organic materials from ocean floors, where the temperature has been essentially constant; in other environments, a variation of 20 degrees C can cause an error of up to 50 percent in determining age.

There is a considerable literature on amino acid dating by J. L. Bada and his associates (e.g., Bada and Protsch 1973). There were a number of efforts made by Bada to date prehistoric human skeletal material in the western United States, principally in California, yielding ages that clearly were far too great. These have been convincingly rebutted with the advent of accelerator mass spectrometry (Stafford et al. 1984; Taylor et al. 1985), and Bada (1985) has himself used this advance in radiocarbon dating to better "calibrate" his efforts with aspartic acid racemization rates. Taylor (1991) has summarized the problems with the use of this technique in the western United States.

The technique still holds potential for archaeological application in the future, however. For example, it has been preliminarily reported (Pope 1990) that the dating of ostrich eggshell, using amino acids, is being developed. Wintle (1996:133) also notes that AAR dating is now working best when applied to shells of the ostrich-emu family. Correlation of radiocarbon dates and AAR ratite eggshell dating has been confirmed at the Border Cave site in South Africa.

Varve Analysis

Baron Gerard de Geer (1937) is credited, in the late nineteenth century, with discovering that the thin clay laminae of certain deposits were annual layers (**varves**) deposited in melt-water basins by retreating glacial ice. Glacial ice-retreat stages back to about 20,000 years can be dated with absolute exactness by varve counts. This method was first applied in the Baltic region by de Geer and in eastern North America by Ernst Antevs. Although the varve counts are exact, human and cultural remains are rarely found in the ancient melt-water basins, so these counts are seldom directly useful in archaeological dating. However, an archaeological deposit may be shown by its associated diatoms or pollen to have occurred when the climate was of a particular nature. The climate substage may then be cross-correlated with the varve chronology, and an indirect varve dating for the site can be determined. All of Antevs's age determinations for remains of early man in North America are ultimately based on the results of his varve counts.

A more recent application in North America of varve analysis has been attempted by Reher and Frison (1980) at the Vore site, a stratified buffalo jump site in Wyoming. Laminated sediments formed at the bottom of what had been an ancient pond at the site. The first five bone levels representing the buffalo jumps at the Vore site were within the varves, and counts by Reher and Frison (1980:55) indicated that these kills occurred from 11 to 34 years apart. By correlating the varves with radiocarbon dates from the site, artifact typology, and tree-ring indices, they concluded that the varve sequence began with the first five years of the sixteenth century! Readers contemplating varve research in North America should consult the study reported by Reher and Frison (1980) as a model.

Other Physical and Chemical Dating Methods

There are several potentially important dating methods that have been briefly reported in the literature and which still remain essentially experimental. **Differential thermal analysis** is a technique applied to pottery from the Amazon region (Enriquez et al. 1979). **Alpha-recoil track dating** is analogous to the fission-track method described earlier (Huang and Walker 1967; Michels 1973:187). Archaeological applications of this approach to the dating of ceramics, fire pits, and burned house floors are reported by Garrison et al. (1978). Yet another fairly new and preliminary chronometric

technique involves the use of **protein diagenesis** to date ostrich eggshells found in Middle Stone Age sites in Africa. The dates appear to be consistent with radiocarbon assays (Brooks et al. 1990).

Wintle (1996) also discusses additional techniques that she believes may be of importance in the next century. One is **single crystal laser fusion** (SCLF), utilizing argon-argon dating (discussed earlier). SCLF involves the targeting of single mineral grains and the use of a high-powered laser to "fuse the grain and drive off the argon for measurement in a super-sensitive mass spectrometer" (Wintle 1996:129). It has been used for dating efforts at Olduvai Gorge, Bed I and of hominids found in Kenya, Ethiopia, and Asia. Another technique is **thermal ionization mass spectrometry** (TIMS), which precisely measures concentration ratios of heavy isotopes such as ^{238}U and ^{234}U (uranium series), as well as ^{232}Th and ^{230}Th (thorium). Applications thus far have involved dating of teeth from sites in Israel (where the dates correlated well with ESR measurements), the dating of ostrich-emu eggshell in an Egyptian site, and improvements in the calibration of radiocarbon analyses to calendar dates (Wintle 1996:134–135).

Association of Dated Historic Materials or Identifiable Sites

We refer briefly here to historic sites and historical archaeology—the investigation of documented archaeological sites (see Chapter 2; Cotter 1968; Deetz 1977; Fontana 1965; Noël-Hume 1969; Schuyler 1978)—where (in North America at least) datable items of European derivation found with aboriginal materials provide a means of determining the age of the deposit. In historic-sites archaeology, absolute dates often can be obtained from such items as glass beads (Kidd and Kidd 1970), coins, ceramic patterns of known manufacturing age, uniform buttons, and distinctive bottle shapes. In addition, the bore diameters of smoking pipes (made of white ball clay, often called kaolin; Walker 1978:22) found commonly in eastern North America can be useful in suggesting a date for colonial occupation. The diameters decreased in linear fashion through time as the technology improved for producing the wire that was used in pipe molds for making the bores in the stems. For many historical artifacts, catalogs still exist that allow the archaeologist to link the item to a catalog entry of a specific date.

When early historic documents—such as journals of explorers, fur traders, missionaries, military reconnaissance parties, and the like—attest to the fact that certain sites were occupied at one time and more recent sources deny or remain silent on their occupation, one can assign the terminal occupation of the sites and the latest cultural manifestation to the time of the documentary record. In this way, using all available records, some definite knowledge of the particular culture type in operation on a certain date or within a definite time span can be determined (see Collier et al. 1942:113; Kidd 1954). Strong (1940:595) summarizes this approach by saying, "Of recent years numerous archaeologists have temporarily shifted their attention from prehistoric horizons of unknown age and affiliations to early historic and documented sites. These have been excavated in order to proceed from the known into the hitherto unknown. Such excavations objectively link history with prehistory and anchor archaeology to meaningful social science." This method, sometimes called the **direct-historical approach,** has been discussed by Steward (1942). Its utility has been demonstrated by Baerreis (1971), Heizer (1941), Valliant (1938), and Wedel (1961). More recent discussions and applications can be found in Rogers and Wilson (1993) and Trigger (1989).

METHODS FOR RELATIVE CHRONOLOGY

In the majority of archaeological investigations, excavators must be content with the relative dating of cultures, where, for example, they can show that culture A is older than cultures B and C, and culture C is younger than culture B. They may be able to estimate the relative duration of each culture and point out that culture B endured for approximately twice as long as culture A. The latest culture (C) may terminate at the historic period and thus be datable, but the actual dating of cultures B and A and the absolute duration of culture A will be a mystery.

There always remains the possibility that some method, whether known but not yet applied or still awaiting discovery, will allow the relative sequence to be made absolute. Dendrochronology was such a method for the American Southwest, and radiocarbon dating allows absolute dating for some of the local sequences based upon imprecise ceramic sequences, obsidian-hydration curves, bone-fossilization, and so forth, elsewhere in the New World.

Some of the more widely used or potentially useful techniques for achieving relative chronology are discussed below.

Stratigraphy

Vertical stratification, revealed by the excavation of occupation sites, is the surest method of determining the order of succession of cultures (see Chapter 10). It is a method borrowed directly from geology (see Grabau 1924), and its regular use by American archaeologists dates from as recently as 1916, when Nelson determined the pottery sequence at the Tano ruins (Nelson 1916; see also Woodbury 1960). About the same time, Kidder used the stratigraphic method at Pecos, and Spier was testing the Trenton argillite culture with vertical sequence in mind (Spier 1916; Wissler 1916). Willey and Sabloff (1974) mention a number of earlier uses of stratigraphy that failed to stimulate other workers to adopt it as part of excavation technique and archaeological interpretation. Petrie used the stratigraphic method at Lachish, Palestine, in 1891 (Wooley 1954:47–48).

The beginnings of archaeological chronology in the American Southwest predate 1916, although this early work was neither appreciated nor exploited. Before 1900, Fewkes saw the connection between Sitkyatki and modern Hopi pottery and interpreted the differences as changes over time (Fewkes 1896a). F. H. Cushing, on the other hand, when he excavated the Los Muertos site in the 1890s, noted two different methods of disposing of the dead (cremations and inhumations), each associated with characteristic types of pottery (Gila

Polychrome and Red-on-yellow). He suggested that the two modes of burial, which he assumed to be contemporaneous, reflected different social positions, interment being a mark of the "priestly class." It was not until 1925, with Schmidt's stratigraphic study of the area, that cremation was shown to be earlier than burial (Schmidt 1927:297–298).

Stratification may be visible, as in the case of some Mississippi Valley mounds that were built and rebuilt successively (Setzler and Jennings 1941:Figure 4), or the stratigraphic sequence may have to be worked out by statistical methods (Beals et al. 1945; Ford and Willey 1949; Kroeber 1940).

Rouse (1939:80–92) points out that most archaeologists assume continuous occupancy of sites and therefore attribute different frequencies of artifact types to temporal changes of fashion. However, the worker should ever be aware of the possibility of intermittent or discontinuous occupation, in itself a feature in which time is an important factor. Such interrupted occupation may be indicated in many ways—intrusive graves or storage pits, superimposed house floors, and the like—and the individual worker must judge the evidence in each case.

Stratigraphy may also be "reversed"—i.e., older layers may lie atop newer ones—as evidenced by the examples presented by Colton (1946:297–299), Coon (1951:33), Crowfoot (1935:191–192), Hawley (1934:31–35, 51–61), and Hole and Heizer (1973:147).

A very useful review of the principles of dating archaeological artifacts through stratigraphy is found in Harris (1989:96–99).

Chemical Analysis of Bone

As has often been pointed out, buried bone is subject to varying conditions of moisture and soil minerals in different parts of the same site. As a result, **fossilization** (replacement of the bone by minerals from the soil; loss of organic matter and addition of mineral material) may take place at very different rates. Consequently, a heavily mineralized bone from one location in a site is not necessarily older than an almost unmineralized bone from another.

However, because fresh or living bone is unfossilized and most ancient bone is fossilized, the general axiom that fossilization is a correlate of time holds true (Cook et al. 1961). Theoretically, therefore, if one were able to secure enough bone samples from an area where the bone was subject to similar soil moisture and temperature conditions over a sufficiently long time span, it should be possible to make quantitative and qualitative chemical tests to determine whether mineralization of bone was random and accidental or proceeded at an orderly pace relative to increasing age. This actually has been done, and the orderly pace does seem on the whole to prevail. Because the curve of fossilization does not invariably conform to the attribution of age as deduced from archaeological evidence, however, it should still be used with caution (Bayle and de Noyer 1939). For the central California area, see the articles by Cook (1951) and Cook and Heizer (1947, 1953a, 1953b, 1965). It is hoped that the anomalies encountered in correlating age and degree of mineralization in central California may yet be explained, and that some tertium quid may be invoked to establish the absolute dating of two or more points on the curve of mineralization.

It may be added here that chemical analysis of bone to achieve relative dating is probably best applied to open sites, is expensive because a laboratory is needed, and has not yet been fully developed. The several factors (e.g., soil minerals, groundwater, and temperature) that cause variability (deceleration or acceleration of the fossilization process) cannot at this time be put into a formula because their individual or joint effects are not fully understood (Cook 1960).

An allied but different technique of bone analysis that may demonstrate relative (not absolute) age differences is called the **fluorine method.** Most groundwaters contain small amounts of fluorine (F). Fluorine ions combine with the hydroxyapatite crystals of the bone to form fluorapatite, a stable mineral resistant to weathering and leaching and having almost no affinity for other materials. A bone buried for a long time will contain more fluorapatite than one buried for a short time. This fact of increasing F-content with age, together with its application for dating bones, was first announced by Middleton (1844), carried further by Carnot

(1892), and revived by Oakley (1964) (see also Heizer [1950]). The F-content method, because of the variability of fluorine content in groundwaters and the relative slowness of uptake of fluorine in bone, cannot be expected to yield an absolute time curve (McConnell 1962). As pointed out by Carnot (1893:192–193) and Heizer (1950) and as demonstrated by Oakley, the F-content method is of value chiefly in determining whether bone implements or human skeletal remains found in association with other bones were or were not buried at the same time. The fluorine method has been applied to some supposedly ancient New World human remains in California (Heizer and Cook 1952), Mexico (Heizer and Cook 1959), and Texas (Oakley and Howells 1961).

Certainly the best-known application of fluorine analysis in relative dating is the case of the Piltdown fossil from England. The cranium and the jaw were analyzed by Oakley (see Oakley 1976), and though it was claimed that they were of the same age, the cranium exhibited .10 percent fluorine and the mandible, less than .03 percent. They were obviously of different ages and could not have come from the same individual. A closer examination of the fossils resulted in the embarrassing discovery that the jaw belonged to an orangutan.

The amount of nitrogen in buried bones tends to decrease with age, and good relative datings have been secured based upon nitrogen determination (Ezra and Cook 1957; Ortner et al. 1972). A similar dating method based on the rate of disappearance of conchiolin in buried shells (Schoute-Vanneck 1960) seems promising but has not been extensively applied.

The combined use of nitrogen and fluorine techniques has been reported in the analysis of prehistoric skeletal materials from the Mississippian period site of Moundville, Alabama (Haddy and Hanson 1982). All of the skeletons had been treated with Alvar (a polyvinyl acetate solution), which had rendered the bone not suitable for radiocarbon dating. The relative ages of the skeletons were thus determined by nitrogen analysis, quantified by a spectrophotometer and by proton-beam fluorine analysis.

Patination and Desert Varnish Analysis

The surface oxidation of artifacts is a tricky kind of evidence for assigning age to the implements. Nevertheless, Rogers (1939:19) argued convincingly for the limited and objective use of this feature to infer relative dating of artifacts:

> Although the processes of patination and oxidation are understood only to a certain degree, and practically nothing is known about the rate of progress, the phenomena, when properly used, can be of aid in establishing an implement sequence in localized fields. When types are suspected of being common to two or more industries, or when an age relation between different types is being sought, the procedure leading to a solution must be conducted with certain controls. Only artifacts of the same lithologic composition which have been subjected to the same natural agencies over varying lengths of time should be used for comparative study. The weakness of the system, of course, lies in the fact that the last-named factors can only be roughly estimated. However, I cannot agree with the many who believe patination and oxidation to be worthless diagnostic factors. The investigator who knows both the causative and tempering factors, and is thoroughly familiar with his field, should certainly make an attempt to employ this methodology.

The best general discussions of patination with reference to archaeology are by Goodwin (1960), Honea (1964), Luedtke (1992), and Rottlander (1975a, 1975b). Investigations of lithic patina and attempts to use such surface oxidation to place stone tools in chronological perspective have been published by Curwen (1940), Hester et al. (1982), Hurst and Kelly (1961), Schmalz (1960), and Van Nest (1985).

An illustration of the problems inherent in using patination as an indicator of age is provided by Benedict (1992). He found that sodium-rich hot springs in the Great Plains can develop, on certain cherts, a white patina in less than a week! Native Americans in the region often left arrow points as offerings to spirits believed to have lived in the springs, and he suggests that they may have deliberately "patinated" the artifacts as part of the ritual process. Desert varnish or rock varnish is a surface alteration, usually a thin film of manganese, iron oxides, and clay minerals that accrues on stone tools after long exposure in a desert environment. This is adequately discussed by Engel and Sharp (1959) and Hunt (1954), and updated by Potter and Rossman (1977) and Taylor (1991:79).

A recent innovative effort by Charles Frederick and his colleagues (Frederick et al. 1994) evaluated the use of patination as a dating technique for chipped stone tools in central Texas. Use of neutron activation analysis, petrographic examination, and measurement of patinas on more than 100 artifacts demonstrated that the "prospects of using chert patination as a dating method are poor" (Frederick et al. 1994:i). At least in central Texas, patination is a progressive process (both in its frequency and its magnitude) and is highly variable on projectile-point types of known temporal spans.

Efforts to date desert-varnished surfaces containing ancient rock art (see Bednarik 1992) have used the techniques of nuclear chemistry (Bard et al. 1978). Similarly, improved radiocarbon dating technology using accelerator mass spectrometry has made it possible to date the varnish on stone surfaces from southern California and Australia (Dorn 1983, 1988). When insufficient organics are available, these researchers have proposed a new chronometric method, **cation-ratio dating,** based on the differences in the rate at which minor chemical elements leach out of desert varnish; these are readily analyzed by x-ray emission techniques (Dorn 1991; Taylor 1991). An application of cation-ratio involves the chronology of eastern California petroglyphs (Whitley and Dorn 1987; see also Francis et al. 1993 regarding Wyoming and Montana rock art). However, Harry (1995:118) has warned that cation-ratio dating is based on untested assumptions and "may not be able to provide accurate dates for most varnished artifacts."

Finally, Clark and Purdy (1979) report their experiments with the weathered surfaces of chert artifacts from Florida. They have used electron microprobe analysis to evaluate the compositional changes in the chert during the weathering process. The leaching of iron minerals from the surface may be a controlled process in which the depth of leaching is proportional to the square root of exposure time—thus offering a possible means of dating some chert artifacts. The amount of fluorine diffusion on the surface of lithic artifacts in southern California has been suggested by Taylor (1975, 1991) as a means of relative dating for some stone tools. The use of diffused nitrogen profiles is suggested by Hedges and Freeman (1994). Near-surface fluorine (^{19}F) diffusion profiles were developed by nuclear resonant reaction techniques and were compared with samples known to be 3,000–4,000 years of age. The similarity of these profiles suggests that the artifacts, from the Buchanan Canyon locality near San Diego, are not of Pleistocene age as had been claimed.

Seriation

Seriation, variously used by American archaeologists, is here defined as the determination of the chronological sequence of styles, types, or assemblages of types by any method or combination of methods. Stratigraphy may be employed, or the materials may be from surface sites. The several methods of seriation may be judged by investigating the classic publications by Brainerd (1951), Dunnell (1970), Ford (1938), Ford and Willey (1949), Kidder (1931), Kroeber (1916, 1948), Michels (1973:66–82), Petrie (1899), Spaulding (1953), and Spier (1917). Spier (1931:283) describes the seriation method: "Remains of a stylistic variable (such as pottery) occurring in varying proportions in a series of sites are ranged, by some auxiliary suggestion, according to the seriation of one element (one pottery type). Its validity is established if the other elements (two or more other pottery types) fall in smooth sequences (e.g., the Zuni ruin series obtained by Kroeber and Spier)." An instructive example of seriation compared with a stratigraphic sequence is contained in Ford and Willey (1949:52). Ford (1962:41–44) has provided an extremely clear and useful manual outlining procedures for developing archaeological chronologies based on surface collections of pottery. More recent treatments of seriation in archaeology have been published by Drennan (1976, 1979), Ester (1981), LeBlanc (1975), Meighan (1977), and a review article by Marquardt (1978).

Rate of Refuse Accumulation

Where no other method suggests itself, some estimate of the rate at which a refuse deposit accumulates may yield estimates of the duration of occupation for a site. Braidwood and Howe (1960: 159) used the life expectancy of, and debris from, dwellings to calculate that the site of Jarmo was probably occupied for about 200 years.

However, rate of refuse accumulation has been used, or efforts have been made to use it, as a method for calculating absolute or relative dates. For example, Cosgrove and Cosgrove (1932:100–103) suggested that, provided that all the variable factors (number of houses and occupants, amount of food eaten, firewood burned, etc.) could be exactly controlled, the time required to amass a specified amount of midden could be calculated. But because these variables can never be raised even to the rank of probabilities, any age estimate derived from this method must be considered to be of extremely limited value.

Nelson (1909:345–346), Gifford (1916), Schenck (1926:205–212), and Cook (1946) all tried to calculate the antiquity of the San Francisco Bay shell mounds by this method; Harrington (1933:171) used the rate-of-increment techniques at Gypsum Cave, and Loud and Harrington (1929:120–123) used this method as supporting evidence for their estimate of the antiquity of Lovelock Cave. Valliant (1935:166–167, 257–258) compared the rate of refuse accumulation at Pecos and certain Valley of Mexico sites. Milne (1881) applied the rate of alluvial soil accumulation in Tokyo Bay to shell mounds. Bird (1948:21, 27–28) suggested the time involved in the building of an artifact-bearing soil profile at Viru. Kubler (1948) determined that the guano composing the "stacks" off the Peruvian coast—stacks that have yielded artifacts of known cultural affiliation from precisely recorded depths—was deposited in annual layers that could be counted but which were of such uniform thickness that depth mea-

surements could be substituted for layer counts. Thus the age of an artifact found at a depth of so many feet could easily be calculated.

The parallel with the glacial-varve-counting method is striking. Kubler's guano dating and Allison's (1926) measurement of the growth rate of stalagmites at Jacob's Cavern might reasonably be included in the preceding section on methods for absolute chronology. Champe (1946:32–33) dated some levels of Ash Hollow Cave by dendrochronology and used the depth of dated levels to estimate the time required for nondated levels to accumulate. Lothrop (1928:197) estimated the population of each district and the total volume of middens to compute the rate at which deposits accumulate in Tierra del Fuego. Strong (1935:236–239) estimated the antiquity of the Signal Butte site by calculating the rate of dune migration. These may be taken as special examples of the rate-of-accumulation method.

A clear demonstration of variable rates of deposition in a single site is found at Modoc Shelter, Illinois (Fowler 1959:19–20). Fowler showed that between 8000 and 5000 B.C. the rate was constant at about 1 foot per 500 years, between 5000 and 3600 B.C. the rate increased markedly to 1.7 feet per 100 years, and between 3300 and 2700 B.C. the rate dropped to 1 foot per 400 years. At Pedra Furada rockshelter in Brazil, Parenti et al. (1990) have suggested a very slow soil formation rate of 0.1 mm/year.

Cross-dating

An artifact type absolutely or relatively dated in one area may provide the lead for pegging down the chronology of material it occurs with elsewhere. J. G. D. Clark (1947:133–136) discusses this source of dating under "synchronisms." American archaeologists are well aware of the cross-dating method and the rich results it often brings. It is the basic technique in Krieger's (1946) classic Texas volume, it was employed at Snaketown (Heizer 1959:368–374), it has assisted Middle American archaeologists (see Kidder et al. 1946:250), and it has long been used in Old World prehistory (Ehrich 1965).

Trade objects, which are the clearest evidence of actual contemporaneity between two geographically separated cultures, may permit an absolute chronology to be extended to a region whose materials have hitherto been only relatively datable. One example is Pring's (1977) dating of Teotihuacan contacts in ancient Belize based on the presence of distinctive Teotihuacan pottery types. Trait *resemblances* between two distant cultures may be so unmistakably the result of diffusion that no reasonable doubt may be entertained. But these similarities are usually to be taken as evidencing not exact synchronisms, but *general* contemporaneity. Thus Kidder et al. (1946:251) and Kidder and Thompson (1938) suggest that the temporally floating Maya Long Count may some day, through the discovery of a chain of cross-finds, be equated and synchronized with the Southwestern dendrochronological time sequence (see Davis 1937). In California, where much of the archaeology was poorly dated, there were pioneering efforts at synchronizing local culture phases with tree-ring-dated cultures of the Southwest by means of shell beads and pottery trade objects (Gifford 1949; Heizer 1946). Patterson (1963) has written a useful survey of methodological principles and precautions to be observed in using archaeological data for cross-dating, and Michels (1973:83–111) discusses paleontological, geomorphological, and cultural cross-dating.

Synchronisms may also be determined from the evidence of natural phenomena. If a fall of volcanic ash covers a wide area, for example, cultural remains can be assigned to periods before and after a given volcanic eruption, according to whether they occur above or below the ash layer (Fryxell 1965; Rapp et al. 1973; Sheets 1992; Wilcox 1965).

Archaeologists must be aware that pieces much older than the general run of artifacts at a site—prehistoric antiques or heirlooms—may be recovered. Any conclusion that these isolated pieces were contemporaneous with the rest could lead to errors in cross-dating (Heizer 1959:367–368; Patterson 1963). The reusing of ancient pieces by modern native groups is a well-documented practice: Poor people in Brazil collect ancient funerary urns and use them to store maize or maioc flour (Laming-Emperaire 1963:70); Persian pilgrims visiting Mos-

lem shrines collected ancient Babylonian cuneiform cylinders and used them as good-luck charms (Rich 1819:58); the Maidu Indians of California reused ancient stone mortars for grinding acorns (Dixon 1905:136); and the Huichol of Mexico used a Paleoindian fluted point in ceremonial activities (Weigand 1970). Similar acts are indicated by prehistoric stone projectile points recovered from historic Seneca graves in New York (Ritchie 1954: 67–68), older Nazca-type pots in Middle Inca–period graves in Peru (Kroeber and Strong 1924: 116), and carved stelae and monuments reused by the people of the Piedras Negras site in Guatemala (Coe 1959:155).

Typology is often an important factor in cross-dating. Artifacts can be grouped into "types" on the basis of similar shapes (morphological or descriptive types) or on the basis of shapes that have meaning in time and space (temporal or cultural types). A good discussion of typology is provided by Thomas (1989). When using temporal or cultural types, care must be taken not to use types defined for specific areas at certain points in time as labels for artifacts of similar shape or design in other, distant regions (see Hester 1986).

The use of types can be very important for constructing relative chronologies based on the stratigraphic occurrences of distinctive temporal or cultural categories. For example, in central Texas, the prehistoric Indians changed the shapes of their projectile points over thousands of years. Excavations have established that certain temporal types are diagnostic of specific time periods. The chronology that has evolved is very useful for cross-dating sites on the fringes of central Texas or in immediately adjacent areas (Turner and Hester 1993; Figure 14.4).

Students interested in the history of types and their use in archaeological research can consult the following references: Adams and Adams (1991), Krieger (1944), Rouse (1960), Thomas (1989), and Turner and Hester (1993).

Geological Methods

Though geological methods have long been used in the dating and interpretation of archaeological deposits, the interrelationship between the two dis-

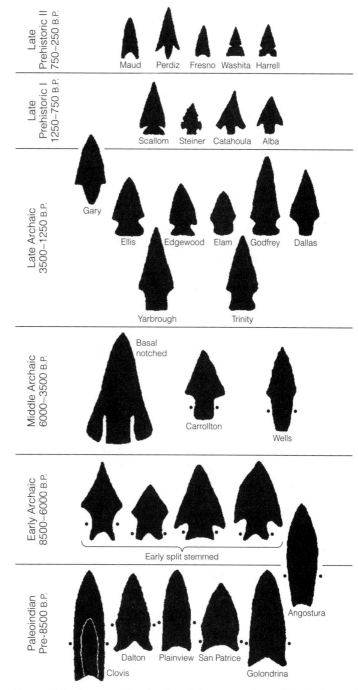

Figure 14.4 A proposed projectile point sequence for north-central Texas. In various parts of North America, such sequences can be used in cross-dating.

ciplines has grown dramatically in recent years. Most common is the use of "geoarchaeology" (Butzer 1982) or "archaeological geology" (Lasca and Donahue 1990) in many different areas of archaeological research, including dating (see Stein 1990:520).

For students of North American archaeology, perhaps the best available reference is Waters's (1992) *Principles of Geoarchaeology: A North American Perspective* (for Europe, see Davidson and Shackley 1976; Richards et al. 1985; and Zangger 1993; see the quarterly journal *Geoarchaeology* to keep up with trends in the field). In Waters's volume, for example, there are detailed discussions of the relative dating of sites buried in alluvial (stream-deposited) soils, along with a substantive discussion of "chronostratigraphy," or "chronosequences" (Holliday, ed. 1992; Stein 1990; see Chapter 10 for further details on stratigraphy).

Any major project, including surveys and excavations, must include a geoarchaeologist or geomorphologist on the staff. These scholars can provide tremendous insights not only into site formation processes (Goldberg et al. 1993; Schiffer 1987), but also on the various factors or rates of sedimentation (Ferring 1986), erosion, and redeposition. These affect relative chronological asssessments, as well as the interpretation of radiocarbon dates from buried deposits.

A specialization within geoarchaeology is **micromorphology,** in which the geologist takes a microscopic look at resin-impregnated thin sections from a soil column. A variety of data on site formation, deposition, erosion, and relative chronology can be obtained (Courty et al. 1989; Goldberg 1992).

The other applications of geoarchaeology and geomorphology to the problems of archaeological dating are many and varied, and some geological applications go back to the early days of archaeology. For example, the geologic aspects of the rise and fall of sea levels and the subsidence of coastlines have been used in relative dating of sites. Along San Francisco Bay, early excavations by Nelson (1909) and Schenck (1926) found that the bases of shell mounds began to form well before modern sea level was achieved. Geologists of that time did not have a rate of subsidence, and no approximate ages of the earliest shell mounds could be determined. Later, with the invention of radiocarbon dating, geologists used that technique to study the history of the shoreline of San Francisco Bay (Nichols and Wright 1971; Wright 1971). Mathiassen (1927), working in the Arctic region, showed that a rising shoreline and a progressively shallower sea at the site of Naujan accounted for the abandonment of that area by whales and thus by the Thule Eskimo, who depended on the animal for food. The house pits of the former Thule settlements are now 5–15 m higher than when the site was originally occupied some centuries ago. For other discussions of the use of sea level change and subsidence for relative-dating, see Bird (1938, 1946), Clark (1947), Deevey (1948), Hopkins (1959), Kraft et al. (1985), Shepard (1964), and Vinton (1962).

In the desert West of North America, shifts in Native American occupation patterns on the borders of pluvial or postglacial lakes were proposed initially by Campbell et al. (1937) for desert valley lakes in southern California. Geologists could provide approximate dates for when the lakes were full, and thus relative ages could be assigned for occupations of shorelines of those now-dry lakes. A later summary of such dating in that region is provided by Pippin (1986). Another early application is seen at George Lake, Ontario, Canada (Greenman and Stanley 1943).

Such lake level fluctuations are related to climatic change. The first effort to develop a fairly exact chronology of climatic change and its effect on the archaeological record (and thus its utility in relative dating) was developed in North America by Ernst Antevs (see Antevs 1955). Among the most controversial of his climatic episodes was the Altithermal, a period of drier and warmer climates between 5,000 and 7,000 years ago. Since Antevs's initial proposals in the late 1930s, the Altithermal has fallen in and out of favor with archaeologists. Sometimes dismissed as a factor in site occupation and relative dating, this concept has enjoyed a resurgence of interest in the 1990s (Reider 1990).

Climatic factors, such as glacial, pluvial, mesic, and arid conditions, all play a major role in the deposition and erosion of deposits in which archaeological sites are incorporated (Bull 1991). Thus, the soil overburden at a site can yield vital clues to a trained geoarchaeologist (Holliday 1992, ed. 1992), who looks at the issues of soil formation and time. The evolution of a broad landscape can be worked out through careful geoarchaeological and geomorphological methods (Butzer and Hansen 1968; Mandel 1992; Nordt 1992). Among the pioneer efforts at correlating archaeological sites of different ages with broad landscape modification were the beach ridges at Cape Krusenstern, Alaska (Giddings 1966) and meander patterns in the lower Mississippi River (Ford and Webb 1956; Phillips et al. 1951).

Soil chemistry has also been used in efforts at relative dating. Especially notable is the use of phosphate analysis (Eidt 1977, 1984; see also Arrhenius 1963). Cook and Heizer (1965) used phosphate concentrations as a method of estimating intensive human occupancy at archaeological sites in California. Isotopic analysis of soils also has the potential to differentiate climatic regimes and thus provide relative dates for archaeological remains buried in soils of distinctive climates (e.g., Bousman 1990).

Geologic dating methods, or geochronology, will continue to be used and developed in archaeological research. Zuener (1958:v) defined **geochronology** as "the science which draws its methods from geology, botany, zoology, and physics. Its chief objective, the development of time scales in years which extend back into the distant past beyond the historical calendar, binds the different methods together." The important point here is that prehistoric chronology is usually the result of several scientific disciplines working together on a single problem. Its importance in modern archaeology is made clear in the volume edited by Rapp and Gifford (1985; see also Hassan 1979; Ritter et al. 1976). Finally, it should be noted that geochronology often encompasses the use of paleontological and zoological methods in dating. A prime example is the association of certain faunas, such as those of the Pleistocene, with human occupations in both the Old and New Worlds (Agenbroad et al. 1990; Haynes and Agogino 1986; Jelinek 1957).

Smaller fauna, such as mollusks, are often climate-sensitive and reflect climatic change; these are especially useful for relative dating (Evans 1972).

CONCLUDING OBSERVATIONS

No part of archaeology is more difficult, generally speaking, than the determination of chronology. Archaeologists must ever be aware of the need for dating their sites and cultures and must collect the materials and make the necessary observations during excavation that will assist them in making time determinations. Because no two archaeological deposits are ever exactly the same, each excavation poses a unique problem. Beyond the routine collecting of charcoal, wood, molluscan remains, vertebrate and invertebrate remains, and soil samples, essential elements in age determination also include the cultural materials themselves and the stratigraphy. Stimulating ideas and fresh approaches to a problem often result from consultation with specialists in the geological, biological, and physical sciences.

GUIDE TO FURTHER READING

General

Sharer and Ashmore 1993; Wintle 1996

Dendrochronology

Douglass 1929; Baille 1982; Stahle and Wolfman 1985

Radiocarbon Dating

Bowman 1990; Taylor 1982; Schiffer 1986; Stuiver et al. 1993; Taylor et al. 1992

Other Absolute Techniques

Aitken 1990; Pourat et al. 1994 (ESR); Aitken 1989, 1990; Wagner et al. 1983 (TL); Wintle 1996 (argon, uranium-series, fission-track); Michels et al. 1983; Freter 1993 (obsidian hydration); Eighmy 1980; Eighmy and Sternberg 1991 (archaeomagnetic); Taylor 1991 (amino acid); Reher and Frison 1980 (varve); Deetz

1977; Kidd and Kidd 1970; Rogers and Wilson 1993 (historic; historic approach)

Relative Chronology

Harris 1989 (stratigraphy); Oakley 1964, 1976; Haddy and Hanson 1982 (chemical); Dorn 1991; Frederick et al. 1994; Harry 1995; Taylor 1991 (patination; desert varnish); Ester 1981; Marquardt 1978 (seriation); Fowler 1959; Parenti et al. 1990 (rates of accumulation); Adams and Adams 1991; Thomas 1989 (typology); Holliday ed. 1992; Rapp and Gifford 1985; Waters 1992 (geologic)

Tables of Equivalents and Conversion Factors

LENGTH/DISTANCE

1 meter	= 1.09361 yards
1 meter	= 39.37 inches
1 meter	= 3.28 feet
1 centimeter	= .3937 inches
1 kilometer	= .62137 miles
1 kilometer	= 1,093.61 yards
1 yard	= .9144 meters
1 foot	= .3048 meters
1 inch	= 2.54 centimeters
1 mile	= 1,609.35 meters

WEIGHT

1 kilogram	= 2.20462 pounds
1 gram	= .0353 ounces
1 ounce	= 28.3 grams
1 pound	= .45359 kilograms
1 metric ton	= 1,000 kilograms
1 ton (long)	= 1,016.05 kilograms
1 short ton	= 907.185 kilograms

AREA

1 hectare	= 2.47104 acres
1 square meter	= 1.19598 square yards
1 square yard	= .836131 square meters
1 square foot	= .09290 square meters
1 square inch	= 645.16 square millimeters
1 acre	= 4,046.9 square meters
1 square mile	= 2.59 square kilometers

VOLUME

1 liter	= 1.05668 quarts
1 liter	= .26417 gallons
1 cubic inch	= .1639 liters
1 cubic foot	= 28.3170 liters
1 cubic yard	= 764.559 liters
1 quart	= .94636 liters
1 gallon	= 3.78543 liters
1 pint	= .95 liters

CONVERSION OF COMPASS POINTS TO DEGREES

	Points	Angular measure °	Angular measure ′		Points	Angular measure °	Angular measure ′
North to East:				*South to West:*			
North	0	0		South	16	180	
N. by E.	1	11	15	S. by W.	17	191	15
NNE.	2	22	30	SSW.	18	202	30
NE. by N.	3	33	45	SW. by S.	19	213	45
NE.	4	45		SW.	20	225	
NE. by E.	5	56	15	SW. by W.	21	236	15
ENE.	6	67	30	WSW.	22	247	30
E. by N.	7	78	45	W. by S.	23	258	45

continued . . .

CONVERSION OF COMPASS POINTS TO DEGREES, *continued*

	Points	Angular measure			Points	Angular measure	
East to South:				*West to North:*			
East	8	90	0	West	24	270	
E. by S.	9	101	15	W. by N.	25	281	15
ESE.	10	112	30	WNW.	26	292	30
SE. by E.	11	123	45	NW. by W.	27	303	45
SE.	12	135		NW.	28	315	
SE. by S.	13	146	15	NW. by N.	29	326	15
SSE.	14	157	30	NNW.	30	337	30
S. by E.	15	168	45	N. by W.	31	348	45
				North	32	360	

CONVERSION FACTORS

Multiply	By	To obtain
cubic centimeters	3.531×10^{-5}	cubic feet
"	6.102×10^{-2}	cubic inches
"	10^{-6}	cubic meters
"	1.308×10^{-6}	cubic yards
"	2.642×10^{-4}	gallons
"	10^{-3}	liters
cubic feet	2.832×10^{-4}	cubic centimeters
"	1728	cubic inches
"	.02832	cubic meters
"	.03704	cubic yards
"	7.48052	gallons
"	28.32	liters
gallons	3785	cubic centimeters
"	.1337	cubic feet
"	231	cubic inches
"	3.785×10^{-3}	cubic meters
"	4.951×10^{-3}	cubic yards
" (water)	8.3453	pounds of water
temperature (°C) + 273	1	absolute temperature (°C)
" (°C) + 17.78	1.8	temperature (°F)
" (°F) + 460	1	absolute temperature (°F)
" (°F) – 32	5/9	temperature (°C)
long tons	2,240	pounds
"	1,016	kilograms
"	1.12000	short tons

continued . . .

CONVERSION FACTORS, *continued*

Multiply	By	To obtain
metric tons	10^3	kilograms
"	2,205	pounds
short tons	2,000	pounds
"	32,000	ounces
"	907.18486	kilograms
"	.89287	long tons
"	.90718	metric tons
centimeter	.3937	inches
cubic inches	16.39	cubic centimeters
"	5.787×10^{-4}	cubic feet
"	1.639×10^{-5}	cubic meters
"	2.143×10^{-5}	cubic yards
cubic meters	10^6	cubic centimeters
"	35.31	cubic feet
"	61,023	cubic inches
"	1.308	cubic yards
cubic yards	7.646×10^5	cubic centimeters
"	27	cubic feet
"	46,656	cubic inches
"	.7646	cubic meters
feet	30.48	centimeters
"	.3048	meters
"	.36	varas
gallons	3785	cubic centimeters
"	.1337	cubic feet
"	231	cubic inches
"	3.785×10^{-3}	cubic meters
"	4.951×10^{-3}	cubic yards
grams	15.43	grains (Troy)
"	10^{-3}	kilograms
"	10^3	milligrams
"	.03527	ounces
"	2.205×10^{-3}	pounds
hectares	1.076×10^5	square feet
inches	2.540	centimeters
kilograms	10^3	grams
"	2.2046	pounds
"	1.102×10^{-3}	tons (short)
kilometers	3,281	feet

continued . . .

CONVERSION FACTORS, *continued*

Multiply	By	To obtain
kilometers	10^3	meters
"	.6214	statute miles
"	1,093.6	yards
meters	3.2808	feet
"	39.37	inches
"	10^{-3}	kilometers
"	1.0936	yards
millimeters	.03937	inches
miles	1,609.35	meters
"	1.6093	kilometers
nautical miles	1.852	kilometers
ounces	28.35	grams
"	.0625	pounds
pounds of water	.01602	cubic feet
"	27.68	cubic inches
"	.1198	gallons
quarts (dry)	67.20	cubic inches
" (liquid)	57.75	cubic inches
rods	16.5	feet
square centimeters	1.076×10^{-3}	square feet
"	.1550	square inches
"	10^{-6}	square meters
square feet	929	square centimeters
"	144	square inches
"	.09290	square meters
"	1/9	square yards
square inches	6.452	square centimeters
"	6.944×10^{-3}	square feet
square meters	10.764	square feet
"	3.861×10^{-7}	square miles
"	1.196	square yards
square miles	27.88×10^6	square feet
"	2.590	square kilometers
"	3.098×10^6	square yards
square kilometers	.3861	square miles
square yards	9	square feet
"	3.228×10^{-7}	square miles

continued . . .

CONVERSION FACTORS, *continued*

Multiply	By	To obtain
square yards	.8361	square meters
varas	2.7777	feet
yards	.9144	meters
hectares	2.471	acres
acres	.4047	hectares
fathoms	1.8288	meters
chains	20.1168	meters
furlongs	201.168	meters

MAP SCALE EQUIVALENTS

Map scale	Inches to mile	Statute miles to an inch	Feet to an inch	Kilometers to an inch
1:600	105.6	.0095	50.	.0153
1:1,200	52.8	.0189	100.	.0305
1:2,400	26.4	.0379	200.	.061
1:2,500	25.34	.0394	208.3	.0635
1:3,600	17.6	.0568	300.	.0914
1:4,800	13.2	.0758	400.	.1219
1:6,000	10.56	.0947	500.	.1524
1:7,200	8.8	.1136	600.	.1829
1:7,920	8.	.125 (i.e., 1/8 mi.)	660.	.2012
1:10,000	6.34	.1578	833.3	.254
1:10,560	6.	.167 (i.e., 1/6 mi.)	880.	.268
1:12,000	5.28	.1894	1,000.	.305
1:15,840	4.	.250 (i.e., 1/4 mi.)	1,320.	.402
1:20,000	3.17	.3156	1,666.	.508
1:21,120	3.	.3333 (i.e., 1/3 mi.)	1,760.	.536
1:25,000	2.53	.3945	2,083.	.635
1:31,680	2.	.5 (i.e., 1/2 mi.)	2,640.	.804
1:62,500	1.01	.986	5,208.	1.587
1:63,360	1.	1.	5,280.	1.609
1:100,000	.634	1.578	8,333.	2.54
1:125,000	.507	1.972	10,416.	3.175
1:316,800	.2	5.	26,400.	8.05
1:500,000	.1267	7.891	41,666.	12.7
1:1,000,000	.063	15.783	83,333.3	25.40

Sources of Supplies and Services

Manufacturers, equipment suppliers, and service providers are listed here for information only. No endorsements or other representations are offered or implied.

GENERAL SUPPLY SOURCES

Forestry Suppliers, Inc.
P.O. Box 8397
Jackson, MS 39284-8397

Ben Meadows Co.
3589 Broad Street
Atlanta, GA 30366

SUPPLIES

Remote Sensing Data (1)

EOSAT imagery

Earth Observation Satellite (EOSAT) Co.
4300 Forbes Blvd.
Lanham, MD 20706

SPOT imagery

Spot Image Corp.
1897 Preston White Drive
Reston, VA 22091

USGS Maps (2)

U.S. Geological Survey (at the following locations):

4230 University Drive, Room 101
Anchorage, AK 99501

Building 3, Room 3128
345 Middlefield Road
Menlo Park, CA 94025

Maps: Box 25286, Bldg. 810
Books: Box 25286, MS 306
Federal Center
Denver, CO 80225

8105 Federal Building
125 South State Street
Salt Lake City, UT 84138

503 National Center, Room 1-C-402
12201 Sunrise Valley Drive
Reston, VA 22092

U.S. Atlas and Gazetteer Series; Street Atlas USA (3)

DeLorme Mapping
P.O. Box 298
Freeport, ME 04032

Stereoviewer (4)

See Forestry Suppliers, Inc. under GENERAL SUPPLY SOURCES.

Template for Map Reading (5)

See Forestry Suppliers, Inc.; Ben Meadows Co. under GENERAL SUPPLY SOURCES.

Base-Plate Compasses (6)

Silva Company compasses

Johnson Camping, Inc.
P.O. Box 1604
Binghamton, NY 13902-1604

Suunto Company compasses

See Forestry Suppliers, Inc. under GENERAL
SUPPLY SOURCES.

Digital Fluxgate Compass
(The Datascope) (7)

KVH Industries
110 Enterprise Center
Middletown, RI 02840

Compass/Rangefinder
(Haglöf Forestor) (8)

See Forestry Suppliers, Inc. under GENERAL
SUPPLY SOURCES.

Right-Angle Prism (9)

See Forestry Suppliers, Inc. under GENERAL
SUPPLY SOURCES.

Hip Chain (10)

See Forestry Suppliers, Inc.; Ben Meadows Co.
under GENERAL SUPPLY SOURCES.

Global Positioning System
(GPS) Units (11)

Garmin International
9875 Widmer Road
Lenexa, KS 66215

Magellan Systems Corp.
Professional Products
San Dimas, CA

Sokkia Corp.
9111 Barton
P.O. Box 2934
Overland Park, KS 66201

Trimble Navigation
Surveying and Mapping Division
P.O. Box 3642
645 North Mary Avenue
Sunnyvale, CA 94088-3642

Atlas GIS (Tiger5; Marco Polo) (12)

Strategic Mapping
3135 Kifer Road
Santa Clara, CA 95051

GIS Database (Etak Map) (13)

Etak, Inc.
1430 O'Brien Drive
Menlo Park, CA 94025

Levels (14)

See Forestry Suppliers, Inc.
under GENERAL SUPPLY SOURCES.

Target Rod Level: (15)

See Forestry Suppliers, Inc.; Ben Meadows Co.
under GENERAL SUPPLY SOURCES.

EDMI (TOPCON DM-A5) (16)

See Forestry Suppliers, Inc. under GENERAL
SUPPLY SOURCES.

Total Stations (17)

Topcon Instrument Corporation of America
65 West Century Road
Paramus, NJ 07652

Two-Way Radio (Maxon FM) (18)

See Forestry Suppliers, Inc.; Ben Meadows Co.
under GENERAL SUPPLY SOURCES.

Contour-Plotting Imaging System (MPS-2 Stereoview) (19)

Adam Technology
Brodie Hall Drive
3/375 Enterprise Unit Complex
W. Australia Tech. Park
Bentley, W. Australia

Cartographic and Computer-aided Design Software (20)

AutoCAD

Autodesk, Inc.
2320 Marinship Way
Sausalito, CA 94965

DesignCAD 2D for Windows

American Small Business Computers, Inc.
One American Way
Pryor, OK 74361

Surfer

Golden Software, Inc.
809 14th Street
Golden, CO 80401-1866

TNTmips

MicroImages, Inc.
201 N. 8th Street
Lincoln, NE 68508-1347

Traverse PC

PC Traverse/Ward Northwest
P.O. Box 105
Florence, OR 97439

GENERAL SERVICES

Aerial Photomapping Services
2929 Larkin
Clovis, CA 93612

Archaeological Mapping Specialists
P.O. Box 80105
Lincoln, NE 68502

References Cited

Acsadi, G. Y., and J. Nemeskeri
1970 *History of Human Life Span and Mortality.* Akademiai Kiado, Budapest, Hungary.

Ad Hoc Committee on Acceptable Field Methods in Mammalogy
1987 Acceptable Field Methods in Mammalogy: Preliminary Guidelines Approved by the American Society of Mammalogists. *Journal of Mammalogy,* Supplement to Vol. 68.

Adams, D. P., and P. J. Mehringer
1975 Modern Pollen Surface Samples: An Analysis of Subsamples. *Journal of Research United States Geological Survey* 3:733–738.

Adams, J. J.
1987 Rio Azul: An Example of an Archaeological Field Camp. In *Rio Azul Reports Number 3, the 1985 Season,* edited by R. E. W. Adams, pp. 222–246. University of Texas at San Antonio.

Adams, K. R.
1980 Pollen, Parched Seeds and Prehistory: a Pilot Investigation of Prehistoric Plant Remains from Salmon Ruin, a Chacoan Ruin in Northwest New Mexico. *Eastern New Mexico Contrib. Anth.* 8, ENMU, Portales.

Adams, K. R., and R. E. Gasser
1980 Plant Microfossils from Archaeological Sites: Research Considerations, and Sampling Techniques and Approaches. *The Kiva* 45(4):293–300.

Adams, R. E. W.
1960 Manuel Gamio and Stratigraphic Excavation. *American Antiquity* 26(1):99.
1971 *The Ceramics of Altar de Sacrificios.* Papers of the Peabody Museum of Archaeology and Ethnology, Vol. 62, No. 1. Harvard University, Cambridge.

Adams, R. E. W., E. Brown, and T. P. Culbert
1981 Radar Mapping, Archaeology, and Ancient Mayan Land Use. *Science* 213:1457–1463.

Adams, W. Y., and E. W. Adams
1991 *Archaeological Typology and Practical Reality.* Cambridge University Press, Cambridge.

Addington, L. R.
1986 *Lithic Illustration: Drawing Stone Artifacts for Publication.* University of Chicago Press, Chicago.

Adkins, L., and R. Adkins
1989 *Archaeological Illustration.* Cambridge University Press, Cambridge.

Adovasio, J. M.
1977 *Basketry Technology: A Guide to Identification and Analysis.* Taraxacum, Washington, D.C.

Adovasio, J. M., and R. C. Carlisle
1988 Some Thoughts on Cultural Resource Management Archaeology in the United States. *Antiquity* 62:72–87.

Adovasio, J. M., J. D. Gunn, J. Donahue, and R. Stukenrath
1978 Meadowcroft Rockshelter, 1977: An Overview. *American Antiquity* 43(4):632–651.

Agenbroad, L. D., J. I. Mead, and L. W. Nelson
1990 *Megafauna and Man: Discovery of America's Heartland.* Scientific Papers 1. The Mammoth Hot Springs, South Dakota.

Agnew, N.
1984 The Use of Silicones in the Preservation of a Field Site, The Lark Quarry Dinosaur Trackways. In *Adhesives and Consolidants,* edited by N. S. Bromelle, E. M. Pye, P. Smith, and G. Thomson, pp. 87–91. International Institute for Conservation of Historic and Artistic Works, London.

Ahlqvist, J., and D. Damsten
1969 A Modification of Kerley's Method for the Microscopic Determination of Age in Human Bone. *Journal of Forensic Sciences* 14:205–212.

Ahmed, F., and D. C. Almond
1983 *Field Mapping for Geology Students.* George Allen & Unwin, London.

Aikens, C. M.
1970 *Hogup Cave.* Anthropological Papers 93. University of Utah, Salt Lake City.

Aitken, M.
1959 Testing for Correlation between Dowsing Response and Magnetic Disturbance. *Archaeometry* 2:58–59.
1970 Magnetic Location. In *Science in Archaeology,* edited by D. Brothwell and E. Higgs, pp. 681–694. Praeger, New York.

Aitken, M. J.
1985 *Thermoluminescence Dating.* Academic Press, Orlando.

1989   Luminescence Dating: A Guide for Non-Specialists. *Archaeometry* 31:147–160.

1990   *Science-Based Dating in Archaeology.* Longman, London.

Akersten, W. A., T. M. Foppe, and G. T. Jefferson

1988   New Source of Dietary Data for Extinct Herbivores. *Quaternary Research* 30:92–97.

Albright, A. B.

1966   The Preservation of Small Waterlogged Wood Specimens with Polyethylene Glycol. *Curator* 9: 228–234.

Alexander, L.

1992   Differential GPS in Operation Desert Storm. *GPS World* 3(6):36–38.

Alexander, R. K.

1970   *Archeological Investigations at Parida Cave, Val Verde County, Texas.* Papers of the Texas Archeological Salvage Project 19, University of Texas at Austin.

Allen, C.

1975   Archaeological Photography. *Journal of Field Archaeology* 2:287–288.

Allen, J.

1978   The Archaeology of Nineteenth Century British Imperialism: An Australian Case Study. In *Historical Archaeology: A Guide to Substantive and Theoretical Contributions,* edited by R. L. Schuyler, pp. 139–148. Baywood, Farmingdale, New York.

Allen, K. M. S., S. W. Green, and E. B. W. Zubrow

1990   *Interpreting Space: GIS and Archaeology.* Taylor & Francis, London.

1993   *Practical Surveying and Computations.* 2nd ed. Butterworth-Heinemann, Oxford and Boston.

Allen, M. J.

1986   A Cleaning Technique for Land Molluscs from Archaeological Contexts. *Circaea* 4(1):51–53.

Allison, J.

1996   Cisco's Ko'an: Educating Archaeologists About Indigenous People's Self-Determination in the Land Use Planning Process for Cultural Resources. *SAA Newsletter* 14(1):14, 15, 26.

Allison, M. J., and A. Pezzia

1974   Preparation of the Dead in Pre-Colombian Coastal Peru. *Paleopathology Newsletter* 5:7–9.

Allison, N.

1990   Hair from Archaeological Sites. *Mammoth Trumpet* 6(1):2–8.

Allison, V. C.

1926   *The Antiquity of the Deposits in Jacob's Cavern.* Anthropological Papers 19, Pt. 6. American Museum of Natural History, New York.

Altschul, J. H.

1990   Red Flag Models: The Use of Modelling in Management Contexts. In *Interpreting Space: GIS and Archaeology,* edited by K. M. S. Allen, S. W. Green, and E. B. W. Zubrow, pp. 226–238. Taylor & Francis, London.

Ambrose, S. H.

1986   Stable Carbon and Nitrogen Isotope Analysis of Human and Animal Diet in Africa. *Journal of Human Evolution* 15:707–731.

American Society of Photogrammetry and Remote Sensing (ASPRS)

1960   *Manual of Photographic Interpretation.* American Society of Photogrammetry, Falls Church, Virginia.

1985   *Close-range Photogrammetry and Surveying: State-of-the-Art; Developing the Art of Application.* American Society of Photogrammetry, Falls Church, Virginia.

1994   *Mapping and Remote Sensing Tools for the 21st Century.* American Society of Photogrammetry and Remote Sensing, Bethesda, Maryland.

Amorosi, T.

1989   *A Postcranial Guide to Domestic Neo-natal and Juvenile Mammals: The Identification and Aging of Old World Species.* BAR International Series No. 533. British Archaeological Reports, Oxford.

Anderson, A. J.

1973   A Critical Evaluation of the Methodology of Midden Sampling. *New Zealand Archaeological Association Newsletter* 16(3):119–127.

Anderson, F. G.

1982   *Southwestern Archaeology: A Bibliography.* Garland, New York.

Anderson, J. M., and E. M. Mikhail

1985   *Introduction to Surveying.* McGraw-Hill, New York.

Andrews, D. H.

1994   Molecular Approaches to the Isolation and Analysis of Ancient Nucleic Acids. In *Theory and Method for Investigating the Peopling of the Americas,* edited by R. Bonnichsen and D. G. Steele, pp. 165–175. Center for the Study of the First Americans, Oregon State University, Corvallis.

Andrews, P.

1990   *Owls, Caves and Fossils.* University of Chicago Press, Chicago.

Andrews, R. L., and J. M. Adovasio

1980   *Perishable Industries from Hinds Cave, Val Verde County, Texas.* Ethnology Monograph 5, Department of Anthropology, University of Pittsburgh, Pittsburgh.

Angress, S., and C. Reed

1962   An Annotated Bibliography on the Origin and Descent of Domestic Mammals 1900–1955. *Fieldiana: Anthropology* 54:1–143.

Antenucci, J. C., K. Brown, P. L. Croswell, M. J. Kevany, and H. Archer

1991   *Geographic Information Systems: A Guide to the Technology.* American Society for Photogrammetry and Remote Sensing, Bethesda, Maryland.

Antevs, E.

1955   Geologic-Climatic Dating in the West. *American Antiquity* 20:317–335.

Anthony, D., and S. L. Black
    1994   Operation 2031: The Main Plaza Excavations. In *Continuing Archaeology at Colha, Belize,* edited by T. R. Hester, H. J. Shafer, and J. D. Eaton, pp. 39–58. Studies in Archeology 16. Texas Archeological Research Laboratory, University of Texas at Austin.

Anyon, R., and S. LeBlanc
    1984   *The Galaz Ruin: A Prehistoric Mimbres Village in Southwestern New Mexico.* University of New Mexico Press, Albuquerque.

Arden, H.
    1989   Who Owns Our Past? *National Geographic* 175: 376–392.

Arkin, A., and R. Colton
    1963   *Tables for Statisticians.* Barnes & Noble, New York.

Armelagos, G. J., D. S. Carlson, and D. P. Van Gerven
    1982   The Theoretical Foundations and Development of Skeletal Biology. In *A History of American Physical Anthropology,* edited by F. Spencer, pp. 305–328. Academic Press, New York.

Armelagos, G. J., and J. R. Dewey
    1970   Evolutionary Response to Human Infectious Disease. *Bioscience* 157:638–644.

Armelagos, G. J., and D. P. Van Gerven
    1980   Sexual Dimorphism and Human Evolution: An Overview. *Journal of Human Evolution* 9:437–446.

Armitage, P. L.
    1975   The Extraction and Identification of Opal Phytoliths from the Teeth of Ungulates. *Journal of Archaeological Science* 2:187–197.
    1989   The Use of Animal Bones as Building Material in Post-Medieval Britain. In *Diet and Crafts in Towns: The Evidence of Animal Remains from the Roman to the Post-Medieval Periods,* edited by D. Serjeantson and T. Waldron, pp. 147–160. BAR British Series No. 199. British Archaeological Reports, Oxford.

Armstrong, D. V.
    1990   *The Old Village and the Great House: An Archaeological and Historical Examination of Drax Hall Plantation, St. Ann's Bay, Jamaica.* University of Illinois Press, Urbana and Chicago.

Arnold, D. E.
    1983   Design Structure and Community Organization in Quinua, Peru. In *Structure and Cognition in Art,* edited by D. K. Washburn, pp. 40–55. Cambridge University Press, Cambridge.

Arnold, J. B., III
    1992   Advances in Underwater Archaeology. *Historical Archaeology* 26(4):1–131.

Arnold, J. B., III (editor)
    1989   *Underwater Archaeology Proceedings from the Society for Historical Archaeology Conference.* Society for Historical Archaeology, Pleasant Hill, California.

Arrhenius, O.
    1963   Investigation of Soil from Old Indian Sites. *Ethnos* 2–4:122–136.

Arroyo de Anda, L. A., M. Maldonado-Koerdell, and P. Martinez del Rio
    1953   *Cueva de la Candelaria.* Memorias del Instituto Nacional de Antropología e Historia 5. Instituto Nacional de Antropología e Historia, Mexico City.

Artz, J. A.
    1980   Inferring Season of Occupation from Fish Scales: An Archaeological Approach. *Plains Anthropologist* 25:47–61.

Asch, D. L.
    1976   *The Middle Woodland Population of the Lower Illinois Valley: A Study in Paleodemographic Methods.* Northwestern University Archeological Program Scientific Papers 1. Northwestern University, Evanston, Illinois.

Asch, N. B., D. L. Asch, and R. I. Ford
    1972   *Paleoethnobotany of the Koster Site: The Archaic Horizons.* Reports of Investigations 24. Illinois State Museum, Springfield.

Ashurst, J., and N. Ashurst
    1988   *Practical Building Conservation.* 3 vols. Halstead Press, New York.

Assad, C., and D. Potter
    1979   *An Intensive Archaeological Survey of Enchanted Rock State Natural Area.* Archaeological Survey Report 84. Center for Archaeological Research, University of Texas at San Antonio.

Aten, L. E.
    1971   *Archaeological Excavations of the Dow-Cleaver Site, Brazoria County, Texas.* Technical Bulletin 1. Texas Archeological Salvage Project, University of Texas at Austin.
    1981   Determining Seasonality of *Rangia cuneata* from Gulf Coast Shell Middens. *Bulletin of the Texas Archeological Society* 52:179–200.

Atkinson, R. J. C.
    1953   *Field Archaeology.* 2nd ed. Methuen, London.

Aufderheide, A. C., F. D. Neiman, L. E. Wittmers, Jr., and G. Rapp
    1981   Lead in Bone II: Skeletal-Lead Content as an Indicator of Lifetime Lead Ingestion and the Social Correlates in an Archaeological Population. *American Journal of Physical Anthropology* 55:285–291.

Auffenberg, W.
    1969   The Fossil Snakes of Florida. *Tulane Studies in Zoology* 10:131–216.
    1976   The Genus *Gopherus* (Testudinidae): Pt. I. Osteology and Relationships of Extant Species. *Bulletin of the Florida State Museum* 20:47–110.

Avery, T. E. and G. L. Berlin
    1992   *Fundamentals of Remote Sensing and Airphoto Interpretation.* 5th ed. Macmillan, New York.

Avery, T. E. and T. R. Lyons
1981 *Remote Sensing: Aerial and Terrestrial Photography for Archaeologists.* Cultural Resources Management Division, National Park Service, U.S. Department of the Interior, Washington, D.C.

Baby, R. S.
1954 Hopewell Cremation Practices. *Ohio Historical Society Papers in Archaeology* 1:1–7.

Bacon, L.
1987 The Care and Protection of Copper Alloy, Silver and Gold Objects on Site. In *In Situ Archaeological Conservation*, edited by H. W. M. Hedges, pp. 138–143. Getty Conservation Institute, Los Angeles.

Bada, J. L.
1985 Amino Acid Racemization Dating of Fossil Bones. *Annual Review of Earth and Planetary Sciences* 13:241–268.

Bada, J. L., and R. Protsch
1973 Racemization Reaction of Aspartic Acid and Its Use in Dating Fossil Bones. *Proceedings of the National Academy of Sciences* 184:791–793.

Baer, N. S., M. Delacorte, and N. Indictor
1977 Chemical Investigations on Pre-Columbian Archaeological Textile Specimens. In *Preservation of Paper and Textiles of Historic and Artistic Value*, edited by J. C. Williams, pp. 261–271. Advances in Chemistry 164. American Chemical Society, Washington, D.C.

Baerreis, D. A.
1971 The Ethnohistoric Approach and Archaeology. *Ethnohistory* 8:49–77.

Bailey, G.
1996 *Boxing Up Your Collections: How Safe Are They?* Conservation Notes 20. Texas Memorial Museum, University of Texas at Austin.

Baille, M. G. L.
1982 *Tree-Ring Dating and Archaeology.* University of Chicago Press, Chicago.

Baker, B. C.
1985 *Handling Waterlogged Artifacts in Preliminary Photographic Documentation Process.* Unpublished Master's thesis, Texas A&M University, College Station.

Baker, B. J., and G. J. Armelagos
1988 The Origin and Antiquity of Syphilis. *Current Anthropology* 29:703–737.

Baker, B. W., and B. S. Shaffer
1991a A Bibliography of Faunal Analysis Coding Systems. *Zooarchaeological Research News* 10(1): 4–5.
1991b Pathological Deer (*Odocoileus* sp.) Elements from a Late Prehistoric Hunter-Gatherer Site (41HR273) in Harris County, Texas. *Texas Journal of Science* 43:217–218.

Baker, B. W., B. S. Shaffer, K. D. Sobolik, and D. G. Steele
1991 Faunal Analysis. Part I: Analysis of the Vertebrate Faunal Remains. In *Alabonson Road: Early Ceramic Period Adaptation to the Inland Coastal Prairie Zone, Harris County, Southeast Texas*, edited by H. B. Ensor and D. L. Carlson, pp. 139–161. Reports of Investigations No. 8. Archeological Research Laboratory, Texas A&M University, College Station.

Baker, C., and G. J. Gumerman
1981 *Remote Sensing: Archeological Applications of Remote Sensing in the North Central Lowlands.* Cultural Resources Management Division, National Park Service, U.S. Department of the Interior, Washington, D.C.

Baker, G.
1960 Hook Shaped Opal Phytoliths in the Epidermal Cells of Oats. *Australian Journal of Botany* 8:69–71.
1961 Opal Phytoliths from Sugarcane, San Fernando, Philippine Islands. *Memoirs of the Queensland Museum* 14:1–12.

Baker, J., and D. Brothwell
1980 *Animal Diseases in Archaeology.* Academic Press, New York.

Bannister, A., and S. Raymond
1984 *Surveying.* 5th ed. Nichols, Pitman, New York.

Bannister, B., and T. L. Smiley
1955 Dendrochronology. In *Geochronology*, edited by T. L. Smiley, pp. 177–195. Bulletin Series 26. University of Arizona, Tucson.

Barber, R., and L. Casjens
1978 Interviews, Library Research, and the Location of Known Sites. In *Conservation Archaeology in the Northeast: Toward a Research Orientation*, edited by A. Speiss, pp. 60–66. Bulletin 3. Peabody Museum of Archaeology and Ethnology, Harvard University, Cambridge.

Barbetti, M., Y. Taborin, B. Schmider, and K. Flude
1980 Archaeomagnetic Results from Late Pleistocene Hearths at Etiolles and Marsangy, France. *Archaeometry* 22:25–46.

Bard, J. C., F. Asaro, and R. F. Heizer
1978 Perspectives on the Dating of Prehistoric Great Basin Petroglyphs by Neutron Activation Analysis. *Archaeometry* 20:85–88.

Barefoot, L., and Hankins, F. W.
1982 *Identification of Modern and Tertiary Woods.* Clarendon Press, Oxford.

Barker, G.
1975 To Sieve or Not to Sieve. *Antiquity* 49:61–63.

Barker, P. A.
1982 *Techniques in Archaeological Excavation.* 2nd ed. Universe Books, New York.

Barnes, J. W.
1990 *Basic Geological Mapping.* 2nd ed. Wiley, New York.

Barnes, R. C.
　1980　Feature Analysis: A Neglected Tool in Archae-
　　　ological Survey and Interpretation. *Man in the
　　　Northeast* 20:101–113.

Barrett, E. C., and L. F. Curtis
　1992　*Introduction to Environmental Remote Sensing.*
　　　3rd ed. Chapman and Hall, London and New York.

Bartlett, R. A.
　1962　*Great Surveys of the American West.* University
　　　of Oklahoma Press, Norman.

Bar-Yosef, O., M. Arnold, N. Mercier, A. Belfer-Cohen,
　　　P. Goldberg, R. Housley, H. Laville, L. Meignen,
　　　J. C. Vogel, and B. Vandermeersch
　1996　The Dating of the Upper Paleolithic Layers in
　　　Kebara Cave, Mt. Carmel. *Journal of Archaeological
　　　Science* 23:297–306.

Bascom, W. R.
　1941　Possible Application of Kite Photography to
　　　Archaeology and Ethnology. *Illinois Academy of Sci-
　　　ence Transactions* 34(2).

Bass, G. F.
　1982　The Excavation. In *Yassi Ada: Volume 1, A
　　　Seventh-Century Byzantine Shipwreck,* edited by
　　　G. F. Bass and F. H. van Doorninck, Jr., pp. 9–31.
　　　Texas A&M University, College Station.

Bass, G. F. (editor)
　1988　*Ships and Shipwrecks of the Americas.* Thames &
　　　Hudson, London and New York.

Bass, G. F., and F. van Doorninck, Jr. (editors)
　1982　*Yassi Ada: Volume 1, A Seventh-Century Byzan-
　　　tine Shipwreck.* Texas A&M University Press, Col-
　　　lege Station.

Bass, W. M.
　1987　*Human Osteology: A Laboratory and Field Man-
　　　ual of the Human Skeleton.* 3rd ed. Missouri Archeo-
　　　logical Society, Columbia.

Baumel, J. J.
　1979　Osteologia. In *Nomina Anatomica Avium: An
　　　Annotated Anatomical Dictionary of Birds,* edited by
　　　J. J. Baumel, A. S. King, A. M. Lucas, J. E. Breazile,
　　　and H. E. Evans, pp. 53–121. Academic Press, New
　　　York.

Bayle, A., and R. de Noyer
　1939　Contribution a l'etude des os en cours de fos-
　　　silisation: Essai de determination de leur age. *Bull.
　　　Soc. Chimique de France,* Ser. 5, Vol. 6:1011–1024.

Beals, R. L., G. W. Brainerd, and W. Smith
　1945　*Archaeological Studies in Northeast Arizona.*
　　　Publications in American Archaeology and Ethnol-
　　　ogy 44:1–236. University of California, Berkeley.

Beaton, J. M.
　1983　Terrestrial Photogrammetry in Australian
　　　Archaeology. In *Australian Field Archaeology: A
　　　Guide to Techniques,* edited by G. Connah, pp.
　　　64–66. Australian Institute of Aboriginal Studies,
　　　Canberra.

Beck, C. W.
　1981　Minimum Requirements for Animal Bone
　　　Reports in Archaeology. *Journal of Field Archaeology*
　　　8:363–365.

　1983　Archaeozoology/Zooarchaeology. *Journal of
　　　Field Archaeology* 10:229–230.

Beck, W. A., and Y. D. Haase
　1974　*Historical Atlas of California.* University of
　　　Oklahoma Press, Norman.

Becker, B., and A. Delorme
　1978　Oak Chronologies for Central Europe and
　　　Their Extension from Medieval to Prehistoric
　　　Times. In *Dendrochronology in Europe,* edited by
　　　J. Fletcher, pp. 59–64. BAR Series 51. British
　　　Archaeological Reports, Oxford.

Bednarik, R. G.
　1992　A New Method to Date Petroglyphs. *Archaeo-
　　　metry* 34:279–291.

Behrensmeyer, A. K.
　1975　The Taphonomy and Paleoecology of Plio-
　　　Pleistocene Vertebrate Assemblages East of Lake
　　　Rudolf, Kenya. *Bulletin of the Museum of Compara-
　　　tive Zoology* 145:473–578. Harvard University, Cam-
　　　bridge.

Behrensmeyer, A. K., and A. P. Hill (editors)
　1980　*Fossils in the Making: Vertebrate Taphonomy and
　　　Paleoecology.* University of Chicago Press, Chicago.

Bell, J. F.
　1978　The Development of the Ordnance Survey
　　　1:25 000 Scale Derived Map. *Cartographic Journal*
　　　15:7–13.

　1993　*Surveying and Setting Out Procedures.* Alder-
　　　shot, Hampshire, United Kingdom.

Bell, L. S.
　1990　Paleopathology and Diagenesis: An SEM
　　　Evaluation of Structural Changes Using Backscat-
　　　tered Electron Imaging, *Journal of Archaeological
　　　Science* 17:85–102.

Bell, R. E.
　1977　Obsidian Hydration Studies in Highland
　　　Ecuador. *American Antiquity* 42:68–78.

Bell, W. H., and C. J. King
　1944　Methods for the Identification of the Leaf
　　　Fibers of Mescal (*Agave*), Yucca (*Yucca*), Beargrass
　　　(*Nolina*), and Sotol (*Dasylirion*). *American Antiquity*
　　　10:150–160.

Bell, W. T.
　1991　Thermoluminescence Dates for the Lake
　　　Mungo Aboriginal Fireplaces and the Implications
　　　for Radiocarbon Dating. *Archaeometry* 33:43–50.

Bement, L. C.
　1985　Spray Foam: A New Bone Encasement Tech-
　　　nique. *Journal of Field Archaeology* 12(3):371–372.

　1991　The Thunder Valley Burial Cache: Group
　　　Investment in a Central Texas Sinkhole Cemetery.
　　　Plains Anthropologist 36:97–109.

Benedict, J. B.
1992   Sacred Hot Springs, Instant Patinas. *Plains Anthropologist* 37(138):1–6.

Bennett, J. A.
1987   *The Divided Circle: A History of Instruments for Astronomy, Navigation, and Surveying.* Phaidon, Christie's, Oxford.

Bennison, G. M.
1990   *An Introduction to Geological Structures and Maps.* Routledge, Chapman & Hall, New York.

Beresford, M. W., and J. K. S. St. Joseph
1979   *Medieval England: An Aerial Survey.* Cambridge University Press, Cambridge.

Berg, R. C., and M. R. Greenpool
1993   *Stack-Unit Geological Mapping: Color-Coded and Computer-Based Methodology.* Department of Energy and Natural Resources, Illinois State Geological Survey, Champaign.

Bernal, I.
1963   *Teotihuacan.* Instituto Nacional de Antropología e Historia, Mexico City.

Bernstein, D. J.
1990   Prehistoric Seasonality Studies in Coastal Southern New England. *American Anthropologist* 92:96–115.

Bettess, F.
1984   *Surveying for Archaeologists.* Durham University Excavation Committee, University of Durham, England.

Biddle, M., and B. Kjolbye-Biddle
1969   Metres, Areas and Robbing. *World Archaeology* 1(2):208–219.

Biek, L. E.
1963   *Archaeology and the Microscope.* Butterworth Press, London.

Binford, L. R.
1962   Archaeology as Anthropology. *American Antiquity* 28:217–225.
1963   An Analysis of Cremations from Three Michigan Sites. *Wisconsin Archeologist* 44:98–110.
1964   A Consideration of Archaeological Research Design. *American Antiquity* 29:425–444.
1965   Archaeological Systematics and the Study of Culture Process. *American Antiquity* 31:203–310.
1971   Mortuary Practices: Their Study and Their Potential. In *Approaches to the Social Dimensions of Mortuary Practices,* edited by J. A. Brown, pp. 6–29. Memoir 25. Society for American Archaeology, Washington, D.C.
1975   Sampling, Judgement, and the Archaeological Record. In *Sampling in Archaeology,* edited by J. W. Mueller, pp. 251–257. University of Arizona Press, Tucson.
1978a   Dimensional Analysis of Behavior and Site Structure: Learning from an Eskimo Hunting Stand. *American Antiquity* 43:330–361.
1978b   *Nunamuit Ethnoarchaeology.* Academic Press, New York.
1981   *Bones: Ancient Men and Modern Myths.* Academic Press, New York.
1982   The Archaeology of Place. *Journal of Anthropological Archaeology* 1:5–31.
1983a   *In Pursuit of the Past.* Thames & Hudson, New York.
1983b   *Working at Archaeology.* Academic Press, New York.

Binford, L. R., and S. R. Binford (editors)
1968   *New Perspectives in Archaeology.* Aldine, Chicago.

Binford, L. R., S. R. Binford, R. Whallon, and M. A. Hardin
1970   *Archaeology at Hatchery West.* Memoir 24. Society for American Archaeology, Washington, D.C.

Binford, L. R., and J. B. Bertram
1977   Bone Frequencies and Attritional Process. In *For Theory Building in Archaeology,* edited by L. R. Binford, pp. 77–153. Academic Press, New York.

Bird, J. B.
1938   Antiquity and Migrations of the Early Inhabitants of Patagonia. *Geographical Review* 28:250–275.
1943   *Excavations in Northern Chile.* Anthropological Papers Vol. 38, Pt. 4. American Museum of Natural History, New York.
1946   The Archaeology of Patagonia. In *Handbook of South American Indians,* edited by J. Steward, pp. 17–24. Bulletin 143, Vol. 1. Bureau of American Ethnology, Smithsonian Institution, Washington, D.C.
1948   *Preceramic Cultures in Chicama and Viru.* Memoir 4. Society for American Archaeology, Washington, D.C.
1968   More About Earth-Shaking Equipment. *American Antiquity* 33:507–509.

Bird, J. B., and J. A. Ford
1956   A New Earth-Shaking Machine. *American Antiquity* 21:399–401.

Bird, R. G.
1989   *EDM Traverses: Measurement, Computation, and Adjustment.* Longman Scientific & Technical, New York.

Black, G. A.
1967   *Angel Site: An Archaeological, Historical, and Ethnological Study.* 2 vols. Indiana Historical Society, Indianapolis.

Black, S. L.
1986   *The Clemente and Herminia Hinojosa Site, 41JW8: A Toyah Horizon Campsite in Southern Texas.* Special Report 18. Center for Archaeological Research, University of Texas at San Antonio.

Black, S. L., K. Jolly, and D. R. Potter
1993   *The Higgins Experiment Field Report.* Wurzbach Project Working Papers. Texas Archeological Research Laboratory, University of Texas at Austin.

Black, S. L., and A. J. McGraw
1985   *The Panther Springs Creek Site: Cultural Change and Continuity Within the Upper Salado Creek Watershed, South-Central Texas.* Archaeological Survey Report No. 100. Center for Archaeological Research, University of Texas at San Antonio.

Black, T. K., III
1978   A New Method for Assessing the Sex of Fragmentary Skeletal Remains: Femoral Shaft Circumference. *American Journal of Physical Anthropology* 48:227–232.

Blackman, E.
1968   The Pattern and Sequence of Opaline Silica Deposition in Rye (*Secale cerale* L.). *Annals of Botany* 32:199–206.
1969   Observations on the Development of the Silica Cells of the Leaf Sheath of Wheat (*Triticum aestivum*). *Canadian Journal of Botany* 47:827–844.

Blake, M., S. A. LeBlanc, and P. E. Minnis
1986   Changing Settlement and Population in the Mimbres Valley, SW New Mexico. *Journal of Field Archaeology* 13:439–464.

Blakely, R. L., and D. S. Mathews
1990   Bioarchaeological Evidence for a Spanish–Native American Conflict in the Sixteenth-Century Southeast. *American Antiquity* 55:718–744.

Blaker, A. A.
1977   *Handbook for Scientific Photography.* W. H. Freeman, San Francisco.

Blandford, P. W.
1991   *Maps and Compasses.* 2nd ed. Tab Books, Blue Ridge Summit, Pennsylvania.

Blangero, J.
1987   *Population Genetic Approaches to Phenotypic Evolution in the Jerels of Nepal.* Ph.D. dissertation, Case Western Reserve University, Cleveland. University Microfilms, Ann Arbor.

Blumenschine, R. J.
1986   *Early Hominid Scavenging Opportunities: Implications of Carcass Availability in the Serengeti and Ngorongoro Ecosystems.* BAR International Series 283. British Archaeological Reports, Oxford.
1988   Reinstating the Early Hominid Scavenging Niche: A Reply to Potts. *Current Anthropology* 29:483–486.

Boaz, N. T., and J. Hampel
1978   Strontium Content of Fossil Tooth Enamel and Diets of Early Hominids. *Journal of Paleontology* 52:928–933.

Bobrowsky, P. T.
1982   Olsen and Olsen's Identity Crisis in Faunal Studies. *American Antiquity* 47:180–183.

Bocek, B.
1986   Rodent Ecology and Burrowing Behavior: Predicted Effects on Archaeological Site Formation. *American Antiquity* 51:589–603.
1992   The Jasper Ridge Reexcavation Experiment: Rates of Artifact Mixing by Rodents. *American Antiquity* 57(2):261–269.

Bock, N. L.
1990   *Global Positioning System: An Overview.* International Association of Geodesy Symposia. Springer-Verlag, New York.

Bocquet-Appel, J. P., and C. Masset
1982   Farewell to Paleodemography. *Journal of Human Evolution* 11:321–333.
1985   Paleodemography: Resurrection or Ghost? *Journal of Human Evolution* 14:107–111.

Bodley, H., and M. Hallas
1978   *Elementary Surveying for Industrial Archaeologists.* Shire Publications, Haverfordwest, England.

Boessneck, J.
1969   Osteological Differences Between Sheep (*Ovis aries* Linne) and Goat (*Capra hircus* Linne). In *Science in Archaeology,* 2nd ed., edited by D. Brothwell and E. S. Higgs, pp. 331–358. Thames & Hudson, London.

Boessneck, J., and A. von den Driesch
1978   The Significance of Measuring Animal Bones from Archaeological Sites. In *Approaches to Faunal Analysis in the Middle East,* edited by R. H. Meadow and M. A. Zeder, pp. 25–39. Bulletin 2. Peabody Museum of Archaeology and Ethnology, Harvard University, Cambridge.

Bogan, A. E., and N. D. Robison (editors)
1978   *A History and Selected Bibliography of Zooarchaeology in Eastern North America.* Tennessee Anthropological Association Miscellaneous Paper 2. Tribute Press, Chattanooga.
1987   *The Zooarchaeology of Eastern North America: History, Method and Theory, and Bibliography.* Tennessee Anthropological Association Miscellaneous Paper 12. UT Graphic Arts Service, University of Tennessee, Knoxville.

Bohrer, V. L.
1968   *Paleoecology of an Archaeological Site near Snowflake, Arizona.* Unpublished Ph.D. dissertation, University of Arizona, Tucson.
1972   Paleoecology of the Hay Hollow Site, Arizona. *Fieldiana: Anthropology* 63:1–30.

Bohrer, V. L., and K. R. Adams
1977   *Ethnobotanical Techniques and Approaches at Salmon Ruin, New Mexico.* Contributions in Anthropology vol. 8, (1). Eastern New Mexico University, Portales.

Bökönyi, S.
1970   A New Method for the Determination of the Number of Individuals in Animal Bone Material. *American Journal of Archaeology* 74:291–292.

Bollong, C. A.
1994   Analysis of Site Stratigraphy and Formation Processes Using Patterns of Pottery Sherd Dispersion. *Journal of Field Archaeology* 21(1):15–28.

Bond, C. L.
1979   *Palo Alto Battlefield: A Magnetometer and Metal Detector Survey.* Cultural Resources Laboratory Report 4. Texas A&M University, College Station.

Bonnichsen, R., and C. W. Bolen
1985   On the Importance of Hair for Pleistocene Studies. *Current Research in the Pleistocene* 2:63–64.

Bonnichsen, R., and D. Sanger
1977   Integrating Faunal Analysis. *Canadian Journal of Archaeology* 1:109–133.

Bonnichsen, R., and M. H. Sorg (editors)
1989   *Bone Modification.* Center for the Study of First Americans, University of Maine, Orono.

Borchers, P. E.
1977   *Photogrammetric Recording of Cultural Resources.* Technical Preservation Services Division, Office of Archaeology and Historic Preservation, National Park Service, U.S. Department of the Interior, Washington, D.C.

Borden, C. E.
1950   A Translucent Shelter for Field Work in Regions with High Precipitation. *American Antiquity* 15:252–253.

Bousman, C. B.
1990   Preliminary Oxygen-Isotope Evidence for Late Pleistocene-Early Holocene Climate Change. *Current Research in the Pleistocene* 9:78–80.

Bower, B.
1988   Skeletal Aging of New World Settlers. *Science News* 133:215.
1989   Modern Humans Take a Spin Back in Time. *Science News* 134:26.

Bowman, B. F.
1990   The Foster Site Cremation: A Single Individual, Partition Cremation in Milam County, Texas. *Plains Anthropologist* 36:31–42.

Bowman, S.
1990   *Radiocarbon Dating.* University of California Press, Berkeley.

Bozarth, S.
1985   Distinctive Phytoliths from Various Dicot Species. Paper presented at the 2nd Phytolith Research Workshop, Duluth, Minnesota.
1986   Morphologically Distinctive *Phaseolus, Cucurbita,* and *Helianthus annuus* Phytoliths. In *Plant Opal Phytolith Analysis in Archaeology and Paleoecology,* edited by I. Rovner, pp. 56–66. Occasional Papers of the Phytolitharien, Raleigh, North Carolina.

Brace, C. L.
1972   Sexual Dimorphism in Human Evolution. *Yearbook of Physical Anthropology* 16:31–49.

Brace, C. L., and K. D. Hunt
1990   A Nonracial Craniofacial Perspective on Human Variations: A(ustralia) to Z(uni). *American Journal of Physical Anthropology* 82:341–360.

Braidwood, R. J.
1974   The Iraq Jarmo Project. In *Archaeological Researches in Retrospect,* edited by G. R. Willey, pp. 61–83. Winthrop, Cambridge, Massachusetts.

Braidwood, R., and B. Howe
1960   *Prehistoric Investigations in Iraq Kurdistan.* Studies in Oriental Civilization 31. Oriental Institute of the University of Chicago, Chicago.
1962   Southwestern Asia Beyond the Lands of the Mediterranean Littoral. In *Course Toward Urban Life,* edited by R. J. Braidwood and G. R. Willey, pp. 132–146. Wenner-Gren, New York.

Brain, C. K.
1974   Some Suggested Procedures in the Analysis of Bone Accumulations from Southern African Quaternary Sites. *Annals of the Transvaal Museum* 29(1):1–5.
1976   Some Principles in the Interpretation of Bone Accumulations Associated with Man. In *Human Origins and the East African Evidence,* edited by G. L. Isaac and E. R. McCown, pp. 97–116. Staples Press, Menlo Park, California.
1981   *The Hunters or the Hunted? An Introduction to African Cave Taphonomy.* University of Chicago Press, Chicago.

Brainerd, G. W.
1951   The Use of Mathematical Formulations in Archaeological Analysis. In *Essays on Archaeological Methods,* edited by J. B. Griffin, pp. 117–127. University of Michigan Press, Ann Arbor.

Brass, D. A.
1994   *Rabies in Bats: Natural History and Public Health Implications.* Livia Press, Ridgeford, Connecticut.

Breaks, T.
1771   *A Complete System of Land-Surveying: Both in Theory and Practice: Containing the Best, the Most Accurate, and Commodious Methods of Surveying and Planning of Ground by All the Instruments Now in Use.* T. Saint for W. Charnley and J. Murray, Newcastle upon Tyne and London.

Breiner, S., and M. D. Coe
1972   Magnetic Exploration of the Olmec Civilization. *American Scientist* 60(5):566–575.

Brewer, D. J.
1987   Seasonality in the Prehistoric Faiyum Based on the Incremental Growth Structures of the Nile Catfish (Pisces: *Clarias*). *Journal of Archaeological Science* 14:459–472.
1992   Zooarchaeology: Method, Theory, and Goals. In *Archaeological Method and Theory,* vol. 4, edited by M. B. Schiffer, pp. 195–244. University of Arizona Press, Tucson.

Brighty, S. G., and D. M. Stirling
1989   *Setting Out: A Guide for Site Engineers.* 2nd ed. rev. BSP Professional, Oxford and Boston.

Brill, R. H.
1961   The Record of Time in Weathered Glass. *Archaeology* 14:18–22.

Brinker, R. C., and R. Minnick
1987   *The Surveying Handbook.* Van Nostrand Reinhold, New York.

Brinker, R. C., and P. R. Wolf
1984   *Elementary Surveying.* 9th ed. Harper & Row, New York.

British Columbia Surveys and Mapping Branch
1975   *Survey Systems Within the Crown Domain: Colonies to Confederation.* Surveys and Mapping Branch, Department of Lands, Forests, and Water Resources, Victoria, British Columbia.

Briuer, F. L.
1976   New Clues to Stone Tool Function: Plant and Animal Residues. *American Antiquity* 41:478–484.

Brooks, A. S., P. E. Hare, J. E. Kokis, G. H. Miller, R. D. Ernst, and F. Wendorf
1990   Dating Pleistocene Archeological Sites by Protein Diagenesis in Ostrich Eggshell. *Science* 248:60–64.

Brooks, S., D. G. Steele, and R. H. Brooks
1990   Formulae for Stature Estimation on Incomplete Long Bones: A Survey of Their Reliability. *Adli Tip Dergïsï (Journal of Forensic Medicine, Istanbul)* 6:167–170.

Brose, D.
1964   Infra-red Photography: An Aid to Stratigraphic Interpretation. *Michigan Archaeologist* 10(4):69–73.

Brothwell, D. R.
1982   *Digging Up Bones.* 3rd ed. Cornell University Press, Ithaca, New York.
1991   Malocclusion and Methodology: The Problem and Relevance of Recording Dental Malalignment in Archaeology. *International Journal of Osteoarchaeology* 1:27–37.

Brothwell, D. R., and A. T. Sandison (editors)
1967   *Diseases in Antiquity.* Charles C. Thomas, Springfield, Illinois.

Brothwell, D. R., K. D. Thomas, and J. Clutton-Brock (editors)
1978   *Research Problems in Zooarchaeology.* Occasional Publication 3. Institute of Archaeology, London.

Browman, D. L.
1981   Isotopic Discrimination and Correction Factors in Radiocarbon Dating. In *Advances in Archaeological Method and Theory,* vol. 4, edited by M. B. Schiffer, pp. 241–295. Academic Press, New York.

Brown, C. L., and C. E. Gustafson
1989   *A Key to Postcranial Skeletal Remains of Cattle/Bison, Elk, and Horse.* Reports of Investigations 57. Laboratory of Anthropology, Washington State University, Pullman.

Brown, D. A.
1984   Prospects and Limits of a Phytolith Key for Grasses in the Central United States. *Journal of Archaeological Science* 11:345–368.

Brown, J. A.
1975   Deep-Site Excavation Strategy as a Sampling Problem. In *Sampling in Archaeology,* edited by J. W. Mueller, pp. 155–169. University of Arizona Press, Tucson.

Brown, J. A. (editor)
1971   *Approaches to the Social Dimensions of Mortuary Practices.* Memoir 25. Society for American Archaeology, Washington, D.C.

Brown, K. M., D. R. Potter, G. D. Hall, and S. L. Black
1982   *Excavations at 41 LK 67, A Prehistoric Site in the Choke Canyon Reservoir, South Texas.* Choke Canyon Series 7. Center for Archaeological Research, University of Texas at San Antonio.

Bruce-Mitford, R. L. S. (editor)
1956   *Recent Archaeological Excavations in Britain.* Routledge & Kegan Paul, London.

Brues, A. M.
1990   The Once and Future Diagnosis of Race. In *Skeletal Attribution of Race: Methods for Forensic Anthropology,* edited by G. W. Gill and S. Rhine, pp. 1–7. Anthropological Papers No. 4. Maxwell Museum of Anthropology, Albuquerque, New Mexico.

Bruseth, J. E., and W. A. Martin (editors)
1986   *Archaeology at the Bird Point Island and Adams Ranch Sites.* Richland Creek Technical Series Vol. 11. Archaeological Research Program, Southern Methodist University, Dallas, Texas.

Bryant, V. M., Jr.
1974a   The Role of Coprolite Analysis in Archaeology. *Bulletin of the Texas Archeological Society* 45:1–28.
1974b   Prehistoric Diet in Southwest Texas: The Coprolite Evidence. *American Antiquity* 39:407–420.
1974c   Pollen Analysis of Prehistoric Human Feces from Mammoth Cave. In *Archaeology of the Mammoth Cave Area,* edited by P. J. Watson, pp. 203–209. Academic Press, New York.

Bryant, V. M., Jr., and J. P. Dering
1994   A Guide to Paleoethnobotany. In *Papers of the Plenary Session of Current Archaeology, Interdisciplinary Approaches,* pp. 23–45. 33rd Annual Meeting of the Manitoba Archaeological Society, University of Winnipeg, Winnipeg, Canada.

Bryant, V. M., Jr., and S. A. Hall
1993   Archaeological Palynology in the United States: A Critique. *American Antiquity* 58:277–286.

Bryant, V. M., Jr., and R. G. Holloway
1983   The Role of Palynology in Archaeology. In *Advances in Archaeological Method and Theory,* vol. 6, edited by M. B. Schiffer, pp. 191–224. Academic Press, New York.

Bryant, V. M., Jr., and D. P. Morris
1986 Uses of Ceramic Vessels from Antelope House: The Pollen Evidence. In *Archaeological Investigations at Antelope House,* edited by D. P. Morris, pp. 489–501. National Park Service, Tucson.

Bryant, V. M., and G. Williams-Dean
1975 The Coprolites of Man. *Scientific American* 232:100–109.

Buettner-Janusch, J.
1954 Use of Infrared Photography in Archaeological Field Work. *American Antiquity* 20: 84–87.

Buikstra, J. E.
1976 *Hopewell in the Lower Illinois River Valley: A Regional Approach to the Study of Biological Variability and Mortuary Activity.* Scientific Papers Number 2. Northwestern University Archaeological Program, Evanston, Illinois.
1981 The Koster Site: Mortuary Practices, Paleodemography, and Paleopathology. A Case Study from Illinois. In *The Archaeology of Death,* edited by R. Chapman, I. Kinnes, and K. Randsborg, pp. 123–132. Cambridge University Press, London and New York.

Buikstra, J. E., and D. C. Cook
1981 Pre-Columbian Tuberculosis in West-Central Illinois: Prehistoric Disease in Biocultural Perspective. In *Prehistoric Tuberculosis in the Americas,* edited by J. E. Buikstra, pp. 115–139. Northwestern University Archaeological Program, Evanston, Illinois.

Buikstra, J. E., S. Frankenberg, J. B. Lambert, and L. Hue
1989 Multiple Elements: Multiple Expectations. In *The Chemistry of Prehistoric Human Bone,* edited by T. D. Price, pp. 155–210. Cambridge University Press, Cambridge.

Buikstra, J. E., and C. C. Gordon
1981 The Study and Restudy of Human Skeletal Series: The Importance of Long-Term Curation. In *The Research Potential of Anthropological Museum Collections,* edited by A. Cantwell, J. B. Griffin, and N. A. Rothchild, pp. 449–465. Annals of the New York Academy of Sciences 376.

Buikstra, J. E., and L. W. Konigsberg
1985 Paleodemography: Critiques and Controversies. *American Anthropologist* 87:316–333.

Buikstra, J. E., L. W. Konigsberg, and J. Bullington
1986 Fertility and the Development of Agriculture in the Prehistoric Midwest. *American Antiquity* 51:528–546.

Buikstra, J. E., and J. H. Mielke
1985 Demography, Diet, and Health. In *The Analysis of Prehistoric Diets,* edited by R. I. Gilbert and J. H. Mielke, pp. 359–422. Academic Press, Orlando.

Buikstra, J. E., and M. Swegle
1989 Bone Modification Due to Burning: Experimental Evidence. In *Bone Modification,* edited by R. Bonnichsen and M. H. Sorg, pp. 247–258. Center for the Study of First Americans, University of Maine, Orono.

Buikstra, J. E., and D. H. Ubelaker (editors)
1994 *Standardized Osteological Database.* Research Series 44. Arkansas Archeological Survey, Fayette-ville.

Buikstra, J. E., and D. H. Ubelaker
1994 *Standards for Data Collection from Human Skeletal Remains.* Arkansas Archeological Survey Research Series No. 44. Arkansas Archeological Survey, Fayetteville.

Bull, W. B.
1991 *Geomorphic Responses to Climatic Change.* Oxford University Press, New York.

Burger, P., and D. Gillies
1989 *Interactive Computer Graphics.* Addison-Wesley Publishing, Reading, Massachusetts.

Burger, R. L., and N. J. van der Merwe
1990 Maize and the Origin of Highland Chavin Civilization: An Isotopic Perspective. *American Anthropologist* 92:85–95.

Burkitt, M. C.
1956 *The Old Stone Age.* Bowes & Bowes, London.

Burlatskaya, S. P., and S. I. Braginsky
1978 The Comparison of Archaeomagnetic Data with the Analytical Representation of the Geomagnetic Field for the Last 2000 Years. *Archaeometry* 20:71–81.

Burnside, C. D.
1985 *Mapping from Aerial Photographs.* Wiley, New York.

Burrough, P. A.
1986 *Principles of Geographic Information Systems for Land Resources Assessment.* Clarendon Press, Oxford.

Butler, V. L., and R. L. Lyman
1996 Taxonomic Identifications and Faunal Summaries: What Should We Be Including in Our Faunal Reports? *Society for American Archaeology Bulletin* 14(1):22.

Butzer, K. W.
1982 *Archaeology as Human Ecology.* Cambridge University Press, Cambridge.

Butzer, K. W., and C. L. Hansen
1968 *Desert and River in Nubia: Geomorphology and Prehistoric Environments at the Aswan Reservoir.* University of Wisconsin Press, Madison.

C&EN
1984 Formation of Fossilized Fabrics Focus of Textiles Research Project. *C&EN,* 10 September: 28–30.

Cadien, J. D., E. F. Harris, W. P. Jones, and L. J. Mandarino
1974 Biological Lineages, Skeletal Populations, and Microevolution. *Yearbook of Physical Anthropology* 18:194–201.

Calamia, M. A.
1986   *Geographic Information System Applications for Cultural Resource Management.* Bureau of Land Management, Denver.

California Department of Transportation
1984   *Code of Safe Surveying Practices.* State of California, Department of Transportation, Sacramento.

Callen, E. O.
1963   Diet as Revealed by Coprolites. In *Science in Archaeology,* edited by D. Brothwell and E. Higgs, pp. 184–194. Praeger, New York.
1967   The First New World Cereal. *American Antiquity* 32:535–538.

Callen, E. O., and T. W. M. Cameron
1960   A Prehistoric Diet Revealed in Coprolites. *New Scientist* 8:35–40.

Calogero, B.
1991   *Macroscopic and Petrographic Identification of the Rock Types Used for Stone Tools in Central Connecticut.* Ph.D. dissertation, University of Connecticut, Storrs. University Microfilms, Ann Arbor.

Camilli, E. L., and L. S. Cordell
1983   *Remote Sensing: Applications to Cultural Resources in Southwestern North America.* Cultural Resources Management Division, National Park Service, U.S. Department of the Interior, Washington, D.C.

Campana, D. V.
1989   *Natufian and Protoneolithic Bone Tools: The Manufacture and Use of Bone Implements in the Zagros and the Levant.* BAR International Series 494. British Archaeological Reports, Oxford.

Campana, D. V., and P. J. Crabtree
1987   Animals—A C Language Computer Program for the Analysis of Faunal Remains and Its Use in the Study of Early Iron Age Fauna from Dun Ailinne. *ArchaeoZoologia* 1(1):57–68.

Campbell, E. W., W. H. Campbell, E. Antevs, C. A. Amsden, J. A. Barbieri, and F. D. Bode
1937   *The Archaeology of Pleistocene Lake Mohave: A Symposium.* Papers 11. Southwest Museum, Los Angeles.

Campbell, J.
1991   *Introductory Cartography.* 2nd ed. W. C. Brown, Dubuque, Iowa.

Campbell, T. N.
1949   The Pioneer Tree-Ring Work of Jacob Kuechler. *Tree-Ring Bulletin* 15(3).

Cannon, D. Y.
1987   *Marine Fish Osteology: A Manual for Archaeologists.* Archaeology Press, Simon Fraser University, Burnaby, British Columbia.

Carbone, V. A.
1977   Phytoliths as Paleoecological Indicators. *Annals of the New York Academy of Science* 288:194–205.

Carlson, D. L.
1988   *Rangia cuneata* as a Seasonal Indicator for Coastal Archaeological Sites in Texas. *Bulletin of the Texas Archeological Society* 58:201–214.

Carlson, D. L., S. B. Carlson, F. L. Briuer, E. Romer, Jr., and W. E. Moore
1986   *Archaeological Survey at Fort Hood, Texas, Fiscal Year 1983: The Eastern Training Area.* Research Report 11. Archaeological Resource Management Series, U.S. Army Fort Hood, Fort Hood, Texas.

Carmichael, D. L.
1990   GIS Predictive Modelling of Prehistoric Site Distributions in Central Montana. In *Interpreting Space: GIS and Archaeology,* edited by K. M. S. Allen, S. W. Green, and E. B. W. Zubrow, pp. 216–225. Taylor & Francis, London.

Carnett, C.
1991   *Legal Background of Archeological Resources Protection.* Archeological Assistance Division Technical Brief 11. U.S. Department of the Interior, National Park Service, Washington, D.C.

Carnot, M. A.
1892   Recherche du fluor dans les os modernes et les os fossiles. *Comptes Rendus de l'Academy des Sciences* 114:1189–1192. Paris.
1893   Recherches sur la composition generale et la teneur en flour des os modernes et des os fossiles des differents ages. *Ann. Mines 3, Series 9, Memoir*:115–195. Paris.

Carr, C. C.
1982   *Handbook on Soil Resistivity Surveying: Interpretation of Data from Earthen Archaeological Sites.* Center for American Archaeology Press, Evanston, Illinois.

Carr, R. F., and J. E. Hazard
1961   *Map of the Ruins of Tikal, El Peten, Guatemala.* Museum Monographs, Tikal Reports 11. University of Pennsylvania Museum, Philadelphia.

Casjens, L., R. Barber, G. Bawden, M. Roberts, and F. Turchon
1980   Approaches to Site Discovery in New England Forests. In *Discovering and Examining Archaeological Sites: Strategies for Areas with Dense Ground Cover,* edited by F. McManamon and D. Ives. American Archaeological Reports 14. University of Missouri, Columbia.

Casteel, R. W.
1972   Some Biases in the Recovery of Archaeological Faunal Remains. *Proceedings of the Prehistoric Society* 38:328–388.
1976   *Fish Remains in Archaeology and Paleoenvironmental Studies.* Academic Press, New York.
1977   Characterization of Faunal Assemblages and the Minimum Number of Individuals Determined from Paired Elements: Continuing Problems in Archaeology. *Journal of Archaeological Science* 4:125–134.

Casteel, R. W., and D. K. Grayson
1977   Terminological Problems in Quantitative Faunal Analysis. *World Archaeology* 9:235–242.

Catling, D., and J. Grayson
1982   *Identification of Vegetable Fibers.* Chapman & Hall, London.

Cazier, L.
1993   *Surveys and Surveyors of the Public Domain, 1785–1975.* Bureau of Land Management, U.S. Department of the Interior, Washington, D.C.

Chadderdon, M. F.
1983   *Baker Cave, Val Verde County, Texas: The 1976 Excavations.* Special Report 13. Center for Archaeological Research, University of Texas at San Antonio.

Champe, J. L.
1946   *Ash Hollow Cave.* Studies, n.s. 1. University of Nebraska, Lincoln.

Chang, C., and H. A. Koster
1986   Beyond Bones: Toward an Archaeology of Pastoralism. In *Advances in Archaeological Method and Theory,* vol. 9, edited by M. B. Schiffer, pp. 97–148. Academic Press, New York.

Chaplin, R. E.
1971   *The Study of Animal Bones from Archaeological Sites.* Seminar Press, New York.

Charles, T.
1995   38GR226: The Pumpkin Site, Greenville County, South Carolina. *Pastwatch* 4(3/4):8–9. Archeological Research Trust, University of South Carolina, Columbia.

Chartkoff, J. L.
1978   Transect Sampling in Forests. *American Antiquity* 43:46–52.

Chartkoff, J. L., and K. K. Chartkoff
1980   The Discovery of Archaeological Sites: A Review of Methods and Techniques. Unpublished manuscript prepared for the U.S. Forest Service.

Chartkoff, J. L., and Childress, J.
1966   *An Archaeological Survey of the Proposed Paskenta-Newville Reservoir in Glenn and Tehama Counties, Northern California.* R. E. Schenck Archives for California Archaeology 24. Society for California Archaeology, San Francisco.

Chenhall, R. G.
1975   Rationale for Archaeological Sampling. In *Sampling in Archaeology,* edited by J. W. Mueller, pp. 3–25. University of Arizona Press, Tucson.

Cheverud, J. M.
1988   A Comparison of Genetic and Phenotypic Correlations. *Evolution* 42:958–968.

Chew, R. M.
1978   The Size Effect: An Explanation of Variability in Surface Artifact Assemblage Content. *American Antiquity* 43:288–293.

Ciolek-Torrello, R., S. D. Shelley, J. J. Altschul, and J. Welch
1990   *Research Design. Roosevelt Rural Sites Study,* vol. 1. Statistical Research Technical Series 28. Statistical Research, Inc., Tucson.

Claassen, C.
1986   Shellfishing Seasons in the Prehistoric Southeastern United States. *American Antiquity* 51:21–37.

Clark, A.
1970   Resistivity Surveying. In *Science in Archaeology,* edited by D. Brothwell and E. Higgs, pp. 695–707. Praeger, New York.

Clark, D. E., and B. A. Purdy
1979   Electron Microprobe Analysis of Weathered Florida Chert. *American Antiquity* 44:517–524.

Clark, D. L.
1961   The Obsidian Dating Method. *Current Anthropology* 2:11–114.
1968   *Analytical Archaeology.* Methuen, London.

Clark, G.
1954   *Excavations at Starr Carr.* Cambridge University Press, Cambridge.

Clark, G., N. R. Hall, G. J. Armelagos, G. A. Borkan, M. M. Panjabi, and F. T. Wetzel
1986   Poor Growth Prior to Early Childhood: Decreased Health and Life-Span in the Adult. *American Journal of Physical Anthropology* 70:145–160.

Clark, G. D.
1974   Prehistoric Europe: The Economic Basis. In *Archaeological Researches in Retrospect,* edited by G. R. Willey, pp. 33–57. Winthrop, Cambridge, Massachusetts.

Clark, J., and K. K. Kietzke
1967   Paleoecology of the Lower Nodular Zone, Brule Formation, in the Big Badlands of South Dakota. *Fieldiana: Geology Memoirs* 5:111–137.

Clark, J. C., Jr.
1974   Rock Art of the Guadalupe Mountains National Park Area. *Bulletin of the Texas Archeological Society* 45:97–120.

Clark, J. G. D.
1947   *Archaeology and Society.* Methuen, London.

Clason, A. T.
1972   Some Comments on the Use and Presentation of Archaeozoological Data. *Helinium* 12:139–153.

Clason, A. T. (editor)
1975   *Archaeozoological Studies.* American Elsevier, New York.

Clason, A. T., and W. Prummel
1977   Collecting, Sieving and Archaeozoological Research. *Journal of Archaeological Science* 4:171–175.

Clausen, C. J., A. D. Cohen, C. Emiliani, J. A. Holman, and J. J. Stipp
1979   Little Salt Spring, Florida: A Unique Underwater Site. *Science* 203:609–614.

Clegg, J.
1983   Recording Prehistoric Art. In *Australian Field Archaeology: A Guide to Techniques*, edited by G. Connah, pp. 87–125. Australian Institute of Aboriginal Studies, Canberra.

Clifton, J. R.
1980   *Stone Consolidating Materials: A Status Report.* NBS Technical Note 1118. National Bureau of Standards, Washington, D.C.

CLIMAP Project Members
1981   *Seasonal Reconstructions of the Earth's Surface at the Last Glacial Maximum.* Chart Series 36. Geological Society of America.

Clutton-Brock, J.
1978   Bones for the Zoologist. In *Approaches to Faunal Analysis in the Middle East*, edited by R. H. Meadow and M. A. Zeder, pp. 49–51. Bulletin 2. Peabody Museum of Archaeology and Ethnology, Harvard University, Cambridge.
1981   *Domesticated Animals from Early Times.* University of Texas Press, Austin.

CNS
1984   *SPOT Satellite-Based Remote Sensing System.* Toulouse, France.

Coale, A., and P. Demeny
1966   *Regional Model Life Tables and Stable Populations.* Princeton University Press, Princeton, New Jersey.

Cochran, W. G.
1963   *Sampling Techniques.* 2nd ed. Wiley, New York.

Cockburn, A., and E. Cockburn (editors)
1980   *Mummies, Disease, and Ancient Cultures.* Cambridge University Press, Cambridge.

Coe, W. R.
1959   *Piedras Negras Archaeology: Artifacts, Caches, and Burial.* Museum Monographs. University of Pennsylvania, Philadelphia.
1962   A Summary of Excavation and Research at Tikal, Guatemala: 1956–61. *American Antiquity* 27:479–507.

Coe, W. R., and J. J. McGinn
1963   Tikal: The North Acropolis and an Early Tomb. *Expedition* 5(2):24–32.

Cohen, M. N., and G. J. Armelagos
1984   *Paleopathology at the Origins of Agriculture.* Academic Press, Orlando.

Cohen, M. R., and I. E. Drabkin
1958   *A Source Book in Greek Science.* Harvard University Press, Cambridge.

Cole, F. C.
1951   *Kincaid, A Prehistoric Illinois Metropolis.* University of Chicago Press, Chicago.

Cole, W. P.
1977   *Using the UTM Grid System to Record Historic Sites.* National Register Bulletin 28. U.S. Department of the Interior, Washington, D.C.

Coles, J. M.
1973   *Archaeology by Experiment.* Scribner's, New York.

Collier, D., A. E. Hudson, and A. Ford
1942   *Archaeology of the Upper Columbia Region.* Publications in Anthropology 9. University of Washington, Seattle.

Collins, M. B.
1969   *Test Excavations at Amistad International Reservoir, Fall, 1967.* Papers 16. Texas Archeological Salvage Project, University of Texas at Austin.

Collins, M. B., B. Ellis, and C. Dodt-Ellis
1990   *Excavations at the Camp Pearl Wheat Site (41KR243), An Early Archaic Campsite on Town Creek, Kerr County, Texas.* Studies in Archeology 6. Texas Archeological Research Laboratory, University of Texas at Austin.

Collins, M. B., T. R. Hester, and F. A. Weir
1969   The Floyd Morris Site (41CF2): A Prehistoric Cemetery Site in Cameron County, Texas. *Bulletin of the Texas Archeological Society* 40:119–146.

Colton, H. S.
1946   *The Sinagua: A Summary of the Archaeology of the Region of Flagstaff, Arizona.* Northern Arizona Society of Science and Art, Flagstaff.

Colwell, R. N. (editor)
1983   *Manual of Remote Sensing.* 2nd ed. Society of Photogrammetry, Falls Church, Virginia.

Comuzzie, A. G., and D. G. Steele
1989   Hypercementosis and Dental Attrition in Populations Along the Texas Coast. *American Journal of Physical Anthropology* 78:9–16.

Condon, K. W., and K. C. Egan
1984   The Use of Power Equipment on Moderately Wooded Sites. *Journal of Field Archaeology* 11: 99–101.

Conkey, M. W., and J. M. Gero
1991   Tensions, Pluralities, and Engendering Archaeology: An Introduction to Women in Prehistory. In *Engendering Archaeology: Women in Prehistory*, edited by J. M. Gero and M. W. Conkey, pp. 3–30. Basil Blackwell, Oxford.

Connah, G.
1991   The Salt of Bunyoro: Seeking the Origins of an African Kingdom. *Antiquity* 65(248):479–494.

Connah, G. (editor)
1983   *Australian Field Archaeology: A Guide to Techniques.* Australian Institute of Aboriginal Studies, Canberra.

Connah, G., and A. Jones
1983   Photographing Australian Prehistoric Sites from the Air. In *Australian Field Archaeology: A Guide to Techniques*, edited by G. Connah, pp. 73–81. Australian Institute of Aboriginal Studies, Canberra.

Conner, M. D.
1990   Population Structure and Skeletal Variation in the Late Woodland of West-Central Illinois. *American Journal of Physical Anthropology* 82:31–43.

Constantine, D. G.
1988   Health Precautions for Bat Researchers. In *Ecological and Behavioral Methods for the Study of Bats,* edited by T. H. Kunz. Smithsonian Institution Press, Washington, D. C.

Cook, D. C., and J. E. Buikstra
1979   Health and Differential Survival in Prehistoric Populations: Prenatal Defects. *American Journal of Physical Anthropology* 51:649–664.

Cook, S. F.
1946   A Reconsideration of Shell Mounds with Respect to Population and Nutrition. *American Antiquity* 12:51–53.
1951   The Present Status of Chemical Methods for Dating Prehistoric Bone. *American Antiquity* 18:354–358.
1960   Dating Prehistoric Bone by Chemical Analysis. *Viking Fund Publications in Anthropology* 28:223–245.

Cook, S. F., S. T. Brooks, and H. C. Ezra
1961   The Process of Fossilization. *Southwestern Journal of Anthropology* 17:355–364.

Cook, S. F., and R. F. Heizer
1947   The Quantitative Investigation of Aboriginal Sites: Analyses of Human Bone. *American Journal of Physical Anthropology,* n.s. 5:201–220.
1951   *The Physical Analysis of Nine Indian Mounds of the Lower Sacramento Valley.* Publications in American Archaeology and Ethnology 40:281–312. University of California, Berkeley.
1953a   Archaeological Dating by Chemical Analysis of Bone. *Southwestern Journal of Anthropology* 9:213–238.
1953b   The Present Status of Chemical Methods for Dating Prehistoric Bone. *American Antiquity* 18:354–358.
1965   *Studies on the Chemical Analysis of Archaeological Sites.* Publications in Anthropology 2:1–102. University of California, Berkeley.

Coon, C. S.
1951   *Cave Explorations in Iran, 1949.* Museum Monographs. University of Pennsylvania, Philadelphia.
1971   *The Hunting Peoples.* Little, Brown, Boston.

Cope, E. D.
1875   On an Indian Kitchen Midden. *Proceedings of the Academy of Natural Sciences* 17:255. Philadelphia.

Cordell, L. S., and V. J. Yannie
1991   Ethnicity, Ethnogenesis, and the Individual: A Processual Approach Toward Dialogue. In *Processual and Postprocessual Archaeologies: Multiple Ways of Knowing the Past,* edited by R. W. Preucel, pp.

96–107. Occasional Paper 10. Center for Archaeological Investigations, Southern Illinois University, Carbondale.

Cornwall, I. W.
1956   *Bones for the Archaeologist.* Phoenix House, London.

Corruccini, R. S.
1973   Size and Shape in Similarity Coefficients Based on Metric Characters. *American Journal of Physical Anthropology* 38:743–753.

Corruccini, R. S., E. M. Brandon, and J. S. Handler
1989   Inferring Fertility from Relative Mortality in Historically Controlled Cemetery Remains from Barbados. *American Antiquity* 54:609–614.

Cosgrove, H. S., and C. B. Cosgrove
1932   *The Swarts Ruin: A Typical Mimbres Site in Southwestern New Mexico.* Papers of the Peabody Museum of Archeology and Ethnology vol. 15, No. 1. Harvard University, Cambridge.

Cotter, J. L.
1968   *Handbook for Historical Archaeology.* Privately printed, Wynecote, Pennsylvania.

Council, R. B., N. Honerkamp, and M. E. Will
1991   *Industry and Technology in Antebellum Tennessee.* University of Tennessee Press, Knoxville.

Courtemanche, M., and V. Legendre
1985   *Os de poissons: Nomenclature codifiée noms français et anglais.* Osteotheque de Montreal, Montreal, Quebec.

Courty, M-A., P. Goldberg, and R. Macphail
1989   *Soils and Micromorphology in Archaeology.* Cambridge University Press, Cambridge.

Cowgill, G. L.
1975   A Selection of Samplers: Comments on Archaeo-statistics. In *Sampling in Archaeology,* edited by James W. Mueller, pp. 258–274. University of Arizona Press, Tucson.

Coy, J.
1978   Comparative Collections for Zooarchaeology. In *Research Problems in Zooarchaeology,* edited by D. R. Brothwell, K. D. Thomas, and J. Clutton-Brock, pp. 143–145. Occasional Paper 3. Institute of Archaeology, London.

Crabb, E. D.
1931   *Principles of Functional Anatomy of the Rabbit.* Maple Press, York, Pennsylvania.

Crabtree, P. J.
1985   Historic Zooarchaeology: Some Methodological Considerations. *Historical Archaeology* 19:76–78.
1990   Zooarchaeology and Complex Societies: Some Uses of Faunal Analysis for the Study of Trade, Social Status, and Ethnicity. In *Advances in Archaeological Method and Theory,* vol. 2, edited by M. B. Schiffer, pp. 155–205. University of Arizona Press, Tucson.

Crabtree, P. J., D. V. Campana, and K. Ryan (editors)
1989   *Early Animal Domestication and Its Cultural Context: Papers in Memory of Dexter Perkins, Jr., and Patricia Daly.* MASCA Research Papers in Science and Archaeology, Special Supplement to Volume 6. University Museum of Archaeology and Anthropology, University of Pennsylvania, Philadelphia.

Cracknell, A., and L. Hayes
1991   *Introduction to Remote Sensing.* Taylor & Francis, New York.

Crader, D. C.
1990   Slave Diet at Monticello. *American Antiquity* 55:690–717.

Creel, D. C.
1989   A Primary Cremation at the NAN Ranch Ruin, with Comparative Data on Other Cremations in the Mimbres Valley, New Mexico. *Journal of Field Archaeology* 16:309–329.
1991   Bison Hides in Late Prehistoric Exchange in the Southern Plains. *American Antiquity* 56:40–49.

Creer, K. M., and J. S. Kopper
1974   Paleomagnetic Dating of Cave Paintings in Tito Bustillo Cave, Asturias, Spain. *Science* 186: 348–350.

Cressman, L. S.
1942   *Archaeological Researches in the Northern Great Basin.* Publication 538. Carnegie Institute of Washington, Washington, D.C.

Cressman, L. S., H. Williams, and A. D. Krieger
1940   *Early Man in Oregon.* Studies in Anthropology 3. University of Oregon Monographs, Eugene.

Croes, D. R., and E. Blinman (editors)
1980   *Hoko River: A 2500 Year Old Fishing Camp on the Northwest Coast of North America.* Reports of Investigations 58. Laboratory of Anthropology, Washington State University, Pullman.

Cross, J. M., C. Hett, and M. Bertulli
1989   *Conservation Manual for Northern Archaeologists.* Archaeology Report 6. Prince of Wales Northern Heritage Center, Yellowknife, Canada.

Crowfoot, J. W.
1935   *Report on the 1935 Samaria Excavations.* Quarterly Statement for 1935. Palestine Exploration Fund, London.

Crowther, L. R.
1994   *Rapid Static Surveying Using the Global Positioning System.* Transportation Research Board, National Research Council, Washington, D.C.

Crumley, C. L., W. H. Marquardt, and T. L. Leatherman
1987   Certain Factors Influencing the Later Iron Age and Gallo-Roman Periods: The Analysis of Intensive Survey Data. In *Regional Dynamics: Burgundian Landscapes in Historical Perspective,* edited by C. L. Crumley and W. H. Marquardt, pp. 121–172. Academic Press, San Diego.

Cully, A. C.
1979   Some Aspects of Pollen Analysis in Relation to Archaeology. *The Kiva* 44:95–100.

Curran, P. J.
1987   *Principles of Remote Sensing.* Longman Group, Essex.

Curwen, E. C.
1940   The White Patination of Black Flint. *Antiquity* 14:435–437.

Cuvigny, H.
1985   *L'arpentage par Especes Dans l'Egypte Ptolemaique d'apres les Papyrus Grecs.* Papyrologica Bruxellensia 20. Fondation Egyptologique Reine Elisabeth, Bruxelles.

Dafoe, T.
1969   Artifact Photography. Archaeological Society of Alberta, *Newsletter* 19:1–17.

Dailey, R. C., and D. Morse
1983   Identification of the Victim. In *Handbook of Forensic Archaeology,* edited by D. Morse, J. Duncan, and J. Stoutmire, pp. 87–123. Rose, Tallahassee, Florida.

Daly, P.
1969   Approaches to Faunal Analysis in Archaeology. *American Antiquity* 34:146–153.

Dancey, W. S.
1981   *Archaeological Field Methods: An Introduction.* Burgess, Minneapolis.

Dart, B. D.
1985   *Principles of Thematic Map Design.* Addison-Wesley, Reading, Massachusetts.

Daugherty, R. D.
1988   Problems and Responsibilities in the Excavation of Wet Sites. In *Wet Site Archaeology,* edited by B. A. Purdy, pp. 15–29. Telford Press, Caldwell, New Jersey.

David, A. R.
1985   The Manchester Mummy Project. *Archaeology* 36:40–47.

Davidson, D. A., and M. L. Shackley (editors)
1976   *Geoarchaeology: Earth Science and the Past.* Duckworth, London.

Davis, E. C.
1937   Tree Rings and the Mayan Calendar. *Science,* n.s., 86(10), Supplement (Nov. 26).

Davis, E. L.
1978   The Non-destructive Archaeologist: How to Collect without Collecting. *Pacific Coast Archaeological Society Quarterly* 14(1):43–55.

Davis, E. M.
1973   Variables Involved in the Use of Radiocarbon Dates. Unpaginated ditto manuscript distributed through University of Texas Radiocarbon Laboratory, Austin.

Davis, E. M., D. Srdoc, and S. Valastro, Jr.
1973   Radiocarbon Dates from Stobi: 1971 Season. *Studies in the Antiquity of Stobi* 23–36. Belgrade.

Davis, E. M., and A. B. Wesolowsky
 1975   The Izum: A Simple Water Separation Device. *Journal of Field Archaeology* 2:271–273.

Davis, F., J. E. Estes, and J. Star
 1991   *Initiative 12: Integration of Remote Sensing and Geographic Information Systems: Report of the Specialist Meeting*. National Center for Geographic Information and Analysis, University of California, Santa Barbara.

Davis, L. B., and B. O. K. Reeves (editors)
 1990   *Hunters of the Recent Past*. Unwin Hyman, London.

Davis, S. J. M.
 1981   The Effects of Temperature Change and Domestication on the Body Size of Late Pleistocene to Holocene Mammals of Israel. *Paleobiology* 7:101–114.
 1987   *The Archaeology of Animals*. Yale University Press, New Haven, Connecticut.

Dawson, M. R.
 1984   John Edward Guilday (1925–1982). In *Contributions in Quaternary Vertebrate Paleontology: A Volume in Memorial to John E. Guilday*, edited by H. H. Genoways and M. R. Dawson, pp. 3–13. Special Publication No. 8. Carnegie Museum of Natural History, Pittsburgh, Pennsylvania.

Deagan, K.
 1991   Historical Archaeology's Contribution to Our Understanding of Early America. In *Historical Archaeology in Global Perspective,* edited by L. Falk, pp. 97–112. Smithsonian Institution Press, Washington, D.C.

Dean, G.
 1993   *In Search of the Rare: Pollen Evidence of Prehistoric Agriculture*. Paper presented at Southwestern Agricultural Symposium, New Mexico Archeological Council Meetings, October 2–4, 1992, Santa Fe.

Dean, M., B. Ferrari, I. Oxley, M. Redknap, and K. Watson (editors)
 1992   *Archaeology Underwater: The NAS Guide to Principles and Practice*. Nautical Archaeology Society. Dorset Press, Dorchester, England.

Debenham, N.
 1994   A Guide to TL Dating Flint Assemblages. In *Stories in Stone,* edited by N. Ashton and A. David, pp. 4–6. Occasional Paper 4. Lithic Studies Society, British Museum, London.

DeBruin, R.
 1970   *100 Topographic Maps Illustrating Physiographic Features*. Hubbard Press, Northbrook, Illinois.

Deetz, J. F.
 1967   *Invitation to Archaeology*. Natural History Press, Garden City, New York.
 1968   Hunters in Archaeological Perspective. In *Man the Hunter,* edited by R. B. Lee and I. DeVore, pp. 281–285. Aldine, Chicago.

 1977   *In Small Things Forgotten: The Archaeology of Early American Life*. Doubleday, New York.
 1991   Introduction: Archaeological Evidence of Sixteenth and Seventeenth Century Encounters. In *Historical Archaeology in Global Perspective*, edited by L. Falk, pp. 1–9. Smithsonian Institution Press, Washington, D.C.

Deetz, J., and E. Dethlefsen
 1965   The Doppler Effect and Archaeology: A Consideration of the Spatial Aspects of Seriation. *Southwestern Journal of Anthropology* 21(3):196–206.

Deevey, E. S.
 1948   On the Date of the Last Rise of Sea Level in Southern New England, with Remarks on the Grassy Island Site. *American Journal of Science* 246:329–352.

Del Bene, T. A.
 1979   Once Upon a Striation: Current Models of Striation and Polish Formation. In *Lithic Use-wear Analysis,* edited by B. Hayden, pp. 167–178. Academic Press, New York.

Deloria, V., Jr.
 1992   Indians, Archaeologists, and the Future. *American Antiquity* 57:595–598.

DeMarcay, G. B., and D. G. Steele
 1986   The Value of Fine Screening on Inland-Based Hunter-Gatherer Habitation Sites. In *Archaeological Investigations at 41LK201, Choke Canyon Reservoir, Southern Texas,* by C. L. Highley, pp. 250–264. Choke Canyon Series vol. 11. Center for Archaeological Research, University of Texas at San Antonio.

DeNiro, M. J., and S. Epstein
 1978   Influence of Diet on the Distribution of Carbon Isotopes in Animals. *Geochimica et Cosmochimica Acta* 42:495–506.

Dent, B. D.
 1993   *Cartography: Thematic Map Design*. 3rd ed. W. C. Brown, Dubuque, Iowa.

DePratter, C. B., and J. D. Howard
 1977   History of Shoreline Changes Determined by Archaeological Dating: Georgia Coast, U.S.A. *Technical Papers and Abstracts, Gulf Coast Association of Geological Sciences* 27:252–258.

Dering, J. P.
 1979   *Pollen and Plant Macrofossil Vegetation Record Recovered from Hinds Cave, Val Verde County, Texas*. Anthropology Research Laboratory, Texas A&M University, College Station.

Dering, J. P., and H. J. Shafer
 1976   Analysis of Matrix Samples from a Crockett County Shelter: A Test of Seasonality. *Bulletin of the Texas Archeological Society* 47:209–229.

Derry, A., H. W. Jandl, C. D. Shull, and I. Thorman (revised by P. C. Parker)

1985   *Guidelines for Local Surveys: A Basis for Preservation Planning.* National Register Bulletin 24. U.S. Department of the Interior, Washington, D.C.

Dever, W. G., and H. D. Lance (editors)
1978   *A Manual of Field Excavation: Handbook for Field Archaeologists.* Hebrew Union College and Jewish Institute of Religion, Cincinnati and Jerusalem.

Dewar, R. E., and K. A. McBride
1992   Remnant Settlement Patterns. In *Space, Time, and Archaeological Landscapes,* edited by J. Rossignol and L. Wandsnider, pp. 227–255. Plenum, New York.

De Wet, E., P. Robertson, and I. Plug
1990   Some Techniques for Cleaning and Degreasing Bones and a Method for Evaluating the Long-term Effects of These Techniques. In *Natural History Collections: Their Management and Value,* edited by E. M. Herholdt, pp. 37–41. Special Publication 1. Transvaal Museum, Pretoria.

Diamant, S.
1979   Archaeological Sieving at Franchthi Cave. *Journal of Field Archaeology* 6:203–219.

Dibble, D. S., and D. Lorrain
1968   *Bonfire Shelter: A Stratified Bison Kill Site, Val Verde County, Texas.* Miscellaneous Papers 1. Texas Memorial Museum, University of Texas at Austin.

Dickel, D. N., and G. H. Doran
1989   Severe Neural-Tube Defect Syndrome from the Early Archaic of Florida. *American Journal of Physical Anthropology* 80:325–334.

Dilke, O. A. W.
1971   *The Roman Land Surveyors: An Introduction to the Agrimensores.* Newton Abbot, David and Charles, London.

Dillehay, T. D.
1974   Late Quaternary Bison Population Changes on the Southern Plains. *Plains Anthropologist* 19:180–196.

Dillon, B. D.
1982   The Archaeological Field Vehicle. In *Practical Archaeology,* edited by B. D. Dillon, pp. 59–89. Archaeological Research Tools 2. Institute of Archaeology, University of California, Los Angeles.

Dillon, B. D. (editor)
1985   *A Student's Guide to Archaeological Illustrating.* Archaeological Research Tools 1. Institute of Archaeology, University of California, Los Angeles.
1989   *Practical Archaeology. Field and Laboratory Techniques and Archaeological Logistics.* Archaeological Research Tools 2. Institute of Archaeology, University of California, Los Angeles.

Dimbleby, G. W.
1985   *The Palynology of Archaeological Sites.* Academic Press, New York.

Dincauze, D.
1968   *Cremation Cemeteries in Eastern Massachusetts.* Papers of the Peabody Museum of Archaeology and Ethnology vol. 59, No. 1. Harvard University, Cambridge.
1976   *The Neville Site: 8000 Years at Amoskeag, Manchester, New Hampshire.* Monographs 4. Peabody Museum of Archaeology and Ethnology, Harvard University, Cambridge.
1978   Surveying for Cultural Resources: Don't Rush Out with a Shovel. In *Conservation Archaeology in the Northeast: Toward a Research Orientation,* edited by A. Speiss, pp. 51–59. Bulletin 3. Peabody Museum of Archaeology and Ethnology, Harvard University, Cambridge.

Dirrigl, F. J., Jr.
1989   Collection Management and Animal Preparation Standards for Vertebrate Collections. *Journal of Middle Atlantic Archaeology* 5:1–28.

Dixon, R. B.
1905   The Northern Maidu. *Bulletin of the American Museum of Natural History* 17:119–346. New York.

Dockall, H. D.
1995   Application of Bement's Spray Sealant Technique to Infant Skeletal Remains. *Journal of Field Archaeology* 22(3):385–387.

Dockall, H. D., J. F. Powell, and D. G. Steele (editors)
1996   *Home Hereafter: Archaeological and Bioarchaeological Investigations at an Historic African-American Cemetery.* Center for Environmental Archaeology, Texas A&M University, College Station.

Dodge, D.
1968   Laboratory Artifact Photography. *Archaeology in Montana* 9(1):17–23.

Dolzani, M.
1987   Blood from a Stone. *Mammoth Trumpet* 3(4):1, 3, 8.

Donahue, J., and J. M. Adovasio
1990   Evolution of Sandstone Rockshelters in Eastern North America, A Geoarchaeological Perspective. In *Archaeological Geology of North America,* edited by N. P. Lasca and J. Donahue, pp. 231–251. Centennial Volume 4. Geological Society of America, Boulder, Colorado.

Donnan, S. G.
1987   Field Conservation of Archaeological Textiles: A Case Study from Pacatnamu, Peru. In *In Situ Archaeological Conservation,* edited by H. W. M. Hodges, pp. 72–77. Getty Conservation Institute, Los Angeles.

Donoghue, D., and I. Shennan
1988   The Application of Remote Sensing in Environmental Archaeology. *Geoarchaeology* 3:275–286.

Doran, G. H.
1975   *Long Bones of Texas Indians.* Unpublished Master's thesis, Department of Anthropology, University of Texas at Austin.

Doran, G. H., and D. N. Dickel
  1988   Multidisciplinary Investigations at the Windover Site. In *Wet Site Archaeology*, edited by B. A. Purdy, pp. 263–289. Telford Press, Caldwell, New Jersey.

Doran, G. H., D. N. Dickel, W. E. Ballinger, Jr., G. F. Agee, P. J. Laipis, and W. W. Hauswirth
  1986   Anatomical, Cellular, and Molecular Analysis of 8,000 Year Old Human Brain Tissue from the Windover Archaeological Site. *Nature* 323: 803–806.

Dorn, R. I.
  1983   Cation-ratio Dating: A New Rock Varnish Age Determination Technique. *Quaternary Research* 20:49–73.
  1988   A Rock Varnish Interpretation of Alluvial-Fan Development in Death Valley, California. *National Geographic Research* 4:56–73.
  1991   Rock Varnish. *American Scientist* 79(6):542–553.

Dorrell, P. G.
  1994   *Photography in Archaeology and Conservation*. 2nd ed. Cambridge University Press, New York.

Douglass, A. E.
  1929   The Secret of the Southwest Solved by Talkative Tree Rings. *National Geographic* 56(Dec.): 737–770.

Dowman, E.
  1970   *Conservation in Field Archaeology*. Methuen, London.

Drager, D. L., and A. K. Ireland (editors)
  1986   *The Seedskadee Project: Remote Sensing in Non-Site Archeology*. Branch of Remote Sensing, Division of Cultural Research, Southwest Cultural Resources Center, Southwest Region, National Park Service, U.S. Department of the Interior, Albuquerque, New Mexico.

Drager, D. L., T. R. Lyons, and J. Livingston
  1985   *Remote Sensing: Photogrammetry in Archaeology: The Chaco Mapping Project*. Branch of Remote Sensing, Cultural Resources Management, National Park Service, U.S. Department of the Interior, Albuquerque, New Mexico.

Drennan, R. D.
  1976   A Refinement of Chronological Seriation Using Nonmetric Multidimensional Scaling. *American Antiquity* 41:290–302.
  1979   How to Succeed in Seriation Without Really Trying. *American Antiquity* 44:171–172.

Driesch, A. von den
  1976   *A Guide to the Measurement of Animal Bones from Archaeological Sites*. Bulletin 1. Peabody Museum of Archaeology and Ethnology, Harvard University, Cambridge.

Driver, J. C.
  1982   Minimum Standards for Reporting of Animal Bones in Salvage Archaeology: Southern Alberta as a Case Study. In *Directions in Archaeology, a Question of Goals*, edited by P. D. Francis and E. C. Poplin, pp. 199–209. Proceedings of the 14th Annual Conference, Archaeological Association of the University of Calgary, Calgary, Alberta.
  1992   Identification, Classification and Zooarchaeology. *Circaea* 9(1)(for 1991):35–47.

Drowser, M. S.
  1985   *Flinders Petrie: A Life in Archaeology*. Gollancz, London.

Drucker, P., R. F. Heizer, and R. Squier
  1959   *Excavations at La Venta, Tabasco, 1955*. Bulletin 170. Bureau of American Ethnology, Washington, D.C.

Duffield, L. F.
  1970   Vertisols and Their Implications for Archaeological Research. *American Anthropologist* 72(5): 1055–1062.

Dunbar, J. S., S. D. Webb, M. Faught, R. J. Anuskiewicz, and M. J. Straight
  1989   Archaeological Sites in the Drowned Tertiary Karst Region of the Eastern Gulf of Mexico. In *Underwater Archaeological Proceedings from the Society for Historical Archaeology Conference*, edited by J. B. Arnold III, pp. 25–31. Society for Historical Archaeology, Baltimore.

Dunn, M. E.
  1983   Phytolith Analysis in Archaeology. *Midcontinental Journal of Archaeology* 8:287–297.

Dunnell, R. C.
  1970   Seriation Method and Its Evaluation. *American Antiquity* 35:305–319.
  1983   The Americanist Literature for 1983: A Year of Contrasts and Challenges. *American Journal of Archaeology* 88(4):489–513.
  1992   The Notion of Site. In *Space, Time, and Archaeological Landscapes*, edited by J. Rossignol and L. Wandsnider, pp. 21–41. Plenum, New York.

Dunnell, R. C., and W. S. Dancey
  1983   The Siteless Survey: A Regional-Scale Data Collection Strategy. *Advances in Archaeological Method and Theory* 6:276–287.

Dye, D. H., and K. H. Moore
  1978   Recovery Systems for Subsistence Data: Water Screening and Water Flotation. *Tennessee Anthropologist* 3:59–69.

Earle, T. K.
  1991   Toward a Behavioral Archaeology. In *Processual and Postprocessual Archaeologies: Multiple Ways of Knowing the Past*, edited by R. W. Preucel, pp. 83–94. Occasional Paper No. 10. Center for Archaeological Investigations, Southern Illinois University, Carbondale.

Eastman Kodak Company
  1972   *Ultraviolet and Fluorescence Photography*. Kodak Publication M-27. Rochester, New York.

1977   *Applied Infrared Photography.* Kodak Publication M-28. Rochester, New York.

Eaton, G. F.
1898   The Prehistoric Fauna of Block Island as Indicated by its Ancient Shell-Heaps. *American Journal of Science* 6:137–159.

Eaton, J. D.
1994   Archeological Investigations at the Main Datum Mound, Colha, Belize. In *Continuing Archeology at Colha, Belize,* edited by T. R. Hester, H. J. Shafer, and J. D. Eaton, pp. 99–108. Studies in Archeology 16. Texas Archeological Research Laboratory, University of Texas at Austin.

Ebert, J.
1992   *Distributional Archaeology.* University of New Mexico Press, Albuquerque.

Ebert, J. I.
1984   Remote Sensing Applications in Archaeology. In *Advances in Archaeological Method and Theory,* vol. 7, edited by M. B. Schiffer, pp. 293–362. Academic Press, New York.

Edwards, K. J.
1979   Palynological and Temporal Inference in the Context of Prehistory with Special Reference to the Evidence from Lake and Peat Deposits. *Journal of Archaeological Science* 6:255–270.

Efremov, J. A.
1940   Taphonomy: A New Branch of Paleontology. *Pan-American Geologist* 74:81–93.

Ehrenberg, R. E.
1987   *Scholars' Guide to Washington, D.C. for Cartography and Remote Sensing Imagery: Maps, Charts, Aerial Photographs, Satellite Images, Cartographic Literature, and Geographic Information Systems.* Smithsonian Institution Press, Washington, D.C.

Ehrich, R. W. (editor)
1965   *Chronologies of Old World Archaeology.* University of Chicago Press, Chicago.

Eidt, R. C.
1973   A Rapid Chemical Field Test for Archaeological Site Survey. *American Antiquity* 38:206–210.
1977   Detection and Examination of Anthrosols by Phosphate Analysis. *Science* 197:1327–1333.
1984   *Advances in Abandoned Settlement Analysis: Application to Prehistoric Anthrosols in Colombia, South America.* Center for Latin America, University of Wisconsin–Milwaukee.

Eighmy, J. L.
1980   *Archaeomagnetism: A Handbook for the Archeologist.* Interagency Archeological Services, National Park Service, Washington, D.C.

Eighmy, J. L., and J. B. Howard
1991   Direct Dating of Prehistoric Canal Sediments Using Archaeomagnetism. *American Antiquity* 56:88–102.

Eighmy, J. L., and P. Y. Klein
1990   *Archaeomagnetic Results from Archaeological Sediments in the Southwest.* Technical Series 1. Colorado State University Archaeometric Lab, Fort Collins.

Eighmy, J. L., and R. S. Sternberg (editors)
1991   *Archaeomagnetic Dating.* University of Arizona Press, Tucson.

Eisele, J.
1994   *Survival and Detection of Blood Residues on Stone Tools.* Technical Report 94–1. Department of Anthropology, University of Nevada, Reno.

Eisenberg, L. E.
1991   Interpreting Measures of Community Health During the Late Prehistoric Period in Middle Tennessee: A Biocultural Approach. In *Health in Past Societies: Biocultural Interpretations of Human Skeletal Remains in Archaeological Contexts,* edited by H. Bush and M. Zvelebil, pp. 115–127. BAR International Series 567. British Archaeological Reports, Oxford.

Elias, S. A.
1994   *Quaternary Insects and Their Environments.* Smithsonian Institution Press, Washington, D.C.

Ellis, L.
1982   *Laboratory Techniques in Archaeology: A Guide to the Literature.* Garland, New York.

El-Najjar, M. Y.
1976   Maize, Malaria, and the Anemias in the Pre-Columbian New World. *Yearbook of Physical Anthropology* 20:329–337.

El-Najjar, M. Y., and K. R. McWilliams
1978   *Forensic Anthropology.* Charles C. Thomas, Springfield, Illinois.

El-Najjar, M. Y., and T. M. Mulinski
1980   Mummies and Mummification Practices in the Southwestern and Southern United States. In *Mummies, Disease, and Ancient Cultures,* edited by A. Cockburn and E. Cockburn, pp. 103–117. Cambridge University Press, Cambridge.

Ember, L. R.
1988   Preserving the Past. *C&EN,* 14 November:10–19.

Emslie, S. D.
1984   Faunal Remains and Archeological Research Designs: A Need for Consistency. *American Archeology* 4:132–139.

Engel, C. G., and R. P. Sharp
1959   Chemical Data on Desert Varnish. *Bulletin of the Geological Society of America* 69:487–518.

Enriquez, C., J. Danon, and M. da C. M. C. Beltrao
1979   Differential Thermal Analysis of Some Amazonian Archaeological Pottery. *Archaeometry* 21:183–186.

Environmental Systems Research Institute (ESRI)
1986   *ARC/INFO Users Manual Version 3.2.* Environmental Systems Research Institute, Redlands, California.

1989a *ARC/INFO Maps 1989*. Environmental Systems Research Institute, Redlands, California.

1989b *ARC/INFO: The Geographic Information System Software*. Environmental Systems Research Institute, Redlands, California.

1990 *Understanding GIS: The ARC/INFO Method*. Environmental Systems Research Institute, Redlands, California.

Ericson, J. E.
1981 *Exchange and Production Systems in California Prehistory: The Results of Hydration Dating and Chemical Characterization of Obsidian Sources*. BAR Series 110. British Archaeological Reports, Oxford.

Erlandson, J. M.
1984 A Case Study in Faunalturbation: Delineating the Effects of the Burrowing Pocket Gopher on the Distribution of Archaeological Materials. *American Antiquity* 49:785–790.

Esarey, D., and T. R. Pauketat
1992 *The Lohmann Site: An Early Mississippian Center in the American Bottom (11-S-49)*. Illinois Department of Transportation and University of Illinois Press, Urbana.

Esarey, D., and S. K. Santure
1990 Archaeological Research at the Morton Site Complex. In *Archaeological Investigations at the Morton Village Site and Norris Farms 36 Cemetery*, edited by S. K. Santure, A. D. Harn, and D. Esarey, pp. 6–10. Reports of Investigations 45. Illinois State Museum, Springfield.

Esau, K.
1965 *Plant Anatomy*. Wiley, New York.

Ester, M.
1981 A Column-Wise Approach to Seriation. *American Antiquity* 46:496–512.

Estopinal, S. V.
1989 *A Guide to Understanding Land Surveys*. Professional Education Systems, Eau Claire, Wisconsin.

Evans, C., and B. Meggers
1959 *Archaeological Investigations at the Mouth of the Amazon*. Bulletin 167. Bureau of American Ethnology, Smithsonian Institution, Washington, D.C.

Evans, J. G.
1972 *Land Snails in Archaeology: With Special Reference to the British Isles*. Seminar Press, New York.

Evans, S. T., and D. L. Webster
in prep. *The Archaeology of Ancient Mexico and Central America: An Encyclopedia*. Garland, New York.

Evershed, R. P., S. Charters, and A. Quye
1995 Interpreting Lipid Residues in Archaeological Ceramics: Preliminary Results from Laboratory Simulations of Vessel Use and Burial. In *Materials Issues in Art and Archeology IV*, edited by P. B. Vandiver, J. R. Druzik, J. L. Galvan Madrid, I. C. Freestone, and G. S. Wheeler, pp. 85–96. Materials Research Society, Pittsburgh.

Evett, J. B.
1991 *Surveying*. 2nd ed. Wiley, New York.

Exon, J. J.
1993 The Future of the U.S. Global Positioning System. *GPS World* 4(7):44–47.

Eyman, C. E.
1965 Ultraviolet Fluorescence as a Method of Skeletal Identification. *American Antiquity* 31:109–112.

Ezra, H. C., and S. F. Cook
1957 Amino Acids in Fossil Human Bone. *Science* 126:80.

Fagan, B. M.
1991a *Ancient North America: Archaeology of a Continent*. Thames & Hudson, London.
1991b *In the Beginning: An Introduction to Archaeology*. HarperCollins, New York.

Fagan, B. (editor in chief)
1996 *Oxford Companion to Archaeology*. Oxford University Press, Oxford.

Falconer, D. S.
1989 *Introduction to Quantitative Genetics*. 3rd ed. Longman Scientific & Technical, Essex, England.

Falk, L. (editor)
1991 *Historical Archaeology in Global Perspective*. Smithsonian Institution Press, Washington, D.C.

Fant, J. F., and W. G. Loy
1972 Surveying and Mapping. In *The Minnesota Messenia Expedition: Reconstructing a Bronze Age Regional Environment*, edited by W. A. MacDonald and G. R. Rapp. University of Minnesota Press, Minneapolis.

Farnsworth, P., J. E. Brady, and M. J. DeNiro
1985 A Re-Evaluation of the Isotopic and Archaeological Reconstruction of Diet in the Tehuacan Valley. *American Antiquity* 50:102–116.

Farnsworth, P., and J. S. Williams (editors)
1992 The Archaeology of the Spanish Colonial and Mexican Republican Periods. *Historical Archaeology* 26(1):1–147.

Fazekas, I. G., and F. Kosa
1978 *Forensic Fetal Osteology*. Akademiai Kiado, Budapest.

Fearn, M. L., and K-B. Liu
1995 Maize Pollen of 3500 B.P. from Southern Alabama. *American Antiquity* 60:109–117.

Feder, K. L.
1981 The Farmington River Archaeological Project: Focus on a Small River Valley. *Man in the Northeast* 22:131–146.
1983 The Avaricious Humour of Designing Englishmen. *Bulletin of the Archaeological Society of Connecticut* 45:89–92.
1988 The Beaver Meadow Complex Prehistoric Archaeological District. National Register of Historic Places Nomination Form. On file, Connecticut Historical Commission, Hartford.

1990a *Frauds, Myths, and Mysteries. Science and Pseudoscience in Archaeology.* Mayfield Publishing Company, Mountain View, California.

1990b Site Survey in the Northwest Uplands of Connecticut. *Bulletin of the Massachusetts Archaeological Society* 51(2): 61–68.

1994 *A Village of Outcasts: Historical Archaeology and Documentary Research at the Lighthouse Site.* Mayfield Publishing Company, Mountain View, California.

Feder, K. L., and M. Banks
1996 Archaeological Survey of the McLean Game Refuge, Granby and Simsbury, Connecticut. *Bulletin of the Archaeological Society of Connecticut.*

Feder, K. L., and M. A. Park
1993 *Human Antiquity: An Introduction to Physical Anthropology and Archaeology.* Mayfield Publishing Company, Mountain View, California.

Feininger, A.
1965 *The Complete Photographer.* Prentice-Hall, Englewood Cliffs, New Jersey.

Ferring, C. R.
1986 Rates of Fluvial Sedimentation: Implications for Archaeological Variability. *Geoarchaeology* 1:258–274.

Feuer, R. C.
1970 Key to the Skulls of Recent Adult North and Central American Turtles. *Journal of Herpetology* 4:69–75.

Fewkes, J. W.
1896a A Contribution to Ethnobotany. *American Anthropologist* 9:16–21.

1896b Pacific Coast Shell from Prehistoric Tusayan Pueblos. *American Anthropologist* 9:359–367.

Fiedel, S. J.
1996 Blood from Stones? Some Methodological and Interpretative Problems in Blood. *Journal of Archaeological Science* 23:139–147.

Findlow, F., V. Bennett, J. Ericson, and S. DeAtley
1975 A New Obsidian Hydration Rate for Certain Obsidians in the American Southwest. *American Antiquity* 40:344–348.

Fish, S. K., and S. A. Kowalewski
1990 *The Archaeology of Regions: A Case for Full-Coverage Survey.* Smithsonian Institution Press, Washington, D.C.

Fisher, E. M.
1942 *The Osteology and Myology of the California River Otter.* Stanford University Press, Stanford, California.

Fisher, J. W., Jr.
1995 Bone Surface Modifications in Zooarchaeology. *Journal of Archaeological Method and Theory* 2(1):7–68.

Fitting, J. E.
1973 An Early Mogollon Community: A Preliminary Report on the Winn Canyon Site. *The Artifact* 11(1/2). El Paso.

Fladmark, K. R.
1978 *A Guide to Basic Archaeological Field Procedures.* Publication 4. Department of Anthropology, Simon Fraser University, Burnaby, British Columbia.

Flannery, K. V.
1973 Archeology with a Capital S. In *Research and Theory in Current Archeology*, edited by C. L. Redman, pp. 47–53. Wiley, New York.

1976a Sampling on a Regional Level. In *The Early Mesoamerican Village*, edited by K. V. Flannery, pp. 131–136. Academic Press, New York.

1976b The Trouble with Regional Sampling. In *The Early Mesoamerican Village*, edited by K. V. Flannery, pp. 159–160. Academic Press, New York.

1976c Sampling by Intensive Surface Collecting. In *The Early Mesoamerican Village*, edited by K. V. Flannery, pp. 51–60. Academic Press, New York.

1982 The Golden Marshalltown: A Parable for the Archaeology of the 1980s. *American Anthropologist* 84(2):265–278.

Flannery, K. V. (editor)
1976 *The Early Mesoamerican Village.* Academic Press, New York.

1986 *Guila Naquitz: Archaic Foraging and Early Agriculture in Oaxaca, Mexico.* Academic Press, New York.

Flannery, K. V., and J. Marcus (editors)
1983 *The Cloud People: Divergent Evolution of the Zapotec and Mixtec Civilizations.* Academic Press, New York and London.

Flannery, K. V., C. L. Moser, and S. Maranca
1986 The Excavation of Guila Naquitz. In *Guila Naquitz: Archaic Foraging and Early Agriculture in Oaxaca, Mexico*, edited by K. V. Flannery, pp. 65–96. Academic Press, New York.

Fleming, S. J.
1977 *Dating in Archaeology: A Guide to the Scientific Techniques.* St. Martin's Press, New York.

Fleming, S. J., and B. Fagg
1977 Thermoluminescent Dating of the Udo Bronze Head. *Archaeometry* 19:86–88.

Fletcher, J. M. (editor)
1978 *Dendrochronology in Europe.* BAR International Series 51. British Archaeological Reports, Oxford.

Fletcher, J. M., and A. Dabrowska
1976 Tree-Ring Examination of Timbers from the Sixth Century Well at Portchester Castle. *Archaeometry* 18:92–106.

Flinn, L., C. G. Turner, II, and A. Brew
1976 Additional Evidence for Cannibalism in the Southwest: The Case of LA4528. *American Antiquity* 41:308–318.

Florian, M. L.
1986 The Freezing Process—Effects on Insects and Artifact Materials. *Leather Conservation News* 3(1): 1–13, 17. Texas Memorial Museum, University of Texas at Austin.

Florian, M. L., and D. Hillman
  1985 A Simple Conservation Treatment for Wet Archaeological Wood. *Studies in Conservation* 30: 39–41.

Foley, R.
  1981 Off-site Archaeology: An Alternative Approach for the Short-Sited. In *Pattern of the Past: Essays in Honour of David Clarke*, edited by I. Hodder, N. Hammond, and G. Isaac, pp. 157–183. Cambridge University Press, Cambridge.

Folk, R. L., and S. Valastro, Jr.
  1976 Successful Techniques for Dating Lime Mortar for Carbon-14. *Journal of Field Archaeology* 3:203–208.

Folsom, F., and M. E. Folsom
  1993 *America's Ancient Treasures.* University of New Mexico Press, Albuquerque.

Fontana, B. L.
  1965 On the Meaning of Historic Sites Archaeology. *American Antiquity* 31:61–65.

Ford, J. A.
  1938 A Chronological Method Applicable to the Southeast. *American Antiquity* 17:250.
  1951 *Greenhouse: A Troyville-Coles Creek Period Site in Avoyelles Parish, Louisiana.* Anthropological Papers 44, Pt. 1. American Museum of Natural History, New York.
  1952 *Measurements of Some Prehistoric Design Developments in the Southeastern United States.* Anthropoligical Papers 44(3). American Museum of Natural History, New York.
  1962 *A Quantitative Method of Deriving Cultural Chronology.* Technical Manual No. 1. Pan American Union, Washington, D.C.
  1963 *Hopewell Culture Burial Mounds near Helena, Arkansas.* Anthropological Papers 50, Pt. 1. American Museum of Natural History, New York.

Ford, J. A., and C. H. Webb
  1956 *Poverty Point, A Late Archaic Site in Louisiana.* Anthropological Papers 46:5–136. American Museum of Natural History, New York.

Ford, J. A., and G. R. Willey
  1949 *Surface Survey of the Viru Valley, Peru.* Anthropological Papers 43(1). American Museum of Natural History, New York.

Ford, P. J.
  1990 Antelope, Deer, Bighorn Sheep and Mountain Goats: A Guide to the Carpals. *Journal of Ethnobiology* 10:169–181.

Ford, R. I.
  1979 Paleoethnobotany in American Archaeology. *Advances in Archaeological Method and Theory*, vol. 2, edited by M. B. Schiffer, pp. 235–236.

Fowler, M. (editor)
  1977 *Explorations into Cahokia Archaeology.* 2nd ed. Bulletin 7. Illinois Archaeological Survey, Urbana.

Fowler, M. L.
  1959 *Summary Report of Modoc Rock Shelter: 1952, 1953, 1955, 1956.* Report of Investigations 8. Illinois State Museum, Springfield.

Fox, A., and T. Hester
  1976 *An Archaeological Survey of Coleto Creek, Victoria and Goliad Counties, Texas.* Archaeological Survey Report No. 18. Center for Archaeological Research, University of Texas at San Antonio.

Francalacci, P.
  1989 Dietary Reconstruction at Arene Candide Cave (Liguria, Italy) by Means of Trace Element Analysis. *Journal of Archaeological Science* 16:109–124.

France, D. L.
  1983 *Sexual Dimorphism in the Human Humerus.* Unpublished Ph.D. dissertation, Department of Anthropology, University of Colorado, Boulder.

Francis, J. E., L. L. Loendorf, and R. I. Dorn
  1993 AMS Radiocarbon and Cation-Ratio Dating of Rock Art in the Bighorn Basin of Wyoming and Montana. *American Antiquity* 58(4):711–737.

Fraser-Taylor, D. R.
  1991 *Geographic Information Systems: The Microcomputer and Modern Cartography.* Pergamon Press, New York.

Frayer, D. W., and M. Wolpoff
  1985 Sexual Dimorphism. *Annual Review of Anthropology* 14:129–173.

Frederick, C. D., M. D. Glasscock, H. Neff, and C. M. Stevenson
  1994 *Evaluation of Chert Patination as a Dating Technique: A Case Study from Fort Hood, Texas.* Research Report 32. Archeological Resource Management Series, U.S. Army Fort Hood, Fort Hood, Texas.

French, D. H.
  1971 An Experiment in Water-Sieving. *Anatolian Studies* 21:59–64.

Freter, A.
  1993 Obsidian-Hydration Dating: Its Past, Present, and Future Application in Mesoamerica. *Ancient Mesoamerica* 4:285–303.

Friedman, A. M., and R. L. Smith
  1960 A New Dating Method Using Obsidian: Part 1, The Development of the Method. *American Antiquity* 25:476–537.

Friedman, I., F. W. Trembour, F. L. Smith, and G. I. Smith
  1994 Is Obsidian Hydration Dating Affected by Relative Humidity? *Quaternary Research* 41:185–190.

Frison, G. C.
  1982 Folsom Components. In *The Agate Basin Site*, edited by G. C. Frison and D. J. Stanford, pp. 37–75. Academic Press, New York.

Frison, G. C., and L. Todd
  1986 *The Colby Mammoth Site: Taphonomy and Archaeology of a Clovis Kill in Northern Wyoming.* University of New Mexico Press, Albuquerque.

Fry, G. F.
1970   Preliminary Analysis of the Hogup Cave Coprolites. In *Hogup Cave*, edited by C. M. Aikens, pp. 247–250. Anthropological Papers 93. University of Utah, Salt Lake City.
1976   *Analysis of Prehistoric Coprolites from Utah.* Anthropological Papers 97. University of Utah, Salt Lake City.
1978   *Prehistoric Diet at Danger Cave, Utah as Determined by the Analysis of Coprolites.* Miscellaneous Papers 23, Anthropological Papers 99. University of Utah, Salt Lake City.
1985   Analysis of Fecal Material. In *The Analysis of Prehistoric Diets,* edited by R. I. Gilbert and J. H. Mielke, pp. 127–155. Academic Press, New York.

Fryxell, R.
1965   Mazama and Glacier Peak Volcanic Ash Layers: Relative Ages. *Science* 147:1288–1290.

Gamble, C.
1978   Optimizing Information from Studies of Faunal Remains. In *Sampling in Contemporary British Archaeology*, edited by J. F. Cherry, C. Gamble, and S. Shennan, pp. 321–353. BAR Series 50. British Archaeological Reports, Oxford.

Gardner, J. S.
1979   Pre-Columbian Textiles from Ecuador: Conservation Procedures and Preliminary Study. *Technology and Conservation* 1:24–30.

Garfinkel, D. M., and U. M. Franklin
1988   A Study on the Feasibility of Detecting Blood Residues on Artifacts. *Journal of Archaeological Science* 15:83–97.

Garrison, E. R., C. M. McGimsey, III, and O. H. Zinke
1978   Alpha-Recoil Tracks in Archaeological Ceramic Dating. *Archaeometry* 20:39–46.

Garrison, E. R., R. M. Rowlett, D. L. Cowan, and L. V. Holroyd
1981   ESR Dating of Ancient Flints. *Nature* 290: 44–45.

Gatto, L. W.
1987   *Benchmark Design and Installation: A Synthesis of Existing Information.* Special Report U.S. Army Cold Regions Research and Engineering Laboratory 87-10. Prepared for the Office of the Chief of Engineers, U.S. Army Corps of Engineers, Cold Regions Research and Engineering Laboratory, Hanover, New Hampshire.

Gautier, A.
1993   Trace Fossils in Archaeozoology. *Journal of Archaeological Science* 20(5):511–523.

Gebhard, D.
1960   *Prehistoric Paintings of the Diablo Region of Western Texas.* Publications in Art and Science No. 3. Roswell Museum and Art Center, Roswell, New Mexico.

Geer, G. de B.
1937   Early Man and Geochronology. In *Early Man,* edited by G. G. MacCurdy, pp. 323–326. Lippincott, Philadelphia.

Gejvall, N. G.
1963   Cremations. In *Science in Archaeology,* edited by D. R. Brothwell and E. S. Higgs, pp. 379–390. Thames & Hudson, London.

Genovés, S.
1967   Proportionality of the Long Bones and Their Relation to Stature Among Mesoamericans. *American Journal of Physical Anthropology* 26:67–77.

Gero, J. M.
1978   Summary of Experiments to Duplicate Post-excavational Damage to Tool Edges. *Lithic Technology* 7:34.

Gero, J. M., and M. W. Conkey (editors)
1991   *Engendering Archaeology: Women and Prehistory.* Basil Blackwell, Oxford.

Gibbon, G.
1984   *Anthropological Archaeology.* Columbia University Press, New York.

Gibbs, B., and S. A. Krajewski
1993   *Mapping Software Update 1992: A Summary of the Mapping Software Update Sessions Held at Geotech '92, Denver, Colorado, September 1992.* Industrial Ergonomics, Inc., Arvada, Colorado.

Giddings, J. L.
1966   Cross-Dating the Archaeology of Northwestern Alaska. *Science* 153:127–135.

Gifford, D. P.
1981   Taphonomy and Paleoecology: A Critical Review of Archaeology's Sister Disciplines. In *Advances in Archaeological Method and Theory*, vol. 4, edited by M. B. Schiffer, pp. 365–438. Academic Press, New York.

Gifford, D. P., and D. C. Crader
1977   A Computer Coding System for Archaeological Faunal Remains. *American Antiquity* 42:225–238.

Gifford, E. W.
1916   *Composition of California Shell Mounds.* Publications in American Archaeology and Ethnology 12:1–29. University of California, Berkeley.
1949   Early Central California and Anasazi Shell Artifact Types. *American Antiquity* 15:156–157.

Gifford, J. C.
1960   The Type-Variety Method of Ceramic Classification as an Index of Cultural Phenomena. *American Antiquity* 25:341–347.

Gifford-Gonzales, D. P., D. B. Damrosch, D. R. Damrosch, J. Pryor, and R. L. Thunen
1985   The Third Dimension in Site Structure: An Experiment in Trampling and Vertical Dispersal. *American Antiquity* 50(4):803–818.

Gilbert, B. M.
1980   *Mammalian Osteology.* B. M. Gilbert, Laramie, Wyoming.

Gilbert, B. M., and T. W. McKern
1973   A Method for Aging the Female Os Pubis. *American Journal of Physical Anthropology* 38:31–38.

Gilbert, B. M., L. D. Martin, and H. G. Savage
1985   *Avian Osteology.* B. M. Gilbert, Laramie, Wyoming.

Gilbert, R., and G. W. Gill
1990   A Metric Technique for Identifying American Indian Femora. In *Skeletal Attribution of Race: Methods for Forensic Anthropology,* edited by G. W. Gill and S. Rhine, pp. 97–99. Anthropological Papers 4. Maxwell Museum of Anthropology, Albuquerque, New Mexico.

Gilbert, R. I.
1985   Stress, Paleonutrition, and Trace Elements. In *The Analysis of Prehistoric Diets,* edited by R. I. Gilbert and J. H. Mielke, pp. 339–358. Academic Press, Orlando.

Gilbert, R. I., and J. H. Mielke (editors)
1985   *The Analysis of Prehistoric Diets.* Academic Press, Orlando.

Giles, E.
1970   Discriminant Function Sexing of the Human Skeleton. In *Personal Identification in Mass Disasters,* edited by T. D. Stewart, pp. 99–109. National Museum of Natural History, Smithsonian Institution, Washington, D.C.

Giles, E., and O. Elliot
1962   Race Identification from Cranial Measurements. *Journal of Forensic Sciences* 7:147–157.

Gill, G. W.
1984   A Forensic Test Case for a New Method of Geographical Race Determination. In *Human Identification,* edited by T. A. Rathbun and J. E. Buikstra, pp. 329–339. Charles C. Thomas, Springfield, Illinois.
1986   Craniofacial Criteria in Forensic Race Identification. In *Forensic Osteology,* edited by K. J. Reichs, pp. 143–159. Charles C. Thomas, Springfield, Illinois.

Gill, G. W., and S. Rhine
1990   *Skeletal Attribution of Race: Methods for Forensic Anthropology.* Anthropological Papers 4. Maxwell Museum of Anthropology, Albuquerque.

Gillespie, R.
1986   *Radiocarbon User's Handbook.* Oxbow Books, Oxford.

Gillio, D. A.
1970   Uses of Infrared Photography in Archaeology. *Colorado Anthropologist* 2(2):13–19.

Gilmore, R. M.
1946   To Facilitate Cooperation in Identification of Mammal Bones from Archeological Sites. *American Antiquity* 12:49–50.

1949   The Identification and Value of Mammal Bones from Archeological Excavations. *Journal of Mammalogy* 30:163–169.

Gladfelter, B. G.
1981   Developments and Directions in Geoarchaeology. In *Advances in Archaeological Method and Theory,* vol. 4, edited by M. B. Schiffer, pp. 343–364. Academic Press, New York.

Glass, B. P.
1951   *A Key to the Skulls of North American Mammals.* 3rd printing. Burgess, Minneapolis.

Gleason, M.
1973   Ozette Project: Summary of Stratigraphic Work (June 1972–Aug. 1973). Unpublished manuscript on file. Texas Archeological Research Laboratory, University of Texas at Austin.

Glock, W. S.
1937   *Principles and Methods of Tree Analysis.* Publications 486. Carnegie Institute of Washington, Washington, D.C.

Godlewska, A.
1988   The Napoleonic Survey of Egypt: A Masterpiece of Cartographic Compilation and Early Nineteenth-Century Fieldwork. Special Number Edited by E. H. Dahl. *Cartographica* 25(1,2), No. 38–39. Winters College, York University, Toronto, Ontario.

Goede, A., and M. A. Hitchman
1987   Electron Spin Resonance Analysis of Marine Gastropods from Archaeological Sites in Southern Africa. *Archaeometry* 29:163–174.

Goetzmann, W. H.
1967   *Exploration and Empire.* Texas State Historical Association, Austin.

Goldberg, P. S.
1974   Sediment Peels from Prehistoric Sites. *Journal of Field Archaeology* 1(3/4):323–328.
1988   The Archaeologist as Viewed by the Geologist. *Biblical Archaeologist* December.
1992   Micromorphology, Soils and Archaeological Sites. In *Soils in Archaeology,* edited by V. T. Holliday, pp. 145–168. Smithsonian Institution Press, Washington, D.C.

Goldberg, P. S., D. T. Nash, and M. D. Petraglia (editors)
1993   *Formation Processes in Archaeological Context.* Prehistory Press, Madison, Wisconsin.

Goldstein, L. G.
1980   *Mississippian Mortuary Practices: A Case Study of Two Cemeteries in the Lower Illinois River Valley.* Northwestern University Archeological Program, Evanston, Illinois.

Goldstein, L., and K. Kintigh
1990   Ethics and the Reburial Controversy. *American Antiquity* 55:585–591.

Goodenough, D. G.
1988 Thematic Mapper and SPOT Integration with a Geographic Information System. *Photogrammetric Engineering and Remote Sensing* 54(2):167–176.

Goodman, A. H.
1993 On the Interpretation of Health from Skeletal Remains. *Current Anthropology* 34:281–288.

Goodman, A. H., and G. J. Armelagos
1988 Childhood Stress and Decreased Longevity in a Prehistoric Population. *American Anthropologist* 90:936–944.

Goodman, A. H., and J. C. Rose
1991 Dental Enamel Hypoplasias as Indicators of Nutritional Status. In *Advances in Dental Anthropology*, edited by M. A. Kelley and C. S. Larsen, pp. 279–293. Wiley-Liss, New York.

Goodman, A. H., R. B. Thomas, A. C. Swedlund, and G. J. Armelagos
1988 Biocultural Perspectives on Stress in Prehistoric, Historical, and Contemporary Populations. *Yearbook of Physical Anthropology* 31:169–202.

Goodwin, A. J. H.
1953 *Method in Prehistory.* 2nd ed. Handbook Series 1. South African Archaeological Society, Capetown.
1960 Chemical Alteration (Patination) of Stone. *Viking Fund Publications in Anthropology* 28: 300–324.

Gordon, B. C.
1984 *Selected Bibliography of Dental Annular Studies on Various Mammals.* Supplement 2. *Zooarchaeological Research News,* New York.
1991 *Archaeological Seasonality Using Incremental Structures in Teeth: An Annotated Bibliography.* A Special Publication of *Zooarchaeological Research News,* New York.

Gordon, C. C., and J. E. Buikstra
1981 Soil pH, Bone Preservation, and Sampling Bias at Mortuary Sites. *American Antiquity* 46: 566–571.

Gordon, E. A.
1993 Screen Size and Differential Faunal Recovery: A Hawaiian Example. *Journal of Field Archaeology* 20:453–460.

Gordon, R. B., and P. M. Malone
1994 *The Texture of Industry: An Archaeological View of the Industrialization of North America.* Oxford University Press, Oxford.

Gould, R. A.
1980 *Living Archaeology.* Cambridge University Press, Cambridge.

Grabau, A. W.
1924 *Principles of Stratigraphy.* 2nd ed. Seiler, New York.

Graham, R. W., and E. L. Lundelius, Jr.
1984 Coevolutionary Disequilibrium and Pleistocene Extinctions. In *Quaternary Extinctions: A Prehistoric Revolution,* edited by P. S. Martin and R. G. Klein, pp. 223–249. University of Arizona Press, Tucson.

Graham, R. W., H. A. Semken, Jr., and M. A. Graham (editors)
1987 *Late Quaternary Mammalian Biogeography and Environments of the Great Plains and Prairies.* Scientific Papers Vol. 22. Illinois State Museum, Springfield.

Grattan, D. W.
1988 Treatment of Waterlogged Wood. In *Wet Site Archaeology,* edited by B. Purdy, pp. 237–254. Telford Press, Caldwell, New Jersey.

Grauer, A. L. (editor)
1995 *Bodies of Evidence: Reconstructing History Through Skeletal Analysis.* Wiley-Liss, New York.

Grayson, D. K.
1973 On the Methodology of Faunal Analysis. *American Antiquity* 39:432–439.
1978 Minimum Numbers and Sample Size in Vertebrate Faunal Analysis. *American Antiquity* 43: 53–65.
1979 On the Quantification of Vertebrate Archaeofaunas. In *Advances in Archaeological Method and Theory,* vol. 2, edited by M. B. Schiffer, pp. 199–237. Academic Press, New York.
1981a A Critical View of the Use of Archaeological Vertebrates in Paleoenvironmental Reconstruction. *Journal of Ethnobiology* 1:28–38.
1981b The Effects of Sample Size on Some Derived Measures in Vertebrate Faunal Analysis. *Journal of Archaeological Science* 8:115–121.
1984 *Quantitative Zooarchaeology: Topics in the Analysis of Archaeological Faunas.* Academic Press, New York.
1987 The Biogeographic History of Small Mammals in the Great Basin: Observations on the Last 20,000 Years. *Journal of Mammalogy* 68:359–375.

Greenman, E. F., and G. M. Stanley
1943 The Archaeology and Geology of Two Early Sites Near Killarney, Ontario. *Papers of the Michigan Academy of Science, Arts and Letters* 28:505–530.

Gregg, J. B., and L. J. Zimmerman
1986 Malnutrition in Fourteenth-Century South Dakota: Osteopathological Manifestations. *North American Archaeologist* 7:191–214.

Griggs, K.
1973 Toxic Metal Fumes from Mantle-Type Camp Lanterns. *Science* 181:842–843.

Grigson, C.
1978 Towards a Blueprint for Animal Bone Reports in Archaeology. In *Research Problems in Zooarchaeology,* edited by D. R. Brothwell, K. D. Thomas, and J. Clutton-Brock, pp. 121–128. Occasional Paper 3. Institute of Archaeology, London.

Grim, M. S.
1992   *An Introduction to MAPGEN.* Books and Open-File Reports Section, U.S. Department of the Interior, U.S. Geological Survey, Denver.

Groeneveld, H. T., and J. A. Kieser
1987   An Evaluation of the M-statistic in Human Odeontomorphometric Analyses. *International Journal of Anthropology* 2:29–36.

Grun, R., and C. B. Stringer
1991   Electron Spin Resonance Dating and the Evolution of Modern Humans. *Archaeometry* 33:153–201.

Gualtieri, M., M. Salvatore, and A. Small
1983   Lo Scavo di S. Giovanni di Ruoti ed il Periodo Tardoantico in Basilicata. *Pubblicazioni del Centro Accademico Canadese* 1. Centro Accademico Canadese in Italia.

Guerreschi, A.
1973   A Mechanical Sieve for Archaeological Excavations. *Antiquity* 47(187):234–235.

Gumerman, G. J., and T. R. Lyons
1971   Archaeological Methodology and Remote Sensing. *Science* 1172:126–132.

Gunn, J., and D. O. Brown
1982   *Eagle Hill: A Late Quaternary Upland Site in Western Louisiana.* Special Report 12. Center for Archaeological Research, University of Texas at San Antonio.

Gustafson, C. E.
1972   *Faunal Remains from the Marmes Rockshelter and Related Archaeological Sites in the Columbia Basin.* Ph.D. dissertation, Washington State University, Pullman. University Microfilms, Ann Arbor.

Haag, W. G.
1986   Field Methods in Archaeology. In *American Archaeology, Past and Future,* edited by D. J. Meltzer, D. D. Fowler, and J. A. Sabloff, pp. 63–76. Smithsonian Institution Press, Washington, D.C.

Haas, H., V. Holliday, and R. Stuckenrath
1986   Dating of Holocene Stratigraphy with Soluble and Insoluble Organic Fractions at the Lubbock Lake Archaeological Site, Texas: An Ideal Case Study. *Radiocarbon* 28(2A):473–485.

Hackett, D.
1976   *Diagnostic Criteria of Syphilis, Yaws, Treponarid (Treponematoses) and of Some Other Diseases in Dry Bone.* Springer-Verlag, Berlin.

Haddy, A., and A. Hanson
1982   Nitrogen and Fluorine Dating of Moundville Skeletal Samples. *Archaeometry* 22:437–444.

Haglund, W. D.
1991   *Applications of Taphonomic Models to Forensic Investigations.* Ph.D. dissertation, University of Washington, Seattle. University Microfilms, Ann Arbor.

1992   Contributions of Rodents to Postmortem Artifacts of Bone and Soft Tissue. *Journal of Forensic Sciences* 37:1459–1465.

Haglund, W. D., D. T. Reay, and D. R. Swindler
1989   Canid Scavenging/Disarticulation Sequence of Human Remains in the Pacific Northwest. *Journal of Forensic Sciences* 34:587–606.

Haines-Young, R., D. R. Green, and S. Cousins
1993   *Landscape Ecology and Geographic Information Systems.* Taylor & Francis, New York and London.

Hall, G. D., M. B. Collins, and E. R. Prewitt
1987   *Cultural Resources Investigations Along Drainage Improvements, Hidalgo and Willacy Counties, Texas: 1986 Investigations.* Reports of Investigations 59. Prewitt and Associates, Inc., Austin.

Hall, G. D., S. M. Tarka, Jr., J. Hurst, D. Stuart, and R. E.W. Adams
1990   Cacao Residues on Ancient Maya Vessels from Rio Azul, Guatemala. *American Antiquity* 55:138–143.

Hall, E. T.
1939   Dendrochronology. *Society for American Archaeology Newsletter* 1:32–41.

Hall, R. L. (editor)
1982   *Sexual Dimorphism in* Homo sapiens: *A Question of Size.* Praeger, New York.

Hamilton, D. L.
1976   *Conservation of Metal Objects from Underwater Sites: A Study of Methods.* Miscellaneous Papers 4, Texas Memorial Museum and Publication 1, Texas Antiquities Committee. Austin.

1984   Preliminary Report on the Archaeological Investigations of the Submerged Remains of Port Royal, Jamaica 1981–1982. *International Journal of Nautical Archaeology and Underwater Exploration* 13(1):11–25.

Hamilton, M. E.
1982   Sexual Dimorphism in Skeletal Samples. In *Sexual Dimorphism in* Homo sapiens: *A Question of Size,* edited by R. L. Hall, pp. 107–163. Praeger, New York.

Hammond, N.
1991   Matrices and Maya Archaeology. *Journal of Field Archaeology* 18:29–41.

Hancox, M. C.
1972   *Biology of Bone.* Cambridge University Press, Cambridge.

Handsman, R.
1990   The Weantinock Indian Homeland Was Not a "Desert." *Artifacts* 18(2):3–7.

Hanna, S. B.
1984   The Use of Organo-silanes for the Treatment of Limestone in Advanced State of Deterioration. In *Adhesives and Consolidants,* edited by N. S. Bromelle, E. M. Pye, P. Smith, and G. Thomson, pp. 171–176. International Institute for Conservation of Historic and Artistic Works, London.

Hanson, D. B., and J. E. Buikstra
1987   Histomorphological Alteration of Buried Human Bone from the Lower Illinois Valley: Implications for Paleodietary Research. *Journal of Archaeological Science* 14:549–563.

Hare, P. E.
1980   Organic Geochemistry of Bone and its Relation to the Survival of Bone in the Natural Environment. In *Vertebrate Taphonomy and Paleoecology,* edited by A. K. Behrensmeyer and A. P. Hill, pp. 208–219. University of Chicago Press, Chicago.

Hargrave, L. L.
1936   The Field Collection of Beam Material. *Tree-Ring Bulletin* 2(3). Tucson.
1938   A Plea for More Careful Preservation of All Biological Material from Prehistoric Sites. *Southwestern Lore* 4(3):47–51 .
1970   *Mexican Macaws: Comparative Osteology and Survey of Remains from the Southwest.* Anthropological Papers 20. University of Arizona Press, Tucson.

Harkonen, T.
1986   *Guide to the Otoliths of the Bony Fishes of the Northeast Atlantic.* Danbui ApS, Denmark.

Harp, E. (editor)
1975   *Photography in Archaeological Research.* University of New Mexico Press, Albuquerque.

Harrar, E. S.
1957   *Hough's Encyclopedia of American Woods.* 16 vols. Robert Speller & Sons, New York.

Harrington, M. R.
1933   *Gypsum Cave, Nevada.* Paper 8. Southwest Museum, Los Angeles.

Harris, B., and M. Batty
1992   *Locational Models, Geographic Information and Planning Support Systems.* National Center for Geographic Information and Analysis, University of California, Santa Barbara.

Harris, E. C.
1979   The Laws of Archaeological Stratigraphy. *World Archaeology* 11:111–117.
1989   *Principles of Archaeological Stratigraphy.* 2nd ed. Academic Press, New York.

Harris, E. C., and M. R. Brown, III
1993   *Practice of Archaeological Stratigraphy.* Academic Press, London.

Harris, E. F., and N. F. Bellantoni
1980   Anthropologic Relationships Among Prehistoric Northeastern Amerindians. *North American Archaeologist* 1:145–159.

Harris, M.
1968   *The Rise of Anthropological Theory: A History of Theories of Culture.* Harper & Row, New York.

Harris, R.
1987   *Satellite Remote Sensing: An Introduction.* Routledge & Kegan Paul, London.

Harry, K. G.
1995   Cation-Ratio Dating of Varnished Artifacts: Testing the Assumptions. *American Antiquity* 60: 118–130.

Harshberger, J. W.
1896   The Purpose of Ethnobotany. *American Antiquarian* 17:73–81.
1898   Uses of Plants Among the Ancient Peruvians. *Bulletin of the Museum of Science and Art* 1:1–3.

Hartl, D. L., and A. G. Clark
1989   *Principles of Population Genetics.* Sinauser, Sunderland, Massachussetts.

Hassan, F. A.
1978   Sediments in Archaeology: Methods and Implications for Paleoenvironmental and Cultural Analysis. *Journal of Field Archaeology* 5(2):197–213.
1979   Geoarchaeology: The Geologist and Archaeology. *American Antiquity* 44:267–270.
1981   Rapid Quantitative Determination of Phosphate in Archaeological Sediments. *Journal of Field Archaeology* 8:384–387.

Hassan, F. A., and D. Ortner
1977   Inclusions in Bone Material as a Source of Error in Radiocarbon Dating. *Archaeometry* 19:131–135.

Hastorf, C. A., and Popper, V. S.
1988   *Current Paleoethnobotany.* University of Chicago Press.

Haury, E. W.
1937   Stratigraphy. In *Excavations at Snaketown,* edited by H. S. Gladwin. Chap. 4, Medallion Papers 25. Gila Pueblo, Globe, Arizona.

Hauser, G., and G. F. De Stafano (editors)
1989   *Epigenetic Variants in the Human Skull.* E. Schweizerbartlsche Verlagsbuchandlung, Stuttgart.

Hauswirth, W. W., C. D. Dickel, G. H. Doran, P. J. Laipis, and D. N. Dickel
1991   8,000-Year-Old Brain Tissue from Windover Archaeological Site: Anatomical, Cellular, and Molecular Analysis. In *Human Paleopathology: Current Syntheses and Future Options,* edited by D. J. Ortner and A. C. Aufderheide, pp. 60–72. Smithsonian Institution Press, Washington, D.C.

Haviland, W. A.
1969   A New Population Estimate for Tikal, Guatemala. *American Antiquity* 34(4):429–433.

Hawken, W. R.
1979   *You and Your Camera.* American Photographic Book Publishing Co., New York.

Hawley, F. M.
1934   *The Significance and the Dated Prehistory of Chetro Ketl.* Monograph Series 1(1). University of New Mexico, Albuquerque.

Hayden, B.
1979   *Paleolithic Reflections: Lithic Technology and Ethnographic Excavations Among the Australian Aborigines.* Academic Press, New York.

Hayden, B. (editor)
1979 *Lithic Use-Wear Analysis.* Academic Press, New York.

Hayes, A. W., D. M. Brugge, and W. J. Judge
1981 *Archaeological Surveys of Chaco Canyon, New Mexico.* Publications in Archaeology 18A, Chaco Canyon Studies. National Park Service, U.S. Department of the Interior, Washington, D.C.

Haynes, C. V.
1988 Geofacts and Fancy. *Natural History* Feb.:4–12.
1990 The Antevs-Bryan Years and the Legacy of Paleoindian Geochronology. In *Establishment of a Geologic Framework for Paleoanthropology,* edited by L. F. Laport, pp. 55–68. Special Paper 242. Geological Society of America, Boulder, Colorado.

Haynes, G.
1980 Evidence of Carnivore Gnawing on Pleistocene and Recent Mammalian Bones. *Paleobiology* 6:341–351.
1983 A Guide for Differentiating Mammalian Carnivore Taxa Responsible for Gnaw Damage to Herbivore Limb Bones. *Paleobiology* 9:164–172.

Haynes, V. C., and G. A. Agogino
1986 *Geoarchaeology of Sandia Cave.* Smithsonian Institution Press, Washington, D.C.

Hearnshaw, H. M., and D. J. Unwin
1994 *Visualization in Geographical Information Systems.* Wiley, New York.

Hedges, R. E. M.
1983 The Accelerator Technique for C14 Measurement: Its Implications for Radiocarbon Dating. In *Archaeology, Dendrochronology and the Radiocarbon Calibration Curve,* edited by B. S. Ottaway, pp. 44–50. Occasional Paper 9. University of Edinburgh, Edinburgh.

Hedges, R. E. M., and S. Freeman
1994 The Possibility of Dating Lithics from Diffused Nitrogen Profiles. In *Stories in Stone,* edited by N. Ashton and A. David, pp. 7–9. Occasional Paper 4, Lithic Studies Society. British Museum, London.

Hedges, R. E. M., and J. A. J. Gowlett
1986 Radiocarbon Dating by Accelerator Mass Spectrometry. *Scientific American* 254:100–107.

Heizer, R. F.
1941 The Direct-Historical Approach in California Archaeology. *American Antiquity* 7:98–122.
1946 The Occurrence and Significance of Southwestern Grooved Axes in California. *American Antiquity* 11:187–193.
1950 *On the Methods of Chemical Analysis of Bone as an Aid to Prehistoric Culture Chronology.* Archaeological Survey Report 7. University of California, Berkeley.
1960 Physical Analysis of Habitation Residues. *Viking Fund Publications in Anthropology* 28:93–157. Chicago.
1967 *Analysis of Human Coprolites from a Dry Nevada Cave.* Archaeological Survey Report 70. University of California, Berkeley.
1970 The Anthropology of Prehistoric Great Basin Coprolites. In *Science in Archaeology,* edited by D. Brothwell and E. Higgs, pp. 244–250. Praeger, New York.

Heizer, R. F. (editor)
1959 *The Archaeologist at Work.* Harper & Row, New York.
1969 *Man's Discovery of His Past.* Peek Publications, Palo Alto, California.

Heizer, R. F., and S. F. Cook
1952 Fluorine and Other Chemical Tests of Some North American Human and Animal Bones. *American Journal of Physical Anthropology* 10:289–304.
1959 New Evidence of the Antiquity of Tepexpan and Other Human Remains from the Valley of Mexico. *Southwestern Journal of Anthropology* 15:36–42.

Heizer, R. F., and J. A. Graham
1967 *Guide to Field Methods in Archaeology.* The National Press, Palo Alto, California.

Heizer, R. F., T. R. Hester, and C. Graves
1980 *Archaeology: A Bibliographical Guide to the Basic Literature.* Garland, New York.

Heizer, R. F., and A. D. Krieger
1956 *The Archaeology of Humboldt Cave, Churchill County, Nevada.* Publications in American Archaeology and Ethnology 47:1–190. University of California, Berkeley.

Heizer, R. F., and L. K. Napton
1969 Biological and Cultural Evidence from Prehistoric Human Coprolites. *Science* 165:563–568.
1970 *Archaeology and the Prehistoric Great Basin Lacustrine Subsistence Regime as Seen from Lovelock Cave, Nevada.* Contributions of the Archaeological Research Facility 10. University of California, Berkeley.

Helbaek, H.
1969 Plant Collecting, Dry Farming and Irrigation in Prehistoric Deh Luran. In *Prehistory and Human Ecology of the Deh Luran Plain: An Early Village Sequence from Khuzistan,* edited by F. Hole, K. V. Flannery, and J. A. Neely, pp. 244–383. Memoirs No. 1. Museum of Anthropology, University of Michigan, Ann Arbor.

Hemion, R. H.
1988 *Field and Laboratory Handbook.* Special Publication 2 (revised). Southern Texas Archaeological Association, San Antonio.

Hempel, C. G.
1965 *Aspects of Scientific Explanation and Other Essays in the Philosophy of Science.* Free Press, New York.

1966   *Philosophy of Natural Science.* Prentice-Hall, Englewood Cliffs, New Jersey.

Henning, G. J., and R. Grun
1983   ESR Dating in Quaternary Geology. *Quaternary Science Reviews* 2:157–238.

Henry, E. (editor)
1991   *Guide to the Curation of Archaeozoological Collections.* Proceedings of the Curation Workshop, 6th International Conference of the International Council of ArchaeoZoology, Washington D.C. Florida Museum of Natural History, Gainesville.

Hepworth, W. G. (editor)
1974   *Identification of the Dorsal Guard Hairs of Some Mammals of Wyoming.* Bulletin 14. Wyoming Game and Fish Department, Cheyenne.

Hesse, B., and P. Wapnish
1985   *Animal Bone Archeology: From Objectives to Analysis.* Taraxacum, Washington, D.C.

Hester, J. J.
1987   The Significance of Accelerator Dating in Archaeological Method and Theory. *Journal of Field Archaeology* 14:445–452.

Hester, T. R.
1969   Human Bone Artifacts from Southern Texas. *American Antiquity* 34:326–328.
1973   A Supplementary Note on Flint Chipping with the Teeth. *Lithic Technology* II(1–2):23.
1981   CRM Publication: Dealing with Reality. *Journal of Field Archaeology* 8(4):493–496.
1983   Late Paleo-Indian Occupations at Baker Cave, Southwestern Texas. *Bulletin of the Texas Archeological Society* 53:101–121.
1986   On the Misuse of Projectile Point Typology in Mesoamerica. *American Antiquity* 51:412–414.

Hester, T. R., and W. I. Follett
1976   Yurok Fish Knives: A Study of Wear Patterns and Adhering Fish Scales. *Contributions of the University of California Archaeological Research Facility* 33:3–23.

Hester, T. R., R. F. Heizer, and J. A. Graham
1975   *Field Methods in Archaeology.* Mayfield Publishing Company, Palo Alto, California.

Hester, T. R., and H. J. Shafer
1984   Exploitation of Chert Resources by the Ancient Maya of Northern Belize, Central America. *World Archaeology* 16(2):157–173.
1992   Lithic Workshops Revisited: Comments on Moholy-Nagy. *Latin American Antiquity* 3:243–248.

Hester, T. R., H. J. Shafer, T. C. Kelly, and G. Ligabue
1982   Observations on the Patination Process and the Context of Antiquity: A Fluted Projectile Point from Belize, Central America. *Lithic Technology* 11(2):29–34.

Hett, C. E. S.
1987   Conservation Measures on Arctic Sites. In *In Situ Archaeological Conservation,* edited by H. W. M. Hodges, pp. 64–71. Getty Conservation Institute, Los Angeles.

Heye, G. G.
1919   *Certain Aboriginal Pottery from Southern California.* Museum of the American Indian, Heye Foundation Indian Notes and Monographs 7. Heye Foundation, New York.

Highley, C. L.
1986   *Archaeological Investigations at 41 LK 201, Choke Canyon Reservoir, Southern Texas.* Choke Canyon Series 11. Center for Archaeological Research, University of Texas at San Antonio.

Hildebrand, M.
1955   Skeletal Differences Between Deer, Sheep, and Goats. *California Fish and Game* 41:327–346.

Hill, J. N.
1966   A Prehistoric Community in Eastern Arizona. *Southwestern Journal of Anthropology* 22(1):9–30.
1970   *Broken K Pueblo: Prehistoric Social Organization in the American Southwest.* Anthropological Papers 18. University of Arizona, Tucson.

Hill, J. N., and R. H. Hevly
1968   Pollen at Broken K Pueblo: Some New Interpretations. *American Antiquity* 33:200–210.

Hillson, S.
1986   *Teeth.* Cambridge University Press, New York.

Hitch, C. J.
1982   Dendrochronology and Serendipity. *American Scientist* 70:300–305.

Hobbs, D.
1983   Surveying Techniques Useful in Archaeology. In *Australian Field Archaeology: A Guide to Techniques,* edited by G. Connah, pp. 43–63. Australian Institute of Aboriginal Studies, Canberra.

Hockett, B. S.
1991   Toward Distinguishing Human and Raptor Patterning on Leporid Bones. *American Antiquity* 56:667–679.

Hodder, I.
1982   *Symbols in Action: Ethnoarchaeological Studies of Material Culture.* Cambridge University Press, Cambridge.

Hodder, I. (editor)
1978   *The Spatial Organization of Culture.* University of Pittsburgh Press, Pittsburgh.
1986   *Reading the Past: Current Approaches to Interpretation in Archaeology.* 2nd ed. Cambridge University Press, Cambridge.

Hodges, H. W. M.
1987   The Conservation Treatment of Ceramics in the Field. In *In Situ Archaeological Conservation,* edited by H. W. M. Hodges, pp. 144–151. Getty Conservation Institute, Los Angeles.

1989   Copper and Copper Alloys. In *Artifacts: An Introduction of Early Materials and Technology*. Duckworth, London.

Hodges, H. W. M. (editor)
1987   *In Situ Archaeological Conservation*. Getty Conservation Institute, Los Angeles.

Hoffman, C.
1990   Red Soils in the Sunset: Close Interval Core Sampling at Southern New England Sites. Paper presented at the annual meeting of the Northeastern Anthropological Association, Burlington, Vermont.
1993   Close-Interval Core Sampling: Tests of a Method for Predicting Internal Site Structure. *Journal of Field Archaeology* 20:461–475.

Hoffman, R.
1989   Seasonality Analysis of Catfish Pectoral Spines from a Southeastern Archaeological Faunal Assemblage. *Tennessee Anthropologist* 14(1):85–92.

Hofmann-Wellenhof, B., H. Lichtenegger, and J. Collins
1994   *Global Positioning System: Theory and Practice*. 2nd ed. Springer-Verlag, New York.

Hole, B. L.
1980   Sampling in Archaeology: A Critique. *Annual Reviews in Anthropology* 9:217–234.

Hole, F.
1978   Changing Directions in Archaeological Thought. In *Ancient North Americans,* edited by J. D. Jennings, pp. 1–23. W. H. Freeman, San Francisco.

Hole, F., K. V. Flannery, and J. A. Neeley
1967   *Prehistoric Human Ecology of the Deh Luran Plain: An Early Village Sequence from Khuzistan, Iran*. Memoirs 1. Museum of Anthropology, University of Michigan, Ann Arbor.

Hole, F., and R. F. Heizer
1965   *An Introduction to Prehistoric Archeology*. Holt, Rinehart & Winston, New York.
1973   *An Introduction to Prehistoric Archeology*. 3rd ed. Holt, Rinehart & Winston, New York.
1977   *Prehistoric Archaeology: A Brief Introduction*. Holt, Rinehart & Winston, New York.

Holliday, V. T.
1992   Soil Formation, Time, and Archaeology. In *Soils in Archaeology: Landscape Evolution and Human Occupation,* edited by V. T. Holliday, pp. 101–118. Smithsonian Institution Press, Washington, D.C.

Holliday, V. T. (editor)
1992   *Soils in Archaeology: Landscape Evolution and Human Occupation*. Smithsonian Institution Press, Washington, D.C.

Holloway, R. G.
1981   *Preservation and Experimental Diagenesis of the Pollen Exine*. Unpublished Ph.D. dissertation, Department of Biology, Texas A&M University, College Station.

1984   Prehistoric Medicinal Uses of Plants by a Late Archaic Population in Culberson County, Texas as Revealed by Coprolite Analysis. *Bulletin of the Texas Archeological Society* 54:319–325.
1986   Macrobotanical Analysis of Charcoal Materials from the Choke Canyon Reservoir Area, Texas. In *Archaeological Investigations at Choke Canyon Reservoir,* edited by G. Hall, T. R. Hester, and S. L. Black, pp. 437–451. Choke Canyon Series 10. Center for Archaeological Research, University of Texas at San Antonio.
n.d.   *Pollen and Plant Macrofossil Analysis of Human Coprolites from Dryden Cave, Nevada*. Manuscript on file, Basin Research Associates, San Leandro, California.

Holman, J. A.
1981   *A Review of North American Pleistocene Snakes*. Publications of the Museum, Michigan State University, East Lansing.

Honea, K. H.
1964   The Patination of Stone Artifacts. *Plains Anthropologist* 9(23):14–17.

Hood, J. S. R.
1977   Photogrammetry and Field Archaeology. *Antiquity* 51 (202):151.

Hope, J.
1983   Recovery and Analysis of Bone in Australian Archaeological Sites. In *Australian Field Archaeology: A Guide to Techniques,* edited by G. Connah, pp. 126–134. Australian Institute of Aboriginal Studies, Canberra.

Hopkins, D. M.
1959   Cenozoic History of the Bering Land Bridge. *Science* 129:1519–1528.

Howell, C. L., and W. Blanc
1992   *A Practical Guide to Archaeological Photography*. Institute of Archaeology, University of California, Los Angeles.

Howell, T. L.
1993   Evaluating the Utility of Auger Testing as a Predictor of Subsurface Artifact Density. *Journal of Field Archaeology* 20:475–485.

Howells, W. W.
1973   *Cranial Variation in Man: A Study of Multivariate Analysis of Patterns of Difference Among Recent Human Populations*. Papers of the Peabody Museum of Archaeology and Ethnology 67. Harvard University, Cambridge.

Howse, D.
1980   *Greenwich Time and the Discovery of Longitude*. Oxford University Press, Oxford.

Huang, W. H., and R. M. Walker
1967   Fossil Alpha-Particle Recoil Tracks: A New Method of Age Determination. *Science* 155: 1103–1106.

Hudson, J. (editor)
1993   *From Bones to Behavior: Ethnoarchaeological and Experimental Contributions to the Interpretation of Faunal Remains*. Occasional Paper 21. Center for Archaeological Investigations, Southern Illinois University, Carbondale.

Huebner, J. A.
1991   Radiocarbon and the North American Archaeologist. *La Tierra* 18(1):15–28. Southern Texas Archaeological Association, San Antonio.

Huelsbeck, D. R.
1989   Zooarchaeological Measures Revisited. *Historical Archaeology* 23:113–117.

Huelsbeck, D. R., and G. Wessen
1982   Thoughts on the Collection, Conservation, and Curation of Faunal Remains. *Northwest Anthropological Research Notes* 16:221–230.

Hughes, R. E. (editor)
1984   *Obsidian Studies in the Great Basin*. Contributions 45. Archaeological Research Facility, University of California, Berkeley.

Hughes, S. S.
1979   *Surveyors and Statesmen: Land Measuring in Colonial Virginia*. Virginia Surveyors Foundation, Virginia Association of Surveyors, Richmond.

Hulbricht, L.
1985   *The Distributions of the Native Land Mollusks of the Eastern United States*. Fieldiana: Zoology, New Series 24. Field Museum of Natural History, Chicago.

Hummert, J. R., and D. P. Van Gerven
1983   Skeletal Growth in a Medieval Population from Sudanese Nubia. *American Journal of Physical Anthropology* 60:471–478.

Hunt, C. B.
1954   Desert Varnish. *Science* 126:183–184.

Hunt, W. J., Jr., and J. Brandon
1990   Using Agricultural Grain Cleaners to Mechanically Screen Earth. *Journal of Field Archaeology* 17:116–121.

Hurley, W. H.
1979   *Prehistoric Cordage: Identification of Impressions on Pottery*. Aldine Manuals on Archaeology 3. Taraxacum, Washington, D.C.

Hurst, V. J., and A. R. Kelly
1961   Patination of Cultural Flints. *Science* 134:251–256.

Hurst, W. J., R. A. Martin, S. M. Tarka, and G. D. Hall
1989   Authentication of Cocoa in Maya Vessels Using High Performance Liquid Chromatographic Techniques. *Journal of Chromatography* 466:279–289.

Huxhold, W. E.
1991   *An Introduction to Urban Geographic Information Systems*. Oxford University Press, Oxford and New York.

Huxtable, J., and M. J. Aitken
1986   Dating of European Flint by Thermoluminescence. In *Proceedings of the 24th International Archaeometry Symposium*, edited by J. S. Olin and M. J. Blackman, pp. 465–472. Smithsonian Institution Press, Washington, D.C.

Hyder, W. D., and M. Oliver
1983   The 35 mm Camera and Rock Art Photography. In *Ancient Images on Stone*, edited by J. A. Van Tilburg, pp. 96–101. Institute of Archaeology, University of California, Los Angeles.

Hyland, D. C., J. M. Tersak, J. M. Adovasio, and M. I. Siegel
1990   Identification of the Species of Origin of Residual Blood on Lithic Material. *American Antiquity* 55:104–112.

Ikeya, M.
1978   Electron Spin Resonance as a Method of Dating. *Archaeometry* 20:147–158.
1986   Electron Spin Resonance. In *Dating and Age Determination of Biological Materials*, edited by M. R. Zimmerman and J. L. Angel, pp. 59–125. Croom Helm, New Hampshire.

Ikeya, M., and T. Miki
1980   Electron Spin Resonance Dating of Animal and Human Bones. *Science* 207:977–979.

Ikeya, M., and A. N. Poulianos
1979   ESR-Age of the Trace of Fire at Petralona. *Anthropos* 6:44–47.

Imboden, O., Jr., and J. N. Rinker
1975   Photography in the Field. In *Photography in Archaeological Research*, edited by E. Harp, Jr., pp. 51–96. University of New Mexico Press, Albuquerque.

Ingbar, E.
1985   A Comparison of Small-Scale Recovery Techniques. In *The Archaeology of Hidden Cave, Nevada*, edited by D. H. Thomas, pp. 74–80. Anthropological Papers 61, Pt. 1. American Museum of Natural History, New York.

Ingersoll, D., J. E. Yellen, and W. MacDonald (editors)
1977   *Experimental Archaeology*. Columbia University Press, New York.

International Committee on Veterinary Gross Anatomical Nomenclature
1983   *Nomina Anatomica Veterinaria*, 3rd ed./*Nomina Histologica*, 2nd ed. World Association of Veterinary Anatomists, Ithaca, New York.

Irish, J. D., and C. G. Turner, II
1987   More Lingual Surface Attrition of the Maxillary Anterior Teeth in American Indians: Prehistoric Panamanians. *American Journal of Physical Anthropology* 73:209–213.

Isaac, G. L.

1978a Food Sharing and Human Evolution: Archaeological Evidence from the Plio-Pleistocene of East Africa. *Journal of Anthropological Research* 34: 311–325.

1978b The Food-Sharing Behavior of Protohuman Hominids. *Scientific American* 238:90–106.

1981 Stone Age Visiting Cards: Approaches to the Study of Early Land Use Patterns. In *Pattern of the Past: Studies in Honor of David Clarke*, edited by I. Hodder, G. Isaac, and N. Hammond, pp. 131–156. Cambridge University Press, Cambridge.

Iscan, M. Y., and K. A. R. Kennedy

1989 *Reconstruction of Life from the Skeleton.* Liss, New York.

Iscan, M. Y., S. R. Loth, and R. K. Wright

1984 Metamorphosis at the Sternal Rib End: A New Method to Estimate Age at Death in White Males. *American Journal of Physical Anthropology* 65: 147–156.

Iversen, J.

1941 Land Occupation in Denmark's Stoneage. *Danmarks Geologiske Undersogelse* 2:1–67.

Jackes, M. K.

1983 Osteological Evidence for Smallpox: A Possible Case from Seventeenth Century Ontario. *American Journal of Physical Anthropology* 60:75–81.

1992 Paleodemography: Problems and Techniques. In *Skeletal Biology of Past Peoples: Research Methods*, edited by S. R. Saunders and A. M. Katzenberg, pp. 189–224. Wiley-Liss, New York.

Jackson, J. B.

1984 *Discovering the Vernacular Landscape.* Yale University Press, New Haven, Connecticut.

Jacob, J. S.

1992 *The Agroecological Evolution of Cobweb Swamp, Belize.* Unpublished Ph.D. dissertation, Texas A&M University, College Station.

1995 Ancient Maya Wetland Agricultural Fields in Cobweb Swamp, Belize: Construction, Chronology, and Function. *Journal of Field Archaeology* 22:175–190.

Jacobson, C.

1988 *The Basic Essentials of Map and Compass.* ICS Books, Merrillville, Indiana.

Jacobson, T. W.

1974 New Radiocarbon Dates from Franchthi Cave: A Preliminary Note Regarding Collection of Samples by Means of Flotation. *Journal of Field Archaeology* 1:303–304.

Jakes, K. A., and H. J. Holter, III

1986 Replacement of Protein and Cellulosic Fibers by Copper Minerals and the Formation of Textile Pseudomorphs. In *Historic Textile and Paper Materials: Conservation and Characterization*, edited by H.

L. Needles, and S. H. Zeronion, pp. 277–290. Advances in Chemistry Series 212. American Chemical Society, Washington, D.C.

Janssens, P. A.

1970 *Paleopathology.* Curwen Press, Great Britain.

Jantz, R. L.

1977 Craniometric Relationships of Plains Populations: Historical and Evolutionary Implications. *Plains Anthropologist Memoir* 13:162–176.

Jantz, R. L., and D. W. Owsley

1984a Temporal Changes in Limb Proportionality Among Skeletal Samples of Arikara Indians. *Annals of Human Biology* 11:157–164.

1984b Long Bone Growth Variation Among Arikara Skeletal Populations. *American Journal of Physical Anthropology* 63:13–20.

Jarman, H. N., A. J. Legge, and J. A. Charles

1972 Retrieval of Plant Remains from Archaeological Sites by Froth Flotation. In *Papers in Economic Prehistory*, edited by E. Higgs, pp. 39–48. Cambridge University Press, Cambridge.

Jedrzejewska, H.

1972 Some New Techniques for Archaeological Textiles. In *Textile Conservation*, edited by J. E. Leene, pp. 235–241. Smithsonian Institution Press, Washington, D.C.

Jelinek, A. J.

1957 Pleistocene Faunas and Early Man. *Papers of the Michigan Academy of Science, Arts and Letters* 42:225–237.

Jelks, E. B.

1975 *The Use and Misuse of Random Sampling in Archaeology.* Jett, Normal, Illinois.

Jelks, E. B., and C. D. Tunnell

1959 *The Harroun Site.* Archaeology Series 2. Department of Anthropology, University of Texas at Austin.

Jennings, J. D.

1980 *Cowboy Cave.* Anthropological Papers 104. University of Utah, Salt Lake City.

Jirikowic, C.

1990 The Political Implications of a Cultural Practice: A New Perspective on Ossuary Burial in the Potomac Valley. *North American Archaeologist* 11:353–374.

Jochim, M.

1976 *Hunter-Gatherer Subsistence and Settlement: A Predictive Model.* Academic Press, New York.

Johanson, D., and M. Edey

1981 *Lucy: The Beginning of Humankind.* Simon & Schuster, New York.

Johansson, L-U.

1987 Bone and Related Materials. In *In Situ Archaeological Conservation*, edited by H. W. M. Hedges, pp. 132–137. Getty Conservation Institute, Los Angeles.

Johnsen, H., and B. Olsen
  1992   Hermeneutics and Archaeology: On the Philosoophy of Contextual Archaeology. *American Antiquity* 57(3):419–436.

Johnson, E.
  1985   Current Developments in Bone Technology. In *Advances in Archaeological Method and Theory*, vol. 8, edited by M. B. Schiffer, pp. 157–235. Academic Press, New York.

Johnson, I.
  1983   Planimetry: Scale Drawings from Photographs. In *Australian Field Archaeology: A Guide to Techniques*, edited by G. Connah, pp. 67–72. Australian Institute of Aboriginal Studies, Canberra.

Johnson, J. S.
  1994   Consolidation of Archaeological Bone: A Conservation Perspective. *Journal of Field Archaeology* 21:221–234.

Johnson, J. S., H. M. Ericson, and H. Iceland
  1995   Identification of Chemical and Physical Change During Acid Cleaning of Ceramics. *Materials Research Society Symposium Proceedings* 352:831–837. Materials Research Society, Pittsburgh.

Johnson, L., Jr.
  1964   *The Devil's Mouth Site.* Archaeology Series 6. Department of Anthropology, University of Texas at Austin.

Johnston, F. E., and L. O. Zimmer
  1989   Assessment of Growth and Age in the Immature Skeleton. In *Reconstruction of Life from the Skeleton*, edited by M. Y. Iscan and K. A. R. Kennedy, pp. 11–21. Liss, New York.

Jolley, R. L.
  1983   North American Historic Sites Zooarchaeology. *Historical Archaeology* 17:64–79.

Jones, D.
  1979   *Visions of Time: Experiments in Psychic Archaeology.* Theosophical Publishing House, Wheaton, Illinois.

Jones, J.
  1994   Pollen Evidence for Early Settlement and Agriculture in Northern Belize. *Palynology* 18: 205–211.

Jones, J. G., and V. M. Bryant, Jr.
  1992   Phytolith Taxonomy in Selected Species of Texas Cacti. In *Phytolith Systematics*, edited by G. Rapp and S. C. Mulholland, pp. 215–238. Plenum Press, New York.

Jones, J. G., and E. Weinstein
  1996   Pollen Analysis of Ceramic Containers from a Late Iron Age II or Persian Period Shipwreck Site near Haifa, Israel. In *Techniques in Palynology*, edited by J. Renn, R. G. Holloway, and V. M. Bryant, Jr., in press. AASP Contribution Series 33. Dallas.

Jones, K. T.
  1984   Small Animal Use by Hunter-Gatherers, and Its Archeological Record: Implications for Early Hominid Diet. In *First International Conference on Bone Modification Abstracts*, pp. 20–21. Center for the Study of Early Man, Orono, Maine.

Jones, V.
  1936   The Vegetal Remains of Newt Kash Hollow Shelter. In *Rock Shelters of Menifee County, Kentucky*, edited by W. S. Webb and W. D. Funkhouser. Reports in Archaeology and Ethnology 3. University of Kentucky, Lexington.

Joukowsky, M.
  1980   *A Complete Manual of Field Archaeology.* Prentice-Hall, Englewood Cliffs, New Jersey.

Jurmain, R.
  1990   Paleoepidemiology of a Central California Prehistoric Population from CA-ALA-329: II. Degenerative Disease. *American Journal of Physical Anthropology* 83:83–94.

Jurney, D. H.
  1986   *A Review and Critique of Tree-Ring Dating of a Possible Spanish Colonial Building in the Proposed Applewhite Reservoir Area.* Report submitted to the Texas Historical Commission, Austin.

Kals, W. S.
  1983   *Land Navigation Handbook: The Sierra Club Guide to Map and Compass.* Sierra Club Books, San Francisco.

Kamminga, J.
  1979   The Nature of Use Polish and Abrasive Smoothing on Stone Tools. In *Lithic Use-wear Analysis*, edited by B. Hayden, pp. 143–158. Academic Press, New York.

Kane, A. E., W. D. Lipe, T. A. Kohler, and C. K. Robinson
  1986   *Dolores Archaeological Program: Research Designs and Initial Survey Results.* U.S. Department of the Interior, Denver.

Kappelman, J.
  1993   The Attraction of Paleomagnetism. *Evolutionary Anthropology* 2(3):89–99.

Keates, J. S.
  1989   *Cartographic Design and Production.* 2nd ed. Longman, London.

Keegan, W. F., and M. J. DeNiro
  1988   Stable Carbon- and Nitrogen-Isotope Ratios of Bone Collagen Used to Study Coral-Reef and Terrestrial Components of Prehistoric Bahamian Diet. *American Antiquity* 53:320–336.

Keeley, L. H.
  1980   *Experimental Determination of Tool Use: A Microwear Analysis.* University of Chicago Press, Chicago.

Keen, J. A.
  1950   A Study of the Differences Between Male and Female Skulls. *American Journal of Physical Anthropology* 8:65–79.

Keepax, C.
1977   Contamination of Archaeological Deposits by Seeds of Modern Origin with Particular Reference to the Use of Flotation Machines. *Journal of Archaeological Science* 4:221–229.

Kehoe, T. F.
1967   *The Boarding School Bison Drive Site. Plains Anthropologist Memoir 4.*

Keleman, P.
1946   Precolumbian Art and Art History. *American Antiquity* 11:145–154.

Keller, C. M.
1973   *Montagu Cave in Prehistory: A Descriptive Analysis.* Anthropological Records 28. University of California, Berkeley.

Kelley, M. A.
1979   Sex Determination with Fragmented Skeletal Remains. *Journal of Forensic Sciences* 24: 154–158.
1989   Infectious Disease. In *Reconstruction of Life from the Skeleton,* edited by M. Y. Iscan and K. A. R. Kennedy, pp. 191–199. Liss, New York.

Kelley, M. A., and C. S. Larsen (editors)
1991   *Advances in Dental Anthropology.* Wiley-Liss, New York.

Kelley, S., O. Williams-Thorpe, and R. S. Thorpe
1994   Laser Argon Dating and Geological Provenancing of a Stone Axe from the Stonehenge Environs. *Archaeometry* 36:209–216.

Kelso, G. K.
1976   *Absolute Pollen Frequencies Applied to the Interpretation of Human Activities in Northern Arizona.* Unpublished Ph.D. dissertation, University of Arizona, Tucson.
1994   Palynology in Historical Rural-Landscape Studies: Great Meadows, Pennsylvania. *American Antiquity* 59:359–372.

Kelso, G. K., and I. L. Good
1995   Quseir Al-Qadim, Egypt, and the Potential of Archaeological Pollen Analysis in the Near East. *Journal of Field Archaeology* 22:191–202.

Kennedy, B. V., and G. M. LeMoine (editors)
1988   *Diet and Subsistence: Current Archaeological Perspectives.* Proceedings of the 19th Annual Conference, Archaeological Association of the University of Calgary, Calgary, Alberta.

Kennedy, K. A. R.
1989   Skeletal Markers of Occupational Stress. In *Reconstruction of Life from the Skeleton,* edited by M. Y. Iscan and K. A. R. Kennedy, pp. 129–160. Liss, New York.

Kent, B.
1988   *Making Dead Oysters Talk: Techniques for Analyzing Oysters from Archaeological Sites.* Maryland Historical Trust, Jefferson Patterson Park and Museum, St. Marys, Maryland.

Kent, S.
1986   The Influence of Sedentism and Aggregation on Porotic Hyperostosis and Anaemia: A Case Study. *Man* 21:605–636.

Kenworthy, M. A., E. M. King, M. E. Ruwell, and T. Van Houten
1985   *Preserving Field Records: Archival Techniques for Archaeologists and Anthropologists.* University Museum, University of Pennsylvania, Philadelphia.

Kenyon, K. M.
1961   *Beginning in Archaeology.* Praeger, New York.

Kerley, E. R., and D. H. Ubelaker
1978   Revisions in the Microscopic Method of Estimating Age at Death in Human Cortical Bone. *American Journal of Physical Anthropology* 49: 545–546.

Key, P. J., and R. L. Jantz
1990   Statistical Assessment of Population Variability: A Methodological Approach. *American Journal of Physical Anthropology* 82:53–59.

Kidd, K. E.
1954   Trade Goods Research Techniques. *American Antiquity* 20:1–8.

Kidd, K. E., and M. A. Kidd
1970   *A Classification System for Glass Beads for the Use of Field Archaeologists.* Canadian Historic Sites Occasional Papers in Archaeology and History. National Historic Sites Service, Ottawa.

Kidder, A. V.
1924   *An Introduction to the Study of Southwestern Archaeology.* Yale University Press, New Haven, Connecticut.
1931   *The Pottery of Pecos.* Papers Vol. 1, No. 5. R. S. Peabody Foundation for Archeology.

Kidder, A. V., and S. J. Guernsey
1921   *Basket Maker Caves of Northern Arizona.* Memoirs 8. Peabody Museum of Archaeology and Ethnology, Harvard University, Cambridge.

Kidder, A. V., J. D. Jennings, and E. M. Shook
1946   *Excavations at Kaminaljuyu, Guatemala.* Publication 561. Carnegie Institute of Washington, Washington, D.C.

Kidder, A. V., and J. E. Thompson
1938   The Correlation of Maya and Christian Chronologies. In *Co-operation in Research,* pp. 493–510. Publications 501. Carnegie Institution of Washington, Washington, D.C.

Kieser, J. A.
1990   *Human Adult Odontometrics: The Study of Variation in Adult Tooth Size.* Cambridge University Press, Cambridge.

Kieser, J. A., H. T. Groenveld, and C. B. Preston
1985   A Metrical Analysis of the South African Caucasoid Dentition. *Journal of the Dental Association of South Africa* 40:121–125.

King, J. E., W. Klippel, and W. Duffield
1975 Pollen Preservation and Archaeology in Eastern North America. *American Antiquity* 40:180–190.

King, T. F.
1978 *The Archeological Survey: Methods and Uses.* Heritage Conservation and Recreation Service, U.S. Department of the Interior, Washington, D.C.

King, T. F., P. P. Hickman, and G. Berg
1977 *Anthropology in Historic Preservation: Caring for Culture's Clutter.* Academic Press, New York.

Kintigh, K. W.
1984 Measuring Archaeological Diversity by Comparison with Simulated Assemblages. *American Antiquity* 49(1):44–54.
1988 The Effectiveness of Subsurface Testing: A Simulation Approach. *American Antiquity* 53: 686–707.

Kissam, P.
1981 *Surveying Practice.* 2nd ed. McGraw-Hill, New York.

Kjellstrom, B.
1994 *Be Expert with Map and Compass.* American Orienteering Service, La Porte, Indiana.

Klein, R. G.
1973 *Ice-age Hunters of the Ukraine.* University of Chicago Press, Chicago.

Klein, R. G., and K. Cruz-Uribe
1984 *The Analysis of Animal Bones from Archeological Sites.* University of Chicago Press, Chicago.

Klepinger, L. L., J. K. Kuhn, and S. Wendell
1986 An Elemental Analysis of Archaeological Bone from Sicily as a Test of Predictability of Diagenetic Change. *American Journal of Physical Anthropology* 70:325–331.

Klesert, A. J., and M. J. Andrews
1988 The Treatment of Human Remains on Navajo Lands. *American Antiquity* 53:310–320.

Kleusberg, A., and R. B. Langley
1990 The Limitations of GPS. *GPS World* 1(2).

Klippel, W. E., and D. F. Morey
1986 Contextual and Nutritional Analysis of Freshwater Gastropods from Middle Archaic Deposits at the Hayes Site, Middle Tennessee. *American Antiquity* 51:799–813.

Knight, H.
1966 The Photography of Petroglyphs and Pictographs. *New Zealand Archaeological Association Newsletter* 19(2).

Knudson, R.
1986 Contemporary Cultural Resource Management. In *American Archaeology, Past and Future,* edited by D. J. Meltzer, D. D. Fowler, and J. A. Sabloff, pp. 395–414. Smithsonian Institution Press, Washington, D.C.

Koch, C.
1989 *Taphonomy: A Bibliographic Guide to the Literature.* Center for the Study of First Americans, University of Maine, Orono.

Konigsberg, L. W.
1985 Demography and Mortuary Practice at Seip Mound One. *Midcontinental Journal of Archaeology* 10:123–148.
1987 *Population Genetic Models for Interpreting Prehistoric Intra-Cemetery Biological Variation.* Ph.D. dissertation, Northwestern University, Evanston, Illinois. University Microfilms, Ann Arbor.
1990 Analysis of Prehistoric Biological Variation Under a Model of Isolation by Geographic and Temporal Distance. *Human Biology* 62:49–70.

Konigsberg, L. W., and J. Blangero
1993 Multivariate Quantitative Genetic Simulations in Anthropology with an Example from the South Pacific. *Human Biology* 65:897–915.

Konigsberg, L. W., J. E. Buikstra, and J. Bullington
1989 A Reply to Corruccini, Brandon, and Handler and to Holland. *American Antiquity* 54:626–636.

Koob, S. P.
1984 The Consolidation of Archaeological Bone. In *Adhesives and Consolidants,* edited by N. S. Bromelle, E. M. Pye, P. Smith, and G. Thomson, pp. 98–102. International Institute for Conservation of Historic and Artistic Works, London.
1986 The Use of Paraloid B–72 as an Adhesive: Its Application for Archaeological Ceramics and Other Materials. *Studies in Conservation* 31:7–14.

Kosa, F.
1989 Age Estimation from the Fetal Skeleton. In *Age Markers in the Human Skeleton,* edited by M. Y. Iscan, pp. 55–70. Charles C. Thomas, Springfield, Illinois.

Kowalewski, S. A.
1976 Review of: *The Prehistory of the Tehuacan Valley, Volume 5: Excavations and Reconnaissance. American Antiquity* 41:581–583.

Kozuch, L., and C. Fitzgerald
1989 A Guide to Identifying Shark Centra from Southeastern Archaeological Sites. *Southeastern Archaeology* 8:146–157.

Kraft, H.
1971 Ammonium Chloride as an Aid in Enhancing the Detail of Lithic Artifacts for Photography and Study. *Man in the Northeast* 1:53–57.

Kraft, J. C., I. Kayan, and S. E. Aschenbrenner
1985 Geological Studies of Coastal Change Applied to Archaeological Settings. In *Archaeological Geology,* edited by G. Rapp, Jr., and J. A. Gifford, pp. 57–84. Yale University Press, New Haven, Connecticut.

Krakker, J. J., M. J. Shott, and P. D. Welch
1983 Design and Evaluation of Shovel-test Sampling in Regional Archaeological Survey. *Journal of Field Archaeology* 10(4):469–480.

Krauskopf, K. B.

1956   Dissolution and Precipitation of Silica at Low Temperatures. *Geochimica et Cosmo Chimica Acta* 10:1–26.

Krieger, A. D.

1944   The Typological Concept. *American Antiquity* 9:271–288.

1946   *Culture Complexes and Chronologies in Northern Texas with Extensions of Puebloan Datings to the Mississippi Valley.* Publications 4640. University of Texas at Austin.

Kroeber, A. L.

1916   *Zuni Potsherds.* Anthropological Papers 28, Pt. 1. American Museum of Natural History, New York.

1940   Statistical Classification. *American Antiquity* 6:29–44.

1948   *Anthropology.* Harcourt, Brace, New York.

Kroeber, A. L., and W. D. Strong

1924   *The Uhle Pottery Collection from Ica.* Publications in American Archaeology and Ethnology 21: 95–133. University of California, Berkeley.

Krogman, W. M., and M. Y. Iscan

1986   *The Human Skeleton in Forensic Medicine.* Charles C. Thomas, Springfield, Illinois.

Krumbein, W. C.

1965   Sampling in Paleontology. In *Handbook of Paleontological Techniques,* edited by B. Kummel and D. Raup, pp. 137–149. W. H. Freeman, San Francisco.

Kubler, G.

1948   *Towards Absolute Time: Guano Archeology.* Memoir 4. Society for American Archaeology, Washington, D.C.

Kunstadter, P.

1972   Demography, Ecology, Social Structure, and Settlement Patterns. In *The Structure of Human Populations,* edited by G. A. Harrison and A. J. Boyce, pp. 313–351. Clarendon Press, Oxford.

Kvamme, K. L.

1989   Geographic Information Systems in Regional Archaeological Research and Data Management. In *Advances in Archaeological Method and Theory,* vol. 1, edited by M. B. Schiffer, pp. 139–203. University of Arizona Press, Tucson.

Kyle, J. H.

1986   Effects of Post-Burial Contamination on the Concentrations of Major and Minor Elements in Human Bones and Teeth—Their Implications for Palaeodietary Research. *Journal of Archaeological Science* 13:403–416.

Lallo, J., G. J. Armelagos, and R. P. Mensforth

1977   The Role of Diet, Disease, and Physiology in the Origin of Porotic Hyperostosis. *Human Biology* 49:471–483.

Lamb, T. R., and L. Newsom

1983   Preservation and Conservation of Organic Ma-terials. In *The Conservation of Archaeological Materials,* edited by C. J. Fairbanks, pp. 19–38. Special Publication 1. *Florida Journal of Anthropology.*

Lamberg-Karlovsky, C. C.

1974   Excavations at Tepe Yahya. In *Archaeological Research in Retrospect,* edited by G. R. Willey, pp. 269–292. Winthrop, Cambridge, Massachusetts.

Lambert, J. B., S. V. Simpson, C. B. Szpunar, and J. E. Buikstra

1984   Ancient Human Diet from Inorganic Analysis of Bone. *Accounts of Chemical Research* 17:298–305.

Lambert, J. B., C. B. Szpunar, and J. E. Buikstra

1979   Chemical Analysis of Excavated Human Bone from Middle and Late Woodland Sites. *Archaeometry* 21:115–129.

Lambert, J. B., J. M. Weydert, S. R. Williams, and J. E. Buikstra

1990   Comparison of Methods for the Removal of Diagenetic Material in Buried Bone. *Journal of Archaeological Science* 17:453–468.

Laming-Emperaire, A.

1963   *L'archéologie préhistorique.* Editions du Seuil, Paris.

Lancaster, J. A., J. M. Pinkley, P. Van Cleave, and D. Watson

1954   *Archeological Investigations in Mesa Verde National Park, Colorado, 1950.* Archeological Research Series 2. National Park Service, Washington, D.C.

Landon, D.

1996   Feeding Colonial Boston: A Zooarchaeological Study. *Historical Archaeology* 30(1):1–153.

Lanford, W. A.

1977   Glass Hydration: A Method of Dating Glass Objects. *Science* 196:975–976.

Langenwalter, P. E., II

1980   The Archaeology of 19th Century Chinese Subsistence at the Lower China Store, Madera County, California. In *Archaeological Perspectives on Ethnicity in America,* edited by R. L. Schuyler, pp. 102–112. Baywood, Farmingdale, New York.

Larsen, C. S.

1982   *The Anthropology of St. Catherine's Island 3: Prehistoric Human Biological Adaptation.* Anthropological Papers 57, Pt. 3. American Museum of Natural History, New York.

Larsen, C. S., and G. R. Milner (editors)

1994   *In the Wake of Contact: Biological Responses to Conquest.* Wiley-Liss, New York.

Larsen, C. S., R. Shavit, and M. C. Griffin

1991   Dental Caries Evidence for Dietary Change: An Archaeological Context. In *Advances in Dental Anthropology,* edited by M. A. Kelley and C. S. Larsen, pp. 179–202. Wiley-Liss, New York.

Lasca, N. P., and J. Donahue (editors)

1990   *Archaeological Geology of North America.* Centennial Special Volume 4. Geological Society of America, Boulder, Colorado.

Laville, H., J. P. Rigaud, and J. Sackett
1980 *Rockshelters of the Perigord*. Academic Press, New York.

Lawlor, D. A., C. D. Dickel, W. W. Hauswirth, and P. Parham
1991 Ancient HLA Genes from 7,500-Year-Old Archaeological Remains. *Nature* 349:785–788.

Lawrence, B.
1951 *Part II. Post-cranial Skeletal Characters of Deer, Pronghorn, and Sheep-Goat with Notes on* Bos *and* Bison. Papers of the Peabody Museum of Archaeology and Ethnology vol. 35, No. 3. Harvard University, Cambridge.

Layton, R. (editor)
1989 *Conflict in the Archaeology of Living Traditions*. One World Archaeology Series, vol. 8. Unwin Hyman, London.

Leach, J. D., H. C. Monger, and R. Mauldin
1994 Eolian Geomorphology, Survey Intensity, and Landscape Patterning in the Surface Archeological Record. Paper presented at the 8th Mogollon Archaeological Conference, El Paso, Texas.

Leakey, M. D.
1971 *Olduvai Gorge, Vol. 3: Excavations in Beds I and II, 1960–1963*. Cambridge University Press, Cambridge.

LeBlanc, S. A.
1975 Micro-seriation: A Method for Fine Chronological Differentiations. *American Antiquity* 40:22–38.

Lee, R. B.
1984 *The Dobe !Kung*. Holt, Rinehart & Winston, New York.

Leechman, D.
1931 Technical Methods in the Preservation of Anthropological Museum Specimens. *Annual Report for 1929, National Museum of Canada Bulletin* 67:127–158. Ottawa.

Legg, C.
1992 *Remote Sensing and Geographic Information Systems: Geological Mapping, Mineral Exploration and Mining*. Ellis Horwood, New York.

Legge, A. J., and P. A. Rowley-Conwy
1991 ". . . Art Made Strong with Bones": A Review of Some Approaches to Osteoarchaeology. *International Journal of Osteoarchaeology* 1:3–15.

Lehmer, D. J.
1960 A Review of Trans-Pecos Archeology. *Bulletin of the Texas Archeological Society* 29 (for 1958): 109–144.

Leick, A.
1990 *GPS Satellite Surveying*. Wiley, New York.

Leigh, D.
1978 *First Aid for Finds*. RESCUE l. Hertford, England.

Leitner-Wild, E., and I. Steffan
1993 Uranium-Series Dating of Fossil Bones from Alpine Caves. *Archaeometry* 35:137–146.

LeMoine, G. M., and A. S. MacEachern (editors)
1983 *Carnivores, Human Scavengers and Predators: A Question of Bone Technology*. Proceedings of the 15th Annual Conference, Archaeological Association of the University of Calgary, Calgary, Alberta.

Lennstrom, H. A., and C. A. Hastorf
1992 Testing Old Wives' Tales in Paleoethnobotany: A Comparison of Bulk and Scatter Sampling Schemes from Pancan, Peru. *Journal of Archaeological Science* 19:205–230.

Leroi-Gourhan, A.
1975 The Flowers Found with Shanidar IV, A Neanderthal Burial in Iraq. *Science* 190:562–564.

Letham, L.
1995 *GPS Made Easy: Using Global Positioning Systems in the Outdoors*. The Mountaineers, Seattle.

Levitan, B.
1983 Reducing the Work-load: Sub-sampling Animal Bone Assemblages. *Circaea* 1(1):7–12.
1984 Reducing the Work-load: A Reply. *Circaea* 2(2):75–76.

Lewis, R.
1979 *Use of Opal Phytoliths in Paleoenvironmental Reconstruction*. Unpublished Master's thesis, University of Wyoming, Laramie.

Lewis, R. H.
1976 *Manual for Museums*. National Park Service, Washington, D.C.

Lewis, T. M. N., and M. K. Kneberg
1946 *Hiwassee Island*. University of Tennessee Press, Knoxville.

Libby, W. F.
1955 *Radiocarbon Dating*. 2nd ed. University of Chicago Press, Chicago.

Lightfoot, K. G.
1979 Food Redistribution Among Prehistoric Pueblo Groups. *The Kiva* 44:319–339.
1986 Regional Surveys in the Eastern United States: The Strengths and Weaknesses of Implementing Subsurface Testing Programs. *American Antiquity* 51:484–504.
1989 A Defense of Shovel-test Sampling: A Reply to Shott. *American Antiquity* 54:413–416.

Lillesand, T. M., and R. W. Kiefer
1987 *Remote Sensing and Image Interpretation*. 2nd ed. Wiley, New York.

Limp, W. F.
1974 Water Separation and Flotation Processes. *Journal of Field Archaeology* 1:337–342.
1989 *The Use of Multispectral Digital Imagery in Archeological Investigations*. Research Series 34. Arkansas Archeological Survey, Fayetteville.

Lindsay, A. J., G. Williams-Dean, and J. Haas
1980 *The Curation and Management of Archaeological Collections*. Department of the Interior, Washington, D.C.

Lippert, D., and E. Shipp
1995   An Examination of the Use of Acetic and Nitric Acids in Cleaning Archaeological Ceramics. Manuscript on file. Materials Conservation Laboratory, Texas Memorial Museum, University of Texas at Austin.

Livingston, S. D.
1987   Prehistoric Biogeography of White-tailed Deer in Washington and Oregon. *Journal of Wildlife Management* 51:649–654.

Lloyd, S.
1963   *Mounds of the Near East*. Edinburgh University Press, Edinburgh.

Logan, W. D.
1952   *Graham Cave: An Archaic Site in Montgomery County, Missouri*. Memoir 2. Missouri Archaeological Society, Columbia.

Logsdon, T.
1992   *The Navstar Global Positioning System*. Van Nostrand Reinhold, New York.

Lothrop, S. K.
1928   *The Indians of Tierra del Fuego*. Heye Foundation Contributions 10. Museum of the American Indian, New York.
1937   *Coclé: An Archaeological Study of Central Panama*. Memoirs 7, Pt. I. Peabody Museum of Archaeology and Ethnology, Harvard University, Cambridge.

Loud, L. L., and M. R. Harrington
1929   *Lovelock Cave*. Publications in American Archaeology and Ethnology 25:1–183. University of California, Berkeley.

Lovejoy, C. O.
1971   Methods for the Detection of Census Error in Paleodemography. *American Anthropologist* 73:101–109.
1985   Dental Wear in the Libben Population: Its Functional Pattern and Role in the Determination of Adult Skeletal Age at Death. *American Journal of Physical Anthropology* 68:47–56.

Lovejoy, C. O., R. S. Meindl, T. R. Pryzbeck, T. S. Barton, K. G. Heiple, and D. Kotting
1977   Paleodemography of the Libben Site, Ottawa County, Ohio. *Science* 198:291–293.

Lovejoy, C. O., R. S. Meindl, T. R. Pryzbeck, and R. P. Mensforth
1985   Chronological Metamorphosis of the Auricular Surface of the Ilium: A New Method for Determining Adult Skeletal Age at Death. *American Journal of Physical Anthropology* 68:15–28.

Lovejoy, C. O., R. P. Mensforth, and G. J. Armelagos
1985   Five Decades of Skeletal Biology as Reflected in the *American Journal of Physical Anthropology*. In *A History of American Physical Anthropology*, edited by F. Spencer, pp. 329–336. Academic Press, New York.

Lovis, W. A.
1976   Quarter Sections and Forests: An Example of Probability Sampling in the Northeastern Woodlands. *American Antiquity* 41:364–371.
1996   Archaeopolitics: Testimony to Oversight Hearing on NAGPRA Implementation. *SAA Bulletin* 14(1):8.

Lowenstein, J. M.
1985   Molecular Approaches to the Identification of Species. *American Scientist* 73:541–547.

Loy, T. H.
1983   Prehistoric Blood Residues: Detection on Tool Surfaces and Identification of Species of Origin. *Science* 220:1269–1270.

Loy, T. H., and D. E. Nelson
1986   Potential Applications of the Organic Residues on Ancient Tools. In *Proceedings of the 24th International Archaeometry Symposium*, edited by J. S. Olin and M. J. Blackman, pp. 175–185. Smithsonian Institution Press, Washington, D.C.

Lucas, A., and J. R. Harris
1962   *Ancient Egyptian Materials and Industries*. E. Arnold, London, England.

Luedtke, B. E.
1992   *An Archaeologist's Guide to Chert and Flint*. Archaeological Research Tools 7. Institute of Archaeology, University of California, Los Angeles.

Lukacs, J. R.
1989   Dental Paleopathology: Methods for Reconstructing Dietary Patterns. In *Reconstruction of Life from the Skeleton*, edited by M. Y. Iscan and K. A. R. Kennedy, pp. 261–286. Liss, New York.

Lukacs, J. R., and B. E. Hemphill
1991   The Dental Anthropology of Prehistoric Baluchistan: A Morphometric Approach to the Peopling of South Asia. In *Advances in Dental Anthropology*, edited by M. A. Kelley and C. S. Larsen, pp. 77–119. Wiley-Liss, New York.

Lundelius, E. L., Jr.
1967   Late Pleistocene and Holocene Faunal History of Central Texas. In *Pleistocene Extinctions: The Search for a Cause*, edited by P. S. Martin and H. E. Wright, Jr., pp. 287–319. Yale University Press, New Haven, Connecticut.
1979   Post-Pleistocene Mammals from Pratt Cave and Their Environmental Significance. In *Biological Investigations in the Guadalupe Mountains National Park, Texas*, edited by H. H. Genoays and R. J. Baker, pp. 239–258. Proceedings and Transactions Series 4. National Park Service, Washington, D.C.
1989   The Implications of Disharmonious Assemblages for Pleistocene Extinctions. *Journal of Archaeological Science* 16:407–417.

Lyman, R. L.
1977   Analysis of Historic Faunal Remains. *Historical Archaeology* 11:67–73.

1979a *Archaeological Faunal Analysis: A Bibliography.* Occasional Papers 31. Idaho Museum of Natural History, Pocatello.

1979b Faunal Analysis: An Outline of Method and Theory with Some Suggestions. *Northwest Anthropological Research Notes* 13:22–35.

1982a Archaeofaunas and Subsistence Studies. In *Advances in Archaeological Method and Theory*, vol. 5, edited by M. B. Schiffer, pp. 331–393. Academic Press, New York.

1982b Nomenclature in Faunal Studies: A Response to Olsen and Olsen. *American Antiquity* 47:179–180.

1984 Bone Density and Differential Survivorship of Fossil Classes. *Journal of Anthropological Archaeology* 3:259–299.

1986 On the Analysis and Interpretation of Species List Data in Zooarchaeology. *Journal of Ethnobiology* 6:67–81.

1987a Archaeofaunas and Butchery Studies: A Taphonomic Perspective. In *Advances in Archaeological Method and Theory*, vol. 10, edited by M. B. Schiffer, pp. 249–337. Academic Press, New York.

1987b On Zooarchaeological Measures of Socioeconomic Position and Cost-Efficient Meat Purchases. *Historical Archaeology* 21:58–66.

1994a Quantitative Units and Terminology in Zooarchaeology. *American Antiquity* 59:36–71.

1994b *Vertebrate Taphonomy.* Cambridge University Press, Cambridge.

Lyman, R. L., and G. L. Fox
1989 A Critical Evaluation of Bone Weathering as an Indication of Bone Assemblage Formation. *Journal of Archaeological Science* 16:293–317.

Lyman, R. L., and S. D. Livingston
1983 Late Quaternary Mammalian Zoogeography of Eastern Washington. *Quaternary Research* 20:360–373.

Lynch, T. F., R. Gillespie, J. A. J. Gowlett, and R. E. M. Hedges
1985 Chronology of Guitarrero Cave, Peru. *Science* 229:864–867.

Lyons, T. (editor)
1977 *Remote Sensing Experiments in Cultural Resource Studies: Non-destructive Methods of Archaeological Exploration, Survey, and Analysis.* National Park Service, Washington, D.C.

Lyons, T., and T. E. Avery
1972 *Remote Sensing: A Handbook for Archaeologists and Cultural Resource Managers.* U.S. Department of the Interior, National Park Service, Washington, D.C.

1977 *Remote Sensing for Archaeologists and Cultural Resource Managers.* National Park Service, Washington, D.C.

Lyons, T., and J. Ebert
1978 *Remote Sensing and Nondestructive Archaeology.* National Park Service, Washington, D.C.

Lyons, T. R., and R. K. Hitchcock
1977 *Aerial Remote Sensing Techniques in Archaeology.* Reports of the Chaco Center 2. Chaco Center, U.S. Department of the Interior, National Park Service, Albuquerque, New Mexico.

Lyons, T. R., and F. J. Mathien
1980 *Cultural Resources: Remote Sensing.* U.S. Department of the Interior, National Park Service, Washington, D.C.

Lyons, T., and D. H. Scovill
1978 Non-destructive Archaeology and Remote Sensing: A Conceptual and Methodological Stance. In *Remote Sensing and Non-destructive Archaeology*, edited by T. R. Lyons and J. I. Ebert, pp. 3–19. National Park Service, Washington, D.C.

McBride, K. A.
1984 *The Prehistory of the Lower Connecticut River Valley.* Archaeological Research Monograph. Public Archaeology Survey Team, Storrs, Connecticut.

McConnell, D.
1962 Dating of Fossil Bone by the Fluorine Method. *Science* 136:241–244.

McDonald, J. N.
1981 *North American Bison: Their Classification and Evolution.* University of California Press, Los Angeles.

MacDonald, L. L.
1974 *Opal Phytoliths as Indicators of Plant Succession in North Central Wyoming.* Unpublished Master's thesis, University of Wyoming, Laramie.

McEntyre, J. F.
1986 *Land Survey Systems.* Landmark Enterprises, Rancho Cordova, California.

McGill, G.
1995 *Building on the Past.* E and FN Spon, London.

McGimsey, C. R., III
1985 "This, Too, Will Pass": Moss-Bennett in Perspective. *American Antiquity* 50(2):326–331.

MacGregor, A.
1985 *Bone, Antler, Ivory and Horn: The Technology of Skeletal Materials Since the Roman Period.* Croom Helm, London.

MacGregor, J. G.
1981 *Vision of an Ordered Land: The Story of the Dominion Land Survey.* Western Producer Prairie Books, Saskatoon, Saskatchewan.

McHargue, G., and M. Roberts
1977 *A Field Guide to Conservation Archaeology in North America.* Lippincott, Philadelphia.

McIntosh, J.
1986 *The Practical Archaeologist.* Facts on File, New York.

McKern, T. W.
1958 *The Use of Short Wave Ultra-Violet Rays for the Segregation of Commingled Skeletal Remains.* U.S. Army Technical Report EP-98. Environmental Pro-

tection Research Division, Quartermaster Research and Development Center, U.S. Army, Natick, Massachusetts.

1970   Estimation of Skeletal Age: From Puberty to About 30 Years of Age. In *Personal Identification in Mass Disasters*, edited by T. D. Stewart, pp. 41–56. National Museum of Natural History, Washington, D.C.

McKern, T. W., and T. D. Stewart

1957   *Skeletal Age Changes in Young American Males Analyzed from the Standpoint of Age Identification.* U.S. Army Technical Report EP-45. Environmental Protection Research Division, Quartermaster Research and Development Center, U.S. Army, Natick, Massachusetts.

McKern, W. C.

1930   The Kletzien and Nitschke Mound Groups. *Bulletin of the Public Museum of the City of Milwaukee* 3(4).

McKinney, C. R.

1977   *An Evaluation of Uranium Series Disequilibrium Dating of Fossil Teeth.* Unpublished Master's thesis, University of Florida, Gainesville.

McKusick, C. R.

1986   *Southwest Indian Turkeys: Prehistory and Comparative Osteology.* Southwest Bird Laboratory, Globe, Arizona.

Maclean, A.

1994   *Remote Sensing and GIS: An Integration of Technologies for Resource Management.* American Society of Photogrammetry and Remote Sensing, Bethesda, Maryland.

MacMahan, H., Jr.

1972   *Stereogram Book of Contours Illustrating Selected Landforms.* Hubbard Scientific Company, Chippewa Falls, Wisconsin.

McManamon, F. P.

1981a   Parameter Estimation and Site Discovery in the Northeast. *Contract Abstracts and CRM Archaeology* 1(3):43–48.

1981b   Probability Sampling and Archaeological Survey in the Northeast: An Estimation Approach. In *Foundations of Northeast Archaeology*, edited by D. Snow, pp. 194–227. Academic Press, New York.

1984a   Discovering Sites Unseen. In *Advances in Archaeological Method and Theory*, vol. 7, edited by M. B. Schiffer, pp. 223–292. Academic Press, New York.

1984b   Method and Techniques for Survey and Site Examination. In *Chapters in the Archaeology of Cape Cod*, vol. 1, edited by F. P. McManamon, pp. 25–44. Cultural Resource Management Study 8. U.S. Department of the Interior, Washington, D.C.

McMillan, R. B.

1991   Paul W. Parmalee: A Pioneer in Zooarchaeology. In *Beamers, Bobwhites, and Blue-Points: Tributes to the Career of Paul W. Parmalee*, edited by J. R. Purdue, W. E. Klippel, and B. W. Styles, pp. 1–13. Scientific Papers Vol. 23. Illinois State Museum, Springfield.

McMillon, B.

1991   *The Archaeology Handbook: A Field Manual and Resource Guide.* John Wiley and Sons, New York.

MacNeish, R. S.

1958   *Preliminary Archaeological Investigations in the Sierra de Tamaulipas, Mexico.* American Philosophical Society Transactions 48, Pt. 6.

1975   *The Prehistory of the Tehuacan Valley, Volume 5: Excavations and Reconnaissance.* University of Texas Press, Austin.

1978   *The Science of Archaeology?* Duxbury Press, North Scituate, Massachusetts.

MacNeish, R. S. (editor)

1970   *The Prehistory of the Tehuacan Valley*, vol. 3. University of Texas Press, Austin.

1972   *The Prehistory of the Tehuacan Valley*, vol. 5. University of Texas Press, Austin.

McWeeney, L.

1989   What Lies Lurking Below the Soil: Beyond the Archaeobotanical View of Flotation Samples. *North American Archaeologist* 10(3):227–230.

Madry, S. L. H.

1989   Geographic Resources Analysis Support System (GRASS): An Integrated, UNIX-Based, Public Domain GIS and Image Processing System for Resource Analysis and Management. In *Proceedings of GIS/LIS '89*, November 1989. Orlando.

1990   The Realities of Hardware. In *Interpreting Space: GIS and Archaeology*, edited by K. M. S. Allen, S. W. Green, and E. B. W. Zubrow, pp. 173–183. Taylor & Francis, London.

Madry, S. L. H., and C. L. Crumley

1990   An Application of Remote Sensing and GIS in a Regional Archaeological Settlement Pattern Analysis: The Arroux Valley, Burgundy, France. In *Interpreting Space: GIS and Archaeology*, edited by K. M. S. Allen, S. W. Green, and E. B. W. Zubrow, pp. 364–380. Taylor & Francis, London.

Magellan Systems Corporation

1992   *Magellan GPS Brain.* Magellan Systems Corporation, San Dimas, California.

Maiorana, V. C., and L. M. van Valen

1985   Terrestrial Isopods for Preparing Delicate Vertebrate Skeletons. *Systematic Zoology* 34:242–245.

Maizlish, A., and W. S. Hunt

1989   *The World Map Directory.* Map Link, Santa Barbara, California.

Makower, J., and L. Bergheim (editors)

1990   *The Map Catalog: Every Kind of Map and Chart on Earth and Even Some Above It.* Rev. ed. Vintage, New York.

Mallouf, R. J.
1987   *A Case Study of Plow Damage to Chert Artifacts.* Report 33. Office of the State Archaeologist, Texas Historical Commission, Austin.

Maltman, A.
1990   *Geological Maps: An Introduction.* Van Nostrand Reinhold, New York.

Mandel, R. D.
1992   Soils and Holocene Landscape Evolution in Central and Southwestern Kansas: Implications for Archaeological Research. In *Soils in Archaeology,* edited by V. T. Holliday, pp. 41–100. Smithsonian Institution Press, Washington, D.C.

Mann, R. W.
1990   *Regional Atlas of Bone Disease: A Guide to Pathologic and Normal Variation in the Human Skeleton.* Charles C. Thomas, Springfield, Illinois.

Mann, R. W., W. M. Bass, and L. Meadows
1990   Time Since Death and Decomposition of the Human Body: Variables and Observations in Case and Experimental Field Studies. *Journal of Forensic Sciences* 35:103–111.

Manning, A. P.
1994   A Cautionary Note on the Use of Hemastix and Dot-Blot Assays for the Detection and Confirmation of Archaeological Blood Residues. *Journal of Archaeological Science* 21:159–162.

Manning, T. G.
1967   *Government in Science: The U.S. Geological Survey, 1867–1894.* University of Kentucky Press, Lexington.

Marchbanks, M. L.
1989   *Lipid Analysis in Archaeology: An Initial Study of Ceramics and Subsistence at the George C. Davis Site.* Unpublished Master's thesis, Department of Anthropology, University of Texas at Austin.

Marks, M. K., J. C. Rose, and E. L. Buie
1985   Bioarcheology of Seminole Sink. In *Seminole Sink: Excavation of a Vertical Shaft Tomb, Val Verde County, Texas,* compiled by S. A. Turpin, pp. 99–152. Research Report 93. Texas Archeological Survey, University of Texas at Austin.

Marquardt, W. H.
1978   Advances in Archaeological Seriation. In *Advances in Archaeological Method and Theory,* vol. l, edited by M. B. Schiffer, pp. 266–314. Academic Press, New York.

Marquardt, W. H., and C. L. Crumley
1987   Theoretical Issues in the Analysis of Spatial Patterning. In *Regional Dynamics: Burgundian Landscapes in Historical Perspective,* edited by C. L. Crumley and W. H. Marquardt, pp. 1–18. Academic Press, San Diego.

Marquardt, W. H., and P. J. Watson
1983   The Shell Mound Archaic of Western Ken-tucky. In *Archaic Hunters and Gatherers in the American Midwest,* edited by J. L. Phillips and J. A. Brown, pp. 323–339. Academic Press, New York.

Marquina, I.
1951   *Arquitectura Prehispanica.* Memorias del Instituto National de Antropología e Historia 1. Mexico City.

Martin, A. C., and Barkley, W. D.
1973   *Seed Identification Manual.* Univ. of California Press, Berkeley, p. 221.

Martin, D.
1991   *Geographic Information Systems and Their Socioeconomic Applications.* Routledge & Kegan Paul, London.

Martin, P. S., G. I. Quimby, and D. Collier
1947   *Indians Before Columbus.* University of Chicago Press, Chicago.

Martin, R., K. Smalley, and B. Sykes
1993   Archaeology and Genetics: Analysing DNA from Skeletal Remains. *World Archaeology* 25:18–28.

Martin, W. A., J. E. Bruseth, and R. J. Huggins
1991   Assessing Feature Function and Spatial Patterning of Artifacts with Geophysical Remote-Sensing Data. *American Antiquity* 56:701–720.

Martini, M., E. Sibilia, and G. Spinolo
1986   TL Dating on Archaeological Ceramics: Discussion on Accuracy Limitations and a Report on the Recent Activity in Milan. In *New Paths of the Use of Nuclear Techniques for Art and Archaeology,* edited by G. Furlan, P. Cassola Guida, and C. Tuniz, pp. 113–123. World Scientific, Singapore.

Mason, J. A.
1961   *The Ancient Civilizations of Peru.* Penguin Books, Harmondsworth, Middlesex, England.

Massey, V. K.
1989   *The Human Skeletal Remains from a Terminal Classic Skull Pit at Colha, Belize.* Papers of the Colha Project 3. Texas Archeological Research Laboratory, University of Texas at Austin, and Department of Anthropology, Texas A&M University, College Station.

Massey, V. K., and D. G. Steele
1982   Preliminary Notes on the Dentition and Taphonomy of the Colha Human Skeletal Material. In *Archaeology at Colha, Belize: The 1981 Interim Report,* edited by T. R. Hester, H. J. Shafer, and J. D. Eaton, pp. 198–202. Center for Archaeological Research, University of Texas at San Antonio, San Antonio, and Centro Studi e Ricerche Ligabue, Venezia.

Mathiassen, T.
1927   *Archeology of Central Eskimos.* Report of the 5th Thule Expedition, 1921–24, Vol. 4, Pt. 1. Glyden Danske Boghandel, Nordisk Forlag, Copenhagen.

Matthiesen, D. G.
1989   The Curation of Avian Osteological Collec-

tions. In *Notes from a Workshop on Bird Specimen Preparation Held at the Carnegie Museum of Natural History in Conjunction with the 107th Stated Meeting of the American Ornithologists' Union, 7 August 1989,* compiled by S. P. Rogers and D. S. Wood, pp. 71–110. Pittsburgh, Pennsylvania.

Mauldin, R., J. D. Leach, and H. C. Monger
1994   Eolian Geomorphology, Artifact Patterning, and Assemblage Composition. Paper presented at the 8th Mogollon Archaeological Conference, El Paso, Texas.

Mayr, E.
1970   *Populations, Species, and Evolution.* Harvard University Press, Cambridge.

Meadow, R. H.
1978   Effects of Context on the Interpretation of Faunal Remains: A Case Study. In *Approaches to Faunal Analysis in the Middle East,* edited by R. H. Meadow and M. A. Zeder, pp. 15–21. Bulletin 2. Peabody Museum of Archaeology and Ethnology, Harvard University, Cambridge.
1980   Animal Bones: Problems for the Archaeologist Together with Some Possible Solutions. *Paléorient* 6:65–77.

Meighan, C. W.
1969   Molluscs as Food Remains in Archaeological Sites. In *Science in Archaeology,* 2nd ed., edited by D. Brothwell and E. Higgs, pp. 415–422. Thames & Hudson, London.
1977   Recognition of Short Time Periods Through Seriation. *American Antiquity* 42:628–629.
1994   Burying American Archaeology. *Archaeology* Nov.–Dec.:64–68.

Meighan, C. W., and B. D. Dillon
1982   Small Boats in Archaeological Exploration. In *Practical Archaeology,* edited by B. D. Dillon, pp. 113–136. Archaeological Research Tools 2. Institute of Archaeology, University of California, Los Angeles.

Meindl, R. S., and C. O. Lovejoy
1985   Ectocranial Suture Closure: A Revised Method for the Determination of Skeletal Age at Death Based on the Lateral-Anterior Sutures. *American Journal of Physical Anthropology* 68:57–66.
1989   Age Changes in the Pelvis: Implications for Paleodemography. In *Age Markers in the Human Skeleton,* edited by M. Y. Iscan, pp. 137–168. Charles C. Thomas, Springfield, Illinois.

Meindl, R. S., C. O. Lovejoy, and R. P. Mensforth
1983   Skeletal Age at Death: Accuracy of Determination and Implications for Human Demography. *Human Biology* 55:73–87.

Meko, D. M., C. W. Stockton, and T. J. Blasing
1985   Periodicity in Tree Rings from the Corn Belt. *Science* 229:381–384.

Melcher, C. L., and D. W. Zimmerman
1977   Thermoluminescent Determination of Prehis-

toric Heat Treatment of Chert Artifacts. *Science* 197: 1359–1362.

Meltzer, D. J.
1986   Clovis Fluted Point Survey. *Bulletin of the Texas Archeological Society* 57:27–68.
1994   *Search for the First Americans.* Smithsonian Press and St. Remy Press, Montreal.

Mensforth, R. P.
1985   Relative Tibia Long Bone Growth in the Libben and Bt-5 Prehistoric Skeletal Populations. *American Journal of Physical Anthropology* 68: 247–262.
1986   *Paleodemography of the Carlston Annis (Bt-5) Skeletal Population.* Unpublished Ph.D. dissertation, Department of Biological Sciences, Kent State University, Kent, Ohio.

Merbs, C. F.
1989   Trauma. In *Reconstruction of Life from the Skeleton,* edited by M. Y. Iscan and K. A. R. Kennedy, pp. 161–189. Liss, New York.

Merbs, C. F., and R. J. Miller (editors)
1985   *Health and Disease in the Prehistoric Southwest.* Anthropological Research Papers 34. Arizona State University, Tempe.

Merriam, C. H.
1928   Why Not More Care in Identification of Animal Remains? *American Anthropologist* 30:731–732.

Merrill, R. H.
1941   Photo-Surveying Assists Archaeologist. *Civil Engineering* 11:233–235.

Michaels, G., and H. J. Shafer
1994   Excavations at Operation 2037 and 2040. In *Continuing Archeology at Colha, Belize,* edited by T. R. Hester, H. J. Shafer, and J. D. Eaton, pp. 117–128. Studies in Archeology 16. Texas Archeological Research Laboratory, University of Texas at Austin.

Michels, J. W.
1973   *Dating Methods in Archaeology.* Seminar Press, New York.
1986   Obsidian Hydration Dating. *Endeavour* n.s. 10(2):97–99.

Michels, J. W., and I. S. T. Tsong
1980   Obsidian Hydration Dating: A Coming of Age. In *Advances in Archaeological Method and Theory,* vol. 3, edited by M. B. Schiffer, pp. 405–444. Academic Press, New York.

Michels, J. W., I. S. T. Tsong, and C. M. Nelson
1983   Obsidian Dating and East African Archaeology. *Science* 219:361–366.

Michie, J. L.
1969   A Mechanical Sifting Device. *Notebook of the Institute of Archaeology and Anthropology* 2(4/5): 15–19. University of South Carolina, Columbia.

Micozzi, M. S.
1991   *Postmortem Change in Human and Animal Re-*

mains: A Systematic Approach. Charles C. Thomas, Springfield, Illinois.

Middleton, J.
1844   On Fluorine in Bones, Its Source and Its Application to the Determination of Geological Age of Fossil Bones. *Proceedings of the Geological Society of London* 4:431–433.

Mihesuah, D. A.
1991   Despoiling and Desecration of Indian Property and Possessions. *National Forum* 71:15–17.

Miksicek, C. H.
1987   Formation Processes of the Archaeobotanical Record. In *Advances in Archaeological Method and Theory,* vol. 10, edited by M. B. Schiffer, pp. 211–247. Academic Press, New York.

Miles, A. E. W., and C. Grigson (editors)
1990   *Colyer's Variations and Diseases of the Teeth of Animals.* Cambridge University Press, Cambridge.

Miller, A.
1980   Phytoliths as Indicators of Farming Techniques. Paper presented at the 45th Annual Meeting of the Society for American Archaeology, Philadelphia.

Millon, R. (editor)
1973   *Urbanization at Teotihuacán, Mexico, Vol. 1: The Teotihuacán Map. Part Two: Maps.* University of Texas Press, Austin.

Milne, J.
1881   The Stone Age in Japan. *Journal of the Royal Anthropological Institute* 10:389–423.

Milner, G. R., and C. S. Larsen
1991   Teeth as Artifacts of Human Behavior: Intentional Mutilation and Accidental Modification. In *Advances in Dental Anthropology,* edited by M. A. Kelley and C. S. Larsen, pp. 357–378. Wiley-Liss, New York.

Minnis, P. E.
1981a   *Economic and Organizational Responses to Food Stress by Non-Stratified Societies: An Example from Prehistoric New Mexico.* Unpublished Ph.D. dissertation, University of Michigan, Ann Arbor.
1981b   Seeds in Archaeological Sites: Sources and Some Interpretive Problems. *American Antiquity* 45:143–152.

Minor, R.
1980   An Obsidian Hydration Rate for the Lower Columbia River Valley. *American Antiquity* 42:616–619.

Mitchell, H. C., and L. G. Simmons
1977   *The State Coordinate Systems: A Manual for Surveyors.* Special Publication, U.S. Coast and Geodetic Survey No. 235. U.S. Department of Commerce, Coast and Geodetic Survey, Rockville, Maryland.

Moffitt, F. H., and H. Bouchard
1991   *Surveying.* 9th ed. Harper & Row, New York.

Moffitt, F. H., and E. M. Mikhail
1980   *Photogrammetry.* Harper & Row, New York.

Molleson, T. I., and P. Cohen
1990   The Progression of Dental Attrition Stages Used for Age Assessment. *Journal of Archaeological Science* 17:363–371.

Monks, G. G.
1981   Seasonality Studies. In *Advances in Archaeological Method and Theory,* vol. 4, edited by M. B. Schiffer, pp. 177–240. Academic Press, New York.

Monmonier, M. S.
1985   *Technological Transition in Cartography.* University of Wisconsin Press, Madison.
1993   *Mapping It Out: Expository Cartography for the Humanities and Social Sciences.* University of Chicago Press, Chicago.

Mook, W. G., and H. T. Waterbolk
1985   *Radiocarbon Dating.* Handbooks for Archaeologists 3. European Science Foundation, Strasbourg.

Moore, K. M., M. L. Murrey, and M. J. Schoeninger
1989   Dietary Reconstruction from Bones Treated with Preservatives. *Journal of Archaeological Science* 16:437–446.

Moorrees, C. F. A., E. A. Fanning, and E. E. Hunt, Jr.
1963a   Formation and Resorption of Three Deciduous Teeth in Children. *American Journal of Physical Anthropology* 21:205–213.
1963b   Age Variation of Formation Stages for Ten Permanent Teeth. *Journal of Dental Research* 42:1490–1502.

Moorrees, C. F. A., and R. B. Reed
1954   Correlations Among Crown Diameters of Human Teeth. *Archives of Oral Biology* 9:685–697.

Morales, A., and K. Rosenlund
1979   *Fish Bone Measurements: An Attempt to Standardize the Measuring of Fish Bones from Archaeological Sites.* Steenstrupia, Copenhagen.

Morey, D. F.
1983   Archaeological Assessment of Seasonality from Freshwater Fish Remains: A Quantitative Procedure. *Journal of Ethnobiology* 3(1):75–95.
1992   Size, Shape, and Development in the Evolution of the Domestic Dog. *Journal of Archaeological Science* 19:181–204.

Morris, E. H., J. Charlot, and A. A. Morris
1931   *The Temple of the Warriors at Chichen Itza, Yucatan.* 2 vols. Publications 406. Carnegie Institution of Washington, Washington, D.C.

Morris, J., and R. B. McMillan
1991   Bibliography of Paul W. Parmalee. In *Beamers, Bobwhites, and Blue-Points: Tributes to the Career of Paul W. Parmalee,* edited by J. R. Purdue, W. E. Klippel, and B. W. Styles, pp. 15–21. Scientific Papers Vol. 23. Illinois State Museum, Springfield.

Morse, D. F.
1973   Dalton Culture in Northeast Arkansas. *Florida Anthropologist* 26(1):23–38.

Morse, D., J. Duncan, and J. Stoutamire
1983   *Handbook of Forensic Archeology and Anthropology.* Rose Publishing Company, Tallahassee, Florida.

Mosley, M., and C. Mackey
1974   *Twenty-Four Architectural Plans of Chan Chan, Peru.* Peabody Museum of Archaeology and Ethnology, Harvard University, Cambridge.

Movius, H. L., Jr.
1974   The Abri Pataud Program of the French Upper Paleolithic in Retrospect. In *Archaeological Researches in Retrospect,* edited by G. R. Willey, pp. 87–116. Winthrop, Cambridge, Massachusetts.

Movius, H. L., Jr. (editor)
1977   *Excavation of the Abri Pataud, Les Eyzies (Dordogne).* Bulletin of the American School of Prehistoric Research 31. Peabody Museum of Archaeology and Ethnology, Harvard University, Cambridge.

Muckelroy, K.
1980   *Archaeology Under Water: An Atlas of the World's Submerged Sites.* McGraw-Hill, New York and London.

Muckle, R. J.
1994   Differential Recovery of Mollusk Shell from Archaeological Sites. *Journal of Field Archaeology* 21:129–131.

Muehrcke, P. C.
1992   *Map Use: Reading, Analysis and Interpretation.* 3rd ed. JP Publications, Madison, Wisconsin.

Mueller, J. W.
1974   *The Use of Sampling in Archaeological Survey.* Memoir 28. Society for American Archaeology, Washington, D.C.
1975   Archaeological Research as Cluster Sampling. In *Sampling in Archaeology,* edited by J. W. Mueller, pp. 33–44. University of Arizona Press, Tucson.

Mueller, J. W. (editor)
1975   *Sampling in Archaeology.* University of Arizona Press, Tucson.

Müller, H.
1991   *Bibliographie zur Archäo-Zoologie und Geschichte der Haustiere (1989–1990).* Zentralinstitut für alte Geschichte und Archäologie, Berlin.

Muller, R. A.
1977   Radioisotope Dating with a Cyclotron. *Science* 196:489–494.

Mundell, R. L.
1975   *An Illustrated Osteology of the Channel Catfish (Ictalurus punctatus).* Occasional Studies in Anthropology 2. Midwest Archeological Center, Lincoln, Nebraska.

Muñiz, A. M.
1988   On the Use of Butchering as a Paleocultural Index: Proposal of a New Methodology for the Study of Bone Fracture from Archaeological Sites. *ArchaeoZoologia* 2:111–150.

Mutunayagam, B. B., and A. Bahrami
1987   *Cartography and Site Analysis with Microcomputers.* Van Nostrand Reinhold, New York.

Nagaoka, L.
1994   Differential Recovery of Pacific Island Fish Remains: Evidence from the Moturakau Rockshelter, Aitutaki, Cook Islands. *Asian Perspectives* 33:1–17.

Nance, J. D., and B. F. Ball
1986   No Surprises? The Reliability and Validity of Test Pit Sampling. *American Antiquity* 51:457–483.
1989   A Shot in the Dark: Shott's Comments on Nance and Ball. *American Antiquity* 54:396–404.

Napton, L. K., and R. F. Heizer
1970   Analysis of Human Coprolites from Archaeological Contexts with Primary Reference to Lovelock Cave, Nevada. In *Archaeology and the Prehistoric Great Basin Lacustrine Subsistence Regime as Seen from Lovelock Cave, Nevada,* edited by R. F. Heizer and L. K. Napton, pp. 87–129. Archaeological Research Faculty Contributions 10. University of California, Berkeley.

Napton, L. K., and G. Kelso
1969   Preliminary Palynological Analysis of Human Coprolites from Lovelock Cave, Nevada. In *Archaeological and Paleobiological Investigations in Lovelock Cave, Nevada,* edited by L. K. Napton. Special Publication 2. Kroeber Anthropological Society, Berkeley, California.

National Aeronautics and Space Administration
1977   *National Geodetic Satellite Program.* NASA SP–365 (2 vols). U.S. Government Printing Office, Washington, D.C.

National Research Council
1982   *Modernization of the Public Land Survey System.* National Academy Press, Washington, D.C.

Nelson, C. M.
1971   *Standard African Site Enumeration System.* Pan African Congress of Prehistory Bulletin 2. University of California, Berkeley.

Nelson, N. C.
1909   *Shell Mounds of the San Francisco Bay Region.* Publications in American Archaeology and Ethnology 7:309–348. University of California, Berkeley.
1916   Chronology of the Tano Ruins. *American Anthropologist* 18:159–180.

Neumann, G. K.
1938   The Human Remains from Mammoth Cave, Kentucky. *American Antiquity* 3:339–353.

Neumann, T. W.
1984   The Opossum Problem: Implications for Human-Wildlife Competition over Plant Foods. *North American Archaeologist* 5:287–313.

1989   Human-Wildlife Competition and Prehistoric Subsistence: The Case of the Eastern United States. *Journal of Middle Atlantic Archaeology* 5:29–57.

Newell, H. P., and A. D. Krieger
1949   *The George C. Davis Site.* Memoir 5. Society for American Archaeology and the University of Texas, Menasha, Wisconsin.

Newell, R. R.
1984   The Archaeological, Human Biological, and Comparative Contexts of a Catastrophically-Terminated Kataligaaq House at Utpiaguik, Alaska (BAR-2). *Arctic Anthropology* 21:5–51.

Newlands, D. L., and C. Breede
1976   *An Introduction to Canadian Archaeology.* McGraw-Hill Ryerson, Toronto.

Newton, P. W., P. R. Zwart, and M. E. Cavill
1992   *Networking Spatial Information Systems.* Belhaven Press, London and New York.

Nichol, C. R.
1989   Complex Segregation Analysis of Dental Morphological Variants. *American Journal of Physical Anthropology* 78:37–59.

Nichols, D. R., and N. A. Wright
1971   *Preliminary Map of Historic Margins of Marshland, San Francisco Bay, California.* Basic Data Contribution 9. U.S. Geological Survey, San Francisco Bay Region Environment and Resources Planning Study, San Francisco.

Nitecki, M. H., and D. V. Nitecki (editors)
1987   *The Evolution of Human Hunting.* Plenum Press, New York.

Noël-Hume, I.
1969   *Historical Archaeology.* Knopf, New York.
1982   *Martin's Hundred: The Discovery of a Lost Colonial Virginia Settlement.* Delta Books, New York.

Noe-Nygaard, N.
1977   Butchering and Marrow Fracturing as a Taphonomic Factor in Archaeological Deposits. *Paleobiology* 3:218–237.

Nordt, L. C.
1992   *Archaeological Geology of the Fort Hood Military Reservation, Ft. Hood, Texas.* Archaeological Resource Management Series Research Report 25. U.S. Army, Ft. Hood.

Oakley, K. P.
1964   *Frameworks for Dating Fossil Man.* Aldine, Chicago.
1976   The Piltdown Problem Reconsidered. *Antiquity* 50:9–13.

Oakley, K. P., and W. W. Howells
1961   Age of the Skeleton from the Lagow Sand Pit, Texas. *American Antiquity* 15:155–156.

Oddy, W. A.
1987   *Problems in the Conservation of Waterlogged Wood.* Monograph 16. National Maritime Museum, London.

Odell, G. H.
1980   Toward a More Behavioral Approach to Archaeological Lithic Concentrations. *American Antiquity* 45(3):404–431.
1992   Bewitched by Mechanical Site-Testing Devices. *American Antiquity* 57:692–703.

Odell, G. H., and F. Odell-Vereecken
1980   Verifying the Reliability of Lithic Use-wear Assessments by "Blind Tests:" The Low-power Approach. *Journal of Field Archaeology* 7:87–120.

Olsen, S. J.
1960   *Post-cranial Skeletal Characters of Bison and Bos.* Papers of the Peabody Museum of Archaeology and Ethnology Vol. 35, No. 4. Harvard University, Cambridge.
1961a   A Basic Annotated Bibliography to Facilitate the Identification of Vertebrate Remains from Archaeological Sites. *Bulletin of the Texas Archeological Society* 30:217–222.
1961b   The Relative Value of Fragmentary Mammalian Remains. *American Antiquity* 26:538–530.
1964   *Mammal Remains from Archaeological Sites. Part 1: Southeastern and Southwestern United States.* Papers of the Peabody Museum of Archaeology and Ethnology Vol. 56, No. 1. Harvard University, Cambridge.
1968a   *Fish, Amphibian and Reptile Remains from Archaeological Sites. Part 1. Southeastern and Southwestern United States.* Papers of the Peabody Museum of Archaeology and Ethnology Vol. 56, No. 2. Harvard University, Cambridge.
1968b   Appendix: The Osteology of the Wild Turkey. In *Fish, Amphibian and Reptile Remains from Archaeological Sites,* by S. J. Olsen, pp. 105–137. Papers of the Peabody Museum of Archaeology and Ethnology Vol. 56, No. 2. Harvard University, Cambridge.
1971   *Zooarchaeology: Animal Bones in Archaeology and Their Interpretation.* Addison-Wesley Module in Anthropology 2. Addison-Wesley, Reading, Massachusetts.
1979a   North American Birds: Postcranial Skeletons. In *Osteology for the Archaeologist,* by S. J. Olsen, pp. 91–186. Papers of the Peabody Museum of Archaeology and Ethnology Vol. 56, Nos. 3–5. Harvard University, Cambridge.
1979b   North American Birds: Skulls and Mandibles. In *Osteology for the Archaeologist,* by S. J. Olsen, pp. 49–89. Papers of the Peabody Museum of Archaeology and Ethnology Vol. 56, Nos. 3–5. Harvard University, Cambridge.
1982   *An Osteology of Some Maya Mammals.* Papers of the Peabody Museum of Archaeology and Ethnology Vol. 73. Harvard University, Cambridge.
1985   *Origins of the Domestic Dog.* University of Arizona Press, Tucson.

Olsen, S. L.
1979   A Study of Bone Artifacts from Grasshopper Pueblo, AZ P:14:1. *The Kiva* 44:341–373.
1989   On Distinguishing Natural from Cultural Damage on Archaeological Antler. *Journal of Archaeological Science* 16:125–135.

Olsen, S. L., and J. W. Olsen
1981   A Comment on Nomenclature in Faunal Studies. *American Antiquity* 46:192–194.

Olsen, S. L., and P. Shipman
1988   Surface Modification on Bone: Trampling versus Butchery. *Journal of Archaeological Science* 15:535–553.

O'Neil, D. H.
1993   Excavation Sample Size: A Cautionary Tale. *American Antiquity* 58(3):523–529.

Orme, B.
1979   *Thermoluminescence Techniques in Archaeology.* Clarendon Press, Oxford.

Orser, C. E., Jr.
1988   The Archaeological Analysis of Plantation Society: Replacing Status and Caste with Economics and Power. *American Antiquity* 53:735–751.

Ortner, D. J.
1991   Theoretical and Methodological Issues in Paleopathology. In *Human Paleopathology: Current Syntheses and Future Options,* edited by D. J. Ortner and A. C. Aufderheide, pp. 1–5. Smithsonian Institution Press, Washington, D.C.

Ortner, D. J., and A. C. Aufderheide (editors)
1991   *Human Paleopathology: Current Syntheses and Future Options.* Smithsonian Institution Press, Washington, D.C.

Ortner, D. J., and W. G. J. Putschar
1981   *Identification of Pathological Conditions in Human Skeletal Remains.* Smithsonian Contributions to Anthropology 28. Smithsonian Institution, Washington, D.C.

Ortner, D. J., N. Tuross, and A. I. Stix
1992   New Approaches to the Study of Disease in Archaeological New World Populations. *Human Biology* 64:337–360.

Ortner, D. J., D. W. Van Endt, and M. S. Robinson
1972   The Effect of Temperature on Protein Decay in Bone: Its Significance in Nitrogen Dating of Archaeological Specimens. *American Antiquity* 37:514–520.

O'Shea, J. M.
1984   *Mortuary Variability: An Archaeological Investigation.* Academic Press, Orlando.

O'Shea, J. M., and P. S. Bridges
1988   The Sargent Site Ossuary (25CV28), Custer County, Nebraska. *Plains Anthropologist* 123:7–20.

Ossenberg, N. S.
1974   Origin and Relationships of Woodland Peoples: The Evidence of Cranial Morphology. In *Aspects of Upper Great Lakes Anthropology: Papers in Honor of Lloyd A. Wilford,* edited by E. Johnson, pp. 15–39. Minnesota Prehistoric Archaeology Series 11. Minnesota Historical Society, St. Paul.
1976   Within and Between Race Distances in Population Studies Based on Discrete Traits of the Human Skull. *American Journal of Physical Anthropology* 45:701–716.

Owsley, D. W., H. E. Berryman, and W. M. Bass
1977   Demographic and Osteological Evidence for Warfare at the Larson Site, South Dakota. In *Trends in Middle Missouri Prehistory: A Festschrift Honoring the Contributions of Donald J. Lehmer,* edited by W. R. Wood, pp. 119–131. Plains Anthropologist Memoir, Lincoln, Nebraska.

Owsley, D. W., and R. L. Jantz (editors)
1994   *Skeletal Biology in the Great Plains: Migration, Warfare, Health, and Subsistence.* Smithsonian Institution Press, Washington, D.C.

Pääbo, S., J. A. Gifford, and A. C. Wilson
1989   Mitochondrial DNA Sequences from a 7000-Year-Old Brain. *Nucleic Acids Research* 16:9775–9787.

Paice, P.
1991   Extensions to the Harris Matrix System to Illustrate Stratigraphic Discussion of an Archaeological Site. *Journal of Field Archaeology* 18(1):17–28.

Palkovitch, A. M.
1980   *Pueblo Population and Society: The Arroyo Hondo Skeletal and Mortuary Remains.* School of American Research Press, Santa Fe, New Mexico.

Pallis, S. A.
1956   *The Antiquity of Iraq.* E. Munksgaard, Copenhagen.

Panshin, A. J., and DeZeeuw, C.
1980   *Textbook of Wood Technology.* McGraw-Hill, New York, p. 722.

Parenti, F., N. Mercier, and H. Valladas
1990   The Oldest Hearths of the Pedra Furada, Brazil: Thermoluminescence Analysis of Heated Stones. *Current Research in the Pleistocene* 7:36–37.

Parham, R. A., and R. L. Gray
1982   *The Practical Identification of Wood Pulp Fibers.* APPI Press, Atlanta, Georgia.

Parmalee, P. W.
1967   *The Fresh-Water Mussels of Illinois.* Popular Science Series Vol. 8. Illinois State Museum, Springfield.
1985   Identification and Interpretation of Archaeologically Derived Animal Remains. In *The Analysis of Prehistoric Diets,* edited by R. I. Gilbert, Jr., and J. H. Mielke, pp. 61–95. Academic Press, New York.

Parmalee, P. W., and W. E. Klippel
1974   Freshwater Mussels as a Prehistoric Food Resource. *American Antiquity* 39:421–434.

Parrington, M.
1983   Remote Sensing. *Annual Review of Anthropology* 12:105–124.

Paterakis, A.
1987   Deterioration of Ceramics by Soluble Salts and Methods for Monitoring Their Removal. In *Recent Advances in the Conservation and Analysis of Artifacts*, compiled by J. Black, pp. 67–72. Jubilee Conservation Conference Papers. Institute of Archaeology, University of London, London.

Patterson, L. W.
1988   Avocational Archaeology in the United States. *Plains Anthropologist* 33(121):377–384.

Patterson, T. C.
1963   Contemporaneity and Cross-Dating in Archaeological Interpretation. *American Antiquity* 28:389–392.

Pattison, W. D.
1979   *Beginnings of the American Rectangular Land Survey System, 1784–1800.* Arno Press, New York.

Payne, S.
1972   On the Interpretation of Bone Samples from Archaeological Sites. In *Papers in Economic Prehistory*, edited by E. S. Higgs, pp. 65–81. Cambridge University Press, Cambridge.
1975   Partial Recovery and Sample Bias. In *Archaeozoological Studies*, edited by A. T. Clason, pp. 7–17. American Elsevier, New York.

Payton, R. (editor)
1992   *Retrieval of Objects from Archaeological Sites.* Archetype Publications, Denbigh, Clwyd, Wales.

Peacock, E. E.
1987   Archaeological Skin Materials. In *In Situ Archaeological Conservation*, edited by H. W. M. Hodges, pp. 122–131. Getty Conservation Institute, Los Angeles.

Pearsall, D. M.
1978   Phytolith Analysis of Archaeological Soils: Evidence for Maize Cultivation in Formative Ecuador. *Science* 199:177–178.
1982a   Phytolith Analysis: Applications of a New Paleoethnobotanical Technique in Archaeology. *American Anthropologist* 84:862–871.
1982b   Maize Phytoliths: A Clarification. *Phytolitharian Newsletter* 1:3–4.
1989   *Paleoethnobotany: A Handbook of Procedures.* Academic Press, San Diego.

Pearsall, D. M., and D. R. Piperno
1993   *Current Research in Phytolith Analysis: Applications to Archaeology and Paleoecology.* MASCA Research Papers in Science and Archaeology 10. University Museum, University of Pennsylvania, Philadelphia.

Pearson, G. W.
1987   How to Cope with Calibration. *Antiquity* 61:98–103.

Peck, W. H.
1980   Mummies of Ancient Egypt. In *Mummies, Disease, and Ancient Cultures,* edited by A. Cockburn and E. Cockburn, pp. 11–28. Cambridge University Press, Cambridge.

Pendleton, M. W.
1979   A Flotation Apparatus for Archaeological Sites. *The Kiva* 44:89–93.

Pennak, R. W.
1989   *Freshwater Invertebrates of the United States: Protozoa to Mollusca.* 3rd ed. Wiley, New York.

Percy, G.
1976   The Use of a Mechanical Earth Auger at the Torreya Site, Liberty County, Florida. *Florida Anthropologist* 29(1):24–32.

Perino, G. H.
1968   The Pete Klunk Mound Group, Calhoun County, Illinois: The Archaic and Hopewell Occupations (with an appendix on the Gibson Mound Group). In *Hopewell and Woodland Site Archaeology in Illinois*, edited by J. A. Brown, pp. 9–124. Bulletin 6. Illinois Archaeological Survey, Urbana.
1981   *Archeological Investigations at the Roden Site, McCurtain County, Oklahoma.* Publication 1. Museum of the Red River, Idabel, Oklahoma.

Peters, J.
1987   Cuboscaphoids, Naviculo-Cuboids, Language Barriers and the Use of Standardized Osteological Nomenclatures in Archaeozoological Studies. *ArchaeoZoologia* 1:43–46.

Peterson, P., F. D. Fracchia, and B. Hayden
1995   A Virtual Computer Imaging Technique for Archaeological Research. *Society for American Archaeology Bulletin* 13(4):30–33. Washington, D.C.

Petrie, W. M. F.
1899   Sequences in Prehistoric Remains. *Journal of the Royal Anthropological Institute* 29:295–301.

Peuquet, J., and D. F. Marble (editors)
1990   *Introductory Readings in Geographic Information Systems.* Taylor & Francis, London and New York.

Phenice, T. W.
1969   A Newly Developed Visual Method of Sexing the Os Pubis. *American Journal of Physical Anthropology* 30:297–301.

Phillips, C. W.
1980   *Archaeology in the Ordnance Survey, 1791–1965.* Council for British Archaeology, London.

Phillips, P., J. A. Ford, and J. B. Griffin
1951   *Archaeological Survey in the Lower Mississippi Alluvial Valley, 1940–1947.* Papers of the Peabody Museum of American Archaeology and Ethnology Vol. 25. Harvard University, Cambridge.

Piggott, S., and M. Murray
1966   A New Photographic Technique at Croft Moraig. *Antiquity* 40:304.

Piperno, D. R.
1984   A Comparison and Differentiation of Phytoliths from Maize and Wild Grasses: Use of Morphological Criteria. *American Antiquity* 49:361–383.
1985   Phytolith Analysis and Tropical Paleoecology: Production and Taxonomic Significance of Siliceous Forms in New World Domesticates and Wild Species. *Review of Paleobotany and Palynology* 45:185–228.
1988   *Phytolith Analysis: An Archaeological and Geological Perspective.* Academic Press, San Diego.

Pippin, L. C.
1986   Paleoenvironmental Modeling and Geoarchaeology. In *Current States of CRM Archaeology in the Great Basin,* edited by C. M. Aikens, pp. 149–189. Cultural Resource Series Monograph 9. Bureau of Land Management, Reno, Nevada.

Plenderleith, H. J., and A. E. Werner
1971   *The Conservation of Antiquities and Works of Art.* 2nd ed. Oxford University Press, Oxford.

Plog, S.
1976   Relative Efficiencies of Sampling Techniques for Archeological Surveys. In *The Early Mesoamerican Village,* edited by K. V. Flannery, pp. 136–158. Academic Press, New York.

Plog, S., F. Plog, and W. Wait
1978   Decision Making in Modern Surveys. In *Advances in Archaeological Method and Theory,* vol. 1, edited by M. B. Schiffer, pp. 383–421. Academic Press, New York.

Polach, D.
1988   *Radiocarbon Dating Literature: The First 21 Years, 1947–1968, An Annotated Bibliography.* Academic Press, London.

Pollach, H. A., and J. Golson
1966   *Collection of Specimens for Radiocarbon Dating and Interpretation of Results.* Manual 2. Australian Institute of Aboriginal Studies, Canberra.

Pollach, H., J. Golson, and J. Head
1983   Radiocarbon Dating: A Guide for Archaeologists on the Collection and Submission of Samples and Age-Reporting Practices. In *Australian Field Archaeology: A Guide to Techniques,* edited by G. Connah, pp. 145–152. Australian Institute of Aboriginal Studies, Canberra.

Pope, G. T.
1990   Egg Times. *Discover* October:38.

Porat, N., H. P. Schwarcz, H. Valladas, O. Bar-Yosef, and B. Vandermeersch
1994   Election Spin Resonance Dating of Burned Flint from Kebara Cave, Israel. *Geoarchaeology* 9(5):393–407.

Porter, C. L.
1967   *Taxonomy of Flowering Plants.* 2nd ed. W. H. Freeman, San Francisco.

Potter, D. R.
1994   Strat 55, Operation 2012 and Comments on Lowland Maya Blood Ritual. In *Continuing Archeology at Colha, Belize,* edited by T. R. Hester, H. J. Shafer, and J. Eaton, pp. 31–81. Studies in Archeology 16. Texas Archaeological Research Laboratory, University of Texas at Austin.

Potter, R. M., and G. R. Rossman
1977   Desert Varnish: The Importance of Clay Minerals. *Science* 196:1446–1448.

Powell, J. F.
1989   *An Epidemiological Analysis of Mortality and Morbidity in Five Late Prehistoric Populations from the Upper and Central Texas Coast.* Unpublished Master's thesis, University of Texas at Austin.
1991   Human Skeletal Remains from Skyline Shelter (41VV930), Val Verde County, Texas. In *Papers on Lower Pecos Prehistory,* edited by S. A. Turpin, pp. 149–173. Studies in Archeology 8. Texas Archeological Research Laboratory, University of Texas at Austin.
1994   Bioarchaeological Analyses of Human Skeletal Remains from the Mitchell Ridge Site. In *Aboriginal Life and Culture on the Upper Texas Coast: Archaeology of the Mitchell Ridge Site, 41GV66, Galveston County, Texas,* edited by R. A. Ricklis, pp. 254–366. Coastal Research Associates, Inc., Corpus Christi, Texas.
1995   *Dental Variation and Affinities Among Middle Holocene Populations in the New World.* Ph.D. dissertation, Texas A&M University, College Station. University Microfilms, Ann Arbor.

Powell, J. F., and D. G. Steele
1993   A Multivariate Craniometric Analysis of North American Paleoindian Remains. *Current Research in the Pleistocene* 9:59–61.

Powell, L. C.
1996   Traditional Narratives and Oral History. In *Home Hereafter: Archaeological and Bioarchaeological Investigations at an Historic African-American Cemetery,* edited by H. D. Dockall, J. F. Powell, and D. G. Steele, in press. Center for Environmental Archaeology, Texas A&M University, College Station.

Powell, L. C., and H. D. Dockall
1995   Folk Narrative and Archaeology: An African-American Cemetery in Texas. *Journal of Field Archaeology* 22:349–353.

Powell, M. L.
1985   The Analysis of Dental Wear and Caries for Dietary Reconstruction. In *The Analysis of Prehistoric Diets,* edited by R. I. Gilbert and J. H. Mielke, pp. 307–338. Academic Press, Orlando.
1988   *Status and Health in Prehistory: A Case Study of the Moundville Chiefdom.* Smithsonian Institution Press, Washington, D.C.

Powell, M. L., P. S. Bridges, and A. M. W. Mires (editors)
1991   *What Mean These Bones? Studies in Southeastern*

Bioarchaeology. The University of Alabama Press, Tuscaloosa.

Praetzellis, A. C.
1993   The Limits of Arbitrary Excavation. In *Practices of Archaeological Stratigraphy,* edited by E. C. Harris, M. R. Brown, III, and G. J. Brown, pp. 68–86. Academic Press, London.

Prat, H.
1948   General Features of the Epidermis in Zea Mays. *Annals of the Missouri Botanical Garden* 35: 343–351.

Press, W. H., B. P. Flannery, S. A. Teukolsky, and W. T. Vettering
1988   *Numerical Recipes in C: The Art of Scientific Computing.* Cambridge University Press, Cambridge.

Preucel, R. W.
1991   Introduction. In *Processual and Postprocessual Archaeologies: Multiple Ways of Knowing the Past,* edited by R. W. Preucel, pp. 1–14. Occasional Paper 10. Center for Archaeological Investigations, Southern Illinois University, Carbondale.

Preucel, R. W. (editor)
1991   *Processual and Postprocessual Archaeologies: Multiple Ways of Knowing the Past.* Occasional Paper 10. Center for Archaeological Investigations, Southern Illinois University, Carbondale.

Preuss, C.
1958   *Exploring with Frémont.* Translated and edited by E. K. and E. G. Gudde. University of Oklahoma Press, Norman.

Prevec, R.
1985   The Advantages of Flotation and Fine Screening to the Faunal Analyst. *Archaeological Notes* 85 (2):22–27.

Prewitt, E. R.
1982   *Archaeological Investigations at the San Gabriel Reservoir District, Central Texas,* vol. 4. Institute of Applied Science, North Texas State University, Denton.

Price, C. A.
1984   The Consolidation of Limestone Using a Poultice of Limestone. In *Adhesives and Consolidants,* edited by N. S. Bromelle, E. M. Pye, P. Smith, and G. Thomson, pp. 160–162. International Institute for Conservation of Historic and Artistic Works, London.

Price, K.
1992   *ABC's of GIS.* American Society of Photogrammetry and Remote Sensing, Bethesda, Maryland.

Price, M. F., and D. I. Heywood (editors)
1994   *Mountain Environments and Geographic Information Systems.* Taylor & Francis, London and New York.

Price, T. D. (editor)
1989   *The Chemistry of Prehistoric Human Bone.* Cambridge University Press, Cambridge.

Price, T. D., M. J. Schoeninger, and G. J. Armelagos
1985   Bone Chemistry and Past Behavior: An Overview. *Journal of Human Evolution* 14:419–447.

Price, W. F., and J. Uren
1989   *Laser Surveying.* Van Nostrand Reinhold, London.

Prikryl, D. J.
1990   *Lower Elm Fork Prehistory, A Redefinition of Cultural Concepts and Chronologies Along the Trinity River, North-Central Texas.* Office of the State Archeologist Report 37. Texas Historical Commission, Austin.

Pring, D. C.
1977   The Dating of Teotihuacan Contact at Altun Ha: The New Evidence. *American Antiquity* 42: 626–628.

Pugh, J. C.
1975   *Surveying for Field Scientists.* University of Pittsburgh Press, Pittsburgh.

Puleston, D.
1974   Intersite Areas in the Vicinity of Tikal and Uaxactan. In *Mesoamerica Archaeology, New Approaches,* edited by N. Hammond, pp. 303–312. University of Texas Press, Austin.

Purdue, J. R.
1983   Methods of Determining Sex and Body Size in Prehistoric Samples of White-tailed Deer (*Odocoileus virginianus*). *Transactions of the Illinois State Academy of Science* 76:351–357.
1986   The Size of White-tailed Deer (*Odocoileus virginianus*) During the Archaic Period in Central Illinois. In *Foraging, Collecting, and Harvesting: Archaic Period Subsistence and Settlement in the Eastern Woodlands,* edited by S. W. Neusius, pp. 65–95. Occasional Paper No. 6. Center for Archaeological Investigations, Southern Illinois University, Carbondale.

Purdy, B. A. (editor)
1988   *Wet Site Archaeology.* Telford Press, Caldwell, New Jersey.

Purdy, B. A., and L. A. Newsom
1985   Significance of Archaeological Wet Sites: A Florida Example. *National Geographic Research* 1: 564–569.

Puterski, R.
1992   *Global Positioning Systems Technology and Its Application in Environmental Programs.* Environmental Monitoring Systems Laboratory, Office of Research and Development, U.S. Environmental Protection Agency, Las Vegas, Nevada.

Pyddoke, E.
1961   *Stratification for the Archaeologist.* Phoenix House, London.

Radliff, D. E.
1964   *Map, Compass and Campfire.* Binford & Mort, Portland, Oregon.

Raemsch, C. A.
1993   Mechanical Procedures Involved in Bone Dismemberment and Defleshing in Prehistoric Michigan. *Midcontinental Journal of Archaeology* 18: 217–244.

Ragir, S.
1975   A Review of Techniques for Archaeological Sampling. In *Field Methods in Archaeology*, by T. R. Hester, R. F. Heizer, and J. A. Graham, pp. 283–302. Mayfield Publishing Company, Palo Alto, California.

Raisz, E.
1962   *Principles of Cartography*. McGraw-Hill, New York.

Raitz, K. B., and J. F. Hart
1975   *Cultural Geography on Topographic Maps*. Wiley, New York.

Randall, G.
1989   *The Outward Bound Map and Compass Book*. Lyons and Burford, New York.

Raper, J.
1989   *Three Dimensional Applications in Geographical Information Systems*. Taylor & Francis, London and New York.

Raphael, B., K. Laitner, and M. Surovik-Bohnert
1982   *BLM Field Conservation Manual*. On file, Texas Archeological Research Laboratory, University of Texas at Austin.

Rapp, G., S. R. B. Cooke, and E. Henrickson
1973   Pumice from Thera (Santorini) Identified from a Greek Mainland Archeological Excavation. *Science* 179:471–473.

Rapp, G., Jr., and J. A. Gifford (editors)
1985   *Archaeological Geology*. Yale University Press, New Haven, Connecticut.

Rapp, G., Jr., and S. C. Mulholland
1992   *Phytolith Systematics: Emerging Issues*. Plenum Press, New York.

Rathbun, T. A., and J. E. Buikstra
1984   *Human Identification*. Charles C. Thomas, Springfield, Illinois.

Rea, A. M.
1986   Verification and Reverification: Problems in Archaeofaunal Studies. *Journal of Ethnobiology* 6: 9–18.

Read, C. E.
1971   *Animal Bones and Human Behavior: Approaches to Faunal Analysis in Archaeology*. Ph.D. dissertation, University of California, Los Angeles. University Microfilms, Ann Arbor.

Read, D. W.
1975   Regional Sampling. In *Sampling in Archaeology*, edited by J. W. Mueller, pp. 45–61. University of Arizona Press, Tucson.

Redman, C.
1974   *Archaeological Sampling Strategies*. Addison-Wesley Module in Anthropology 55. Addison-Wesley, Reading, Massachusetts.

Redman, C. L.
1987   Surface Collection, Sampling, and Research Design: A Retrospective. *American Antiquity* 52(2): 249–265.

Redman, W. C., and P. J. Watson
1970   Systematic, Intensive Surface Collection. *American Antiquity* 35(3):279–291.

Reed, R.
1972   *Ancient Skins, Parchments, and Leathers*. Seminar Press, London.

Reher, C. A., and G. C. Frison
1980   *The Vore Site, 48CK302, A Stratified Buffalo Jump in the Wyoming Black Hills*. Plains Anthropologist Memoir 16.

Reichel-Dolmatoff, G., and A. Reichel-Dolmatoff
1956   Momil, Excavaciones en el Sinu. *Revista Colombiana de Antropologia* 5:109–333. Bogota.

Reichs, K. (editor)
1986   *Forensic Osteology*. Charles C. Thomas, Springfield, Illinois.

Reider, R. G.
1990   Late Pleistocene and Holocene Pedogenic and Environmental Trends at Archaeological Sites in Plains and Mountain Areas of Colorado and Wyoming. In *Archaeological Geology of North America*, edited by N. P. Lasca and J. Donahue, pp. 335–360. Geological Society of America, Boulder, Colorado.

Reinhard, K. J., and V. M. Bryant, Jr.
1992   Coprolite Analysis: A Biological Perspective in Archaeology. In *Archaeological Method and Theory*, vol. 4, pp. 245–288. University of Arizona Press, Tucson.

Reitz, E. J.
1987   Zooarchaeological Theory and Method. In *The Zooarchaeology of Eastern North America: History, Method and Theory, and Bibliography*, edited by A. E. Bogan and N. D. Robison, pp. 27–65. Tennessee Anthropological Association Miscellaneous Paper No. 12. UT Graphic Arts Service, University of Tennessee, Knoxville.

1993   Zooarchaeology. In *The Development of Southeastern Archaeology*, edited by J. K. Johnson, pp. 109–131. University of Alabama Press, Tuscaloosa.

Reitz, E. J., T. Gibbs, K. Cargill, and L. S. Lieberman
1980   Nutrition in a Slave Population: An Anthropological Examination. *Medical Anthropology* 4:175–262.

Relethford, J. H.
1994   Craniometric Variation Among Modern Human Populations. *American Journal of Physical Anthropology* 95:53–62.

Relethford, J. H., and J. Blangero
1990   Detection of Differential Gene Flow from Pat-

terns of Quantitative Variation. *Human Biology* 62:5–25.

Relethford, J. H., and H. C. Harpending
1994   Craniometric Variation, Genetic Theory, and Modern Human Origins. *American Journal of Physical Anthropology* 95:249–270.

Relethford, J. H., and F. C. Lees
1982   The Use of Quantitative Traits in the Study of Human Population Structure. *Yearbook of Physical Anthropology* 25:113–132.

Renfrew, C.
1983   Divided We Stand: Aspects of Archaeology and Information. *American Antiquity* 48:3–16.

Renfrew, C., and P. Bahn
1991   *Archaeology: Theories, Methods, and Practice.* Thames & Hudson, New York.

Rhine, S.
1990   Non-metric Skull Racing. In *Skeletal Attribution of Race: Methods for Forensic Anthropology,* edited by G. W. Gill and S. Rhine, pp. 9–20. Anthropological Papers No. 4. Maxwell Museum of Anthropology, Albuquerque, New Mexico.

Rice, D. S., and D. E. Puleston
1981   Ancient Maya Settlement Patterns in the Peten, Guatemala. In *Lowland Maya Settlement Patterns,* edited by W. Ashmore, pp. 121–156. University of New Mexico Press, Albuquerque.

Rice, G. E.
1990   *A Design for Salado Research: Roosevelt Platform Mound Study, Arizona State University.* Roosevelt Monograph Series 1, Anthropological Field Studies 22. Arizona State University, Tempe.

Rich, C.
1819   *Second Memoir on Babylon.* London.

Richards, K. S., R. P. Arnett, and S. Ellis
1985   *Geomorphology and Soils.* G. Allen & Unwin, London.

Richie, P. R., and J. Pugh
1963   Ultra-violet Radiation and Excavation. *Antiquity* 37:259–263.

Rick, J. W.
1996   The Use of Laser Tools in Archaeology. *Bulletin, Society for American Archaeology* 14(2):8–10.

Ricklis, R. A. (editor)
1994   *Aboriginal Life Culture on the Upper Texas Coast: Archaeology of the Mitchell Ridge Site, 41GV66, Galveston County, Texas.* Coastal Research Associates, Inc., Corpus Christi, Texas.

Ricklis, R. A., M. D. Blum, and M. B. Collins
1991   *Archeological Testing at the Vera Daniel Site (41TV1364), Zilker Park, Austin, Texas.* Studies in Archeology 12. Texas Archeological Research Laboratory, University of Texas at Austin.

Ridings, R.
1991   Obsidian Hydration Dating: The Effects of Mean Exponential Ground Temperature and Depth

of Artifact Recovery. *Journal of Field Archaeology* 18:77–85.

Riley, D. N.
1987   *Air Photography and Archaeology.* Duckworth, London.

Ripple, W. J. (editor)
1989   *Fundamentals of Geographic Information Systems: A Compendium.* American Society for Photogrammetry and Remote Sensing, Falls Church, Virginia.

Riskind, D. A.
1970   Pollen Analysis of Human Coprolites from Parida Cave. In *Archeological Excavations at Parida Cave, Val Verde County, Texas,* edited by R. K. Alexander, pp. 89–101. Papers of the Texas Archeological Salvage Project 19, University of Texas at Austin.

Ritchie, W.
1988   *Surveying and Mapping for Field Scientists.* Wiley, New York.

Ritchie, W. A.
1954   *Dutch Hollow, An Early Historic Period Seneca Site in Livingston County, New York.* Transcripts and Researches of the New York State Museum 13(1).

Ritter, E. S., B. W. Hatoff, and L. A. Payen
1976   Chronology of the Farmington Complex. *American Antiquity* 41:334–341.

Robbins, L. M.
1971   A Woodland "Mummy" from Salts Cave, Kentucky. *American Antiquity* 36:201–206.

Robertson, B. P., and L. B. Robertson
1978   The Generation of Location Models in an Inductive Framework. In *Conservation Archaeology in the Northeast: Toward a Research Orientation,* edited by A. Speiss, pp. 27–36. Bulletin 3. Peabody Museum of Archaeology and Ethnology, Harvard University, Cambridge.

Robinson, A. H., R. D. Sale, J. L. Morrison, and P. C. Muehrcke
1984   *Elements of Cartography.* 5th ed. Wiley, New York.

Robinson, C. K., G. T. Gross, and D. A. Breternitz
1986   Overview of the Dolores Archaeological Program. In *Dolores Archaeological Program: Final Synthetic Report,* edited by D. A. Breternitz, C. K. Robinson, and G. T. Gross, pp. 3–52. U.S. Department of the Interior, Bureau of Reclamation, Engineering and Research Center, Denver.

Robison, N. D.
1978   Zooarchaeology: Its History and Development. In *A History and Selected Bibliography of Zooarchaeology in Eastern North America,* edited by A. E. Bogan and N. D. Robison, pp. 1–22. Tennessee Anthropological Association Miscellaneous Paper No. 2. Tribute Press, Chattanooga.

Rock, J. T.
1974   The Use of Social Models in Archaeological Interpretation. *The Kiva* 46(1–2):81–91.

Roemer, A. S.
1956   *Osteology of the Reptiles.* University of Chicago Press, Chicago.

Rogan, P. K., and J. J. Salvo
1990   Study of Nucleic Acids Isolated from Human Remains. *Yearbook of Physical Anthropology* 33:195–214.

Rogers, J. D., and S. M. Wilson (editors)
1993   *Ethnohistory and Archaeology, Approaches to Postcontact Change in the Americas.* Plenum Press, New York.

Rogers, M. J.
1939   *Early Lithic Industries of the Lower Basin of the Colorado River and Adjacent Areas.* Papers 3. San Diego Museum, San Diego.

Rohl, A. N., M. Langer, and G. Moncure
1982   Endemic Pleural Disease Associated with Exposure to Mixed Fibrous Dust in Turkey. *Science* 216:518–520.

Rojo, A. L.
1991   *Dictionary of Evolutionary Fish Osteology.* CRC Press, Boston.

Rolando, V. R.
1992   *200 Years of Soot and Sweat: The History and Archeology of Vermont's Iron, Charcoal and Lime Industries.* Vermont Archaeological Society, Burlington.

Romero, J.
1970   Dental Mutilation, Trephination, and Cranial Deformation. In *Handbook of Middle American Indians, Vol. 9: Physical Anthropology,* edited by T. D. Stewart, pp. 50–67. University of Texas Press, Austin.

Roosevelt, A. C.
1980   *Parmana: Prehistoric Maize and Manioc Subsistence Along the Amazon and Orinoco.* Academic Press, New York.
1991   *Moundbuilders of the Amazon.* Academic Press, San Diego.

Rose, J. C. (editor)
1985   *Gone to a Better Land: A Biohistory of a Rural Black Cemetery in the Post-Reconstruction South.* Research Series 25. Arkansas Archeological Survey, Fayetteville.

Rose, J. C., K. W. Condon, and A. H. Goodman
1985   Diet and Dentition: Developmental Disturbances. In *The Analysis of Prehistoric Diets,* edited by R. I. Gilbert and J. H. Mielke, pp. 281–305. Academic Press, Orlando.

Rose, J. C., and L. G. Santeford
1985   Burial Descriptions. In *Gone to a Better Land: A Biohistory of a Rural Black Cemetery in the Post-Reconstruction South,* edited by J. C. Rose. Research Series 25. Arkansas Archeological Survey, Fayetteville.

Rosen, A. M.
1986   *Cities of Clay: The Geoarchaeology of Tells.* University of Chicago Press, Chicago.

Rosencrantz, D. M.
1975   Underwater Photography and Photogrammetry. In *Photography in Archaeological Research,* edited by E. Harp, pp. 265–310. University of New Mexico Press, Albuquerque.

Roth, E. A.
1992   Applications of Demographic Models to Paleodemography. In *Skeletal Biology of Past Peoples: Research Methods,* edited by S. R. Saunders and A. M. Katzenberg, pp. 175–188. Wiley-Liss, New York.

Rothenberg, J.
1995   Ensuring the Longevity of Digital Documents. *Scientific American* January:42–47.

Rothschild, B. M.
1992   Advances in Detecting Disease in Earlier Human Populations. In *Skeletal Biology of Past Peoples: Research Methods,* edited by S. R. Saunders and A. M. Katzenberg, pp. 131–151. Wiley-Liss, New York.

Rothschild, B. M., and L. D. Martin
1993   *Paleopathology: Disease in the Fossil Record.* CRC Press, London.

Rottlander, R.
1975a   The Formation of Patina on Flint. *Archaeometry* 17:106–110.
1975b   Some Aspects of the Patination of Flint. Second International Symposium on Flint. *Staringia* 3. Nederlandse Geologische Vereniging.

Rouse, I.
1939   *Prehistory in Haiti: A Study of Method.* Publications in Anthropology 21. Yale University, New Haven, Connecticut.
1960   The Classification of Artifacts in Archaeology. *American Antiquity* 25:313–323.

Rovner, I.
1980   The History and Development of Plant Opal Phytolith Analysis. Paper presented at the 45th Annual Meeting, Society for American Archaeology, Philadelphia.
1983   Plant Opal Phytolith Analysis: Major Advances in Archeobotanical Research. In *Advances in Archaeological Method and Theory,* vol. 6, edited by M. B. Schiffer, pp. 225–268. Academic Press, New York.
1986   *Plant Opal Phytolith Analysis in Archaeology and Paleoecology.* Occasional Papers 1 of the Phytolitharien, Raleigh, North Carolina.

Rowe, M. W.
1986   Archaeological Dating. *Journal of Chemical Education* 63(1):16–20.

Rowell, R. M., and R. J. Barbour (editors)

1990   *Archaeological Wood-Properties, Chemistry and Preservation*. Advances Series 225. American Chemical Society, Washington, D.C.

Rowlett, R. M., and J. P. Tandarich
1985   Thermoluminescence Dating of Loess in Northwest Missouri. *American Antiquity* 51: 137–141.

Russ, J., M. Hyman, H. J. Shafer, and M. W. Rowe
1990   Radiocarbon Dating of Prehistoric Rock Paintings by Selective Oxidation of Organic Carbon. *Nature* 348:710–711.

Russ, J. C.
1992   *The Image Processing Handbook*. CRC Press, Boca Raton, Florida.

Ryder, M. L.
1969   *Animal Bones in Archaeology: A Book of Notes and Drawings for Beginners*. Mammal Society Handbooks, Oxford, Edinburgh.
1980   Hair Remains Throw Light on Early British Prehistoric Cattle. *Journal of Archaeological Science* 7:389–392.

Rye, O. S.
1981   *Pottery Technology: Principles and Reconstruction*. Manuals on Archaeology No. 4. Taraxacum, Washington, D.C.

SAA Executive Committee
1986   Statement Concerning the Treatment of Human Remains. *Bulletin of the Society for American Archaeology* 4:7–8.

Sabloff, J. A., and G. Tourtellot
1991   *The Ancient Maya City of Sayil: The Mapping of a Puuc Region Center*. Publications No. 60. Middle American Research Institute, Tulane University, New Orleans.

Sage, R. J.
1990   Geographic Information Systems: The Marriage of Mapping and Computer Graphics. *Proceedings of the 76th Annual Road School, 1990*. Purdue University, Purdue, Indiana.

Salo, W. L., A. C. Aufderheide, and J. Buikstra
1994   Identification of *Mycobacterium tuberculosis* in a Pre-Columbian Peruvian Mummy. *Proceedings of the National Academy of Sciences* (USA) 91: 2091–2094.

Sampson, E. H., S. J. Fleming, and W. Bray
1972   Thermoluminescent Dating of Colombian Pottery in the Yotoco Style. *Archaeometry* 14:119–126.

Sampson, G.
1975   The Caddington Site, England. Paper presented at the Society for American Archaeology Annual Meeting, Dallas, Texas.

Samuel, L. H., and D. D. McGeehan
1990   *A Methodology for Conducting Underwater Archaeological Surveys: Final Report*. Virginia Transportation Research Council, Charlottesville.

Samuels, R.
1965   Parasitological Study of Long Dried Fecal Samples. *American Antiquity* 31:165–179.

Sandford, M. K.
1992   A Reconsideration of Trace Element Analysis. In *Skeletal Biology of Past Peoples: Research Methods*, edited by S. R. Saunders and A. M. Katzenberg, pp. 153–174. Wiley-Liss, New York.

Sandford, M. K. (editor)
1993   *Investigation of Ancient Human Tissues*. Food and Nutrition in History and Anthropology, vol. 10. Gordon and Breach, Amsterdam.

Sandison, A. T.
1980   Diseases in Ancient Egypt. In *Mummies, Disease, and Ancient Cultures*, edited by A. Cockburn and E. Cockburn, pp. 11–44. Cambridge University Press, Cambridge.

Sanger, D.
1975   Laboratory Photography. In *Photography in Archaeological Research*, edited by E. Harp, pp. 15–48. University of New Mexico Press, Albuquerque.

Santulli, M. A., M. K. Sanford, J. E. Buikstra, and J. F. Powell
1996   Bioarchaeological Applications of Imaging: A Comparative Investigation. Poster presented at the 61st Annual Meeting of the Society for American Archaeology, New Orleans.

Santure, S. K.
1990   Field and Laboratory Methods. In *Archaeological Investigations at the Morton Village and Norris Farms 36 Cemetery*, edited by S. K. Santure, A. D. Harn, and D. Esarey, pp. 11–13. Reports of Investigations 45. Illinois State Museum, Springfield.

Sattenspiel, L., and H. Harpending
1983   Stable Populations and Skeletal Age. *American Antiquity* 48:489–498.

Saul, F. P.
1972   *The Human Skeletal Remains of Altar de Sacrificios*. Papers of the Peabody Museum of Archaeology and Ethnology Vol. 63, No. 2. Harvard University, Cambridge.

Saul, F. P., and J. M. Saul
1989   Osteobiography: A Maya Example. In *Reconstruction of Life from the Skeleton*, edited by M. Y. Iscan and K. A. R. Kennedy, pp. 287–302. Liss, New York.

Saunders, S. R., and A. M. Katzenberg (editors)
1992   *Skeletal Biology of Past Peoples: Research Methods*. Wiley-Liss, New York.

Savage, S. H.
1990   GIS in Archaeological Research. In *Interpreting Space: GIS and Archaeology*, edited by K. M. S. Allen, S. W. Green, and E. B. W. Zubrow, pp. 22–32. Taylor & Francis, London.

Saxe, A. A.
1971   Social Dimensions of Mortuary Practices in

the Mesolithic Population from Wadi Halfa, Sudan. In *Approaches to the Social Dimensions of Mortuary Practices,* edited by J. A. Brown, pp. 39–57. Memoir 25. Society for American Archaeology, Washington, D.C.

Sayles, E. B.
1937   Disposal of the Dead. *Medallion Papers* 25: 91–100. Gila Pueblo, Globe, Arizona.

Scarborough, V., R. Connolly, and S. Ross
1994   The Pre-Hispanic Maya Reservoir System at Kinal, Peten, Guatemala. *Ancient Mesoamerica* 5(1): 97–106.

Schanfield, M. S.
1992   Immunoglobulin Allotypes (GM and KM) Indicate Multiple Founding Populations of Native Americans: Evidence of at Least Four Migrations to the New World. *Human Biology* 64:381–402.

Schanfield, M. S., M. H. Crawford, J. B. Dossetor, and H. Gershowitz
1990   Immunoglobulin Allotypes in Several North American Eskimo Populations. *Human Biology* 62:773–789.

Schenck, W. E.
1926   *The Emeryville Shellmound.* Publications in Archaeology and Ethnology 23:147–282. University of California, Berkeley.

Schiffer, M. B.
1972   Archaeological Context and Systemic Context. *American Antiquity* 37:156–165.
1975a   Behavioral Chain Analysis: Activities, Organizations, and the Use of Space. In *Chapters in the Prehistory of Eastern Arizona IV,* pp. 103–119. Fieldiana: Anthropology 65.
1975b   Archaeology as a Behavioral Science. *American Anthropologist* 77:836–849.
1976   *Behavioral Archeology.* Academic Press, New York.
1983   Towards the Identification of Site Formation Processes. *American Antiquity* 48(4):673–706.
1986   Radiocarbon Dating and the "Old Wood" Problem: The Case of the Hohokam Chronology. *Journal of Archaeological Science* 13:13–30.
1987   *Formation Processes of the Archaeological Record.* University of New Mexico Press, Albuquerque.

Schiffer, M. B., and G. J. Gumerman (editors)
1977   *Conservation Archaeology: A Guide for Cultural Resource Management Studies.* Academic Press, New York.

Schiffer, M. B., and J. H. House (editors)
1975   *The Cache River Archeological Project: An Experiment in Contact Archaeology.* Archeological Research Series No. 8. Arkansas Archeological Survey, Fayetteville.

Schiffer, M. B., A. P. Sullivan, and T. C. Klinger
1978   The Design of Archaeological Surveys. *World Archaeology* 10(1):1–28.

Schmalz, R. F.
1960   Flint and the Patination of Flint Artifacts. *Proceedings of the Prehistoric Society* 26:44–49.

Schmid, E.
1972   *Atlas of Animal Bones for Prehistorians, Archaeologists and Quaternary Geologists.* Elsevier, Amsterdam.

Schmidt, E. F.
1927   A Stratigraphic Study in the Gila Salt Region, Arizona. *Proceedings of the National Academy of Science* 13:291–298.
1928   *Time Relations of Prehistoric Pottery Types in Southern Arizona.* Anthropological Papers 30, Pt. 5. American Museum of Natural History, New York.

Schmitt, D. N., and K. E. Juell
1994   Toward the Identification of Coyote Scatological Faunal Accumulations in Archaeological Contexts. *Journal of Archaeological Science* 21:249–262.

Schmitt, D. N., and K. D. Lupo
1995   On Mammalian Taphonomy, Taxonomic Diversity, and Measuring Subsistence Data in Zooarchaeology. *American Antiquity* 60:496–514.

Schmucker, B. J.
1985   Dental Attrition: A Correlative Study of Dietary and Subsistence Patterns in California and New Mexico Indians. In *Health and Disease in the Prehistoric Southwest,* pp. 275–323. Anthropological Research Papers 34. Arizona State University, Tempe.

Schoeninger, M. J.
1979   *Dietary Reconstruction at Chalcatzingo, A Formative Period Site in Morelos, Mexico.* Technical Report 9. Museum of Anthropology, University of Michigan, Ann Arbor.

Schoeninger, M. J., and M. J. DeNiro
1984   Nitrogen and Carbon Isotopic Composition of Bone Collagen from Marine and Terrestrial Animals. *Geochimica et Cosmochimica Acta* 48: 625–639.

Schoeninger, M. J., M. J. DeNiro, and H. Tauber
1983   Stable Nitrogen Isotope Ratios of Bone Collagen Reflect Marine and Terrestrial Components of Prehistoric Human Diet. *Science* 220:1381–1383.

Schoenwetter, J.
1962   The Pollen Analysis of Eighteen Archaeological Sites in Arizona and New Mexico. In *Chapters in the Prehistory of Eastern Arizona,* edited by P. S. Martin, pp. 168–209. Fieldiana: Anthropology 43.
1974   Pollen Analysis of Human Paleofeces from Upper Salts Cave. In *Archaeology of the Mammoth Cave Area,* edited by P. J. Watson, pp. 49–58. Academic Press, New York.

Schour, I., and M. Massler
1940   Studies in Tooth Development: The Growth Pattern of Human Teeth. Part II. *Journal of the American Dental Association* 27:1918–1931.

1944   *Chart-Development of the Human Dentition.* 2nd ed. American Dental Association, Chicago.

Schoute-Vanneck, C. A.
1960   A Chemical Method for the Relative Dating of Coastal Shell Middens. *South African Journal of Science* 56:67–70.

Schramm, E.
1982   Towards a Rational Nomenclature in Faunal and Ecological Studies. *American Antiquity* 47: 178–179.

Schuldenrein, R.
1991   Coring and the Identity of Cultural-Resource Environments: A Comment on Stein. *American Antiquity* 56(1):131–137.

Schulman, R. D.
1991   Portable GIS: From the Sands of Desert Storm to the Forests of California. *Geographic Information Systems,* September.

Schulz, P. D., and S. M. Gust
1983   Faunal Remains and Social Status in 19th Century Sacramento. *Historical Archaeology* 17:44–53.

Schuyler, R. L. (editor)
1978   *Historical Archaeology: A Guide to Substantive and Theoretical Contributions.* Baywood, Farmingdale, New York.

Schwarcz, H. P.
1980   Absolute Age Determinations of Archaeological Sites by Uranium Series Dating of Travertine. *Archaeometry* 22:2–24.
1982   Applications of U-Series Dating to Archaeometry. In *Uranium Series Disequilibrium: Applications to Environmental Problems,* edited by M. Ivanovich and R. S. Harmon, pp. 302–325. Clarendon Press, Oxford.

Schwarcz, H. P., and B. A. Blackwell
1992   Archaeological Applications. In *Uranium-series Disequilibrium: Applications to Earth, Marine, and Environmental Sciences,* edited by M. Ivanovich and R. S. Harmon, pp. 513–552. Clarendon Press, Oxford.

Schwarcz, H. P., and R. Grun
1988   ESR Dating of Level L 2/3 at La Micoque (Dordogne), France: Excavations of Debenath and Rigaud. *Geoarchaeology* 3(4):293–296.

Schwarcz, H. P., and M. J. Schoeninger
1991   Stable Isotope Analyses in Human Nutritional Ecology. *Yearbook of Physical Anthropology* 34: 283–321.

Schwartz, G. T.
1964   Stereoscopic Views Taken with an Ordinary Single Camera—A New Technique for Archaeologists. *Archaeometry* 7:36–42.

Schwartz, G. T., and G. Junghans
1967   A New Method for Three-Dimensional Recording of Archaeological Finds. *Archaeometry* 10: 57–63.

Schwartz, S.
1978   *The Secret Vaults of Time: Psychic Archaeology and the Quest for Man's Beginnings.* Grosset & Dunlap, New York.
1983   *The Alexandria Project.* Delacorte Press, New York.

Sciulli, P. W.
1990a   Deciduous Dentition of a Late Archaic Population of Ohio. *Human Biology* 62:221–245.
1990b   Cranial and Metric Discrete Trait Variation and Biological Differentiation in the Terminal Late Archaic of Ohio: The Duff Site Cemetery. *American Journal of Physical Anthropology* 82:19–29.

Sciulli, P. W., L. Piotrowski, and D. Stothers
1984   The Williams Cemetery: Biological Variation and Affinity with Three Glacial Kame Groups. *North American Archaeologist* 5:139–170.

Scollar, I., A. Tabbagh, A. Hesse, and I. Herzog
1990   *Archaeological Prospecting and Remote Sensing.* Cambridge University Press, Cambridge.

Scott, D. A.
1983   The Deterioration of Gold Alloys and Some Aspects of Their Conservation. *Studies in Conservation* 28:194–203.

Scott, D., R. Fox, Jr., M. Conner, and D. Harmon
1989   *Archaeological Perspectives on the Battle of the Little Bighorn.* University of Oklahoma Press, Norman.

Scott, E. C.
1979   Dental Wear Scoring Techniques. *American Journal of Physical Anthropology* 51:213–218.

Sears, W. H.
1961   The Study of Social and Religious Systems in North American Archaeology. *Current Anthropology* 2:233–246.

Sease, C.
1994   *A Conservation Manual for the Field Archaeologist.* 3rd ed. Archaeological Research Tools 4. Institute of Archaeology, University of California, Los Angeles.

Sebert, L. M.
1985   *Mapping with Simple Instruments: A Manual for Canadian Map-Makers.* Round Table Books, Ramsey, Isle of Man.

Secrist, J.
1979   High Resolution Photography for Archeology. *Bulletin of the Texas Archeological Society* 50:141–146.

Seeman, M. F.
1988   Ohio Hopewell Trophy Skull Artifacts as Evidence for Competition in Middle Woodland Societies Circa 50 B.C.–A.D. 350. *American Antiquity* 53:565–577.

Selner, G. I., and R. B. Taylor
1992   *System 8: GSMAP, GSMEDIT, GSMUTIL, GSPOST, GSDIG, and Other Programs for the IBM PC and Compatible Microcomputers, to Assist Workers*

in the Earth Sciences. Version 8. U.S. Department of the Interior, Geological Survey, Books and Open-File Reports Section, Denver.

Selner, G. I., R. B. Taylor, and B. R. Johnson
1986   *GSDRAW and GSMAP: Prototype Programs for the IBM PC or Compatible Microcomputers to Assist Compilation and Publication of Geologic Maps and Illustrations.* U.S. Department of the Interior, Geological Survey, Denver.

Selwitz, C.
1988   *Cellulose Nitrate in Conservation.* Getty Conservation Institute, Los Angeles, California.

Setzler, F. M., and J. D. Jennings
1941   Peachtree Mound and Village Site. Cherokee County, North Carolina. *Bulletin of American Ethnology* B 131.

Shackley, M. L.
1975   *Archaeological Sediments.* Wiley, New York.
1985   *Environmental Archaeology.* Batsford, London.

Shafer, H. J.
1982   Classic Mimbres Phase Households and Room Use Patterns. *The Kiva* 48(1–2):17–37.
1986   *Ancient Texans: Art and Lifeway Along the Lower Pecos.* Texas Monthly Press, Austin.

Shafer, H. J., and V. M. Bryant, Jr.
1977   *Archeological and Botanical Studies at Hinds Cave, Val Verde County, Texas.* Special Series 1. Anthropology Laboratory, Texas A&M University, College Station.

Shafer, H. J., J. E. Dockall, D. Owsley, and T. Ellzey
1994   The Canyon Creek Site (41OC13): A Component of the Equestrian Nomad Archeological Complex. *Bulletin of the Texas Archeological Society* 65: 291–340.

Shafer, H. J., and T. R. Hester
1983   Ancient Maya Chert Workshops in Northern Belize, Central America. *American Antiquity* 48: 519–543.

Shafer, H. J., and R. G. Holloway
1979   Organic Residue Analysis in Determining Stone Tool Function. In *Lithic Use-wear Analysis,* edited by B. Hayden, pp. 385–399. Academic Press, New York.

Shafer, H. J., M. Marek, and K. J. Reinhard
1989   A Mimbres Burial with Associated Colon Remains from the NAN Ranch Ruin, New Mexico. *Journal of Field Archaeology* 16:17–30.

Shafer, H. J., and A. J. Taylor
1986   Mimbres Mogollon Pueblo Dynamics and Ceramic Style Change. *Journal of Field Archeology* 13(1):43–68.

Shaffer, B. S.
1990   The Modified Rabbit Pelvis: A Newly Discovered Tool Type for the Mimbres. *The Artifact* 28:7–13.
1991   *The Economic Importance of Vertebrate Faunal Remains from the NAN Ruin (LA15049), a Classic*

Mimbres Pueblo Site, Grant County, New Mexico. Unpublished Master's thesis, Department of Anthropology, Texas A&M University, College Station.
1992a   The Interpretation of Gopher Remains in Southwestern Archaeological Assemblages. *American Antiquity* 57:683–691.
1992b   Quarter-Inch Screening: Understanding Biases in Recovery. *American Antiquity* 57(1):129–136.

Shaffer, B. S., and B. W. Baker
1992   *A Vertebrate Faunal Analysis Coding System with North American Taxonomy and dBase Support Procedures (Version 3.3).* Technical Report 23. Museum of Anthropology, University of Michigan, Ann Arbor.

Shaffer, B. S., and J. A. Neely
1992   Intrusive Anuran Remains in Pit House Features: A Test of Methods. *The Kiva* 57:343–351.

Shaffer, B. S., and J. L. J. Sanchez
1994   Comparison of 1/8" and 1/4" Mesh Recovery of Controlled Samples of Small to Medium-Sized Mammals. *American Antiquity* 59:525–530.

Sharer, R. J., and W. Ashmore
1979   *Fundamentals of Archaeology.* Benjamin/Cummings, Menlo Park, California.
1987   *Archaeology: Discovering Our Past.* Mayfield Publishing Company, Palo Alto, California.
1993   *Archaeology: Discovering Our Past.* 2nd ed. Mayfield Publishing Company, Mountain View, California.

Shaw, L. C.
1994   Improved Documentation in Shell Midden Excavations: An Example from the South Shore of Cape Cod. In *Cultural Resource Management: Archaeological Research, Preservation Planning, and Public Education in the Northeastern United States,* edited by J. E. Kerber, pp. 115–138. Bergin and Garvey, London.

Sheets, P. D.
1992   *The Ceren Site.* Harcourt Brace College Publishers, Fort Worth.

Sheets, P. D. (editor)
1983   *Archaeology and Volcanism in Central America: The Zapotitan Valley of El Salvador.* University of Texas Press, Austin.

Sheets, P. D., and D. Grayson (editors)
1979   *Volcanic Activity and Human Ecology.* Academic Press, New York.

Sheets, P. D., and B. R. McKee (editors)
1994   *Archaeology, Volcanism, and Remote Sensing in the Arenal Region, Costa Rica.* University of Texas Press, Austin.

Sheets, P., and T. Sever
1988   High-tech Wizardry. *Archaeology* 41(6): 28–35.

Shepard, A.
1976   *Ceramics for the Archaeologist.* Publication 609. Carnegie Institute of Washington, Washington, D.C.

Shepard, F. P.
1964   Sea Level Changes in the Past 6000 Years: Possible Archaeological Significance. *Science* 143: 574–576.

Shetrone, H. C.
1930   *The Mound Builders.* D. Appleton and Co., New York.

Shipman, C.
1981   *Understanding Photography.* HP Books, Tucson, Arizona.

Shipman, P.
1981   *Life History of a Fossil: An Introduction to Taphonomy and Paleoecology.* Harvard University Press, Cambridge.
1986   Scavenging or Hunting in Early Hominids: Theoretical Framework and Tests. *American Anthropologist* 88:27–43.

Shipman, P., G. Foster, and M. Schoeninger
1984   Burnt Bones and Teeth: An Experimental Study of Color, Morphology, Crystal Structure, and Shrinkage. *Journal of Archaeological Science* 11: 307–325.

Shott, M.
1989   Shovel Test Sampling in Archaeological Survey: Comments on Nance and Ball and Lightfoot. *American Antiquity* 54:396–404.

Shutler, R., Jr., D. C. Anderson, L. S. Tatum, and H. A. Semken, Jr.
1980   Excavation Techniques and Synopsis of Results Derived from the Cherokee Project. In *The Cherokee Excavations,* edited by D. C. Anderson and H. A. Semken, Jr., pp. 1–20. Academic Press, New York.

Sibley, L. R., and K. A. Jakes
1986   Characterization of Selected Prehistoric Fabrics of Southeastern North America. In *Historic Textiles and Paper Materials: Conservation and Characterization,* edited by H. L. Needles and S. H. Zeronion, pp. 253–276. Advances in Chemistry Series 212. American Chemical Society, Washington, D.C.

Siegal, B. S., and A. R. Gillespie
1980   *Remote Sensing in Geology.* Wiley, New York.

Siegel, J.
1976   Animal Paleopathology: Possibilities and Problems. *Journal of Archaeological Science* 3:349–384.

Sigler-Eisenberg, B.
1985   Forensic Research: Expanding the Concept of Applied Archaeology. *American Antiquity* 50: 650–655.

Silimperia, D. R., W. L. Alward, J. C. Feeley, W. W. Myers, and W. L. Heyward
1984   Microbiologic Investigations of the Barrow Eskimo Specimens. *Arctic Anthropology* 21:117–121.

Sillen, A., and M. Kavanagh
1982   Strontium and Paleodietary Research: A Review. *Yearbook of Physical Anthropology* 25:67–90.

Sillen, A., J. C. Sealy, and N. J. van der Merwe
1989   Chemistry and Paleodietary Research: No More Easy Answers. *American Antiquity* 54:504–512.

Silverman, S., and N. J. Parezo
1992   *Preserving the Anthropological Record.* Wenner-Gren, New York.

Simmons, H. C.
1969   *Archaeological Photography.* New York University, New York.

Simmons, T., R. L. Jantz, and W. M. Bass
1990   Stature Estimation from Fragmentary Femora: A Revision of the Steele Method. *Journal of Forensic Sciences* 35:628–636.

Simpson, B. B., and M. C. Ogorzaly
1986   *Economic Botany: Plants in Our World,* McGraw-Hill Co., New York, p. 640.

Singh, I. J., and D. L. Gunberg
1970   Estimation of Age at Death in Human Males from Quantitative Histology of Bone Fragments. *American Journal of Physical Anthropology* 33: 373–381.

Singleton, T. A.
1985   *The Archaeology of Slavery and Plantation Life.* Academic Press, New York.

Singley, K. R.
1981   Caring for Artifacts After Excavation, Some Advice for Archaeologists. *Historical Archaeology* 15:36–48.

Skinner, M., and A. H. Goodman
1992   Anthropological Uses of Developmental Defects of Enamel. In *Skeletal Biology of Past Peoples: Research Methods,* edited by S. R. Saunders and A. M. Katzenberg, pp. 153–174. Wiley-Liss, New York.

Skinner, S. A.
1971   Prehistoric Settlement of the DeCordova Bend Reservoir, Central Texas. *Bulletin of the Texas Archeological Society* 42:149–269.

Skinner, S. A., F. L. Briuer, G. B. Thomas, and I. Show
1981   *Initial Archaeological Survey at Fort Hood, Texas: Fiscal Year 1978.* Archaeological Resource Management Series Report 1. United States Army, Fort Hood, Texas.

Skinner, S. A., H. Haas, and S. L. Wilson
1980   The ELCOR Burial Cave: An Example of Public Archeology from West Texas. *Plains Anthropologist* 25:1–15.

Slama, C. C.
1980   *Manual of Photogrammetry.* 4th ed. American Society for Photogrammetry and Remote Sensing, Bethesda, Maryland.

Smart, T. L., and E. S. Hoffman
1988   Environmental Interpretations of Archaeological Charcoal. In *Current Paleoethnobotany,* edited by C. A. Hastorf and V. S. Popper, pp. 167–206. University of Chicago Press, Chicago.

Smith, A. L.
1950   *Uaxactun, Guatemala: Excavations of 1931–1937.*

Publication 588. Carnegie Institution of Washington, Washington, D.C.

1972   *Excavations at Altar de Sacrificios.* Papers of the Peabody Museum of Archaeology and Ethnology Vol. 62, No. 2. Harvard University, Cambridge.

Smith, A. L., and A. V. Kidder
1943   *Explorations in the Montaqua Valley, Guatemala.* Publication No. 546, Contribution 41. Carnegie Institute of Washington, Washington, D.C.

Smith, B. D.
1975   *Middle Mississippi Exploitation of Animal Populations.* Anthropological Papers 57. Museum of Anthropology, University of Michigan, Ann Arbor.
1976   "Twitching": A Minor Ailment Affecting Human Paleoecological Research. In *Cultural Change and Continuity: Essays in Honor of James Bennett Griffin*, edited by C. E. Cleland, pp. 275–318. Academic Press, New York.

Smith, B. W., E. J. Rhodes, S. Stoker, N. A. Spooner, and M. J. Aitken
1990   Optical Dating of Sediments: Initial Quartz Results from Oxford. *Archaeometry* 32:19–32.

Smith, C. E.
1971   *Preparing Specimens of Vascular Plants.* Agricultural Information Bulletin 348. ARS, U.S. Department of Agriculture, Washington, D.C.
1985   Recovery and Processing of Botanical Remains. In *The Analysis of Prehistoric Diet*, edited by R. I. Gilbert and J. W. Mielke. Academic Press, New York, pp. 97–127.

Smith, F. H.
1984   Legal Aspects and Suggested Protocol in Dealing with Human Remains Found in an Archaeological Context in Alaska. *Arctic Anthropology* 21:141–147.

Smith, M. E.
1979   A Further Criticism of the Type-Variety System: The Data Can't Be Used. *American Antiquity* 44: 822–826.

Smith, P. R., and M. T. Wilson
1990   Detection of Haemoglobin in Human Skeletal Remains by ELISA. *Journal of Archaeological Science* 17:255–268.

Smith, R. E.
1955   *Ceramic Sequence at Uaxactun, Guatemala.* 2 vols. Publication 20. Middle American Research Institute, Tulane University, New Orleans.

Sobolik, K. D.
1990   A Nutritional Analysis of Diet as Revealed in Prehistoric Human Coprolites. *Texas Journal of Science* 42:23–36.
1993   Direct Evidence for the Importance of Small Animals to Prehistoric Diets: A Review of Coprolite Studies. *North American Archaeologist* 14(3): 227–244.

Sobolik, K. D. (editor)
1994   *Paleonutrition: The Diet and Health of Prehistoric Americans.* Occasional Paper 22. Center for Archaeological Investigations, Southern Illinois University, Carbondale.

Sokal, R., and J. Rohlf
1971   *Introduction to Biostatistics.* W. H. Freeman, San Francisco.

Solecki, R. S.
1957   Practical Aerial Photography for Archaeologists. *American Antiquity* 22(4):337–351.
1963   The Prehistory of Shanidar, Iraq. *Science* 139: 179–193.
1975   Shanidar IV, a Neanderthal Flower Burial in Northern Iraq. *Science* 190:880–881.

South, S. (editor)
1977a   *Research Strategies in Historical Archeology.* Academic Press, New York.
1977b   *Method and Theory in Historical Archeology.* Academic Press, New York.

Southworth, M., and S. Southworth
1982   *Maps: A Visual Survey and Design Guide.* Little, Brown, Boston.

Spaulding, A. C.
1953   Statistical Techniques for the Discovery of Artifact Types. *American Antiquity* 18:305–313.

Spector, J. D.
1994   Working Together: Collaboration at *Inyan Ceyaka Antonwan* (Village at the Rapids). *SAA Bulletin* 12(3):8–10.

Spencer, E. W.
1993   *Geologic Maps: A Practical Guide to the Interpretation and Preparation of Geologic Maps for Geologists, Geographers, Engineers, and Planners.* Macmillan, New York.

Spier, L.
1916   New Data on the Trenton Argillite Culture. *American Anthropologist* 18:181–189.
1917   *Outline of Chronology of the Zuni Ruins.* Anthropological Papers 18:209–331. American Museum of Natural History, New York.
1931   N. C. Nelson's Stratigraphic Technique in the Reconstruction of Prehistoric Sequences in Southwestern America. In *Methods in Social Science*, edited by S. A. Rice, pp. 275–283. University of Chicago Press, Chicago.

Spier, R. F. G.
1970   *Surveying and Mapping: A Manual of Simplified Techniques.* Holt, Rinehart & Winston, New York.

Sprague, R.
1968   A Suggested Terminology and Classification for Burial Descriptions. *American Antiquity* 33: 479–485.

Spuhler, J. N.
1988   Evolution of Mitochondrial DNA in Monkeys,

Apes, and Humans. *Yearbook of Physical Anthropology* 31:15–48.

Stafford, C. R.
1995   Geoarchaeological Perspectives on Paleolandscapes and Regional Subsurface Archaeology. *Journal of Archaeological Method and Theory* 2(1):69–104.

Stafford, T. W., Jr., A. J. T. Tull, T. H. Zabel, D. J. Donahue, R. C. Duhamel, K. Brendel, C. V. Haynes, Jr., J. L. Bischoff, L. A. Payen, and R. E. Taylor
1984   Holocene Age of the Yuha Burial: Direct Radiocarbon Determinations by Accelerator Mass Spectrometry. *Nature* 308:446–447.

Stahl, P. W.
1982   On Small Mammal Remains in Archaeological Context. *American Antiquity* 47:822–829.

Stahle, D. W.
1979   Tree-Ring Dating of Historic Buildings in Arkansas. *Tree-Ring Bulletin* 39:1–29. University of Arizona, Tucson.
1990   *The Tree-Ring Record of False Spring in the Southcentral USA.* Unpublished Ph.D. dissertation, Arizona State University, Tempe.

Stahle, D. W., M. K. Cleaveland, and J. G. Hehr
1988   North Carolina Climate Changes Reconstructed from Tree Rings: A.D. 372 to 1985. *Science* 240:1517–1519.

Stahle, D. W., E. R. Cook, and J. W. C. White
1985   Tree-Ring Dating of Baldcypress and the Potential for Millenia-Long Chronologies in the Southeast. *American Antiquity* 50:796–802.

Stahle, D. W., and D. Wolfman
1985   The Potential for Archaeological Tree-Ring Dating in Eastern North America. In *Advances in Archaeological Method and Theory*, vol. 8, edited by M. B. Schiffer, pp. 279–302. Academic Press, New York.

Stampfli, H. R., and J. Schibler
1991   *Bibliography of Archaeozoology.* Seminar für Ur- und Frühgeschichte, Switzerland.

Stanley, D. R.
1952   The Microptic Alidade. *Surveying and Mapping* 12:25–26.

Stanley Price, N. P. (editor)
1984   *Conservation of Archaeological Excavations with Particular Reference to the Mediterranean Area.* ICCROM, Rome.

Starbuck, D. R.
1994   Industrial Archeology. *Federal Archeology* 7(2):15.

Starrett, W. C.
1971   *A Survey of the Mussels (Unionacea) of the Illinois River: A Polluted Stream.* Illinois Natural History Survey Bulletin Vol. 30, Article 5. Department of Registration and Education, Illinois Natural History Survey Division, Urbana.

Steele, C. W., and J. W. Hissong
1984   Caving. In *Fieldbook*, 3rd ed., pp. 415–423. Boy Scouts of America, Irving, Texas.

Steele, D. G.
1970   Estimation of Stature from Fragments of Long Limb Bones. In *Personal Identification in Mass Disasters*, edited by T. D. Stewart, pp. 85–97. National Museum of Natural History, Smithsonian Institution, Washington, D.C.
1979   The Estimation of Sex on the Basis of the Talus and Calcaneus. *American Journal of Physical Anthropology* 45:581–588.
1988   Utilization of Marine Mollusks by Inhabitants of the Texas Coast. *Bulletin of the Texas Archeological Society* 58:215–248.
1989   Zooarchaeology, Taphonomy and Preservation of the Fossil Faunal Assemblage. In *Interdisciplinary Workshop on the Physical-Chemical-Biological Processes Affecting Archeological Sites*, edited by C. C. Mathewson, pp. 65–84. U.S. Army Corps of Engineers, Washington, D.C.
1990   Taphonomic Provenience and Mammoth Bone Modification. In *Hunters of the Recent Past*, edited by L. B. Davis and B. O. K. Reeves, pp. 87–102. Unwin Hyman, London.

Steele, D. G., and C. A. Bramblett
1988   *The Anatomy and Biology of the Human Skeleton.* Texas A&M University Press, College Station.

Steele, D. G., K. E. Byrd, L. McNatt, and G. Veni
1984   Human and Non-human Skeletal Remains Recovered from Sorcerer's Cave, Terrell County, Texas. *Texas Journal of Science* 36:169–184.

Steele, D. G., J. D. Eaton, and A. J. Taylor
1980   The Skulls from Operation 2011 at Colha: A Preliminary Examination. In *The Colha Project Second Season, 1980 Interim Report*, edited by T. R. Hester, J. D. Eaton, and H. J. Shafer, pp. 163–172. Center for Archaeological Research, University of Texas at San Antonio, San Antonio, and Centro Studi e Ricerche Ligabue, Venezia.

Steele, D. G., and T. W. McKern
1969   A Method for Assessment of Maximum Long Bone Length and Living Stature from Fragmentary Long Bones. *American Journal of Physical Anthropology* 31:215–228.

Steele, D. G., and J. F. Powell
1992   Peopling of the Americas: Paleobiological Evidence. *Human Biology* 64:303–336.
1994   Paleobiological Evidence of the Peopling of the Americas: A Morphometric View. In *Theory and Method for Investigating the Peopling of the Americas*, edited by R. Bonnichsen and D. G. Steele, pp. 141–163. Center for the Study of the First Americans, Oregon State University, Corvallis.

Stein, J. K.
1986   Coring Archaeological Sites. *American Antiq-*

uity 51:505–527.

1987 Deposits for Archaeologists. *Advances in Archaeological Method and Theory*, vol. 11, edited by M. B. Schiffer, pp. 337–395. Academic Press, New York.

1990 Archaeological Stratigraphy. In *Archaeological Geology of North America*, edited by N. P. Lasca and J. Donahue, pp. 512–523. Centennial Special Vol. 4. Geological Society of America, Boulder, Colorado.

Stein, J. K. (editor)

1992 *Deciphering a Shell Midden.* Academic Press, San Diego.

Stein, J. K., and W. R. Farrand (editors)

1985 *Archaeological Sediments in Context.* Center for the Study of Early Man, Orono, Maine.

Stein, J. K., K. D. Kornbacher, and J. L. Tyler

1992 British Camp Shell Midden Stratigraphy. In *Deciphering a Shell Midden*, edited by J. K. Stein, pp. 95–133. Academic Press, San Diego.

Steinbock, R. T.

1976 *Paleopathological Diagnosis and Interpretation: Bone Disease in Ancient Human Populations.* Charles C. Thomas, Springfield, Illinois.

Sterud, E. L., and P. P. Pratt

1975 Archaeological Intra-Site Recording with Photography. *Journal of Field Archaeology* 1(2):152–168.

Steward, J.

1937 *Ancient Caves of the Great Salt Lake Region.* Bulletin 116:9–10, 91–93, 107. Bureau of American Ethnology, Smithsonian Institution, Washington, D.C.

Steward, J. H.

1942 The Direct-Historical Approach to Archaeology. *American Antiquity* 7:337–343.

Stewart, F. L.

1991 Floating for Fauna: Some Methodological Considerations Using the Keffer Site (AK Gv-14) Midden 57 Faunal Sample. *Canadian Journal of Archaeology* 15:97–115.

Stewart, M.

1977 Pits in the Northeast: A Typological Analysis. In *Current Perspectives in Northeastern Archaeology*, edited by R. Funk and C. F. Hayes, III. Researches and Transactions of the New York State Archaeological Association 18(1).

Stewart, T. D.

1973 *The People of America.* Scribner's, New York.

1979 *Essentials of Forensic Anthropology.* Charles C. Thomas, Springfield, Illinois.

Stewart-Macadam, P. L.

1989 Nutritional Deficiency Diseases: A Survey of Scurvy, Rickets, and Iron-Deficiency Anemia. In *Reconstruction of Life from the Skeleton*, edited by M. Y. Iscan and K. A. R. Kennedy, pp. 201–222. Liss, New York.

1992 Porotic Hyperostosis: A New Perspective. *American Journal of Physical Anthropology* 87:39–47.

Stewart-Macadam, P. L., and S. Kent (editors)

1992 *Diet, Demography, and Disease: Changing Perspectives on Anemia.* Aldine de Gruyter, New York.

Stiner, M. C. (editor)

1991 *Human Predators and Prey Mortality.* Westview Press, San Francisco.

St. Joseph, J. K. S.

1977 *The Uses of Air Photography.* 2nd ed. Baker, London.

Stock, J. A.

1980 Laboratory Procedures at Colha, 1980 Season. In *The Colha Project Second Season, 1980 Interim Report*, edited by T. R. Hester, J. D. Eaton, and H. J. Shafer, pp. 251–256. Center for Archaeological Research, University of Texas at San Antonio, and Centro Studi e Ricerche Ligabue, Venezia.

1983 *The Prehistoric Diet of Hinds Cave, Val Verde County, Texas: The Coprolite Evidence.* Unpublished Master's thesis, Texas A&M University, College Station.

Stockton, C. W., and D. M. Meko

1983 Drought Recurrence in the Great Plains as Reconstructed from Long-Term Tree-Ring Records. *Journal of Climate and Applied Meteorology* 22:17–29.

Stockton, E. D.

1973 Shaw's Creek Shelter: Human Displacement of Artifacts and Its Significance. *Mankind* 9: 112–117.

Stockton, J.

1974 Earth Moving Equipment in Archaeological Excavation. *Archaeology and Physical Anthropology in Oceania* 9:238–241.

Stone, E. N.

1928 Roman Surveying Instruments. *University of Washington Publications in Language and Literature* 4(4):215–242. University of Washington Press, Seattle.

Stone, T., D. N. Dickel, and G. H. Doran

1990 The Preservation and Conservation of Waterlogged Bone from the Windover Site, Florida: A Comparison of Methods. *Journal of Field Archaeology* 17:177–186.

Stoneking, M., K. Bhatia, and A. C. Wilson

1986 Rate of Sequence Divergence Estimated from Restriction Maps of Mitochondrial DNAs from Papua, New Guinea. *Cold Spring Harbor Symposia on Quantitative Biology* 51:433–439.

St-Onge, M. R.

1990 *NATMAP, Canada's National Geoscience Mapping Program: Report of a Workshop Held March 8–10, 1990.* NATMAP Committee, Geological Survey of Canada, Ottawa.

Storch, P. S.

1983 *Field and Laboratory Methods for Handling Osseous Material.* Conservation Notes 6. Texas Memorial Museum, University of Texas at Austin.

1986a Conservation Report. In La Villita Earthworks (41BX677), San Antonio, Texas. In *A Preliminary Report of Investigations of Mexican Siege Works at the Battle of the Alamo*, edited by J. H. Labadie, pp. 172–177. Archaeological Survey Report 159. Center for Archaeological Research, University of Texas at San Antonio.

1986b *Curatorial Care and Handling of Ceramic Objects.* Conservation Notes 15. Texas Memorial Museum, University of Texas at Austin.

1987 *Curatorial Care and Handling of Skin Materials, Part II: Semi-Tanned Objects.* Conservation Notes 18. Texas Memorial Museum, University of Texas at Austin.

1988 Recommendations for the Conservation of Shell Materials. *Bulletin of the Texas Archeological Society* 58:267–274.

Storey, R.
1990 A Human Cremation from the De Soto Winter Encampment, Tallahassee, Florida (abstract). *American Journal of Physical Anthropology* 81:302.

Story, D. A.
1972 *A Preliminary Report of the 1968, 1969, and 1970 Excavations at the George C. Davis Site, Cherokee County, Texas.* Report submitted to the National Science Foundation and the Texas Historical Survey Committee. University of Texas at Austin.

1982 *The Deshazo Site, Nacogdoches County, Texas.* Vol. 1. Texas Antiquities Committee Permit Series 7, Austin.

Straffin, D.
1971 A Device for Vertical Archaeological Photography. *Plains Anthropologist* 16(53):232–243.

Strong, W. D.
1935 *An Introduction to Nebraska Archaeology.* Miscellaneous Collections 93(10). Smithsonian Institution, Washington, D.C.

1940 What Is Pre-Amerindian? *Science* 91:594–596.

Struever, S.
1968a Flotation Techniques for the Recovery of Small-scale Archaeological Remains. *American Antiquity* 33:353–362.

1968b Problems, Methods and Organization: A Disparity in the Growth of Archeology. In *Anthropological Archeology in the Americas*, edited by B. Meggers, pp. 131–151. Anthropological Society of Washington, Washington, D.C.

Stuckenrath, R., J. M. Adovasio, J. Donahue, and R. Carlisle
1982 The Stratigraphy, Cultural Features and Chronology at Meadowcroft Rockshelter, Washington County, Southwestern Pennsylvania. In *Meadowcroft: Collected Papers on the Archaeology of Meadowcroft Rockshelter and the Cross Creek Drainage*, edited by R. C. Carlisle and J. M. Adovasio, pp. 69–90. University of Pittsburgh, Pittsburgh.

Stuiver, M.
1990 Timescales and Telltale Corals. *Nature* 345:387–389.

Stuiver, M., A. Long, and R. S. Kra (editors)
1993 *Calibration. Radiocarbon,* University of Arizona, Tucson.

Styles, B. W.
1981 *Faunal Exploitation and Resource Selection: Early Late Woodland Subsistence in the Lower Illinois Valley.* Scientific Papers 3. Northwestern University Archeological Program, Evanston, Illinois.

Styles, S.
1970 *The Forbidden Frontiers: The Survey of India from 1765 to 1949.* Hamilton, London.

Suchey, J. M., P. A. Owings, D. V. Wiseley, and T. T. Noguci
1984 Skeletal Aging of Unidentified Persons. In *Human Identification: Case Studies in Forensic Anthropology,* edited by T. A. Rathbun and J. E. Buikstra, pp. 278–297. Charles C. Thomas, Springfield, Illinois.

Suchey, J. M., D. V. Wiseley, R. F. Green, and T. T. Noguci
1979 Analysis of Dorsal Pitting in the Os Pubis in an Extensive Sample of Modern American Females. *American Journal of Physical Anthropology* 51:517–540.

Suess, R. E.
1980 Bristlecone-Pine Calibrations of the Radiocarbon Time-Scale, 5200 B.C. to the Present. In *Radiocarbon Variations and Absolute Chronology,* edited by I. U. Olsson, pp. 303–309. Nobel Symposium 12. Wiley Interscience, New York.

Sullivan, G.
1980 *Discover Archaeology: An Introduction to the Tools and Techniques of Archaeological Fieldwork.* Penguin, New York.

Sutcliffe, A. J.
1985 *On the Track of Ice Age Mammals.* British Museum of Natural History, London.

Sutton, M. Q.
1988 *Insects as Food: Aboriginal Entomophagy in the Great Basin.* Anthropological Papers 33. Ballena Press, Novato, California.

1995 Archaeological Aspects of Insect Use. *Journal of Archaeological Method and Theory* 2(3):253–298.

Swartz, B. K., Jr.
1963 Aluminum Powder: A Technique for Photographically Recording Petroglyphs. *American Antiquity* 29:400–401.

Swedlund, A. C. (editor)
1975 *Population Studies in Archaeology and Biological Anthropology: A Symposium.* Memoir 30. Society for American Archaeology, Washington, D.C.

Szabo, B. J., and D. Collins
1975 Age of Fossil Bones from British Interglacial Sites. *Nature* 254:680–682.

Szathmary, E. J. E.

1985   Peopling of North America: Clues from Genetic Studies. In *Out of Asia*, edited by R. L. Kirk and E. J. E. Szathmary, pp. 79–104. Canberra Journal of Pacific History, Australian National University, Canberra.

1994   Modelling Ancient Population Relationships from Modern Population Genetics. In *Theory and Method for Investigating the Peopling of the Americas*, edited by R. Bonnichsen and D. G. Steele, pp. 117–130. Center for the Study of the First Americans, Oregon State University, Corvallis.

Szuter, C. R.

1988   Small Animal Exploitation Among Desert Horticulturists in North America. *ArchaeoZoologia* 2:191–200.

Tarleton, K. S., and M. T. Ordonez

1995   Stabilization for Textiles from Wet Sites. *Journal of Field Archaeology* 22:81–96.

Tarling, D. H.

1985   Archaeomagnetism. In *Archaeological Geology*, edited by G. Rapp, Jr., and J. A. Gifford, pp. 237–264. Yale University Press, New Haven, Connecticut.

Taylor, J. V., and R. DiBennardo

1984   Discriminant Function Analysis of the Central Portion of the Innominate. *American Journal of Physical Anthropology* 64:315–320.

Taylor, R. E.

1975   Flourine Diffusion: A New Dating Method for Chipped Lithic Materials. *World Archaeology* 7(2): 125–135.

1987   *Radiocarbon Dating*. Academic Press, San Diego.

1989   Radiocarbon Dating: Potential Applications in Archaeology and Paleoanthropology. In *Archaeological Chemistry IV*, edited by R. O. Allen, pp. 321–335. American Chemical Society, Washington, D.C.

1991   Frameworks for Dating the Late Pleistocene Peopling of the Americas. In *The First Americans: Search and Research*, edited by T. D. Dillehay and D. J. Meltzer, pp. 77–112. CRC Press, Boca Raton, Florida.

Taylor, R. E. (editor)

1976   *Advances in Obsidian Glass Studies*. Noyes Press, Park Ridge, New Jersey.

Taylor, R. E., D. J. Donahue, T. H. Zabel, P. E. Damon, and A. J. T. Tull

1984   Radiocarbon Dating by Particle Accelerators: An Archaeological Perspective. In *Advances in Archaeological Chemistry III*, edited by J. B. Lambert, pp. 333–356. Advances in Chemistry Series 205. American Chemical Society, Washington, D.C.

Taylor, R. E., A. Long, and R. Kra (editors)

1992   *Radiocarbon After Four Decades: An Interdisciplinary Perspective*. Springer-Verlag, New York.

Taylor, R. E., L. A. Payen, C. A. Prior, P. J. Slota, Jr., R. Gillespie, J. A. J. Gowlett, R. E. B. Hedges, A. J. T. Jull, T. H. Zabel, D. J. Donahue, and R. Berger

1985   Major Revisions in the Pleistocene Age Assignment for North American Human Skeletons by C-14 Accelerator Mass Spectrometry; None Older Than 11,000 C-14 Years B.P. *American Antiquity* 50:136–140.

Taylor, W. W.

1948   *A Study of Archaeology*. Memoirs 69. American Anthropological Association, Menasha, Wisconsin.

Tchernov, E., and J. K. Horwitz

1991   Body Size Diminution Under Domestication: Unconscious Selection in Primeval Domesticates. *Journal of Anthropological Archaeology* 10:54–75.

Teaford, M. F.

1991   Dental Microwear: What Can It Tell Us About Diet and Dental Function? In *Advances in Dental Anthropology*, edited by M. A. Kelley and C. S. Larsen, pp. 341–356. Wiley-Liss, New York.

Tennant, N. H., and J. Baird

1985   The Deterioration of Molluscan Collections: Identification of Shell Efflorescence. *Studies in Conservation* 30:73–85.

Thomas, D. H.

1969   Great Basin Hunting Patterns: A Quantitative Method for Treating Faunal Remains. *American Antiquity* 34:392–401.

1971   On Distinguishing Natural from Cultural Bone in Archaeological Sites. *American Antiquity* 36:366–371.

1973   An Empirical Test for Steward's Model of Great Basin Settlement Patterns. *American Antiquity* 38:155–176.

1978   The Awful Truth About Statistics in Archaeology. *American Antiquity* 42(2):231–244.

1983   *The Archaeology of Monitor Valley: Gatecliff Shelter*. Anthropological Papers 59. American Museum of Natural History, New York.

1985   *The Archaeology of Hidden Cave, Nevada*. Anthropological Papers 61. American Museum of Natural History, New York.

1986   *Refiguring Anthropology: First Principles of Probability and Statistics*. Waveland Press, Prospect Heights, Illinois.

1987   *The Archaeology of Mission Santa Catalina de Guale 1. Search and Discovery*. Anthropological Papers 63(2):47–161. American Museum of Natural History, New York.

1989   *Archaeology*. 2nd ed. Holt, Rinehart & Winston, Fort Worth.

Thomas, P. A.

1978   Indian Subsistence and Settlement Patterns in Non-coastal Regions: Early Historic Massachusetts. In *Conservation Archaeology in the Northeast: Toward a Research Orientation*, edited by A. Speiss, pp. 17–26.

Bulletin 3. Peabody Museum of Archaeology and Ethnology, Harvard University, Cambridge.

Thompson, D. D.
1979   The Core Technique in the Determination of Age at Death in Skeletons. *Journal of Forensic Sciences* 44:902–915.

Thompson, M. M.
1988   *Maps for America: Cartographic Products of the U.S. Geological Survey*. U.S. Geological Survey, Reston, Virginia.

Thoms, A. V. (editor)
1994   *The Valley Branch Archeological Project: Excavations at an Archaic Site (41MU55) in the Cross Timbers Uplands, North Central Texas*. Reports of Investigations 15. Archaeological Research Laboratory, Texas A&M University, College Station.

Thuesen, I., and J. Engberg
1990   Recovery and Analysis of Human Genetic Material from Mummified Tissue and Bone. *Journal of Archaeological Science* 17:679–689.

Tolstoy, P.
1958   *Surface Survey of the Northern Valley of Mexico: The Classic and Post-Classic Periods*. Transactions of the American Philosophical Society 48, Pt. 5.

Tomlin, C. D.
1990   *Geographic Information Systems and Cartographic Modelling*. Prentice-Hall, Englewood Cliffs, New Jersey.

Toriabara, T. Y., and D. A. Jackson
1982   X-ray Fluorescence Measurement of the Zinc Profile of a Single Hair. *Clinical Chemistry* 28: 650–654.

Torres, V. R. P., A. A. Enciso, and E. G. Porras
1986   *The Osteology of South American Camelids*. Translated by E. Sandefur. Archaeological Research Tools Vol. 3. Institute of Archaeology, University of California, Los Angeles.

Torroni, A., T. G. Schurr, M. F. Cabell, M. D. Brown, J. V. Neel, M. Larsen, and D. G. Smith
1993   Asian Affinities and Continental Radiation of the Four Founding Native American mtDNAs. *American Journal of Human Genetics* 53:563–590.

Toscano, P.
1991   The Gunter's Chain. *Surveying and Land Systems Information* 51(3):155–161. Bethesda, Maryland.

Toumey, C. P.
1979   Techniques for Photographing Artifacts. *Journal of Field Archaeology* 6:122–123.

Traverse, A.
1988   *Paleopalynology*. Unwin Hyman Pub. Co., Boston.

Trefil, J. S.
1985   Concentric Clues from Growth Rings Unlock the Past. *Smithsonian* 16(4):47–54.

Trigger, B. G.

1989   *A History of Archaeological Thought*. Cambridge University Press, Cambridge.

Trimm, L.
1966   *The California Coordinate System: Its Growth and Application*. State of California, Transportation Agency, Department of Public Works, Division of Highways, Right of Way Engineering, Sacramento.

Trinkaus, E.
1983   *The Shanidar Neanderthals*. Academic Press, New York.

Trotter, M.
1970   Estimation of Stature from Intact Limb Bones. In *Personal Identification in Mass Disasters*, edited by T. D. Stewart, pp. 71–83. National Museum of Natural History, Washington, D.C.

Trotter, M., and G. C. Gleser
1952   Estimation of Stature from Long Bones of American Whites and Negroes. *American Journal of Physical Anthropology* 10:463–514.
1958   A Re-Evaluation of Estimation of Stature Based on Measurements of Stature Taken During Life and of Long Bones After Death. *American Journal of Physical Anthropology* 16:79–123.
1977   Corrigenda to "Estimation of Stature from Long Bones of American Whites and Negroes, *American Journal of Physical Anthropology* (1952)." *American Journal of Physical Anthropology* 47: 355–356.

Trubowitz, N.
1976   *Instrument and Chemical Methods of Site Survey and Testing in the Allegheny and Genesee River Valleys*. Reports of the Archaeological Survey Vol. 5(3), No. 13. Department of Anthropology, SUNY, Buffalo.
1981   The Use of the Plow in Archaeological Site Survey: An Experimental Example from Western New York. *American Center for Conservation Archaeology Reports* 8(5 and 6):16–22.

Tuniz, C.
1986   Archaeological Dating with Accelerators. In *New Paths in the Use of Nuclear Techniques for Art and Archaeology*, edited by G. Furlan, P. Cassola Guida, and C. Tuniz, pp. 113–124. World Scientific, Singapore.

Turgeon, D. D., A. E. Bogan, E. V. Coan, W. K. Emerson, W. G. Lyons, W. L. Pratt, C. F. E. Roper, A. Scheltema, F. G. Thompson, and J. D. Williams
1988   *Common and Scientific Names of Aquatic Invertebrates from the United States and Canada: Mollusks*. Special Publication No. 16. American Fisheries Society, Bethesda, Maryland.

Turkel, S. J.
1989   Congenital Abnormalities in Skeletal Populations. In *Reconstruction of Life from the Skeleton*, edited by M. Y. Iscan and K. A. R. Kennedy, pp. 109–127. Liss, New York.

Turner, A.
1984   Sub-sampling Animal Bone Assemblages: Reducing the Work-load or Reducing the Information? *Circaea* 2(2):69–74.

Turner, C. G., II
1985   The Dental Search for Native American Origins. In *Out of Asia,* edited by R. Kirk and E. Szathmary, pp. 31–78. Journal of Pacific History, Australian National University, Canberra.
1986   Dentochronological Separation Estimates for Pacific Rim Populations. *Science* 23:1140–1142.
1987   Late Pleistocene and Holocene Population History of East Asia Based on Dental Variation. *American Journal of Physical Anthropology* 73: 305–321.
1990   The Major Features of Sundadonty and Sinodonty, Including Suggestions About East Asian Microevolution, Population History, and Late Pleistocene Relationships with Australian Aboriginals. *American Journal of Physical Anthropology* 82:295–317.

Turner, C. G., II, and L. M. C. Machado
1983   New Dental Wear Pattern and Evidence for High Carbohydrate Consumption in a Brazilian Archaic Skeletal Population. *American Journal of Physical Anthropology* 61:125–130.

Turner, C. G., II, C. R. Nichol, and G. R. Scott
1991   Scoring Procedures for Key Morphological Traits of the Permanent Dentition: The Arizona State University Dental Anthropology System. In *Advances in Dental Anthropology,* edited by M. A. Kelley and C. S. Larsen, pp. 13–31. Wiley-Liss, New York.

Turner, C. G., II, and J. A. Turner
1992   The First Claim for Cannibalism in the Southwest: Walter Hough's 1901 Discovery at Canyon Butte Ruin 3, Northeast Arizona. *American Antiquity* 57:661–682.

Turner, E. S., and T. R. Hester
1993   *A Field Guide to Stone Artifacts of Texas Indians.* 2nd ed. Gulf, Houston.

Tuross, N.
1994   Archaeological Artifacts and Biomolecule Affiliation: Testing the Consequences of Cleaning. In *Material Issues in Art and Archaeology IV:*41–50. Materials Research Society, Pittsburgh.

Tuross, N., and M. L. Fogel
1994   Exceptional Molecular Preservation in the Fossil Record: The Archaeological, Conservation, and Scientific Challenge. In *Archaeometry of Pre-Columbian Sites and Artifacts,* edited by D. Scott and P. Meyers, pp. 367–380. Getty Conservation Institute, Los Angeles.

Turpin, S.
1982   *Seminole Canyon: The Art and the Archaeology. Val Verde County, Texas.* Research Report 83. Texas Archeological Survey, University of Texas at Austin.

Turpin, S. A. (editor)
1985   *Seminole Sink: Excavation of a Vertical Shaft Tomb, Val Verde County, Texas.* Research Report 93. Texas Archeological Survey, University of Texas at Austin.

Turpin, S., M. Hennenberg, and D. H. Riskind
1986   Late Archaic Mortuary Practices of the Lower Pecos River Region, Southwest Texas. *Plains Anthropologist* 31:295–315.

Turpin, S., R. P. Watson, S. Dennett, and H. Muessig
1979   Stereophotogrammetric Documentation of Exposed Archaeological Features. *Journal of Field Archaeology* 6(3):323–338.

Twiss, P. S., E. Suess, and R. M. Smith
1969   Morphological Classification of Grass Phytoliths. *Soil Science Society of America Proceedings* 33:749–751.

Tyner, J. A.
1992   *Introduction to Thematic Cartography.* Prentice-Hall, Englewood Cliffs, New Jersey.

Ubelaker, D. H.
1974   *Reconstruction of Demographic Profiles from Ossuary Skeletal Samples: A Case Study from the Tidewater Potomac.* Contributions to Anthropology 18. Smithsonian Institution, Washington, D.C.
1979   Skeletal Evidence for Kneeling in Prehistoric Ecuador. *American Journal of Physical Anthropology* 51:679–685.
1989a *Human Skeletal Remains: Excavation, Analysis, and Interpretation.* 2nd ed. Manuals on Archaeology 2. Taraxacum, Washington, D.C.
1989b The Estimation of Age at Death from Immature Human Bone. In *Age Markers in the Human Skeleton,* edited by M. Y. Iscan, pp. 55–70. Charles C. Thomas, Springfield, Illinois.

Ubelaker, D. H., and L. G. Grant
1989   Human Skeletal Remains: Preservation or Reburial. *Yearbook of Physical Anthropology* 32:249–287.

Ubelaker, D. H., and N. D. Sperber
1988   Alterations in Human Bones and Teeth Due to Restricted Sun Exposure and Contact with Corrosive Agents. *Journal of Forensic Sciences* 33:540–546.

Ubelaker, D. H., and P. Willey
1978   Complexity in Arikara Mortuary Practice. *Plains Anthropologist* 23:69–74.

Uerpmann, H. P.
1973   Animal Bone Finds and Economic Archaeology: A Critical Study of "Osteo-archaeological" Method. *World Archaeology* 4:307–332.

U.S. Department of the Interior, Bureau of Land Management (USDI/BLM)
1973   *Manual of Instructions for the Survey of the Public Lands of the United States, 1973.* U.S. Government Printing Office, Washington, D.C.

1991a *Satellite Positioning System Work Group Report.* Satellite Positioning System Work Group. U.S. Department of the Interior, Bureau of Land Management, Cheyenne, Wyoming.

1991b *Cadastral Survey.* U.S. Department of the Interior, Bureau of Land Management, Washington, D.C.

U.S. Department of the Interior, Geological Survey (USDI/GS)

1989 *Cartography at the U.S. Geological Survey: The National Mapping Division's Cartographic Programs, Products, Design, and Technology.* U.S. Department of the Interior, U.S. Geological Survey, National Mapping Division, Reston, Virginia.

1991 *Geographic Information Systems.* U.S. Geological Survey, U.S. Department of the Interior, Washington, D.C.

U.S. Government, Superintendent of Documents

1991 *Surveying and Mapping.* U.S. Government Printing Office, Washington, D.C.

Uzes, F. D.

1977 *Chaining the Land: A History of Surveying in California.* Landmark Enterprises, Sacramento.

Valdez, F., Jr., and P. J. Buttles

1991 G-103: A Late Preclassic Monumental Structure at Rio Azul, Guatemala. Paper presented at the Annual Meeting of the Society for American Archaeology, New Orleans.

Valladas, H., and G. Valladas

1987 Thermoluminescence Dating of Burnt Flint and Quartzite: Comparative Results. *Archaeometry* 29:214–220.

Valladas, H., J-L. Joron, G. Valladas, B. Arensburg, O. Bar-Yosef, A. Belfer-Cohen, P. Goldberg, H. Laville, L. Meignen, Y. Rak, E. Tchernov, A-M. Tillier, and B. Vandermeersch

1987 Thermoluminescence Dates for the Neanderthal Burial Site at Kebara in Israel. *Nature* 330:159–160.

Valliant, G. C.

1935 *Excavations at El Arbolillo.* Anthropological Papers 35, Pt. 2. American Museum of Natural History, New York.

1938 Correlation of Archaeological and Historical Sequence in the Valley of Mexico. *American Anthropologist* 40:535–578.

Van der Veen, M., and N. Fieller

1982 Sampling Seeds. *Journal of Archaeological Science* 9:287–298.

Van Gerven, D. P., and G. J. Armelagos

1983 "Farewell to Paleodemography?" Rumors of Its Death Have Been Greatly Exaggerated. *Journal of Human Evolution* 12:353–360.

Van Horn, D.

1988 *Mechanized Archaeology.* Wormwood Press, Calabasas, California.

Van Horn, D. M., and J. R. Murray

1982 A Method for Effectively Screening Some Clay Matrices. In *Practical Archaeology,* edited by B. Dillon, pp. 23–31. Archaeological Research Tools 2. Institute of Archaeology, University of California, Los Angeles.

Van Horn, D. M., J. R. Murray, and R. S. White

1986 Some Techniques in Mechanical Excavation in Salvage Archaeology. *Journal of Field Archaeology* 13:239–244.

Van Nest, J.

1985 Patination of Knife River Flint. *Plains Anthropologist* 30(110):325–339.

van Vark, G. N., and W. W. Howells (editors)

1984 *Multivariate Statistical Methods in Physical Anthropology: A Review of Recent Advances and Current Developments.* D. Reidel, Hingham, Massachusetts.

Van West, C. R.

1993 *Modeling Prehistoric Agricultural Productivity in Southwestern Colorado: A GIS Approach.* Reports of Investigations 67. Department of Anthropology, Washington State University, Pullman.

Varner, D. M.

1968 The Nature of Non-buried Archaeological Data: Problems in Northwestern Mexico. *Bulletin of the Texas Archeological Society* 38:51–65.

Vaughan, P. C.

1985 *Use-Wear Analysis of Flaked Stone Tools.* University of Arizona Press, Tucson.

Vaught, K. C.

1989 *A Classification of the Living Mollusca.* American Malacologists, Melbourne, Florida.

Vehik, S. C.

1977 Bone Fragments and Bone Grease Manufacturing: A Review of Their Archaeological Use and Potential. *Plains Anthropologist* 22:169–182.

Verano, J. W., and D. H. Ubelaker (editors)

1994 *Disease and Demography in the Americas.* Smithsonian Institution Press, Washington, D.C.

Verosub, K. L., and P. J. Mehringer, Jr.

1984 Congruent Paleomagnetic and Archaeomagnetic Records from the Western United States: A.D. 750 to 1450. *Science* 224:387–389.

Vigo, T. L.

1977 Preservation of Natural Textile Fibers: Historical Perspectives. In *Preservation of Papers and Textiles of Historic and Artistic Value,* edited by J. C. Williams, pp. 189–207. Advances in Chemistry Series 164. American Chemical Society, Washington, D.C.

Villa, P.

1982 Conjoinable Pieces and Site Formation Processes. *American Antiquity* 47:276–290.

Villa, P., and J. Courtin

1983 The Interpretation of Stratified Sites: A View

from Underground. *Journal of Archaeological Science* 10:267–282.

Vinton, K. W.
1962   Carbon-dated Ocean Level Changes Offer a New System of Correlating Archaeological Data. *Akten des 34 Internationalen Amerikanistenkongresses, Wien 1960*:390–395. Vienna.

Vita-Finzi, C.
1978   *Archaeological Sites in Their Setting*. Thames & Hudson, London.

Vogel, J. C., and N. J. van der Merwe
1977   Isotopic Evidence for Early Maize Cultivation in New York State. *American Antiquity* 42:238–242.

Volman, K. C.
1981   *Paleoenvironmental Implications of Botanical Data from Meadowcroft Rockshelter, Pennsylvania*. Unpublished Ph.D. dissertation, Texas A&M University, College Station.

Vreeland, J. M., and A. Cockburn
1980   Mummies of Peru. In *Mummies, Disease, and Ancient Cultures*, edited by A. Cockburn and E. Cockburn, pp. 135–174. Cambridge University Press, Cambridge.

Wagner, G. A., M. J. Aitken, and V. Mejdahl
1983   *Thermoluminescence Dating*. Handbooks for Archaeologists No 1. European Science Foundation, Strasbourg.

Wagner, G. E.
1988   Comparability Among Recovery Techniques. In *Current Paleoethnobotany*, edited by C. A. Hastorf and V. S. Popper, pp. 17–35. University of Chicago Press, Chicago.

Wakefield, E. F., and S. C. Dellinger
1936   Diet of the Bluff Dwellers of the Ozark Mountains and Its Skeletal Effects. *Annals of Internal Medicine* 9:1412–1418.

Walker, I. C.
1978   Binford, Science and History: The Probabilistic Variability of Explicated Epistemology and Nomothetic Paradigms in Historical Archaeology. In *Historical Archaeology*, edited by R. L. Schuyler, pp. 223–239. Baywood, Farmingdale, New York.

Walker, J. W.
1993   *Low Altitude, Large Scale Reconnaissance: A Method of Obtaining High Resolution Vertical Photographs for Small Areas*. Interagency Archeological Services, National Park Service, Denver.

Walker, P. L.
1985   Anemia Among Prehistoric Indians of the American Southwest. In *Health and Disease in the Prehistoric Southwest*, edited by C. F. Merbs and R. J. Miller, pp. 139–161. Anthropological Research Papers No. 34. Arizona State University, Tempe.
1989   Cranial Injuries as Evidence of Violence in Prehistoric Southern California. *American Journal of Physical Anthropology* 80:313–323.

Walker, P. L., G. Dean, and P. Shapiro
1991   Estimating Age from Tooth Wear in Archaeological Populations. In *Advances in Dental Anthropology*, edited by M. A. Kelley and C. S. Larsen, pp. 169–178. Wiley-Liss, New York.

Walker, R.
1985   *A Guide to Post-Cranial Bones of East African Animals*. Hylochoerus Press, Norwich, England.

Wandsnider, L., and C. Dore
1995   Creating Cultural Resource Data Layers: Experiences from the Nebraska Cultural Resources GIS Project. *Society for American Archaeology Bulletin* 13(4):25–26. Washington, D.C.

Warren, R. E., and M. J. O'Brien
1981   Regional Sample Stratification: The Drainage Class Technique. *Plains Anthropologist* 26:213–228.

Waselkov, G. A.
1987   Shellfish Gathering and Shell Midden Archaeology. In *Advances in Archaeological Method and Theory*, vol. 10, edited by M. B. Schiffer, pp. 93–210. Academic Press, New York.

Waterlogged Wood Working Group Conference
1984   *Waterlogged Wood: Study and Conservation*. Second International Council of Museums, Waterlogged Wood Working Group Conference, Grenoble.

Waters, M. R.
1986   *The Geoarchaeology of Whitewater Draw, Arizona*. Anthropological Papers 45. University of Arizona, Tucson.
1992   *Principles of Geoarchaeology: A North American Perspective*. University of Arizona Press, Tucson.

Watson, K., and D. H. Knepper, Jr. (editors)
1994   *Airborne Remote Sensing for Geology and the Environment; Present and Future*. U.S. Geological Survey Bulletin, Washington, D.C.

Watson, P. J.
1991   A Parochial Primer: The New Dissonance as Seen from the Midcontinental United States. In *Processual and Postprocessual Archaeologies: Multiple Ways of Knowing the Past*, edited by R. W. Preucel, pp. 265–274. Occasional Paper No. 10. Center for Archaeological Investigations, Southern Illinois University, Carbondale.

Watson, P. J., S. A. LeBlanc, and C. Redman
1971   *Explanation in Archaeology*. Columbia University Press, New York.
1984   *Archaeological Explanation: The Scientific Method in Archaeology*. Columbia University Press, New York.

Wauchope, R.
1966   *Archeology Survey of Northern Georgia: With a Test of Some Cultural Hypotheses*. Memoir 23. Society for American Archaeology, Washington, D.C.

Weakley, W. F.
1971   *Tree-Ring Dating and Archaeology in South*

Dakota. Memoir 8. *Plains Anthropologist.*

Webb, C. H.
1959   *The Belcher Mound, A Stratified Caddoan Site in Caddo Parish, Louisiana.* Memoir 16. Society for American Archaeology, Washington, D.C.

Webb, W. S.
1946   *The Indian Knoll: Site OH-2, Ohio County, Kentucky.* Reports in Archeology and Anthropology 4:115–365. University of Kentucky, Lexington.

Webb, W. S., and D. L. DeJarnette
1942   *An Archaeological Survey of the Pickwick Basin in the Adjacent Portions of the States of Alabama, Mississippi, and Tennessee.* Bulletin 29. Bureau of American Ethnology, Smithsonian Institution, Washington, D.C.

Webster, W. J. E.
1962   Techniques of Field Photography for Archaeological Purposes. *Oceania* 33:139–142.
1964   Ultra-violet Photography of Australian Rock Paintings. *Antiquity* 40:144.

Wedel, W. R.
1961   *Prehistoric Man on the Great Plains.* University of Oklahoma Press, Norman.

Weeks, J. M.
1994   *Ancient Caribbean.* Garland, New York.

Weide, D. L., and G. D. Webster
1967   Ammonium Chloride Powder Used in the Photography of Artifacts. *American Antiquity* 32:104–105.

Weigand, P. C.
1970   Huichol Ceremonial Reuse of a Fluted Point. *American Antiquity* 35:365–367.

Weigelt, J.
1989   *Recent Vertebrate Carcasses and Their Paleobiological Implications.* Translated by J. Schaefer. University of Chicago Press, Chicago.

Weir, F. A.
1985   An Early Holocene Burial at the Wilson-Leonard Site in Central Texas. *Mammoth Trumpet* 2:1–3.

Weir, G. H.
1976   *Palynology, Flora and Vegetation of Hovenweep National Monument: Implications for Aboriginal Plant Use on Cajon Mesa, Colorado and Utah.* Unpublished Ph.D. dissertation, Texas A&M University, College Station.
1982   Analysis of Mammalian Hair and Plant Fibers in Cordage from a Texas Archaic Shelter. *Bulletin of the Texas Archeological Society* 53:131–149.

Weiss, K. M.
1972   On the Systematic Bias in Skeletal Sexing. *American Journal of Physical Anthropology* 37:239–250.
1973   *Demographic Models for Anthropology.* Memoir 27. Society for American Archeology, Washington, D.C.

1975   Demographic Disturbance and the Use of Life Tables in Anthropology. In *Population Studies in Archaeology and Biological Anthropology: A Symposium,* edited by A. C. Swedlund, pp. 46–56. Memoir 30. Society for American Archaeology, Washington, D.C.

Wells, D.
1986   *Guide to GPS Positioning.* Canadian GPS Associates, Fredericton, New Brunswick, Canada.

Wells, W., D. E. Wells, and A. Kleusberg
1992   *Global Positioning System Bibliography.* Technical Report DRP-92-2. U.S. Army Engineer Waterways Experiment Station, Vicksburg, Mississippi.

Werner, R., and J. Young
1991   A Checklist to Evaluate Mapping Software. *Journal of Geography* 90(3):118–120.

Werner, S. B.
1974   Coccidioidomycosis Among Archaeology Students: Recommendations for Prevention. *American Antiquity* 39:367–370.

Werner, S. B., D. Pappagianis, I. Heindl, and A. Mickel
1972   An Epidemic of Coccidioidomycosis Among Archeology Students in Northern California. *New England Journal of Medicine* 286:507–512.

Wesolowsky, A. B.
1973   The Skeletons of Lerna Hollow. *Hesperia* 42:340–351.

Westervelt, J., W. Goran, and M. Shapiro
1986   Development and Applications of GRASS: The Geographic Resources Analysis Support System. In *Geographic Information Systems in Government,* vol. 2, edited by B. K. Opitz, pp. 605–624. A. Deepak Publishing, Hampton, Virginia.

Weymouth, J. W.
1986   Geophysical Methods of Archaeological Site Surveying. In *Advances in Archaeological Method and Theory,* vol. 9, edited by M. B. Schiffer, pp. 311–395. Academic Press, Orlando.

Whalen, M. E.
1990   Sampling Versus Full-Coverage Survey: An Example from Western Texas. In *The Archaeology of Regions: A Case for Full-Coverage Survey,* edited by S. Fish and S. Kowalewski, pp. 219–236. Smithsonian Institution Press, Washington, D.C.
1994   *Turquoise Ridge and Late Prehistoric Residential Mobility in the Desert Mogollon Region.* Anthropological Papers 118. University of Utah Press, Salt Lake City.

Wheat, C. I.
1957–1963   *Mapping the Transmississippi West, 1540–1861.* 6 vols. Institute of Historical Cartography, San Francisco.

Wheat, J. B.
1972   *The Olsen-Chubbuck Site: A Paleo-Indian Bison Kill.* Memoir 26. Society for American Archaeology, Washington, D.C.

Wheeler, A., and A. K. G. Jones
1989   *Fishes.* Cambridge Manuals in Archaeology. Cambridge University Press, New York.

Wheeler, E. A., R. G. Pearson, C. A. LaPasha, T. Zack, and W. Hatley
1986   *Computer-aided Wood Identification.* Bulletin 474. North Carolina Agricultural Research Service, North Carolina State University, Raleigh.

Wheeler, R. E. M.
1954   *Archaeology from the Earth.* Clarendon Press, Oxford.

White, C. A.
1983   *A History of the Rectangular Survey System.* Bureau of Land Management, U.S. Department of the Interior, Washington, D.C.

White, T. D.
1986   Cutmarks on the Bodo Cranium: A Case of Prehistoric Defleshing. *American Journal of Physical Anthropology* 69:503–509.
1991   *Human Osteology.* Academic Press, San Diego.
1992   *Prehistoric Cannibalism at Mancos 5MTUMR-2346.* Princeton University Press, Princeton, New Jersey.

White, W. S.
1992   *Geological Maps: Portraits of the Earth.* U.S. Geological Survey, U.S. Department of the Interior, Reston, Virginia.

Whitley, D. S., and R. I. Dorn
1987   Rock Art Chronology in Eastern California. *World Archaeology* 19:150–164.

Whittaker, J. C.
1994   *Flintknapping: Making and Understanding Stone Tools.* University of Texas Press, Austin.

Whittlesey, J. H.
1966   Photogrammetry for the Excavator. *Archaeology* 19:273–276.
1967   Balloon over Sardis. *Archaeology* 29:67–68.
1970   Tethered Balloon for Archaeological Photos. *Photogrammetric Engineering* 36(2)181–186.
1975   Elevated and Airborne Photogrammetry and Stereo Photography. In *Photography in Archaeological Research,* edited by E. Harp, Jr., pp. 223–258. University of New Mexico Press, Albuquerque.
1977   Interdisciplinary Approach to Archaeology. *Journal of Field Archaeology* 4:135–137.

Whittlesey, S. M.
1978   *Status and Death at Grasshopper Pueblo: Experiments Toward an Archaeological Theory of Correlates.* Unpublished Ph.D. dissertation, Department of Anthropology, University of Arizona, Tucson.

Wienker, C. W.
1984   A Case of Mistaken Assumption. In *Human Identification,* edited by T. A. Rathbun and J. E. Buikstra, pp. 229–243. Charles C. Thomas, Springfield, Illinois.

Wijngaarden-Bakker, L. H. van (editor)
1986   *Database Management and Zooarchaeology.* Pact 14, Journal of the European Study Group on Physical, Chemical and Mathematical Techniques Applied to Archaeology, Strasbourg.

Wilcox, D. R.
1975   A Strategy for Perceiving Social Groups in Puebloan Sites. In *Chapters in the Prehistory of Eastern Arizona,* IV, edited by P. S. Martin, E. B. W. Zubrow, D. C. Bowman, D. A. Gregory, J. A. Hanson, M. B. Schiffer, and D. R. Wilcox, pp. 120–159. Fieldiana: Anthropology 65. Chicago.

Wilcox, R. C.
1965   Volcanic-ash Chronology. In *The Quaternary of the United States,* edited by H. E. Wright and D. G. Frey, pp. 809–816. Princeton University Press, Princeton, New Jersey.

Wilding, L. P.
1967   Radiocarbon Dating of Biogenic Opal. *Science* 156:66–67.

Wilding, L. P., and L. R. Drees
1974   Contributions of Forest Opal and Associated Crystalline Phases to Fine Silt and Clay Fractions of Soils. *Clays and Clay Minerals* 22:295–306.

Wilford, J. N.
1981   *The Mapmakers.* Vintage Books, Random House, New York.

Wilk, R. R., and W. L. Rathje
1982   Archaeology of the Household: Building a Prehistory of Domestic Life. *American Behavioral Scientist* 25(6):611–728.

Wilkenson, K.
1968   A Method of Preparing Translucent Artifacts for Photography. *Reporter, Nevada Archaeological Survey* 2(2):10–11.

Willey, G. R.
1953   *Prehistoric Settlement Patterns in the Viru Valley, Peru.* Bulletin 153. Bureau of American Ethnology, Washington, D.C.

Willey, G. R., and J. Sabloff
1974   *A History of American Archaeology.* W. H. Freeman, San Francisco.
1993   *A History of American Archaeology.* 3rd ed. W. H. Freeman, New York.

Williams, D.
1973   Flotation at Siraf. *Antiquity* 47:288–292.

Williams, S.
1991   *Fantastic Archaeology: The Wild Side of North American Archaeology.* University of Pennsylvania Press, Philadelphia.

Williams, S. R., J. L. Longmire, and L. A. Beck
1990   Human DNA Recovery from Ancient Bone (abstract). *American Journal of Physical Anthropology* 81:318.

Williams-Blangero, S., and J. Blangero
1989   Anthropometric Variation and the Genetic

Structure of the Jirels of Nepal. *Human Biology* 62: 131–146.

Williams-Dean, G.
1978   *Ethnobotany and Cultural Ecology of Prehistoric Man in Southwest Texas.* Unpublished Ph.D. dissertation, Texas A&M University, College Station.

Wilson, D. R.
1983   *Air Photo Interpretation for Archaeologists.* St. Martin's Press, New York.

Wilson, B., C. Grigson, and S. Payne (editors)
1982   *Ageing and Sexing Animal Bones from Archaeological Sites.* BAR British Series 109. British Archaeological Reports, Oxford.

Wilson, D. R.
1982   *Air Photo Interpretation for Archaeologists.* St. Martin's Press, New York.

Wilson, G. L.
1924   *The Horse and the Dog in the Hidatsa Culture.* Anthropological Papers Vol. 15, Pt. 2, pp. 123–311. American Museum of Natural History, New York.

Wilson, J. G.
1985   *Follow the Map: The Ordnance Survey Guide.* A & C Black and the Ordnance Survey, London and Southhampton.

Wilson, M. A.
1990   *Geographic Information Systems: A Partially Annotated Bibliography.* Council of Planning Librarians, Chicago.

Wilson, R. L.
1982   *Elementary Forest Surveying and Mapping II.* Rev. ed. Oregon State University Bookstore, Corvallis.
1985   *Elementary Forest Surveying and Mapping.* Rev. ed. Oregon State University Bookstore, Corvallis.

Wing, E. S.
1983   *A Guide for Archeologists in the Recovery of Zooarcheological Remains.* Special Publication 3. *Florida Journal of Anthropology,* Gainesville.

Wing, E. S., and A. B. Brown
1979   *Paleonutrition: Method and Theory in Prehistoric Foodways.* Academic Press, New York.

Wing, E. S., and I. R. Quitmyer
1985   Screen Size for Optimal Data Recovery: A Case Study. In *Aboriginal Subsistence and Settlement Archaeology of Kings Bay Locality, Vol. 2: Zooarchaeology,* edited by W. H. Adams, pp. 49–57. Reports of Investigations 2. Department of Anthropology, University of Florida, Gainesville.

Wintemberg, W. J.
1919   Archeology as an Aid to Zoology. *Canadian Field-Naturalist* 33:63–72.

Winter, M. C.
1976   The Archaeological Household Cluster in the Valley of Oaxaca. In *The Early Mesoamerican Village,* edited by K. V. Flannery, pp. 25–31. Academic Press, New York.

Wintle, A. G.
1996   Archaeologically-relevant Dating Techniques for the Next Century. *Journal of Archaeological Science* 23:123–138.

Wiseman, J.
1983   Conflicts in Archaeology: Education and Practice. *Journal of Field Archaeology* 10(1):1–9.

Wissler, C.
1916   The Application of Statistical Methods to the Data on the Trenton Argillite Culture. *American Anthropologist* 18:190–197.

Wolfenden, G. E.
1961   *Postcranial Osteology of the Waterfowl.* Bulletin Vol. 6, No. 1. Florida State Museum, Gainesville, Florida.

Wolfman, D.
1984   Geomagnetic Dating Methods in Archaeology. In *Advances in Archaeological Method and Theory,* vol. 7, edited by M. B. Schiffer, pp. 363–458. Academic Press, New York.

Wood, J. W., G. R. Milner, H. C. Harpending, and K. M. Weiss
1992   The Osteological Paradox: Problems in Inferring Prehistoric Health from Skeletal Samples. *Current Anthropology* 33:343–370.

Wood, W. R.
1969   Two House Sites in the Central Plains: An Experiment in Archaeology. Memoir 6, *Plains Anthropologist.*

Wood, W. R., and D. L. Johnson
1978   A Survey of Disturbance Processes in Archaeological Site Formation. In *Advances in Archaeological Method and Theory,* vol. 1, edited by M. B. Schiffer, pp. 315–381. Academic Press, New York.

Wood, W. R., R. K. Nickel, and D. E. Griffin
1984   Remote Sensing the American Great Plains. In *Remote Sensing: A Handbook for Archaeologists and Cultural Resource Managers.* Supplement No. 9. Cultural Resources Division, National Park Service, U.S. Department of the Interior, Washington, D.C.

Woodbury, R. B.
1960   Nels C. Nelson and Chronological Archaeology. *American Antiquity* 25:400–401.

Wooley, L.
1954   *Digging Up the Past.* Benn, London.

Word, J. H., and C. L. Douglas
1970   *Excavations at Baker Cave, Val Verde County, Texas.* Bulletin 16. Texas Memorial Museum, University of Texas at Austin.

Wright, R. H.
1971   *Miscellaneous Field Studies Map MF-317, Basic Data Contribution 33.* Map Showing Location of Samples Dated by Radiocarbon Methods in the San Francisco Bay Region. U.S. Geological Survey, San Francisco Bay Region Environment and Resources Planning Study, San Francisco.

Wylie, A.
1992   The Interplay of Evidential Constraints and Political Interests: Recent Archaeological Research on Gender. *American Antiquity* 57(1):15–35.

Wylie, H. G.
1975   Artifact Processing and Storage Procedure: A Note of Caution. *Lithic Technology* 4(1–2):17–19.

Yellen, J. E.
1977a   *Archaeological Approaches to the Present: Models for Predicting the Past.* Academic Press, New York.
1977b   Cultural Patterning in Faunal Remains: Evidence from the !Kung Bushmen. In *Experimental Archaeology*, edited by D. Ingersoll, J. E. Yellen, and W. MacDonald, pp. 271–331. Columbia University Press, New York.

Yerkes, R. W.
1987   Seasonal Patterns in Late Prehistoric Fishing Practices in the North American Midwest. *Archaeo-Zoologia* 1:137–148.

Yohe, R. M., II, M. E. Newman, and J. S. Schneider
1991   Immunological Identification of Small-Mammal Proteins on Aboriginal Milling Equipment. *American Antiquity* 56(4):659–666.

Young, J. C.
1992   The State of the Art and the Artifact: A Regional Survey of Museum Collections. *Technology and Conservation*, Summer–Fall:10–16.

Zangger, E.
1993   *The Geoarchaeology of the Argolid.* Gebr. Mann Verlag, Berlin.

Ziegler, A. C.
1973   *Inference from Prehistoric Faunal Remains.* Addison-Wesley Module in Anthropology 43. Addison-Wesley, Reading, Massachusetts.
1975   Recovery and Significance of Unmodified Faunal Remains. In *Field Methods in Archaeology*, edited by T. R. Hester, R. F. Heizer, and J. A. Graham, pp. 183–205. Mayfield Publishing Company, Palo Alto, California.

Zierhut, N. W.
1967   Bone Breaking Activities of the Calling Lake Cree. *Alberta Anthropologist* 1:33–36.

Zimmerman, D. W., and J. Huxtable
1971   Thermoluminescence Dating of Upper Paleolithic Fired Clay from Dolni Vestonice. *Archaeometry* 13:53–57.

Zimmerman, L. J.
1977   *Prehistoric Locational Behavior: A Computer Simulation.* Report 10. Office of the State Archaeologist, University of Iowa, Iowa City.
1994   Sharing Control of the Past. *Archaeology* 47(6):65–68.

Zimmerman, L. J., T. Emerson, P. Willey, M. Swegle, J. B. Gregg, P. Gregg, E. White, C. Smith, T. Haberman, and P. Bumstead
1980   *The Crow Creek Site (39BF11) Massacre: A Preliminary Report.* Archeology Laboratory, University of South Dakota, Vermillion.

Zimmerman, M. R., and M. A. Kelley
1982   *Atlas of Paleopathology.* Praeger, New York.

Zimmerman, M. R., E. Trinkaus, M. Lemay, A. C. Aufderheide, T. A. Rayman, G. R. Marrocco, R. E. Shultes, and E. A. Coughlin
1981   Trauma and Trephination in a Peruvian Mummy. *American Journal of Physical Anthropology* 55:497–501.

Zingg, R. M.
1940   *Report on the Archaeology of Southern Chihuahua.* Contributions 1. Center of Latin American Studies, University of Denver, Denver.

Zivanovic, S.
1982   *Ancient Diseases: The Elements of Paleopathology.* Pica Press, New York.

Zubrow, E. B. W.
1990   The Fantasies of GIS Software. In *Interpreting Space: GIS and Archaeology*, edited by K. M. S. Allen, S. W. Green, and E. B. W. Zubrow, pp. 184–193. Taylor & Francis, London.

Zuener, F. E.
1958   *Dating the Past.* 4th ed. Hutchinson, London.

Zulick, C. A.
1986   Application of a Geographic Information System to the Bureau of Land Management's Resource Management Planning Process. In *Geographic Information Systems in Government*, vol. 1, edited by B. K. Opitz, pp. 309–328. A. Deepak Publishing, Hampton, Virginia.

ABOUT THE CONTRIBUTORS

Richard E.W. Adams is Professor of Anthropology and Director, Rio Azul Archaeological Project at The University of Texas at San Antonio. Professor Adams is a specialist in the culture of the ancient Maya and is the author of 4 books, including *Prehistoric Mesoamerica*; 85 papers; and has edited 5 volumes.

Barry W. Baker is a doctoral student in anthropology at Texas A & M University. His research focuses on zooarchaeology, taphonology and Quaternary vertebrate paleontology. He is co-author, with Brian Shaffer, of *A Vertebrate Faunal Analysis Coding System*.

Michael B. Collins is Associate Director and Head of Sponsored Projects at the Texas Archeological Research Laboratory, The University of Texas at Austin. He is the author of dozens of papers and monographs on geoarchaeology, Paleoindian studies, and lithic analysis. He is currently editing the multivolume report on the Wilson-Leonard site in central Texas.

Kenneth L. Feder is Professor of Anthropology at Central Connecticut State University. In addition to his ongoing research and excavations in the Northeastern United States, he has authored *Frauds, Myths, and Mysteries; A Village of Outcasts; The Past in Perspective*; and is the co-author of *Human Antiquity*.

Elizabeth A. Greathouse is Coordinator of the Central California Information Center/California Historical Resources Information System. She has participated in archaeological work in California, Nevada, and Australia.

Thomas R. Hester is Professor of Anthropology and Director of the Texas Archeological Research Laboratory at The University of Texas, Austin. He has done fieldwork in Texas, Belize, the western United States, Mexico, and Egypt. Professor Hester has authored and edited 8 books as well as more than 400 other publications reflecting research in these areas in addition to lithic analysis, trace element studies, and ancient technologies.

Richard G. Holloway is a paleobotanist at Quaternary Services, Flagstaff, Arizona. He has done fieldwork for more than 20 years in the Southwest, Southeast, and Pacific Northwest. Among many other publications, he is co-editor of *Pollen Records of Late-Quaternary North American Sediments*.

L. Kyle Napton is Professor of Anthropology and Director of the Institute for Archaeological Research at California State University, Stanislaus. His areas of research include desert environments in North America and Australia. Professor Napton has done pioneering research on subsistence patterns in the western Great Basin, especially with data from the site of Lovelock Cave.

Joseph F. Powell is Assistant Professor of Anthropology and Curator of Human Osteology, Maxwell Museum of Anthropology at the University of New Mexico. Dr. Powell has done extensive osteological and bioarchaeological analysis. He has published numerous papers, including several on his work with Paleoindian human remains.

Harry J. Shafer is Professor of Anthropology at Texas A & M University. He specializes in lithic technology (he received the Society for American Archaeology Award for Excellence in Lithic Studies in 1995) and the archaeology of the Mimbres culture in the American Southwest. The author of more than 100 papers and monographs, he has also authored *Ancient Texans: Rock Art and Lifeways along the Lower Pecos* and coedited *Maya Stone Tools*.

Brian S. Shaffer is the Director of the Zooarchaeology Laboratory at the Institute of Applied Sciences, University of North Texas. He is an anthropology doctoral student at Texas A & M University. His research interests, on which he has authored a number of publications, include subsistence, taphonomy, and site formation processes.

D. Gentry Steele is Professor of Anthropology at Texas A & M University. As a physical anthropologist, he has conducted extensive studies on the ancient peoples of the New World. His research, with Joseph Powell, has involved the analysis of the health and diet of Paleoindian cultures. Dr. Steele is also the coauthor of *The Anatomy and Biology of the Human Skeleton*.

Fred Valdez, Jr., is Associate Professor of Anthropology at the University of Texas, Austin and Director, Programme for Belize Archaeological Project. His fieldwork in Belize involves a long term documentation and excavation of Maya sites in the northwestern part of that country. Professor Valdez has published numerous papers and is a specialist in Mayan ceramic analysis.

Credits

p. xiiii, Robert F. Heizer; **Chapter 1** Fig. 1.1, Thomas R. Hester; **Chapter 2** Fig. 2.1, (c) Copyright Institute of Nautical Archaeology, Fig. 2.2, Harry.J. Shafer, Texas A&M University, Fig. 2.3, Center for Archaeological Research, University of Texas, San Antonio, Fig. 2.4, D.L. Hamilton/Institute of Nautical Archaeology, Fig. 2.5, American Museum of Natural History, Anthropological Papers 44(3), Fig. 2.6 From D.L. Clark, Analytical Archaeology, Methuen, London, 1968, Fig. 2.7, Texas Archaeological Research Laboratory; **Chapter 3** Fig. 3.1, From Robert J. Sharer and Wendy Ashmore, Archaeology: Discovering Our Past, 2nd Edition, (c) 1993 Mayfield Publishing Company. Used by permission of the publisher, Figs. 3.2-3.5, Plog, S., 1976, "Relative Efficiencies of Sampling Techniques for Archaeological Surveys" in The Early Mesoamerican Village, ed. K.V. Flannery, pp. 136-158. Academic Press, Inc., By permission of the publisher, Fig. 3.6, Courtesy of U.S. Army, III Corps and Fort Hood, Fig. 3.7, From N. Hammond, ed., MesoAmerican Archaeology, Gerald Duckworth and Company Ltd. By permission of the publisher, Fig. 3.8, Hill, J.N., 1970 Broken K Pueblo: Prehistoric Social Organization in the American Southwest, Anthropological Papers 18. Copyright (c)1970 The University of Arizona Press, Fig. 3.9, Courtesy of The Witte Museum, San Antonio, Texas; **Chapter 4** Figs. 4.1-4.3, 4.5-4.8, Kenneth L. Feder, Fig. 4.9, From K.W. Kintigh, The Effectiveness of Subsurface Testing: A Simulation Approach, American Antiquity 53:686-707, 1988. Used with permission of the publisher, Fig. 4.11, Courtesy of B.L. Turner, Fig. 4.15, Courtesy of the Connecticut Historical Commission; **Chapter 5** Fig. 5.2a, Courtesy of the Wilson-Leonard project, Texas Archaeological Research Lab and Texas Department of Transportation, Figs. 5.2b, 5.3, David Van Horn, Fig. 5.4, Courtesy of Illinois Transportation Archaeological Research Program, Fig. 5.5 Alston Thomas and Center for Environmental Archaeology, Texas A&M University, Fig. 5.6, Texas Archaeological Research Laboratory, University of Texas, Austin, Fig. 5.7, David Hurst Thomas, Courtesy of The American Museum of Natural History, Fig. 5.8, Colha Project, photo by Daniel R. Potter, Fig. 5.11, Kenneth M. Brown, Center for Archaeological Research, University of Texas, San Antonio, Fig. 5.12, Thomas R. Hester, Fig. 5.13, Texas Archeological Research Laboratory, University of Texas, Austin, photo by Dee Ann Story, Fig. 5.14, Thomas R. Hester, Fig. 5.15, Linda Donley, Fig. 5.16, Kenneth M. Brown, Center for Archaeological Research, University of Texas, San Antonio, Fig. 5.17, Texas Archaeological Research Laboratory, University of Texas, Austin, photo by Dee Ann Story, Fig. 5.18, Texas Archaeological Research Laboratory, University of Texas, Austin, Fig. 5.19, 5.20, Thomas R. Hester, Fig. 5.21, Kenneth M. Brown, Center for Archaeological Research, University of Texas, San Antonio, Fig. 5.22, News and Information, University of Texas, Austin, photo by Larry Murphy, Fig. 5.23, Thomas R. Hester, Fig. 5.24, 5.25, With permission of Journal of Field Archaeology and the Trustees of Boston University, Fig. 5.26, Colha Project, photo by Thomas R. Hester, Fig. 5.27, Thomas R. Hester, Fig. 5.28, Thomas R. Hester, Fig. 5.29, Colha Project, Fig. 5.30, David Hurst Thomas, Courtesy of The American Museum of Natural History, Fig. 5.31, (c) Robert S. Peabody Museum of Archaeology, Phillips Academy, Andover, MA. All Rights Reserved, Fig. 5.32, Texas Archaeological Research Laboratory, University of Texas, Austin, photo by Darrell Creel, Fig. 5.33, Thomas R. Hester, Fig. 5.34-5.37, Colha Project; **Chapter 6** Figs. 6.5b, 6.6, 6.9a, 6.11, 6.13, 6.15, 6.17, 6.19, 6.20, Kenneth L. Feder, Fig. 6.10, From Ivor Noel Hume, Martin's Hundred, Alfred A. Knopf, Inc. 1982. With permission of the publisher. Fig. 6.18, Deborah Pearsall, Fig. 6.21, Courtesy of Centro Camuno di Studi Preistorici; **Chapter 7** Fig. 7.1, Used with permission, Archaeological Research Facility, University of California, Berkeley, Fig. 7.2, Colha Project, Fig. 7.3, Payson Sheets, University of Colorado, Boulder, Fig. 7.4, Colha Project, Fig. 7.5, 7.6, Dr. Dan Hamilton,

Texas A&M University, Fig. 7.7, Paul Storch and the Materials Conservation Laboratory, Texas Memorial Museum, Fig. 7.8, Texas Archaeological Research Laboratory, University of Texas, Austin; **Chapter 8**, Figs. 8.1, 8.2, 8.4, 8.5, H.J. Shafer, Fig. 8.3, Thomas R. Hester; **Chapter 9** Fig. 9.1 Earth Observation Satellite Company, Figs. 9.2-9.4, 9.6-9.8, 9.12, USDI/USGS, Figs. 9.9-9.11, 9.13, USDI/BLM, Figs. 9.15, 9.16, Suunto Company, Fig. 9.24, Trimble Navigation, Figs. 9.25-9.27, CSUS Institute for Archaeological Research, Fig. 9.28, Courtesy K&E, Fig. 9.29a, TOPCON Corporation, Fig. 9.33, Lewis R. Binford, An Alywara Day: Making Men's Knives and Beyond. Reproduced by permission of the Society for American Archaeology from American Antiquity 51(3), 1986, Fig. 9.34, CSUS/IAR; **Chapter 10** Fig. 10.1 From Archaeology and Volcanism in Central America: The Zapotitan Valley of El Salvador, edited by Payson D. Sheets, (c)1983. Courtesy of the University of Texas Press, Fig. 10.2, Texas Archaeological Research Laboratory, University of Texas, Austin, photo by David S. Dibble, Fig. 10.3a, Fred Valdez, Fig. 10.3b, Thomas R. Hester, Fig. 10.3c, Reprinted by permission of Graham Connah and Antiquity Publications Ltd., Fig. 10.4, From Cultural Resource Management: Archaeological Research, Preservation Planning and Public Education in the Northeastern United States, ed. Jordan E. Kerber, 1994, Bergin & Garvey, London, an imprint of Greenwood Publishing Group, Inc., Westport, CT, Fig. 10.5, Peabody Museum, Harvard University, Cambridge, Fig. 10.6, Department of Anthropology, University of Texas, Austin, Fig. 10.7, Colha Project, Fig. 10.8, Carnegie Institute, Washington, D.C., Fig. 10.9, 10.10, Peabody Museum, Harvard University, Cambridge; **Chapter 11** Fig. 11.1, J.F. Powell, 1989, unpublished Master's thesis, University of Texas, Austin, Fig. 11.2, From Advances in Dental Anthropology, eds. M.A.Kelley and C.S. Larsen, (c)1991 Wiley-Liss, Inc. Reprinted by permission of the publisher, a subsidiary of John Wiley & Sons, Inc., Fig. 11.3, Don Hamilton, Texas A&M University, Fig. 11.4, James W. Lyle, Fig. 11.5, Thomas R. Hester, Fig. 11.6, R. A. Ricklis, Figs. 11.7, 11.11, 11.13, From Douglas E. Ubelaker, Human Skeletal Remains: Excavation, Analysis, and Interpretation, 2nd Ed., Manuals on Archaeology 2, pp. 168, 53, 65. With permission of Taraxacum Press, Fig. 11.8, J.F. Powell, Fig. 11.9, Thomas R. Hester, Texas Archaeological Research Laboratory, Austin, Fig. 11.10, Harry J. Shafer, Texas A&M University, Fig. 11.12, From R.C. Dailey and Dan Morse, Identification of the Victim, pp. 87-123 in Handbook of Forensic Archaeology, , Dan Morse, Jack Duncan, James Stoutmire, eds. Rose Printing Co., Fig. 11.14, From Jane E. Buikstra and Douglas H. Ubelaker, Standards for Data Collection from Human Skeletal Remain, 1994, Arkansas Archaeological Survey Research Series No. 44, Arkansas Archaeological Survey, Figs. 11.15-11.17, J.F. Powell; **Chapter 12** Figs. 12.1-12.3, John G. Jones, Texas A&M University, Figs. 12.4-12.6, Harry J. Shafer; **Chapter 13** Fig. 13.1 Buda Project, Texas Archaeological Research Laboratory, The University of Texas, Austin and Texas Department of Transportation, Austin, Fig. 13.2, Choke Canyon Project and the University of Texas, San Antonio, photo by Thomas R. Hester, Fig. 13.3, Barry Baker, Brian Shaffer, UMMA; **Chapter 14** Fig. 14.1, E. Mott Davis, The University of Texas at Austin, Fig. 14.2, Center for Archaeological Research, The University of Texas, San Antonio, Fig. 14.3, Joseph W. Michels, Pennsylvania State University, Fig. 14.4, Office of the State Archaeologist, Texas Historical Commission.

Text Credits

Chapter 13 Tables 13.1, 13.2, From B.S. Shaffer and J.L.J. Sanchez, Comparison of 1/8" and 1/4 " Mesh Recovery of Controlled Samples of Small to Medium-Sized Mammals, American Antiquity 59:525-530, Used with permission of the publisher; **Chapter 14** page 328, Dr. Donald R. Lewis, University of Texas, San Antonio.

INDEX